MAGILL'S
LITERARY ANNUAL
2011

MAGILL'S
LITERARY ANNUAL
2011

Essay-Reviews of 200 Outstanding Books
Published in the United States During 2010

With an Annotated List of Titles

Volume One
A-L

Edited by
JOHN D. WILSON
STEVEN G. KELLMAN

SALEM PRESS
Pasadena, California   Hackensack, New Jersey

LIBRARY OF CONGRESS CATALOG CARD NO
ISBN (set): 978-1-58765-815-0
ISBN (vol. 1): 978-1-58765-816-7
ISBN (vol. 2): 978-1-58765-817-4

FIRST PRINTING

PRINTED IN CANADA

CONTENTS

CONTENTS

PUBLISHER'S NOTE

Magill's Literary Annual, 2011 is the fifty-seventh publication in a series that began in 1954. Critical essays for the first twenty-two years were collected and published in the twelve-volume *Survey of Contemporary Literature* in 1977; since then, yearly sets have been published. Each year, *Magill's Literary Annual* seeks to evaluate critically 200 major examples of serious literature, both fiction and nonfiction, published during the previous calendar year. The philosophy behind our selection process is to cover works that are likely to be of interest to general readers, that reflect publishing trends, that add to the careers of authors being taught and researched in literature programs, and that will stand the test of time. By filtering the thousands of books published every year down to 200 notable titles, the editors have provided busy librarians with an excellent reader's advisory tool and patrons with fodder for book discussion groups and a guide for choosing worthwhile reading material. The essay-reviews in the *Annual* provide a more academic, "reference" review of a work than is typically found in newspapers and other periodical sources.

The reviews in the two-volume *Magill's Literary Annual, 2011* are arranged alphabetically by title. At the beginning of each volume is a complete alphabetical list, by category, of all covered books that provides readers with the title, author, and a brief description of each work. Every essay is approximately four pages in length. Each one begins with a block of reference information in a standard order:

- Full book title, including any subtitle
- *Author:* Name, with birth and death years
- *First published:* Original foreign-language title, with year and country, when pertinent
- Original language and translator name, when pertinent
- Introduction, Foreword, etc., with writer's name, when pertinent
- *Publisher:* Company name and city, number of pages, retail price
- *Type of work:* (chosen from standard categories)

Anthropology	Essays	Literary criticism
Archaeology	Ethics	Literary history
Autobiography	Film	Literary theory
Biography	Fine arts	Media
Current affairs	History	Medicine
Diary	History of science	Memoir
Drama	Language	Miscellaneous
Economics	Law	Music
Education	Letters	Natural history
Environment	Literary biography	Nature

Novel	Psychology	Sociology
Novella	Religion	Technology
Philosophy	Science	Travel
Poetry	Short fiction	Women's issues

- *Time:* Period represented, when pertinent
- *Locale:* Location represented, when pertinent
- Capsule description of the work
- *Principal characters* [for novels, short fiction] or *Principal personages* [for biographies, history]: List of people, with brief descriptions

The text of each essay-review analyzes and presents the focus, intent, and relative success of the author, as well as the makeup and point of view of the work under discussion. To assist readers further, essays are supplemented by a list of additional "Review Sources" for further study in a bibliographic format. Every essay includes a sidebar offering a brief biography of the author or authors. Thumbnail photographs of book covers and authors are included as available.

Four indexes can be found at the end of volume 2:

- Biographical Works by Subject: Arranged by subject, rather than by author or title. Readers can locate easily reviews of biographical works—memoirs, diaries, and letters in addition to biographies and autobiographies—by looking up the name of the person covered.
- Category Index: Groups all titles into subject areas such as current affairs and social issues, ethics and law, history, literary biography, philosophy and religion, psychology, and women's issues.
- Title Index: Lists all works reviewed in alphabetical order, with any relevant cross references.
- Author Index: Lists books covered in the annual by each author's name.

A searchable cumulative index, listing all books reviewed in *Magill's Literary Annual* between 1977 and 2011, as well as in *Magill's History Annual* (1983) and *Magill's Literary Annual, History and Biography* (1984 and 1985), can be found at our Web site, **www.salempress.com**, on the page for *Magill's Literary Annual, 2011*.

Our special thanks go to the editors for their expert and insightful selections: John D. Wilson is the editor of *Books and Culture* for *Christianity Today*, and Steven G. Kellman is a professor at the University of Texas at San Antonio and a member of the National Book Critics Circle. We also owe our gratitude to the outstanding writers who lend their time and knowledge to this project every year. The names of all contributing reviewers are listed in the front of volume 1, as well as at the end of their individual reviews.

COMPLETE ANNOTATED LIST OF TITLES

VOLUME 1

COMPLETE ANNOTATED LIST OF TITLES

A study of expectations regarding reasons for and the purposes and responsibilities of Great Britain and its empire—from its vast size in the early twentieth century to its minuscule extent within sixty years—especially in terms of the leadership of Winston Churchill

This book focuses on prominent Americans in London before and during U.S. involvement in World War II, putting a new spin on a well-documented era of the twentieth century

Brandon's novel about a small county in Florida and three characters who are isolated in their own worlds and about the desperate and appalling act by one of them that will change all of their lives forever

The author describes her quest for a meaningful life in the harsh, often solitary, expanses of the American West

An intellectual biography of the eminent French anthropological theorist Lévi-Strauss

Harris's second novel about the life and times of Cicero continues the story of his public career, covering the momentous half-decade that followed his election to the office of consul

This book is the story of two sisters, Emily and Jessamine Bach, their love affairs, and their work

Reproduced in this volume is the hitherto unpublished correspondence between the two giants of post-World War II German poetry, Bachmann and Celan, documenting their often stormy artistic, spiritual, and sensual relationship

COMPLETE ANNOTATED LIST OF TITLES

VOLUME 2

COMPLETE ANNOTATED LIST OF TITLES

COMPLETE ANNOTATED LIST OF TITLES

COMPLETE ANNOTATED LIST OF TITLES

CONTRIBUTING REVIEWERS

Michael Adams
*City University of New York
Graduate Center*

Richard Adler
*University of Michigan-
Dearborn*

Emily Alward
College of Southern Nevada

Andrew J. Angyal
Elon University

Jacob M. Appel
*The Mount Sinai Medical
School*

Dean Baldwin
*Penn State Erie, The
Behrend College*

Carl L. Bankston III
Tulane University

Jane Missner Barstow
University of Hartford

Milton Berman
University of Rochester

Cynthia A. Bily
Macomb Community College

Margaret Boe Birns
New York University

Nicholas Birns
*Eugene Language College,
The New School*

Franz G. Blaha
*University of Nebraska-
Lincoln*

Pegge Bochynski
Beverly, Massachusetts

Harold Branam
*Savannah State University
(retired)*

Peter Brier
*California State University,
Los Angeles*

William S. Brockington, Jr.
University of South Carolina

Faith Hickman Brynie
Bigfork, Montana

Byron Cannon
University of Utah

Henry L. Carrigan, Jr.
Northwestern University

Sharon Carson
University of North Dakota

Dolores L. Christie
*Catholic Theological Society
of America (CTSA)
John Carroll University*

C. L. Chua
*California State University,
Fresno*

Richard Hauer Costa
Texas A&M University

Frank Day
Clemson University

Francine A. Dempsey
College of Saint Rose

Robert P. Ellis
Northborough, Massachusetts

Thomas R. Feller
Nashville, Tennessee

Roy C. Flannagan
*South Carolina Governor's
School for Science and
Mathematics*

Robert J. Forman
*St. John's University, New
York*

Kathryn E. Fort
*Michigan State University
College of Law*

Jean C. Fulton
Landmark College

Ann D. Garbett
Averett University

Janet E. Gardner
Falmouth, Massachusetts

Sheldon Goldfarb
*University of British
Columbia*

Sidney Gottlieb
Sacred Heart University

Karen Gould
Austin, Texas

Lewis L. Gould
University of Texas, Austin

Jay L. Halio
University of Delaware

Diane Andrews Henningfeld
Adrian College

Carl W. Hoagstrom
*Ohio Northern University
(retired)*

John R. Holmes
*Franciscan University of
Steubenville*

Robert Jacobs
*Central Washington
University*

Jeffry Jensen
*Glendale Community
College*

Steven G. Kellman
*University of Texas, San
Antonio*

xxxvii

Howard A. Kerner
Polk Community College

Grove Koger
*Albertsons Library, Boise
State University*

Wendy Alison Lamb
South Pasadena, California

James B. Lane
*Indiana University
Northwest*

Timothy Lane
Louisville, Kentucky

Eugene Larson
Los Angeles Pierce College

L. L. Lee
*Western Washington
University*

Leon Lewis
Appalachian State University

Thomas Tandy Lewis
*St. Cloud Community and
Technical College*

Bernadette Flynn Low
*Community College of
Baltimore County-
Dundalk*

R. C. Lutz
CII Group

Janet McCann
Texas A&M University

Joanne McCarthy
Tacoma, Washington

Andrew Macdonald
Loyola University

S. Thomas Mack
*University of South
Carolina-Aiken*

David W. Madden
*California State University,
Sacramento*

Mira N. Mataric
*University of Belgrade,
Serbia*

Charles E. May
*California State University,
Long Beach*

Laurence W. Mazzeno
Alvernia University

Michael R. Meyers
Pfeiffer University

Timothy C. Miller
*Millersville University of
Pennsylvania*

Robert Morace
Daemen College

Daniel P. Murphy
Hanover College

John Nizalowski
Mesa State College

Holly L. Norton
*University of Northwestern
Ohio*

Lisa Paddock
*Cape May Court House, New
Jersey*

Robert J. Paradowski
*Rochester Institute of
Technology*

David Peck
Laguna Beach, California

Marjorie J. Podolsky
*Penn State Erie, The
Behrend College*

Cliff Prewencki
Delmar, New York

Maureen Puffer-Rothenberg
Valdosta State University

Tony Rafalowski
University of Missouri

Christopher Rager
San Dimas, California

Thomas Rankin
Concord, California

R. Kent Rasmussen
Thousand Oaks, California

Rosemary M. Canfield
Reisman
*Charleston Southern
University*

Betty Richardson
*Southern Illinois University,
Edwardsville*

Dorothy Dodge Robbins
Louisiana Tech University

Carl Rollyson
*City University of New York,
Baruch College*

Joseph Rosenblum
*University of North
Carolina, Greensboro*

John K. Roth
Claremont McKenna College

Elizabeth D. Schafer
Loachapoka, Alabama

Barbara Schiffman
Vanderbilt University

Reinhold Schlieper
*Embry-Riddle Aeronautical
University*

Barbara Kitt Seidman
Linfield College

R. Baird Shuman
*University of Illinois at
Urbana*

Paul Siegrist
Fort Hays State University

Tom Sienkewicz
Monmouth College

Narasingha P. Sil
Western Oregon University

Charles L. P. Silet
Iowa State University

Amy Sisson
Houston Community College

Jan Sjåvik
*University of Washington,
Seattle*

CONTRIBUTING REVIEWERS

Roger Smith
Portland, Oregon

Ira Smolensky
Monmouth College

Maureen Kincaid Speller
*University of Kent at
   Canterbury*

Theresa L. Stowell
Adrian College

Gerald H. Strauss
Bloomsburg University

Paul Stuewe
Green Mountain College

Paul B. Trescott
Southern Illinois University

William L. Urban
Monmouth College

Ronald G. Walker
Western Illinois University

Shawncey Webb
Taylor University

Thomas Willard
University of Arizona

John Wilson
Editor, Christianity Today

James A. Winders
Appalachian State University

Scott D. Yarbrough
*Charleston Southern
   University*

AUTHOR PHOTO CREDITS

Martin Amis: *Cheryl A. Koralik*; Aharon Appelfeld: ©*Jerry Bauer/Courtesy, Weidenfeld & Nicolson, New York*; Paul Auster: ©*Jerry Bauer*; James Baldwin: ©*John Hoppy Hopkins*; Roland Barthes: *Holtz/Sygma*; Thomas Bernhard: *Courtesy, Teos*; T. Coraghessan Boyle: *Courtesy, Allen & Unwin*; George W. Bush: *Eric Draper, White House/Courtesy, DOD*; Peter Carey: ©*Miriam Berkley*; René Char: ©*Irisson*; Michael Connelly: *Courtesy, Allen & Unwin*; William Dalrymple: *Nina Subin/ Courtesy, Allen & Unwin*; Edwidge Danticat: ©*Arturo Patten*; Don DeLillo: *Thomas Victor*; Louise Erdrich: *Michael Dorris/Courtesy, Harper & Row*; William Gibson: *Karen Moskowitz/Putnam*; Allegra Goodman: *Nina Subin/Courtesy, Allen & Unwin*; Seamus Heaney: *Courtesy, Allen & Unwin*; Edward Hirsch: ©*Miriam Berkley*; Sebastian Junger: *Michael Kamber/Courtesy, W. W. Norton & Company*; Milan Kundera: ©*Vera Kundera*; Anne Lamott: ©*Scott Braley/Courtesy, Riverhead Books*; John le Carré: *The Douglas Brothers*; Alexander McCall Smith: *Chris Watt/Library of Congress*; Ian McEwan: ©*Miriam Berkley*; Thomas McGuane: ©*Marion Ettlinger/Courtesy, Houghton Mifflin*; David Malouf: *Jane Bown/Courtesy, Pantheon Books*; Sue Miller: *Courtesy, Allen & Unwin*; Ngugi wa Thiong'o: *David Mbiyu*; Gina Ochsner: ©*Fritz Liedtke/Courtesy, Houghton Mifflin Harcourt*; Kenzaburō Ōe: *Courtesy, Allen & Unwin*; Cynthia Ozick: ©*Nancy Crampton/Courtesy, Houghton Mifflin Company*; Philip Roth: ©*Nancy Crampton/Courtesy, Simon & Schuster*; Gary Shteyngart: *Brigitte Lacombe/Courtesy, Allen & Unwin*; Leslie Marmon Silko: *University Press of Mississippi*; Charles Simic: ©*Kevin Wells*; Robert Stone: ©*Phyllis Rose/Courtesy, Houghton Mifflin Harcourt*; Scott Turow: ©*Skrebneski*; Mark Twain: *Library of Congress*; Anne Tyler: *Diana Walker*; Richard Wilbur: *Stathis Orphanos*; Simon Winchester: ©*Marion Ettlinger/Courtesy, Picador, USA*

THE ABYSS OF HUMAN ILLUSION

Author: Gilbert Sorrentino (1929-2006)
Publisher: Coffee House Press (Minneapolis). 168 pp.
 $14.95
Type of work: Novel
Time: Mostly the present but with some reference to the
 personally remembered past
Locale: Various locations in the United States, often the
 West Coast or Brooklyn, New York

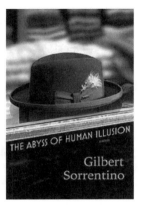

This posthumously published work, composed of fifty short narratives, revisits many of Sorrentino's earlier thematic concerns and showcases some of his characteristic literary devices

In the realm of experimental fiction, Gilbert Sorrentino is an important figure. During a career spanning five decades, he established a significant critical reputation as a writer who helped redefine the novel as an art form. Published four years after the author's death in 2006, *The Abyss of Human Illusion* serves to reinforce Sorrentino's reputation as a writer who tested the traditional parameters of fiction.

As is the case with his earlier work, Sorrentino's last novel places primary emphasis on structure rather than plot or character. *The Abyss of Human Illusion* has no overarching narrative and no principal characters. Instead, the reader is confronted with fifty short, nonchronological sections, each one identified by a roman numeral and each one essentially self-contained. The first twenty-five are only a few hundred words each, while the second twenty-five average around one thousand words each. In its overall structure, the book resembles some of the author's other works such as *Little Casino* (2002) and *A Strange Commonplace* (2006), each composed of fifty-two short chapters.

Examined individually, each section or chapter of *The Abyss of Human Illusion* provides a glimpse into the lives of a single character or a small group of characters, some captured in a single moment and others reflecting on a past, real or imagined. As with all metafiction, most of the tales are self-conscious, making overt reference to themselves as narratives. In section XXIV, for example, the narrator (or, more precisely, the storyteller) comments on the situation of his protagonist: "Let's assume that Vince's wife, had he a wife, never brought home from the store a particular brand of cereal that Vince liked." The content of section XXVII the narrator labels as "banal" if indeed "it can be called a story at all."

Sorrentino's manipulation of language is just as intentionally explicit as his narrative strategy. The reader is compelled to confront the author's word choice because he frequently places particular words or phrases in quotation marks or in italics, often highlighting his wry, subversive use of clichés. A good example can be found in sec-

∿

*Gilbert Sorrentino taught creative
writing at Stanford University for
seventeen years. He won two
Guggenheim Fellowships, was twice
named a PEN/Faulkner Award for
Fiction finalist, and received a Lannan
Literary Lifetime Achievement Award.*

∿

tion XXI, which focuses on how Martha invents her own content for her husband Larry's utterances, converting their marriage into her personal "improvisatory fantasia" characterized by the illusion that they are both "deeply respectful of each other's feelings."

Sorrentino is especially attuned to word choice and syntax, perhaps because he began his literary career as a poet; He published seven volumes of poetry before 1979, when his novel *Mulligan Stew* brought him to the attention of mainstream critics and caused him to redirect his principal focus to fiction.

Furthermore, sometimes because of their specific meaning in a given historical period and sometimes because of their discrete usage in the context of Sorrentino's narrative, some words and phrases are placed at the end of the book following the text proper in a section marked "commentaries." In essence, this conclusion to the novel is a glossary of more than 160 bits of text, ranging from a disquisition on the "weirdly orange" color of Kraft French dressing referred to in section I to a 1930's synonym for "white rayon underpants," referred to in section XIX as "step-ins."

Each section or mininarrative can be read on its own, but taken collectively, they underscore one overarching theme of the book, which is indicated by the title, quoted from a passage in the short story "The Middle Years" (1893) by Anglo-American novelist Henry James. In essence, according to James's tale, beneath the "surface and twinkle" of human existence lies a yawning gulf of self-generated illusion, which is "the real, the tideless deep."

In "The Middle Years," an author named Dencombe, somewhat resentful that his fiction has not reached a larger public, acknowledges in his final illness that the work alone matters, not the hope of public recognition. This idea obviously resonated with Sorrentino. Though critically acclaimed, like James, Sorrentino failed to gain a mass readership, but, also like James, he was nourished by his own personal devotion to the art of fiction.

It is not surprising, therefore, that a number of sections of the novel should be devoted to writers and their respective fates. Some, like the third-rate versifier who somehow still manages to become a "great success in the small, almost always weaselly world of poetry" (section XXXIII) and the "translator of late nineteenth century French poets" who in a "vaguely deluded way" thinks of himself as an artist (section XXXVI), are depicted as self-serving careerists, a term that Sorrentino reserves for those whose reputations are based not so much on their work but on their personal politicking. These writers—perhaps modeled after academic colleagues he had encountered over the years—are all essentially poseurs, and Sorrentino takes almost devilish delight in satirizing their inflated self-importance.

Of the eight mininarratives devoted to writers and artists in general, section XLIII may come closest to capturing the author's perception of his own situation at the time that he was writing his final novel. According to his son, the novelist Christopher Sorrentino, who wrote the preface to the book, Gilbert Sorrentino, diagnosed with cancer in 2005, persisted in the composition of what he called his "last book" despite his illness. After fifty years of work, just like Sorrentino, the old novelist in section XLIII continues to write because he is "doomed to blunder through the shadows of this pervasive twilight, until finally, perhaps, he would get said what could never be said."

Ironically, even those literary practitioners who come closest to replicating Sorrentino's own situation do not escape the author's relentlessly withering gaze. Each is in thrall to some essential illusion. The old writer in section XLVI, for example, is bored to tears by his work and skeptical of the enthusiastic encouragement of his new publisher, but he persists in "this foolishness" because he is "not quite ready to disappear into dead silence" and there may be a PEN/Faulkner Award for Fiction "waiting!"

Other patterns emerge as the reader navigates the stream of seemingly random stories. There is, for example, the return of characters from the author's earlier works. In section II, a boy listening to the "Philco floor-model radio" equates the "unearthly laughter" of the Shadow, the crime-fighting alter ego of pulp-fiction protagonist Lamont Cranston in a score of popular novels written by Walter B. Gibson during the 1930's and 1940's, to that of his dead grandmother. Readers are reminded of the twelve-year-old title character in Sorrentino's *Red the Fiend* (1995) who is terrorized by Grandma, who beats him daily.

Section XVI is essentially a reworking of the major elements of a railway car seduction described in the poem "A Dream for Winter" (1870) by the nineteenth century French poet Arthur Rimbaud, who inspired much of Sorrentino's novel *Splendide-Hotel* (1973). Given the poetic roots of Sorrentino's own literary career, it is therefore not surprising that poets, particularly such iconoclasts as Rimbaud, should figure prominently and repeatedly in his work.

In this particular section, which ends not with the sex act as in the Rimbaud original but with the young woman's refusal to acknowledge acquaintance with the young man after their night of erotic exploration, Sorrentino converts his protagonist to a soldier on leave. Three other tales in the book focus on soldiers and former soldiers, which also serve as staple characters in some of the author's earlier fiction. His repeated use of soldiers in his work may also spring from autobiographical sources; Sorrentino himself was drafted into the Army in the early 1950's and served as a medic in the United States during the Korean War. The commentary following section XXVI identifies the setting as a beer hall at Fort Hood, Texas, and the misadventures of the medic in section XLVII occur while he is on a weekend pass from the Medical Field Service School at Fort Sam Houston; Sorrentino was familiar with both locations from his days in the Army.

Sorrentino's repeated use of people and objects from his past highlights what might appear to be, on the surface, a contradiction in his compositional method. Although he begins each work with a preconceived form, such as the decision to write a novel composed of fifty mininarratives, Sorrentino then passively exposes himself to the currents of memory and dream, letting the content of each individual narrative be determined by largely unconscious forces. The overall process is a curious interplay of the intentional and unintentional.

In essence, Sorrentino's authorial stance informs one of the principal messages of this novel. While people strive for control and meaning in their lives, they end up with neither. Consider, in this regard, the author's refusal to assign objects any significance beyond their physical existence. Individuals may try to project value on these objects, such as the glass bottle of Kraft French dressing in Section I, but as the narrator asserts: "There is no meaning. These things will evoke nothing."

The illusion of meaning, just like all the other erroneous concepts and beliefs that people cling to in order to create order out of chaos, is a recurring theme in this collage of vignettes. What spares the reader from the cumulative effect of fifty sad stories, however, is the fact that Sorrentino leavens his pessimism with comedy, albeit dark. The painter whose life is encapsulated in section XLII, for example, is so "choked with misery" that before he finally succeeds in securing a "regular dealer or gallery" he chooses to become a waiter so that he can be "shouted at by the chefs, the head waiters, the bartenders" and "treated contemptuously by so many of the diners." In short, he delights in his masochistic choice of temporary livelihood because it mirrors his low self-image. In section XLIX, Audrey, a "large, hefty, yet rawboned woman of startling homeliness" clings stubbornly to her vegetarian habits and to the illusion that her faithless husband Billy will return to their unhappy marriage; in the final paragraph of the narrative, she is smoking a "cigarette made of some sort of rank legume," which envelopes her in a "cloud of smoke that smelled very like a burning barn."

This subversively comic overtone, most critics agree, makes the depressing situation of many of Sorrentino's characters somehow bearable, just as their generally stubborn persistence despite the bleakness of their lives adds the only modicum of dignity that they possess. The protagonist named Al in section XLI, for example, repaints his whole apartment, including the walls and ceilings of each room, after his wife leaves him, taking their two daughters with her. He himself acknowledges that the color, which he identifies as forest green, is "so gloomy and bleak that it seemed the representation of utter despair, a suicidal color, if one can call it a color, for it was somehow blacker than black." To the few friends that he has left, Al explains that "he was not yet dead if he could survive this tomb."

S. Thomas Mack

Review Sources

Contemporary Fiction 30, no. 1 (Spring, 2010): 246-247.
Literary Review 53, no. 3 (Spring, 2010): 207-213.
The New York Times Book Review, February 28, 2010, p. L7.
Review of Contemporary Fiction 30, no. 1 (Spring, 2010): 246-47.

ADAM SMITH
An Enlightened Life

Author: Nicholas Phillipson
Publisher: Yale University Press (New Haven, Conn.).
   345 pp. $32.50
Type of work: Biography, history, economics
Time: 1723-1790
Locale: Kirkcaldy, Edinburgh, and Glasgow, Scotland;
   and London

*Phillipson traces the career of a major figure of the Scot-
tish Enlightenment, an original thinker who wrote* Theory
of Moral Sentiments *(1759) and* Wealth of Nations *(1776)
and who coined the metaphor of the "invisible hand" to describe the rational behavior of free markets*

Principal personages:
> ADAM SMITH (1723-1790), an early promoter of free markets, but with
>   regulations
> FRANCIS HUTCHESON (1694-1746), his tutor at Glasgow University, and
>   a lifelong influence
> DAVID HUME (1711-1776), a brilliant philosopher and close friend of
>   and major influence on Smith

In *An Enlightened Life*, Nicholas Phillipson traces the life of Adam Smith, whose
parents were members of the Presbyterian gentry, on June 5, 1723, in the small town
of Kirkcaldy, a narrow strip of village on the Firth of Forth, ten miles north of Edinburgh, Scotland. His father, Adam Smith, Sr., held several significant appointments,
culminating in the post of controller of customs at Kirkcaldy. His mother, Margaret
Smith, née Douglas, was the elder Smith's second wife and the daughter of a well-to-
do fife laird. The younger Smith never married and was close to his mother, spending
long periods of his life with her.

Smith studied at the burgh school from 1731 to 1737, benefiting from the attention
of the school's master, David Miller, known for his practice of promoting civic education through drama. Classical texts such as Epictetus's *Encheiridion* (c. 138 C.E.;
English translation, 1567) and Cicero's *De Officiis* (44 B.C.E.; *On Duties*, 1534) were
probably supplemented by the *Spectator* essays of Joseph Addison and Sir Richard
Steele, all in service to the intertwined values of philosophy and public life. Phillipson
believes that these classics gave Smith a "simple but sophisticated way of looking at
the social world" and that Addison's essays revealed to him the "modern" commercial city as a complex pluralistic entity that had the power to improve as well as to
corrupt human nature.

Smith matriculated at Glasgow University in 1737 when he was fourteen and left

~

Nicholas Phillipson is a scholar of the Scottish Enlightenment, an Honorary Research Fellow in History at the University of Edinburgh, and an associate editor of The New Oxford Dictionary of National Biography.

~

there in 1740 to spend six years at Balliol College, Oxford. Almost nothing is known of Smith's activities in these years, but Phillipson sketches the intellectual climate of the time and speculates on what influences Smith must have encountered. Foremost among the teachers he certainly met was Francis Hutcheson, chair of moral philosophy, who regarded knowledge of human nature and the natural world as the foundation of study in theology. Hutcheson reacted against the teachings of the German Samuel von Pufendorf, whose Augustinian view of human nature Hutcheson rejected. Hutcheson admired the third earl of Shaftesbury, whose influential *Characteristicks of Men, Manners, Opinions, and Times* (1711) argued that human beings are basically benevolent. In this respect, Shaftesbury's vision ran counter to that of the satirist Bernard Mandeville, whose *The Fable of the Bees: Or, Private Vices, Publick Benefits* (1714) sneered at all standards as mere delusions masking humankind's natural depravity. Hutcheson instead posited a natural moral sense grounded in the love of God and the enabling of a society of virtuous citizens. Smith never accepted Hutcheson's belief in a moral sense, but he took to heart Hutcheson's emphasis on sociability and everyday social interaction.

Smith left Oxford in May, 1740, and after visiting his mother in Kirkcaldy, went on to Oxford, where he studied privately for six years. He taught himself French and probably read the fashionable French philosophers of the day, but, says Phillipson, he found their grim outlook on human nature "uncongenial and even silly." For example, he called Blaise Pascal a "whining moralist." The novelist Marivaux, however, was a thinker whose concerns for the problems of ordinary people impressed Smith. Far more important than the influence of French thinkers, however, was that of David Hume, which provided the "decisive event in Smith's intellectual development." Hume insisted that all "knowledge originated in the imagination," and his skepticism extended even to the source of mathematical thought. Smith "never forgot the fundamental human principle that theology . . . was a product of the imagination and one that was capable of breeding delusions that could be particularly destructive of society." Hume taught that what humans call knowledge is more a form of understanding developed from daily ideas and sentiments. Philosophy, then, should study how humans acquire these ideas and sentiments and why they create elaborate intellectual and aesthetic systems. The human capacity for sociability derives from a sensibility that is not innate but is instead traceable to an acquired sense of justice, a state of affairs that obligates government to administer justice and preserve lives and property. "It was a theory that was built on the belief that the progress of society depended on the efforts of individuals to better their lot, rather than on radical exercises in political engineering."

Between 1748 and 1751, Smith delivered a series of lectures on rhetoric and jurisprudence at the University of Edinburgh. Rhetoric, he taught, encourages a sense of propriety vital to social discourse, and a theory of jurisprudence underpins a system of justice. The progress of opulence was a key to Smith's understanding of the central significance of the division of labor, a division dependent on the market. The content of these lectures is not recorded, but Phillipson surmises that Smith was working out ideas that would appear in *Wealth of Nations*, such as this passage copied down by his colleague Dugald Stewart: "Little else is requisite to carry a free state to the highest degree of opulence from the lowest barbarism, but peace, easy taxes, and a tolerable administration of justice." Elsewhere Smith would make it clear that the "invisible hand" relied on peace and a just system of regulation.

Smith published *Theory of Moral Sentiments* in 1759. It was his explanation for how humans learn the principles of morality from everyday experience. Crucial to this education was the sympathy for others that enables humans to live peacefully, and only by the imagination can humans feel sympathy. Furthermore, this sympathy led Smith to political conclusions: If one can feel sorrow for sufferers, one should also feel joy for the rich and prosperous. By deferring to these happy few, people strengthen political stability, and by working hard to get ahead and emulate them, humans advance the whole global community. Smith explains why people seek this material gratification: "To be observed, to be attended to, to be taken notice of with sympathy, complacency, and approbation, are all the advantages we can propose to derive from it. It is the vanity, not the ease, or the pleasure, which interests us."

Smith then asked why it is that citizens feel it necessary to follow the precepts of justice. He concluded that, besides shame and fear, many people suffer cruel feelings of remorse, "of all the sentiments which can enter the human breast the most dreadful." To flesh out this theory, Smith rejected Jean-Jacques Rousseau's argument that humans' moral sensibilities are shaped by the opinions of others, postulating instead an impartial spectator, a "man within the breast, whose voice counsels and guides us to virtue." Smith was persuaded, in Phillipson's words, "that the satisfaction of being able to live sociably under the direction of the impartial spectator was enough for humankind."

In his lectures at Glasgow University between 1759 and 1763, Smith stressed two points that were central to his philosophy. From Hume he took his conviction that without property there can be no government, which arises from the need to protect wealth, guarding the rich from the poor. However, he taught that the inheritance laws had, as Phillipson notes, "more to do with perpetuating the power of the nobility than with facilitating the workings of a market economy," and he trusted the nobility only insofar as they had an enlightened education. At this time, Smith also outlined his arguments for the division of labor as the foundation of opulence, an important theme in *Wealth of Nations*. With these two important tenets—the vital role of property and the stimulus provided by the division of labor—by 1763, Smith had transformed European thinking.

Smith's growing reputation as a teacher prompted Charles Townshend, the young duke of Buccleuch's stepfather and guardian, to give him a generous salary to serve as Buccleuch's tutor and companion. Smith had already served several months at Glasgow as tutor to Thomas Fitzmaurice, son of a wealthy Anglo-Irish peer, and found the work congenial enough to accept Townshend's offer. Smith met Buccleuch in London in January, 1764, and they traveled to France the next month, soon settling in Toulouse to begin the education Smith was to provide. A highlight of their stay was a two-month visit to Geneva, where Smith greatly enjoyed the company of Voltaire. From Geneva, they went to Paris, where Hume introduced Buccleuch to French intellectual society, a social life that Smith reveled in. The most stimulating of Smith's acquaintances was to be François Quesnay, the centerpiece of the group of thinkers known as the *économistes*. Despite their many points of accord, Smith could not wholeheartedly accept Quesnay's teachings on land as the key to political economy.

The sudden death of Buccleuch's brother ended the European tour in 1766. Smith then returned to London but only until the spring of 1767, when he settled down in Kirkcaldy for six years while drafting *Wealth of Nations*. He had already worked out his theory of the division of labor, and he shaped this into a labor-based analysis of value and price focused on the natural and market price of commodities. Crucial to his arguments was the central importance he gave to a system of free markets and free exchange in stimulating economic growth. Quesnay's teachings were often on Smith's mind, but the French thinker's vision of economics becoming a mathematically exact science was completely foreign to Smith's mentality. In this respect he remained Hume's disciple, rejecting absolute knowledge in favor of subjective understanding. Competing philosophical systems would rise and fall on the strength and appeal of their proponents' rhetorical prowess. In the spring of 1773, Smith returned to London to finish *Wealth of Nations* and enjoy some satisfying socializing with Edmund Burke and Edward Gibbon.

An Inquiry into the Nature and Causes of the Wealth of Nations was published in two volumes on March 9, 1776. Smith's discerning readers soon realized that his opus was, as Phillipson observes, "deeply embedded in a system of moral philosophy, jurisprudence and politics about which most of his readers knew nothing." Much of the book's substance, such as the claim that labor and not money determined price and value, had been outlined in earlier works, but it needed refinement. The three determinants of price—rent, wages, and profits—required attention, as did the landowners, wage earners, and manufacturers and merchants, whom he identified as "the three great, original and constituent orders of every society, from whose revenue that of every other order is ultimately derived." None of these orders, however, was without weakness. Landowners were too rich and indolent to understand public regulation, wage earners were cramped by their poverty, and merchants and manufacturers, in Phillipson's words, "had no hesitation in using [their superior understanding] to gull others into believing that their interests were the same as their own." These men have often both "deceived and oppressed the public." Smith expressed great confidence in the thrift of individuals intent on improving their lot but called governments the greatest spendthrifts in society and a government of merchants "the worst of all governments." In supporting domestic industry the individual is, in effect, being guided by an "invisible hand" that unintentionally advances the broad public interest.

In January, 1778, Smith moved with his mother to Edinburgh, where he took up a seat on the board of customs. He published a final, third edition of *Wealth of Nations* in 1784, the year his mother died, and managed, despite failing strength, to complete a new edition of *Theory of Moral Sentiments* in 1788. He told a friend that his body was "breaking down," however, and he died on July 17, 1790.

Smith is often cited by conservative economists in support of their free-trade absolutism, but his ultimate purpose was always to strengthen sociability through the rules of justice, and his supporters should not overlook his conviction that the invisible hand could easily pick the citizens' pockets in the absence of peace and just regulation. Phillipson has written a fine book.

Frank Day

Review Sources

The Economist 396, no. 8694 (August 7, 2010): 84.
Library Journal 135, no. 16 (October, 2010): 80.
London Review of Books 32, no. 19 (October 7, 2010): 21-23.
National Review 62, no. 21 (November 15, 2010): 46-48.
New Statesman 139, no. 5014 (August 16, 2010): 48-49.
The New Yorker 86, no. 32 (October 18, 2010): 82-87.
The Spectator 314, no. 9507 (November 13, 2010): 55-57.

ALL THE WHISKEY IN HEAVEN
Selected Poems

Author: Charles Bernstein (1950-   )
Publisher: Farrar, Straus and Giroux (New York).
   300 pp. $26.00
Type of work: Poetry

*A startling and inventive selection of poems that show-
cases Bernstein as a giant of postmodern poetry*

Charles Bernstein has been stimulating and confounding the poetry world since the publication of his first collection *Asylums* (1975). He is considered one of the central
figures in the rise of Language poetry during the 1970's
and the 1980's. He has played an integral role in show-
casing a more radical style of poetics for more than thirty
years. Language is essential to all poetry, but for the Language poets, the arrangement
of words, and the very words themselves, become the journey and the focal point.

For Bernstein's poetry the reader can essentially throw subject matter and structure out the window. The beauty of the words becomes more radiant by how phrases
crash into one another. In reality, art can only happen through collision. The final creative product can be considered a maze that entices the reader to take the journey.
Bernstein describes how he is driven by "The sense of music in poetry" and the desire
to push any "composition to the very limits of sense, meaning, to that razor's edge
where judgment/aesthetic sense is all I can go on (know-how)." The poet becomes a
conductor of various elements, such as shapes, sounds, and the measurement of many
objects. This bizarre sort of orchestration sparks the creation of an end product that
can be called a poem. The finished poem may work even when the poet is not really
sure how or why. Bernstein has stated that he attempts to stretch his mind as far as it
will go in order to push a poem into being. His willingness to experiment, to prod, and
to write outside the lines has established him as one of the most important postmodern
poets working in the United States.

Bernstein has been identified as both a poet and an antipoet. Over the years, he has
made much of molding language like one would a pretzel. It is not merely words that
are placed on his examination table; more times than not, letters must stand on their
own. It is almost like he is a modern-day Dr. Frankenstein, busily working in his basement, breathing life into various parts that he has gathered together. Bernstein is well
aware that not all experiments will succeed, but there is a learning curve that will
come into play for the next time.

During the late 1960's, Bernstein attended Harvard University and protested against
the Vietnam War. He was a philosophy major and wrote his senior thesis on Ludwig
Wittgenstein and Gertrude Stein. These events were the building blocks for a poet with

subversive tendencies. He and Bruce Andrews started the magazine $L=A=N=G=U=A=G=E$ in 1978. Although the magazine lasted only until 1981, it was an influential Language publication. Pushing boundaries, whether poetic, cultural, or sociopolitical, was at the heart of what Bernstein was after. Since the 1980's, he has taught at various institutions. He joined the faculty of the University of Pennsylvania in 2003 as the Donald T. Regan Professor of English and Comparative Literature.

Charles Bernstein is the author of more than thirty stimulating and experimental works in a number of genres, including poetry, essays, librettos, and translations. He has established himself as one of the most prominent postmodern poets and thinkers of his generation.

Taking inspiration from Ezra Pound's approach to poetics, Bernstein has challenged mainstream poetry. It has been his mantra to expand what poetry, language, and words in general can accomplish. Words have weight, value, and baggage. A particular word may have been manipulated—even exploited—over the centuries by those who wished to promote a certain mythology or history. For Bernstein, words must be freed of the roles that they have been assigned. All of these inventive avenues are employed in order to free words and to free poetry from the shackles of the past.

Bernstein has instituted the radical idea that the product or poem is more important than the identity of the poet. The poet serves as the assembler of the text. The radical idea for a poet such as Bernstein is that it is left to the reader to piece together a meaning for the poem. This is not necessarily an easy task. For Bernstein, the poet is merely the presenter. The serious, committed reader becomes the translator and the final arbiter of what the text means. As a political act, this is a democratic exercise. Words do have consequence, and they are in need of close examination. Each person involved in the process must be willing to invest energy and critical purpose in what text they are reading. Past conclusions and historical assumptions cannot win the day or be taken at face value.

Since the 1970's, Bernstein has been requiring readers to join in an adventure that risks much but rewards even more. The selected poems that have been gathered together to make *All the Whiskey in Heaven* give the reader a wildly adventurous poetic sojourn. As an introduction to what Bernstein has had up his sleeve for as long as his radical impulse has been active stands as an extraordinary statement. He has put it bluntly, stating that he wanted "to put the art part back in poetry, which means considering many different ways that one word can follow another, one phrase can collide or merge with the next."

Bernstein readily admits that his approach to poetry is not for everyone. Although poetry holds a marginal place in society at best, Bernstein thinks of poetry "as a fundamental activity within our culture." In this collection that attempts to house a career, the reader is presented with how the poet became himself. It is an evolution of thought and imagination that has been brought together for public consumption. With nineteen volumes being drawn from for *All the Whiskey in Heaven*, there is much to be challenged by and much to take the conscientious reader out of complacency. For his 1979 collection *Poetic Justice*, Bernstein includes the poem "AZOOT D'PUUND," which appears to be no more than a jumble of typographical experiments. It opens with "iz wurry ray aZoOt de puund in reducey ap crrRisLe ehk nugkinj/ sJuxYY senshl." What is the reader supposed to do with such a baffling text? Can any meaning be established upon a close reading? This may seem to be no more than nonsense or, at worst, some sort of sabotage perpetrated upon an innocent public. The challenge is not to throw it away or to give up on the exercise. Bernstein can be considered a mischievous devil looking to corrupt all innocent consumers of true poetry, but he is honestly hoping that he will find a select few willing to take the plunge, willing to reconsider their preconceived ideas of what poetry must deliver. He appears to be the alternative to what has been identified as "respectable" poetry.

While a poem such as "AZOOT D'PUUND" may stand at the most radical end of the spectrum, Bernstein does not always inhabit that realm. He is a poet of vast possibilities. He has always argued for broadening the boundaries of poetry and not merely setting constraints as to what poetry should look like. Bernstein's 1980 collection *Controlling Interests* brings together poems that are rich in their excess of free-flowing words. In the long poem "Matters of Policy," the words seem to tumble from poet to reader. The poem opens with "On the broad plain in a universe of/ anterooms, making signals in the dark, you/ fall down on your waistband &, carrying your/ own plate, a last serving, set out for/ another glimpse of a gaze." Though the reader may want more of a glimpse of this Bernstein as opposed to the poet of "AZOOT D'PUUND," the poem continues to be a true smorgasbord of images, wit, fancy, and meditations as it advances toward an ending in which a "captain gently/ chides farewell to us with a luminous laugh." Such a laugh is not uncommon in a Bernstein creation. He revels in the merely amusing, the darkly sinister, the totally absurd. "Matters of Policy" ends with "The surrounding buildings have a stillness/ that is brought into ironic ridicule by the pounding/ beats of the bongo drums emanating from the candy/ store a few blocks away." What the reader ends up taking away from this poem is primarily up to what the reader is willing to invest. Again and again, Bernstein emphasizes the two-way street that exists between poet and reader.

The relationship between poet and reader becomes even more evident with Bernstein's 2001 collection *With Strings*. There is a poem, "The Boy Soprano," that employs an obvious rhyme scheme; the last stanza presents teachers who "teach the grandest things/ Tell how poetry's words on wings/ But wings are for Heaven, not for earth/ Want my advice: hijack the hearse."

Irreverence and playfulness are crucial to Bernstein. The craft should not take control of a poem. For Bernstein it is "the extremity, the eccentricity, even the didacticism, that shakes things up." Poetry must not become too "normalized" or too "oriented toward craft." When poetry goes down that establishment road "it loses the point." Another poem from *With Strings* contains only a title. On the page there is nothing but the title "This Poem Intentionally Left Blank." For this poem enough has been said. More defiance can be found in *Girly Man* (2006). Bernstein takes on the subject of the terrorist attacks of September 11, 2001, and the Iraq War. As a postmodernist poet who has taken jabs at all the sacred cows, Bernstein was not going to be silenced by the crisis that the United States was facing. He was still going to respond to what he views as "illogical" pronouncements and actions taken in the name of patriotism. The poem "War Stories" consists of one statement after another about what war truly is. It begins with "War is the extension of prose by other means./ War is never to say you're sorry./ War is the logical outcome of moral certainty." After several pages of provocative statements, Bernstein ends the poem with "War is 'over here.'/ War is the answer./ War is here./ War is this./ War is now./ War is us."

All the Whiskey in Heaven represents more than thirty years of stimulating postmodern poetry that Bernstein has published. The collection proves how, at his best, Bernstein is a positive force for change on many fronts. What language can and cannot accomplish in a poem is provocatively on display in *All the Whiskey in Heaven*. The title poem closes out the collection with an emphatic pronouncement that he will "never stop loving" his wife Susan to whom this collection is dedicated. He will not change how he feels. "Not even for all the whiskey in heaven," "all the flies in Vermont," "all the tears in the basement," or "a million trips to Mars." He has the strength of character not to be distracted by things that are not important. Bernstein has adhered to that mantra in his creative life as well.

Jeffry Jensen

Review Sources

Entertainment Weekly 257, no. 8 (April 16, 2010): 75.
Forward 113 (March 26, 2010): 15.
The New York Times Book Review, April 11, 2010, p. 20.
Publishers Weekly 257, no. 8 (February 22, 2010): 47.

AMERICA AND THE PILL
A History of Promise, Peril, and Liberation

Author: Elaine Tyler May (1947-   )
Publisher: Basic Books (New York). 214 pp. $25.95
Type of work: History, women's issues
Time: The late nineteenth century to 2010
Locale: United States

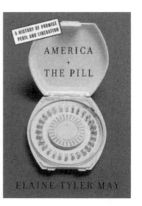

On the fiftieth anniversary of Food and Drug Administration (FDA) approval of an oral contraceptive for women, May examines the birth control pill's origins, the expectations of its developers and proponents, and its social impact

Principal personages:
MARGARET SANGER (1879-1966), an early
  feminist and a birth-control advocate
KATHERINE DEXTER MCCORMICK (1875-1967), the heiress who funded
  research that developed the pill
JOHN ROCK, the director of the Brookline, Massachusetts, Reproductive
  Study Center and pioneer in reproductive studies
GREGORY GOODWIN PINCUS (1903-1967), another researcher
  instrumental in the pill's development
EDWARD TYLER, the author's father, involved in clinical trials of the pill
ESTELLE GRISWOLD (1900-1981), the executive director of the Planned
  Parenthood League of Connecticut

In 1993, *The Economist* hailed oral conception as one of the seven wonders of the modern world. In *America and the Pill*, Elaine Tyler May offers a more nuanced view. A scholar who writes about family and women's issues, she describes how the pill affected women's lives in ways that its developers never envisioned. She warns against attributing these societal changes solely to the pill, though. For example, the pill is available in Saudi Arabia, but women there may not drive cars.

One of May's earlier books, *Barren in the Promised Land: Childless Americans and the Pursuit of Happiness* (1995), deals with infertility. This issue is connected to her work because, ironically, the pill was initially developed, at least in part, to combat infertility. *America and the Pill* is of personal and academic interest to May, and she dedicated the book to her parents. Her mother, Lillian B. Tyler, set up birth-control clinics in Los Angeles, where she distributed the pill free to her patients. Overseeing these clinics was May's father, Edward Tyler, who participated in clinical trials of the pill and influenced the FDA's decision to license the first oral contraceptive.

As May points out, the pill was hardly the first contraceptive device. For millennia, women have practiced birth control through abstinence, coitus interruptus, condoms, spermacides, and abortion. In Philip Roth's 1959 novel *Goodbye, Columbus*, Brenda

Patimkin goes to a clinic to be fitted for a dia-
phragm so she can have sex with her boyfriend, Neil Klugman, without fear of pregnancy. In Mary McCarthy's 1954 "Dottie
Makes an Honest Woman of Herself," the
sexually liberated heroine also secures a dia-
phragm. May writes that well before the pill,
between 1800 and 1900, the U.S. birthrate declined by 50 percent. By the latter half of the
nineteenth century men sought to restrict access to contraception, even to bar knowledge
about it. The 1873 Comstock Act, named for
postal inspector Anthony Comstock, banned
dissemination of contraceptive information through the mail. The women's rights
movement of the late nineteenth century fought not only for the right to vote but also
for reproductive freedom. Margaret Sanger, at the forefront of the women's movement, coined the term "birth control" in 1915.

*Elaine Tyler May teaches at the
University of Minnesota. Her books
include* Homeward Bound: American
Families in the Cold War Era *(1998),*
Barren in the Promised Land: Childless
Americans and the Pursuit of
Happiness *(1995), and* Great
Expectations: Marriage and Divorce in
Post-Victorian America *(1980).*

Sanger's Catholic mother had given birth to eleven children and had died at the age
of fifty. Sanger, a nurse, saw many women similarly exhausted from multiple pregnancies or dying as a result of back-alley abortions. She also believed that women
would enjoy sex more if they were freed from the fear of pregnancy. Sanger and her
husband repeatedly challenged the Comstock Act and were repeatedly arrested for
their efforts, but in 1936, they triumphed when the U.S. Circuit Court of Appeals
granted doctors the right to distribute birth-control information. In 1916, Sanger was
jailed when she opened the country's first birth-control clinic. However, by 1942,
more than eight hundred such facilities were serving women across the nation.

In 1917, Sanger met the wealthy Katherine Dexter McCormick, wife of the heir to
the International Harvester Company fortune. McCormick used her wealth to under-
write research on the pill; as late as 1959, the U.S. government refused to fund such
work. The person McCormick chose to lead this project, Gregory Goodwin Pincus,
was seeking a cure to infertility. To assist with human trials of the drug Pincus turned
to obstetrician and gynecologist John Rock, who shared Pincus's interest in alleviating sterility. Much of the testing was done in Puerto Rico, which had no laws against
contraception and maintained sixty-seven birth-control clinics. In 1957, the FDA approved the pill to treat infertility, and only three years later, the agency licensed it for
preventing pregnancy.

May emphasizes that many of the pill's early supporters cared little about giving
women control over their bodies. Even by the 1950's, Sanger regarded the pill as a
means of furthering the eugenics movement. Many others envisioned the pill as a
weapon in the Cold War against communism. In the immediate post-World War II
period, the birthrate of developing countries was twice that of the developed nations.
Overpopulation led to poverty, which bred discontent, which in turn could foster
communism. Books such as Edward Stockwell's *Population and People* (1958) and

Paul R. Ehrlich's *The Population Bomb* (1958) warned of dire consequences if the birthrate did not decline. Ehrlich helped found the organization Zero Population Growth. Even in the United States failure to curb the population increase—the United States was in the midst of a baby boom—would, it was feared, lead to increased crime (juvenile delinquency was a major concern during the 1950's), urban violence, and higher taxes to pay for welfare. The Dwight D. Eisenhower administration had opposed government funding for birth control, but under U.S. presidents John F. Kennedy and Lyndon B. Johnson this policy changed. By 1969, the federal government was spending $56.3 million at home and another $131.7 overseas for family planning.

Population growth slowed, but, May argues, not because of the pill. Among the reasons she cites are coercive government policies in Asia, which included forced sterilization in India and China's one-child policy. Increased education and employment opportunities, especially in the West, encouraged women to get out of the house. May acknowledges that the pill helped these women, but it was a tool for, not a cause of, their liberation.

May also rejects the contention that the pill created the sexual revolution of the 1960's. According to her, most of the pill's early users were married women planning their pregnancies. Also, despite Philip Larkin's tongue-in-cheek claim in "Annus Mirabilis" that "Sexual intercourse began/ In nineteen sixty-three/ . . . / Between the end of the *Chatterley* ban/ And the Beatles' first LP," by the early 1950's, one-half of American women were engaging in sex before marriage. This figure did not change much in the next decade. Sociologist Ira Reiss reported in 1968 that 60 percent of women graduating from college were virgins, about the same figure as before the introduction of the pill. Also, the pill did not change attitudes toward premarital sex. A 1964 survey of women at the University of Kansas found an overwhelming 91 percent opposed to premarital sex except with a fiancé. Moreover, most sexually active, single, young women did not take the pill. A 1972 national survey found that 75 percent of these women never or rarely used any form of contraception.

The pill has nonetheless affected society, serving as a flashpoint for women's challenges to authority. Estelle Griswold, executive director of Connecticut's Planned Parenthood League, joined by Charles Lee Buxton of the Yale School of Medicine, sued to overturn her state's ban on contraception. The Supreme Court ruling that ensued struck down such prohibitions across the country (*Griswold v. Connecticut*, 1965). Catholic John Rich, one of the pill's developers, urged his church's leaders to alter their opposition to birth control. In 1964, Pope Paul VI appointed a committee to review the Catholic Church's position. A majority favored lifting the ban, but in 1968, the pope's encyclical *Humanae Vitae* restated the traditional view. Catholic women in the West, at least, rejected the Church's doctrine, which served only to contribute to the rift between the papacy and the laity and to the erosion of the Vatican's authority.

Although the medical profession created the pill, it, too, was subject to opposing its use. The first report on the pill's side effects appeared in 1961, just one year after the FDA approved the drug. These side effects included blood clots, strokes, nausea, diarrhea, headaches, weight gain, depression, and diminished libido. In 1969, Barbara Seaman published *The Doctor's Case Against the Pill*, which set out the pill's health risks. The 1998 edition of *Our Bodies, Ourselves*, published by the nonprofit group of the same name, urged women to choose another form of birth control. Such concern contributed to the development of lower-dose and therefore safer versions of the pill. These objections showed that women would no longer passively accept the dictates of doctors and scientists any more than they would necessarily heed those of church and state.

Men as well as women were liberated by the pill. They no longer had to struggle with condoms or practice coitus interruptus to avoid possible pregnancy, and women freed from this fear could respond to sex more passionately. *Playboy* magazine endorsed the pill because it allowed women to engage in sex more freely. However, May writes, not all men responded positively to the pill. Some resented women's greater reproductive freedom. Psychiatrist Rollo May blamed the pill for increased male impotence, and fellow psychiatrist Andrew Ferber said that women's use of the pill lowered men's sex drive.

Additionally, men have not shown much enthusiasm for their own version of the pill. May discusses the quest for such a drug. Enovid, the first female oral contraceptive, also worked for men by stopping sperm production, but it erased male sexual desire and impaired the ability to achieve erection. China's experiments with Gossypol revealed other problems with a male pill, including heart attacks and permanent sterility. A scientific challenge to a male version of the pill is the constant production of sperm, whereas women ovulate only once a month. May is correct, however, in attributing much of the problem to cultural bias, which places the burden of contraception on women. It is revealing that scientists have developed a pill to reduce female fertility and others to heighten male potency. Moreover, men are less accepting of side effects. They would not tolerate the bloating, headaches, and nausea that women accept from oral contraception.

An Internet survey that May conducted shows that women remained ambivalent about the pill fifty years after its introduction. Many claimed to be liberated by it. Some found that it helped with acne problems, reduced menstrual cramps, and gave them larger breasts. Women reported that the pill fostered open discussions with partners and friends about sex and birth control and so brought them closer together. Others objected to its side effects. Another complaint was that doctors pressured women, even lesbians, into taking the pill. Whereas in 1960 the most feared consequence of sex was pregnancy, in the twenty-first century, for many the greatest fear is sexually transmitted diseases, against which the pill offers no protection.

For all its limitations, the pill, according to May, has liberated women in ways that its early proponents could not have imagined. By giving women greater control over reproduction than they had ever enjoyed before, the pill allowed them to pursue educational and employment opportunities that child rearing would have denied them. Feminism, rather than the pill, created these options, but the pill facilitated women's ability to take advantage of them. The concerns that the pill raised also encouraged women to challenge bastions of male authority, thus strengthening the women's movement.

Joseph Rosenblum

Review Sources

Booklist 106, no. 16 (April 15, 2010): 7.
Culture and Books 21 (May, 2010): 50.
Library Journal 135 (May 1, 2010): 86.
Nature 465, no. 7295 (May 13, 2010): 164.
Publishers Weekly 257 (March 15, 2010): 45.
Reason 42, no. 3 (July, 2010): 61-63.

AMERICAN TALIBAN

Author: Pearl Abraham (1960-　　)
Publisher: Random House (New York). 258 pp. $25.00
Type of work: Novel
Time: August, 2000-May, 2002
Locale: Washington, D.C.; Pakistan; Outer Banks, North
　　Carolina; and New York City

*Abraham's novel chronicles a young man's spiritual
journey as he moves from a tentative encounter with the
quasi-spiritual writings of Bob Dylan through a more serious rumination on spiritual traditions such as Taoism to a
full embrace of a militant branch of Islam*

Principal characters:
　　JOHN JUDE PARISH, protagonist
　　BARBARA PARISH, his mother
　　BILL PARISH, his father
　　KATIE, his girlfriend
　　KHALED, his friend
　　YUSEF, his friend

Pearl Abraham's *American Taliban* begins in August, 2000, as nineteen-year-old
surfer and skateboarder John Jude Parish is hanging out on the Outer Banks of North
Carolina with his girlfriend, Katie, and two other girls in search of some big waves.
Parish has deferred his freshman year at Brown simply because he is not ready to give
up his freedom—surfing, skating, and reading—to sit in college classrooms and be
forced to read books outside his interests. John's mother, Barbara, and his father, Bill,
are former 1960's radicals who evolved into solid, middle-class citizens in Washington, D.C. They are still active in various liberal political causes, though socially and
religiously they have become more conservative. Neither of John's parents is entirely
happy with their son's decision to defer college for a year of reading and thinking, but
both seem willing to accept it as long as John keeps up with a reading list he has made
for himself. However, his parents play a small role in the novel and are not fully
drawn characters; therefore, there is little sympathy for their concerns, even at the end
of the novel, when almost the entire narrative is devoted to them and their worries
about their son.

　　John's summer moves along languorously until the middle of August when fate
turns against him momentarily. One day he is watching his wahines—the group of
girl surfers with whom he spends his time—compete in a surfing competition. John
has little recollection of the end of the contest, though, for the next morning he wakes
up in a hospital bed in a series of casts, having crashed his skateboard. The once free-
and-easy John finds himself confined and limited to a hospital bed. During this early

~

Pearl Abraham is an assistant professor of English at Western New England College, where she teaches creative writing and fiction. She is the author of three previous novels: The Romance Reader *(1995),* Giving Up America *(1998), and* The Seventh Beggar *(2006).*

~

crisis, John decides to start living like a mystic, and he composes a ten-week reading list that includes the *Tao Te Ching*, Walt Whitman's "Song of Myself" (1855), Ralph Waldo Emerson's *Nature* (1836), Elaine Pagels's *The Gnostic Gospels* (1979), Anthony Scaduto's *Bob Dylan: An Intimate Biography* (1971), Søren Kierkegaard's *Frygt og Bæven: Dialektisk lyrik* (1843; *Fear and Trembling: A Dialectical Lyric*, 1939), the Qurʾān, and Ibn al-ʿArabī's mystical poems, among other works. In bed for twelve weeks, John commences his journey into the mystic, a quest aided by his chat room conversations about Islam with various members of his Internet community. While the conversations in the chat room revolve around the differences and similarities among Christianity, Judaism, and Islam, John is more interested in the mystical poetry of the Sufis and whether or not Western translations of the poetry have been faithful to the Arabic. One of the newest members in the chat room is a young Muslim woman named Noor, who responds to John's questions about aesthetics and poetry and with whom John starts to correspond outside the chat room by e-mail. The two discuss the freedom that Muslim law allows women and the kind of freedom that most westerners experience. John is incredulous that a woman subject to her father and the men in her society can speak so boldly about the powerful freedom that she experiences in her culture. Attracted by Noor's ideas, John itches to escape his bedroom hermitage in Washington, D.C., for the Brooklyn Sharia School of Classical Arabic.

While John's parents are perplexed by their son's sudden interest in Islam and classical Arabic poetry, they nevertheless help him move to Brooklyn to get settled in his new apartment. Thus begins John's spiritual quest that takes him from the Sharia school in Brooklyn to Islamia College in Peshawar, Pakistan, to a retreat in the mountains of Kashmir. The retreat turns out to be a militant training camp, and while John is initially reluctant to participate in the activities of the camp, he eventually embraces the discipline so strongly that he joins Taliban fighters in Afghanistan.

Once John joins the Afghan Taliban, he disappears from the view of his parents, and the story takes a new and not-so-convincing turn. Abraham weaves into the novel the true story of John Walker Lindh, a young American man arrested by American forces in Afghanistan for fighting against American forces. Because John Jude Parish was incommunicado for several months and because Lindh's story and Parish's story are so similar, Barbara Parish is certain that Lindh is her son. Her voice dominates the last third of the novel and considerably weakens an otherwise fast-paced and engrossing narrative dominated by John's quest to find himself. In spite of these final chapters, the novel nevertheless demonstrates powerfully how easily one individual can be caught up in a journey to move beyond the strictures and confinement of one social and religious tradition and embrace a new one that more clearly articulates his understanding of others, the world, and the divine.

The themes of freedom and subjection dominate the novel, and Abraham weaves them subtly throughout this coming-of-age tale. From the beginning of the novel, when he spends his days surfing and skateboarding, John experiences a kind of artificial freedom; in spite of the fact that he seems not to be limited by the rules of society while on either of his boards, he is still subject to the laws of nature and, more broadly, to the laws of a society that regulate the spaces (beaches and sidewalks) in which he plies his trade. Moreover, his freedom is only a temporary one; for as much as he would like to spend the rest of his days surfing, he has merely deferred his subjection to a college curriculum and to a way of life imposed upon him by his parents and his society. After his accident, John is literally subjected to the confinement of his room, but he experiences a new kind of freedom in his conversations with Noor and others. He can discuss any aspect of Islam that he wishes as an anonymous contributor to this chat room, and his discussions with Noor encourage him to explore freely the history and nature of Islam.

Once John enters the Brooklyn school, he encounters a different kind of subjection: He is not only subject to his schoolmasters but also to the derogatory comments of his classmates who believe that this American is only playing at being Muslim. Once John moves beyond this school to Pakistan and to the militant camp, the conflict between freedom and subjection comes to a climax. The book poses the questions of whether or not John has achieved true freedom by so deeply embracing the laws of a new religion and whether or not he has been molded into a person that he did not want to be. Abraham examines whether or not John has discovered a freedom beyond freedom—that is, in so deeply embracing the laws of the new religion has he moved beyond its details and its stricter interpretations? Other issues of freedom remain, and the reader is left to wonder if John's role as a fighter for the Taliban was a choice or not. While John's mother, and much of American society, is ready to accuse Islam of robbing her son of his freedom, Abraham demonstrates superbly that the answers are not simple ones and that John's decisions grow not out of blind acceptance of a particular religious teaching but out of an honest struggle to understand the teachings of Islam and to understand how these teachings might inform his own life.

Most reviewers of *American Taliban* offer generous praise for Abraham's efforts, but many criticize the novel for its unwarranted lapse into a narrative dominated by John's mother. While most critics agree that John's search to find himself and his identity is the core of the book and its most interesting and engrossing story, at least one reviewer concludes that the sympathy of readers will be for John's confused and scared mother. Abraham's novel, however, is more successful than some others—most notably, John Updike's *Terrorist* (2006)—in exploring the fragility of youthful identity and the yearnings of a young person to feel accepted and to belong. Even more than that, Abraham takes seriously John's struggles with a religion not his own and his spiritual journey in general; she refuses to treat John's quest as merely another phase in his life or as a shallow attempt to belong to a larger group. Her portrayal of John provides readers with a sympathetic character whose struggles mirror those of real people. John Jude Parish's name is an interesting combination of Christian references to John the Apostle; Jude, the writer of the shortest New Testament book, which deals with imprisonment; and parish (which could also echo the word "perish"), which describes a particular area under the care of the Catholic Church. Abraham captures cannily the young protagonist's fascination with Islam, his progressive acceptance of its teachings, and his active participation in an Islamic jihadist movement in Afghanistan. Her portrait demonstrates convincingly the unease that Americans continue to harbor about Islam after September 11, 2001. She portrays superbly the faltering steps that a young person might take toward making a decision to adopt a religious tradition and the uncertain effects that such a decision might have on his family.

Henry L. Carrigan, Jr.

Review Sources

Booklist 106, no. 14 (March 15, 2010): 18.
Kirkus Reviews 78, no. 4 (February 15, 2010): 95.
Library Journal 135, no. 3 (February 15, 2010): 84.
Publishers Weekly 257, no. 2 (January 11, 2010): 27.
USA Today, April 29, 2010, p. 5D.

ANGELOLOGY

Author: Danielle Trussoni (1973-   )
Publisher: Viking (New York). 452 pp. $27.95
Type of work: Novel
Time: September, 1939-Christmas Day, 1999
Locale: New York City, the Hudson River Valley, Paris, and Bulgaria

A nun discovers that the powerful offspring of angels and humans have been plotting to gain control of the world

Principal characters:
    SISTER EVANGELINE CACCIATORE, a young nun
    GABRIELLA LÉVI-FRANCHE VALKO, her grandmother
    ANGELA CACCIATORE, her mother
    ABBY (ABIGAIL) ALDRICH ROCKEFELLER, a wealthy philanthropist
    MOTHER INNOCENTA, the former abbess of St. Rose's Convent
    V. A. VERLAINE, an art historian and researcher
    PERCIVAL GRIGORI, Verlaine's mysterious client
    SISTER CELESTINE, a frail, elderly nun
    DR. SERAPHINA and DR. RAPHAEL VALKO, leading angelologists
    FATHER CLEMATIS, leader of the First Angelological Expedition

Danielle Trussoni's remarkable first book, *Falling Through the Earth* (2006), is a memoir detailing her difficult relationship with her father, a war veteran who never recovered from his experience in the tunnels of Vietnam. In it Trussoni explains why, as a young woman, she was compelled to go to Vietnam herself. Moving freely back and forth between her father's stories and her own life, she stitches these episodes together skillfully with the continuous thread of her visit to Vietnam.

This flexible structure works to Trussoni's advantage in the memoir, but *Angelology* is a longer, more complex book in which it is easy to become confused. Although the action of the novel spans only forty-eight hours, a lengthy, sometimes awkward, flashback to Germany's 1939 invasion of Poland and to World War II takes place in the second section. Later, brief scenes shift rapidly from the American present to the European past, and from the luxurious apartments of New York City's upper East Side to the rugged mountains of Bulgaria.

Sister Evangeline Cacciatore, a Franciscan Sister of Perpetual Adoration in her early twenties, handles all correspondence for St. Rose Convent. She denies a written request from V. A. Verlaine, a young artist and historian, to view some private letters between the order's former abbess, Mother Innocenta, and its affluent patron, Abby Aldrich Rockefeller (1874-1948), the wife of philanthropist John D. Rockefeller, Jr. Earlier, Verlaine had recovered four undocumented letters written by Mother Inno-

~

Danielle Trussoni attended the University of Wisconsin and the Iowa Writers' Workshop. Her memoir Falling Through the Earth *was named one of the ten best books of 2006 by* The New York Times Book Review.

~

centa to Mrs. Rockefeller (a historical figure who is never actually seen) and is seeking the remaining correspondence; however, unlike the convent's distinguished collection of angel figures and paintings, these letters are not available to the public.

Unaware of Sister Evangeline's refusal, Verlaine agrees to a meeting in Central Park with his wealthy client, Percival Grigori, to discuss his findings. He does not realize that Percival is a Nephilim, a descendant of the angels in Genesis who mated with human daughters; these creatures move unrecognized through the human population. Tall and pale, Percival is far older than he appears. He suffers from a degenerative disease that has shriveled and blackened his wings (usually hidden under his clothing) and coughs up "drops of luminous blue blood, vivid as chipped sapphires in snow," but nobody seems to notice. Unimpressed by the nineteenth century architectural drawings of St. Rose Convent that Verlaine has brought him, Percival directs Verlaine to go there in person to obtain further information about the letters.

When Verlaine reaches the convent, he notices that the architectural drawings do not correspond to the existing structure and learns that a terrible fire in 1944, which resulted in the death of Mother Innocenta, destroyed most of the original buildings. Confronted by Sister Evangeline, he explains his mission, also noting that the lyre pendant she wears, which originally belonged to her grandmother, is identical to a rare design on the drawings. Her suspicions allayed, Evangeline allows him to copy a similar letter, from Mrs. Rockefeller to the abbess, but when Verlaine returns to his parked car, he sees two tall figures breaking in to steal his papers. He manages to elude them by escaping on foot to Milton, the nearest town, where by chance Sister Evangeline encounters him again. They quickly determine to work together. Presumably a romance is destined to develop between these two.

Returning to the convent, Evangeline visits the simple room of Sister Celestine, wheelchair-bound and ill with cancer. The elderly nun reveals to her the existence of the Nephilim and the scholarly group of angelologists that formed to thwart them. She explains that, in Bulgaria's Rhodope Mountains, a gorge called the Devil's Throat was believed to be the legendary opening to the Greek underworld, where Orpheus entered to reclaim his wife Eurydice. It was there that those disobedient angels who had coupled with mortal women to produce the Nephilim were condemned to eternal imprisonment in an underground cavern. Struck with pity for their fall, the Archangel Gabriel reportedly threw them his lyre as a consolation, a symbol that the angelologists later adopted.

Angelology's long central flashback is primarily exposition, narrated in the teenage Celestine's deliberate voice and includes her life at the Angelology Academy of Paris just before World War II; her former, close friendship with Gabriella Lévi-Franche, who would become Sister Evangeline's grandmother; and an expedition to the Rhodope Mountains. Both Gabriella and Celestine studied angelology with their mentor, Dr. Seraphina Valko. Her husband, Dr. Raphael Valko, had previously unearthed and translated the account of an ancient lyre that was discovered in a Bulgarian cave by Father Clematis, the tenth century priest who led the doomed First Angelological Expedition to search for it, warning of its potentially destructive power. After Raphael successfully located the legendary cave, Celestine was permitted to join the Second Angelological Expedition, funded by Rockefeller, to recover the lyre, in spite of the danger posed by the imprisoned "dark angels." The details of her adventure become nearly as horrific as those of poor Clematis.

The flashback continues as Sister Celestine reviews her memories of Gabriella, the angelologists, and occupied France. The two young women, both at the top of their class, had become acquainted with a more detailed history of the disobedient angels, also called Watchers, in the Book of Enoch. (These were not the same as the rebel angels led by Lucifer, who refused to serve God.) The Watchers were sent to Earth as observers of God's creation before the Flood, but many of them, attracted by the daughters of humans, fell from grace. Their hybrid children, the angel-human Nephilim, were fair, tall, and strong, but they soon grew coldly intellectual and hungry for power.

In 1944, near the end of World War II, Celestine, by then a nun, brought the rescued lyre from Europe to St. Rose for safekeeping. Mother Innocenta in turn entrusted it to Rockefeller, who successfully hid it but later died without revealing its location. The fear was that the Nephilim would somehow confiscate the lyre and use its seductive power to dominate humans. At this point, Sister Celestine informs Evangeline that her grandmother is still alive, directs her to the trunk where letters from Gabriella rest, and sends her off to read them. Evangeline learns that her mother Angela, Gabriella's daughter and a brilliant angelologist, was murdered by the Nephilim to prevent her research into the powerful physical effects of celestial music.

In the meantime, Verlaine takes the midnight train returning to New York City, having lost his car and most of his research to Percival Grigori's messengers. He watches in horror as two immense, red-winged, red-eyed figures fly just outside his train window, matching the speed of the train. These are Gibborim, the Nephilim warrior class, beautiful but soulless, and they are hunting him.

The novel soon dissolves into an extended chase and a series of escapes involving Gabriella, Verlaine, Evangeline, and several angelologists, all pursued by the Nephilim. The various plot twists and multiple recognitions that occur in the search for the hidden lyre, which will involve the Museum of Modern Art and even the ice rink at Rockefeller Center, seem endless. Surprisingly, Sister Celestine, feeble as she is, proves to be heroic.

Trussoni, who has obviously done her research, incorporates numerous Biblical references into her novel, documenting them for the curious. Although a reader might easily assume that the aforementioned Book of Enoch is a fictitious device, it is not. This ancient book has been a historical and controversial influence on both Jewish mysticism and Christian apocrypha. The young Gabriella informs Celestine that the book is "an apocryphal prophecy written by a direct descendant of Noah." Enoch is even identified in some versions of the Bible as the patriarch's descendant, "the seventh from Adam" (Jude 1:14).

Most of the name symbolism used here is obvious. Several angelologists bear appropriate names: Angela, Gabriella, Seraphina, Raphael. The convent's oldest nun, a centenarian, has memorized the whole of John Milton's epic poem *Paradise Lost* (1667), from which she frequently quotes, while the neighboring town also bears his name. Evangeline's Italian surname, Cacciatore, means "hunter," and a hunter is in fact what she becomes and may continue to be, for several critics have predicted that this book will have a sequel.

Regrettably, the mechanics of Trussoni's writing are too often creaky. There is far too much exposition, interminably narrated by a single character or revealed in various letters, rather than occurring as an integral part of the action. A different choice of narrative structure might have helped, and as in any lengthy and complex novel with an intricate plot, questions are raised. One of the most obvious occurs when the young Celestine finds a naked Nephilim in her bathroom. Why is it that she cannot see his wings? Excessive length can also lead to unnecessary repetition, and *Angelology* is guilty of this too. The pacing is uneven—at times almost leaden, yet truly terrifying at others.

Difficult to classify, *Angelology* is a mixture of fact, fantasy, and legend. Trussoni takes pains to avoid the impression that Christianity alone is at the heart of her novel. The nuns of St. Rose are obviously Catholic, Gabriella is Jewish, and the scientist Seraphina is an agnostic, but all work together toward a common goal. Essentially the book is a thriller, though several scenes are redundant. The appearance of Gabriella's final letter to her granddaughter is obviously orchestrated to arrive in the nick of time, thus destroying any illusion of reality. The conclusion, unexpected as it should be, is nevertheless unsatisfying.

Joanne McCarthy

Review Sources

Kirkus Reviews 78, no. 1 (January 1, 2010): 16.
Los Angeles Times, March 13, 2010, p. D8.
The New York Times, March 1, 2010, p. C1.
The New York Times Book Review, March 7, 2010, pp. 1-2.
People 73, no. 10 (March 15, 2010): 61.
Publishers Weekly 257, no. 4 (January 25, 2010): 92.
Time 175, no. 10 (March 15, 2010): 55.
Library Journal 135, no. 1 (January 1, 2010): 95.

ANTEROOMS
New Poems and Translations

Author: Richard Wilbur (1921-   )
Publisher: Houghton Mifflin Harcourt (Boston). 63 pp.
   $20.00
Type of work: Poetry

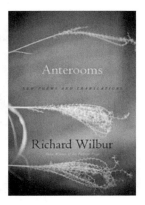

In this collection, particularly in the first section, Wilbur uses metrical and formal patterns, connecting what he is doing with the long history of such poetry written in English

The allusive functions, the balances of idea and sound, the music of the lines, and the concreteness of Richard Wilbur's images in *Anterooms* give his verse a richness and an intellectual density, involving both mind and body. His poetry is, at bottom, a celebration of life, of the natural world, and of human language, but behind it can be felt a subtle and complex religious worldview. Although the four sections into which *Anterooms* is divided can be rather wildly different from one another, and the works in the individual sections are often unrelated among themselves, those differences do demonstrate the comprehensiveness of Wilbur's interests and his abilities. Nevertheless, the title of the book suggests a thematic center for the poems in the first section, poems that make up almost all the personal, lyric works of the collection—that is, the present moment is the anteroom, a waiting room. What follows, what awaits, is problematic.

The introductory poem, "The House," precedes the first section, a positioning that sets it off not only as different but also as particularly meaningful to the poet because it poses a bewildering question that lingers over many of the poems that follow. "Too It" is a personal work, Wilbur's restrained lament on the loss of his wife; at the same time, it closes as a love poem addressed to her. In iambic pentameter, rhyming *abba*, its music is quiet and moving. It begins with the speaker describing his loved one's speaking of the "house" of which she had repeatedly dreamed, a New England house with a "widow's walk," a delicate and moving way of bringing in the idea of death. What is the house? Is it where, in a sense, she has gone? Is heaven merely death itself? The poem ends with that implied question, a bafflement.

A later poem in the book, "Galveston, 1961," is another love poem, but this time it is a celebration of life. The woman, swimming in the Gulf of Mexico, is seen almost as the Nereid Panope—beautiful, changeable, and mysterious—but who, when she comes to shore, is the singular and loved woman. The poem looks backward to an earlier, happier time.

The short first poem of the opening section, "A Measuring Worm," offers a development of the theme of what life and its end mean. Beautifully imagistic, it presents a

Richard Wilbur received the Pulitzer Prize in poetry in 1957 and 1989. In 1987, he was named poet laureate of the United States. He has received the National Book Award and the National Arts Club medal of honor for literature.

"yellow-striped green/ Caterpillar" climbing up a screen. The caterpillar, lacking feet in its middle, progresses by humping its back so that its back feet can be drawn up against its front feet, making an omega of itself; this is the guiding allusion to Revelation 1:8, "I am Alpha and Omega, the beginning and the ending, saith the Lord." The worm does not know its future—that, coming out of the sleep of its chrysalis, it will have changed into something startlingly beautiful. The implied question is, will the human speaker be transformed in the same pattern? The stanzas are tercets, rhyming "aba"; the meter is a variable mixture of iambs and trochees—with occasional other feet—almost as if imitating the worm's movements. The worm does not progress absolutely smoothly, hence the multiple kinds of poetic feet. Thus, the worm's movements, echoing its life as well as giving an image of human life, cannot be entirely smooth and regular.

A following poem, "Psalm," is in its way yet another reenactment of life. At the same time, it is a poem of thanksgiving, and so a direct celebration of life, but also a reminder that life is filled with difficulty and, inevitably, death. Its five stanzas, tercets again, ask the reader to "give thanks" on the lute, the harp, and the horn for "All things," for having been "born," but the poem closes with two stanzas in which, first, the "deep drum" is asked "to make/ Pandemonium," for life is not simply sweet order. Lastly, the voice says, on the cello, "to praise . . . our sorrows . . . of shared grief"—for death is part of life.

The later "Terza Rima," in which Wilbur uses Dante's three-line, interlinking stanza, seems to turn "Psalm" and "A Measuring Worm" on their heads, for Wilbur announces that the form, as in the "Inferno," can depict and create the most horrifying of scenes; Wilbur uses a terrible image from World War II, in which he served. The jeep in which the speaker is riding skids into the head of a dead German soldier, "bumping a little," and "then fl[ying] on as if towards Paradise." The irony of the poem is contained in this line, for the poem is no celebration.

The title poem, "Anterooms," would seem by right to be the introductory poem, but Wilbur inserts it well into the first section. Its place allows him to talk again of time, of before and after, and of how moments can contain past, present, and future. Nevertheless, the poem is one more elegy, a delicate lament. It begins with the image of a sundial "lift[ing]" out of the snowdrift that had covered it, which is an image of rebirth and new movement, even though, paradoxically, a sundial does not move and yet exists to tell time. Humans experience time peculiarly. Humans are in time, but it never stops; therefore, all times are forever past and forever future: "Still, it strains be-lief/ How an instance can dilate/ Or long years be brief."

"A Pasture Poem" is one more examination of time, life, and death, even as it is on the surface, merely the description of a thistle that grows old and ends in seed. Again, Wilbur uses short lines arranged in triplets. The young thistle is all "barb and bristle," resisting attack and so protecting butterfly eggs laid in the angles of its leaves, pro-tecting, in short, new life. However, the thistle cannot, in the end, resist time, old age, and death.

The second section offers a number of translations—from Stephane Mallarmé, *Les Poémes d'Edgar Poe* (1888); to Paul Verlaine; Horace's *Odes*, (23 B.C.E., 13 B.C.E.; English translation, 1621) book 2, 10, the ode on the golden mean; and two "Nativity" poems of Joseph Brodsky. The Mallarmé is a monster of a poem to translate. It is a slight variant on the Petrarchan sonnet in both the original and the translation. Wilbur translates it into an intriguing and almost clear English poem and so, despite the diffi-culties, makes it a success. Horace's poem, much-translated, still seems fresh and wise—the underlying blank-verse pattern of the translation offers an English replica-tion of the original Latin, which is formally structured yet still a voice speaking, not a chant. In Wilbur's collection, it is presented in five four-line stanzas, each stanza made up of three iambic-pentameter lines followed by a closing two-beat line, both musical and colloquial. The two Russian poems are poems on the Nativity, and the reader, believer in the Christ story or not, cannot ignore their emotion and beauty.

Section 3 seems to be a mixed bag, a combination of song lyrics, wordplay, self-criticism, and a touch of satire; most of the poems are comic in the end. "The Censor" in (almost) heroic couplets satirizes a certain type of egoist, the man who listens to others for "signs of egoism and self-regard,/ Reacting . . . / With . . . / A wince . . . " that is directed toward the "Egomaniac within his breast." This is not the external sat-ire of John Dryden and Alexander Pope—and would almost seem as if aimed at the poet (Wilbur) himself. Certainly the following poem, "A Reckoning," is aimed at himself, although the faults to which the "I" confesses are hardly great sins but rather stupidities and fatuities. What the narrator really regrets is having made a fool of him-self, making a social error, not a moral one. The voice asks "how can I repent/ From mere embarrassment?" Not too oddly, the jog-trot rhythms of the poem do not help the idea behind it—there is little wit here.

Following is "A Prelude," a rather packed mockery of another poet, the often too humorless Matthew Arnold; a small satire of Arnold's "Dover Beach"; and a nod to Wilbur's friend Anthony Hecht and his poem "The Dover Bitch." Arnold is pictured as looking across the English Channel to the French coast, where he sees the French poet Gérard de Nerval—who once, in his madness, went for a walk in Paris with a lobster on a leash—walking, perhaps, the same lobster and "enjoying his *vacances./ Alas for gravitas . . . Hélas for France.*" Arnold, that serious man, "left in a hurry,/ Foreseeing a night of worry." There is a delightful insouciance in the mixture of line lengths as well as in the lighthearted rhymes: for example, "Aiguille" and "sea," "panicky" and "anarchy."

Here, too, is a song that Wilbur composed for a musical version of Jean Giraudoux's *La Folle de Chaillot* (pr., pb. 1945; *The Mad Woman of Chaillot*, 1947). The song is a rollicking concoction, a satire on the idea of the capitalist's desire for an essentially robotic workforce. The "President" sings: "What a luscious conception, far sweeter than babas or tarts . . . / A standardized laboring man with replaceable parts." Wilbur rarely offers a take on political or economic positions so that this poem may seem an anomaly, but the very sprightliness of this song suggests a heartfelt stance. In other poems are the plays on and with words and the discoveries of words that give the reader insights into society and economics: For example, the realization that "homeowner" has a "meow" in its center says something about the American love of cats—and calls into question who really owns the home.

The final section does not add much to the collection, except to be fun. It is made up of translations of thirty-seven of the riddles of the second or third century c.e. Latin poet Symphosius. The reader is given only the English versions, but the general meaning of the Latin and even an aspect of the form is carried over. The form uses tercets, all three lines rhyming in Wilbur's version, a difficult task considering that the original Latin hexameters do not use rhyme. Of course the translations can hardly be literal, but they are always beautifully clear, and the individual verses make good riddles in English. The title to each riddle is its answer, but in Latin and not translated until the end of the section. Although Wilbur's verses are always clear, those answers will probably be necessary for most readers.

L. L. Lee

Review Sources

Library Journal 135, no. 18 (November 1, 2010): 66.
Publishers Weekly 257, no. 42 (October 25, 2010): 31.
Weekly Standard 16, no. 9 (November 15, 2010): 34-35.

APPARITION AND LATE FICTIONS
A Novella and Stories

Author: Thomas Lynch (1948-   )
Publisher: W. W. Norton (New York). 216 pp. $24.95
Type of work: Novella, short fiction
Time: The second half of the twentieth century and the
early twenty-first century
Locale: Northern and western Michigan; Mackinac
Island, Michigan; a small town in Ohio; and a coastal
resort area in Connecticut

*In four short stories and a novella, Lynch traces the
progress of characters through loss to the discovery of
truth or even of some form of grace*

Principal characters:
> DANNY, the narrator of "Catch and Release," a man in his late twenties
> and an expert fishing guide
> MARGARET, his stepmother and an understanding woman
> MARTIN, a funeral director in "Bloodsport" and a dedicated,
> compassionate man
> ELENA, a beautiful young woman, loved from afar by Martin but, at
> twenty, the victim of her husband's rage
> MRS. DELANO, Elena's grieving mother
> HAROLD KEEHN, a lonely, retired casket sales representative in
> "Hunter's Moon"
> AISLING BLACK, in "Matinée de Septembre," a widow, a poet, a
> University of Michigan professor, and a mature woman infatuated
> with a young girl
> BINTALOU, a beautiful Jamaican teenager and a waitress at Mackinac
> Island's Grand Hotel
> BLAKE SHIELDS, Bintalou's white boyfriend
> ADRIAN LITTLEFIELD, in *The Apparition*, a young Methodist minister
> and later a successful author and lecturer
> CLARE LITTLEFIELD, Adrian's wife and the mother of their two children,
> later his former wife
> FR. FRANCIS ASSISI CONCANNON, a Roman Catholic priest and
> Littlefield's friend
> MARY DE DONA, a kindly Italian Catholic and briefly Littlefield's lover

Thomas Lynch received critical acclaim for the three books of poetry and the three
volumes of essays that preceded his venture into fiction. In his earlier works, it was evident that Lynch was firmly rooted in reality, whether he was reflecting upon his Irish
heritage, as in *Booking Passage: We Irish and Americans* (2005), or drawing upon his
experiences as a funeral director in a small Michigan town. Lynch did not flinch from

~

Thomas Lynch has published three
books of poetry and three books of
essays. The Undertaking: Life Studies
from the Dismal Trade *(1997) won the*
1998 American Book Award and was a
finalist for the National Book Award.

~

gritty truths about death and dissolution, though often he proceeded to suggest the possibility of grace. Critics have pointed out that Lynch's fiction has the same virtues as his essays and his poetry: meticulous workmanship, precise use of detail, the acknowledgment that suffering is a part of everyday life, and the suggestion that out of suffering may come not merely acceptance but transformation.

In the short story "Catch and Release," for example, Danny is devastated by the death of his father, who is also his favorite fishing companion. His father's influence helped Danny become a professional fishing guide; his father insisted that Danny should do what he loved, not what others expected of him. It was from his father that Danny learned that nature should be treated with reverence. Thus, as his father had taught him to do, Danny keeps just one fish out of a day's catch; he expects his clients to do the same, releasing all the other fish unharmed. It is this practice from which the title of the short story is drawn.

The plot of "Catch and Release" is simple: After her husband's sudden, unexpected death, Danny's stepmother Margaret distributes his ashes among his four children, each of whom is to make appropriate use of them. She puts Danny's portion into a thermos, which he stows in his boat as he sets off on a fishing trip, accompanied only by his constant companion, his dog Chinook. With him, Danny has his father's treasured fishing tackle, which Margaret has also given him. As he moves along the river, Danny recalls instances of his father's influence upon him. After Chinook was run over and crippled, for example, Danny planned to shoot him; however, because his father believed so strongly that even less-than-perfect creatures have a right to life, Danny spared the dog's life. In the end, Danny releases most of the ashes into the river but, in a Eucharistic gesture, reserves a remnant of his father to live on in him.

In "Hunter's Moon," the protagonist also has the habit of looking to nature for consolation. During his lifetime, Harold Keehn has lost three wives, one to another woman, one because of his own neglect, and the third to cancer. His only daughter turned against him then was killed in an accident when she was a teenager. Harold threw himself into his job as a casket salesman, which he found both challenging and aesthetically satisfying. However, after the casket business became modernized and, in his view, cheapened, Harold was more than willing to retire. He is alone with his memories. His only pleasure is his nightly walks, at least until one particular night, when he is forced to recognize not only his isolation but also his own mortality. What he has still to notice as the story ends is that he has gained a companion, the dog he has loathed for so long has followed him home and curled up beside him.

Lynch's belief that being a funeral director is a vocation much like the ministry or the priesthood is reflected in many of his works. In "Bloodsport," funeral director Martin prepares the body of a young woman for burial. He treats her with respect, unlike the husband who killed her with as little compunction as he had shown when he shot a fawn that wandered up to their doorstep. Martin cannot forget his first glimpse of Elena at her father's funeral, his response to her beauty then, and his continuing interest in her over the years, when he was often called upon to comfort her mother, Mrs. Delano, who had come to regard him as a friend. Twenty years later, Martin is still haunted by those memories and by his conviction that Elena died betrayed by men, perhaps even by him, because all he could do for her was to bury her.

"Matinée de Septembre" is the only work in this collection written from a woman's perspective. It also has a more luxurious setting than the other short stories: the Grand Hotel on Mackinac Island, where for generations wealthy Americans have spent their summer vacations. The central character in the story, Aisling Black, can well afford to stay there, for she has family money and a substantial inheritance from her late husband as well as her own income as an internationally known poet and a tenured professor at the University of Michigan. On her flight back to Ann Arbor after a summer in the British Isles, Black realizes that she needs a rest, and since she still has two weeks before she must take up her duties at the university, she catches a flight to northern Michigan and checks in at the Grand Hotel.

Though Aisling believes firmly that she no longer has sexual needs, there are indications that she does not know herself as well as she thinks she does. If she had lost her interest in sex, she would hardly take such pride in the fact that she has kept her figure, nor would she need to assure herself that audiences think of her as a young woman. There is a brief, revealing moment during her flight when she takes note of the good-looking, male flight attendant who adjusts her seat. The fact that she immediately thinks to herself that he must be gay suggests that Aisling feels it necessary to suppress her sexual impulses. Her preoccupation with sex is reflected even in her plans for a new course. Aisling tells herself that she will begin with an account of the romantic relationship between the Irish poet William Butler Yeats and Maud Gonne, because in that way she can capture the interest of students in their early twenties, whose sexual appetites are at their height.

Aisling may be right about her students, but she is wrong about herself. At the Grand Hotel she falls in love at first sight with Jamaican teenager, Bintalou, who is a waitress there. Although Aisling makes every effort to attract the girl's attention, to Bintalou she is never more than another hotel guest, to be served politely and then forgotten. Helplessly and hopelessly in love with this embodiment of beauty, Aisling overstays her vacation and abandons her students in order to pursue vicarious satisfaction through her glimpses or her visions of Bintalou in the arms of her boyfriend.

In the novella *The Apparition*, Clare Littlefield begins her search for a new life by first being unfaithful to her husband, Adrian Littlefield, a Methodist minister in the small town of Findley, Ohio, and then by permanently abandoning him and their two young children. However, Clare is a relatively minor character in the novella. The author's focus is on Adrian. In the course of the story, Adrian moves from despair and disillusionment to what he describes as an "apparition," a new view of the world and the people in it, which comes to him through grace. At the beginning of the novella, however, there is no hint that the story will have a religious dimension. Adrian is described as a man who has become a popular lecturer, thanks to his best-selling book, *Good Riddance—Divorcing for Keeps*. At one of the conferences where he speaks, he decides to make a tour of Block Island, the site of Clare's first infidelity twenty years before. He recalls the agony of the divorce, the pain his children endured, and his own sense of betrayal when the members of his congregation and his clerical superiors seemed interested only in eliminating the scandal from their presence, which meant avoiding Adrian as if he had a communicable disease and then getting rid of him as soon as possible.

The only person who sympathizes with Adrian is a Roman Catholic priest, Father Francis Assisi Concannon. Francis does not deluge Adrian with theology; he brings him companionship and poetry. When he senses that Adrian is at his lowest, Francis brings him a motherly Italian woman, Mary De Dona, to babysit his children. In a car reeking of marijuana, Adrian and the priest drive across the border to Windsor, Ontario. There they have steaks and wine and then make their way to a topless-bottomless bar, where they can gaze at naked women. Back home, the priest pronounces an absolution, and Adrian goes off to bed. However, what he first thinks is a dream, turns out to be reality: The babysitter makes love to him, then matter-of-factly puts on her clothes and leaves. A few hours later, Adrian faces his congregation. He has no prepared sermon; in fact, he cannot think of anything to say to them. Instead, he sings the familiar popular song with the refrain "Let it be, let it be." Later he tells Francis that as he sang, he had an epiphany: The people in the congregation all looked angelic to him.

The ongoing romance with Mary De Dona leads Adrian to doubt St. Paul's equation of sex with sin. For him, she is a redemptive force, a means of grace. She inspires him to write his book, which brings him financial security and a new career. On Block Island twenty years later, Adrian accepts the fact that he was never meant for a conventional marriage. However, he is content. As he tells his readers, divorce can indeed enrich one's life.

Just as Lynch did in his poems and his essays, in his fiction he explores the meaning of life and death, one character at a time. Although he is scrupulously realistic, describing human body parts as carefully as he does living, breathing fish or aesthetically pleasing caskets, he never ignores the possibility of redemption. The haunting beauty of his language, his gift for creating convincing characters, and his insight into the possibilities of human existence combine to make Lynch one of the most impressive new fiction writers of the year.

Rosemary M. Canfield Reisman

Review Sources

Booklist 106, no. 12 (February 15, 2010): 32.
The Christian Century 127 (May 4, 2010): 45-46.

The Daily Telegraph, February 27, 2010, p. 11.
Kirkus Reviews 77, no. 20 (October 15, 2009): 29.
Library Journal 134, no. 17 (October 15, 2009): 72.
Los Angeles Times, February 14, 2010, p. E6.
The New York Times Book Review, February 21, 2010, p. 7.
Sunday Times, February 21, 2010, p. 47.

THE ASK

Author: Sam Lipsyte (1968-   )
Publisher: Farrar, Straus, and Giroux (New York).
  296 pp. $25.00
Type of work: Novel
Time: Present
Locale: New York City and the borough of Queens

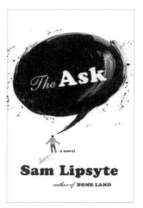

Lipsyte's story concerns a hapless fund-raiser for a small university whose life begins to fall apart; his only chance at saving his career—and possibly his family—is to "ask" for a large donation from a former college friend who has become rich and famous

Principal characters:
  MILO BURKE, a fund-raiser for a small
    university
  VARGINA, his supervisor
  HORACE, one of his coworkers
  BERNIE, his son
  MAURA, his wife
  PURDY STUART, a college friend of his who became a multimillionaire
  DON, Purdy's illegitimate son and an Iraq War veteran

Sam Lipsyte has established himself as a satirical observer of the American scene, or at least the New York scene, and his fourth book *The Ask* is another biting look at twenty-first century cultural conventions, trends, and fads. *The Ask* tells the story of Milo Burke, a former artist turned fund-raiser for a small New York university. Advancing steadily toward middle age, Milo is married to Maura, a marketing consultant. They live in Queens with their three-year-old son, Bernie, who is enrolled in a particularly whimsical and "progressive" preschool that is itself a satirical study in modern urban parenting.

Milo's story is, in many ways, the story of a loser, and from the beginning of the novel, he understands that he is a failure. While Milo is unable to land any significant donations, his colleague Lewellyn is always scoring large "asks": gifts, donations, or favors universities need to succeed. As Milo puts it, "An ask could be a person, or what we wanted from that person. If they gave it to us, that was a give."

Figuratively speaking, the title and the titular term used throughout the novel indicate both Milo's defining characteristic and the author's take on modern society. In essence, Milo is in search of meaning. Without explicitly stating so, he is "asking" the universe for a purpose, for a sense of identity, and for a path to happiness. Indeed, the questioning tone of the title is continuously refrained by Milo's unspoken "Why?" and "Why me?" Despite setting himself up for failure repeatedly, he is also continuously surprised at how events transpire.

In his student days, Milo planned to be an artist. However, despite his technical proficiency, his work lacked innovation and never made any headway in the New York art world. Former friends, on the other hand, went on to big reputations and acclaim. Milo and Maura have settled into lives of quiet complacency in Queens. Milo does not take any satisfaction from his employment; he knows that he is not particularly good at his

Sam Lipsyte was an editor for the influential Internet magazine Feed *and became a cult favorite with his novels* The Subject Steve *(2001) and* Home Land *(2004). He received a Guggenheim Fellowship in 2008. He teaches at Columbia University.*

job, and his boss, Vargina, has sentenced him to sharing desk space with Horace, a young man whom Milo regards as especially ill-suited to the task of fund-raising. Bored and unhappy with his work, Milo refers internally to the small New York university of his employment as "the Mediocre University at New York City." Events spiral slowly out of control for Milo as he realizes his wife has little use for him, his son's babysitters and educators are useless and perhaps even dangerous, and his old friends and college acquaintances (such as wealthy magnate Purdy Stuart) have become famous or rich while he has wallowed in mediocrity. Things come to a head when he loses his patience and tells off a student whose father is a major donor to the university; in no time Milo has lost his job. Maura is less inclined to be supportive than to lament his loss of income, and so Milo is forced to try to find a new job; true to form, he fails miserably at that endeavor as well.

Milo's chance for redemption comes when the university attracts the interest of Purdy, Milo's college friend. Purdy, we are told, has made a fortune with an online music site, which he sold, afterward becoming a venture capitalist. The development office at Mediocre University hopes to use Milo to ask for a donation or gift from Purdy; in essence, Purdy becomes "the ask." Milo has to swallow whatever is left of his pride. On one hand, he has to accept this humiliating assignment from the employers who just fired him, and, on the other, he has to ask a successful classmate for a handout in order to save his job.

The novel's primary mode is satirical. The dialogue is typically more ironic than realistic, making use of non sequiturs and over-the-top reactions from characters throughout the novel. Lipsyte effectively skewers the world of academic art programs, of fund-raising, and of postslacker, white-collar workers who hold sadly onto dreams of artistic preeminence. The blade of his wit's scalpel glints especially keenly when describing the Happy Salamander, a nouveau preschool where the teachers feel that children are not respected properly; therefore, all parents are referred to in the context of their children only—thus, Milo is not Milo, or Mr. Burke, but "Bernie's dad." The Happy Salamander school will eventually experience a schism in which some of its believers move north, forming the "Blue Newt Faction." Characters such as Horace react to every circumstance in ways that are geared to elicit laughs. For example, when Milo is being fired, Horace accuses him of sexual harassment as a prank, not caring that the school will take the accusation seriously. Similarly, after her split with his father, Milo's mother decides to become a lesbian and is completely caught up in her new-age lifestyle. She has no interest in Milo's son, since she does not feel she should be reduced to the status of "grandmother."

Lipsyte further demonstrates the artificial quality of Milo's failed career by juxtaposing it with a more traditional role when Milo joins his babysitter's strange brother, Nick, in building wooden decks for back yards. Milo realizes immediately that he is in no shape to engage in manual labor; additionally, he lacks the simple skills that would make the work go smoothly. At the same time, Nick is no poster boy for the blue-collar world. Even as he works as a carpenter, he informs Milo of his plan for a reality show about celebrity chefs who cook last meals for death-row inmates.

Milo's life is falling apart in other ways as well. As Maura avoids physical contact with him and spends more and more time at the office, he begins to suspect she may be having an affair. His mother flatly refuses to loan him money and, like Maura, has little sympathy for his tailspin. Milo's pathos is highlighted by numerous flashbacks to earlier and equally pathetic times, and the reader comes to understand that Milo's latest series of catastrophes is a culmination of a lifetime of disappointments.

As the novel progresses, Purdy asks Milo to do more and more for him if Milo expects him to donate, all of which Milo must do to preserve his job. Purdy explains to Milo that as a young man he had a brief affair with a woman, which resulted in a son, now twenty-one years old. Purdy's son, Don, has served in Iraq, where he has lost both legs from an explosion; he uses prosthetic limbs to walk.

Purdy's life is interestingly contrasted to Milo's. Rather than failing to live up to his early potential, Purdy far exceeded his. Purdy is in love with his young wife and dedicated to her even as Milo's marriage is falling apart. At the same time, Milo's love for Bernie is profound and is far and away the most important factor of his life, whereas Purdy hardly knows Don and employs Milo to buy off his bitter and disenfranchised son.

The luckless nature of Milo's life becomes increasingly apparent throughout the novel. Many chapters are flashbacks to earlier times in Milo's life. The same central story continues to emerge: Milo has a chance to rise to an occasion, and fails to do so; as a result, he doubts and questions himself for years afterward. In one flashback episode, armed thieves rob Milo and his college roommates, and Purdy and his friend, Michael Florida, attack the robbers to protect a woman in the group, as Milo sits paralyzed. In another scene, Milo leaves behind in a rental house the ceremonial knife from Spain his father gave to him; when he tries to recover it at a party, he cannot stand up to the challenge of the new tenants who disregard his story of ownership.

In some ways the novel is a commentary on fatherhood. As a veteran and a double amputee, Don seems to be suffering from post-traumatic stress syndrome. He uses various kinds of drugs, and he simultaneously longs for his father's company and bitterly resents him. Purdy had been unaware of Don for some time and has had nothing to do with his upbringing; their relationship is further complicated because Don believes that Purdy ceased paying his mother's hospital bills, leading to her death, which resulted from complications ensuing from her transfer to another facility. Don is obsessed with his rich father not because of his wealth but because Purdy has never truly been a father to him. Similarly, in his own memories of his suicidal and unhappy father, related in painful and awkward flashbacks, Milo realizes how much of his own ineffectual nature is a result of his father's lack of presence in his own life. In contrast to his father and Purdy, Milo is determined to be a good father to Bernie.

Although Lipsyte's insights are shrewd and his wit is often biting, the novel does have a central flaw. Milo allows himself to be abused throughout the novel. Horace mocks him at work, his employer scorns and derides him, and Vargina fails to respect him in any way. Instead of firing back at these various insults, Milo makes excuses and asks for forgiveness. It takes him a long time to realize that Maura wants more than distance from him; she wants his absence. Instead of standing up for himself and growing angry with her, he tolerates her treatment of him and believes he is to blame for it. He allows Purdy and Purdy's friend, Michael Florida, to push him around as well. Although Milo is doubtlessly rendered as a realistic and rounded character, the reader nevertheless grows frustrated with his ineffectiveness and inertia. When Milo does show flashes of integrity, they are often too little and too late.

Scott D. Yarbrough

Review Sources

Booklist 106, no. 7 (December 1, 2009): 21.
Kirkus Reviews 77, no. 21 (November 1, 2009): 1134.
Library Journal 134, no. 17 (October 15, 2009): 67-70.
Literary Review 53, no. 2 (Winter, 2010): 203-206.
The Nation, June 28, 2010, p. 32-35.
The New York Review of Books, April 8, 2010, p. 16.
The New Yorker 86, no. 5 (March 22, 2010): 71.
People 73, no. 10 (March 15, 2010): 63.
Virginia Quarterly Review 86, no. 3 (Summer, 2010): 192.

ATLANTIC
Great Sea Battles, Heroic Discoveries, Titanic Storms, and a Vast Ocean of a Million Stories

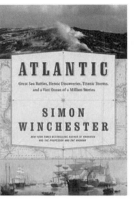

Author: Simon Winchester (1944-   )
Publisher: Harper (New York). 495 pp. $27.99
Type of work: History, history of science, environment, natural history
Time: 540 million years ago to 2010
Locale: Atlantic Ocean

A geological, biological, and sociological history of the Atlantic Ocean, particularly of the ways in which humans have interacted with it

> *Principal personages:*
> JOHN CABOT (c. 1450-c. 1498), an Italian navigator and explorer
> RACHEL CARSON (1907-1964), an American biologist and writer; one of the first to warn of the importance of protecting the environment
> CHRISTOPHER COLUMBUS (1451-1506), an Italian navigator and explorer; an early and important explorer of North America
> LEIF ERIKSSON (c. 970-c. 1035), a Norse navigator and explorer; probably the first European to reach North America
> ANGUS CAMPBELL MACINTYRE, the first mate of the South African tugboat *Sir Charles Elliott*
> MATTHEW FONTAINE MAURY (1806-1873), an oceanographer with the U.S. Navy, who charted the floor of the Atlantic Ocean
> WILLIAM SHAKESPEARE (1564-1616), an English playwright

As the full title *Atlantic: Great Sea Battles, Heroic Discoveries, Titanic Storms, and a Vast Ocean of a Million Stories* promises, Simon Winchester's book is thick and rich, interesting, moving, and occasionally exciting; if it does not actually contain one million stories, it comes as close as one could in five hundred pages. Winchester calls his project a biography of the Atlantic Ocean, using the term much as fellow polymath Philip Ball did in his own *Life's Matrix* (2000), to emphasize his subject's vitality and changeability. Through most of his book, Winchester focuses on human interaction, showing how human civilizations have been influenced by the Atlantic and how humans are beginning to exert measurable influence back on it.

To organize his vast subject, Winchester takes his structure from William Shakespeare's play *As You Like It* (pr. c. 1599-1600, pb. 1623); he quotes the famous "All the world's a stage" monologue delivered by the character Jacques, in act 2, scene 7, in which Jacques describes the seven ages of a man's life: infant, school boy, lover, soldier, justice, pantaloon, and finally a man in an old age, which is a stage reminis-

cent of a second childhood, "Sans teeth, sans
eyes, sans taste, sans everything." The prologue and the seven subsequent chapters of
Winchester's book use pieces of Jacques's
speech as epigraphs, guiding and focusing on
what is to come.

Before the seven chapters and their seven
ages comes the prologue, "The Beginnings of
Its Goings On," which Winchester uses to introduce his major character, the Atlantic, and
to demonstrate the wide variety of material
he will bring to his exploration. As he does
throughout the book, he devotes several pages
to a story from his own travels. He begins at
his favorite spot for gazing at the ocean, the
Faeroe Islands in the northern reaches of the
Atlantic, "where all is cold and wet and bleak.
In its own challenging way, it is entirely beautiful." With an unfailing eye for the telling
detail, Winchester describes the sheer basalt

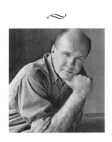

*British-born Simon Winchester is the
author of twenty books, including the
best sellers* The Professor and the
Madman: A Tale of Murder, Insanity,
and the Making of the Oxford English
Dictionary *(1998) and* Krakatoa: The
Day the World Exploded, August 27,
1883 *(2003).*

cliffs on the western edges of the islands and the extraordinary efforts Faeroese
sheepherders go through each spring to deposit one lamb on each small grassy out-
cropping of these cliffs. The author is a thoroughly engaged narrator in sequences like
these, capable of being fascinated and fascinating at the same time. His descriptions
of the climate, the landscape, and the islanders and their cliff-side religious service
are detailed and lovely, and his references to Homer and Arthur C. Clarke enrich his
telling; all of these details serve his larger purpose of creating a narrative space in
which to smoothly work in the history and science that shape the biography.

Winchester studied geology in college at Oxford, and several of his previous
books—*The Map That Changed the World: William Smith and the Birth of Modern
Geology* (2001), *A Crack in the Edge of the World: America and the Great California
Earthquake of 1906* (2005), and others—have drawn on that expertise. Here, his
training serves him well. From his adventure in the Faeroes, Winchester moves
seamlessly to the geologic history of the Atlantic, casting backward millions of years
to the supercontinent known as Ur, then forward to a time some 540 million years ago
when a familiar-looking ocean began to appear. The Atlantic Ocean is about halfway
through its expected life, he explains; the tectonic plates that moved apart to create the
ocean basin are still drifting slowly around the Earth's spherical surface, and in another 200 million years or so the Atlantic will no longer be a discrete body of water.

With chapter 1, the book's passage through the ages of man begins in earnest. The
first age is infancy; here "infancy" refers not to the earliest days of the ocean itself but
rather to the dawn of human interaction with it. According to the fossil record, as
Winchester relates it, it took "a mere thirty thousand years" for humans to extend their

domain from the grassy plains of what is now known as Kenya and Ethiopia to the southern tip of the African continent, where the Indian Ocean and the Atlantic meet. These waters proved to be abundant with sea life and provided a bountiful source of protein for early seaside inhabitants. However, finding the ocean and crossing it were vastly different challenges. With stereotypical British understatement, the author notes, "I have sailed in these waters and know them to be very trying." For thousands of years, Winchester points out, most seaside humans lived along the eastern shores of the ocean, gradually expanding their range to include offshore islands and finally to include what is called the Western Hemisphere. The Phoenicians were the first to build ships large enough for trading along ocean routes, in the fifth century B.C.E., followed by the Romans, the Arabs, and others. Winchester blends the history of trading and commerce with clear explanations of ocean currents and the technological advances necessary to exploit and struggle against them, narrating the expansion of human civilizations westward and northward along the Atlantic.

Finally, he takes on the question of who it was that first crossed the Atlantic to reach North America. With a fascinating tale of a priceless ancient map (probably a forgery), Viking ships, Norwegian scholars, a local fisherman, and buried ruins at L'Anse aux Meadows, Newfoundland, Canada, Winchester demonstrates convincingly that Leif Eriksson was the first to make the crossing. He continues the story on through Christopher Columbus, who never realized what he had found, and Amerigo Vespucci, "the first to realize that the Americas formed a continent between Europe and Asia—and therefore that the Atlantic was a discrete and separate body of water, an ocean." With the "discovery" of the ocean and its first appearance on maps, the Atlantic's first age, its infancy, was concluded.

In subsequent chapters, Shakespeare's seven ages provide thematic, rather than chronological, underpinnings. Chapter 2, based on the "whining schoolboy," explores the mapping of the Atlantic. The International Hydrographic Organization, based in Monaco, is the official body charged with delineating the boundaries of oceans and seas, and with supervising the standardization of navigational charts. However, before the days of Global Positioning System (GPS) and satellite imaging, there were only men in ships, venturing out to see new things and attempting to record what they saw. This chapter traces hundreds of years of measurement and mapping, describing the efforts of familiar explorers (Vasco da Gama, Ferdinand Magellan, Charles Darwin) and the lesser known (U.S. Navy officer Matthew Fontaine Maury, who discovered and charted the submarine mountain chain known as the Mid-Atlantic Ridge).

In chapter 3, devoted to the "lover," Winchester takes a meandering rumination through the Atlantic's influence on art, including Anglo-Saxon poetry and the poetry of Edmund Spenser, Shakespeare, and John Donne; Norse and pre-Columbian depictions of sea monsters; and the paintings of Pieter Bruegel the Elder, J. M. W. Turner, and Winslow Homer, and he also describes the great cities that have sprung up along the Atlantic coast. The fourth chapter, based on "a soldier," describes the evolution of naval warfare, while the fifth, titled "They That Occupy Their Business on Great Waters," concerns the "justice" and analyzes the Atlantic as a foundation for laws, order, and commerce.

After delivering on the heroics, the storms, and the stories promised in his title, Winchester takes a darker turn with his last two chapters, the final two ages, the "pantaloon" and the "second childishness and mere oblivion;/ Sans teeth, sans eyes, sans taste, sans everything." Here he describes the gradual discovery that the Atlantic, for all its vastness, is not infinitely capable of absorbing pollution and is not a limitless provider of food. In "Change and Decay All Around the Sea," he acknowledges the prescience of Rachel Carson, who warned of the dangers of pollution during the 1950's and 1960's, and writes emotionally and poetically of what came after:

> "One cannot but hang one's head in shame and abject frustration: we pollute the sea, we plunder the sea, we dishonor the sea that appears like a mere expanse of hammered pewter as we fly over it in our air-polluting planes—forgetting or ignoring all the while that the sea is the source of all the life on earth, the wellspring of us all."

Technology, he explains, has made crossing the ocean by plane or by ship easy, and the pollution created by these transatlantic machines is increasing and accumulating. Other innovations have made fishing easier, but less precise, providing cheap food at a tremendous environmental cost. Winchester contrasts the Grand Banks off the coast of Newfoundland, once one of the richest fishing grounds in the world but now overfished to virtual emptiness, with a fishery near the South Georgia Island and South Sandwich Islands successfully managed by the British to provide great quantities of fish in a sustainable way. Surprisingly, the book's discussion of pollution includes the British Petroleum (BP) oil spill that occurred in the summer of 2010, just a few months before *Atlantic* arrived in bookstores.

If Winchester is a believer in the evils of humans and their pollution, he seems agnostic on the question of whether humans are causing global warming, though he is certain of its effects. "The Storm Surge Carries All Before" is his analysis of global warming, the clearly shifting and melting sea ice, and its implications for the animals and humans who live in and near the ocean. "It is clear," he concludes, "that some exceedingly strange things are happening in today's Atlantic Ocean, and no one is quite sure why."

One of Winchester's greatest strengths is his ability to bring both wide-angle and zoom lenses to his material—to show the expansiveness of the great ocean as well as the struggles and achievements of individual human beings. In *Atlantic* he frequently enhances his explanations of history and science with accounts of his own travels, and he does seem to have left few corners of the ocean unexplored. He opens the book with an account of his own first Atlantic crossing, at the age of eighteen, on the ocean liner *Empress of Britain*. To his description of the well-managed fisheries in the South Atlantic Ocean he adds a relatively recent visit he made to the Falkland Islands, where an old school friend is deputy governor; his description of the 1982 war between Great Britain and Argentina over the Falklands includes a mention of the author's own presence there during the conflict, and his unfounded arrest for espionage, which is told more fully in his third book, *Prison Diary: Argentina* (1983). In other chapters he remembers visits to the Faeroe Islands, Cape Town, Hong Kong, the Grand Banks, the north of Scotland, the Gulf coast, and Greenland. He closes the book with the moving story of Angus Campbell Macintyre, the heroic World War II tugboat first mate to whom the book is dedicated, and with Winchester's own journey to find the remains of Macintyre's wrecked ship on the Skeleton Coast in northern Namibia.

One always wishes for maps in a book such as this, and Winchester helpfully provides them: In addition to beautiful illustrations of ships and fish and artwork, there are a political map, a physical map, a map showing the routes of the great explorers, a map of the Gulf Stream current drawn by Benjamin Franklin, a map of shrinking Antarctic ice, and even a map showing where commercial airplanes cross the Atlantic. Readers, most of whom will not come to the book with Winchester's firsthand familiarity with the globe, will find themselves constantly flipping back to the maps to remind themselves where the Faeroes and the Cape Verde Islands are, or how far Cape Horn is from the Cape of Good Hope. For all his experience as a world traveler, Winchester has an uncanny sense of what the reader has forgotten—or never knew— about where things are. These images enrich the narrative, but it is Winchester's skill at turning history and science into beautiful and compelling stories that makes for a compelling history of the Atlantic Ocean.

Cynthia A. Bily

Review Sources

Booklist 107, no. 1 (September 1, 2010): 23.
The Economist 397 (October 30, 2010): 92.
Kirkus Reviews 78, no. 15 (August 1, 2010): 720.
Library Journal 135, no. 14 (September 1, 2010): 122.
National Geographic Traveler 27, no. 8 (November/December, 2010): 43.
Nature 468 (November 4, 2010): 33.
Publishers Weekly 257, no. 35 (September 6, 2010): 31.
The Spectator 314, no. 9506 (November 6, 2010): 49.
USA Today, December 16, 2010, p. 10B.
The Wall Street Journal, November 1, 2010, p. A19.

THE AUTOBIOGRAPHY OF AN EXECUTION

Author: David R. Dow (1959-   )
Publisher: Hachette Book Group (New York). 271 pp.
   $24.99; paperback $14.99
Type of work: Memoir, law
Time: 1989-2010
Locale: Texas

Part autobiography, part polemic, and part history, the book is an examination of the death penalty by a Texas lawyer and teacher

David R. Dow's *The Autobiography of an Execution* is an unusual book for two reasons: In order to protect client confidentiality, including the confidentiality of the dead, Dow has scrambled the facts of the cases he discusses and the names of the clients, judges, and lawyers involved. Consequently, there is no way to check or verify his facts. Moreover there are events in Dow's story that are out of the ordinary: In the midst of one of Dow's cases the judge, a woman, comes on to him; a state trooper lets him out of a 100-mile-per-hour-plus speeding ticket when he learns that Dow is hurrying to prison to try to stave off an execution; and some of the lawyers the state provides for defense of the indigent are either stupid, drunk, or negligent, sometimes all three. None of these things is implicitly unbelievable, but the reader has to accept Dow's reputation for integrity in order to credit his statements.

The second unusual feature of this book is its moving discussion of Dow's constant recourse to his family. The narrative frequently switches between his case and his family relationships. His wife, Katya, and his six-year-old son, Lincoln, ease the strains and disappointments of his death-sentence work. They also teach him important lessons about human behavior and caring that serve him well as he works on his cases. If readers are to take him at face value, they see that he is fortunate in his family life. His occasional despair makes him testy; he fears that he is an inadequate parent and husband. Katya and Lincoln help him through these periods. He also draws sustenance from exercise. He and his dog run together and this quasi solitude also calms him.

The case around which *The Autobiography of an Execution* revolves is the imminent execution of the man Dow calls "Henry Quaker." Although the pseudonym is evocative, Dow is no "bleeding heart" when it comes to his clients. He says that of the more than one hundred death penalty cases on which he has worked, he has only doubted the guilt of seven of the defendants. He recognizes that nearly all of his clients are bad people and gives examples of some of the dreadful things they have done.

However, Quaker is one of the seven. Dow thinks he may have been innocent. The evidence in the case is ambiguous. Had Quaker had a decent defense at trial it is possible that a jury could have acquitted him. Unfortunately for Quaker, his trial lawyer

~

David R. Dow teaches law at the University of Houston Law Center. He has written or edited several books on law and the death penalty, including Executed on a Technicality: Lethal Injustice of America's Death Row *(2005) and* Machinery of Death *(2002).*

~

was a drunk who actually slept through much of the trial. To make it worse, his first appellate lawyer failed to raise several crucial issues, the most important of which would have been the claim that Quaker was inadequately represented at trial.

Quaker was accused of murdering his wife, Dorris, from whom he had been separated for several months, and their two children, twelve-year-old Daniel and eight-year-old Charisse. In 1995, a neighbor found Dorris, Daniel, and Charisse shot to death in their home. According to the police reports no gun was found at the scene. Investigation revealed that Quaker owned a .22-caliber pistol. This pistol was never found, but .22-caliber bullets were found in the bodies of his murdered family. Blood, which deoxyribonucleic acid (DNA) analysis proved to belong to Daniel, was found in Quaker's truck. Dorris and the children were covered by a life-insurance policy worth $500,000. That was the sum of the evidence that emerged against Quaker at trial.

Quaker's trial lawyer, "Jack Gatling," slept through part of the trial. He failed to challenge any of the circumstantial evidence, put on no witnesses, and advised Quaker not to testify on his own behalf. Many defense opportunities were lost. For example, Dow later learned that Daniel suffered frequent nose bleeds. Had Gatling bothered to discover this and put it in evidence it would have undercut one of the major pieces of circumstantial evidence against Quaker.

Even in the absence of any defense, it took the jury six hours to decide to convict Quaker. Under Texas law if a defendant is convicted of capital murder, there is then a separate punishment hearing before the jury to decide whether the defendant should be executed. In the punishment hearing Gatling did not even bother to make a plea for mercy and brought no evidence whatever in mitigation. After three further hours of jury deliberation Quaker was condemned to death. Gatling died of cirrhosis of the liver not long after the trial.

A new attorney represented Quaker in the appellate process. Like all other states, Texas has fairly rigid rules about the content of appeals in criminal cases. Courts will not entertain appeals that the jury got the facts wrong. Only procedural defects can be appealed. The defendant is entitled to one trip through the state appellate processes; if he loses in the state courts, he may bring any federal issues before federal courts, but he can only raise the issues that have been decided at the state court level. Given these rules, it is crucial that all available issues be raised on the first appeal in the state courts. Quaker's second attorney unaccountably failed to raise the matter of the incompetent representation that Quaker had received. Quaker's state court appeal was denied. Dow points out that both the trial judge and the prosecutor must have known perfectly well that Quaker was not being adequately defended. The system, he argues, is geared to disposing of cases rather than discovering the truth.

Dow and his colleagues in the Texas Defender Service entered the case after the state court denied Quaker's appeal. An execution date had been set for Quaker. Working with short deadlines is characteristic of death-penalty appellate cases. Dow alludes to frequent all-night sessions to prepare last-minute appeals as the moment of execution approaches. The strain is immense.

In this case, the immediate problem for Dow was finding some ground on which Quaker's case could be brought before a court again. The only available avenue appeared to be to find new evidence. Under narrow circumstances new evidence, not available at trial, can be the gravamen of a new appeal. As Dow and his colleagues looked into the facts of the case two theories emerged. The first was that Dorris killed the children and then committed suicide. In order to demonstrate this it had to be shown that the blood droplets between the couch where Dorris was found and the rooms in which the children were found belonged to the children, proving that they had been killed first. It also had to be shown that the investigating detective had in fact found a gun at the site of the killing and had lied. Neither fact was demonstrable; indeed, there seemed no conceivable reason that a detective would have lied about the gun, as its presence at the scene would have closed the case easily and quickly. Moreover, the blood evidence showed that Dorris had died first.

Dow turned to the question of whether some other person might have been the murderer. Here some murky evidence emerged. "Ezekiel Green," another death-row inmate, somewhat demented, told Dow that a man named "Ruben Cantu" had done it and had told Green about it. There were two problems with Green's statement. Under the rules of evidence it was "hearsay." Hearsay is normally inadmissible. The second problem was that Green himself was to be executed shortly and thus be unavailable for any future proceedings. Dow interviewed Cantu and learned that the police had questioned him at the time of the murder. Dow reasoned that there must have been some ground to suspect Cantu.

Dow dealt with Green's imminent death by taking a deposition and having him take a polygraph test. Polygraph test results are normally excluded in legal proceedings, but Dow thought that the results might strengthen his application for a stay and possibly a new trial. Green passed the polygraph test. Two days later he was executed.

An application for a stay was filed, and the trial judge who had signed Quaker's death warrant withdrew the execution date; the prosecution responded by arguing to the Texas appeals court that she did not have the power to withdraw the date as no appeal was pending in her court. The appeals court agreed with the prosecutor. Last-minute attempts to get the U.S. Supreme Court to intervene failed, and Quaker was put to death.

The bare recitation of Quaker's case does not really do justice to Dow's book. Many other death-penalty cases that he knows about are discussed. *The Autobiography of an Execution* is well written. One of Dow's great strengths as a writer is his ability to convert legal and jurisdictional procedures into clear lay language. He has great contempt for legal technicalities, as he believes that the objective of saving lives is more important than maintaining a set of rules whose purpose is to maintain a smoothly running system of justice in which cases can be closed. Most lawyers and judges would disagree with this controversial view. Many of the incidents Dow discusses also show a deplorable want of skill, intelligence, and even humanity among judges and attorneys. He is particularly critical of the U.S. Court of Appeals for the Fifth Circuit which, as he sees it, is largely staffed by cronies of the Texas political establishment, nearly all of whom are proponents of the death penalty.

The greatest strength of *The Autobiography of an Execution* is its loving portrayal of Dow's family. His wife, Katya; his son, Lincoln; and his dog, Winnie, provide him with sustenance in the demanding and tense work that he does. If it is true, as he himself says, that he is bookish, plodding, unforgiving, short-tempered, surly, and unpleasant to be around, his family both forgives and humanizes him. Even if, as one suspects, he is not quite so intransigent and narrow-minded as his own description avers, it is clear that the warmth and sensitivity of his family relationships keep him centered. The light he casts on these relationships is the most rewarding part of what is a wonderful book.

Robert Jacobs

Review Sources

The Economist 395, no. 8680 (May 1, 2010): 85.
Kirkus Reviews 77, no. 22 (November 15, 2009): 1188-1189.
Library Journal 135, no. 9 (May 15, 2010): 52.
The New York Review of Books 57, no. 18 (November 25, 2010): 31-33.
The New York Times, February 14, 2010, p. 10.
Publishers Weekly 256, no. 41 (October 12, 2009): 39.

AUTOBIOGRAPHY OF MARK TWAIN, VOLUME 1

Author: Mark Twain (Samuel Langhorne Clemens; 1835-1910)
Edited by Harriet Elinor Smith
Publisher: University of California Press (Berkeley). 736 pp. $95.00
Type of work: Memoir
Time: 1835-1910
Locale: United States

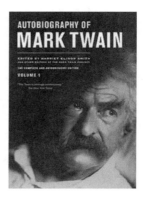

This first of three volumes of Twain's vast autobiographical writings is a significant publishing event; several Twain autobiographies have been published before, but none can rival the completeness and meticulous editing and annotating standards of this version prepared by the Mark Twain Project at the University of California at Berkeley

Principal personages:
 MARK TWAIN (SAMUEL LANGHORNE CLEMENS; 1825-1910), an American author
 OLIVIA CLEMENS (1845-1904), his wife, whom he married in 1870
 SUSY CLEMENS (1872-1896), his oldest daughter, whose biography of him he frequently quotes in his own autobiography
 ULYSSES S. GRANT (1822-1885), a Civil War general and former U.S. president

It is a testament to the enduring popularity of Mark Twain, one of the most iconic American writers, that fully one hundred years after his 1910 death, a 736-page book that constitutes merely the first of three volumes of his autobiography should top national best-seller lists. That any work by such a long-dead author should achieve such sales success is remarkable. More remarkable still is that this has happened despite the fact that most of the text in this volume has already been published in earlier versions of Twain's autobiography. To appreciate the significance of this new edition, it is necessary to review the history of Mark Twain autobiography—a subject thoroughly covered in editor Harriet Elinor Smith's thoughtful, fifty-eight-page introduction to *Autobiography of Mark Twain*.

An introspective writer who always questioned his own honesty, Twain had a lifelong fascination with autobiography as a literary form. He expressed that fascination in an 1887 letter to his wife, Olivia, stating that "apparently no narrative that tells the facts of a man's life in the man's own words, can be uninteresting." Not surprisingly, perhaps, he regarded his own life as exceptionally interesting—as, indeed, it was—and he burned with a desire to put those facts into words. As early as 1870, the year he married Olivia and before he was even thirty-five years old, he began experimentally

Mark Twain is best known for his most widely read novels, The Adventures of Tom Sawyer *(1876),* The Prince and the Pauper *(1881),* Adventures of Huckleberry Finn *(1884),* A Connecticut Yankee in King Arthur's Court *(1889), and* The Tragedy of Pudd'nhead Wilson *(1894).*

writing his autobiography. However, although he was a prolific writer comfortable in a variety of prose forms, he had great difficulty finding an autobiographical form that suited him. Over the following thirty-five years, he dabbled at autobiography, rarely sustaining his efforts for any substantial period. Part of his problem was doubtless his inability to express uncomfortable truths about himself—a fact he admitted in a 1904 letter to his close friend author William Dean Howells. In that letter, he described an autobiography as

the truest of all books; for while it inevitably consists mainly of extinctions of the truth, shirkings of the truth, partial revealments of the truth, with hardly an instance of plain straight truth, the remorseless truth *is* there, between the lines, where the author-cat is raking dust upon it which hides from the disinterested spectator neither it nor its smell.

Throughout the nineteenth century, as Twain struggled to find an autobiographical form, he published fiction, sketches, essays, and travel books. His travel writings are especially interesting; as accounts of his own real-life experiences, they might be read as autobiography. However, with the partial exception of *Following the Equator* (1897), a comparatively straightforward account of his around-the-world lecture tour in 1895-1896, all his travel books are so highly embellished with exaggerations, deliberate distortions, and outright fiction that it is difficult even to regard their firsthand narrators as Twain himself. Indeed, when it comes to extinctions, shirkings, and partial revealments of truth with few instances of plain straight truth, *The Innocents Abroad* (1869), *Roughing It* (1872), *A Tramp Abroad* (1880), and major parts of *Life on the Mississippi* (1883) cannot be seriously regarded as autobiography.

Meanwhile, most of the experiments in straight autobiography that Twain wrote between 1870 and 1905 are essentially anecdotal memoirs about subjects that happened to be on his mind at the time he wrote about them. Examples include a huge tract of land in Tennessee bequeathed by his father that became a family albatross; General Ulysses S. Grant, whose Civil War memoirs his own company published during the 1880's; and an experience he had in Hawaii during the 1860's that enhanced his reputation as a journalist.

Twain finally found a form that satisfied him in 1906, when he discovered that dictating to a stenographer made it easy for him to express himself spontaneously. He concluded that the best way to compose autobiography was to start at no particular time of your life; wander at your free will all over your life; talk only about the thing which interests you for the moment; drop it the moment its interest threatens to pale, and turn your talk upon the new and more interesting thing that has intruded itself into your mind meantime.

Over the following two and one-half years, Twain dictated autobiographical passages almost daily. In addition to freely talking about a wide range of subjects—many of which had little to do with his own life—he injected clippings from newspapers and long passages from the manuscript his daughter Susy had written about him when she was very young. Well before this time, Twain had determined that his autobiography should not be published until a century after he died, so that he would, in effect, be "speaking from the grave." He thought that this liberating point of view would combine with his newly discovered technique of discursive dictating to free him to tell the whole truth about himself. In reality, however, he is rarely more revealing than most authors of autobiographies.

Earlier published editions of Twain's autobiography have incorporated some of his "experimental" passages as integral parts of his autobiography proper. However, Smith and her colleagues opted not to regard them as such after discovering evidence that helped determine exactly what Twain wanted to include. The experimental writings nevertheless occupy about 140 pages of *Autobiography of Mark Twain* but are labeled "Preliminary Manuscripts and Dictations, 1870-1905." The "Autobiography" proper does not formally begin until page 203. This latter section fills the next 268 pages of the book, followed by nearly 300 pages of detailed and fascinating explanatory notes, appendixes, bibliographical references, and a wonderfully detailed index.

Some readers may regard the editors' distinction between "Preliminary Manuscripts and Dictations" and "Autobiography" as petty and perhaps even pedantic. However, this distinction reflects a fundamental principle underlying this and all Mark Twain editions prepared by the Mark Twain Project, namely the goal of presenting Twain's works exactly as he intended. In the case of new editions of such previously published books as *The Adventures of Tom Sawyer* (1876), *Roughing It*, and *Adventures of Huckleberry Finn* (1884), that objective was achieved by meticulously examining every surviving scrap of Twain's manuscripts, typescripts, and galley pages personally corrected by Twain and other pieces of evidence that helped reveal what Twain intended for those books. The process is broadly similar to producing what is called a "director's cut" in modern filmmaking: After directors finish their films, the producers often have the films recut and reedited before they are released. Much later, if the directors are lucky, they are allowed to recut their own films to restore their original conceptions. What the Mark Twain Project editors try to do is akin to inviting Twain himself to come back to supervise "recutting" his books. The result is editions that general readers, students, and scholars can confidently regard as being as close to definitive as is possible in the absence of Twain's personal supervision.

Although the Mark Twain Project's goal of publishing Twain's autobiography as he intended it to be is identical to its goal for all his books, the challenges presented by the autobiography are vastly different because no complete edition of the work was ever published under Twain's supervision. When he died in 1910, he left about 500,000 words of autobiographical writings and dictations with no clear instructions on how they should be organized or even what should and should not be included. As a consequence, every previous published version of this material has been radically different and less than satisfactory.

Although Twain more than once declared that his autobiography should not be published until he had been dead for one hundred years, this new University of California Press edition is actually the fifth, not the first, published version of his autobiographical writings. In fact, Twain himself violated his dictum several years before he died. Motivated primarily by his need for money, he published about 100,000 words of autobiographical material in twenty-five installments titled "Chapters from My Autobiography" in the *North American Review* (1906-1907). Most of that money he used to build his final home—an Italianate mansion outside Redding, Connecticut, that he fittingly dubbed "Autobiography House" (he later changed its name to "Stormfield").

The *North American Review* articles constitute the only portions of Twain's autobiography that Twain personally saw through publication, but he made no effort to present them as anything more than extracts from the much larger work that was to be published after his death. Many years later, after the magazine articles had fallen into the public domain, they were reprinted in books titled *Mark Twain's Own Autobiography* (1990), *Chapters from My Autobiography* (1996), and *My Autobiography* (1999). Before then, however, three more ambitious autobiographical publications had appeared.

After Twain died in 1910, the only person to have access to his unpublished manuscripts was his official biographer, literary executor, and editor, Albert Bigelow Paine, an author and former magazine editor. Over the following twenty-five years, Paine organized and cataloged Twain's huge mass of unpublished manuscripts and drew upon them to publish new volumes of Twain speeches, letters, sketches, short stories, essays, and notebooks. In 1924, he published 195,000 words—including much of what had already appeared in the *North American Review*—in two volumes titled *Mark Twain's Autobiography*. In the absence of any independent oversight of how he selected and edited this material, Paine's version stood as the standard edition of Twain autobiography for thirty-five years. Although he obviously ignored Twain's request that his autobiography not be published until a century after his death, Paine did attempt to follow Twain's instruction that the material be arranged in the chronological order in which it was created. Not until much later was it discovered that Paine had taken great liberties in rewriting and expurgating Twain's words, partly so as not to offend Twain's sole surviving daughter, Clara Clemens Gabrilowitsch.

After Paine died in 1935, editorship of Twain's papers passed to Bernard DeVoto, the first professional scholar to gain unrestricted access to the manuscript collection that Paine had long sheltered from outside eyes. DeVoto soon undertook to correct what he regarded as the deficiencies of Paine's edition of the autobiography—not by redoing the work but by adding to it. He collected about 100,000 words of previously unused material in *Mark Twain in Eruption: Hitherto Unpublished Pages About Men and Events* in 1940. In sharp contrast to Paine's edition, this new volume was organized by subject matter under nine headings, with titles such as "Theodore Roosevelt," "Andrew Carnegie," "The Plutocracy," "Hannibal Days," and "Various Literary People." Like Paine, DeVoto acted as a censor by omitting material he regarded as too scandalous or simply insufficiently interesting, and he was not shy about editing Twain's punctuation to conform to his own standards.

The next major version of the autobiography was published in 1959 as *The Autobiography of Mark Twain*, edited by Charles Neider, a freelance writer who would go on to edit more than a dozen volumes of Twain's writings. Radically different from its predecessors, Neider's edition of the autobiography drew freely on previously published portions, to which some new material was added, but rearranged it in a form that attempted to mimic the chronological structure of more traditional autobiographies. Although the resulting book separated passages intended to be read in sequence and ripped many passages out of their original contexts, it won acceptance as the standard version of the autobiography through the next sixty years.

With the publication of the University of California Press's *Autobiography of Mark Twain* in 2010, all previous versions can be permanently retired. Thanks to what was published in those earlier versions, only a small portion of Mark Twain's texts appear in this new edition for the first time. Readers already familiar with those earlier versions may not find much that surprises in this new edition. However, for the first time, they can be confident that nothing—even including canceled text—has been left out, that nothing has been altered, and that everything is arranged as Twain intended it. Moreover, with the wealth of annotation material assembled by the editors, *Autobiography of Mark Twain* offers one of the richest sources of information on Twain ever assembled in a single volume.

R. Kent Rasmussen

Review Sources

Library Journal 135, no. 15 (September 15, 2010): 74.
Publishers Weekly 257, no. 38 (September 27, 2010): 50.
Booklist 107, no. 2 (September 15, 2010): 16.
Commentary 130, no. 4 (November, 2010): 59-62.
First Things: A Monthly Journal of Religion and Public Life, no. 207 (November, 2010): 73-76.
People 74, no. 17 (November 18, 2010): 47.
Time 176, no. 21 (November 22, 2010): 103-105.

THE AXE AND THE OATH
Ordinary Life in the Middle Ages

Author: Robert Fossier (1927-   )
First published: Ces gens du Moyen Âge, 2007, in France
Translated from the French by Lydia G. Cochrane
Publisher: Princeton University Press (Princeton, N.J.).
   384 pp. $35.00
Type of work: History

A leading medievalist summarizes a lifetime of academic study in a nonacademic volume

The Axe and the Oath offers a broad-brush account of ordinary people's lives in medieval Europe, based on its author's studies during sixty years as a medievalist, educator, and historical curator. More than this, the book sums up the French scholar Robert Fossier's lifelong personal reflections, which often have run counter to the conventional wisdom of his profession.

Despite being the work of a disciplined scholar and educator, *The Axe and the Oath* is not a classroom textbook, nor does it supply a scholarly apparatus of references, footnotes, bibliography, and index to identify sources of evidence supporting his arguments. Having labored long under those constraints, Fossier undertakes to soar freely above them toward a panoramic view of his subject.

In some ways this work could be likened to W. Somerset Maugham's *The Summing Up* (1938), which is not a conventional autobiography but a disciplined novelist's endeavor to organize his thoughts on subjects of lifelong interest to him, subjects that would not necessarily fit into a fictional narrative. Similarly, certain of Fossier's personal interests—or at least his way of considering them—could not necessarily be expounded in academic fashion, and as a result, *The Axe and the Oath* is a different kind of book from others he has produced. Still, it may have been those personal concerns that drew him into an academic study of medieval history in the first place. In this book he reverts, perhaps, to those original concerns and the conclusions he has reached about them.

Fossier's stated goal in *The Axe and the Oath* is to "follow very ordinary [medieval] people in their daily lives and daily cares, their material concerns in particular." This perspective leads him to scorn abstract historical "certitudes," as he has done in the past. For example: "Was this a segment of time in which the economy and society had certain distinct traits—'feudalism,' as [Karl] Marx would have it? But, really, did people eat 'feudally'?"

The way ordinary folk actually did eat is one of the subjects he discusses at length. Their simple meals of "bread . . . , a piece of cheese, a bit of meat" are contrasted with the elaborate, days-long, conspicuously wasteful feasts of the upper classes. The author notes that common folk would normally wipe their mouths on their sleeves except on holidays, when linen was used. He even itemizes the after-dinner portions left to dogs.

Common people's beverages, too, receive meticulous attention. They often avoided water, especially from rivers, which was not sanitary and was likely to cause disease. Instead, most common people drank beer rather than the fine wines available to the nobility. As an example of the rich detail offered in this book, Fossier reports that the production of

Robert Fossier began his career as curator at the historical library of Paris. In 1971, he received the silver medal of Le Centre National de la Recherché Scientifique (CNRS, or National Centre for Scientific Research). In 1993, he became professor emeritus of medieval history at the Sorbonne.

beer increased markedly in the thirteenth century, but that it was "not the beer that we know. The Celtic *cervoise* and the Saxon *al* were bitter and brownish" and made from oats, whereas Germanic beer was made from barley, with hops added later in the Middle Ages.

With similar generosity of detail, Fossier describes the evolution of clothing and hairstyles during the thousand-year period of the Middle Ages. He notes wryly that "medieval clothing had no pockets, an inconvenience sometimes shared with women's clothing today." He also describes medieval practices and attitudes regarding marriage, sex, children, work, illness and health, nature, and religion. Also, although he purports to focus on "their material concerns in particular," he also examines how ordinary people perceived and experienced medieval society, culture, and matters of the spirit.

Fossier holds that "all of those [medieval] men, no matter what their origin, clearly ate, slept, walked, defecated, copulated, and even thought in the same ways that we do." As one of his major conclusions in this book, he declares that medieval people were more similar than dissimilar to people of the early twenty-first century, or, as he puts it, "in spite of the convictions brandished by almost all medieval historians, I am persuaded that medieval man is us."

Despite his insistence on sticking to the concrete facts of medieval life, Fossier's narrative in *The Axe and the Oath* almost never descends into the lives of individuals. Perhaps wishing to distill decades of immersion in his subject, he is far more inclined toward general observations such as "Control over animals indicated rank and placed the individual. The horseman physically dominated the pedestrian." Occasionally, his meditations take on a romantic tone: "As with nautical sports and oceanic competitions today, people of those centuries saw the sea as fully charged with marvellous and dreamlike qualities."

In his earlier works, too, Fossier concentrated on everyday people of the Middle Ages and the actual trends—as opposed to abstract historical concepts—that shaped everyday life. In *Enfance de l'Europe: Xe-XIIe siècle—aspects économiques et sociaux* (1982), to maintain this focus and to counter abstract theories of feudalism and serfdom, he originated the concept of *encellulement* (translated as "encellment" in

The Axe and the Oath), referring to the tenth century decentralization of power into local seigneuries, or lordships, giving the affiliation between lord and vassal primacy among human relationships.

Fossier deplores the abuses that the "encellment" process often entailed. Indeed, many of his generalizing comments serve to indict the political trends of the time, both as injustices and as futile attempts to establish impenetrable security for the ruling class. He and others have published detailed research on the destructive influence of predatory nobles who oppressed the peasantry and seized resources for their own castles. His generalizations demonstrate his view, expressed abundantly throughout the book, that all forms of social organization to guard against the inescapable dangers of illness, political chaos, and natural disaster are illusory.

It should not be surprising that a book expressing such views, and failing to fit into an established literary genre, has met with an uneven critical reception. Many reviewers confessed they did not know what to make of the book's English title, *The Axe and the Oath*, which the author never explains. The French title of the book, originally published in 2007, was *Ces gens du Moyen Âge*, which may be translated "these people of the Middle Ages"—a title giving its subject a certain immediacy. Indeed, Fossier takes every opportunity to emphasize the similarities between common medieval folk and modern-day people. As he clearly believes that medieval political organization was a futile attempt to avoid hardship, he seems to imply that modern political organization is likewise futile.

Although his publisher described the book as being for general readers, Fossier himself wondered in his conclusion whether the book would be too "simplistic for the erudite, confusing for the student, obscure for the non-initiate?" Judging by several of the critical responses, he had cause for concern. Clearly, some reviewers were expecting a different book. Scholars had anticipated an academic book, and other reviewers, perhaps, looked for a politically correct book. A work that cannot be easily categorized may run into critical difficulties.

One college-affiliated reviewer, Brian Renvall, noted that the absence of reference notes, bibliography, and index would constitute a serious concern for academic libraries, though not necessarily for other organizations or individuals. Nonetheless, Renvall commended the book on all other criteria.

The lack of footnotes, references, and bibliography, however, led another reviewer to suggest that Fossier has behaved autocratically. The complaint was that this lack leaves skeptical readers unable to verify Fossier's claims in the book unless they do the research themselves. This reviewer expressed irritation that "Fossier tells you his unvarnished opinion and that is his sole objective." Nonetheless, one wonders how an author can provide references for an assertion such as this: "All culture, even all civilization, is a struggle against fear. . . . Only among humans does fear take on a metaphysical dimension."

The same reviewer, Juanita Feros Ruys, also charged Fossier with misogyny and neglect of women in his narrative. To his comment that "Women did not write" in the Middle Ages, she responded that three decades of feminist research has revealed the works of both individual women writers and female monastic communities. It may be fair to suggest that Fossier has underestimated the significance of a renowned medieval author such as Christine de Pizan (1365-c. 1430), though he does show familiarity with her work. However, the assertion by this critic that Fossier is guilty of "old-fashioned misogyny . . . an indulgent paternalistic smile at their inherent coquetry, or their slyness, or their ability to manipulate men" does not appear to be supported anywhere in the text of *The Axe and the Oath*.

On the contrary, Fossier seems to take every opportunity to acknowledge the important role of women in all aspects of medieval life and to reproach medieval society itself for failing to recognize the existence of women, let alone their achievements. As one example, Fossier laments "the female sex, so poorly treated in the texts" of what is known as demographic reporting—that is, the enumeration of medieval women was faulty, as was that of "the new born, the extremely old . . . the miserably poor." He sharply criticizes "men of the church" who "haughtily ignored" women. Fossier scathingly condemns the misogyny of medieval thinkers who held women responsible for Adam's fall. His primary point is that the judgments handed down to posterity about women are those of "men without women, and this was all the Christian world heard."

As to Fossier's treatment of sex in the Middle Ages, Ruys compares *The Axe and the Oath* most unfavorably with James Brundage's *Law, Sex, and Christian Society in Medieval Europe* (1990) on the grounds that Brundage's seven-hundred-page work is "closely argued . . . , with masses of supporting material." In *The Axe and the Oath*, however, Fossier clearly did not have the same goals in mind. He declares in his conclusion that he has nothing to "demonstrate." He does, however, reflect at length on the misunderstanding and frustration that existed between the sexes during the Middle Ages.

Fossier, then, is describing attitudes of the Middle Ages, not defending them, and there seems to be a critical misunderstanding: Ruys makes a personal attack on what she sees as Fossier's contempt and condescension toward women, when in fact he is explicitly critiquing misogyny in the medieval society he examines. The misconstruction of Fossier's intent points up an issue common in contemporary book reviewing: the tendency to ascribe base motives to one's intellectual antagonists rather than stick to evaluation of their work.

These are among the dangers confronting a hard-to-classify work such as Fossier's, which led him to wonder whether the book would be too "simplistic . . . , confusing . . . , [and] obscure." Still, although some reviewers shared this uncertainty, the disappointment they felt has not kept even the harshest critics from acknowledging that Fossier's perspective on the Middle Ages is intriguing and invigorating. Fossier's own final declaration is, "I felt like saying all this, and that is enough." As the fruit of more than six decades in the study of historical documents and artifacts, this is an engrossing and thought-provoking volume of deeply personal reflections.

Thomas Rankin

Review Sources

ForeWord 13, no. 5 (September/October, 2010): 47.
History Today 60, no. 11 (November, 2010): 58-59.
Library Journal 135, no. 14 (September 1, 2010): 120.
Times Higher Education, no. 1971 (October 28, 2010): 58.
The Times Literary Supplement, no. 5612 (October 22, 2010): 27.

THE BARS OF ATLANTIS
Selected Essays

Author: Durs Grünbein (1962-   )
Translated from the German by John Crutchfield,
   Michael Hofmann, and Andrew Shields
Publisher: Farrar, Straus and Giroux (New York).
   323 pp. $35.00
Type of work: Essays
Locale: Dresden, Germany; Italy; and the depths of the
   ocean

*A major contemporary German poet shares his passion
for deep-sea diving, German philosophy and literature, the
fine arts, and Roman satirists*

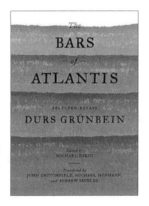

Durs Grünbein's *Ashes for Breakfast*, a selection of po-
ems ably translated by Michael Hofmann, made a strong impression on major American poets and critics when it appeared in 2005. John Ashbery called Grünbein "one of
the most intelligent poets writing in German today," and Helen Vendler, the dean of
American critics of poetry, was kept up all night by her first reading of Grünbein's
"sardonic humor, the savagery, [his] violent candor—all expressed in lines of cool
formal elegance." Seldom does a foreign-language poet arouse such attention, but
Grünbein is an extraordinary literary phenomenon. The author of eight volumes of
poetry, as well as essays and translations from the Greek and Latin and *The Bars of
Atlantis*, he is the recipient of a host of major German literary prizes, including the
most prestigious, the Georg Büchner Prize, which he won at the age of thirty-three.

If the poet in Grünbein tends toward the sardonic and grim diet of the everyday, the
essayist is a gentler soul that feeds on reflection, nostalgia, and the pleasures of aesthetic experience. Grünbein was born in Dresden, famous for its devastating fire
bombing in late World War II, but his childhood memories are not overshadowed by
the suffering his city experienced a generation before his birth. He recalls as a child
rummaging in a huge garbage dump for obscure refuse and wandering half asleep in the
predawn hours in the deserted street in front of his home. Recalling a class visit with his
primary-school peers to the famous baroque Zwinger Museum in Dresden, Grünbein
remembers that the fuss made over the museum's Raphael Madonna could not keep
him from being far more absorbed by the sensuous Titian nude on the adjacent wall.

Grünbein celebrates the perceiving "eye." He cites the objective instrument of physical perception glorified by Charles Darwin in his research and marvels at the fact that
the same remarkably intricate physical organ is used by fish probing the deepest channels of the ocean. There is something of Ralph Waldo Emerson's famous "transparent
eyeball" in Grünbein's celebration of the imaginative eye of the painter and the poet
who see their way into the deepest recesses of the human mind and into the mysteries of

~

*Durs Grünbein, author of twelve
volumes of poetry and four collections
of essays, has been awarded many
major German literary prizes.*

~

the natural world. "Personally, " he writes in the essay, "The Poem and Its Secret," "I believe that what is expressed in poems is the human devotion to the transcendental—together with a concomitant fidelity to this world's prodigious wealth of detail."

In the essay that gives this collection its title—"The Bars of Atlantis"—Grünbein sees in the mythic sea voyages of discovery celebrated in Homer, Dante, and Romantic poetry, a trope for poetry itself. One step ahead of the great mariners and sea dogs of battle and commerce, the poets explore the real world primarily to go beyond its confines. Atlantis, the lost world of antique mythology, beckons the poet and lures him to a kind of shipwreck on its hidden sandbars far out at the edge of the known world.

In a passage rich in metaphors and ideas that bring together his love of travel, the discovery of antiquity, immersion in works of art (particularly painting), and the growth of the poet's mind, Grünbein recalls a journey in his youth to the remote and impressive Doric temples of Paestum south of Naples. These Greek architectural remains are not really ruins in the traditional sense because of their remarkable state of preservation. Deep in what was once a swamp, they escaped decay and plunder and seem to rise out of the ground like the vestiges of a lost world. Indeed the well-preserved columns seem to resemble vegetative trunks in a verdant jungle. In "The Poem and Its Secret," Grünbein noted that "Only among the poets does one come across . . . those successful moments of reconciliation between something purely ideal and its unexpectedly concrete manifestations." Even as he describes the effect of Paestum on his "eyes," Grünbein is sharing with his readers the growth of his poetic imagination.

This becomes even more dramatic when he recounts his visit to a small anthropological museum at the edge of Paestum. Here Grünbein encounters a haunting painting on the lid of a tomb erected to memorialize a young athlete. The Tomb of the Diver depicts the dead man as diving into the sea—from the land of the living into the unknown land of the dead. With his life ahead of him, Grünbein nevertheless intuitively grasps the connection between the poet's readiness to embrace the unknown in the very act of experiencing the known; to imagine a continuum in which life and death are reconciled. With characteristic humility, Grünbein recounts that at the time he was not ready to shoulder the poet's tragic mantle. Instead he translated his fascination with the Greek diver in the painting into a yearning for the same kind of intimacy with the sea.

Grünbein immediately took up deep-sea diving, which became the hobby of a lifetime and took him to reefs and depths Charles Darwin would have envied. There is a humorous account of Grünbein's stumbling on a school of "peripatetic" shrimp in conclave in the depths below the entrance to the Blue Grotto in Capri.

The reader will no doubt wonder what drives Grünbein's need to share the evolving and growing spirit of his poetic imagination as a process in tandem with his personal history and curiosity about nature. Ultimately, he comes to understand that philosophy and poetry share a strange history of their own and that the deference of the one to the other is not an open-and-shut case. Grünbein is a classical scholar and at home in all aspects of the classical heritage in philosophy and literary criticism. He takes umbrage at the "usurpation" of poetry by philosophy in Plato's Socratic dialogues. In the dialogue "Ion," the poet, or rhapsode, who gives the dialogue its title, is ridiculed by Socrates as a performer and reciter of Homer without any clear *techne* or methodology and incapable of defending the integrity or pragmatic value of what he does. In his zeal to establish the ascendancy of reason, in its inductive and deductive schemes of logical analysis and argument, Plato obscures the fact that before him philosophy was identified with imagery, meter, and the inspiration of the "Muses, who inspire all knowledge." This was true of both Parmenides and Heraclitus, the pre-Socratic philosophers. Poetry has never recovered from being "demoted to a mere pastime," says Grünbein, and this is true despite "such occasional counteroffensives as Friedrich Schiller's project of an 'aesthetic education' of mankind . . . and Holderlin's philosophical hymns." Grünbein's dissatisfaction with the "demotion" of poetry by traditional philosophy explains his falling back on personal experience as a strategy of refutation.

Grünbein's recollections of childhood, his experiences as a deep-sea diver, his intensive and exotic travels all serve as "fragments" akin to the impressions and shards of thought that remain from the pre-Socratic thinkers. This kind of bold revisionism returns the stuff of poetry to its legitimate place in the hierarchy of knowing. Grünbein does not allude to Martin Heidegger, but there is much of this famous philosopher's idea of being and *Dasein* in Grünbein's moments of high perception. Like Heidegger, Grünbein is attracted to great works of art as objects of empathy through which the imagination can discover truth.

In his essay on Friedrich Nietzsche, Grünbein is finally able to pull out all stops and restore poetry to its pre-Socratic eminence. Nietzsche's "winged words," his uniquely poetic prose, were organically connected to his philosophical ideas. There was no separation of the two in all that Nietzsche wrote. "It is his voice—one recognizes it from the first note—that word for word manifests itself as bundled semantic energy; voice, understood as the instrument of reason, instinct, musicality, judgment, personal strategy, and eros." Everything that Nietzsche had to tell of the will to power was filtered through a rejoining of poetry and philosophy, a love match that had been "betrayed," as Grünbein puts it, by Plato's contempt. Nietzsche never denied Apollo his power over Dionysus. True poetry does not forsake the "light" of reason merely to indulge human drives and emotions for their own sake. Nonetheless, without the "enormous capacity for wonder" that poetry releases in the human mind, there would be no philosophy to speak of; there would be no Aristotelian logic or Kantian metaphysics.

Although Grünbein takes delight in poetry's ability to balance the real and the ideal, nature and the transcendental, he is also intrigued by the bias toward one or the other in the great poets of the German tradition. Johann Wolfgang von Goethe is "confessional/private" while Friedrich Hölderlin is "liturgical/public." The difference between these two actually rose to a profound antipathy that kept one from appreciating the other. Grünbein does little more than merely cite this split, but its broader implications of a kind of dissociation of sensibility in the German poetic character is almost haunting. The psychological health of a sensibility like Goethe's is often touted as a model for the perfectly adjusted human being. Holderlin's projection of a lost cultural perfection through his beautiful evocations of an imaginary and perfect Hellenic world eventually cost him his sanity. Grünbein seems to wonder if the German imagination is fated to sacrifice the individual's robust psyche to hallucinatory myths of collective deliverance.

Whereas Grünbein remains aloof to any binding judgments on the German poetic character, he closes this collection with a series of essays on the great Roman satirists that suggest a perfect fit between what the Roman world was actually like and what poetic satire, as a literary genre, can reveal. Each was meant for the other. Though the Greeks are the source of the first satires, traceable to the cynic Menippos, the "expression" of the form reached a perfection in Rome that has never been surpassed. Petronius, Horace, and Juvenal are the great names associated with satire and are still the touchstones for excellence in the genre.

The often outrageous fluidity of Roman society (despite the rigid distinctions among patrician, plebeian, and slave) provided an opening for both satirical reduction and moral judgment that has never been equaled. "The collapse of Republican values and the attrition of moral boundaries at every level of society" deflated heroic, tragic, and lyrical forms. Trimalchio, the host of the banquet in the *Satyricon* of Petronius, is a slave "who within a generation rises from bedpan washer to millionaire." In a telling sentence Grünbein sums up the perfect union of poet and world: "Where a foundling could rise from the gutter to being sole heir, silver-plate everything he owns, make a killing in wholesale, and thereupon withdraw to his own private Tusculum—there now the perfect aristocrat, to lounge about in idleness—it would be difficult not to write satires. Juvenal got it right: as the last and most cunning of the Roman satirists, he simply struck the balance on his everyday experience."

Grünbein as a poet is essentially a dark lyricist, but his world view is Juvenalian. There is much irony in the fact that this urbane, modest, and cordial essayist is at heart a sardonic poet. True to his aesthetic, he balances worldliness and a transcendent satirical-moral vision in his literary voice(s). In this regard one must give him credit for bridging the historical gap in German sensibility (Goethe versus Hölderlin). A German poet from the old East Germany comes to the West and points the way toward a higher integration.

Peter Brier

Review Sources

Library Journal 135, no. 6 (April 1, 2010): 75.
The New Republic 241, no. 10 (June 24, 2010): 28-32.
The New York Review of Books 57, no. 15 (October 14, 2010): 53-57.

THE BATTLE OF MARATHON

Author: Peter Krentz (1953-   )
Publisher: Yale University Press (New Haven, Conn.).
    230 pp. $27.50
Type of work: History
Time: 490 B.C.E.
Locale: Asia Minor and Greece

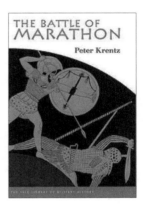

An investigation of the pivotal battle of Marathon, fo-
cusing on reevaluations of Greek armor and tactics and
demonstrating the potential accuracy of Herodotus's nearly
contemporary account

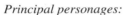

Principal personages:
 DARIUS THE GREAT (550-486 B.C.E.), a
  Persian king, insistent on expanding his empire into mainland Greece
  in order to punish disobedient city-states such as Athens and Eretria
 ARISTAGORAS (d. 497 B.C.E.), the grasping Greek overlord of the Ionian
  city Miletus
 ARTAPHERNES (fl. sixth-fifth centuries B.C.E.), a close relative of Darius
  the Great and the governor of a rebellious province in eastern Asia
  Minor; he cocommanded the Persian forces at Marathon
 DATIS (fl. fifth century B.C.E.), along with Artaphernes, one of the
  commanders of Persian expeditionary forces; primarily a naval
  commander
 MILTIADES (c. 550-489 B.C.E.), a Greek general with a history of fighting
  with and against the Persians; one of the commanders of the Athenian
  forces at Marathon

  Most historians describe the Battle of Marathon, the subject matter of Peter
Krentz's *The Battle of Marathon*, as a pivotal moment in the conflict between Greece
and Persia. Strategically, Marathon demonstrated the resolve of Athens, the leading
Greek city, to remain free despite long odds. Tactically, it demonstrated that under the
right circumstances a properly motivated force of Greek citizen-soldiers could defeat
the experienced Persian military.

  For such an important battle, however, there are remarkably few contemporary
sources. The earliest account was written about sixty years after the event by Herodotus (c. 485-425 B.C.E.). Since then, most historians, beginning with Thucydides
(c. 459-394 B.C.E.), have rejected either parts or the entirety of Herodotus's work.
Published on the twenty-five hundredth anniversary of the event, *The Battle of Marathon* uses a synthesis of ancient and modern evidence and differs significantly from
this trend in historiography.

  Since mid-490 B.C.E., a Persian expeditionary force had been conducting an island-
hopping campaign to subjugate Greek islands in the Aegean Sea. With that phase

*Peter Krentz is a recognized expert in
Greek military history, publishing both
books and peer-reviewed articles in the
field. His work has earned grants from
the National Endowment for the
Humanities.*

concluded, the Persian force turned its attention to mainland Greece. In mid-August, it landed on a relatively open plain surrounded by low hills, about twenty or so miles from Athens. Overall, the Persian campaign was designed to pay back the Greeks for what the Persians considered to be treason.

About twenty years before, Athenian emissaries had approached the Persian governor in Asia Minor and sworn submission in exchange for the king's protection. Athens was tired of years of political turmoil and interference from Sparta, the most powerful military city-state in Greece. Infighting between two powerful Athenian families in the sixth century B.C.E. had led to Spartan interference in city politics, including the exile of the city's tyrant Hippias of Athens (c. 550-c. 490 B.C.E.). Afterward, the Spartans continued to interfere, and the Athenians resented it. The submission to Persia was a clear warning to the Spartans to keep their hands off.

From the Persian perspective, almost immediately after their submission, the Athenians proved treacherous. Ionian Greek cities in western Asia Minor had been part of the Persian Empire for several generations but were not well integrated into it. The popularity of Persian rule in any given Ionian city probably depended on the personal popularity of the individual Greek strongman who governed it.

In 499 B.C.E., a popular Greek tyrant of Miletus, Aristagoras, accompanied a Persian naval expedition to conquer the free Greek island of Naxos. For various reasons it was unsuccessful. Historians suggest that immediately after the defeat, Aristagoras, expecting to be blamed by the Persians, encouraged Miletus's citizens to revolt. Soon, other Ionian Greek cities joined the revolt. Athens was quick to lend support with both money and warriors, even helping the rebels to burn the regional capital, Sardis. By 492 B.C.E. the revolt was crushed, and as historians report, the Persian king Darius the Great appointed a court functionary to remind him three times per day of the treachery of the Athenians.

Two years later, the Persians, as vigorous as ever, landed on the Greek coast. In response, Athens sent emissaries throughout southern Greece, asking for help as quickly as possible. Ironically, the Athenians even asked for Spartan help. Krentz suggests that Sparta was having domestic troubles of its own at the time, perhaps including a slave revolt. In any event, Sparta promised to send help within a few weeks. In fact, on the day Athenian and Persian forces finally clashed, Spartan troops had just reached the outskirts of Athens. Of all the Greek cities, however, only a small town named Plataea immediately sent a force of soldiers to help.

No historian is sure exactly how many Persians landed at Marathon or how many Greeks marched to confront them. Estimates suggest that the Persians may have numbered around twenty-five thousand to thirty thousand; the Greeks may have had one-half to one-third as many. For almost a week, the two armies stared at each other across the fields of Marathon. Finally, early one morning, after a pivotal vote by its commanders, the Greek army crossed the open field, attacking their Persian adversaries.

In Herodotus's account, the Greeks sprinted across the field, running almost a mile before reaching the Persian infantry. Most historians consider this to be either an exaggeration or an outright falsehood based on the fact that the average Athenian citizen-soldier wielded an eight- or nine-foot-long spear, wore a thick suit of bronze armor, and carried a massive shield. The traditional view is that this equipment weighed about seventy pounds. Given this load, a sprint of any distance would have exhausted the average Athenian.

Another reason for skepticism is the traditionalists' belief that at Marathon the Athenians had to have used a phalanx, the customary Greek infantry formation. Basically, a phalanx is a columnar formation of tightly packed warriors. As a phalanx moves forward, warriors in the front ranks lock their shields together and level their spears, projecting the tips three to four feet beyond the shield wall. The middle and back ranks push the front ranks forward. The strength of this formation was its relentless forward push. It could literally thrust enemy formations aside. Amateur warriors, such as the Athenians, would not have been able to maintain a phalanx formation while running.

Krentz's view of Greek tactics and equipment is somewhat different, and it is essentially the highlight of his book. The plain of Marathon was fertile, with rich annual harvests. Negotiating a landscape of vineyards, orchards, and wheat fields would have required a looser formation than the traditional phalanx. Obviously, a more open formation can move faster than a tightly packed one. In addition, the average Greek warrior might not have been as heavily loaded as previously thought. Using modern reproductions, Krentz argues that Greek equipment may have weighed about half as much as believed. Moreover, only the richest Athenians would have been fully armored. Most Greeks would have had only a shield, a spear, and a helmet. A more lightly equipped force could have moved rapidly. Besides, there were at least two reasons for the Athenians to sprint: the needs to negate both the Persian archers and cavalry.

In contrast to the Greek reliance on the spear, Persians infantry relied on missile weapons to defeat their enemies. Krentz suggests that only about 10 percent of the Persian infantry would have been equipped for melee combat, with wicker shields and short spears. Individually, these soldiers would have had more training and experience than their Greek counterparts, but their relatively small numbers and inadequate weapons would have put them at a disadvantage in close combat.

The remaining 90 percent of the Persian infantry carried sophisticated compound bows. Although they were worthless in hand-to-hand combat, they could launch volley after volley of arrows at approaching enemies. Against lightly armored or unarmored forces in the ancient Near East, Persian archers would have been devastating. Against poorly motivated enemies, the sheer number of arrows would certainly have caused panic. The Greeks at Marathon, however, were highly motivated and even their light armor was impervious to arrows at greater than about fifty yards. Within fifty yards, the Persian bows had enough kinetic force to penetrate Greek armor. A sprint across such a kill zone would have been necessary.

Besides contending with archers, the Greeks also had to face the Persian cavalry. Herodotus's account neglects to mention the cavalry in the battle, which many traditional historians interpret as evidence that the cavalry was engaged in some other task, such as a raid. In his book, Krentz supports Herodotus while departing from other historians: The Persian cavalry might have been present at Marathon and still have had little impact.

Mounted on the fastest horses in the Middle East, Persian cavalry was versatile and well trained. In battle, Persian cavalry used bows or javelins to disrupt enemy infantry and then used spears to run down and kill enemies who broke ranks. One significant weakness of cavalry, however, is the relatively long time horses need to get ready for battle. To keep their horses from wandering at night, the Persians tied their hooves loosely together. These bindings had to be removed each morning. After being let loose, the horses had to be fed and watered. They might have needed additional preparation, depending on the amount of armor each horse was expected to carry. Finally, after all the other preparation was completed, the cavalry still had to mount and get to the location of the battle, which might have been a considerable distance.

Like other ancient armies, the Persians zealously protected their horses by encamping them in the most secure location possible. Krentz suggests they may have been stationed across a small lagoon well in the rear of the Persian force. The cavalry would have had to work its way around the margin of the lagoon before reaching open land where they could deploy. The Persians may not have had nearly enough time to get ready before the Greek and Persian infantry were in hand-to-hand combat. At that point, Persian cavalry may have been only of limited use.

From his analysis of the causes of the battle to his shrewd calculations about Greek armor, Krentz's account is both interesting and informative, especially for the nonhistorian. However, he spends little time afterward describing the phases of the battle and the amazing actions the Greeks took in it. This lack of sustained attention to the entire battle is one of the few problems with Krentz's book: After convincing the reader that the Greek force was not a phalanx, creeping glacially under an avalanche of Persian arrows, but a lightly armored mob rushing into combat, the historian's next responsibility might be to show how that mob demonstrated the command and control necessary to destroy a veteran Persian army.

From other historians one learns that the Persians stationed their best troops in the center of their line and flanked them with relatively inexperienced troops. Miltiades chose the opposite approach, weakening his center and strengthening his wings. After several hours of fighting, the Persian wings collapsed, leaving their center—which had initially been winning—abandoned. Remarkably, instead of pursing their fleeing enemies, the Greeks on either end of the line turned inward, surrounding the still-fighting Persian center and completing the destruction of the Persian force. This encirclement suggests an incredible level of cohesion, discipline, and tactical savvy. It would be interesting to learn where an amateur Greek mob might have learned this. Short of another shrewd account by Krentz or another similarly minded historian, readers are unlikely to find out.

Michael R. Meyers

Review Sources

The Wall Street Journal, September 24, 2010, p. W10.
The Washington Times, September 17, 2010, p. B6.

THE BERLIN-BAGHDAD EXPRESS
The Ottoman Empire and Germany's Bid for World Power

Author: Sean McMeekin (1943-   )
Publisher: Belknap Press of Harvard University Press
(Cambridge, Mass.). Illustrated. 460 pp. $29.95
Type of work: History
Time: 1889-1918
Locale: Eastern and southeastern Europe, Anatolia, Iran,
Afghanistan, and India

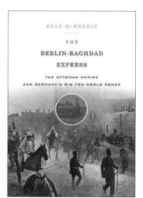

*A detailed financial, political, and military account of
the origins of the Ottoman-German alliance in World
War I, with emphasis on jihad as a propagandistic tactic*

Principal personages:

MAX FREIHERR ("BARON") VON
OPPENHEIM (1860-1946), the main (often controversial) architect of
Germany's "Great Game" scheme of imperial expansion via its
Ottoman wartime alliance

ENVER PAŞA (1881-1922), a "Young Turk" strong man who played a key
role in allying Germany and the Ottomans in World War I

SULTAN MEHMED V (1844-1918), the sultan who launched the call for
an all-Islamic jihad against the Entente powers

OSKAR VON NIEDERMAYER (1885-1948), one of several German or
Austrian travelers and agents who tried to forge anti-Entente
movements

Sean McMeekin's *The Berlin-Baghdad Express* offers a detailed account of not only the origins but also the evolving importance of a famous railroad building project that seemed destined to play a critical transcontinental role in World War I. Although the author does not delve extensively into the broader seventeenth to nineteenth century historical background of what historians have labeled the "Eastern Question," his account of the major importance of the Berlin-to-Baghdad railway clearly places his subject in, and develops it as a key issue for, the latter-day stages of the Eastern Question.

Because the book concerns an international railroad, the geographical context, in which a much broader story unfolds, comprises a vast territory running from Berlin (or more accurately from the major port city of Hamburg) to the Persian Gulf port of Basra. In the nineteenth century, all lands between the two port cities were under the rule of three great empires: Imperial Germany, unified by Otto von Bismarck in 1871; the Habsburg Austro-Hungarian Empire; and the Ottoman Empire.

Since at least 1700, when Habsburg and czarist Russian desires to end the centuries-long ruling presence of the Ottomans in the Balkans seemed close to realization (after an Ottoman military defeat in 1689, followed by a decade of retreat down the Danube), a recurring strategic and diplomatic question crossed the desks of policy makers in all major European capitals: What diplomatic and territorial fallout would occur if the Ottoman Empire met full defeat? Some of the issues in McMeekin's book, which focuses mainly on the period from the 1890's to the end of the Ottoman Empire between 1918 and 1923, can be understood in a broader context of the long historical pull of the Eastern Question prevalent in the previous two centuries. As the Ottomans became increasingly vulnerable to European military advances, diplomatic concerns focused mainly on preventing one or another of the European powers from gaining unilateral advantages (territorial or political) from a piece-by-piece dismantling of the Ottoman Empire itself. Most notably in the Crimean War of 1853-1856, Great Britain and France worked jointly to stem the influence of the Ottomans' immediate neighbors, Russia and the Austro-Hungarian Empire.

Sean McMeekin is assistant professor of international relations at Bilkent University in Ankara, Turkey. He was a guest of the International Security Studies' Brady-Johnson Program in Grand Strategy, and School of Management, Yale University.

The situation changed when Bismarck's newly united Germany entered into the "traditional" Eastern Question after 1871. Even as early as the Congress of Berlin of 1878, early lines of an Ottoman-German alliance against Russia, Britain, and France began to emerge. By the time of the Balkan Wars (1912 and 1913) there was an ever stronger likelihood that Germany might be considering an actual alliance with the Ottomans with military implications. McMeekin's coverage of this immediate pre-World War I phase is not as developed as it could be, particularly given the clearly rising level of German military aid that played a big role in achieving better terms for the Ottomans in the Second Balkan War.

Thus, as Germany became more and more involved in Ottoman affairs—which included the ambitious scheme that became the Berlin-to-Baghdad railway—European powers worried about effects this could bring to the future, specifically in the Near East. However, as McMeekin's work shows clearly, at some point, Germany's attraction to working closely with Istanbul moved beyond plans for the railway, as Germany began to perceive the advantages to be gained if it could—through the Ottomans—strike at French, Russian, and British imperial influence in places beyond the core of the Near East—such as in Egypt, the Maghrib region of North Africa, and sub-Saharan quasi colonies—and in Asia east of Suez, notably in India. McMeekin's original historical research helps fill in the details (indeed, many readers will find that details are so numerous that they "spill over") of Germany's use of certain aspects of what one might call Ottoman paranoia to chart a wartime strategy that could implant its influence in far-flung non-Ottoman, but Muslim, areas "claimed" by its European enemies during the course of the nineteenth century.

The book provides not only a number of different perspectives on the origins, financing, and long-term aims of the Berlin-to-Baghdad railroad when compared with, for example, an early study by Edward M. Earle, *Turkey, the Great Powers, and the Baghdad Railway* (1924), but also it develops a variety of political repercussions stemming from that particular aspect of Imperial German foreign policy that carried forward prior to and during World War I. McMeekin acknowledges his debt to an earlier researcher, Peter Hopkirk, who was the first to explore Turkish-German "Great Game" perceptions of jihad as part of World War I strategy. Hopkirk's 1994 book on the subject bears the title *On Secret Service East of Constantinople: The Plot to Bring Down the British Empire*. McMeekin also gained insight from Jonathan McMurray's study of the Baghdad railway, *Distant Ties: Germany, the Ottoman Empire, and the Construction of the Baghdad Railway* (2001), and, especially for the jihad issue, original documents in Mustafa Aksakal's article "The Trained Triumphant Soldiers of the Prophet Muhammad: Holy War and Holy Peace in Modern Ottoman History."

By any normal definition, declaration of jihad, sometimes translated as "Holy War," rested with a responsible Islamic leader, certainly not with the German kaiser or his diplomatic agents. Nonetheless, if Germany could succeed in gaining the Ottoman Sultan Mehmed V (r. 1909-1918) as a wartime ally, that sultan's call to jihad could draw any Islamic leader in any area under the yoke of Christians to the cause of fighting Istanbul's enemies—namely France, Britain, and Russia—who "happened" to be enemies of Germany as well.

This is in fact what Germany adopted as an essential part of its wartime strategy. A chief architect of that policy and one who tied that policy to strategic rail construction is one of the main protagonists in several sections of McMeekin's book: Max Freiherr von Oppenheim. The adventurous Oppenheim left the German "regular" civil service in 1892 to dedicate himself to a multifaceted career that took him all over the Near East. His reports to the German Foreign Office helped form policy bases for what later became a famous slogan: *Drang nach Osten* (eastward expansion), beginning with the Berlin-to-Baghdad rail scheme. His ideas in a propagandistic tract, translated as "Revolutionizing of the Islamic Territories of Our Enemies" became the cornerstone of an operation he ran (until falling out with the German Foreign Office): a heavily subsidized jihad bureau in wartime Berlin.

At several levels, different factors, less easily traceable than German involvement in rail projects in the Ottoman empire, contributed to the World War I *Drang nach Osten*. Sometimes, as McMeekin's findings show, contributions came from only marginally known figures and appear to be the product of chance circumstances operating far from the locus of "official" policy makers. This is certainly one of the main strengths of *The Berlin-Baghdad Express*: It uncovers original information on the "missions" of individuals sent by Berlin to carry out aspects of the "global jihad" policy. These, although ultimately unsuccessful, cast quite new light on a number of subtopics of World War I history.

In addition to recognizing the value of McMeekin's broad analysis of the German-Ottoman jihad, original contributions appear in his treatment of several individual Germans or Austro-Hungarians who, like the near-legendary T. E. Lawrence, traveled, often in "native" garb, into desert expanses to try to forge local alliances with potential enemies of their enemies. These include the fairly well known 1914 travels to Arabia of Alois Musil and the lesser known 1915 German-Ottoman jihadist endeavors of Oskar von Niedermayer to carry word of German-Ottoman promises of "liberation" (from Russia and Britain) as far as Afghanistan and "to the Gates of India."

In these cases of German-supported "fifth column" operations in and beyond Arabia, new light is thrown on older images of what other histories (particularly of Lawrence in the Hejaz) have tended to view as the "main actors" in inciting local opposition to the Ottoman-German alliance in World War I. For example, McMeekin's detailed account of the extraordinary career of Leo Frobenius (also known as Abdul Kerim Pasha), who was assigned the task of fomenting jihadist movements in Sudan and Abyssinia (Ethiopia), reveals German efforts to recruit Arab tribal support along the same strategic Hejaz rail route to and from Mecca that is associated with Britain's (ultimately more successful) mission under Lawrence.

As would be expected in a carefully organized history book, McMeekin's chapters change focus as identifiably different circumstances affecting the main subject emerge. Thus, once the key role of Sultan Abdul Hamid II (r. 1876-1908)—including his involvement in railway concessions and international politics—is covered, events of the era of the Committee of Union and Progress (CUP, or "Young Turk") government—the regime that carried the Ottomans into World War I—necessarily become the primary target of interest. Since the clearly secularist wartime strongman Enver Paşa and several of his closest CUP colleagues played more of a role than Sultan Mehmed V in laying the bases, succeeding chapters rightly focus on the CUP policies toward a number of issues that the German ally identified as priorities. These include (in addition to the Baghdad railway project): the Suez Canal and Gallipoli Peninsula campaigns, the dilemma and tragedy of the Armenian cause, and efforts to secure key areas of the Caucasus (especially oil-rich Baku) claimed by the Russian enemy.

To look at not only the goals but also the tactical methods of Ottoman-German jihadist propaganda beyond Ottoman borders in World War I requires some idea of identifiable groupings in distant regions that might respond with actual programs for action against Istanbul's enemies. This need is met in some of the areas covered in McMeekin's book (particularly Sanussi-controlled zones in North Africa), but the reader should be aware that necessary reliance on diplomatic archival sources makes it difficult to provide adequate analysis of "grassroots" conditions in all cases.

Byron Cannon

Review Sources

The New York Review of Books 57, no. 19 (December 9, 2010): 42-44.
The Spectator 313, no. 9491 (July 24, 2010): 29-30.
The Wall Street Journal 256, no. 45 (August 23, 2010, p. A13.

BETSY ROSS AND THE MAKING OF AMERICA

Author: Marla R. Miller (1966-   )
Publisher: Henry Holt and Company (New York).
  467 pp. $30.00
Type of work: Biography, history
Time: 1752-1836
Locale: Philadelphia, Pennsylvania

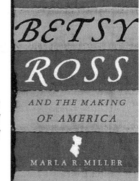

*The story covers the seamstress to whom legend credits
the creation of the first American flag and the roles played
by craftsmen and artisans in the early history of the United
States*

Principal personages:

ELIZABETH "BETSY" GRISCOM ROSS (1752-
    1836), the seamstress often credited with creating the first American
    flag
SAMUEL GRISCOM, a Philadelphia carpenter and the father of Betsy Ross
JOHN ROSS, an upholsterer and the first husband to Betsy Ross; died
    early in the American Revolution
GEORGE WASHINGTON (1732-1799), the commander of the colonial
    army and the first president of the United States
JOSEPH ASHBURN, a privateer and the second husband to Betsy Ross;
    died in British captivity
JOHN CLAYPOOLE, an upholsterer and the third husband of Betsy Ross
JANE CLAYPOOLE CANBY, daughter of Betsy Ross Claypoole
WILLIAM CANBY, Betsy Ross's grandson and the source for much of the
    Ross legend
CLARISSA CLAYPOOLE WILSON, the oldest daughter of Betsy and John
    Claypoole

The name "Betsy Ross" is arguably among the most familiar of early American heroes/heroines outside the realm of politics and the military. Surprisingly, other than in extensive children's literature, little has been written about Betsy and the role she played in early American life. An accomplished seamstress, she is generally credited with making the first American flag at the behest of General George Washington, who, according to legend, visited her home specifically to make that request. In *Betsy Ross and the Making of America* author Marla R. Miller addresses that question, attempting to separate legend and myth from facts. The question of Betsy's role in producing the first flag aside—there is no doubt she did fulfill requests from the government for flags and other forms of ensigns—there has been a paucity of research into Betsy herself, including her life and the story of her family against the background of early American history.

Betsy Ross, which was the name she held for only four years of her long life, was born Elizabeth Griscom on January 1, 1752, "the first day of the first week of the first month of the first year of a new era." She was the eighth child of seventeen born into to a well-to-do Quaker family, artisans extending back to her great-grandfather, Andrew Griscom, the first relative to immigrate to the colonies. Inspired by the teachings of George Fox, Griscom joined the "Society of Friends," more commonly known as the Quakers. Griscom took advantage of the offer to members of the "Friends" from William Penn for land on the western bank of the Delaware River, the future Pennsylvania, and acquired five hundred acres in what eventually became downtown Philadelphia. An accomplished carpenter, Griscom began the family fortune while helping to build homes for immigrant English families.

Marla R. Miller is director of the public history program at the University of Massachusetts, Amherst. She previously wrote The Needle's Eye: Women and Work in the Age of Revolution *(2006).*

Griscom's grandson, Samuel, Betsy's father, continued the family trade, participating in the construction of thousands of homes in the city during the mid-seventeenth century, including a large house for his growing family. Betsy's mother, Rebecca James, was the daughter of George James, a successful Quaker shopkeeper. James's life was a microcosm of the times in which spouses and children often died early, and remarriages produced extended families of half siblings. James had already buried his first wife and seven children before remarrying.

Rather than marrying within the Quaker community, Samuel Griscom and Rebecca James eloped in 1741 in New Jersey. The reason is unknown. The author notes that their "mutual attraction was so strong that their public displays of affection attracted comments of disapproval." Miller tempts the reader with the possibility of a pregnancy, though no child was recorded as born; eighteen months later, they returned to the church. More important for their future, the Griscoms became part of a large, extended, and influential Philadelphia family.

Betsy entered the workforce about the age of fifteen in a time of change both within the family and in the general political environment. According to one story, Betsy was visiting a sister working in the shop of upholsterer John Webster near the Griscom home. Betsy demonstrated her ability to carry out a difficult piece of work and was hired, spending some six years in Webster's employ. During these years, political changes in the colonies embroiled the extended Griscom family.

While describing Betsy's life and the development of her craftsmanship during this period, Miller also presents the larger context in which this work was being carried out. The upholstery profession was one of the most important, and most lucrative, during this period. Unlike the twenty-first century view of the profession, in the 1760's, the trade encompassed production of high-quality furniture; accoutrements for the home, including the furniture for the bedroom, often the most important region of the home, and bed covers; and anything that involved textiles. Women were at the core of much of this trade, which could vary from performing fine needlework to wrestling sixty-pound feather mattresses.

The 1760's represented the beginning of a period of significant change between the American colonies and England. After winning what Americans call the French and Indian War—actually a much more widespread conflict between the French and English antagonists—England found itself with a national debt that had doubled over the course of the war, a debt largely carried by the English taxpayer in England. Believing it fair for the colonies to pay a share of costs, the English Parliament passed a series of acts taxing the American colonies. The first of these, the Stamp Act of 1765, resulted in a successful colonial boycott of British goods, particularly among the more elite merchants in the colonies. The colonists were not reacting to the tax but rather to the fact that such taxes were not initiated by their own elected officials. When a second series of charges, the 1767 Townshend Acts, was imposed on materials used by the trades—including paper, glass, paint, and even tea—the response created a political movement that evolved into revolution a decade later. Artisans, including Betsy's father Samuel, entered directly into the political changes taking place.

Other changes were also taking place in Betsy's life, both politically and personally. In 1773, she married John Ross, her coworker for several years in Webster's shop. The couple eloped in New Jersey, violating both her parents' wishes and the rules of the Friends. Betsy was disowned when she refused to "atone" and never returned to the "Friends" in its institutionalized form. Politically, she found herself in the middle of the coming conflict. At this point in the narrative, Miller intersperses the developing political scene with the increasing involvement of the Ross family—no easy task given the large family and the diversity of its views. As Quakers, the Griscom family attempted to remain apolitical as long as possible. Betsy's maternal uncle, Abel James, and his business partner, Henry Drinker, owners of a business selling East India Company tea, a British company, preferred to ignore the new boycott on English goods until pressured by the radicals, at which point they still retained a reluctant loyalty to the England. The Ross side became increasingly identified with the rebel position. Three of Betsy's husband's uncles—George Ross; John Ross, the namesake of her husband; and George Read—were signers of the Declaration of Independence.

The developing conflict became tragically personal for Betsy when her husband died early in 1776. The circumstances of his death have muddled over time. John Ross had joined the Committee of Safety and likely the local militia as well. The story that emerged was that he was killed in an explosion of a munitions cache. However, no record of either such an explosion or his accidental death has been found. Family stories hint of a developing dementia, perhaps not unlike that which had afflicted his mother, and that his death resulted from some form of hemorrhage. Regardless, Betsy was a childless widow twenty-six months after marrying.

Regarding Betsy's involvement with the creation of the American flag, Miller develops the legend with which Betsy is associated. On May 29, 1777, Betsy was paid by the Pennsylvania navy board for "making ship's colours," one of many dozens she is known to have stitched. Two weeks later, the Continental Congress passed a resolution establishing the appearance of the nation's flag. The family story related that General Washington, Robert Morris, and George Ross, Betsy's late husband's uncle, visited her at her shop, bringing a sketch of the model of the flag they envisioned: square with six-pointed stars. Betsy suggested a rectangular flag with five-pointed stars, arranged in a circle. Only one account of the story survived, that of Betsy's daughter Rachel. More problematic is there is no known written record confirming such a visit in 1776. At that time, Morris was deeply conflicted over independence and appears unlikely to have participated in such a visit. The story might be true, but absence of any supporting evidence makes it questionable at best.

As an eligible young widow, Betsy remained single only a short time, marrying mariner Joseph Ashburn in June, 1777. Little is known of Ashburn, even his place of birth. Also, it is unclear how the two met. With the advent of war, Ashburn entered the conflict as a member of the crew on a privateer preying on British shipping, while Betsy contributed in a manner similar to many women of the city, helping produce munitions in addition to the consignment work in her business. In September, 1779, she gave birth to her first child, a daughter Aucilla; the child lived less than one year. A second daughter, Eliza, was born in February, 1781. In June of that year, Ashburn was captured by a British frigate and transported to Mill Prison in England. Betsy did not learn of her husband's fate until April, 1782, when a list of men imprisoned was published. By then she was widowed a second time.

Among the prisoners released at the end of the war was John Claypoole, a captive of the British and an acquaintance of Joseph Ashburn. In May, 1783, Betsy married for the third time, becoming Betsy Claypoole. John Claypoole entered the upholstery business and appears to have been quite successful. In 1785, Betsy gave birth to her third daughter, Clarissa, the first of five daughters the couple would have. Clarissa eventually succeeded her mother in the upholstery business, and Betsy lived her final years at Clarissa's home.

John Claypoole's health deteriorated during the later years of his marriage to Betsy; he likely suffered a stroke before dying in 1817. Betsy moved in with her children, maintaining her upholstery business with Clarissa until age took its toll. The upholstery industry changed over time, and what had been piecework was gradually replaced by a manufacturing industry. Much of the Philadelphia Betsy knew was, or shortly would be, gone when she died in 1836. Miller conveys this change poignantly.

The question of whether Betsy really created the first flag is left open by Miller. Original sources that might have shed light on the question were lost, some in a fire in the Department of War in 1800, and others belonging to the family were mistakenly destroyed in the 1880's. Betsy's 1836 obituary made no mention of the first flag story. Miller provides a strong argument that were it not for Betsy's daughter Clarissa and grandson William Canby, the name Betsy Ross might well have been no more than a footnote in American history. As she was preparing to move to Iowa late in life in 1857, Clarissa told the story to her nephew Canby who, in an 1870 speech to the Historical Society of Pennsylvania, repeated what his aunt had dictated. The context for each was suspicious. During the 1850's greater recognition was being paid to the women of the American Revolution. Betsy certainly knew some of these women, and it was logical for her daughter to add her name to the list. That Betsy had personally met General Washington was likely true, and her "adoration" for the man was not unusual among those in that generation. The admiration ran in two directions. When Eleanor Parke Custis Lewis, Martha Washington's granddaughter, visited Philadelphia in 1820, Custis made a point of wishing to visit Betsy.

Perhaps the question of fact or myth in this specific example becomes moot. Betsy Ross represented the "common" woman of her time, using her skills in overcoming adversity to survive and support a growing family and to do her part in helping the colonies win their independence.

Richard Adler

Review sources

Booklist 106, no. 16 (April 15, 2010): 19.
American History 45, no. 2 (June, 2010): 66.
Interdisciplinary Quarterly 33, no. 3 (Summer, 2010): 584-585.
Kirkus Reviews 78, no. 5 (March 1, 2010): 186.
Library Journal 135, no. 3 (February 15, 2010): 101.
The New York Times Book Review, May 9, 2010, p. 21.
Publishers Weekly 257, no. 11 (March 15, 2010): 44-45.

BEYOND KATRINA
A Meditation on the Mississippi Gulf Coast

Author: Natasha Trethewey (1966-   )
Publisher: University of Georgia Press (Athens). 127 pp.
$22.95
Type of work: Memoir, history, poetry
Time: 1900-2008
Locale: Mississippi gulf coast

Pulitzer Prize-winning poet Trethewey describes the ef-fects of Hurricane Katrina on the African American com-munity living along the Mississippi gulf coast

Principal personages:
    NATASHA TRETHEWEY, a poet and a
      memoirist
    JOE, her brother
    LERETTA, her grandmother
    WILLIE "SON" DIXON, her granduncle

The floodwaters of Hurricane Katrina had barely receded from New Orleans and the Mississippi gulf coast when another "tidal wave" began to swell—the flood of books and papers about the storm and its aftermath. It seems that anyone with even the most tangential connection to New Orleans found it necessary to weigh in on the issue, largely to catalog thousands of personal tragedies or indict various government officials and agencies for contributing to the problem through ineffectual response ef-forts. Among the more notable books about the disaster is New Orleans *The Times-Picayune* reporter Chris Rose's *One Dead in Attic: After Katrina* (2007), a poignant exposé of the suffering of people displaced by the storm and its aftermath and, at times, a caustic critique of the ineffective efforts by government officials to deal with the disaster. *Times-Picayune* metro editor Jed Horne's *Breach of Faith: Hurricane Katrina and the Near Death of a Great American City* (2006) offers a similar assess-ment. Michael Eric Dyson's *Come Hell or High Water: Hurricane Katrina and the Color of Disaster* (2006) indicts government officials for, among other issues, ignor-ing the large African American population in New Orleans that suffered most from the flooding. Christopher Cooper's *Disaster: Hurricane Katrina and the Failure of Homeland Security* (2006) offers an extended critique of the U.S. Department of Homeland Security for its many missteps and its general inability to respond quickly and effectively to the unfolding catastrophe in New Orleans. One of the best personal accounts, Tom Piazza's *Why New Orleans Matters* (2005), reads like an extended love story between a sensitive writer and a city he has come to call home. Most reports skipped over the devastation in Mississippi, but Natasha Trethewey's brilliantly writ-ten memoir and meditation, *Beyond Katrina: A Meditation on the Mississippi Gulf*

Coast, goes a long way to giving voice to this nearly forgotten community.

~

Natasha Trethewey is an award-winning writer and teacher. She is the author of several volumes of poetry, including the collection Native Guard *(2006), for which she won the Pulitzer Prize in poetry in 2007.*

~

Lost in all the accusations about ineffective prevention efforts by the U.S. Army Corps of Engineers and recriminations against city, state, and federal officials; absentee landlords; and virtually anyone else in a position of responsibility in New Orleans, is the fact that the full force of Hurricane Katrina did not hit the city. The center of the storm made landfall an hour east of New Orleans near the Mississippi gulf coast hamlets of Waveland, Bay St. Louis, Pass Christian, Gulfport, and Biloxi. Wind and water damage in New Orleans on the evening of August 29 was notable but modest. The real catastrophe occurred two days later when, weakened in the storm, the levees protecting many of the neighborhoods in New Orleans broke, sending water swirling down city streets and into homes, driving thousands onto rooftops and destroying entire neighborhoods—most notably the city's Lower Ninth Ward, a predominantly African American community that had always been the victim of benign neglect, which was thrust into the national limelight and kept there by a continuous stream of stories about bodies found inside flooded homes after the waters receded.

By contrast, the devastation caused by Katrina's winds and storm surge along the shoreline of the Mississippi Sound was catastrophic. Residences and commercial establishments, including major hotels and gambling casinos, simply disappeared. For several miles inland the thirty-foot tidal wave smashed residences that were already leaking from wind-driven rains. The people of southern Mississippi suffered as much as their neighbors in Louisiana, but the media concentrated in New Orleans, leaving Mississippians to recover as best they could in relative obscurity.

A native of Gulfport, Trethewey is able to provide some historical perspective on the region so that her account becomes a before-and-after look at the people whose lives were forever changed by the hurricane. Blending poetry, personal accounts, historical background, statistical analysis, and speculation, Trethewey manages to convey a sense of what happened to people in Gulfport and other communities along the coast after that fateful day in August, 2005, when the lives of virtually everyone in her hometown changed overnight.

On one level, Trethewey's book is similar to other personal narratives about Katrina and other natural disasters. She writes of devastation, loss, and regeneration—both physical and psychological. Her detailed descriptions of the Gulf coast before and after the storm give one a sense of what was lost when the floodwaters swept ashore, wiping out whole communities, many of which had been rebuilt less than four decades earlier after Hurricane Camille ravaged the area in 1969. *Beyond Katrina* is especially valuable as documentary history because Trethewey writes principally about the African American community along the Mississippi gulf coast, a population often invisible to the mostly white outsiders who had been coming to the region for seven decades to enjoy surf, sand, and gaming. Trethewey also provides a brief account of the changes to the region that occurred even before Katrina struck, most notably the demise of the fishing industry and the rise of tourism and gambling as economic drivers. Her stories of people who have had to adapt to these changing conditions in order to remain living on the Gulf coast hint at the effects of the long history of racial and economic discrimination that has plagued the region and, even in the twenty-first century, hinders recovery efforts in many subtle and not-so-subtle ways.

Trethewey is at her best, however, in telling family stories. With a poet's sensitivity to detail and imagery, she provides readers a glimpse of what it was like to grow up in the segregated South. In an era when "whites only" signs were everywhere, entrepreneurs such as Trethewey's uncle, Willie "Son" Dixon, managed to set up successful businesses through entrepreneurial efforts in the hospitality and housing industries. Largely through his own efforts, Son Dixon opened a popular bar in the city's North Gulfport section, where most African Americans lived, and erected a row of houses that he rented out at reasonable rates to people who needed places to live. His sister Leretta, Trethewey's grandmother, managed to keep her family together by working at odd jobs. Leretta's devotion to her church becomes an important theme in *Beyond Katrina*, suggesting how a faith community serves as a nexus for those who need reassurance and support in tough times. Trethewey writes lovingly about bringing her grandmother back to Gulfport after Katrina from the Atlanta home where she was living when the storm hit and about Leretta's funeral in the heavily damaged church where she had devoted so much of her time and talent over the years.

If *Beyond Katrina* is part tragedy, then its tragic hero is certainly Trethewey's brother Joe. Younger than Natasha by several years, Joe seemed set for success as a rental-property owner, having taken over his granduncle Son's properties just before the storm. Joe had invested his life savings and taken out a substantial mortgage to renovate these properties, completing the work just weeks before Katrina hit. Essentially destitute after the storm, he spent months moving from job to job, trying to scrape together enough money to support himself and his girlfriend. Eventually he was tempted to earn quick money by becoming a courier for drug dealers. That career did not last long, however. Joe had made only a few runs when he was arrested, tried, and sent to prison—a lesson in how even good people can be brought to ruin by circumstances over which they have little control. To heighten readers' sympathy for Joe, Trethewey reproduces several letters she received from her brother while he was in prison. His straightforward, unembellished account of what went wrong and why he should have known better is as effective as any of the emotionally charged poems that set off sections of narrative in conveying the psychological toll that Katrina took on residents of the Gulf coast.

Trethewey's title is itself a bit of poetry, as the term "beyond" carries multiple meanings. The tales she tells of her brother and others in confronting life after the storm are a narrative about getting "beyond" the disaster and rebuilding their lives. At the same time, however, Trethewey wants to get "beyond" her immediate story to offer reflections on a larger topic: the way in which "history," especially cultural history, is constructed through individual and collective memory. With an awareness shaped by postmodern theories of narratology, Trethewey exposes ways people create what she calls a "preferred narrative." For example, she recounts how her brother's girlfriend spoke to her of people pulling together to help one another—but failed to mention that she had been evicted from her apartment to make room for her landlord, who lost his own home in the storm. Creating accounts that are "full of omissions, partial remembering, and purposeful forgetting" are not only coping mechanisms to deal with immediate trauma, Trethewey suggests, but also ways of rebuilding. How a community creates memories is as important to its recovery as its attempts to put up new physical structures and restore jobs.

Combining her poet's insight with keen skill as a postmodern theorist, Trethewey manages to read with a critic's eye for incongruities and subtle signs of power and oppression. For example, as she gazes over the generalized destruction she sees along the coast two years after the storm, she notes that the natural landscape offers a metaphor of hope: "In the years after the storm, as the leaves have begun to return, the trees seem a monument to the very idea of recovery." On the other hand, "Man-made monuments tell a different story. Never neutral, they tend to represent the narratives and memories of those citizens with the political power and money to construct them"—a narrative that celebrates a past filled with racism and discrimination. Trethewey sees the recovery being driven by similar "contests" over control of narratives past, present, and future: "These contests, rooted in power and money, undergird the direction of the rebuilding efforts as well—how the past will be remembered, what narratives will be inscribed by the rebuilding." For her, the possibility of a future that puts aside past wrongs is possible but doubtful, unless people consciously construct a narrative of recovery that is inclusive and truly communal.

Seen in this light, *Beyond Katrina* is truly a meditation—akin to those of the Roman emperor Caracalla (also known as Marcus Aurelius Antoninus), whose writings provided him a way to reflect on life as a means of self-improvement. The larger theme of the book is expressed succinctly in the quotation from another southern writer, Flannery O'Connor, used by Trethewey to introduce her narrative: "Where you came from is gone. Where you thought you were going to never was there. And where you are is no good unless you can get away from it." In *Beyond Katrina*, the twin temptresses of memory and desire that drive everyone are exposed for what they are—alluring chimeras that mask the sobering reality that what happens in the present is what really makes a difference in people's lives.

Laurence W. Mazzeno

Review Sources

Atlanta Magazine, September, 2010, p. 30.
Books & Culture, September, 2010, "Web Exclusives: Book Notes." http://www
　.booksandculture.com.
ForeWord Reviews, September/October, 2010. http://www.forewordreviews.com.

THE BIG SHORT
Inside the Doomsday Machine

Author: Michael Lewis (1960-   )
Publisher: Norton (New York). 266 pp. $27.95
Type of work: Economics
Time: 2007-2008
Locale: Wall Street, New York City

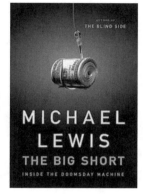

Lewis explains what was happening on Wall Street in 2007-2008 when financial markets began collapsing under the weight of subprime mortgages, credit default swaps, and so-called collateralized debt obligations

Principal personages:
 STEVE EISMAN, shrewd observer who knew something was not right on Wall Street
 MIKE BURRY, master of credit default swaps

One of the first Wall Street speculators to take a close look at what was going on with the mortgage bond market was Steve Eisman, an honors graduate from Harvard Law School who delighted in scanning the Talmud searching for contradictions. Lewis's story begins with the flourishing of subprime mortgages in the 1990's and 2000's, especially in 2004 and 2005. Subprime mortgages enabled the growth of the mortgage bond market and later a new invention, the collaterized debt obligation (CDO). A mortgage bond was created by pooling hundreds of home loans and then dividing the payments made by homeowners into so-called tranches with interest rates varying according to the likelihood of the tranche being paid off early. When a mortgage is paid off early, the bondholder's investment dries up; therefore he is left with money to invest (probably at a lower rate) but no bond. These bonds initially enjoyed government guarantees covering defaults, but the trouble began when subprime mortgages were extended to borrowers with dubious credit. Lewis cites the instance of a Mexican strawberry picker in California making only $14,000 a year but being granted a mortgage for $724,000.

In 2002, Eisman learned how the lending giant Household Finance Corporation (HFC) was cheating its customers, convincing them they were paying 7 percent interest when they were really paying "something like 12.5 percent." Eisman's campaign against this fraud led to a class-action suit settled out of court, a $484 million fine, and the sale of HFC's bloated portfolio of subprime loans to a British conglomerate for $15.5 billion. HFC's chief executive officer bailed out with $100 million. Eisman's discoveries converted him from a "strident" Republican to a harsh critic of the party. "When you're a conservative Republican, you never think people are making money by ripping other people off. I now realized there was an entire industry, called consumer finance, that basically existed to rip people off."

~

*Michael Lewis is the best-selling
author of* Liar's Poker *(1989),*
Moneyball *(2003),* The Blind Side
(2006), and Home Game *(2009). He
lives in Berkeley, California.*

~

The subprime mortgage industry mush-roomed into $625 billion in loans by 2005, $507 billion of which existed in mortgage bonds. In 2004, a neurologist-turned-investor, Michael Burry, the founder of the immensely successful Scion Capital, was already puz-zling over how to short subprime mortgage bonds. Shorting stocks usually means bor-rowing, for example, one thousand shares worth $10 each, selling them, and then when the share price drops to $8 replacing the $10 shares with $8 ones and keeping a profit. Burry wondered how he could short these new inventions. The answer was not in the usual shorts but in credit default swaps (CDS), which were not really swaps at all but insurance policies, usually on corporate bonds. Lewis offers an example: "For instance, you might pay $200,000 a year to buy a ten-year CDS on $100 million in General Electric bonds. The most you could lose was $2 million: $200,000 a year for ten years." However, if General Elec-tric were to default in the following ten years, you would receive $100 million. Burry's problem became finding a Wall Street firm that would sell insurance on a subprime mortgage bond.

In 2005, when Burry approached Goldman Sachs, Morgan Stanley, Deutsche Bank, Bank of America, UBS, Merrill Lynch, and Citigroup, only Deutsche Bank and Goldman Sachs paid any attention to him. Despite the initial indifference of these banks, within three years CDS on subprime mortgage bonds had become a trillion-dollar market, and these same big firms would soon lose hundreds of billions of dollars. Burry worried increasingly that some sharp Wall Street observer would catch on to the risks in subprime mortgages, but no one did. He soon realized that he needed to formalize his purchase of CDS in some kind of contract; after months of negotiating with Wall Street lawyers and traders, an agreement was reached through the International Swaps and Derivatives Association (ISDA). One problem to be set-tled was what to do when defaults occurred sporadically rather than all at once, and the answer lay in the insurers being paid incrementally as individual homeowners defaulted.

With this groundwork laid, Burry made his first venture into subprime mortgage speculation in May, 2005, purchasing from Deutsche Bank $10 million in "naked" CDS on six different bonds. (In a "naked" CDS the buyer does not own the bond—called the "reference security"—but only the insurance on it.) Burry's ultimate suc-cess at this new form of speculation resulted from the hours of careful scrutiny he de-voted to studying dozens of prospectuses to find what Lewis calls "the dodgiest pools" of mortgages. He was surprised that Deutsche Bank apparently did not care which bonds he chose to bet against; their price for insurance was determined by the rating of the bond by Moody's and Standard and Poor's (S&P's). The triple-B-rated tranches were the riskiest, and Goldman Sachs unwittingly obliged him by providing a long list of "crappy" mortgage bonds for him to choose from. By mid-2005, Burry's

Scion Capital had amassed more than one billion dollars in CDS on subprime mortgage bonds, and Burry told his investors that the entire economy was dependent on
the stability of the mortgage bond market.

While Burry had been making a fortune, a bond trader from Deutsche Bank named
Greg Lippmann was explaining to Eisman the intricacies of "shorting home equity
mezzanine tranches," Lippmann's language for buying CDS on the worst triple-B
mortgage bonds. At the same time, Eisman was looking for the reason that so many
subprime borrowers paid off their loans so fast: "They were making loans to lower-
income people at a teaser rate when they knew they could not afford to pay the go-to
rate. They were doing it so that when the borrowers got to the end of the teaser rate
period, they'd have to refinance, so the lenders can make more money off them." By
2004, the "consumer loans" that Goldman Sachs and other firms asked AIG Financial
Products to insure jumped to 98 percent subprime mortgages.

The stage was then set for the next act in this comedy of investor naïveté: the invention of the synthetic subprime mortgage bond-backed CDO. The usual CDO was
created by collecting one hundred mortgage bonds—preferably the riskiest ones—
and then contriving to get the product rated triple-A. (Lewis calls it "a machine that
turned lead into gold.") Finding a source of triple-B-rated bonds ceased to be a problem with the invention of the synthetic CDO, a CDO made up wholly of credit default
swaps (CDS). Goldman Sachs was buying up CDS as fast as possible while at the
same time peddling its risky bonds to its customers.

In January, 2007, Eisman, Lippmann, and other subprime mortgage entrepreneurs attended the profession's big conference in Las Vegas. Eisman was seated at
dinner beside a man named Wing Chau, who introduced himself as the CDO manager of Harding Advisory. Chau shocked Eisman by confessing that he held no
subprime bonds himself and that the more trades Eisman could do, the better it would
be for his business. Eisman then realized that the CDOs were using CDS to replicate
bonds based on real home loans and that his money paid for synthesizing these CDOs.
He left vowing to buy CDS only on Chau's CDOs. Eisman's friend Vinny Daniel
says of the convention: "There were more morons than crooks, but the crooks were
higher up."

Cracks in Wall Street's facade began showing when in February, 2007, HSBC announced heavy losses on its subprime loans and a month later dumped its portfolio.
Then in July, Merrill Lynch confessed that it had suffered significant losses in
subprime bonds. Eisman and his team then began what they named "The Great Treasure Hunt," a search for hidden subprime risk. When Eisman listened to a talk by the
chief executive officer of Bank of America, Ken Lewis, he said he had an "epiphany":
"Oh my God, he's dumb." With this revelation Eisman shorted Bank of America,
UBS, Citigroup, Lehman Brothers, and other investment banks. Even as more and
more loans went bad, Moody's and S&P's stuck to their ratings of them. When
Eisman pestered the bond people at Goldman Sachs and Morgan Stanley for information about what the ratings agencies were doing, he said his only answer was a
"smirk." The information available to Eisman from the agencies was only "pool-level

data" that told him nothing about individual loans. What Eisman eventually learned was that the agencies had no more data than he had. Therefore he concluded, as Lewis observes, that "It was impossible to determine how badly the Wall Street firms had gamed the system."

The mystery remained of what was inside a CDO. Jim Grant, the editor of *Grant's International Rate Observer*, assigned his assistant, Dan Gertner, a chemical engineer with an MBA, to solve this mystery. Gertner decided that nobody, especially investors, could penetrate this conundrum, and so Grant wrote a series of articles accusing the ratings agencies of failing their responsibilities. Grant and Gertner were then called into the S&P headquarters for a stiff rebuke. Gertner reported that the rebukers did not like Grant's term "alchemy."

Meanwhile, Burry was holed up meditating about why, in Lewis's words, "Complicated financial stuff was being dreamed up for the sole purpose of lending money to people who could never repay it." Burry's investors were becoming increasingly restive with him, not understanding exactly what was going on with the dollars they had tied up in CDS. Finally, as Bear Stearns collapsed and the situation for subprime mortgage bonds worsened, Goldman Sachs seemed to be suffering a nervous breakdown. Henry Paulson, secretary of the Treasury, and Ben Bernanke, the chairman of the Federal Reserve, had fatuously proclaimed there was no threat of "contagion" from subprime mortgage losses, but by August, 2007, the total number of loans in default had reached 37.7 percent and the Wall Street titans were panicking. In late 2007, adjustable rate mortgages were defaulting at record rates.

In the denouement to this drama of greed and ignorance, the American taxpayer proved to be the deus ex machina. In September, 2008, Paulson midwifed the Troubled Asset Relief Program and got Congress to agree to provide $700 billion to buy subprime mortgage assets from banks. Once he got the money he began doling out billions to Citigroup, Morgan Stanley, Goldman Sachs, and others. Thus, the $13 billion AIG owed Goldman Sachs for subprime mortgage insurance was paid completely by the U.S. government. When $700 billion proved too little, the Federal Reserve started buying up subprime mortgage bonds; by early 2009, the U.S. taxpayer had assumed more than one trillion dollars' worth of sour investments from Wall Street. Lewis sums it up this way: "The world's most powerful and most highly paid financiers had been entirely discredited; without government intervention every single one of them would have lost his job; and yet those same financiers were using the government to enrich themselves."

Frank Day

Review Sources

Business Week, no. 4171 (March 22, 2010): 94-96.
The Economist 394, no. 8674 (March 20, 2010): 92-93.

Fortune 161, no. 4 (March 22, 2010): 18-18.
Library Journal 135, no. 7 (April 15, 2010): 91.
The New York Review of Books 57, no. 10 (June 10, 2010): 37-39.
The New York Times Book Review, April 18, 2010, p. 14.
Publishers Weekly 257, no. 18 (May 3, 2010): 44-46.

THE BLACK MINUTES

Author: Martín Solares (1970-   )
First published: Los minutos negros, 2006, in Mexico
Translated from the Spanish by Aura Estrada and John
   Pluecker
Publisher: Black Cat (New York). 436 pp. $14.00
Type of work: Novel
Time: Late 1970's and late 1990's
Locale: Fictional Mexican gulf port city of Paracuán,
   Tamaulipas; briefly, rural northern Tamaulipas and
   Ciudad Victoria, capital of Tamaulipas

   *In this noir mystery two detectives from different de-
cades, both mired in endemic corruption and high-level
cover-ups, investigate the sensational case of a serial sexual molester and killer of girls*

> *Principal characters:*
> BERNARDO BLANCO, investigative journalist and murder victim
> RAMÓN CABRERA RUBIALES (EL MACETON, "the big flowerpot"),
>   detective assigned to investigate Blanco's murder
> JOAQUÍN TABOADA (EL TRAVOLTA), Cabrera's police chief
> RUFINO CHÁVEZ MARTÍNEZ (EL CHANEQUE, "the Duende"), Cabrera's
>   police-force rival
> MARIANA, Cabrera's wife, known in 1977 as La Chilanga, and a
>   newspaper photographer
> JOHNNY GUERRERO, a pushy newspaper reporter and columnist
> PADRE FRITZ TSCHANZ, a Jesuit priest and teacher
> RODRIGO MONTOYA, the director of the Paracuán archives
> EL CHACAL ("the Jackal"), the media nickname for the serial sexual
>   molester/killer
> RENÉ LUZ DE DIOS LÓPEZ, the deliveryman charged and imprisoned as
>   "the Jackal"
> VICENTE RANGEL GONZÁLEZ, the detective assigned in 1977 to
>   investigate "the Jackal" case
> CHIEF PEDRO GARCÍA GONZÁLEZ, the chief of police in 1977
> JOHN "JACK" WILLIAMS, JR., the dissolute son of a rich local
>   businessman
> DR. RIDAURA, a forensic doctor and biology professor
> JORGE ROMERO (EL CIEGO, "the Blind Man"), a lackey/assistant to Rangel
> LUIS CALATRAVA (EL BRUJO, "the Wizard"), a gunned-down checkpoint
>   guard
> LIEUTENANT MIGUEL RIVERA GONZÁLEZ, Rangel's detective uncle and
>   role model
> DR. ALFONSO QUIROZ CUARÓN, a world-famous criminologist

The setting of Martín Solares's debut novel *The Black Minutes* is the fictional Mexican gulf port city of Paracuán, Tamaulipas. The "neighboring city of Tampico" is said to be "a few minutes north of Paracuán," which gives Paracuán a somewhat problematic location, possibly even offshore under water, since Tampico is the southernmost city in the state of Tamaulipas. However, one can hardly blame Solares for disguising his hometown of Tampico and thereabouts as Paracuán. After all, the author might want to return home some day. If the fate of the investigative reporter in his novel is any indication, Solares's invention of a fictional setting is only discreet.

Martín Solares holds a doctorate in Iberian and Latin American Studies from the University of Paris I. The Black Minutes, his first novel, was a finalist for the Grand Prix de Littérature Policière and the Rómulo Gallegos Prize.

Another reason for inventing the fictional city of Paracuán might be to make it a generic slice of Mexico, a microcosm representing all the crime and corruption troubling that country, much like the mythical town of Macondo, in Gabriel García Márquez's *Cien años de soledad* (1967; *One Hundred Years of Solitude*, 1970), recapitulates the troubled history of Latin America generally. In *The Black Minutes*, the character Dr. Alfonso Quiroz Cuarón (in real life, a renowned criminologist) links the story to Mexico's modern history: "The way I see it, everything went downhill starting with President Miguel Alemán [in office 1946-1952]. The bureaucrats were only looking out for their own advancement, there was endless fraud."

As is already apparent, *The Black Minutes* is more than a straightforward police procedural. Other real-life people making brief appearances in the novel include politicians, film directors, rock stars, other writers, and even the author himself as one of four Boy Scouts who discover a girl's decaying corpse. The novel features two main detectives (in different decades) and has so many other characters, most sporting colorful nicknames, that it starts with a three-page listing of the cast. Although most of the novel is told from the points of view of the two detectives, a few chapters are from the point of view of the police chief; other chapters are presented as testimony, statements, or reports from such characters as the priest, the criminologist, the blind man, and an earlier incarnation of the archivist as a young beatnik into New Journalism. Finally, there are numerous references to popular culture and a few excursions into magical realism, usually as drunken or dream sequences but in one instance as a postmortem message from the other side.

Some reviewers have thought that Solares plays around too much in the novel, includes too much gratuitous material, repeats himself, and dilutes suspense. Nonetheless, much of what Solares does can be justified: First of all, he provides atmosphere—a taste of Mexico—which helps to explain why both his detective protagonists exhibit psychosomatic symptoms (Cabrera has gastritis, and Rangel's hands itch, sweat, crack, and bleed). Aside from drinking too much coffee (Cabrera) and losing too much sleep (Rangel), they deal with enough in their daily lives to give anyone nervous problems.

Book one of the novel begins in the late 1990's in medias res, or even close to the plot's end, with Cabrera on a bus ride south, where he meets a young journalist who, inexplicably, has quit a fine job and left his beautiful girlfriend in San Antonio to return home to Paracuán. The omens are not good: "They knew they were getting into Mexico because the air on the bus was too thick to breathe." When they cross the Río Muerto and reach Dos Cruces, the bus is stopped by the judicial police. The police pull the young journalist from the bus, rough him up, and take his jacket, sunglasses, and one thousand pesos. He is saved from a worse fate only by Cabrera's intervention. Finally they reach Paracuán, where "two gigantic billboards welcomed them to the city: the first was an ad for Cola Drinks" (an omnipresent symbol of corporate domination), and the second is a bullet-riddled message from Mexico's president promising "A GOOD LIFE FOR YOUR FAMILY."

Some time later, the young journalist is found murdered, and Cabrera is assigned to the case. The journalist has "a Colombian necktie"—a euphemism meaning his throat has been slit from ear to ear and his tongue pulled through the slit—to cast suspicion on the Colombian drug cartel operating in the port. However, as Cabrera investigates, he discovers that the young journalist had been researching a book on a psychopath, known in the media as "the Jackal," who committed a string of gruesome sexual violations and murders of schoolgirls in the Paracuán area twenty years earlier. The police eventually arrested a deliveryman of cold cuts for the crimes. However, because the detective investigating the earlier case, Rangel, disappeared and the string of sexual violations and murders of girls continued in the north of the state, Cabrera also deduces that the deliveryman serving time as "the Jackal" is innocent, that the identity of the actual perpetrator was covered up, and that the journalist was killed because he was close to discovering the cover-up.

Cabrera's deductions seem to be confirmed by several people, including an old priest, who warn him about also digging too deep, messing with dangerous matters, and riling important folk. Before Cabrera can follow up on his deductions, however, he is sidetracked by a fight with another detective, his nemesis Rufino Chávez, who mockingly tells him, "'But if *you* want to find Rangel, go ask your wife." Then, as Cabrera is driving home, he is bushwhacked on the street by a pickup truck driven by a drug dealer's twelve-year-old son, whose monogrammed gun Cabrera had confiscated a few days before. After the violent collision, book one ends as the pickup truck shoots into the path of an oncoming double tractor trailer and Cabrera is taken to the hospital with multiple injuries.

Book two goes back to the original investigation of "the Jackal" in the late 1970's, led by the young Rangel. Straightforward chronologically, book two focuses on the initial mystery of the case and the gradual buildup of evidence but also the increase of public panic fanned by a sensational press as the body of each girl is found. ("The Jackal" seems to strike on a monthly basis, as if affected by the full moon.) In book two the link between Rangel and Cabrera's future wife is established: Back then she was known as La Chilanga, a beautiful, idealistic newspaper photographer who seems to have no trouble falling into Rangel's bed. Rangel is also eventually successful in tracking down and apprehending "the Jackal," who stays in jail all of five minutes.

Book three picks up twenty years later where book one left off. It begins with Chief Taboada recalling how he got his job in exchange for cooperating with the "Federal Safety Administration, the personal police force of President Echavarreta," in "the Jackal" case: He was complicit in the arrest of an innocent man, release of the real "Jackal," and retaliation against fellow officers who apprehended "the Jackal." With a political and media uproar over the young journalist's death, the chief fears he will lose his job. Sure enough, he is called to the state capital that day and fired: There is uproar about not only the young journalist but also the hacked-up body of another girl that has been found that morning on the city outskirts.

The novel ends with Cabrera, in a neck brace and tailed by the drug dealer's associates, continuing to pursue his leads. He learns that the journalist had been a childhood playmate of one of the little girls killed by "the Jackal," that his police-force rival Rufino Chávez has been found dead and that he is the suspect, and that the chief has been ousted and that he is the prime candidate as replacement. Finally, he tracks down Rangel, who has been hiding out all these years, and they discuss their shared experiences, including the woman they both have loved.

Cabrera and Rangel stand out as honest, highly capable detectives in a rotten system, like Rangel's uncle before them, as if there is at least one honorable investigator in each generation. This positive theme balances the novel's overall depiction of Mexico as a cesspool of corruption. These generational themes help explain the reasons for the novel's structure and complexity, which also gradually unlayer the levels of cover-up and present the crime as a metaphor for Mexico itself.

It is a shame that the novel suffers from either poor translation or editing, or both. There are irritating problems with proofreading, bits of syntax, and untranslated terms, and it would help to have notes explaining such things as Spanish surnames (the paternal followed by the maternal), floor numbering, and the various Mexican police forces. Also, there are inconsistencies in whether the events recounted happened twenty years apart or twenty-five (most references are to twenty) and in the spelling of President Luis Echeverría's name. The spelling "Echaverreta" might be a form of discretion, but if so, it should be consistent. (The fact that Echeverría, who held office from 1970 to 1976, was no longer president in 1977 is not necessarily an inconsistency, since he continued to exercise great power and influence after leaving office.)

A final way *The Black Minutes* differs from the typical police procedural is that both of the culprits are still at large at the novel's end. Besides culprits on the loose, other unfinished business remains. Possibly Solares is planning a sequel.

Harold Branam

Review Sources

Booklist 106, no. 17 (May 1, 2010): 20.
Library Journal 135, no. 11 (June 15, 2010): 64-68.
The Nation 291, no. 20 (November 15, 2010): 34-36.
The New York Times, June 1, 2010, p. C6.
Publishers Weekly 257, no. 12 (March 22, 2010): 48.

BLOOMS OF DARKNESS

Author: Aharon Appelfeld (1932-   )
First published: Pirhe ha-afelah, 2006, in Israel
Translated from the Hebrew by Jeffrey M. Green
Publisher: Schocken Books (New York). 279 pp. $25.95
Type of work: Novel
Time: 1941-1944
Locale: Ukraine

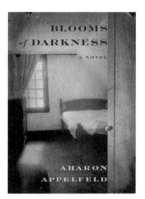

A coming-of-age story in which a Jewish boy is separated from his family as the German army marches toward Moscow during World War II

Principal characters:
HUGO MANSFIELD, a boy living in the
  Ukraine
JULIA MANSFIELD, his mother
HANS MANSFIELD, his father
UNCLE SIGMUND, Julia Mansfield's brother
MARIANA PODGORSKY, a prostitute
VICTORIA, a cook
NATASHA, a prostitute

Since the translation of *Badenheim, 'ir nofesh* (1975; *Badenheim 1939*, 1980) from the Hebrew to English, novelist Aharon Appelfeld has been a major international voice among Jewish writers. A Romanian Jew who, as a child, witnessed from inside a concentration camp the Nazi atrocities perpetrated on his people, Appelfeld has made the Holocaust and the plight of Europe's Jews a constant theme in his fiction. His latest novel, *Blooms of Darkness*, is set in the Ukraine during the period when German soldiers swept through the countryside on their ill-fated trek toward Moscow, only to retreat in disarray before the advancing Russian armies. The story, a kind of coming-of-age tale, is told through the consciousness of Hugo Mansfield, a boy whose mother decides shortly after his eleventh birthday that the family must go into hiding. The Germans have already arrived at their town and are rounding up Jews; Hugo's father and uncle have already been taken away. There are clear signs that it is only a matter of time before the entire Jewish population of the city is carted off—to labor camps, or worse, to installations where Adolf Hitler's henchmen are carrying out the "final solution" to what Hitler called the "Jewish problem." Unable to smuggle him out to the countryside, Hugo's mother decides to place him with a childhood friend, Mariana Podgorsky, a Ukrainian who lives at The Residence, the town's local brothel.

Still naive at the age of eleven, Hugo is not aware of what Mariana does in the evenings while he is hiding away in her closet. Hugo has little to do to occupy his time.

Aharon Appelfeld is an Israeli novelist who writes frequently about the Holocaust and World War II. He is the author of fifteen novels, including the acclaimed Badenheim, 'ir nofesh *(1975;* Badenheim 1939, *1980).*

Instead of reading and doing mathematics, as he had promised his mother, he spends most of his waking hours listening to the activities going on in Mariana's room. When not occupied in this manner, he daydreams about his life before the war and fantasizes about impending reunions with family and friends. His nights are often restless, and in his dreams the people who have meant so much to him, especially his parents and his Uncle Sigmund, visit with him and share their wisdom. In fact, the only presence Hugo's father and uncle have in the novel is through these dreams and in the recollections Mariana and other townspeople have of them. Readers will realize, if Hugo does not, that Sigmund was a frequent client of Mariana's before the war. She confirms Hugo's impressions of this happy-go-lucky ne'er-do-well as a man much to be admired despite his failings, recalling that he treated her handsomely and seemed to care for her genuinely.

Only gradually does Hugo realize the kind of work Mariana and the other women living in the house are doing, but despite constant danger to herself and her housemates, Mariana keeps Hugo safe from German Jew hunters and local snitches who will sell out their Jewish neighbors for a few packs of cigarettes. Eventually others in the house learn of Hugo's presence there, and for a time he lives in fear that the cook, Victoria, will inform on him to the Nazis. To add to his distress, when Mariana is forced to leave The Residence temporarily, he is left in the care of Natasha, one of Mariana's friends, who sneaks off one day and commits suicide.

Hugo remains hidden away at The Residence for more than one year, and as he grows, he begins to feel the urges of his oncoming manhood. That proves a serious complication for Mariana, who is in the habit of expressing her frustrations about the contempt with which she is treated by her customers to the sympathetic and inquisitive boy. Aware of what is happening to Hugo, she decides to initiate him into the joys of sexual pleasure. At first their contact seems like that of mother and son, but after awhile, subtle hints lead readers to understand that Hugo and Mariana have become lovers. The budding sexual relationship between the growing youngster and the older woman may seem troubling, but in the context of the war it makes sense, if anything does in this nightmare scenario.

Although there are virtually no descriptions of the fighting taking place in the Ukraine while Hugo is in hiding, hints from Mariana's German customers and from the other prostitutes allow Hugo (and readers) to get a sense of larger issues playing out on the eastern front. Gradually the braggadocio that characterizes Mariana's German customers turns to apprehension as rumors spread of German retreat and Russian advance toward the city where Hugo lives. The Soviet army drives the Germans from the town before anyone reveals Hugo's whereabouts to the Germans; hence, one might think the novel would have a happy ending. Instead, Mariana and the others living at the brothel are forced to escape from their liberators. She and Hugo wander about the countryside for weeks before Ukrainian partisans working for the Communists find the two of them and take them back into town. There, Hugo learns a harsh lesson: The liberators turn out to be almost as vengeful as the Germans. The Russians round up suspected Nazi collaborators, including all of the prostitutes, and conduct sham trials before executing them. At the end of the tale, Hugo is left alone among other refugees. He seems to be safe. No one will kill him and someone will feed him. It would be hard to say, however, that his future looks bright.

Thematically, Appelfeld is concerned with the nature and causes of anti-Semitism, but he poses questions about society's unreasoned discrimination against Jews in a larger context: the curious social phenomenon of the outcast. In *Blooms of Darkness* the Jews are not the only people persecuted simply for being who they are. The prostitutes, whose presence in the community is tolerated and secretly supported by some of the town's leading citizens, are also victims of discrimination and hatred. One of Hugo's discoveries at The Residence is that most of the women living there have not chosen that lifestyle so much as had it forced upon them. While none of them are saints, few are simply stereotypes of sinful women who revel in debauchery. Most of them express a strong belief in God, acknowledging somewhat sorrowfully that the life they lead is displeasing to the deity. In a particularly telling episode, the young women in the house take up a collection to pay medical expenses of a fellow prostitute who is in the hospital without any way to pay for her care. The more Hugo interacts with these women, the more he comes to realize that they were once school children like himself; they care deeply about their families; and, especially important for him, they have good hearts and a depth of courage that allows them to keep his presence among them secret even at the risk of their own lives.

Gradually Hugo comes to understand what his mother had meant when she told him that Mariana had fallen on hard times; circumstances, not character, have driven her into this profession.

The same might be said of the Jews. Although Appelfeld does not dwell on the historical problems Jews have had in being accepted in Christian communities, he makes clear that their status as outsiders is largely artificial. As Hugo learns from Mariana and the other prostitutes, Jews come in all stripes—some good, some bad, some gentle, some stubborn, some learned, some avaricious, and some incredibly charitable. (Hugo's parents are the prime examples of Jews who care deeply about other people.) If Jews are special in any way, Appelfeld seems to say, it is because of their collective hope for a better future and their determination to survive whatever atrocities might be perpetrated against them. At first, Hugo has great difficulty understanding why the Nazis choose to persecute the Jews simply for being who they are. Gradually, he learns that there are some things that defy reason. There is some solace for him among the Jewish refugees who take him in after the Russians have driven away the Germans. In the refugee camp, people who knew his parents tell him that they will care for him because the Jews have a collective responsibility to look after one another. It is their only hope of survival as a people.

Blooms of Darkness is certain to remind some readers of Elie Wiesel's *Un di Velt hot geshvign* (1956; *Night*, 1960), a story about the effect on an impressionable boy of the Germans' persecution of the Jews. In Appelfeld's novel, however, one never sees the horrors of the concentration camps directly, no physical harm comes to Hugo, and no acts of violence are described. Instead, the specter of the Holocaust looms constantly in the background, driving the action and creating a state of constant anxiety not only for Hugo and his fellow Jews but also for the Ukrainians who suffer under German occupation. In some ways *Blooms of Darkness* is more akin to Anne Frank's *Het Achterhuis* (1947; *The Diary of a Young Girl*, 1952), although Frank is significantly more astute than Hugo about matters of the world and considerably more articulate at expressing both her concerns over Nazi horrors and her optimism for the human race. By creating a naive but reasonably reliable narrator, Appelfeld is able to suggest rather than depict directly both the insanity of the Germans' campaign to eradicate the Jews and the essential goodness of the Ukrainians who defy their German occupiers and assist hundreds of their Jewish neighbors in evading the clutches of the Nazis.

Ultimately, despite these small blooms of hope, a sense of unrelieved anxiety and wholesale suffering permeates *Blooms of Darkness*. Appelfeld's decision to narrate his tale through the eyes of a child and tell the story in present tense makes the catastrophe of World War II seem even more immediate and poignant. As a consequence, the novel is likely to linger in the mind long after the last page is turned. Many readers will probably find it troubling—principally because it is meant to be.

Laurence W. Mazzeno

Review Sources

Booklist 106, no. 14 (March 15, 2010): 18.
Kirkus Reviews 78, no. 2 (February 15, 2010): 95-96.
Library Journal 135, no. 6 (April 1, 2010): 66.
The New York Review of Books 57, no. 7 (April 29, 2010): 23-24.
The New York Times Book Review, March 21, 2010, p. 16.
Publishers Weekly 257, no. 1 (January 4, 2010): 28.

BOB DYLAN IN AMERICA

Author: Sean Wilentz (1951-   )
Publisher: Doubleday (New York). 390 pp. $28.95
Type of work: Biography, music, history
Time: Primarily 1941-2009, also the 1920's and 1930's
Locale: United States

A fascinating and thoughtful discussion of the imprint that Dylan has left on the musical and cultural history of the United States

> *Principal personages:*
> BOB DYLAN (1941-   ), a brilliant singer-songwriter who altered the face of popular music
> JOAN BAEZ (1941-   ), a folk singer and political activist
> WOODY GUTHRIE (1912-1967), an important and influential singer-songwriter
> PETE SEEGER (1919-   ), an important folk singer
> AARON COPLAND (1900-1990), an American composer who combined folk music with contemporary classical trends
> BLIND WILLIE MCTELL (1901-1959), an influential African American blues singer-songwriter
> ALLEN GINSBERG (1926-1997), an influential Beat poet

Sean Wilentz, the author of *Bob Dylan in America*, is a highly respected historian and has written several striking studies of American democracy and the people who have shaped it. His first book, *Chants Democratic: New York and the Rise of the American Working Class*, was published in 1984. As a social and political historian, Wilentz has written passionately about how the common person has been affected by major American events. He was given the Albert J. Beveridge Award by the American Historical Association for *Chants Democratic*. In 2005, he authored *The Rise of American Democracy: Jefferson to Lincoln*. It was considered an extraordinary chronicle of how democracy became the lifeblood of the United States. Always the tenacious researcher, Wilentz produced a supremely authoritative study, and for his efforts, *The Rise of American Democracy* won the prestigious Bancroft Prize.

Truly fascinated with what the United States was and has become, Wilentz next produced the provocative study *The Age of Reagan: A History, 1974-2008* (2008). While this subject may seem outside his realm of expertise and/or interest, he felt compelled to examine Ronald Reagan's impact on the United States with the same thoroughness of purpose that he had brought to all of his projects. Although not a supporter of Reagan, Wilentz proved that it was possible for a trained historian to write a clearheaded portrait. For his next project, he decided to examine the world of American popular

*Sean Wilentz is the author of several
critically acclaimed historical studies,
including the award-winning* The Rise
of American Democracy: Jefferson to
Lincoln *(2005). He also is the Sidney
and Ruth Lapidus Professor in the
American Revolutionary Era at
Princeton University.*

culture. With *Bob Dylan in America*, Wilentz has made good use of his training as a historian in order to produce a striking discussion of the sometimes inscrutable Bob Dylan.

Many other writers also have taken on the challenge of piecing together a credible portrait of Dylan. With varying degrees of success, such writers as Greil Marcus, Robert Shelton, Tim Riley, Clinton Heylin, Howard Sournes, Dylan's former girlfriend Suze Rotolo, and Dylan himself have delivered their vision of the man. Few would argue about Dylan's genius or that he has transformed several forms of popular music with his startling poetic songs. Growing up in 1950's America, Dylan was fascinated by what was taking place in contemporary music and literature. It was a time for youthful exploration, and Dylan—who was still known by his given name, Robert Zimmerman—took the time to listen, read, and experiment on his own.

Bob Dylan in America became Wilentz's chance to flesh out not only who Dylan is but also how the man fits into American cultural history. As a historian, Wilentz does not see events happening in a vacuum. How Robert Zimmerman became Bob Dylan, therefore, becomes a larger American story. If it takes a village to raise a child, then it must take an entire country to create a Dylan. Wilentz had no intention to write a conventional biography. He wanted to focus almost exclusively on "[Dylan's] influences and the way he has drawn from different aspects of American culture." Over the length of his career, Dylan has reinvented himself on several occasions. He can be thought of as the Pablo Picasso of American music. He has refused to sit still or to have one approach to his art. While a great number of other artists and musicians have been perfectly content not to alter what they do, Dylan has taken the "road less traveled" at almost every turn. In a sense, this restlessness and need to change his stripes periodically make him truly part of the American experiment.

Wilentz states in his introduction to *Bob Dylan in America* that it is somewhat of a "fluke" that he ever entertained the idea of writing about American music in general and Dylan specifically. When Wilentz was a child growing up in Brooklyn Heights, his father and uncle ran the 8th Street Bookshop in Greenwich Village. Wilentz points out that this bookshop was important to the Beat poets of the 1950's and the folk music revival of the early 1960's. He felt lucky to witness the rise of the "counterculture." The young Wilentz would hear stories about the poets, musicians, and activists who frequented the shop. It was at his uncle's apartment above the bookshop that Dylan first met Allen Ginsberg in 1963. With this social and cultural history happening right under his nose, it seemed that it was just a matter of time before he would turn his attention to what was going on in the United States during these turbulent decades.

For Wilentz, *Bob Dylan in America* would contain more than merely an analysis of historical events and musical developments, it would also tell a personal story, one that is close to his heart. In addition to his introduction, he has divided the book into five parts and a coda. The five parts are named for stages in Dylan's career: "Before," "Early," "Later," "Interlude," and "Recent." Each of the parts has two chapters except the last part, which has three chapters. The first chapter, "Music for the Common Man: The Popular Front and Aaron Copland's America," details how powerful an influence Aaron Copland was on the American musical landscape during the 1930's and the 1940's. A connection between Copland and Dylan may seem like a stretch, but the author points out that Copland incorporated many styles of music into his finished compositions. He took inspiration from both the cowboy and folk tradition in order to establish his own unique style. This desire to create his own modernism out of an amalgam of various traditions places him as a direct precursor to Dylan's approach to music decades later. While other experts have rightly linked Dylan to Woody Guthrie and Guthrie's "paeans to the common man," Wilentz boldly establishes the connection to Copland "whose orchestral work raises some of the same conundrums that Dylan's songs do—about art and politics, simplicity and difficulty, compromise and genius, love and theft." The uncanny nature of Dylan's accomplishment lies in his ability to shape the songs of others into a body of work that was "all his own." Dylan's massive absorption of everything American did not stop with Copland and Guthrie. In the second chapter of part 1, "Penetrating Aether: The Beat Generation and Allen Ginsberg's America," it becomes clear that the Beats offered Dylan a "play of language" and a "spiritual estrangement that transcended conventional politics." In the Dylan song "Desolation Row," there is a "carnival of fragments" that can be compared to such great modernist poems as T. S. Eliot's *The Waste Land* (1922) and Ginsberg's *Howl, and Other Poems* (1956). Dylan's ability to shape a song out of various influences has served him well. Other compositions such as "Mr. Tambourine Man" and "It's Alright, Ma" contain "bits and pieces" that were "gathered from hither and yon." The tease, the obscure references, and the magic trick all seemingly apply to a successful Dylan song.

Wilentz emphasizes the making of songs and the making of image through performing and recording in part 2. In chapter 3, he discusses how Dylan would play songs in concert that the audience knew by heart as well as introduce new songs that the audience found "baffling." The New York Philharmonic Hall concert in 1964 could be called a "summation of past work" as well as a "summons to an explosion for which none of us, was fully prepared." He was more than willing to be the singer behind a "mask." The audience was within their rights to expect a "great entertainer," but anything beyond that was too much to ask or require of anyone. Dylan did not want to accept the "burden" of being "the voice of a generation." For him it was the songs that mattered. The "astounding" words and images should be enough for the public, but it was becoming obvious that no one would leave it at just that.

In chapter 4, Wilentz takes the reader on a fascinating journey through the making of the seminal album *Blonde on Blonde*. Dylan did not want to do "anything twice." This was the impression that he gave the record's producer, Bob Johnson, and the brilliant musicians who were chosen to sit in at the recording sessions. There was a need to be perfect yet also capture the spontaneous moment. Dylan has had many "peaks" and "valleys" in his career, and *Blonde on Blonde* was a major peak. The two chapters of part 3 describe Dylan after his 1966 motorcycle accident. He took time to "reassess" his life. The accident did not stop him from being creative, though.

Chapter 5 examines the period leading up to the Rolling Thunder Revue of 1975. Reinvention would once again pull him through to the other side. Wilentz makes the point that Dylan found a way of looking forward by listening to the musicians and musical styles of the past. He always was ready to learn, evolve, and move on to something different. The Dylan found in chapter 6 takes inspiration from the blues musician Blind Willie McTell. McTell had been active from the late 1920's until the late 1950's. Like Dylan, McTell wrote songs that had "strong roots" in older musical forms, yet his songs were still contemporary. Dylan recorded a song titled "Blind Willie McTell" in 1983 but did not release it until 1991.

Part 4 of *Bob Dylan in America* pulls Dylan into the 1990's. He barely survived the various personal troubles of the 1980's. During the early 1990's, he released the traditional folk song albums *Good as I Been to You* (1992) and *World Gone Wrong* (1993). Dylan remained rooted in the American songbook, the rich tradition that came before him. He was determined to keep it alive. In Part 5, Dylan is in fine form for the turn of the century. The music found on *Love and Theft* (2001) gives the listener a history lesson. As usual, but perhaps more overtly in this case, the United States is the topic at hand. In an attempt to be as current as possible Wilentz includes a coda at the end of the book that mentions Dylan's 2009 Christmas album *Christmas in the Heart*. Always the alchemist, this compilation may have seemed puzzling to many.

While Wilentz presents an inventive and—at times—frustrating portrait of Dylan, there is much to relish in *Bob Dylan in America*. Since 2001, Wilentz has served as the "historian-in-residence" of Dylan's official Web site, and many of the chapters first appeared on the site. Although Wilentz may not always seem to be a dispassionate historian, he is never less than fascinating in his attempt to get at the heart of Dylan's complicated love affair with America.

Jeffry Jensen

Review Sources

Chicago Tribune, September 9, 2010, p. 3.
Independent, October 15, 2010, p. 22.
Kirkus Reviews 78, no. 12 (June 15, 2010): 562.
Los Angeles Times, September 8, 2010, p. D1.
New Statesman 139 (October 4, 2010): 69.
The New York Review of Books 57, no. 18 (November 25, 2010): 34.
The New York Times, September 10, 2010, p. C1.
The Observer, September 12, 2010, p. 38.
The Washington Post, September 5, 2010, p. B6.

BOMBER COUNTY
The Poetry of a Lost Pilot's War

Author: Daniel Swift (1977-   )
Publisher: Farrar, Straus and Giroux (New York).
   268 pp. $26.00
Type of work: History, poetry
Time: 1939-1943 and 2007-2009
Locale: Netherlands, Germany, and England

Swift begins his search for the poetry of World War II by visiting the cemeteries that hold the remains of Allied flyers, including those of his grandfather, a pilot in the Bomber Command of the Royal Air Force, and then expands his inquiry to encompass a brief history of the air war and some analysis of the poetry, both British and American, that deals with that air war

   Principal personages:
      W. H. AUDEN (1907-1973), a British poet
      JOHN CIARDI (1916-1986), an American poet and translator
      JAMES DICKEY (1923-1997), an American poet
      T. S. ELIOT (1888-1965), an Anglo-American poet
      RANDALL JARRELL (1914-1965), an American poet
      CECIL DAY LEWIS (1904-1972), a British poet
      STEPHEN SPENDER (1909-1995), a British poet
      JAMES ERIC SWIFT, the grandfather of the author and World War I
         bomber pilot
      DYLAN THOMAS (1914-1953), a Welsh poet

In *Bomber County* Daniel Swift looks at some of the poets of World War II. However, twentieth century war poets and war poetry in English usually refer to those British poets who fought in World War I and bring to mind the awfulness of trench warfare and the slaughter on the Western front. These included Allied writers who had served in combat such as Siegfried Sassoon, Rupert Brooke, Harold Rosenberg, Alan Seeger, and, especially, Wilfred Owen, whose "Dolce et Decorum Est," with its graphic description of a gas attack, became perhaps the most famous of all the war poems. The conclusion of World War I left numb a civilian population that had not been prepared for the horrors of a modern, mechanized war and its use of aircraft, tanks, and dreadnoughts; the enormity of the loss of life; and the destruction of civilian property. The worldwide disillusionment and exhaustion over the enormity of the material and human waste that followed the conclusion of the hostilities produced a generation receptive to the antiwar message of writers, in both poetry and fiction, which had an unprecedented impact.

∽

*Daniel Swift writes essays, profiles,
and reviews for such periodicals as the*
Financial Times Magazine, The New
York Times Book Review, Bookforum,
The Nation, *the* Times Literary
Supplement, *and the* Daily Telegraph.

∽

In retrospect, World War II seemed to have produced few poets and less poetry, or, at any rate, poets and poetry of lesser importance than those that emerged from World War I. In part, this was because of different attitudes toward the wars. World War I was fought for ideological reasons. It was the "war to end all wars" and produced a generation of disillusioned writers. World War II was less ideological and more pragmatic; the world simply needed to be rid of expansionist dictators. The post-World War II literature reflected a less disillusioned, more cynical group of writers, writers who were more successful at getting their ideas across in fiction than in poetry. Having already experienced an earlier world war, perhaps the public, too, was less moved or receptive to the antiwar message that followed World War II. The poetry and novels that came out of the latter conflict were less poignant and tougher; the readers were less sentimental and more resigned.

Furthermore, even the publications during the war, such as the *Times Literary Supplement* (TLS) in the early months of the war, called on British poets to become involved in the conflict in "To the Poets of 1940." However, the literary establishment somehow felt that the response was disappointing, and that sense of disappointment carried over into the postwar world. Therefore, after the war, Edmund Blunden could declare that Owen's place was still secure, as the poetry from World War II did not rival that from World War I.

In *Bomber County*, Swift sets out to redress the impression that World War II did not inspire great poetry by making the claim that bombers and the bombing war provided the same poetic inspiration for World War II that the trenches did during World War I. He supports this claim with examples of poetry written during and after the war, on both sides of the Atlantic, which belie the contemporary criticism that the poets did not rise to the occasion the way their earlier compatriots had. Swift argues that, at the time, the literary establishment, such as the TLS and the prominent prewar poets, were not ready for the kind of poetry brought forth by World War II, a poetry called forth from the new conditions of warfare, in this instance, the war in the air. Like the trench war of World War I, the air war raised the level of both the scope and the intensity of the carnage and had a more profound effect on the civilian population than had been experienced in World War I. Also, it provided a dual perspective, the bombers and their crews above and the civilians and soldiers below. As Swift notes, the crews who did not return from their missions left a lack of an ending, at least their ending, and the indiscriminate killing of a civilian population consisting mostly of women, children, and old men made the action of the air raids seem less than heroic, robbing the Bomber Command of any sense of nobility or goodness.

Bomber County is an attempt to reframe the war and the experience of those who fought in it in ways that can illuminate the literary responses to it. Swift argues that the poetry that came out of World War II can hold its own against that poetry from World War I. He also expands the definition of "war poetry" to include the extensive poetry written by the general population, who also were responding to the war, often in ways only recognized after the conflict.

Swift begins his reclamation of the poetry of World War II with a search for the grave of his paternal grandfather, who perished over the English Channel during his return from a bombing mission on the European continent. James Eric Swift was a pilot of a Lancaster bomber whose plane crashed into the ocean off the coast of Holland on June 12, 1943, after a night raid over Münster, Germany. His body washed up on the beach at Callantsoog five days later. He was buried initially at Huisduinen, and in 1946, his remains were moved 100 miles south to a cemetery at Bergen op Zoom. Of the six men on his plane only one other body was ever recovered, that of the rear gunner, Sergeant J. J. Anderton, who was found later and interred in a different graveyard.

Bomber County follows three trajectories: The story of James Eric Swift, his past and military service; some of the history of World War II, particularly involving the British Bomber Command; and the presentation and analysis of the poetry of the war. Readers learn that the author's grandfather went by his middle, not first, name and so was known as Eric Swift throughout most of his life. His father was a partner in a rubber-importing firm, when rubber was an important commodity and before it was made synthetically. Eric went to work at the company, but family gossip holds that he disliked the work and that was one of his reasons for enlisting. In any event, he had been taking flying lessons during the 1930's, and the fact that he could already fly expedited his participation in combat once hostilities began. Using official sources and privately written memoirs in the Imperial War Museum, Swift takes his readers through his grandfather's induction and his training and the Bomber Command's initial offensives in the spring of 1940, even though it was another year before Eric Swift actually began his bombing missions. Since he knows little of his grandfather's actual military experience, Swift must rely on knowledge that is not firsthand and that leads him to intertwine the war career of his grandfather with the broader outlines of the war, especially the air war.

Herein Swift sets up the pattern he employs throughout the book, intersecting the search for his grandfather with the historical material about the war; this pattern is interrupted from time to time with discussions of various war poets and their poetry. So, for example, while recounting his grandfather's early training with the Royal Air Force, Swift intercuts an analysis of the poetry and the biographical data of the American poet Randall Jarrell, who joined the U.S. Air Force, trained with the Second Air Force, and came into contact with bomber pilots but never saw combat. Nevertheless, his "The Death of a Ball Turret Gunner" became one of the more memorable American poems to come out of the war. It was an imaginative rendering of the death and unceremonious disposal of the body of a gunner on a bomber. It is an image as graphic as anything from World War I. This coalescence of the imagination with history and literature is what Swift's book is all about.

Swift deals primarily with well-known writers such as W. H. Auden, Cecil Day Lewis, Jarrell, Dylan Thomas, James Dickey, T. S. Eliot, and others, most of whom never experienced combat. However, his concluding chapter, "Bomber Poets," is devoted to exploring the writings of those men who were actually in the air war. Their names remain unfamiliar; their poetry immediate and poignant. In this chapter, Swift also reconstructs the final days of his grandfather's life.

Bomber County is an engaging study of World War II from the perspective of some of the literary responses the war called forth. Swift is especially interested in the writing that was the result of the extensive air campaign, of those who fought in it, and of those who experienced it on the ground. Swift's observations about the dual perspective brought about by bombing, both above and below, helps to illuminate at least some of the creative impetus behind the poetry emanating from the war. It explores some of the same issues pursued in other studies of the impact of the extensive World War II bombing, especially on the nonmilitary populations, such as the historian W. G. Sebald's work on the impact of Allied strikes and the near total destruction of German cities on postwar German literature. However, *Bomber County* is more than a literary study because it provides a new look at the war itself. Also, it has a personal touch because of Swift's engagement in the search for his grandfather, not only his grave, which in any case he finds early in the narrative, but also for the experiences of a man he never met but who is nevertheless a part of his life through his father and family. *Bomber County* is a fine piece of literary and historical research and a heartfelt memoir.

Charles L. P. Silet

Review Sources

Booklist 106, no. 22 (August 1, 2010): 17.
New Statesman 139, (August 16, 2010): 53-54.
The New York Times, September 1, 2010, p. 1.
The New York Times Book Review, September 26, 2010, p. 19.
The Spectator 313, no. 9495 (August 21, 2010): 32-34.

BONHOEFFER
Pastor, Martyr, Prophet, Spy

Author: Eric Metaxas (1963-   )
Foreword by Timothy J. Keller
Publisher: Thomas Nelson (Nashville). 591 pp. $29.99
Type of work: Biography, history, religion
Time: 1896-1945
Locale: Europe and the United States

A narrative of the life of Dietrich Bonhoeffer, and many of his contemporaries, from his birth into a patrician family to his death at Flossenbürg concentration camp, with consideration of his theological studies and his contrapuntal relationship to the national-socialist state

Principal personages:
> DIETRICH BONHOEFFER (1906-1945), a Lutheran theologian, pastor, and politically engaged opponent of the national-socialist regime
> EBERHARD BETHGE, a student and his close confidante
> KARL BONHOEFFER, his father and a prominent psychiatrist in Breslau then Berlin
> HANS VON DOHNANYI (1889-1945), his brother-in-law and his collaborator in the Abwehr, a counterespionage agency
> ADOLF VON HARNACK (1851-1930), a theologian and one of his first teachers
> REINHOLD NIEBUHR (1892-1971), a German American theologian and his teacher at Union Theological Seminary
> MARTIN NIEMÜLLER (1892-1984), a German Submarine Commander turned theologian and his collaborator in the Bekennende Kirche (witnessing church)
> MARIA VON WEDEMEYER, his wife
> ELISABETH ZINN (BORNKAMM), a fellow student of theology and, perhaps, his love interest
> KARL BARTH (1886-1968), a Swiss theologian who taught in Germany until his refusal to sign an oath of allegiance motivated his return to Switzerland

Eric Metaxas's account of the life of Dietrich Bonhoeffer, entitled simply *Bonhoeffer*, begins with the meeting and subsequent marriage of Karl Bonhoeffer, a promising psychiatrist, and Paula von Hase, a teacher with strong Christian faith. The book ends with the same two people turning off the radio after listening to the memorial service for Bonhoeffer at Holy Trinity Brompton, where George Bell, bishop of Chichester, had honored the memory of their son. Between these two events, Metaxas packs an account of Bonhoeffer's attempt to live a life of one practicing a responsible

~

Eric Metaxas has written a variety of children's books, biographies, and Christian apologetics. His writing has appeared in the Atlantic Monthly, The New York Times, The Washington Post, *the* Regenerative Quarterly, Christianity Today, *and other publications.*

~

Christian morality in a time filled with serious challenges and unfathomably difficult moral controversies.

The reader follows Bonhoeffer through a childhood in an affluent patrician family in Berlin. His father was a prominent psychiatrist in a strongly empirical tradition, and his mother took charge of his and his siblings' religious development in the tradition of the Herrnhuter Brethren, a group advocating a personal relationship with God. These two polar opposites synthesized in the thinking of Bonhoeffer.

The first key stage of Bonhoeffer's life takes place in Tübingen, where he begins his studies in theology, much to the surprise of his family. He continues his studies in Berlin with a subsequent internship at an expatriate German church in Barcelona. With an important quote from Bonhoeffer's diary, Metaxas illuminates a key characteristic of Bonhoeffer's reasoning: He does not force decisions but lets them ferment in his mind until moral clarity occurs. Later, Bonhoeffer uses that same process to answer important dilemmas, such as whether one should be a pacifist and conscientious objector or whether one should find the assassination of a dictator morally permissible. In both cases, Bonhoeffer appears to find moral clarity for himself without taking a stand on how others should act, except to practice the same process of moral deliberation under terms of one's relationship to God. Metaxas shows quite well that Bonhoeffer offers responsibility, not easy answers.

Bonhoeffer spent one year at Union Theological Seminary in New York. While he was lukewarm about and sometimes outright critical of the quality of American theological studies and Union Theological Seminary, specifically, Bonhoeffer made important contacts in the African American community, gaining a particular appreciation for the religious music of that community and of the racial issues in American society. Metaxas states that Bonhoeffer's strong sense of opposition to racism had him turn down a teaching appointment at Harvard; he feared being infected by American racism.

The greater part of the biography focuses on Bonhoeffer's confrontation with Nazi doctrines and practices. In anticipation of Hannah Arendt's "consensus iuris," Bonhoeffer published in the *Kreuzzeitung* (newspaper of the cross) an admonition that the leader principle can work only if the leader heeds the ultimate authority of the ones he leads, something that Adolf Hitler did not do, finding instead a moral compass in preconceived ideologies of his own. Hitler's leadership polarized the German people and its churches. When the so-called Aryan paragraph excluded all persons of Jewish descent from holding posts in public-service jobs, the Prussian synod of the Lutherans decided to abide by the rule, although churches had been expressly excluded from this requirement. That action on the part of the mainstream church effectively motivated Bonhoeffer's departure from that church to found the Bekennende Kirche (Metaxas prefers "confessing church"; perhaps a better translation would be the "witnessing church"). Bonhoeffer saw the secession from the mainstream church as the only morally responsible act.

With increasing hostilities on the part of the Nazi government toward the Bekennende Kirche, Bonhoeffer's safety was at risk. With the help of friends in the United States, he returned to Union Theological Seminary. Seeking moral clarity by way of his personal focus on God, Bonhoeffer came to the conclusion that he had to return to Germany. He decided to leave for Germany after only twenty-six days in New York. With help from his brother-in-law Hans von Dohnanyi, Bonhoeffer began working for the Abwehr (antiespionage department). Admiral Wilhelm Canaris's department had the task of protecting the secrecy of the clandestine collection of documentation of the Nazi atrocities. As part of his work for this department, Bonhoeffer was able to travel abroad, making important connections and exchanging information with his international contacts. Metaxas seems to cover this phase of Bonhoeffer's life well; however, by virtue of the secret operations in which Bonhoeffer was involved, Metaxas has to work with a certain amount of conjecture.

Metaxas spends one chapter on Bonhoeffer's relationship with his eventual wife, Maria von Wedemeyer, who, as an eighteen-year-old, adored the impressive intellect of the thirty-seven-year-old Bonhoeffer. Despite misgivings of the family and requests for a one-year cooling-off period, the two eventually announced their engagement. The actual relationship, however, was mainly by way of letters, with a few visits by Maria to Berlin Tegel prison, where Bonhoeffer was incarcerated. After the failed Stauffenberg plot to assassinate Hitler, Dohnanyi and Canaris were jailed also. Bonhoeffer's name appeared in the records of Dohnanyi, thus raising suspicions of his connections to the conspiracy. That suspicion sealed his fate. After a brief trial at Flossenbürg concentration camp in Bavaria, Bonhoeffer was hanged.

Metaxas's style is fluid and easily read. He uses narrative techniques from fiction writing; that is, one often knows what goes on in the thoughts of the personages of the biography. What this technique adds in readability, it takes away in reliability. Many such lines rely on conjecture without evidence; however, the overall effect clearly enhances readability, even though it also often includes untested popular assumptions, thereby made stronger in the uncritical reader's thoughts. A proofreader might have enhanced Metaxas's work. There are about forty orthographic errors in German quotations, including some name errors. In addition, the book contains some outright factual errors: Theodor Storm might have been unhappy about being referred to as a Danish German; he clearly had sided with Prussia and had written sharply critical comments in the daily press about Denmark. Also, the young man who took aim at a member of the German embassy in Paris and so gave reason for the Kristallnacht (Night of Broken Glass) in 1938 did decidedly not do so because "his father had recently been put in a crowded boxcar and deported to Poland." After all, the war against Poland did not begin until August of 1939. There would have been little point in such a boxcar transport in 1938.

In addition, no mention is made of Bonhoeffer's ethical theory of the "mandates," a key issue in his relationship to the Nazi state and the core of Bonhoeffer's attempt to resolve the dilemma of obedience to the state as required by Romans 13 while maintaining a simultaneous obedience to God. Also, Metaxas seems to miss a clear understanding of Hitler's ideological roots in the Stoa, the view that the universe is morally motivated and will leave hints of being properly aligned to the individual from providence (*Vorsehung*). Metaxas sees Hitler as a cynical pragmatist, but that is too much of a simplification and ignores the kind of strange religiosity that ruled him and led him eventually to a most baroque interest in the occult.

Finally, Metaxas also misinterprets the metaphor of the "spoke to be tossed into the wheel," a misunderstanding or a mistranslation that seems to revive itself in every new work about Bonhoeffer. The actual quote comes from Bonhoeffer's essay "Die Kirche vor der Judenfrage" (1933; the church in the face of the Jewish question). In it, Bonhoeffer insists on three stages of analysis regarding the German government's actions against Jews, the first being public questioning of the state's legitimacy in its action, the second being the active assistance rendered to the victims of the state's action, and the third being "dem Rad selbst in die Speichen zu fallen" (to fall into the spokes of the wheel). The metaphor should be clear to any teamster. When a wagon goes downhill or uphill and when the beasts of burden cannot hold the wagon, then it is the task of the teamster to hold or to push the spokes by hand to slow the progress or to advance the progress appropriately; the teamster should by no means break the wheel by tossing a spoke into it. Bonhoeffer goes on to explain that he means to encourage political activity on the part of the church where the state has failed its tasks. The four divine mandates of state, church, family, and labor hold state and church apart; but where one institution fails, the other must engage to control and to interact with the development of the other. In other words, where churches fail, the state may have a similar obligation; at any rate, such a reciprocal action would certainly be consistent with Bonhoeffer's theory of the mandates.

Reinhold Schlieper

Review Sources

America 202, no. 20 (June 21, 2010): 23-25.
The Christian Century 127, no. 21 (October 19, 2010): 34-39.
First Things: A Monthly Journal of Religion & Public Life, no. 206 (October, 2010): 77-78.
Kirkus Reviews 78, no. 8 (April 15, 2010): 346.
Library Journal 135, no. 10 (June 1, 2010): 88.
National Review 62, no. 11 (June 21, 2010): 46-47.
The Wall Street Journal, April 22, 2010, p. A21.

THE BOOK IN THE RENAISSANCE

Author: Andrew Pettegree (1957-   )
Publisher: Yale University Press (New Haven, Conn.).
    421 pp. $40.00
Type of work: History, literary history
Time: 1450-1600
Locale: Europe

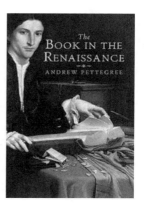

Pettegree surveys the first 150 years of printing in Europe, examining the ways books influenced and were affected by economic, religious, and cultural forces

Principal personages:
> Matthias I Corvinus, the book-collecting
> 　　king of Hungary
> Johann Gutenberg (1394/1399-1468),
> 　　the inventor of printing from movable type
> Anton Koberger, a fifteenth century Nürnberg printer
> Nicolas Jenson, a fifteenth century Venetian printer
> Aldus Manutius (c. 1450-1515), a humanist Venetian printer and
> 　　publisher
> Christophe Plantin (c. 1520-1589), a sixteenth century Dutch printer
> Desiderius Erasmus (1466?-1536), a Dutch scholar
> Martin Luther (1483-1546), a church reformer
> John Calvin (1509-1564), a Protestant leader
> Sir Thomas Bodley (1545-1613), the founder of Oxford's Bodleian
> 　　Library

The history of the book as a discipline may be dated from 1958, when Lucien Febvre and Henri-Jean Martin published *L'Apparition du livre* (1958; *The Coming of the Book: The Impact of Printing, 1450-1800*, 1976). Febvre and Martin argued that Johann Gutenberg's invention of printing from movable type transformed European society. As the study of the history of the book has widened, scholars have adopted a more nuanced view. Print culture has come to be seen not just as a force for change but also as a reflection of economic, religious, political, and technological developments. Andrew Pettegree's study, *The Book in the Renaissance*, drawing on his directorship of the Universal Short Title Catalogue Project, illustrates many of the ways the press shaped and was affected by its milieu.

Pettegree's first chapter briefly describes the medieval handwritten book and its readers. Pettegree observes that the advent of print did not at once destroy the scribal world. In the Netherlands the production of manuscripts reached its peak in the 1490's, well after Gutenberg had invented printing from movable type about 1450. Scribes also found employment decorating early printed books, since printing in color, though technically possible, was expensive and time consuming. Also, the

~

Andrew Pettegree is the director of the
Universal Short Title Catalogue
Project. His books include The Early
Reformation in Europe *(1992),* Marian
Protestantism: Six Studies *(1996), and*
Reformation and the Culture of
Persuasion *(2005).*

~

early purchasers of printed works wanted their books to look like manuscripts, with marginal flourishes and decorations that were beyond the capacity of the fifteenth century press. Scribes nonetheless feared and objected to printing technology, and with good reason: Scribal culture waned after 1500.

Although the press produced books for scholars and publishers such as Aldus Manutius belonged to the world of Renaissance humanism, Pettegree notes that printing in the West was invented and sustained by entrepreneurs. Gutenberg and those who followed sought to make a profit, without which they and their presses could not survive. Gutenberg was not only Europe's first printer but also Europe's first printer to go bankrupt. His magnificent forty-two-line Bible enjoyed a welcome reception; all 180 copies quickly sold despite their high price of twenty gulden for a paper copy, fifty for one on vellum. Twenty gulden was a year's salary for a master craftsman in Mainz in 1450.

A perennial problem with printing is the investment required, not only in paper (which until the nineteenth century made up about one-half the cost of production) but also in type, presses, and workers, before any money can be recovered through the sale of the finished product. Gutenberg's Bible required years to complete. To finance his project he borrowed money from Johann Fust, who sued to recover his investment. Money from the sale of the Bible did not come in quickly enough, and Fust gained control of Gutenberg's presses. Fust then engaged Gutenberg's foreman, Peter Schoeffer, who became Mainz's (and Europe's) second printer. Fust was a better businessman than Gutenberg. His press continued to print religious works but also printed broadsheets and certificates that could be produced and sold quickly to finance larger books.

Printing reduced the price of books, a development that displeased some. In 1473, the Benedictine monk Filippo de Strata urged the doge of Venice to ban printing because the flood of books allowed anyone to own them. Scholars, too, complained that printed texts were inaccurate. A more serious challenge to print came from its technological success: Too many books were produced. Whereas scribes created individual texts to order, printers ran off hundreds of copies in the hope that customers would buy them. In 1472, Konrad Sweinheim and Arnold Pannartz, Italy's protoprinters, petitioned the pope for money because they had not sold enough of the twenty thousand books they had produced. Despite a papal subvention, they went out of business in 1473. In that year, eight of Venice's dozen printers ceased operating, and Florence, which had seen its first press established in 1471, lost all of its printers.

To limit risk, publishers might agree not to compete. They often asked for payment from authors to help finance an edition and also shared risk through consortiums. In addition, they sought regulations to protect their investments. In 1496, Manutius secured a twenty-year monopoly from Venice for his Greek type. This restriction did not apply beyond the reach of Venetian law, so printers elsewhere were free to copy his letter forms and did so. In England, the London Stationers' Company cooperated with the government to restrict pirating of books.

Despite financial hazards, print spread quickly, reaching Bamberg and Strasbourg by 1460, Cologne by 1464, Basel and Augsburg in 1468, Venice in 1469, Nürnberg and Paris in 1470, Buda (now part of Budapest) in 1473, Kraców (Cracow) in 1474, Lübeck in 1475, London in 1476, and Vienna in 1481. Highlighting the importance of trade for the industry are the locations where presses thrived: commercial rather than intellectual centers. Tübingen and Heidelberg both housed universities, but printers did not settle there. London, not Oxford or Cambridge, became England's publishing capital. Italy's first books were printed at the monastery of Subiaco, but after two years, that press relocated to Rome. Venice emerged as Europe's major fifteenth century source for books because of its commercial ties, and in the sixteenth century, it out-produced Rome and Florence. Between 1564 and 1600, three-fourths of all Italian books were printed in Venice. Paris and Lyon dominated French book production in the sixteenth century, and Basel became a center of scholarly publishing because printers there could readily reach markets across the continent. The Lyon publisher Symphorien Beraud dealt with booksellers in Florence, Naples, Sienna, Turin, Venice, Piacenza, Milan, Barcelona, Zaragoza, Medina del Campo, and Salamanca. Dutch publishers produced more than five hundred editions in Spanish for Iberian readers.

Christophe Plantin provided more than fifty-two thousand liturgical works for the Spanish Church and supplied his English customers with books printed in Basel, Geneva, Lyon, and Zürich. Venice printed many books for the Slavic market. Although eighty cities in Italy in the fifteenth century had a press at least briefly, four produced 80 percent of the output because these were major centers of commerce. Book fairs played an important role in the book trade. The most important such event occurred in Frankfurt in the spring during Lent and in the fall at Michaelmas. Michael Harder of Augsburg sold more than five thousand books at one fair. Leipzig and Lyon sponsored fairs at Easter; Lyon held others in August and at the Feast of All Souls. Basel had a fair in October. This international trade in books allowed the collector Fernando Colón, son of Christopher Columbus, to acquire more than one thousand French books outside that country.

Religion, like commerce, affected the book trade. Because it was the focal point of the German Reformation, Wittenberg, despite its small population and its distance from major trade routes, became one of Germany's, indeed Europe's, chief centers of book production. Martin Luther's *Sermons on Indulgences and Grace* (1518) went through fourteen editions in its first year, three printed in Wittenberg, the rest in Leipzig, Nürnberg, Augsburg, and Basel. Luther's polemical writings were brief, so printers could produce and sell an edition rapidly and realize a quick profit. In 1519, Luther invited the Leipzig printer Melchior Lotter to set up a press in Wittenberg. In 1520, Lotter's son, who established a press in the town, published Luther's *To the Christian Nobility of the German Nation* and *On the Babylonian Captivity of the*

Church. The 4,000 copies of the former sold out in five days, and fifteen further editions followed. Lotter also profited from printing thousands of copies of Luther's translation of the New Testament. At least 100,000 copies of this work were printed in Wittenberg during Luther's lifetime. Between 1520 and 1525, Wittenberg's printers produced 600 editions, many of them related to the Reformation. German presses overall turned out 7,764 editions.

Printing began or was reintroduced in at least thirty-four German towns as a consequence of the demand for texts that Luther's Reformation created. The Reformation's impact on print spread to Switzerland, the Netherlands, Scandinavia, and eastern Europe. In Zürich, Christopher Froschauer and his family produced some thirteen hundred editions, including twenty-eight editions of the Bible. Königsberg emerged as an important center of Protestant publishing in the east. Under the reform-minded regime of Edward VI, London printing doubled between 1546 and 1548; most of the works issued dealt with religion. When Edward's Catholic sister, Mary, succeeded him in 1553, the English publishing industry contracted. The Reformation helped even Catholic printers, as polemicists responded to Luther and his followers. However, religious controversy proved a mixed blessing to the press because Catholic and Protestant rulers banned books supporting the rival confession. Lists of banned books cited not only individual works but also authors' and even printers' entire output. Religious wars also threatened printing. Plantin's presses in Antwerp were nearly destroyed during the fighting between Catholic Spanish and Protestant Dutch forces. He left for the safety of Leiden, as did others, markedly lowering the number of books printed at Antwerp.

Political controversies also provided fodder for printers. Pettegree found more than four thousand editions of French royal edicts published between 1560 and 1600. In 1565, Robert Estienne became France's first royal printer, a coveted position because it guaranteed business. Town councils also subsidized printers by paying for the publication of ordinances, and the crown selected provincial royal printers. Jacques Garnier of Bourges was one of many printers who relied on government work to remain solvent. James I supported the small Scottish printing establishment. Henry IV of France proved particularly adept at using the press to stimulate loyalty. England remained an exception to the European pattern; English rulers did not use the press to shape public opinion. Between 1632 and 1638, Charles I banned the printing of all news, foreign and domestic. Only after the English Civil War broke out did he belatedly try to foster a provincial press to bolster his position.

Pettegree examines conditions for authors in the early era of print. Writers received little profit. They were more likely to have to pay to get their books into print than to make money from their work, though there were rare exceptions, such as in the case of Desiderius Erasmus. Authors who were not wealthy relied on patronage, and publication could advance a writer's career. Consequently, books were dedicated to a rich or powerful person in the hope of reward. To encourage generosity, Pietro Aretino published the sums he received, highlighting the generosity or stinginess of his dedicatees.

Pettegree estimates that more than 345,000 editions were published between 1450 and 1600. This explosion in the number of books prompted attempts to establish order to the world of print. In 1545, Conrad Gesner published his *Bibliotheca universalis*, an effort to record all titles in Greek, Latin, and Hebrew. Encyclopedic works such as Sebastian Münster's *Cosmographia* (1544); Leonhard Fuchs's history of plants, *De Historia stirpium* (1542); and Gesner's *Historiae animalium* (1551-1558) sought to summarize the wealth of accumulating knowledge. Cosimo de' Medici and Colón tried to build universal libraries. Sir Thomas Bodley founded Oxford's library. Individual colleges had their own books, but Bodley wanted to build a comprehensive collection for the university.

Despite their proliferation, sixteenth century imprints have survived in limited numbers. For more than one-half of the books produced in France during this century, only one copy is known to exist. Of all the publications in the 1500's, about 1 percent remains. Pettegree provides an accessible scholarly tribute to these works that shaped and reflected the thinking of the early modern era, and he reveals the intimate relationship among politics, religion, economics, and the printed word.

Joseph Rosenblum

Review Sources

Booklist 106, no. 18 (May 15, 2010): 8.
Library Journal 135, no. 11 (June 15, 2010): 47.
The New York Times Book Review, August 15, 2010, p. 15.
Times Higher Education Supplement, June 24, 2010, p. 47.
The Times Literary Supplement, October 1, 2010, p. 25.

BOURGEOIS DIGNITY
Why Economics Can't Explain the Modern World

Author: Deirdre N. McCloskey (1942-   )
Publisher: University of Chicago Press (Chicago).
    571 pp. $35.00
Type of work: Economics, history

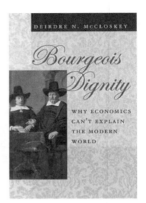

The economic transformation that created the modern world originated in the seventeenth and eighteenth centuries with a change in rhetoric, as common discourse came to depict the middle class—the "bourgeoisie"—as being dignified and free; numerous myths about this transformation are evaluated and dismissed

The subtitle of *Bourgeois Dignity: Why Economics Can't Explain the Modern World* is a bit misleading— Deirdre N. McCloskey is not undertaking directly to unhorse Gary S. Becker, Steven D. Levitt, or others who have enjoyed showing people how basic economics can help people understand marriage, education, crime, or other modern phenomena. Her objective is to explain the economic miracle that began in the West around 1700. The economic changes that began with the Industrial Revolution brought qualitative changes in consumption but also in work, social relationships, values, and morality. The process is often identified as "economic growth," but that fails to capture the qualitative element.

To be sure, modern people have more stuff, but that is only a small part of the story. The average American and European consumes amounts of goods and services roughly sixteen times as large as the average westerner of two centuries ago—the average per-capita consumption in modern Bangladesh or Haiti. However, two chapters of McCloskey's book explore the impressive qualitative benefits of modern economic life, reviewing with skepticism many of the criticisms thereof. Life in a modern, advanced economy offers "a uniquely enlarged scope to be fully realized human beings."

The economic miracle did not merely raise average incomes; it spread benefits throughout the range of incomes. As Joseph Schumpeter noted, the logic of mass production lay in providing inexpensive items for mass consumption. The "poor" in the West have vastly better jobs than those in underdeveloped regions of the world, judged by weekly hours, physical and emotional stress, and pay. Surprisingly, McCloskey does not highlight American immigration experience. Migrants from the truly low-income sectors of the world have made quantum leaps in their income and life opportunities by moving to North America.

McCloskey is a professor of economics, history, English, and communication and has a good time interweaving these elements. Since she published an earlier book entitled *The Rhetoric of Economics* (1998), it is not surprising to read that "ideas, or 'rhetoric,' enriched us. . . . A change in rhetoric about prudence, and about the other and peculiarly human virtues, exercised in a commercial society, started the material and spiritual progress. Since then the bourgeois rhetoric has been alleviating poverty worldwide, and enlarging the spiritual scope of human life." Below the rhetoric lies ideas and

Bourgeois Dignity is Deirdre N. McCloskey's twenty-first book. Her breadth of vision is reflected in her position as Distinguished Professor of Economics, History, English, and Communication at the University of Illinois in Chicago.

attitudes. Crucial elements for the bourgeoisie were dignity and liberty.

Some readers will identify bourgeois rhetoric with the platitudes of service clubs, parodied by the figure of George Babbitt, from Sinclair Lewis's novel *Babbitt* (1922). McCloskey's emphasis is really directed toward "innovation backed by liberal economic ideas." "In northwestern Europe around 1700 the general opinion shifted in favor of the bourgeoisie, and especially in favor of its marketing and innovating." The bourgeoisie are "the hiring or owning or professional or educated class." However, McCloskey is praising entrepreneurs rather than intellectuals. According to Schumpeter, intellectuals commonly have a low opinion of entrepreneurs. Schumpeter helped highlight the prominence of innovation as a driver of economic improvement and seems to receive inadequate credit from McCloskey. At least he is mentioned, however. Other hard-working chroniclers of entrepreneurship such as Samuel Smiles and Stewart Holbrook do not appear at all.

Social scientists, and perhaps economists most of all, tend to downplay the possible independent role of ideas in economic life. However, as McCloskey notes, such ideas as racism, religion, environmentalism, nationalism, and socialism have had pervasive economic impacts.

McCloskey envisages this book as simply one of a series. It follows a brilliant exposition of *The Bourgeois Virtues: Ethics for an Age of Commerce* (2006). Much of this book is devoted to refuting unsatisfactory explanations of the modern economic miracle—explanations that neglect its revolutionary character, which do not explain why the miracle happened when and where it did. The reader is promised two further volumes concentrating on the positive evidence, although much of that is introduced in this volume.

An important element in McCloskey's analysis is the fact, established relatively recently, that until the eighteenth century many parts of the world were as prosperous as Western Europe. Market economy, private property, trade, and commerce had existed for many centuries and in many areas before the modern economic miracle. However, in older times, merchants were condemned as, at best, unproductive middlemen or, at worst, lying tricksters. The Marxist myth that the person who hires workers for productive purposes is "exploiting" them replicates the same kind of prejudice. Mao Zedong and Fidel Castro have kept these attitudes alive in modern times. China's economic miracle since Mao's death reflects the permissive role of free markets. In McCloskey's view, emphasis needs also to be placed on a shift in attitude that elevated the status and self-regard of innovative entrepreneurs. Part of the benefit of the shift in rhetoric, ideas, and attitudes has been to reduce the impediments to enterprise and innovation. The ethical element was central, supplemented by the functional and the analytical.

Appropriately, late twentieth century and early twenty-first century developments in China and India receive a lot of notice. During the 1940's, both countries adopted policies and attitudes that retarded beneficial economic innovation, then underwent a subsequent rapid liberalization. During China and India's dark economic times, innovation in the rest of the world was moving ahead. Relaxing the restrictions opened the way to rapidly adopting those innovations. Germany and Japan after 1945; South Korea and Taiwan after 1953; and Ireland, Chile, and New Zealand at various times all exhibited the same process.

McCloskey devotes most of the book to a lengthy roster of supposed explanations that have been tested and found inadequate. There is no documented evidence of a rise in saving ("thrift"). Similarly, the economic miracle cannot be attributed merely to increase in capital. Much of the Industrial Revolution involved machinery that did not absorb a lot of capital (textile equipment). Capital as such, in the absence of innovation, is subject to diminishing marginal productivity. Great Britain during the Industrial Revolution saved a smaller proportion of output than other major countries. If anything, innovation helps to enlarge the proportional level of investment, particularly when the profits from successful innovation are reinvested.

It is also not true that the age of the economic miracle was one of increased greed. Greed is a constant element in human nature and human history, although its avenues of realization are constantly changing. (McCloskey might have noted that productive innovations are not always the result of greed—there is something to Thorstein Veblen's "instinct of workmanship" and David McClelland's "achievement motive.") Max Weber's sometime hypothesis that the Protestant ethic, and especially the social content of Calvinism, significantly contributed to the economic miracle is shown to be unpersuasive (without, however, giving attention to the fact that the rise of Protestant persuasion went hand-in-hand with book publishing, literacy, and schooling for the young).

Karl Marx assigned a special role to "primitive accumulation," the idea that some treasure trove bequeathed from the past helped get modern economic life moving rapidly. The enclosure movement, the slave trade, and the inflow of treasure from the New World have all been cited as contributors to this accumulation, and all fail the test of available evidence. Mostly they were not big enough to be significant. Furthermore, the accumulation of human capital through schooling became a big deal prior to the middle of the twentieth century.

A popular view among noneconomists is that abundance of natural resources has been an important factor in development. Such abundance (of good land per worker) helps explain the migrations that followed 1840 and the high wages of American labor that attracted many of the migrants. Various analysts have stressed climate, sea-coast, coal, and oil. These all contribute to productivity, but they lack relevance when one asks why a high rate of economic innovation and improvement occurred when and where it did. "Hong Kong and Singapore and Japan, with little in the way of natural resources, and Denmark with nothing but land for cows, leapt into the modern world."

Among economists there is much support for the view that trade, particularly international trade, has been a driver of rapid development—for example, for the "Asian tigers." However, the magnitudes simply do not support anything beyond small incremental gains. McCloskey takes considerable space to refute claims that "imperialism" somehow made the imperialists rich (without crediting John Atkinson Hobson who documented a similar refutation a century ago).

The view that rhetoric matters is effectively advanced in sections illustrating and denouncing the many "marxoid" usages that have become part of the unexamined baggage of intellectuals and their students. Notable is the assumption that each person's ideas and attitudes are predictably and uniformly dictated by that person's "social class"—the latter construct being itself a remarkably sloppy element for analysis. For McCloskey, ideas have a life of their own and thus potential influence of their own. More specifically:

> ". . . the change [the economic miracle following 1700] was not genetic (as [Gregory] Clark argues) or psychological (as Weber argued) or economic (as Marx argued) or legal (as [Douglass] North argues) but sociological and political. Literacy, printing, a free press, and free conversation make technology available. . . . What mattered was a radical change 1600-1776, 'measurable' in every play and pamphlet, in what English people honored, wanted, paid for, revalued."

Becker, Levitt, and others do get raked over the coals somewhat in chapter 33. The caricature of human nature emphasized in modern mainstream economics is painfully inadequate for many purposes. McCloskey is building an argument in which people's conditioning as they grow up in a particular society develops a particular way of perceiving right and wrong and a particular basis for self-regard, guilt, and shame or the contrary. This kind of analysis requires more dimensions than one finds in the fixation on "Max-U"—the utility-maximizing protagonist. Neoclassical devotees such as North have "explained" Western economic growth in ways that would yield only gradual, routine changes. "But the astounding growth after 1800 needs an astounding explanation." North's claim that property rights in England received a quantum improvement around 1689 is examined in detail and found unpersuasive. Security of private property was the rule rather than the exception over a wide range of earlier time and space.

After devoting most of the book to rejecting numerous inadequate explanations for the modern economic miracle, positive explanations are more prominent in the final chapters. A sample: "By adopting the respect for deal-making and innovation and the liberty to carry out the deals which Amsterdam and London pioneered around 1700, the modern world was born." Changes in law and politics, art, literature, philosophy, and commerce and finance all contributed. The Luddite attitude, which often worked against mechanical investment and innovation, faded away.

The book is much longer than it needs to be, if judged simply as a scholarly treatise—North and Robert Paul Thomas limned *The Rise of the Western World* (1973) in a mere 167 pages. For an author preoccupied with words and rhetoric, McCloskey does not always respect them. There are a lot of zigzag sentences and passages with excessive name-dropping or appositives. For example, what is the reader to make of this sentence?

> "Nor does Clark show an interest in his and my ancestors in Ireland, who, when they crossed the Irish Sea to staff the cotton and wool mills he has investigated in past decades with such empirical imagination, became rapidly the good workers (his father and mother, for example) who couldn't of course ever arise from such a turbulent and non-bourgeois and demographically unsound place as John Bull's troublesome Other Island—which in most parts did not have an industrial revolution."

Poor Clark is pilloried for much of three chapters—way too much space. However, the leisurely exposition, with all its digressions and repetitions, is intended to be read for enjoyment as well as intellectual instruction, and for the most part this intention is fulfilled. The book offers rewards to many classes of readers, to economists and (for different reasons) to intellectuals in general. The author's erudition is awesome and is usually offered in a lighthearted manner. The thirty-seven-page index shows exceptional care. Almost every entry has a helpful descriptor with it. The book comes at a good time, with its tone of optimism regarding the continuation of, and benefits from, economic improvement.

Paul B. Trescott

Review Sources

Globe and Mail, November 27, 2010, p. F4.
New Statesman 140, no. 5035 (January 17, 2011): 44-45.

THE BRIDGE
The Life and Rise of Barack Obama

Author: David Remnick (1958-   )
Publisher: Alfred A. Knopf (New York). 656 pp. $29.95
Type of work: Current affairs, history, biography
Time: 1961-2008
Locale: United States

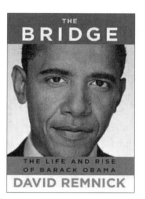

An account of the life and times of Obama from his birth until his election as president of the United States in 2008

Principal characters:
> BARACK HUSSEIN OBAMA (1961-   ),
> president of the United States
> BARACK HUSSEIN OBAMA, SR. (1936-1982),
> his father
> ANN DUNHAM (1942-1995), his mother
> MICHELLE OBAMA (1964-   ), his wife
> JOHN LEWIS (1940-   ), a civil rights leader

In *The Bridge: The Life and Rise of Barack Obama*, David Remnick discusses the career of Barack Obama from his birth to an African father and a Midwest American mother to his election as president in 2008. The title refers to the "bloody Sunday" confrontation at the Edmund Pettus Bridge in Selma, Alabama, on March 7, 1965, between African American civil rights demonstrators and Alabama state troopers. It was one of the iconic events of the Civil Rights movement. If the generation of the 1960's was the Moses generation of the Civil Rights movement, then Obama, the author argues, can be said to be the Joshua, the African American who reached the "promised land"—the White House—even though Obama was a generation younger than those involved in the Civil Rights movement, raised in Hawaii and Indonesia, and had no direct or personal connections with the movement.

The overarching theme in *The Bridge* is race, including Obama's understanding of himself, his relationship with other African Americans, and his reception by the white majority in the United States. Much of Obama's story was told in his own writings, *Dreams of My Father* (1995) and *The Audacity of Hope* (2006). Remnick has fleshed out that picture with hundreds of interviews. Obama's father, Barack Obama, Sr., was from a middle-class background in Kenya. Bright and ambitious, the senior Obama left Kenya and enrolled in the University of Hawaii in 1959. Obama's mother, Ann Dunham, was the daughter of a middle-class Kansas couple, who moved to multicultural and multiethnic Hawaii. Obama, Sr., met Dunham in a class. After she became pregnant, they married in 1961, although he had a wife and children in Kenya. The future president was born on August 4, 1961, in Honolulu's Kapi'olani Medical Center. After graduating, Obama, Sr., accepted a scholarship to Harvard, leaving Ann and his

~

David Remnick's Lenin's Tomb: The
Last Days of the Soviet Empire *(1994)
was awarded the 1994 Pulitzer Prize.
He has written and edited other works
on Russia and on such varied topics as
the boxers Muhammad Ali and Mike
Tyson and the culture of New York.*

~

young son behind. Obama's parents divorced in 1964, and there was little contact between father and son for a decade. Eventually Obama, Sr., returned to Kenya, but his government career never reached the top levels that he expected. He visited his son once, then in school in Honolulu. Obama, Sr., died in an automobile accident in Kenya in 1982.

Dunham's second marriage was to an Indonesian geologist, Lolo Soetoro. Obama's half sister, Maya, was born in 1970. Remnick notes that living in a multiethnic family in a foreign clime, Obama did not have a typical road to the White House. Ever receptive to new things, Dunham prospered in Indonesia, but the marriage suffered. She and the children returned to Honolulu, and Obama enrolled in the esteemed private school Punahou. As one of the few black students, he felt initially like an outsider, but "Barry," as he was known, integrated himself in school affairs, becoming a varsity basketball player.

In his memoir Obama admits to using drugs, he said to compensate in part for his broken family and his father's failures; many of his schoolmates also used drugs without his excuses. In 1979, he enrolled at Occidental College, a highly regarded, small, liberal arts institution in the suburbs of Los Angeles. Most of the students at Occidental were Caucasian, but the school had a liberal reputation—it had elected an African American as student-body president during the 1950's. In addition to Obama's academic studies, his "curriculum" also included drugs and rock and roll. Then later, Obama moved easily among the various ethnic and social groups on campus. While at Occidental, Obama began to go by his given name of Barack instead of Barry—a step, Remnick suggests, toward his acceptance of his African heritage. Occidental was small—sixteen hundred students—and, eventually, Barack desired both a university experience with an urban focus and engagement with more African Americans; therefore, he transferred to New York's Columbia University.

After graduating, he worked briefly as an economic analyst with Business International Corporation and the New York Public Interest Group, a consumer and environmental organization. An advertisement in *Community Jobs* for a community organizer led Obama to Chicago. Obama was a person between two racial worlds, but, Remnick argues, by the time he reached Chicago, Obama had become comfortable with his racial identity as a black man: In the traditional racial distinctions of the United States there was no halfway house, and inevitably, he could be only "black." Chicago had elected an African American as mayor, which, the author claims, was an inspiration to Obama and his political ambitions. He joined Trinity United Church of Christ, ministered by the Reverend Jeremiah Wright, who had embraced black liberation theology with its commitment to social justice. Obama had been exposed to various religious traditions by his mother and by his sojourn in Indonesia but had never joined an organized religion before. Obama's decision to join a Christian church is understandable on several levels, including as a political maneuver.

Obama entered Harvard Law School in 1988. A lawyer had more economic potential than a community organizer, but the law was also a better platform from which to pursue his political ambitions. Obama's confidence, his skill in mediating differences, his open-mindedness, and his ability to relate to different groups led him to election as editor of the prestigious *Harvard Law Review*. His reputation at Harvard was that of a progressive or liberal but not an ideologue. In 1989, while serving as a summer associate in a Chicago law firm, he met Michelle Robinson, a Harvard law graduate. Robinson's commitment to her black heritage was greater than Obama's somewhat outsider stance. Although they differed over Michelle's desire for stability and Obama's political ambitions, they married in 1992.

After law school, Obama returned to Chicago, where he accepted a position with a civil rights law firm. He also became an adjunct instructor at the University of Chicago and began writing what would become *Dreams of My Father*. It was reviewed in the major newspapers but failed to become a best seller until after Obama's breakout speech at the 2004 Democratic Convention. In a chapter entitled "A Narrative of Ascent," Remnick summarizes brilliantly Obama's racial trek from his white mother and white Kansas grandparents to his African father's relatives and claims that, while *Dreams of My Father* is not a great book, few politicians have exposed themselves more personally that did the young Obama. Not necessarily intended to be a political campaign biography, by 2008, *Dreams of My Father* had become exactly that.

Obama's first campaign for political office occurred in 1996 when he was elected to the Illinois state senate. As a freshman state senator he was not eagerly embraced by other African Americans who saw him as too ambitious, too influenced by the Ivy League, and not black enough. However, Obama's goal was to reach Congressman Bobby L. Rush, a onetime Black Panther, who had been badly defeated in a run for mayor of Chicago and seemed vulnerable. President Bill Clinton backed Rush, who easily defeated Obama in the Democratic primary. Michelle hoped that his flirtation with elective politics was at an end, but, as Remnick notes, his addiction had not waned.

In late 2002, Obama spoke at a Chicago rally against the looming U.S. invasion of Iraq. It was a measured speech, opposing the invasion but not against using force in other circumstances: He did not want to be labeled a pacifist. In the 2004 Illinois U.S. senatorial election the Republican incumbent chose not to stand for reelection. Although not having as much money or experience as some other candidates, Obama won the Democratic nomination easily. The Republican nominee, involved in a nasty divorce, withdrew from the campaign, and was replaced by a conservative and unelectable candidate. In November, Obama received 70 percent of the vote. Remnick points out that at times Obama's political ascent depended upon luck, and 2004 was one of those times.

By the summer of 2004, Obama, as a young, charismatic African American, was receiving national attention and was chosen to deliver the keynote address at the

Democratic Convention. The speech was a great success, with his appeal to "a politics of hope," and it made him a viable presidential candidate for the future instantly. When asked about his presidential ambitions, Obama denied that he would be a candidate in 2008. Whatever his ambitions, he attempted to keep a relatively low profile, which befitted a freshman senator. As far as policy was concerned, Remnick places Obama in the middle of the Democratic Party, generally progressive on domestic and foreign matters, but more deliberative than passionate. Moral absolutism was not Obama's way.

The 2006 publication of *The Audacity of Hope* brought him more attention. The unpopularity of President George W. Bush, frustrations over the war in Iraq, and the economic downswing suggested that 2008 would not be a Republican year, and although Hillary Clinton would be a strong candidate, perhaps the voters would be willing to opt for a fresh face with fewer negatives. The lack of experience would be an issue for Obama, as would be the question of timing: He was still young for the presidential sweepstakes. Michelle was unenthusiastic. Also, the issue of race arose as some wondered whether the country was ready for a black president. In February, 2007, he launched his presidential campaign in symbolically significant Springfield, Illinois, Abraham Lincoln's hometown.

Remnick rightfully devotes considerable discussion to the 2008 election. Obama's race was always a concern to his campaign managers, and the issue was ignored as much as possible. Controversial African American figures such Jesse Jackson and Al Sharpton were not invited to share platforms with Obama. Hillary Clinton's campaign was unsure how to deal with Obama, the "outsider" as one adviser expressed it. Bill Clinton had been popular among African Americans, and Hillary Clinton hoped that a significant number would support her candidacy. Prominent African Americans were also divided: Obama was black, but the Clintons had always been strong supporters of African Americans.

In January, 2008, Obama came in first in the Iowa caucuses, with Clinton finishing third behind John Edwards. For many, by carrying an overwhelmingly white state Obama proved his electability. However, in March, the American Broadcasting Company (ABC) broadcast clips from Reverend Wright's sermons, including the statement "God damn America" for its failures to ensure justice and equality. Obama condemned Wright's comments and, pointing to his own interracial background, appealed for a forward rather than a backward vision of the United States.

By June the primary campaign was over. Before November's general election, some supporters of the Republican nominee, Arizona Senator John McCain, attempted to connect Obama with Louis Farrakhan and the Nation of Islam and the socialist revolution of Venezuela's Hugh Chávez. However, Obama won the November election, earning 53 percent of the popular vote to McCain's 46 percent, a significant margin in presidential elections. McCain carried the white vote, 55 percent to 43 percent, but was victorious only in the South. At the January 20, 2008, inauguration, John Lewis, who led the march at the Edmund Pettus Bridge in 1965, sat on the platform near the new president, and the benediction was given by Reverend Joseph

Lowery, a colleague of Martin Luther King, Jr., in the Southern Christian Leadership Conference. Remnick claims that Obama did not believe that his election ended the issue of race in the United States, but it had moved the journey along the road.

Incredibly ambitious, as Remnick shows, Obama had the genius to be many things to all people. A brilliant speaker but also an excellent listener, a political moderate with liberal inclinations, Obama and his outsider origins seemed to transcend the issue of race. *The Bridge* is an engrossing read, and although it does not add a great deal to the Obama saga, it will likely remain one of the seminal studies of Obama before he reached the presidency.

Eugene Larson

Review Sources

Booklist 106, no. 14 (March 15, 2010): 4.
Commentary 130, no. 1 (July/August, 2010): 99 -102.
Commonweal 137, no. 14 (August 13, 2010): 23-25.
Kirkus Reviews 78, no. 6 (March 15, 2010): 239.
Library Journal 135, no. 5 (March 15, 2010): 83-87.
National Review 62, no. 10 (June 7, 2010): 4.
New Statesman 139, no. 5001 (May 17, 2010): 50-52.
The New York Times, April 6, 2010, p. C1.
The New York Times Book Review, April 11, 2010, p. 1.
Newsweek 155, no. 15 (April 12, 2010): 2.
Publishers Weekly 257, no. 16 (April 19, 2010): 11.
The Spectator 313, no. 9480 (May 8, 2010): 33.
Time 175, no. 14 (April 12, 2010): 22.

THE CHANGELING

Author: Kenzaburō Ōe (1935-   )
First published: Torikaego: Chenjiringu, 2000, in Japan
Translated from the Japanese by Deborah Boliver Boehm
Publisher: Grove Press (New York). 468 pp. $26.00;
    paperback $15.95
Type of work: Novel
Time: 1997-1999, with flashbacks as far back as 1952
Locale: Tokyo, Matsuyama, and Ehime prefecture, Japan

Nobel Prize-winning Japanese author Ōe successfully
mixes autobiography and magical realism to explore
meaningfully the ideas of friendship, identity, trauma, ar-
tistic creation, and the problem of suicide; his characters
struggle with some key issues arising from contemporary
human existence

> *Principal characters:*
> KOGITO CHOKO, a novelist thrown into crisis by the suicide of his close
>   friend Goro
> GORO HANAWA, a film director who commits suicide at the beginning of
>   the novel and is considered a changeling by his sister, Chikashi
> CHIKASHI CHOKO, Kogito's wife and sister of Goro
> DAIO, the one-armed leader of a band of young, right-wing disciples
>   whom he inherited from Kogito's late father in 1945
> PETER, a homosexual U.S. Army officer serving in Japan in 1952
> MITSU AZUMA-BÖME, a mysterious older Japanese woman who seeks
>   out Kogito in Berlin
> AKIRA CHOKO, Kogito's son and slightly mentally handicapped
>   composer
> URA SHIMA, Goro's teenage lover in Berlin one year before his suicide

The Changeling offers readers an intellectually rich portrayal of the friendship between a film director and a novelist that is cut short by the director's tragic suicide.
Even though the novel is built on a strong autobiographical link to its Japanese author,
Kenzaburō Ōe, who won the Nobel Prize in Literature in 1994, with key characters
modeled on himself and his real friends and family, it can be enjoyed as a literary
work of considerable stature on its own. A certain dose of magical realism, familiar
from other works by Ōe and stemming from the influence of Gabriel García Márquez,
gives a certain unreal, and often darkly humorous, flair to some sections. With
Deborah Boliver Boehm's graceful and attentive translation, *The Changeling* is accessible to an English-speaking readership. Readers are likely to enjoy this novel for
its literary quality and scope of intellectual inquiry.
    Beginning on the night when film director Goro Hanawa commits suicide by

jumping to his death from the roof of his eight-story office building, *The Changeling* follows the process by which his friend and brother-in-law, Kogito Choko, and Goro's sister, Chikashi Choko, try to make sense of Goro's desperate act. Early on, the novel hints that at least one important key to Goro's suicide may lie in the past, when he and Kogito were high school students in the years immediately following World War II. In due course, Ōe sets before the reader an intricate pattern of inquiry into the souls of Kogito, Goro, and their families and friends, all of whom occupy a place in the artistic scene of contemporary Japan.

Kenzaburō Ōe is an internationally acclaimed Japanese novelist who won the 1994 Nobel Prize in Literature. His works generally look at the condition of contemporary humanity through the lens of an autobiographical narrator and often include elements of magic realism.

Coincidentally, on the night of Goro's suicide, Kogito is listening to the last of more than thirty cassette tapes filled with Goro's musings that he had sent Kogito over the previous few years. Kogito has been listening to these tapes with an outdated tape recorder. The shape of its two huge black headphones, Kogito explains, each "bore a curious resemblance to the giant medieval-armored water beetles known as *tagame*—pronounced "taga-may"—that Kogito used to catch . . . as a boy." For this reason, Kogito refers to the machine as Tagame. On the last tape, Goro announces "I'm going to head over to the other side now." After a loud thud, his voice resumes, promising to continue to communicate to Kogito through Tagame, that is, his tapes.

Indicative of the fine line between the magical world and reality that Ōe treads in *The Changeling*, the brief resumption of Goro's last recording after the thud may hint at a posthumous message. For a realistic explanation, Kogito wonders if Goro jumped to his death while recording. Because his wife insists he should not view the corpse at Goro's wake, Kogito cannot find out if Goro's face bears an imprint from headphones, which would have proved he continued his last message after his fall, just before dying from his injuries. However, throughout the remainder of the novel, there are no more messages from Goro. His communication with Kogito comes through the prerecorded tapes alone. Ōe hints here at the possibility that the friendship between Kogito and Goro has become mutually solipsistic.

Kogito quickly becomes obsessed with this peculiar way of conversing with his dead friend. Ensconcing himself in his study at night, he picks up one of the tapes and inserts it into the Tagame machine. He listens to his friend's musings, and when he feels compelled to reply, he presses the pause button and speaks his own words before resuming the tape. Ōe uses Kogito's obsession to develop a series of philosophical dialogues on the meaning of death, friendship, memory, and artistic creation. Ōe gives

Kogito the conviction that he is playing a mind game related by Kogito to the real-life theories of Russian philosopher Mikhail Bakhtin about such an endeavor. This insight deliberately links the action of the novel to concepts from literary theory.

On the realistic side of *The Changeling*, Kogito's wife and their mildly mentally handicapped son, Akari, who successfully composes contemporary music, ask Kogito to stop his disturbing conversations via Tagame. For as low as Kogito responds, his voice is still audible in Chikashi and Akari's rooms below Kogito's second-floor study. In response, Kogito submits himself to what he calls a "Tagame-free quarantine in Berlin." Goro actually suggested this to him on one of his last tapes. Agreeing to a one-term lectureship at the Free University of Berlin, an actual school, Kogito leaves without taking Tagame.

Ōe uses Kogito's stay in Berlin both to develop *The Changeling* as a substantial novel of ideas and to have his protagonist pursue possible motives for Goro's suicide. This makes for interesting reading across different genres of writing. One possible reason for the suicide becomes evident: It may have been in response to a tabloid threatening to expose Goro's involvement in a sex scandal that began a year before his suicide when he was in Berlin. This might fit with Kogito being accosted there by the mysterious older Japanese expatriate woman Mitsu Azuma-Böme, who may be the mother of the young girl involved in the scandal. On the other hand, Kogito reveals that Goro had been attacked and slashed in the face by *yakuza* thugs a few years earlier. The thugs objected to Goro's satirical treatment of the *yakuza* in one of his films. However, *The Changeling*, in a rare moment of certainty, through the character of Kogito's police officer brother, Chu, rejects the idea that the *yakuza* killed Goro and faked his suicide.

Chikashi, Goro's sister and Kogito's wife, offers a third explanation. Goro's suicide may be the direct, logical result of a change occurring in him after a traumatic experience he had, alongside Kogito, when he was eighteen years old in 1952. With this clue, *The Changeling* offers its first interlude of magical realism. Kogito reveals a surrealist phenomenon that may parallel Goro being attacked for his work. Whenever Kogito had written something critical of a group of right-wing paramilitarists in his home province of Ehime, on Japan's southwest island of Shikoku, he was attacked by three local thugs. Each time, one of them dropped an antique "miniature cannonball onto the second joint of his big toe" as punishment. Continuing his musings in this vein, Kogito tells how, as a high school student in 1952, he was accosted by one-armed Daio, leading a band of youthful right-wingers. Daio inherited the group from the original leader, Kogito's father. The older Kogito died in a surreal, botched bank robbery the day after Japan's surrender in World War II on August 16, 1945.

Mirroring Goro's ridicule of the *yakuza* in his film, *The Changeling* paints an absurd picture of a bizarre right-wing group. Goro's resentment is linked to a traumatic event in Goro's and Kogito's past, somewhat overominously referred to as "THAT" by the two characters in the novel. Daio befriends Kogito and Goro because of the latter's friendship with Peter, an officer in the U.S. Army occupying Japan after World War II. Inviting Peter and the boys to his forest training camp, Daio hopes to persuade

Peter to provide him with some broken weapons for a suicidal mock attack on the American base in Matsuyama. *The Changeling* reveals that both Peter and Daio are pederasts who try to molest Goro and Kogito. Thwarted, Daio has his disciples throw a freshly cut calf skin over the two boys that leaves them bloody and traumatized.

Deliberately ambiguous, Ōe provides two possible endings for the incident through the technique of a text within a text. Goro's unfinished last screenplay, which is delivered to Kogito in Japan, contains two versions. In one, Goro is sent home by Daio as Peter engaged in sexual intercourse with minors. In the other, Peter is murdered by Daio's disciples. Chikashi acknowledges that the truth could have been found if the boys had asked the Americans "whether Peter had returned safely, but perhaps they could not bring themselves to go back there," thus keeping the ending open.

Chikashi believes that this incident in 1952 turned her brother Goro into a changeling, a belief based on a folk myth about goblins exchanging human babies for one of their own. By supporting Goro's lover from Berlin, young Japanese student Ura Shima, in carrying her pregnancy to term, Chikashi believes Goro will be reborn.

Readers not familiar with Ōe's work and life can still enjoy *The Changeling* without following up on all its superabundant autobiographical and historical references. Most important, Kogito represents Ōe himself. Goro is modeled closely on Ōe's friend, Japanese filmmaker Jūzō Itami (pseudonym of Yoshihiro Ikeuchi). Itami committed suicide on December 20, 1997, in the fashion described in *The Changeling*. In the United States, Itami's best-known film is *Tampopo* (1985; also released as *Dandelion*). It is mentioned in the novel along with his other films, some with slightly different titles, as is done in the case of Kogito's/Ōe's novels. Like Goro, who shares his first name with the protagonists of *Tampopo* and a later Itami film, Itami was attacked by a gang of *yakuza* in 1992 for his satirical film *Minbo no Onnna* (1992; *Minbo: Or, The Gentle Art of Japanese Extortion*). However, the magical realist parts of *The Changeling* are clearly fiction; also, Ōe's father died in 1944 and not in the manner of Kogito's father at all.

At the end of *The Changeling*, Ōe reflects on his technique of writing the novel according to the theory voiced by Kogito that "meaning emerges from the progression of slight variations." For the novel, it means that by slightly and also drastically changing events from his own life and work and that of his friends, Ōe seeks to arrive at some profound truths about contemporary human existence and the plight of the artistic soul. *The Changeling* offers a disarming self-awareness of many of its literary techniques and methods. About Kogito's unusual, nontraditional Japanese name, for example, the novel has Daio state the obvious implication: Kogito's grandfather named him for Rene Descartes' famous lines, "Cogito, ergo sum." As cogito means "I think" in Latin, it is an apt, tongue-in-cheek name for Ōe's deep-thinking protagonist. Kogito reappeared in Ōe's later novel *Sayonara, watashi no hon yo!* (2005; farewell, my books).

Critical reception of *The Changeling* has been positive. Some critics noticed that Ōe's books have not attracted the huge international readership of the novels of his

Japanese contemporary Haruki Murakami. *The Changeling* itself comments at various times on the loss of readership of Kogito's books in Japan. This is an autobiographical hint that Ōe's politically committed, antinationalistic, and philosophically minded books often mixing magical realism and realist observations about contemporary Japanese culture may be uncomfortable for some readers. As the rich substance of *The Changeling* demonstrates, this is a pity and a loss for those disinclined to engage with Ōe's powerful work. *The Changeling* shows Ōe again as a leading, if challenging, contemporary master storyteller from Japan.

R. C. Lutz

Review Sources

Booklist 106 (March 1, 2010): 48.
Library Journal 135 (April 1, 2010): 69.
The New York Times Book Review, May 16, 2010, p. 28.
The New Yorker 86 (March 29, 2010): 101.
Publishers Weekly 256 (November 30, 2009): 26.
The Times Literary Supplement, June 18, 2010, p. 19.

CHARLIE CHAN
The Untold Story of the Honorable Detective and His Rendezvous with American History

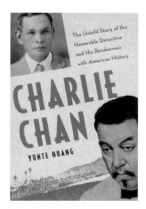

Author: Yunte Huang (1969-   )
Publisher: W. W. Norton (New York). 354 pp. $26.95
Type of work: History, literary biography, literary history

Huang presents a richly involving narrative of his encounter with the famous fictional detective Charlie Chan, his creator Earl Derr Biggers, and Chang Apana, the Hawaiian detective who may have inspired the character

Principal personages:
  CHANG APANA (1871-1933), a Chinese
    American detective in Hawaii
  EARL DERR BIGGERS (1884-1933), the
    mystery writer who created Charlie Chan
  WARNER OLAND (1879-1938), an actor who
    played Charlie Chan in many films

Yunte Huang's *Charlie Chan: The Untold Story of the Honorable Detective and His Rendezvous with American History* is an affectionate meditation on a fictional character whom time has made politically suspect. Charlie Chan, the famous sleuth created in 1924 by mystery writer Earl Derr Biggers, was the hero of six novels and forty-seven films. Mystery aficionados rank Charlie Chan with such American cultural icons as Ellery Queen, Sam Spade, and Philip Marlowe. However, the portly Asian American detective appeared at a time when racial sensitivities were much less finely tuned than in later decades. The Charlie Chan of Biggers's novels and the films speaks an idiosyncratically lyrical pidgin English, incessantly delivering such mock-Confucian aphorisms as "Murder like potato chip—cannot stop at just one."

A Chinese actor never played Charlie Chan in the American film series; the most famous portrayals were given by white men in "yellowface." Consequently, many Asian American writers have reacted against the character, seeing him as a Chinese "Uncle Tom," embodying a noxious brew of racist stereotypes about Asians. Jessica Hagedorn's groundbreaking 1993 anthology of Asian American fiction was titled *Charlie Chan Is Dead*. In 2003, when the Fox Movie Channel announced that it was going to air a festival of Charlie Chan films, protests by Asian American groups led to the festival being canceled. Many guardians of approved American culture would prefer that Charlie Chan was forgotten. In the face of this consensus, Huang mounts a spirited defense of the great detective. Even if he does not restore Charlie Chan to the literary and cinematic canon, his book will lead thousands of readers back to Biggers's novels and to the films, victory enough for a beloved fictional character, who, in Huang's opinion, will deservedly enjoy new life as a result.

Yunte Huang is a professor of English at the University of California, Santa Barbara. He is the author of Transpacific Imaginations: History, Literature, Counterpoetics *(2008).*

Huang might seem an unlikely champion for a dated Asian American detective. He was born in China during the reign of Mao Zedong. As a college student, he took part in the 1989 prodemocracy protests in Tiananmen Square. This political daring worried his family. A telegram that his mother was deathly ill tore him away from the protests. He arrived home to find his mother well and relieved that he was out of harm's way. This familial deception saved him from the tanks that crushed the student demonstrations on June 4. However, it could not save him from disillusionment with the repressiveness of modern China. In 1991, Huang moved to the United States and the University of Alabama at Tuscaloosa. Huang felt out of place in the southern heartland, aware of its legacy of racial division yet distanced from it by his own race. To support himself, he became a partner in a Chinese restaurant and pondered his role as a new stereotype, a culinary ambassador of a faux orientalism, fortune cookies and all. Huang left this behind for graduate school in English at SUNY-Buffalo.

While pursuing his doctorate, Huang supported himself working as a deliveryman for a Chinese restaurant and as a security guard for a Korean wig shop. On weekends, Huang amused himself by shopping for used books at estate sales. In an old Victorian home that was being emptied, he came across two 1940's omnibuses of Charlie Chan novels. He picked them up for a dollar a piece, began reading, and was immediately hooked. Soon Huang was hunting down variant editions of the novels and renting video tapes of the films. His obsession with Charlie Chan did not dim as he earned his Ph.D., taught at Harvard, and became a professor of English at the University of California, Santa Barbara.

As a native of China, Huang acknowledges that Charlie Chan emerged at a time of rampant nativism and racism in the United States, when Chinese immigration was precluded by law. As an American, he sees Charlie Chan as an expression of a distinctively American creativity. While many modern critics denounce the corpulent and invariably polite detective as an unmanned expression of white racism, Huang argues that Charlie Chan can be understood as a trickster figure, simultaneously embodying and subverting social hierarchy. Understood this way, Charlie Chan takes his place with such characters as China Aster in Herman Melville's *The Confidence Man: His Masquerade* (1857) and Jim in Mark Twain's *Adventures of Huckleberry Finn* (1884).

As a detective, Charlie Chan operates in a moral universe in which being Chinese could be seen as a badge of inferiority. Despite this, he always gets his man, usually a white man. It is important to remember that in the novels and in the films, Charlie Chan is in command of his situation; his gnomic pronouncements and air of exoticism only imperfectly mask his steely determination to bring murderers to justice. Charlie Chan challenges the racial order of his day, even as he conforms to expectations about the inscrutability of the Chinese.

Huang follows the critic Stanley Crouch in seeing a doubleness in figures such as Uncle Tom, Aunt Jemima, and Charlie Chan. Inhabiting the intersection of race and culture, they exemplify the enduring syncretic fertility of American culture; they are the products of "cultural miscegenation." As such they are symptoms of the continuous renewal of what it means to be American. Huang is emphatic that Charlie Chan is an authentically American character. The superficiality of the detective's Chinese trappings ensures this. For Huang, Charlie Chan is as American as apple pie and chop suey. Given this, Huang's quest for the origins of Charlie Chan is a metaphor for his own journey from birth in China to American citizenship. He uses his exploration of the wider cultural context of Charlie Chan to comment on the experience of the Chinese in the United States. Along the way he discusses the nineteenth century conjoined twins Chang and Eng Bunker, the building of the Central Pacific Railroad, Bret Harte's poem "The Heathen Chinee," the Chinese Exclusion Act of 1882, and the Chinese American actor Anna May Wong. Huang's enterprising eclecticism is one of the chief delights of his book.

Charlie Chan began his sleuthing career as a detective with the Honolulu Police Department. Huang spends much of his book reconstructing the life of a man who may have been the real-life inspiration for the fictional crime fighter. Like Charlie Chan and Huang himself, his life reflected an ongoing process of cultural accommodation and reinvention. In the early nineteenth century, skilled Chinese labor helped establish the sugar industry in Hawaii. Soon, large numbers of Chinese workers were imported to tend the fields of sugarcane. Among these were the parents of Chang Apana, who was born in 1871 near Honolulu. When Apana was three, his parents took him back to China and to his father's home village near Canton (Guangzhou), where Apana experienced the poverty of a region of China ravaged by the Opium Wars and the Taiping Rebellion. At the age of ten, he returned to Hawaii with his uncle. He never saw China again. In Hawaii, he found work on the plantation of the wealthy Wilder family. Here he became a *paniolo*, a Hawaiian cowboy. This wild, outdoor life shaped Apana's character. Physically rugged, dashing, and fearless, Apana favored cowboy hats as headgear and always carried a five-foot-long bullwhip that he had crafted himself. This whip became his trademark weapon of choice when he became a policeman. Apana's skill with horses impressed his patrons in the Wilder family; they saw to it that he was appointed the first enforcement officer of the Hawaiian Humane Society. He was so effective that in 1898, he became the first Chinese member of the Honolulu Police Department.

Apana soon became a legendary figure in Hawaiian law enforcement. Unlike Charlie Chan, Apana was a man of action rather than a ratiocinator. He infiltrated the Hawaiian underworld in a variety of disguises and physically overpowered malefactors when necessary, along the way, picking up an impressive array of scars. So bold was Apana, and so fearsome his reputation with lawbreakers, that he once single-handedly arrested more than forty gamblers, armed only with his whip. As a Honolulu police detective, Apana won for himself a position of respect and regard in an intensely race-conscious society.

Biggers grew up a world away from Apana. He was born in Warren, Ohio, in 1884, the son of a factory engineer. Raised in middle-class comfort, Biggers attended Harvard University and wrote for the famous *Harvard Lampoon*. Upon graduation, Biggers attempted to make a career as a newspaperman. After being fired from a job, he sat down and wrote a mystery novel, *Seven Keys to Baldpate*, that when published in 1913 became a phenomenal success. George M. Cohan turned Biggers's book into a Broadway hit. The novel inspired seven films. Biggers had found his vocation as a mystery writer.

Plagued by ill-health before his premature death at the age of forty-eight, Biggers visited Hawaii on a vacation in 1920. He decided to write a mystery set in the islands. It took several years to bring this to fruition. Biggers later claimed that in 1924, while perusing a Honolulu paper in the New York Public Library, he came across an item describing an arrest by Apana and another Chinese detective. This was the inspiration for the character of Charlie Chan in his 1924 novel *The House Without a Key*. Huang has found no such reference in the 1924 Honolulu newspapers. The origins of Charlie Chan may not be as simple as Biggers asserted. What is indisputable is that Charlie Chan became a sensation, earning Biggers an enduring place in the history of mystery fiction.

The three silent films based on Biggers's books did not make much of an impression. Then, in 1931, Twentieth Century-Fox released *Charlie Chan Carries On* starring Warner Oland, a Swedish-born actor who, because of features inherited from his Russian mother, specialized in Asian roles. Oland had played Fu Manchu, the villainous master criminal created by the novelist Sax Rohmer. Until Charlie Chan, Fu Manchu was the most visible Chinese character in American film. Charlie Chan changed that. The Charlie Chan series proved so successful that after Oland died, the role was carried on by Sidney Toler and Roland Winters, the last film appearing in 1949. Huang notes with irony that Charlie Chan was enormously popular in China. The Chinese authorities were sensitive to racial slights in American films and banned Fu Manchu. However, when Oland visited China in 1936, he was treated as a hero. The Chinese even made their own Charlie Chan films. The ersatz Chinese American detective, so much a product of the American milieu, became a cultural icon in his putative Asian homeland.

Apana loved to watch films. In 1931, when Fox filmed *The Black Camel* in Hawaii, he was delighted to visit the set and meet Oland. In 1933, first Biggers then Apana died. Seventy-four years later, during a visit to Hawaii, Huang attempted to find Apana's burial place. In the cemetery, a sign directed him to the grave of "Detective Charlie Chan (Chan Apana)." Even in death the doughty Hawaiian policeman is still identified with the legendary detective. The sign, with its mixing of fact and fiction and telling misspelling, is a measure of the complex allure and legacy of Charlie Chan.

Daniel P. Murphy

Review Sources

Booklist 106, no. 21 (July 1, 2010): 12.
The Chronicle of Higher Education 57, no. 8 (October 15, 2010): B12-13.
Kirkus Reviews 78, no. 11 (June 1, 2010): 506.
Library Journal 135, no. 12 (July 1, 2010): 90.
The New Republic 241, no. 14 (September 2, 2010): 28-31.
The New York Review of Books 57, no. 16 (October 28, 2010): 16-17.
The New York Times, August 11, 2010, p. 1.
The New York Times Book Review, September 5, 2010, p. 12.
The New Yorker 86, no. 23 (August 9, 2010): 70-74.
Publishers Weekly 257, no. 25 (June 28, 2010): 122.
Time 176 (September 6, 2010): 65.
Weekly Standard 15, no. 47 (August 30, 2010): 35-37.

THE CHARMING QUIRKS OF OTHERS

Author: Alexander McCall Smith (1948-   )
Publisher: Pantheon Books (New York). 256 pp. $24.95
Type of work: Novel
Time: The twenty-first century
Locale: Edinburgh and environs, Scotland

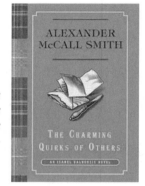

The seventh volume of McCall Smith's Isabel Dalhousie series, featuring an inquisitive editor with a mind for ethics and a penchant for sleuthing, centers on the suspicious backgrounds of three final candidates for the post of headmaster at a prestigious Scottish boys' school

Principal characters:
> ISABEL DALHOUSIE, a quietly wealthy,
>> forty-something editor of the *Review of Applied Ethics*
> JAMIE, her fiancé who is fourteen years younger than she; a bassoonist
> CHARLIE, their toddler son
> GRACE, her no-nonsense housekeeper and the caretaker of Charlie
> CAT, her niece, Jamie's former girlfriend, and a delicatessen owner
> HAROLD SLADE, the outgoing principal of the Bishop Forbes School
> ALEX MACKINLAY, the chairman of the board of governors, Bishop Forbes School
> JILLIAN MACKINLAY, Alex's wife
> PROFESSOR LETTUCE, the previous chairman of the editorial board of the *Review of Applied Ethics*
> PROFESSOR CHRISTOPHER DOVE, her nemesis and Lettuce's longtime collaborator
> PRUE, Jamie's cellist colleague, afflicted with illness and aberrant romantic designs
> GUY PEPLOE, an art connoisseur

In this seventh installment of a mystery series that began with *The Sunday Philosophy Club* (2004) and has been followed by *Friends, Lovers, Chocolate* (2005); *The Right Attitude to Rain* (2006); *The Careful Use of Compliments* (2007); *The Comforts of a Muddy Saturday* (2008); and *The Lost Art of Gratitude* (2009), Alexander McCall Smith's moral philosopher Isabel Dalhousie grapples with her own imperfections as she conducts an informal investigation of career academics. As ever, the small events of her life prompt an ongoing interior monologue on everyday ethics; Isabel wonders continually how one should behave, what people's legitimate duties and obligations toward others are, and how people can embrace humanity when people can be ruthless.

Consistent with the previous six volumes of the series, Dalhousie's sleuthing in *The Charming Quirks of Others* is as much about Scotland's landscape and character as it is about untangling various intrigues that garner her attention in the concert halls, cafes, art galleries, and dining rooms of her beloved Edinburgh, with its "moral capital of Presbyterian rectitude." Musings on soft green hills, the changeable Edinburgh sky, and the legacy of clans and kings are woven into the narrative more often than actual clues to the mystery, as are manifestations of national character. The pivotal information that Isabel gleans from an impecunious septuagenarian, for example, pales in comparison to the man's demeanor; Isabel sees in Iain Alexander a generation of Scots for whom "indigence was borne with fortitude; solvency with modesty." Indeed, in *The Charming Quirks of Others*, all things Scottish—from Macpherson plaid rugs and Scotch pies to Gaelic expressions, portraits by Sir Henry Raeburn, and the dignified bearing of a traditional countryman—

Alexander McCall Smith became famous as a fiction writer with The No. 1 Ladies' Detective Agency *(1998). He is also author of the* Portuguese Irregular Verbs *series and the* 44 Scotland Street *series, both set in Edinburgh.*

link the country's innocents, suspects, schemers, and philosophically minded sleuths alike. Isabel considers the homeland mix with goodwill.

In *The Charming Quirks of Others*, Isabel accepts a new case with notable reluctance, lacking the personal connection and feelings of urgency that usually compel her involvement. In the first book of the series, for example, Isabel investigates the death of a man she witnesses falling (or was he pushed?) from a theater balcony; in the second, she volunteers to help an anxious heart-transplant patient probe the mystery of his disturbing, postsurgical memories. In subsequent volumes, Isabel's curiosity, kindness, or heightened sense of moral obligation draws her willingly into the dilemmas of family, friends, and acquaintances. In the seventh book, however, the editor with a son, a husband-to-be, and a decidedly steady job (Isabel has become owner, as well as editor, of the *Review of Applied Ethics*) agrees to act as professional detective in the hallowed realm of private education. Moreover, she does so for an imperious woman who is unnaturally breezy about confidentiality in a city like a village.

Specifically, Jillian Mackinlay, an affiliate of the Bishop Forbes School, asks Isabel to look into the backgrounds of three candidates vying for the post of principal because current headmaster Harold Slade is set to leave for a post in Singapore. An anonymous letter has warned that one of the three candidates on the short list to replace him—the letter does not specify which candidate—harbors a secret past that could embarrass the school and cause scandal if the questionable applicant were to be appointed. Formal inquiries by hired agents might worry parents and jeopardize school enrollment. Despite her own reservations and Jamie's frequent warnings against meddling, Isabel acquiesces: "Isabel found it very difficult indeed—

practically impossible—to say to somebody in need of help that they would get no assistance from her." Isabel's weakness for saying yes affects the careers of three educators and subjects the situational detective to a conflict of interest.

As it turns out, one of the candidates for principal is dating Isabel's niece, Cat. Senior mathematics teacher Gordon Leafers is a seemingly upright addition to a string of Cat's boyfriends that has included an emotionally volatile tightrope walker, a philandering wine dealer, and an Italian lothario. For all his promise, however, Gordon Leafers may be using the headmaster competition as leverage to secure a promotion from his current employer, Firth College.

The skeleton in a rival applicant's closet is dubious behavior on a mountaineering expedition in northern Scotland. Did candidate John Fraser cut the safety rope that linked him to a fellow climber falling to certain death? Does self-preservation, or perhaps a secret crime, haunt his past? A third applicant, Tom Simpson, claims to have earned a master's degree that a member of the selection committee suspects is fraudulent. To sort fact from rumor, Isabel seeks out relatives and colleagues of the candidates, making small talk and asking strategic, but polite, questions. The investigation takes her to a parapsychology lecture, a fundraiser in Sir Walter Scott's historic home, a Scotch Malt Whisky Society party, a school cricket match, and a crumbling country abode.

Among the slow-paced mysteries of the Isabel Dalhousie series, *The Charming Quirks of Others* may be the slowest: It is heavy on rumination and slight on plot-driving certainties. The opening conversation of the book serves as illustration. Isabel's scholarly repartee with art expert Guy Peploe abounds in the sophisticated heroine's witty remarks, asides, and humorous understatements—seven pages of them—before the two focus on a practical matter: Isabel's bid on *Portrait of Mrs. Alexander and Her Granddaughter*, a nineteenth century painting up for auction. It is true that their banter about Scottish leaders, Edinburgh gossip, school principals, and royal love gone awry aptly sets the stage for the school-related mystery, as well as for Isabel's romantic missteps and a complication involving ancestral art. Nevertheless, the repartee is uncharacteristically long and pedantic—and somehow not as believable as Isabel's and Jamie's shared plays on words or as the evocative lines that sift though Isabel's mind from the works of Saint Augustine, W. H. Auden, and Robert Burns. Furthermore, Isabel's hunches and sixth senses lead to little solid evidence in the seventh novel. There is, in fact, little evidence to find. The case has been invented, and Isabel is being misled. As Isabel eventually realizes, she "had been asked to find things wrong with three people with whom there was essentially not much wrong: they were simply human."

The most startling discovery that Isabel makes is personal. She learns secondhand that Jamie, who has been lending a compassionate ear to a terminally ill colleague, went to the cinema in an unfamiliar neighborhood on a night set aside for music rehearsal. Oddly, he has mentioned nothing about the excursion to Isabel. Although she is even-tempered as a journal editor—Isabel rises above the urge to exact revenge against Professors Lettuce and Dove, petty academics bent on discrediting her and using her philosophical publication for their selfish ends—Isabel is quickly overcome with worry about the fidelity of her attractive and young husband-to-be. Prue, the dying cellist, must have preyed on Jamie's sympathies and lured him to the cinema and to bed, fears Isabel. Isabel and Jamie discuss the strange circumstances of the film date—but not before Isabel has spoken ugly, regrettable words. Truth, learns Isabel, can be easily misconstrued.

Clues in most Dalhousie mysteries crop up at fairly regular intervals during kitchen conversations, bowls of pasta, and architecturally rich walks across Edinburgh, but key revelations are reserved for the eleventh hour of *The Charming Quirks of Others*. On the afternoon that Isabel is due to report her findings, a cricketer tells her about the tangled web of illicit affairs among staff and faculty at the Bishop Forbes School, and an administrator's color blindness suddenly points to the identity of the anonymous letter writer. Apparently, Harold Slade's lover set in motion a scheme to discredit his potential replacements and keep the favored teacher on native soil; individual and shared blunders, academic territorialism, guilt, and the arrogance of privilege further derailed the appointment of a new headmaster. Unwittingly, Isabel has played a part in the scheme, and a man accustomed to lording over underlings has allowed her to do so. In the end, Isabel keeps a disquieting part of the truth from proud Alex Mackinlay.

Ultimately, understanding and forgiveness prevail, as they usually do in McCall Smith's work. Isabel manages to empathize with characters in the sorry drama of the Bishop Forbes School: "They were schemers, she felt; schemers in a small and contained society. But then, were we not all like that, whatever circles we moved in. . . . Did we not all have flaws of greater or less magnitude—all of us?" Isabel's own quirks ("I tend to over-complicate matters," she admits) allow her to find common ground with other fallible people, even conniving people, and her abiding love of Scotland and Scots nourishes her magnanimity. Not surprisingly, the novel's final scene is idyllic. Jamie, Isabel, and Charlie enjoy a sleepy backyard picnic, with the couple exchanging sweet words as Charlie plays contentedly. Such love, suggests McCall Smith, begets forgiveness—and moves beyond misguided ploys for recognition.

One critic of the seventh Dalhousie book, such as Grace within the novel, takes issue with Isabel's incessant mental gymnastics, claiming that the moral philosopher-turned-detective overthinks everything. Indeed, the Sunday philosophy club—a hypothetical discussion group and the title of the first Dalhousie installment—still has not materialized by volume seven of the series. Although Grace, Jamie, and other members of Isabel's inner circle provide her with valuable, commonsense perspectives, they hardly constitute a club. Neither do Willy the postman and the cab driver, who offer equally sound advice on the worries and ethical concerns of Isabel's life. The club, insofar as it exists, remains entirely in Isabel's mind, where various sides of an issue—be it the nature of goodness, the experience of God, or the development of a moral conscience—are examined alone, often with wry humor.

Within the mystery genre, *The Charming Quirks of Others* is light fare, at the civilized end of a mystery spectrum opposite hard-boiled criminal tales in seedy, underworld settings. Like her literary precursor Precious Ramotswe, the plucky Botswanian heroine of McCall Smith's *The No. 1 Ladies' Detective Agency* (1998), Dalhousie gets to the root of mysteries over cups of tea, sharp observation, and thoughtful reflection. Precious may investigate suitors and unscrupulous maids in Africa, while Isabel probes the shady behavior of Scottish miscreants; both detectives are memorable for their insights on human nature, not for jailing notorious lawbreakers. For readers, McCall Smith's philosophizing lady detectives offer amiable counterpoints to the tough-talking gumshoes of other kinds of mysteries.

The gentility of the Dalhousie mysteries has given rise to lighthearted humor for radio audiences. On October 16, 2010, days after *The Charming Quirks of Others* was published in the United States, author McCall Smith played himself in a detective sketch poking fun at the refinement of the popular mystery series. On Garrison Keillor's *A Prairie Home Companion*, a radio variety show broadcast that day from St. Paul, Minnesota, McCall Smith played a mystery writer gathering material for an action-filled book for hunters and other tough men. "I want to write a book in which there is shooting," proclaimed the earnest author, prodigiously taking notes as dangerous American gangsters maneuver around him, "lots of shooting and car chases. . . . Not Isabel Dalhousie drinking tea with her lady friends." Spoofs notwithstanding, critics and readers worldwide have welcomed the seventh installment of the acclaimed series that transports them to Isabel Dalhousie's kind, quirk-forgiving world of twenty-first century Edinburgh.

Wendy Alison Lamb

Review Sources

Booklist 107, no. 1 (September 1, 2010): 39.
Kirkus Reviews 78, no. 18 (September 15, 2010): 894.
Library Journal 135, no. 11 (June 15, 2010): 5.
People 74, no. 15 (October 25, 2010): 48.
Publishers Weekly 257, no. 32 (August 16, 2010): 29.

CHURCHILL'S EMPIRE
The World That Made Him and the World He Made

Author: Richard Toye (1973-   )
Publisher: Henry Holt (New York). Illustrated. 423 pp.
   $32.00
Type of work: History, biography
Time: Late nineteenth to twentieth-first century
Locale: Global, focusing on Great Britain and the British
   Empire

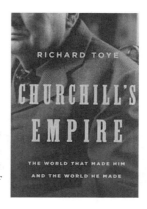

*A study of expectations regarding reasons for and the
purposes and responsibilities of Great Britain and its empire—from its vast size in the early twentieth century to its
minuscule extent within sixty years—especially in terms of
the leadership of Winston Churchill*

Principal personages:
   L. S. Amery (1873-1955), a British journalist and Tory/Conservative
      Party politician who campaigned tirelessly for military preparedness
      and for the preservation of the British Empire
   Lord Randolph Churchill (1849-1895), the aristocratic father of
      Winston Churchill who stood for Tory democracy but whose political
      folly thrust him into the netherworld of British politics
   Winston Churchill (1874-1965), a British soldier, politician (cabinet
      minister and prime minister), author, artist, and bon vivant
   Éamon de Valera (1882-1975), an American-born Irish nationalist
      who fought successfully for complete separation of Ireland from the
      United Kingdom and who later served a number of terms as the
      political leader of the Republic of Ireland
   Mohandas Karamchand Gandhi (1869-1948), the Indian spiritual
      and ideological leader who endeavored to speak for all Indians during
      his crusade for swaraj (struggle for Indian independence) and who
      defeated his adversaries through satyagraha (nonviolent civil
      disobedience)
   William Lyon Mackenzie King (1874-1950), the Canadian Liberal
      Party leader who dominated Canadian politics from the 1920's to the
      1940's and who often challenged Britain's (and Churchill's) imperial
      ideas
   Jawaharlal Nehru (1889-1964), a political leader of the Indian
      Congress Party, who, along with Gandhi, championed Indian
      independence and who, following Gandhi's assassination, served as
      India's first prime minister (1947-1964)
   Franklin D. Roosevelt (1882-1945), the thirty-second president of the
      United States (1933-1945), who was elected to four terms and led his
      country during the Great Depression and World War II

~

*Richard Toye is an associate professor
at the University of Exeter. He was
selected as the Young Academic Author
of the Year in 2007 by the* Times
Higher Education *magazine for* Lloyd
George and Churchill: Rivals for
Greatness *(2008).*

~

Neoimperialism describes the late nineteenth century period when every great European power undertook a frenzied drive to acquire control of alien peoples, territories, and resources. At that time, a nation's prestige and power were gauged by quantifiable factors: industrial strength (requiring raw materials and markets), strategic/tactical military capabilities, and imperial size. By 1914, most of the world was controlled by imperialist, Eurocentric powers, and Great Britain maintained its preeminent imperial status; it not only maintained control over its earlier, largely American and oceanic empire but also acquired a host of additional territories. At its zenith, Great Britain dominated the world's seas, controlled one-quarter of the landforms of Earth, and ruled one-quarter of its inhabitants. The aphorism that "the sun never sets on the British Empire" was essentially true, and, in *Churchill's Empire*, author Richard Toye surveys this period with Britain's leader as his centerpiece.

In England, just as imperialist rivalries were intensifying, at Blenheim Palace (the ducal residence of the Churchill/Marlborough family), a son—Winston Churchill—was born to Lord Randolph Churchill and his American wife. Over the course of an incredibly long, active, and relevant career spanning six of the most tumultuous decades in world history, the younger Churchill was one of the most influential and powerful (within a constitutional framework) Englishmen of the twentieth century. He was the face of England—at least until the Beatles emerged during the 1960's. To him, the British Empire was an essential vehicle for sharing English civilization with less fortunate peoples, for maintaining stability in the world, and for ensuring a continued role as a major world power for the United Kingdom.

Soldier, politician, author, artist, and bon vivant, Churchill had his "finest hour" in his tenacious and unrelenting opposition to totalitarianism during World War II. Throughout Churchill's life, however, the British Empire, its raison d'être, and its relationship with the mother country, was a dilemma about which Churchill continually agonized and over which he was often concerned. Despite his efforts, by the time of his death in 1965, the empire that he had helped to create and maintain had virtually disappeared.

In many ways, Churchill's life and career paralleled Britain's twentieth century imperial rise and fall. Toye—a young and brilliant English historian—set for himself the daunting task of discerning—from what is without question a prodigious mass of data pertaining to Churchill and the British Empire—elucidations of how and why Churchill's imperialist attitudes and behavior were shaped and how changing circumstances, both at home and abroad, affected his guiding principles.

Churchill's Empire: The World That Made Him and the World He Made is a well-researched and exceptionally well-written opus that proffers an analytical cross section of not only Churchill's deep involvement with the acquisition and maintenance of the British Empire but also his evolving imperialist attitudes during his roller-coaster journey through much of the twentieth century. Toye boldly asserts that Churchill's parents instilled certain values in their offspring, that Churchill's Harrovian education prepared him for imperialist tasks, and that his absorption of late nineteenth century, proimperialist popular culture provided the foundation for his imperial point of view. This background, plus Churchill's firsthand experiences of fighting in and reporting from diverse parts of the British Empire, further refined his appreciation for and belief in that which the mother country could and should do for and with the colonies and dominions. Furthermore, Toye postulates that Churchill's beliefs, words, and actions show a more flexible, more compromising, and less predictable person than has heretofore been presented.

Until Toye's explication, Churchill's imperial viewpoint has often been summarized by citing his own public declaration (uttered in the midst of World War II): "I have not become the King's First Minister to preside over the liquidation of the British Empire." Alternatively, since Churchill's imperialist pronouncements seemingly fluctuated according to political expediency, credence is given to the acerbic quip by Lord Beaverbrook (whose given name was William Maxwell Aitken and who was no real friend of Churchill), that Churchill held every opinion on every subject. Churchill's mercurial political life, which witnessed personal triumph superseded by political disaster followed by resurrection, gave to him a reputation for impetuosity and opportunism. These, coupled with Churchill's predilection for derogating people of color, make it almost too easy to portray Churchill as a bigoted, Machiavellian, arch-conservative.

To his credit, Toye refutes such simplisms by sifting through the vast literature—various archives and collections, diaries, popular culture materials (especially newspapers), and secondary sources—by collating and filtering the data and then by presenting his findings in palatable form. To summarize Toye, Churchill was guided by English constitutionalism, by nineteenth century British liberalism, and by the tenets of social Darwinism. Churchill firmly believed in responsible government of, by, and for those who had earned the right. Human rights were for those who embraced civilization, that is, those who accepted the superiority of English civilization and acted to re-create England overseas.

Toye's task was monumental: interpolating and interpreting the imperialist weltanschauung of a multifaceted individual who was not only in and out of government—at high levels—for decades but also had to deal with events and issues of incredible complexity. The only practical way to accomplish this is to presume that a reader has a working knowledge of the history of the period and of the complexity of the topic, thereby allowing Toye to address Churchill's positive and negative roles over sixty years through a chronological, highly documented narrative.

While space constraints do not allow an exhaustive directory of that which Toye did or did not include, perhaps the following suggestions will help. Context is crucial when analyzing how and why historical events occur and how, why, and in what way societies (or cultural entities) interact with one another. In his speech to the parliament of South Africa, on February 3, 1960, in Cape Town, then British prime minister Harold Macmillan noted that: "The wind of change is blowing through this continent. Whether we like it or not, this growth of national consciousness is a political fact." Not to disparage Macmillan's observation, but it was not a newly discovered fact; it merely recognized the changes that took centuries to evolve, coalesce, and emerge.

"Winds" had been blowing for centuries—witness the American Revolution, which resulted in the transformation of that which is called the First British Empire. Colonial reformers such as Adam Smith and Edward Gibbon Wakefield advocated preparing colonials for eventual independence and giving responsible government to colonies that had earned the privilege. How could this be earned? English masters had a ready answer—to become English. For Churchill there was a pecking order: English, British, Europeans, civilized non-Caucasians, and, at the bottom, non-Caucasians recently acquired. Tempering this was Churchill's certitude that non-white peoples, though inferior, were capable of advancement.

As this component of Churchill's convictions, which is documented at great length, is considered throughout *Churchill's Empire*, it is quite appropriate to wonder if Churchill was really a racist. The answer is simple: It is neither the right nor the privilege of a responsible historian to abjure or to absolve; Toye makes a valiant effort to follow this maxim. However, he must be faulted for omitting any significant reference to social Darwinism or for failing to investigate its clear influence on Churchill's thinking.

The hypotheses put forward in Charles Darwin's *On the Origin of Species by Means of Natural Selection: Or, The Preservation of Favoured Races in the Struggle for Life* (1859) were misapplied to human societies. The pseudosciences of social Darwinism and eugenics provided an intellectual underpinning for imperialism and racism. Social Darwinists held that the "struggle for existence" and the "law of the jungle" were the very foundations of the operation of nature. Those victorious in competition demonstrated superiority over a beaten opponent. Therefore, they were more fit and had not only the right but also the duty to impose themselves on lesser groups. This rationalized both colonialism in its most naked form and the gross injustices of imperialism.

Ironically, Toye essentially disproves a portion of the title of his own book. Churchill's world was turned upside down because of factors over which no one person could have any long-term control or influence. Nonetheless, Toye provides a portrait of one person who, in numerous ways, confirms the best that the British Empire offered. A testament to Churchill's steadfast belief in Britain's constitutional system as providing the best alternative to dictatorship can be witnessed in such diverse nation-states as India, Jamaica, South Africa, and the United States. It may be said that, during World War II, Churchill mobilized the English language and sent it forth into battle; but far more significantly, the length and breadth of the British Empire resulted in English becoming the world's lingua franca. Without the unifying language of the colonizer, there could be no India or Nigeria.

Rudyard Kipling's "The White Man's Burden" (1899) was actually a clarion call to Liberal Imperialists such as Churchill. The poem, often misinterpreted, was not a paean to imperialism; it was an appeal for imperial service. The colonial master's responsibility was to "Send forth the best ye breed. . . . To serve your captives' need." Within the stability that only colonial rule could provide, British rule ended "savage wars," ended "Famine" and "bid the sickness cease." Despite his English hauteur and his various statements to the contrary, Churchill firmly believed in progress for all peoples and in hope for the world. This is the man portrayed in *Winston's Empire*; without question, it is a far better world for his having been here.

William S. Brockington, Jr.

Review Sources

Booklist 106, no. 21 (July 1, 2010): 20.
Contemporary Review 292, no. 1698 (Autumn, 2010): 404-405.
History Today 60, no. 6 (June, 2010): 69-70.
Kirkus Reviews 78, no. 8 (May 1, 2010): 408.
The New York Times Sunday Book Review, August 15, 2010, p. BR11.
Publishers Weekly 257, no. 21 (May 24, 2010): 45.
The Spectator 312, no. 9473 (March 20, 2010): 34-35.
World War II 25, no. 4 (November/December, 2010): 76.

CITIZENS OF LONDON
The Americans Who Stood with Britain in Its Darkest, Finest Hour

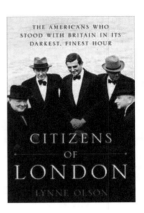

Author: Lynne Olson (1952-   )
Publisher: Random House (New York). 471 pp. $28.00
Type of work: History
Time: 1939-1945
Locale: London

This book focuses on prominent Americans in London before and during U.S. involvement in World War II, putting a new spin on a well-documented era of the twentieth century

Principal personages:
  JOHN G. WINANT (1889-1947), the U.S. ambassador to Britain, 1941-1946
  WILLIAM AVERELL HARRIMAN (1891-1986), an American diplomat in Britain and the Soviet Union during World War II
  EDWARD R. MURROW (1908-1965), an American correspondent in London during World War II
  FRANKLIN D. ROOSEVELT (1882-1945), the president of the United States, 1933-1945
  WINSTON CHURCHILL (1874-1965), the prime minister of Britain, 1940-1945

During World War II the populace of London was subjected to a series of bombings that killed thousands, left hundreds of thousands homeless, and devastated the economic and cultural life of one of the world's most important capitals. The story of Londoners' courage and tenacity in coping with this constant threat to their safety has been told by several historians. In *Citizens of London*, veteran journalist and historian Lynne Olson provides a different perspective on these bombings, using them as an entry point to examine the important alliance between the British government and its sometimes reluctant partner, the United States.

In hindsight, it is apparent that the Anglo-American partnership was a key factor in the defeat of Adolf Hitler and the Axis forces that threatened to bring an especially cruel brand of dictatorial rule to Europe and virtually every other part of the world. At the time, however, there was no guarantee that a successful alliance could be forged or that it would eventually succeed in stopping Hitler's relentless march on Europe. To explain how the two countries eventually overcame significant political obstacles to make their partnership work, Olson chooses to focus her narrative on three Americans who were present in London during much of the war: John G. Winant, U.S. ambassador to the United Kingdom; William Averell Harriman, coordinator of Lend-Lease Act operations for the United States; and Edward R. Murrow, chief of the

London office of the Columbia Broadcasting
System (CBS).

*Lynne Olson is the author of several
historical studies, including* Freedom's
Daughters *(2001) and* Troublesome
Young Men *(2008), and coauthor with
her husband, Stanley Cloud, of* The
Murrow Boys *(1996) and* A Question
of Honor *(2007).*

Moving back and forth among the stories
of her principal figures, Olson provides a
gripping account of the gradual movement of
the United States toward full-scale participation as a combatant in World War II. As
Olson notes repeatedly, where Winston Churchill had almost dictatorial powers from the
moment he became prime minister in 1940,
Roosevelt and the supporters of American intervention in the war had to deal with a
recalcitrant and often obstructionist Congress that repeatedly challenged the president's every move to aid Britain and other Allied Powers fighting the Axis Powers.
Roosevelt was forced to outmaneuver critics by devising programs to support the
British while officially preserving the noncombatant status of the United States. One
of those programs, the Lend-Lease Act, has come to be viewed as a brilliant stroke of
political legerdemain, providing Britain war materiel while keeping the United States
officially neutral.

In 1941, however, lend-lease was a much-debated program on both sides of the
Atlantic. To facilitate the transfer of equipment to Britain and protect American interests in the exchange, Roosevelt selected an ambitious businessman, Harriman. The
son of a rich railroad baron, Harriman was close to Roosevelt's trusted adviser Harry
Hopkins, who convinced the president to send Harriman to London as the government's watchdog. The alliance was anything but smooth. Harriman discovered that
he often had to badger his own government for more supplies and equipment, and
Churchill was repeatedly forced to swallow his considerable pride and agree to draco-
nian terms for payment, including key concessions on commercial air and naval
rights that he knew would make the United States a formidable world presence at the
end of the conflict. In describing the operations of the lend-lease policy and other initiatives undertaken by the two governments, Olson follows the lead of other historians in portraying Roosevelt as a crafty politician who held back on commitments as
long as he could, demanded much for American help, and seemed to know just how
far he could push Congress and the American people without causing either to
retaliate against him and jeopardize the inevitable entry of the United States into the
conflict.

Among her principal characters, Olson chooses to make the lesser known Winant
her hero, repeatedly emphasizing his selflessness and courage. Born into a relatively
privileged household, Winant chose a life of public service that included two terms as
governor of New Hampshire. Though a Republican, he supported Roosevelt's New
Deal policies and was eager to serve as his country's ambassador in London. Winant
could not have arrived in London at a more auspicious time for someone who wanted
to help the Allied cause. His predecessor, Joseph P. Kennedy, father of future president John F. Kennedy, had been urging Americans to leave Britain and had counseled

Roosevelt that England was doomed to fall to Hitler's forces. Winant quickly asserted his faith in the Allied cause and immediately endeared himself to the British people. For the following five years he worked tirelessly in what some saw as a reversal of roles, pleading England's case to the American government and eventually helping to smooth over problems caused by the arrival of millions of American soldiers beginning in 1942.

If Winant is the hero of this tale, Harriman is certainly the villain. Born to privilege, Harriman seems never to have let an opportunity for self-promotion slip by. Olson suggests he orchestrated his appointment as coordinator of the lend-lease policy when he could get no better appointment from Roosevelt, but that upon arrival in London he began acting as a kind of minister-without-portfolio. Olson describes him as wheedling his way into Churchill's inner circle and then taking on tasks that were rightfully the ambassador's, repeatedly putting Winant in the awkward position of having to learn about important decisions thirdhand. Harriman was able to operate in this way because Roosevelt had a habit of using special envoys to carry out missions directly for him; Hopkins was often thrust into that role, and Harriman reveled in having direct access to both the president and the British prime minister. Olson is quick to point out the deleterious effects of Harriman's behavior on Winant, who behaved admirably despite being treated shabbily. On the other hand, she seems to take special pleasure in describing Harriman's tenure as ambassador to the Soviet Union—a position he did not seek, and one that caused him the same kind of frustration Winant felt when Harriman was operating behind his back.

Journalist Murrow seems to get less attention than the other principal members of the story, perhaps because Olson had already written extensively about him in *The Murrow Boys* (1996), a book coauthored with her husband, Stanley Cloud. She does underscore Murrow's importance in helping Americans understand the plight of the British and discusses his relationships with Winant, Harriman, Roosevelt, and Churchill. If Winant was responsible for helping Britons understand and accept the loud, cantankerous, and often rude young Americans who had come to England to liberate them, Murrow was the person who did the most to get Americans in the United States to see that Britain's fight was the United States' as well. Like Winant, he risked his life on numerous occasions to help bombing victims even while attacks were still in progress or when the threat of falling buildings made rescue efforts dangerous. He also made a dozen flights with Allied aircraft engaged in their own bombing missions over Germany. His passionate broadcasts about the horrors inflicted by the German Luftwaffe on England's capital city and his open calls for the United States to join Britain in fighting the Nazis were heard by millions, many of whom considered him a trusted eyewitness to the conflict.

The principal figures in *Citizens of London* were not always in the public eye, and Olson reports on their many marital troubles and extramarital affairs that occurred during the war years. She provides an insightful discussion of Murrow's relationship with his wife, Janet, who had accompanied him to London, and his affair with Pamela Digby Churchill Harriman (known as Pamela Churchill at the time), the prime minister's daughter-in-law. Pamela Churchill first took up with Harriman, whose wife had remained in the United States, turning to Murrow when Harriman was sent to the Soviet Union as U.S. ambassador. She also had affairs with Englishmen and other Americans. Her quieter sister-in-law, Sarah Churchill, the prime minister's daughter, became a close confidante and evening partner of Winant, although he had a wife and family in the United States. The point Olson seems to be making is that, in times of great stress, men in power often turn to women for solace and companionship—not always for love, but frequently as a form of stress relief.

Citizens of London also includes brief sketches of other key figures in the Allied war effort: Field Marshal Alan Francis Brooke, British chief of the Imperial General Staff; Roosevelt's key confidant, Hopkins; William J. "Billy" Fiske III, the first American casualty of the war; and Tommy Hitchcock, the renowned American polo player and fighter pilot who persuaded military leaders in the United States to adopt the British Mustang as the model for the American P-51 fighter. Olson's portrait of Dwight D. Eisenhower's generalship is particularly flattering. While acknowledging his many limitations, she repeatedly demonstrates why Eisenhower was the right man to lead the Allies in the final months of the conflict with Germany. The future president's ability to work closely with British commanders—many of whom were openly disdainful of his intellectual acumen and leadership abilities—and to smooth over problems caused by American soldiers in Britain were essential to the success of the massive invasion of the European continent on D day (June 6, 1944). Eisenhower's ability to keep the military focus on defeating Hitler and off various political objectives sought by Allied governments proved vital to the success of subsequent operations.

By carefully weaving the story of Winant, Harriman, and Murrow into the larger fabric of Allied efforts to stymie German advances throughout Europe and in North Africa and eventually to conquer Hitler's forces, Olson offers her readers a comprehensive, if abbreviated, survey of the war. While her descriptions of battlefield operations are limited, her assessments of the politics behind military decision making is insightful and detailed. Specialists in the history of World War II may discover that Olson offers little new factual information about either her principal subjects or the conflict as a whole. What she does superbly, however, is make the story come alive through her vivid writing style and careful assimilation of available details. Reading her book gives one the same feeling CBS tried to convey by the title of its popular 1950's television show that took viewers back in time to relive many of these important historical moments: "You Are There." That sense of immediacy makes *Citizens of London* appealing to a wide audience interested in learning more about the personalities of men and women who shaped the world's history at one of its moments of crisis.

Laurence W. Mazzeno

Review Sources

Booklist 106, no. 11 (February 1, 2010): 16.
Kirkus Reviews 77, no. 21 (November 1, 2009): 1152.
Library Journal 134, no. 16 (October 1, 2009): 59.
Publishers Weekly 256, no. 46 (November 16, 2009): 44.
Virginia Quarterly Review 86, no. 3 (Summer, 2010): 191.
Weekly Standard 15, no. 38 (June 21, 2010): 32-33.

CITRUS COUNTY

Author: John Brandon (1976-   )
Publisher: McSweeney's (San Francisco). 215 pp.
   $22.00
Type of work: Novel
Time: Present
Locale: Central Florida

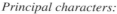

   Brandon's novel about a small county in Florida and
three characters who are isolated in their own worlds and
about the desperate and appalling act by one of them that
will change all of their lives forever

   Principal characters:
      TOBY MCNURSE, a fourteen-year-old
         student and orphan, raised by an isolated, uncaring uncle
      SHELBY REGISTER, his classmate, a recent transplant to Citrus County
      MR. HIBMA, a teacher at Shelby and Toby's school
      BEN REGISTER, Shelby's father
      KALEY, Shelby's younger sister
      MRS. CONNER, an English teacher and colleague of Mr. Hibma

Citrus County is John Brandon's second novel. The story is set in the county of the title, a sparsely populated, real county on the Gulf coast in central Florida. The novel's narrative is focused through three characters whose lives have been shaped in various ways by trauma and isolation, and the third-person point of view rotates among their three perspectives. The first character to whom the reader is introduced, Toby McNurse, has been raised—somewhat—by his uncle Neal. Rather than acting as Toby's father, Neal continually threatens suicide, explains to Toby how little he cares about him, and drinks hemlock (the same poisonous brew that was given in ancient Athens to Socrates) daily in dilute amounts as an ongoing ritual in recognition of his fascination with death. Raised in this environment, Toby not only fails to fit in but also has no interest in fitting in. In truth, Toby only has occasional intersections with the world of normal human endeavors.

Toby's new classmate, Shelby Register, does come from a loving home, but it is a home unmade by grief. At the time of the novel, Shelby's mother has been dead for two years, and her father, Ben, works hard to provide an active and interesting family life for Shelby and her four-year-old sister, Kaley, taking them on boat expeditions to find manatees and dreaming up other activities. Like Toby, Shelby has no interest in being a member of the crowd and intends to go her own way, refusing to court the favor of the popular girls in her class.

Mr. Hibma, Toby and Shelby's teacher, has much in common with his two students. As a newborn, he was stolen from the hospital by a nurse for several hours.

~

John Brandon published his first novel,
Arkansas, *in 2009. He is the John and*
Renee Grisham Writer-in-Residence at
the University of Mississippi.

~

Brandon draws an overt connection between Hibma's past and Toby when he provides Toby with the last name of "McNurse." Later, Hibma would inherit $190,000, but he has managed to spend it in only a few years, traveling in Europe. By his late twenties he has spent his inheritance and finds himself a geography teacher in a middle school in Citrus County, Florida, choosing the city by throwing a dart at a map of the United States. Hibma feels trapped by his new life and is an almost aggressively bad instructor. He eschews textbooks, instead holding trivia contests and requiring presentations on anything but the subject at hand. He is reluctant to coach the middle school girls' basketball team and typically refuses to administer discipline when called for or to fairly adjudicate grades, once giving a flagrantly false autobiographical presentation by Toby an "A." His attitude is perceptible to some other teachers and leads him into conflict with Mrs. Connor, a retirement-aged, by-the-book English teacher.

Shelby almost immediately senses in Toby's weird rebelliousness a kindred spirit and decides to make an ally of him, going out of her way to speak to him and to be around him. Before long they almost casually fall into a relationship. While they are not a conventional boyfriend and girlfriend in many ways—Shelby has a difficult time enticing Toby to kiss her, and Toby is almost congenitally incapable of small talk, flattery, or flirtation—they do become a kind of couple. What Shelby does not know, however, is that Toby has decided for quite some time to commit some form of evil act that will force the world to take notice of him. When he meets Shelby, he also sees her sister Kaley, and he decides to kidnap her and hide her in an underground room on his uncle's property he calls "the bunker."

The text makes it clear that Toby does not intend to abuse Kaley physically or sexually (although keeping a four-year-old girl captive in an underground bunker for weeks obviously will cause emotional and psychological trauma). Rather, his act is an attempt to gain some agency in the world. He is excited by the news coverage of the event yet outraged when search teams give up looking for her after just a few days.

Initially, Shelby reacts to her sister's abduction with a sense of numb irritation toward the media and community members who seem to thrive on the sensationalism of the event. She is particularly angered by church members who seem to regard the abduction as an incentive or even an excuse to proselytize to Shelby and her father. At the same time, her father is shocked to his core and is unable to eat or sleep. He spends every waking moment searching for Kaley, and Shelby almost has to force him to eat and rest. Shelby's world is even further spun off its axis because of the gentle treatment she now receives from her schoolmates; she has endured this before, with her mother's death, and the repetition of the sympathetic glances and hushed speech around her is almost more than she can bear. Her attraction to Toby is heightened even further because he is so poorly socialized that he is unsure of how to act toward her. Shelby does not understand Toby's culpability, and takes his diffidence—which in some ways may be masking his unacknowledged guilt—as a sign of his uniqueness.

The connections between Mr. Hibma's search for purpose and Toby's own destructive quest is further amplified when Mr. Hibma finds out about Shelby's aunt Dale. Aunt Dale is the sister of Shelby's father; she lives in Iceland and writes a Web-based review journal titled "WhatWouldTheyThink?," which, in its reviews of music, literature, restaurants, and so on, posits as its central gimmick that the reviewers are extraterrestrial aliens visiting Earth for the first time. Shelby's reaching out to Aunt Dale by e-mail messages serves as a clear indication of her need for a mother in her time of crisis and need. She tries to persuade Aunt Dale to come visit them but eventually is unable to do so, and thus reinforces her suspicion that, ultimately, she can only rely upon herself. Mr. Hibma, on the other hand, has long been a fan of Aunt Dale's Web site, and to her he finally puts in writing something that has only been an unspoken thought so far: He is considering killing Mrs. Connor. Aunt Dale treats both Shelby and Mr. Hibma the same, seeming to show favor and interest when, in reality, she has no intention of taking part in either's life.

The novel is told in the third-person limited point of view, with the narrative shifting, as stated above, among the three characters' perspectives. Although the novel delves deeply into Shelby's and Mr. Hibma's consciousnesses—so that readers may feel they come to understand the characters' opinions, motives, and actions—the sections filtered through Toby's perspectives are more minimalist in style. In Toby's sections, particularly the latter ones, Toby's thoughts are more focused on his actions and the events around him; they are not introspective, and they do not provide complete insight into Toby's state of mind.

Perhaps the novel's greatest strength is in its ability to make the reader feel some sympathy for Toby at an almost granular level. Brandon refuses to make use of any of the more shopworn clichés when it comes to promoting an antihero; the reader does not see Toby's suffering, as such, nor does the reader bear witness to silent acts of compassion or heroism that the reader recognizes but that go unacknowledged by the various characters in the novel. Instead, although there is a certain attraction to his stark refusal to act the part of the typical American teenager in any recognizable way, Brandon makes it clear that Toby is not a particularly positive or nice character and that he may well be capable of causing great harm.

The novel's chief flaw is that, at times, the writing lacks vitality. Although Shelby is a sympathetic character, Hibma is a misanthrope and Toby a kidnapper. Use of unsympathetic characters in novels—particularly novels that center on crimes, such as Fyodor Dostoevski's *Prestupleniye i nakazaniye* (1866; *Crime and Punishment*, 1886) or Theodore Dreiser's *An American Tragedy* (1925)—are nothing new. More snap and more energy in Brandon's prose, on the other hand, would make the plots and characters less significant than the writing and ideas in themselves. Similarly, the plot becomes a bit murky at times; for example, as the search for Kaley intensifies, it often becomes difficult to tell how many days have passed and how often Shelby and Toby have seen each other.

However, as the narrative unfolds and the reader becomes more acquainted with Toby's past and realizes how bereft of human companionship he has been, the reader comes not so much to empathize with Toby but to feel some sympathy and compassion for him. Just as Toby keeps Kaley in a physical bunker, he too is trapped in a mental and emotional one, borne out of a life of isolation and loneliness. Both Mr. Hibma and Shelby are more fully realized and developed characters, just as they are more fully functioning human beings than Toby seems to be. Shelby has had to deal with true emotional traumas through the losses of her mother and then her sister, yet she has also had the love of her father—and her love for him—to sustain her. Similarly, although he seems in some ways to be a slightly more socialized, adult version of Toby, Mr. Hibma is able on his own to withdraw from the downward spiral of his descent, largely through his attempts to reach out to Shelby and Toby in an unconscious recognition of his similarity to them.

Throughout the first sections of the novel, Mr. Hibma seems just as isolated as Toby, if less a victim of a traumatic upbringing. Slowly, however, almost with an act of will, he begins to reach out to others. His coaching of the middle school girls' basketball team becomes less of a painful chore and more of a rewarding challenge, and Mr. Hibma is shocked to find that he is good at it. Additionally, he realizes how much easier his life can be when, instead of withdrawing from people and creating enemies, he actually reaches out to people he dislikes (such as Mrs. Conner) and finds that they respond to his overtures. Through channeling his antisocial impulses into positive energy—first through his coaching and then through his efforts to help Toby—Hibma shows the path out of isolation and self-destruction.

Scott D. Yarbrough

Review Sources

Atlanta Journal and Constitution, September 26, 2010, p. E6.
The New York Times Book Review, July 18, 2010, p. 1.
Publishers Weekly 257, no. 19 (May 10, 2010): 28-29.
St. Petersburg Times, October 17, 2010, p. L-4.

CLAIMING GROUND

Author: Laura Bell (1954-   )
Publisher: Alfred A. Knopf (New York). 244 pp. $24.95
Type of work: Memoir
Time: 1977-2004
Locale: Western states, primarily Wyoming and Utah

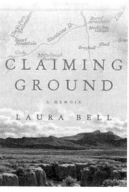

*The author describes her quest for a meaningful life in
the harsh, often solitary, expanses of the American West*

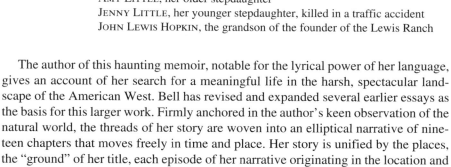

Principal characters:
LAURA BELL, a sheepherder, cattle rancher,
naturalist in Wyoming and Utah
JOE LITTLE, her husband, whom she
divorces
BELL'S FATHER, a minister and theologian
BELL'S MOTHER, a social worker
AMY LITTLE, her older stepdaughter
JENNY LITTLE, her younger stepdaughter, killed in a traffic accident
JOHN LEWIS HOPKIN, the grandson of the founder of the Lewis Ranch

The author of this haunting memoir, notable for the lyrical power of her language, gives an account of her search for a meaningful life in the harsh, spectacular landscape of the American West. Bell has revised and expanded several earlier essays as the basis for this larger work. Firmly anchored in the author's keen observation of the natural world, the threads of her story are woven into an elliptical narrative of nineteen chapters that moves freely in time and place. Her story is unified by the places, the "ground" of her title, each episode of her narrative originating in the location and the season that prompt her reflections.

The first nine chapters describe Bell's three years as a sheepherder in Wyoming. She reveals little of her early life, describing herself as a solitary child given to fantasy, the fourth of five children of unconventional parents. Her story begins in 1977, when as a recent college graduate, she is troubled by indecision and unable to move forward in her life. A lover of horses, she imagines a romantic life as a cowgirl. She leaves her home in Kentucky to visit her sister in the West, where, on impulse, she signs on as sheepherder in the Big Horn Basin of Wyoming. As the only woman in a crew of older men, she lives a solitary life in a small trailer, a primitive sheep wagon equipped with only the bare necessities. Her companions are her horse, her sheepdogs, and the man who brings her weekly supplies to the summer camp in the high ground. In her first summer she endures a near rape by a drunken herder; a frightening night on the range, in which she has lost her way in wild country; and the temporary loss of her horse, which runs away with a band of wild horses. The unimaginable privations and loneliness of this existence will inspire her reflections about her life.

~

Laura Bell has received two literature fellowships from the Wyoming Arts Council, the Neltje Blanchan Memorial Award, and the Frank Nelson Doubleday Memorial Award. She works as an administrator for the Nature Conservancy.

~

The male sheepherders in the crew are loners and misfits, many of them alcoholics. After ten months of hard physical labor and solitude, most will lose their money in the brothels and bars of Western towns. Bell is generous in her description of these men, refusing to pass judgment. Sterling, an elderly herder, brings her an unexpected gift of strawberries and a six-pack of beer; he will later commit suicide by shooting himself with his rifle. Murdi, born in the Basque country, will die of a self-treated leg injury, leaving one hundred thousand dollars to be used for his burial with the rest given to charity. John Lewis Hopkin, the grandson of the original owner of the ranch, serves as her mentor; she will later mourn his death. Some of these men behave badly by conventional standards; nevertheless, Bell characterizes them with empathy, acknowledging the generosity with which they have welcomed her, understanding in the final chapters of her story that their kindness is a form of love that has transformed her life.

Readers are drawn into the story by the author's poetic description of the landscape and its inhabitants, both human and animal. The sheep in the moonlight are "restless for green feed, a luminous, drifting mass that spills in rivulets through gullies and rises up hillsides, conforming intricately to the imperfect shape of earth." Later she describes an abandoned winter camp: "Across the meadow to the east, where just the day before we'd sunbathed on warm rock slabs by the hot springs, white steam rises in the cold air and the silvered trunks of burned trees catch the snow." The dogs and horses who serve her in her work are often her only companions, sharing both physical warmth and a mystical sense of communication.

Bell's writing style is distilled and restrained. While she is often praised for her honest self-revelations, there are gaps in her narrative that leave unanswered questions. There are lovers who appear in oblique references without explanation. At one point she reveals without further comment that she is pregnant and plans an abortion. Perhaps the most notable omission is any reference to her childhood in Nashville; her sense of alienation seems incompatible with her description of her warm, supportive family.

Following the three years of sheepherding, Bell moves her story forward to 1990, when she recalls the previous ten years. In 1980, she begins her work as a cattle hand on the Diamond Tail Ranch. Here she learns from a female colleague that women who work with cattle cannot match male physical strength and must depend on their wits. At the ranch she meets Joe Little, the charming, book-loving ranch hand with whom she falls in love and marries. Little, who had recently lost his wife in a fall from a horse, has two small daughters, Amy and Jenny, who are being raised by their grandparents in Minnesota. Although Bell is well aware that Joe is drowning his grief in alcohol, his obvious charm and his love for her overcome her reservations. Her parents, who had traveled west to visit her in her sheepherding years, show their support again, joining in the wedding celebration.

Before deciding to marry Joe, she had already met and formed an emotional attachment to eighteen-month-old Jenny and four-year-old Amy. She persuades Joe that the girls must come to live with them. Although Bell expresses no blame for Little's shortcomings as a provider, she leaves the Diamond Tail Ranch to take a position with the Big Horn National Forest as an administrator of public lands, a job that will guarantee health insurance and benefits for the family. The four begin their life together in their new home on Beaver Creek. The marriage lasts for nearly ten years until Bell, in a wrenching decision, and after testing her husband with her own admitted infidelity, divorces him. She demands that he decide which is more important: his life with her or his addiction to alcohol, which has poisoned their marriage. She accepts his admission that he cannot change his ways to meet her expectations. With profound regret and a sense of guilt, she leaves her husband and stepdaughters.

Throughout the story, Bell's parents, despite their disappointment in their daughter's unusual choice of lifestyle, remain solid in their emotional support. Her father is a minister and theologian; her mother earns her master's degree at the age of sixty, becoming a social worker who treats Alzheimer's patients. To Bell, the usefulness of her parents' lives is evidence of her own failure. Although her mother criticizes her for the divorce, her father reminds her that she can count on their continuing love.

After leaving her job and her marriage, Bell moves to Salt Lake City and trains as a masseuse. Feeling the absence of her estranged family and learning of the death of her former sheepdog, Louise, she takes a new companion, Grace, an Australian sheepdog that comforts her with its devoted companionship. In one moving passage, Laura and Grace share the consoling experience of gazing out together at the passing landscape as they drive through the badlands of Wyoming.

While working as a masseuse in the winter, Bell takes on a summer job at a bookstore and art gallery in an old schoolhouse near her former home in Beaver Creek. Amy and Jenny, who at this point in the narrative are teenagers, are frequent visitors, sharing the stories of their lives at school and becoming again a regular part of Bell's life. For the next five years she follows the seasons, wintering in Utah and returning to the Wyoming schoolhouse in summer.

The last four chapters of Bell's memoir describe her coming to terms with the losses of her life. Jenny, her beloved stepdaughter, dies at the age of eighteen in a single car accident on a deserted western road. In a phone call attempting to console Amy, Bell grieves that she is more skilled in comforting a frightened animal than in helping Amy cope with her loss. After Jenny's burial, Bell finds her only consolation again on horseback, as a guide for tourists camping in the mountains of Yellowstone National Park. A fortunate opportunity comes with a job opening with the Nature Conservancy.

Bell's memoir ends five years later, with the joint celebration of the three families—Amy's maternal grandparents, Joe, and Bell's mother and father—at Amy's graduation from the University of Wyoming. In a touching moment of reconciliation, Joe expresses his gratitude for the part Bell has played in his daughters' lives. As the celebration ends, Bell endures yet another loss: Her current lover tells her that he is leaving her for another woman. She finds consolation in the words of Ani Pema Chödrön, the American-born woman ordained as a Tibetan Buddhist nun, who teaches that fully embracing one's grief is the path that will lead one forward.

Readers have been delighted by Bell's poetic descriptions of her sensuous experiences in the American West. There is the total darkness of a night in the badlands, the relief of cool water poured over the head in the unrelenting heat of the desert sun. There is the intuitive understanding of the mind of animals: an orphaned lamb and a ewe tricked into accepting each other, the companionship of the horse as Bell leans against the warmth of his neck, and the companionship of her dog, Grace, sharing the front seat of her pickup truck.

The places named in her cryptic titles of the nineteen chapters—Burnt Mountain, Shell Creek, Heart Mountain—are the ground that prompts her memory and establishes her claim. Believing in midlife that her goals have lacked coherence and that she has often failed, she finds spiritual release in the wisdom of her father. Her redemption, he tells her, rests in her work as a conservationist, a freeing of the land for future generations.

Bell's concludes her memoir with hope. She acknowledges the love of all those people who have supported her, especially her parents, who, although often disappointed by her choices, have traveled to share with her all the important times in her life. In her isolation and closeness to the natural world that have fueled her writing, she has found a kind of transcendence that allows her to move graciously into whatever future is in store for her. Her valediction for the first fifty years of her life provides an eloquent conclusion to her memoir: "And if we're supple of heart, we get to gather our bones together and walk on in the world with our noses to the wind, bright-eyed for the days ahead."

In contrast to the confessional style of many memoirs, Bell writes with emotional restraint. Even in the face of her terrible losses, she invites the reader to fill in the blanks that she has left. Her memoir, frequently praised for its lyrical descriptions of the land and its inhabitants, human and animal, links her to the tradition of the literature of the American West. Her work has been compared to that of Wallace Stegner, E. Annie Proulx, Terry Tempest Williams, and Gretel Ehrlich, among others.

Marjorie Podolsky

Review Sources

Booklist 106 (March 1, 2010): 44.
Kirkus Reviews 78, no. 1 (January 1, 2010): 24.
Library Journal 134, no. 20 (December 15, 2009): 114.
Minneapolis Star Tribune, April 25, 2010, p. E12.
Nature Conservancy 60, no. 2 (Summer, 2010): 77.
Publishers Weekly 257 (February 1, 2010): 43

CLAUDE LÉVI-STRAUSS
The Poet in the Laboratory

Author: Patrick Wilcken
Publisher: Penguin Press (New York). Illustrated.
  404 pp. $29.95
Type of work: Biography

  An intellectual biography of the eminent French anthropological theorist Lévi-Strauss

      Principal personages:
        CLAUDE LÉVI-STRAUSS (1908-2009), a
          French anthropologist known for his
          work on mythology and the structures of
          thought
        DINA DREYFUS LÉVI-STRAUSS (c. 1910-c.
          1999), an anthropologist and
        philosopher; the first wife of Claude Lévi-Strauss, who made the
        expedition into Brazil with him
        CURT NIMUENDAJÚ (1883-1945; born CURT UNCKEL), a German-born
        anthropologist who later became a Brazilian citizen; the foremost
        authority on the indigenous people of Brazil
        ANDRÉ BRETON (1896-1966), a French writer and theorist of the
        Surrealist movement who spent time in New York during World
        War II
        MAX ERNST (1891-1976), a German Surrealist artist who was active in
        the intellectual life of New York during World War II
        ROMAN JAKOBSON (1896-1982), a Russian linguist whose structural
        analysis of language influenced the ideas of Lévi-Strauss
        JACQUES LACAN (1901-1981), a French psychoanalyst whose work had
        implications for philosophy and literary theory

    Claude Lévi-Strauss, the subject of Patrick Wilcken's *Claude Lévi-Strauss*, may well have been the most influential anthropologist of the late twentieth century. More than any other intellectual figure, he gave rise to the theoretical approach to the humanities and social sciences known as structuralism and to its successor, poststructuralism. His fundamental idea, derived primarily from the structural analysis of language, was that human kinship relations and mythological accounts expressed systems of thinking driven by the need to order the world according to binary systems of oppositions.

    Although he generally expressed his theories in complex and difficult literary works, Lévi-Strauss also achieved a wider renown among members of the general reading public. His bittersweet, elegiac memoir *Tristes tropiques* (1955; *A World on the Wane*, 1961; better known as *Tristes Tropiques*), about his field work in Brazil,

~

Australian-born Patrick Wilcken writes for The Times Literary Supplement *and the* Guardian *on Brazilian affairs. His first book,* Empire Adrift: The Portuguese Court in Rio de Janeiro, *was published in 2005.*

~

established him as one of the great commentators on the labors of anthropology, the questionable benefits of modernity, and the nature of the disappearing life of tribal people. Ironically, as Wilcken points out in his fascinating account of the anthropologist's life and work, Lévi-Strauss was not much of a fieldworker; the explorer of the preliterate mind always felt most at home in libraries.

Born into a family of secular Jews of Alsatian origin, Lévi-Strauss, from his youth, found himself at the boundaries of different cultural worlds in the frequently anti-Semitic society of France. His father, Raymond, was a portrait painter just at the time when the adventurous movements of artistic modernism and the rise of mass photography were making realistic portrait painting outmoded. From his father, Lévi-Strauss acquired a strong aesthetic sense and perhaps also an old-fashioned fondness for tradition that would lie behind the anthropologist's inclination toward tribal societies and that would come to the surface in the social conservatism of his later years.

As a student, Lévi-Strauss became involved in socialist politics and studied law and philosophy. After teaching secondary school for a time and marrying Dina Dreyfus, he accepted an offer to go with his wife to Brazil as part of a French cultural mission. The two were appointed visiting professors at the University of São Paulo. Although most French expatriate intellectuals formed insular communities, Lévi-Strauss and his wife became friends with Brazilian writers and artists, and they conceived the idea of a journey of ethnographic exploration into the vast inland region of Mato Grosso.

The first forays into the indigenous cultures of Brazil brought Lévi-Strauss into contact with the Caduveo and the Bororo. Prefiguring his later fascination with structural forms in cultures, he became intrigued with the elaborate facial designs of women in the former and the expressions of social relations through housing patterns in the latter. The early studies on these groups helped to establish Lévi-Strauss as an anthropologist. However, his approach to fieldwork was far from ideal. His stays with his subjects were brief. He did not speak their languages or have deep grounding in their cultures. The great journey into Mato Grosso that followed also showed these shortcomings, since it was more of a caravan of exploration than an immersion in indigenous cultures.

In 1938, the Lévi-Strausses and a well-supplied team set out to follow the Rondon line, the remains of a telegraph line that had been strung earlier in the century, making contact with the indigenous people who lived along the way. Lévi-Strauss had corresponded with the anthropologist Curt Unckel, who had adopted the Brazilian name Nimuendajú. He tried to get Nimuendajú, the foremost expert on the peoples of the region, to accompany them, but the authority was too busy working on his field notes. Although the expedition that followed was amateurish in many respects, Lévi-Strauss proved to be an assiduous note taker and a talented photographer. Although he would never again do fieldwork after this trek, his Brazilian adventure did inspire some of the ideas that helped to form his theories and it supplied the material for his 1955 memoir.

Lévi-Strauss might well have enjoyed a distinguished career if he had spent the rest of his life in France after the Brazilian expedition, but World War II sent him to another exotic location, where he came into contact with some of the great minds of his time. When the war broke out, he was drafted into the French army. The German invasion and the rapid collapse of France left Lévi-Strauss, as a Jew, vulnerable to Nazi anti-Semitism. At first, he was so unaware of the danger that he requested an appointment to teach in Paris, which was within the German occupied zone. However, he soon learned the insecurity of being Jewish even in the unoccupied zone governed by the French administration in Vichy when he was fired under an anti-Jewish statute. The reputation he had made in Brazil earned him an offer of a teaching position at the New School for Social Research in New York, which was taking in German refugee intellectuals. Although he offered to bring Dina, from whom he had divorced by that time, with him, Lévi-Strauss made his way alone to the United States.

New York enabled Lévi-Strauss to flourish in one of the most vibrant intellectual hothouses of the twentieth century. War and oppression drove many of Europe's most notable artists and scholars across the Atlantic, and New York held the greatest concentration. On board the ship, Lévi-Strauss formed a friendship with the surrealist André Breton, and once in New York, he associated with Breton and the Surrealist artist Max Ernst. Lévi-Strauss and the Surrealists shared interests in mythological expressions of the subconscious mind, and they became collectors of tribal artifacts in the shops in New York. This environment encouraged Lévi-Strauss to move away from the specialized study of particular human groups and toward patterns of thought underlying all the mythologies and artifacts he and his associates were collecting.

The most important of his contacts in New York may have been the Russian linguist Roman Jakobson, who argued that languages should be understood not as ways of representing the world but as systems of structural relations, expressing mental patterns. Drawing on structural linguistics, Lévi-Strauss developed the concept of an abstract system of oppositions and linkages lying behind specific cultural relations. This led to a doctoral thesis and to a first major book, *Les Structures élémentaires de la parenté* (1949; *The Elementary Structures of Kinship*, 1969) that presented kinship as a code of relations among people.

As Wilcken presents the life, New York provided the foundation for the rest of Lévi-Strauss's career. The time in New York not only brought him into the currents of thought of the midcentury but also helped to bring him into the intellectual establishment. Once back in France, he became an able administrator. As he produced a steady stream of erudite works, he became recognized as part of the postwar intellectual elite of France. He became particular friends with the psychoanalyst Jacques Lacan. Although Lévi-Strauss wrote only a little about psychoanalysis and the unconscious directly, the idea of an unconscious was clearly part of his structural anthropology. In turn, Lacan incorporated some of Lévi-Strauss's ideas into elaborate and often incomprehensible psychoanlytic theories.

Being Jewish continued to be a barrier to Lévi-Strauss's acceptance in the inner circle of France. However, the old prejudices were weakening. After the war, he had almost been elected to membership in one of the most selective circles of the French academic hierarchy, the Collège de France. He had, though, been repeatedly blocked, apparently by the unwillingness of some members to accept a Jewish colleague. In 1960, though, he finally achieved this honor. By the early 1970's, his public appearances and his popular memoir had made him almost an intellectual celebrity, while he had become enough of an established figure that many of the post-structuralists had begun to define themselves in contrast to him. In 1973, Lévi-Strauss reached the pinnacle of French intellectual life, when he was elected to the French Academy.

Ironically, as Lévi-Strauss moved into the center of his own tribal group, he became ever more a loner. In his own work, he assembled examples and illustrations of his theories from the reports of ethnographers and travelers, some of which were not always accurate. While many were influenced by his writings, he had no close students or successors who would carry on his tradition. Also ironically, as French intellectuals in general tended to move sharply to the left politically, Lévi-Strauss became more socially conservative, even opposing the election of Marguerite Yourcenar, the first woman to become a member of the French Academy, on grounds of tradition.

The biography portrays Lévi-Strauss as a polite but distant and standoffish figure. In interviews with the biographer, Lévi-Strauss refused to provide much information on his personal life. His first wife, Dina, appears in these pages largely because of her role in the Brazilian expedition. His second wife, from whom he was also divorced, and his third receive only a few lines of text. Although it does not give an intimate portrait of a man who apparently did not take readily to intimacy, it gives an engaging account of the development of the ideas of one of the foremost anthropological theorists of modern times. Wilcken's critical discussion of these ideas is somewhat limited. He does not, for example, give much consideration to the question of how much tribal people actually do think in terms of abstract binary oppositions, rather than in terms of coming up with practical solutions to the material and social problems that face them daily. Wilcken also does not discuss the problem of how the theories of Lévi-Strauss might be verified or refuted, or, if they cannot be refuted, what use the theories might have beyond giving readers pleasurable contemplation.

This book is not a detailed critical analysis of the thinker, but it is an excellent introduction to the thinking. Even readers who are already familiar with the work will enjoy seeing the work connected to the life. Whatever their ultimate judgment on Lévi-Strauss's structural anthropology, readers of Wilcken's biography will find this an excellent, well-written account of the intellectual progress of one the masters of modern social science. For readers who would like to continue their study of Lévi-Strauss's work, Wilcken includes a concise bibliographical essay on suggestions for further reading at the end of the book.

Carl L. Bankston III

Review Sources

New Statesman 139, no. 5025 (November 1, 2010): 46.
The New York Times, October 18, 2010, p. C7.
The New Yorker 86, no. 37 (November 22, 2010): 135.
Science 330, no. 6008 (November 26, 2010): 1180.
The Times Literary Supplement, nos. 5621/5622 (December 24, 2010): 11.

CONSPIRATA
A Novel of Ancient Rome

Author: Robert Harris (1957-   )
First published: Lustrum, 2009, in England
Publisher: Simon & Schuster (New York). 341 pp.
    $26.00
Type of work: Novel
Time: 63 B.C.E.-58 B.C.E.
Locale: Rome

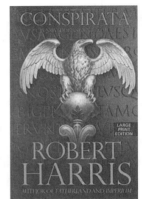

Harris's second novel about the life and times of Cicero continues the story of his public career, covering the momentous half-decade that followed his election to the office of consul

Principal characters:
>   MARCUS TULLIUS CICERO (106-43 B.C.E.),
>   Roman lawyer, politician, and statesman
>   TIRO (c. 104-c. 4 B.C.E.), his slave and secretary; later his biographer
>   TERENTIA (98 B.C.E.-4 C.E.), his wife, the mother of his two children
>   JULIUS CAESAR (100-44 B.C.E.), an ambitious politician, supported by
>   plebeians
>   CATALINA (108-62 B.C.E.), leader of a conspiracy to overthrow the
>   republic
>   CLODIUS (c. 93-53 B.C.E.), a vain young patrician with political
>   ambitions
>   CATO THE YOUNGER (95-46 B.C.E.), unrealistic mouthpiece of old
>   Roman ideals
>   POMPEY (106-48 B.C.E.), Rome's most powerful general, conqueror of its
>   eastern provinces

   In September, 2006, as Americans debated the pros and cons of the five-year-old Patriot Act, the British novelist Robert Harris wrote an op-ed piece for *The New York Times.* He pointed out that Rome had its own terrorist attack, when pirates burned the Roman harbor of Ostia in 68 B.C.E. and destroyed a fleet of war ships. Backers of the ambitious general Pompey exploited the occasion and the fear it generated. They persuaded the senate to repeal provisions in the constitution that prevented a single person from amassing too much power. Pompey rousted the pirates within the year, but the individual rights of the old republic were never restored. Pompey was soon the most powerful person in Rome, returning from his conquests in the Middle East as Pompey the Great. Within a generation, Rome was an empire with an emperor.

   In 2006, Harris had just released the first in what he said would be a trilogy of historical-fiction books. Its central character was Cicero, arguably Rome's greatest orator and political thinker, and its narrator was Tiro, his faithful secretary. Tiro is said to have outlived his master by several decades and to have written a long biography, cited by ancient authors but no longer extant. *Imperium* (2006) tells the story of Cicero's early years as Tiro might have told it, extending from Cicero's successful prosecution of a corrupt official to his election as a magistrate and his achievement of supreme political power (*imperium*), when he is elected consul at the

Robert Harris began writing political fiction with novels about Nazi Germany and Stalinist Russia and continued with The Ghost *(2007), which he adapted for the screen in Roman Polanski's* The Ghost Writer *(2009).*

age of forty-two. By the end, he has overcome the prejudice of aristocrats who consider him a "new man" to become the presiding officer in the Roman senate at the youngest possible age.

The re-created biography was quite successful. Some of the best dialogue came straight out of Cicero's speeches, which had been recorded by Tiro, who was the inventor of a shorthand systems with symbols still in use (such as "i.e.," "e.g.," and "etc.") and Rome's first court recorder. Tiro was such a devoted servant that his master would quite naturally be the hero of any tale he wrote, but he was also close enough to the great moments of intrigue to note any quirks that Cicero exhibited or any gossip he relished. *Imperium* is a modern novel about the quest for political power, but it is cast in the form of a biography. Cicero would have termed it a Greek or Hellenistic biography because it paints the real man, warts and all.

The second novel in the series, *Cospirata*, covers the half-decade (*lustrum*) that followed Cicero's ascension to the rank of consul. The year of his consulate was marked by the conspiracy (*conspiratia*) of Catalina. An ally of Julius Caesar and an outspoken voice of dissent in the senate, Catalina shared Caesar's hopes of consolidating power through a populist campaign against Rome's ruling elite. His rebellion was followed by continued threats of civil war, during which Cicero worked resolutely to maintain order.

In the novel's brief preface, Harris explains that he has not let the facts (or the absence of clear evidence) stand in the way of a good story. The details of Catalina's involvement in the conspiracy that bears his name, and of Cicero's speeches about him at the time, are reconstructed from fragmentary evidence, about which neither ancient historians nor contemporary scholars agree. As Harris tells it, there are really two conspiracies.

The first conspiracy begins to unfolds on the day before the newly elected senate convenes. After a ritually mutilated body is found near the city, Cicero makes inquiries and discovers a plot to kill key members of the senate, himself included. The conspirators will then create terror in Rome, discard the constitution, and establish a new political order. Suspecting that the leaders come from inside the senate, and represent the old patrician order that feels threatened by upstarts like himself, Cicero moves quickly to make deals and to prepare a speech that will expose the plot before the whole senate. Blame is affixed on Catalina, a disaffected and outspoken patrician senator whose loyalty to the constitution has already come into question. Catalina is exiled, but later returns, and still later raises an army. By the time that Catalina's rebellion is quashed, Cicero's term in office has ended and he is the most celebrated man in town. For his part in saving the republic he has been declared father of the country.

Catalina's conspiracy turns out to be part of a second, broader conspiracy that reaches still higher in the Roman establishment and poses a greater threat to the seven hundred-year-old republic. Cicero learns about it gradually, during the years after his consulate, but he can only slow its progress. The chief conspirators are too careful to be implicated and too ambitious to cede power. In a series of ironic reversals, Cicero's expedient compromises come back to haunt him. Old allies become new enemies, laws are enacted through trickery that would make a modern politician blush, and the father of the country is publicly discredited as an enemy of the state.

Compared to its predecessor, *Conspirata* has nothing to match the oratorical fireworks of Cicero's speech against Verres, the corrupt official whom he prosecuted as a young lawyer. That is not Harris's fault. Cicero's style changes as he ascends to power. He makes concessions and compromises; he sets aside his youthful ideals in what he considers to be the larger interest of Rome; he has less time to prepare his speeches as he faces increasing pressure from friends and rivals alike. Perhaps the most stirring speech in *Conspirata* is delivered by Cato the Younger, sounding like his famous ancestor and refusing to take stock of his audience on the occasion. Tiro admires the speech as he takes it down for posterity, while Cicero complains that Cato talks as though he is living in Plato's republic rather than cutthroat Rome. In a delicious irony, Cicero finds that he must defend a governor who is quite as corrupt as Verres was and must suffer the innuendos of a young prosecuting lawyer whom he once mentored. Here as elsewhere the great orator knows how to make a crowd laugh at his opponent's expense.

The humor gets dark when it comes to the outrageous corruption in Roman society. Cicero's dull but faithful wife, Terentia, tells him that his young patrician friend Clodius has broken into a women's religious festival and exposed himself before the Vestal Virgins—a crime punishable by death or banishment for life. Cicero refuses to defend the obviously guilty man. However, he uses his family's wealth, and his lascivious sister's body, to buy off jurors. Showing no shame, he announces his plan to become a plebeian and build a power base among the masses. His first actions lead to the law that forces Cicero into exile.

In one of the final scenes, when Cicero is about to go into exile, he visits the triumphant Julius Caesar, who has just had his command in Gaul doubled in size and quintupled in duration. Caesar says he can restore Cicero to a position of power and influence but demands total personal loyalty. Cicero refuses the offer, saying he finds it strange "that I should be the one driven from Rome for seeking to be a king." Caesar agrees and tries once more to win Cicero's support, at which point Cicero drops all courtesy and speaks with the bluntness of Cato. He calls Caesar a more "wicked" person than Catalina or any other convicted conspirator, remarking that Caesar wants everyone in Rome to be under his foot.

A former political reporter, Harris has the reputation of doing for politicians what

John le Carré has done for spies: making them credible characters in tense and consequential intrigues. He has invented postwar Nazi leaders, in *Fatherland* (1992); a loyal postwar Stalinist, in *Archangel* (1998); and a former prime minister accused of war crimes, in *The Ghost* (2007). Staying closer to the historical facts, he has told the stories of the effort to crack the Nazi's secret code, in *Enigma* (1995), and of the eruption of Mount Vesuvius in 79 C.E., in *Pompei* (2003). He does not idolize the "Roman way," as other authors have done, nor does he idolize his protagonist. Roman *imperium* was clearly based on brutal conquests, harsh rule, and punitive taxation. Political careers owed more to family connections than to study or devotion to civic ideals. Cicero could not have managed even the small household of his youth without an army of slaves, and he realizes only on the eve of exile how little he knows about the personal life and dreams of his slave Tiro. Indeed, their evolving relationship could prove a fruitful theme for the final novel in the trilogy.

Though part of a trilogy, *Conspirata* holds up well on its own. There are no teasing references back to the earlier novel and no hints about what is to come. Harris tells the story of Cicero at midlife as Tiro must have done. If the story of his life were made into a drama in three acts, *Imperium* would contain the rising action, and *Conspirata* the climax. When Cicero is at the peak of his political career, he makes what Tiro calls an error in judgment. He buys the sort of villa that he thinks the father of the country should own. To pay for it, he accepts gifts that will later embarrass him. The house goes up in smoke as he leaves the city to go into exile, presumably burned by an angry mob. The last act will showcase his political rehabilitation and his tragic end. The reader has only to await the arrival of Brutus. Perhaps the only questions are how Harris will show Cicero's development as a political thinker during the long years away from civic life.

Reviewers on both sides of the Atlantic have admired the novel's technique. When they differ, the British reviewers are more comfortable with the details of Roman names and offices, while their American counterparts would like more coaching. To this end, the publisher provides maps of Rome and its provinces in 63 B.C.E., a glossary of Roman legal and political terms, and a list of thirty-three leading people in the story with their full names and brief descriptions.

Thomas Willard

Review Sources

The Economist, November 17, 2009, p. 99.
Library Journal 135, no. 3 (February 15, 2010): 87.
The New York Times Book Review, February 21, 2010, p. 14.
Publishers Weekly 256, no. 51 (December 21, 2009): 37-38.
The Spectator, October 10, 2009, pp. 39-40.

THE COOKBOOK COLLECTOR

Author: Allegra Goodman (1967-   )
Publisher: Dial Press (New York). 394 pp. $26.00.
Type of work: Novel
Time: Fall, 1999, to May, 2002
Locale: Northern California and New England

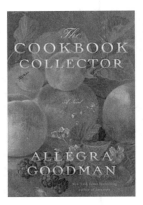

*This book is the story of two sisters, Emily and Jessa-
mine Bach, their love affairs, and their work*

> *Principal characters:*
> EMILY BACH, the young chief executive
>   officer of Veritech, a start-up computer
>   company
> ALEX ZASLOVSKY, Veritech's chief
>   technology officer
> JESSAMINE (JESS) BACH, a graduate student at the University of
>   California
> RICHARD BACH, the father of Emily and Jessamine
> GILLIAN BACH, Richard's deceased wife, mother of Emily and Jess
> HEIDI BACH, Richard's second wife
> JONATHAN TILGHMAN, the cofounder of ISIS and Emily's fiancé
> ORION STEINER, the cofounder of ISIS and Emily's childhood friend
> MEL MILLSTEIN, the director of human resources at ISIS
> DAVE, the chief executive officer of ISIS
> OSKAR FEUCHTWANGLER, the senior scientist at ISIS
> GEORGE FRIEDMAN, the proprietor of Yorick's bookstore, Jess's
>   employer
> LEON, the founder of "Save the Trees"
> MOLLY EISENSTAT, Orion's lover, a hardworking nurse
> RABBI HELFGOTT, the Bialystoker rabbi in Berkeley
> MRS. GIBBS, a convert to Judaism, Jess's friend
> SANDRA MCCLINTOCK, the inheritor of her uncle's cookbook collection
> RABBI ZYLBERFENIG, the Bialystoker rabbi in Canaan, Massachusetts
> CHAYA, Rabbi Zylberfenig's wife
> SOREL FISHER, a programmer at ISIS

Allegra Goodman's novel *The Cookbook Collector* opens in Berkeley, California,
just before Thanksgiving. Emily and her sister Jess meet for dinner on a rainy night
and spend the evening together. Emily, older than Jess, is protective of her twenty-
three year-old sister, who is doing graduate work in philosophy at the University of
California. Emily is the successful chief executive officer (CEO) of Veritech, a company about to go public, which will make Emily rich. She wants her sister to invest in
the company, too, although to do so Jess would have to borrow money to buy shares.
She dislikes asking her father, with whom she does not get along well. He lives in

New England and has sent for his daughters to come for the Thanksgiving holiday.

Emily is willing to make the trip, as her fiancé, Jonathan, works in nearby Cambridge, Massachusetts, at another start-up computer company, ISIS, also about to go public. Their long-distance romance is difficult for both of them. When they finally get together during the holiday and make love, Emily tells him a secret plan, the details of which her chief technology officer, Alex, had confided in her. The project involves fingerprinting data, a security technology that raises certain ethical and possibly legal issues that make Emily uncomfortable. She therefore decides not to pursue the project, although her decision angers Alex. Jonathan promises to keep her secret, and he does, until much later in the novel.

Allegra Goodman is the author of two collections of short stories and several novels, including Kaatterskill Falls *(1998),* Paradise Park *(2001),* Intuition *(2006), and* The Other Side of the Island *(2008).*

Meanwhile, Jess has gone to work at Yorick's, a bookstore owned and operated by George Friedman, who got rich working for Bill Gates at Microsoft and subsequently retired. He has used his wealth to buy an expensive mansion in the Berkeley hills, to collect rare books, and to live well, if somewhat reclusively. Although sixteen years older than Jess, he eventually falls in love with her, despite some personality differences between them, among other issues. However, Jess is having an affair with Leon, the founder of the "Save the Trees" movement. She knew Leon slightly at Brandeis University when she was a student. She engages in his movement by "leafleting," but she is too frightened of heights to "tree sit," like other members of his group do. At one point later in the novel, she tries to conquer her fear of heights and climb a tall tree, but her attempt, successful at first, frightens her considerably, and she needs to be rescued. The episode also leads to the end of her affair with Leon.

The initial public offering (IPO) for Veritech, at eighteen dollars per share, is wildly successful. (In 1999 "dot-coms" were extremely popular on the stock exchanges). Emily makes half a billion dollars, and the other people at her company also become rich. Even Jess profits. Unable to borrow from anyone else, she is lent $1,800 by Rabbi Helfgott, whom she had met while both were distributing leaflets (of different kinds) around Sproul Plaza. Helfgott, a Bialystoker rabbi, was sent to Berkeley by his rabbi as an evangelist to the Jews. Among his congregants is Mrs. Gibbs, a convert and Jess's friend, who warmly endorses the rabbi and his activities. In fact, it is she who brings Jess to Rabbi Helfgott to help her with her problem. The Messianic rabbi, who also happens to love computers and dabbles in stocks, decides to help Jess with an interest-free loan. He says: "Just return the eighteen hundred after the IPO. If you want to give me anything more, then you decide however to repay me. Give to *tzedakah*—a gift to charity. Give to the Bialystock Center. Or give nothing. This is an investment. You are investing in Veritech. I am investing in you." It turns out to be a good investment for both.

While everything runs smoothly at Veritech as far as the IPO is concerned, things are not quite so well at ISIS. During the Thanksgiving break, for example, when Emily and Jonathan meet Orion, an excellent programmer who works with Jonathan and helped found ISIS, and Orion's girlfriend, Molly, some friction develops between the two men. It was Orion who actually introduced Jonathan to Emily. Though Orion and Emily had been childhood sweethearts, their romance faded, and Emily took up with Jonathan. Complicating matters, when Orion meets Sorel Fisher, a new programmer at ISIS, he begins to fall in love with her, despite still living with Molly. Their relationship begins when he helps Sorel track down and solve a programming problem that has caused Lockbox, the stellar program that ISIS has developed, to crash for several hours. Orion knows that Lockbox has serious problems, a fact that Jonathan refuses to acknowledge.

The IPO for ISIS stock goes through, nevertheless, and everyone makes a huge profit, most of all the officers of the company: Jonathan, the chief technology officer; Dave, the CEO; Oskar Feuchtwangler, the senior scientist, who had been Jonathan's adviser before Jonathan dropped out of the Massachusetts Institute of Technology; Mel Millstein, the director of human resources; and others. As the company prospers, Jonathan puts pressure on Mel to hire more programmers—and quickly, too— causing Mel much mental anguish. This leads first to Mel's gastric problems and then a serious back ailment. Orion, son of a poet and himself a visionary of sorts, also feels growing discomfort working with Jonathan and the others; at top level meetings, it is clear that he is not in harmony with them. Although he continues to work for the firm, he repeatedly tells Molly that he wants to leave.

During the Thanksgiving holiday, Emily and Jess meet Rabbi Helfgott's brother-in-law, Rabbi Zylberfenig, also a Bialystoker rabbi, who lives in Canaan, Massachusetts. He has his eye on a piece of property adjacent to Richard's home that he wants to develop as a Bialystok center. His wife, Chaya, seems to recognize in the sisters a resemblance to her own relatives back in London, from where the girls' mother also came. Only at the end of the novel does the significance of the resemblance emerge, if not for Jess, certainly for Emily, who insists on tracking down their mother's family and the events that led to her marriage with Richard.

One day, Sandra McClintock enters Yorick's with two old cookbooks that she wants to sell to George. He recognizes their value and buys them, hoping that she will return with more. She does, and George is at last able to persuade her to let him see all of the books her uncle had bequeathed to her. He takes Jess along, too, since he knows she has a good way of dealing with people such as Sandra; so it is that through Jess George manages to buy the whole collection at a bargain price. He then offers Jess the job of cataloging the books, many of which are eighteenth century editions or otherwise rare. Sandra's uncle had also left numerous notes, annotations, and drawings in the books, which Jess finds more than simply curious, especially the drawings of a woman, usually nude. Like Chaya trying to plumb the mystery of the Bach sisters origins, Jess tries to discover who the woman in the drawings is, and she finally does, with surprising results.

For Jess, cataloging the cookbook collection is fascinating, as she settles into George's home where the books are housed. She works most afternoons while George is at Yorick's. However, one day, when he returns early, she and he become more intimate and eventually become lovers. During this period—the spring and summer of 2001—after the dot-com bubble had burst, many shareholders lost money on their stocks. However, some, such as Mel and Emily, had earlier sold enough of their stock to remain wealthy. Problems arise, however, for both Veritech and ISIS. New projects need to be conceived and developed, and both Emily and Jonathan go to work, separately, to try to find what would help renew everyone's faith in their companies. Adding to Jonathan's problems at ISIS, Lockbox had been hacked into, just as Orion had warned him it might.

It is then that Jonathan decides to take advantage of the idea Emily had privately mentioned to him during the Thanksgiving holiday in 1999. Unaware of its source, everyone thinks it is a great idea, even Orion, who at his own request becomes the leader of the "Fast Track" group assigned to develop the program. The project is kept secret, but Dave, Oskar, and the others at top management think it is just what the company needs. At Veritech work has also begun on a new product, which Emily dubs Verify, unaware of Jonathan's plans.

As the affair between Jess and George grows and as Jess becomes increasingly confident of her abilities as a historian, Jess grows increasing disturbed about her relationship with Leon. He had been away from Berkeley for many weeks doing "Save the Trees" work when she decides to conquer her fear of heights and climb one of the gigantic redwoods Leon's group are trying to save from a lumber company. Against George's advice and exhortations, she goes along with the group and even makes it to the tree platform, where she plans to spend a week on her own. However, her courage soon fails her, and she has to be rescued by Leon, whose disappointment in her is obvious. George pursues Jess and finally persuades her to leave the traumatic experience she has had. His apology for speaking against her wishes makes an impression on Jess, but she is even more impressed by the sincere concern and love he manifests.

Disaster strikes on September 11, 2001, when one of the planes that hits the towers in New York carries both Jonathan and Mel to their deaths. At the memorial service in Cambridge soon afterward, Emily gathers from some of the eulogies what Jonathan had been working on, and his betrayal destroys any feelings of love she has had for him. At the same time, she becomes increasingly determined to get to the bottom of her dead mother's history, especially after Chaya identifies Gillian Bach as the runaway sister of the Gould family in London. As Jonathan had concealed his plans for the future, so too had Gillian concealed her past, Emily mused. "She had loved them both, and this news made her feel entirely alone. Or had she loved them? She had loved aspects of Jonathan, and tested and adored him; adored her idea of Gillian, and studied her. She doubted now that she had known either."

It is too late to get to know Jonathan any better, but Emily feels compelled to know her mother—or at least her mother's past—better. Hence, she flies to London and makes contact with her newly discovered relatives. Before that, she also presses her father to reveal who and what her mother was. By contrast, Jess feels no such compulsion. Her marriage to George under a chuppah at the end of the novel, presided over by Rabbi Helfgott, is a great celebration, not only of the love the two have found for each other but also of much else, including, indirectly, Orion's union with Sorel and the founding of the Melvin Millstein Center for Jewish Life in Canaan.

Jay L. Halio

Review Sources

Booklist 107, no. 3 (July 1, 2010): 30.
Bookmarks, September/October, 2010, p. 20.
Harper's Magazine 321, no. 1925 (October, 2010): 75-76.
Kirkus Reviews 78, no. 12 (June 15, 2010): 534.
Library Journal 135, no. 5 (March 15, 2010): 94.
The New York Times Book Review (July 25, 2010): 10.
The New Yorker 86, no. 21 (July 26, 2010): 77.
People Weekly 73, no. 28 (July 19, 2010): 53.
Publishers Weekly 257, no. 10 (March 8, 2010): 36.

CORRESPONDENCE:
INGEBORG BACHMANN AND PAUL CELAN
With the Correspondences Between Paul Celan and Max Frisch and Between Ingeborg Bachmann and Gisèle Celan-Lestrange

Authors: Ingeborg Bachmann (1926-1973) and Paul
   Celan (1920-1970)
*First published: Herzzeit: Ingeborg Bachmann-Paul
   Celan, Briefwechsel*, 2008, in Germany
Translated from the German by Wieland Hoban
Edited by Bertrand Badiou, Hans Höller, Andrea Stoll,
   and Barbara Wiedeman
Photos, reproductions, a time line, and commentaries by
   the editors
Publisher: Seagull Books (New York). 373 pp. $24.95
Type of work: Letters
Time: 1948-1967

Reproduced in this volume is the hitherto unpublished correspondence between the two giants of post-World War II German poetry, Bachmann and Celan, documenting their often stormy artistic, spiritual, and sensual relationship

> *Principal personages:*
> PAUL CELAN (1920-1970), a Jewish, German-language poet
> INGEBORG BACHMANN (1926-1973), an Austrian poet
> MAX FRISCH (1911-1991), a Swiss writer
> GISÈLE LESTRANGE (1927-1991), Celan's wife
> YVAN GOLL (1891-1950), a French German poet
> CLAIRE GOLL (1890-1997), Goll's wife and a writer

"Waiting for letters is difficult," Paul Celan writes to Ingeborg Bachmann in an October, 1950, letter from Paris, published in *Correspondence: Ingeborg Bachmann and Paul Celan*. It is a sentiment that was certainly shared by German literary scholars, knowing that the correspondence between the two most influential poets of the post-World War II period had been sealed by Bachmann's heirs until 2023, no doubt because even this long after both the protaganists' deaths, their conservative Austrian sense was averse to making public the unmarried young woman's early affair with a Jew. That there had, indeed, been such an affair was not secret: It is well documented in letters and biographies of some of their contemporaries and in *Unvollendete Symphonie* (1950; unfinished symphony), a roman à clef by Hans Weigel, whom Bachmann left when she first met Celan. Further evidence of her lifelong attachment to Celan can be found in her last autobiographical novel, *Malina* (1971; English translation, 1989), to which she added a fairy-tale chapter, "Die Geheimnisse der Prinzessin von Kagran" (the secrets of the princess of Kagran), as

∽

*Ingeborg Bachmann was a member of
the famous German avant-garde
Gruppe 47 (Group 47) and was
awarded the Literature Prize of the
Federal Association of German
Industry (1955) and the Georg Büchner
Prize (1960). Paul Celan was awarded
the Literature Prize of the Federal
Association of German Industry (1957)
for his early poetry. He did extensive
translation work, mainly of French and
Russian poems.*

∽

an homage to Celan shortly after his death.

Despite all these secondary sources, the details of their relationship were the subject of much speculation among scholars and fans of the two poets; thus, the lifting of the publishing injunction by the Bachmann estate in 2008, allowing the publication of around two hundred letters, notes, and telegrams—as well as the correspondence between Celan and Max Frisch and Bachmann's exchange of letters with Paul's wife, Gisèle Lestrange— created a publishing sensation in Germany. Indeed, the correspondence between these two doomed geniuses reads more like a tragic, often pathetic, epistolary novel, tugging at the readers' heartstrings and making them hope against hope that the couple's struggle for mutual affection, friendship, and the right words to express their feelings for each other would lead to a happy end instead of despair and premature death: Celan drowned himself in the Seine River in 1970 at the age of forty-nine; Bachmann died of the consequences of a fire in her Rome apartment, caused by a cigarette that set her bed ablaze.

How promising, in contrast, had their relationship been when they first met in a friend's house in Vienna on May 17, 1948, an event Bachmann describes to her parents in separate letters, relating that Celan had, "splendidly enough," fallen in love with her and inundated her room with poppies. However, one of the letters states, Celan would have to leave for Paris in a month, which Celan, in fact, did on June 25, 1948. This ominous separation, so shortly after their first meeting, was made necessary by Celan's past: His German-Jewish parents had been murdered in a Nazi extermination camp in Romania, where he had himself spent some time in labor camps. Celan's departure from Soviet-occupied, postwar Vienna, with all its vestiges of the Nazi past and its still rampant anti-Semitism, seemed necessary, and there is no evidence that Bachmann ever attempted to persuade him to stay. In addition, Celan knew that Bachmann's father had been a Nazi before the war and that Bachmann was, as far as their different ethnic backgrounds were concerned, a "stranger." Celan's first letter to her is thus a love poem, "In Egypt," probably attached to a gift. The speaker in the poem, who finds himself in exile in Egypt, like the Hebrews in the Bible, addresses some Jewish women, presumably drowned, to accept the "stranger" with whom he is sleeping.

Nothing in the correspondence that follows indicates why there was no communication between the two lovers, except for a letter that was never sent, in which Bachmann touchingly asks herself and Celan what their brief encounter had really meant and whether Celan would even want her to come and visit him in Paris. Their letters during the first two years of their separation deal almost exclusively with this question, and it is Bachmann who is clearly desperate to hear that Celan wants to see her again, whereas he concentrates on the details of getting her a visa. Her letters are longer, more emotionally charged, and much more frequent, while his sometimes sound almost cold and evasive. Most foreboding is a passage in a letter by Celan (from August, 1949), in which he attempts to excuse himself for not having written for so long by stating that "my silence is perhaps more understandable than yours, for the darkness that imposes it on me is older." This appears to refer to the darkness related to his background as a Jewish Holocaust survivor and the psychological burdens it imposes on him.

Thus this early part of their correspondence is an attempt to find a modus operandi for their relationship, given that they discover that those happy weeks together in Vienna are irretrievably lost as the result of their physical separation, despite a brief visit by Bachmann to Paris in 1950. Eventually she comes to the conclusion that her lover will not emotionally commit himself to her to the same degree she is prepared to risk, and she recognizes (in a February 21, 1952, letter) that she has "put all her eggs in one basket and lost." Celan's marriage to Lestrange in December of 1952 appears to have devastated Bachmann, but she continued tirelessly to champion Celan's work. While her letters are full of praise and encouragement for Celan's work, he rarely comments on her own meteoric rise to fame as a poet, except in the most cursory fashion. So, in spite of all the turmoil in their lives—Bachmann had left Austria for good and moved to Italy with the composer Hans Werner Henze; Celan's first son died one day after his birth—there are only five letters between 1953 and 1957, most of them brief, almost impersonal. However, just as it appeared that both protagonists had resigned themselves to lives without the other, their love affair was rekindled with even greater intensity when they met at a literary conference in Germany.

During the relatively brief time of their renewed passion for each other—as is clear from her letters, Lestrange was informed of the affair and, perhaps wisely, chose to let it run its course and even met Bachmann during that time—it is Celan who seems transformed from his former cautious and self-centered attitude. He sent Bachmann a number of poems, took interest in and praised her work, made every effort to be with her as much as he could, and seemed completely smitten. His letters outnumber hers greatly from 1957 to 1958 and continue for almost year, even after Bachmann had told him that she had decided to move in with the famous Swiss playwright Max Frisch, with whom she lived from 1958 to 1962. The correspondence does not make clear why this renewed love affair lasted only until the summer of 1958, although there are several references by Celan to "Troubled, eerie times." It is unlikely that, as the editors assert, this was merely a reference to the strained political situation in both Germany and France at the time, although both Celan and Bachmann were concerned with the stationing of nuclear weapons in Germany under the North Atlantic Treaty Organization auspices. There are more frequent references to telephone conversations between the two—both trusted the spoken word more than the written one—and some cryptic references in the correspondence may refer to things said on the phone, but it is also evident that Celan was becoming more and more troubled about what he perceived, mostly correctly, as anti-Semitic attacks on him and other Jewish artists and intellectuals.

The first incident that pushed Celan toward his eventual nervous breakdown and suicide was a review of his collection *Sprachgitter* (1959; *Speech-Grille*, 1971), which Celan viewed rightly as anti-Semitic and which led to a rather heated exchange of letters with Frisch, who appeared to suggest that Celan was using his tragic experiences with concentration and labor camps as a ploy to attract attention and sympathy. What Frisch did suggest was that an artist should be able to simply ignore such vile attacks, a stance Celan found contemptible and dangerous. Bachmann was put into the unenviable position of having to choose to support either the man she still loved or the man with whom she was living. Her unwillingness to show more than what he considered token support led to some angry and hurtful letters by Celan and Bachmann's exhausted response on February 19, 1960, indicating that she could no longer bear the strain of this "conflict of interest."

Worse was to come. In May of 1960, an article by Claire Goll, the widow of the poet Yvan Goll, renewed her accusations, first vented in 1953, that Celan had plagiarized from the work of her husband. These renewed accusations were published to coincide with the awarding of the prestigious Georg Büchner Prize to Celan and set off an extensive press campaign, in which many journalists took the side of Goll without considering the evidence. Indeed, it has since been shown that Goll herself had plagiarized from Celan's translations of her dead husband's work. Celan saw this accusation and the support it received by many in the German press as further evidence of rampant anti-Semitism, although many friends and fellow poets rushed to his defense, heroically mustered by Bachmann, whose own relationship and health was beginning to crack under the strain of her efforts, which eventually also led to her breaking up with Frisch. When the Goll affair had substantially subsided by 1961, it had taken its toll on both Bachmann and Celan. Increasingly paranoid, Celan twice attempted to kill Lestrange and himself and spent considerable time in mental hospitals between 1962 and 1969, before committing suicide in April of 1970.

Bachmann's last letter to Celan, on December 5, 1961, already indicates her own increasingly depressive state and mentions her inability to write letters but still has kind, encouraging words for the man who was the love of her life. As Frisch had done in much coarser form, she gently tells Celan that he should realize how much control he does in fact have over his own life and that he should get better once he assumes this control. Except for some short letters in which Celan begs her in vain to write him a few lines, a thirteen-year tempestuous relationship, mainly conducted by correspondence, came to an unhappy end.

The brief correspondences between Celan and Frisch and between Celan and Lestrange give the reader additional insight into this complex relationship. It must have been difficult for both Frisch and Lestrange to see that the partner they were living with was primarily committed to another person; their letters show remarkable forbearance and tact.

Correspondence: Ingeborg Bachmann and Paul Celan is a fascinating document of a relationship between two doomed geniuses who would not even let a strong attraction come between them and their poetic calling. Even American audiences, to whom neither protagonist is readily recognizable, can appreciate the unveiling of all-too-common postmodern relationship problems, including the man's failure to cope with the greater professional success of his beloved woman and the inability of these masters of language to give adequate expression to the powerful feelings that were locked up inside them.

Franz G. Blaha

Review Source

The Times Literary Supplement, nos. 5621/5622 (December 24, 2010): 35.

COUNTRY DRIVING
A Journey Through China from Farm to Factory

Author: Peter Hessler (1969-   )
Publisher: HarperCollins (New York). 438 pp. $27.99
Type of work: Travel, economics, sociology
Time: 2001-2009
Locale: China

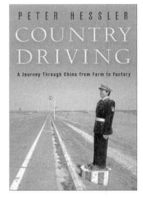

In part I, the author describes his drive following the Great Wall from east to west; part II examines life in Sancha, a small village north of Beijing; and part III looks at the rapidly changing industrial economy and society in Zhejiang Province

This is the third of a successful series of deceptively low-key and subtle studies of life in modern China, following *River Town* (2001) and *Oracle Bones* (2006). Hessler is equipped with a knowledge of the Chinese language and the skills of a sympathetic listener sufficient to win the confidence of a vast number of ordinary Chinese. He effectively sketches their personalities and current life situations in a way that gives a lot of insight into what life is like in a society that has experienced unprecedented rapid economic growth and change. The pace of change clearly leaves many Chinese bewildered and groping for criteria to guide their behavior and feelings.

Some time early in 1984 Chinese news media heralded the first example (since the 1950's) of an automobile being owned by a private individual. In 2009, more new cars were sold in China than in the United States. The twenty-first century has brought a highway boom imitating, in many respects, the creation of the American interstate system during the 1950's. Hessler brings this down to the personal level, describing his own experience getting a driver's license and quoting liberally from the more than six hundred sample questions given to examinees. For example:

352. If another motorist stops you to ask directions, you should
    a) not tell him
    b) reply patiently and accurately
    c) tell him the wrong way

Renting a car in harvest season, Hessler soon encounters the long-standing practice of spreading grain on the highway to let it be threshed by passing vehicles. Hessler ignores the rules against driving his rental car outside the Beijing area: "In China, much of life involves skirting regulations, and one of the basic truths is that forgiveness comes easier than permission." He recounts vividly the bad driving in a nation of rookie drivers. "It's hard to imagine another place where people take such joy in driving so badly." There's an entire language of horn blowing. Would-be Chinese drivers must undergo a relatively expensive fifty-eight-hour driving class, which Hessler describes in painful detail, including its lack of attention to seatbelts or turn signals.

Hessler touches base with the Great Wall at many points, noting the diversity of materials and the frequency with which bricks were removed to use in private construction. Most of the villages near the Great Wall have expe-

Peter Hessler's River Town *(2001) won the Kiriyama Book Prize. His* Oracle Bones *(2006) was a finalist for the National Book Award. He received the 2008 National Magazine Award for excellence in reporting.*

rienced rapid depopulation as young people have moved to the cities. At one village, officials praise an ambitious World Bank tree-planting project, but the villagers actually working on it note that, after they dig holes, no trees are planted and "local officials embezzle the money." Farther west, the author encounters the growing area of desertification, much of it accelerated by past, misguided efforts to irrigate and grow crops.

A constant theme is the widespread bewilderment in the face of rapid change. "The place changes too fast; nobody can afford to be overconfident in his knowledge, and there's always some new situation to figure out." In another passage he states, "Long-term planning made no sense: the goal was to gain some profit today before you found yourself overwhelmed by the next wave of change." Hessler found the remaining rural residents affable and hospitable: "It was standard for them to invite me in for tea or a meal." Hessler fears these qualities will not survive urbanization. At least his travels were facilitated by good cell-phone coverage and by the availability of filling stations, invariably staffed by female attendants. However, most Chinese are baffled by maps.

While book I is travelogue, without much commentary on individual Chinese people, book II is different. Hessler sought a quiet, peaceful place to live and work and rented a deserted dwelling in a tiny village named Sancha, along the Great Wall north of Beijing. Here the reader meets Wei Ziqi, the rent collector, and his family. Wei was highly literate and widely traveled. He had tried city life and a factory job and did not like either. He has hopes the village may develop tourist attractions. Hessler became close to Wei's five-year-old son, Wei Jia. The reader shares with them the traumas of Wei Jia's starting school—as the last child in Sancha he had little exposure to other children—and his hospital visit to test for possible leukemia. From that episode the reader learns that Chinese hospitals are often inhospitable to people from the countryside and that middle-aged authorities often lack flexibility and pragmatism, a remnant of the Cultural Revolution. Hessler's extensive contacts with medical personnel in China and in the United States help him through an emotional confrontation with an obstinate female doctor. After a transfusion, Wei Jia regains his health, but slowly. Hessler finds his assistance in the crisis has enhanced his status in the eyes of the villagers and Wei Ziqi's family.

Wei Ziqi opens a restaurant and guesthouse and begins to take advantage of the highway improvements and expanded auto use. The family prospers, but at the cost of great increase in psychological stress. Both Wei Ziqi and his wife had joined the Falun Gong when it was gaining popularity in 1999, primarily as a sensible routine of exercise and meditation. The central government's paranoia soon targeted the group, and intense persecution followed. Participants in Sancha quickly withdrew. Wei Ziqi's wife next finds solace in Buddhism, inspired by some tourist visitors. By 2004, Wei Ziqi has the highest income in the village and celebrates by remodeling his home, joining the Communist Party, and successfully obtaining a driver's license. Party membership will help with business, where connections (*guanxi*) are crucial.

After an inauspicious beginning, Wei Jia emerges from first grade as an excellent student. Hessler praises the emotional dedication of the teachers and the universal support given by parents to schooling. Nonetheless, he is appalled by what Wei Jia studies: "the most incredible collection of unrelated factors and desystematized knowledge that had been ever been crammed into a child with a lung capacity of 1,400 milliliters."

As the family prospers, their health deteriorates, a response to poor eating habits and too much television watching. Wei Ziqi smokes and drinks more than he had before. Hessler fears that many Chinese "grasp instinctively at the worst of both worlds: the worst modern habits, the worst traditional beliefs." More fundamentally, "many people were searching; they longed for some kind of religious or philosophical truth, and they wanted a meaningful connection with others." Marital problems are widespread. Surprisingly, Hessler scarcely mentions the rapid spread of Christianity in response to these needs. Self-help literature abounds, often suggesting gamesmanship. Hessler encounters a lot of "white lies" involved in worker-employer negotiations.

In 2007, Wei Ziqi agrees to stand for party secretary against the incumbent, who is suspected of financial misconduct. There is no overt campaign, no debates, no issues. However, the higher authorities disapprove, and he is defeated—with some relief. Hessler accompanies him on efforts to buy a car, visiting the Beijing Old Car Transaction Market, which may offer as many as twenty-thousand vehicles. In general, secondhand markets are relatively new in China, and this is notably true for automobiles: "[N]obody in the market had the faintest idea what he was doing."

Book III changes pace abruptly again. The locale shifts to southern Zhejiang Province, a three-hour drive south of Shanghai and site of furious industrial development. Hessler is looking for insights about what life is like for the pioneering factory owners and workers. He discovers a world of one-product communities—270 manufacturers of playground equipment in the town of Xiaxie, for example. The region is anchored by the city of Wenzhou, famous for entrepreneurship, almost all private. The business model involves low investment, low-quality products, and low profit margins. Most workers have migrated from rural households. Wenzhou produces 70 percent of the world's cigarette lighters. It also produces a lot of plastic leather, a nasty polluter.

Hessler settles on the newly developing town of Lishui and follows the development of a new factory producing the tiny rings that adjust the straps on brassieres. He watches Boss Gao and his uncle, Boss Wang, design a 21,000-square-foot factory layout in about one hour. On Hessler's return after three months, the managers are struggling to adjust "the Machine," for which they have paid $65,000. It is computer controlled, coating a steel ring with nylon.

The labor market swarms with newcomers. Both employers and workers are inexperienced with this kind of job market. There is rampant discrimination—looks matter, some points of origin provoke negative reactions, and women are paid less than men. Lishui has a statutory minimum wage (about forty U.S. cents per hour), and fortunate workers can earn $120 a month—"excellent money for an uneducated migrant." After watching the interviewing process, Hessler is persuaded that, among job candidates, strong personalities matter and persistence pays. A fifteen-year-old girl, Tao Yufeng, bluffs her way on to the payroll, misrepresenting her age and experience, then shoehorns her older sister in as well. Their parents have also moved to town from a rural background; they operate a small shop, and the mother does clothing alterations.

Once "the Machine" is operational, the firm quickly acquires a pretentious name, a Web site, and a logo. They seek customers, a process which requires gifts and banquets. Officials must be cultivated the same way, otherwise the firm will encounter obstacles. Boss Wang is quick to agree to employ an accountant recommended by a tax official.

Hessler reflects on differences between the modern Chinese boomtown settlement patterns and those in the nineteenth century United States. The Chinese developments are all business, while in the United States, there was usually a newspaper, churches, lawyers, and a courthouse in each town. Government in China appears mainly to seek shakedowns. However, private schools and tutorials abound, especially those helping workers to upgrade their skills. In the United States, scarcity of labor stimulated technological innovation and high capital intensity. China's abundance of labor inhibits such developments.

Hessler studies the Tankeng Dam, designed to provide hydroelectric power for the rapidly expanding industrial region. He watches the dismantling of the town of Beishan, scheduled for inundation. He tracks some of the displaced residents, finding their relocation communities extremely depressing. He wryly commends the government for creating a host of little rules for compensation, which serve to distract people from the real injustices: lack of public meetings, prohibitions against journalistic coverage, and the absence of property rights.

As the book winds up, Boss Gao and Boss Wang decide to move their operation to another city with a lower rent. They keep the plan a secret until the last minute, at which point most of the workers quit. Heavy negotiations with Mr. Tao and his daughters ultimately break down. The parents decide not to move, but the daughters are willing to go to the new location. However, they soon return, find different jobs, and plan optimistically to set up their own retail business.

Hessler does not try to present a general view of the Chinese economy. If there is a general move toward high-tech products and processes, he does not show it. The only technically sophisticated person is Luo Shouyun, who is basically self-taught. His opportunistic job changes move him up the income scale rapidly, if not always consistently. What is impressive is the extent of entrepreneurship. However, in the end, this is a book about people, not impersonal trends. Hessler clearly cares about the people, and the reader is likely to end up feeling the same way, wondering how all the characters have made out since the book ended.

Paul B. Trescott

Review Sources

Booklist 106, no. 7 (December 1, 2009): 8.
China Economic Review 21, no. 6 (June, 2010): 43.
The Economist 394, no. 8671 (February 27, 2010): 88.
Kirkus Reviews 77, no. 24 (December 15, 2009): 1270.
Library Journal 134, no. 19 (November 15, 2009): 76.
The New York Times Book Review, February 18, 2010, p. 6.
Publishers Weekly 256, no. 42 (October 10, 2009): 44.
The Times Literary Supplement, no. 5589 (May 14, 2010): 30.

CREATE DANGEROUSLY
The Immigrant Artist at Work

Author: Edwidge Danticat (1969-   )
Publisher: Princeton University Press (Princeton, N.J.).
    189 pp. $19.95
Type of work: Essays

This book is a medley of interlocking essays by an out-spoken Haitian American on the woes besetting her native land and on her own ambiguous status writing between two cultures

Even before the catastrophic 7.0-magnitude earthquake that struck the country on January 12, 2010, leaving more than 230,000 dead and obliterating its infrastructure, Haiti, the poorest country in the Western Hemisphere, had long been beset by oppression, corruption, storms, and diseases. Since attaining its independence in 1804 after a successful slave rebellion against France, Haiti has been what, in Creole, Edwidge Danticat, the author of *Create Dangerously*, calls "*tè glise*, slippery ground.*" Pointing to the political and meteorological upheavals that have rendered life in her hurricane-prone native land so precarious, she explains that: "Even under the best of circumstances, the country can be stable one moment and crumbling the next."

The most prominent Haitian living in the United States, Danticat speaks out frequently and forcefully on behalf of the luckless island that she left behind in 1969, when she was twelve years old. Her parents had immigrated to the United States ten years before, leaving her in the custody of her aunt and uncle. Beginning with her first book, the novel *Breath, Eyes, Memory* (1994), Haitian culture and identity have been a central preoccupation of Danticat's fiction. In her 2007 memoir, *Brother, I'm Dying*, she recounts the death of Joseph, the uncle who raised her, while he was detained by immigration officials in Miami after fleeing for his life from Haiti. *Create Dangerously*, which is based in part on the Toni Morrison Lectures that Danticat delivered at Princeton University in 2008, reflects on life and death in Haiti and on the ambiguous position of a writer who attempts to serve as a bridge between her native and adopted lands. A translingual person who comes to English as her third language, Danticat, "writing in this language that is not mine," nevertheless shapes her thoughts in a graceful, engaging style. Her book is less a coherent argument than a series of loosely connected, but vivid, incidents and reflections.

Danticat announces her artistic credo in her title: *Create Dangerously*. It is an injunction she acknowledges borrowing from Albert Camus, whose play *Caligula* (wr. 1938-1939, pb. 1944, pr. 1945; English translation, 1948) she notes, was performed in Haiti clandestinely, as an act of defiance against the brutal dictatorship of François

Edwidge Danticat is the author of the novels Breath, Eyes, Memory *(1994) and* The Farming of Bones *(1998); the story collections* Krik? Krak! *(1995) and* The Dew Breaker *(2004); and the family memoir* Brother, I'm Dying *(2007).*

"Papa Doc" Duvalier. "Create dangerously," Danticat urges herself and others, "for people who read dangerously. This is what I've always thought it meant to be a writer. Writing, knowing in part that no matter how trivial your words may seem, someday, somewhere, someone may risk his or her life to read them." For Danticat, as for Camus, who defied the Nazi occupation of France by editing an underground newspaper, creating dangerously "is creating as a revolt against silence, creating when both the creation and the reception, the writing and the reading, are dangerous undertakings, disobedience to a directive." In the United States, which enjoys constitutional safeguards for freedom of expression, writing does not usually entail a mortal risk, but Danticat pays tribute to Haitian writers and artists who put their lives in jeopardy in order to bear witness to injustice. She salutes Daniel Morel, a courageous photojournalist who became the target of assassination attempts because he showed the world images of Haiti's harsh realities. Conversations with Morel persuade Danticat that "to create dangerously is also to create fearlessly, boldly embracing the public and private terrors that would silence us, then bravely moving forward even when it feels as though we are chasing or being chased by ghosts." Morel dared to photograph the bodies of Marcel Numa and Louis Drouin, two gifted young men who gave up comfortable lives in the United States to try to liberate Haiti. They were put to death by firing squad because of their opposition to the Duvalier regime. *Create Dangerously* begins with an account of their public execution on November 12, 1964, and it uses that gruesome scene as a touchstone for much of Danticat's insistence on the urgency of art and on the obligations of Haitian expatriates.

Despite its subtitle, *The Immigrant Artist at Work*, the book is not a generic study of creativity in exile nor does it provide an historic overview of the phenomenon. Instead, Danticat's focus is personal, her method anecdotal. While she does discuss the experiences of other displaced Haitians such as the writers Jacques Stephen Alexis, Louis-Philippe Dalembert, Dany Laferrière, and Marie Vieux-Chauvet; the radio commentator Jean Dominique; and Morel, Danticat mentions only in passing immigrant artists from other times and other places such as Frantz Fanon, Wole Soyinka, and Isabel Allende. The book is an expression of its author's privileged, unstable, and awkward position within what, using the Creole term, she calls the Haitian *dyaspora*.

One of Danticat's cousins, whom in this book she calls Marius, was living in exile in Miami when he died of AIDS. She recounts how Marius's mother, whom she calls Tante Zi, implores her to arrange for the return of his body for burial in Port-au-

Prince. Because Marius entered the United States surreptitiously by boat and never obtained legal papers, Danticat struggles against bureaucratic obstacles to his posthumous repatriation to Haiti. However, she eventually succeeds in fulfilling her grieving aunt's request to have her dead son sent back home. However, when Danticat arrives in Haiti, Tante Zi is suspicious of her literary niece. "People talk," says the aunt. "They say that everything they say to you ends up written down somewhere." Danticat is troubled by the accusation she faces repeatedly: "You are a parasite and you exploit your culture for money and what passes for fame." However, as she admits to her aunt: "the immigrant artist, like all other artists, is a leech, and I needed to latch on. . . . I wanted to ask her forgiveness for the essay that in my mind I was already writing." Without abandoning her essay or even apologizing for planning it, she does promise Tante Zi that she will disguise her name and Marius's name when she writes about them. However, Danticat also recounts an arduous trek into the mountains in 1999 to see her seventy-five-year-old Tante Ilyana, who, though illiterate, beams with pride in the knowledge that her visitor is a writer.

There is an element of the vampire in all writers, who obtain sustenance for their art from the human lives they encounter, but Danticat suggests that artists who relocate abroad are particularly vulnerable to the charge of being foreign expropriators of native lives. They are gifted with a valuable double consciousness; Danticat can bring to her writing the perspective of a Haitian who spent her first dozen years under the ruthless tyranny of the Duvaliers, but she also sees through the eyes of the American she has been for most of her life. When Hurricane Katrina wreaks havoc on the American Gulf coast, she is able to observe that, like Haiti, even the United States is not immune to humanitarian and ecological disaster. However, immigrant artists also suffer the alienation of dislocation. Divided loyalties can make them question any loyalty. Danticat seems to express some of her own anxieties of identity when she quotes an immigrant photographer: "I have no country now," states Jean Daniel, trying to eke out a living after moving to the United States. "I can't live in Haiti and I can't live in the U.S. In Haiti they called me *jounalis la, atis la*, the journalist, the artist. . . . Here, I feel like I have little value."

Create Dangerously provides valuable witness to the rich culture and dreadful tribulations of its author's native land. Long before its misery in the aftermath of the devastating 2010 earthquake, Haiti was burdened with onerous debts as the immediate price for independence from France. It has endured vicious dictatorships, violent coups, exploitation by foreign corporations, and a nineteen-year military occupation by the United States. Danticat describes her return to Haiti for the burial of her beloved, vibrant cousin Maxo, a victim of the 2010 earthquake. She also recalls the funeral in 2000 of Dominique, who was assassinated in the parking lot of the radio station from which he broadcast his provocative views. However, the most heartrending section of the book, chapter 5, is devoted to an account of her encounter with Alèrte Bélance, a Haitian refugee in her late twenties living in New Jersey with her husband and three young children. In 1991, paramilitary men working for the latest junta abducted, slashed, and dismembered Bélance, a supporter of the ousted President Jean-

Bertrand Aristide. Left for dead, she survived to describe her ordeal, how they sliced her up with machete strokes, cutting out her tongue, slashing through an eye and ear and severing her right arm. "She looked like chopped meat," her young son explains. Nonetheless, Bélance is undaunted. Pregnant again, she declares: "They tried to take my life away, but not only couldn't they do that, I'm producing more life."

While pained and appalled by her condition, Danticat clearly admires Bélance's tenacity and defiance, finding in it a model for the immigrant artist who, spanning two worlds but at home in neither, is particularly well positioned to speak truth to both her nation of origin and her nation of residence. Danticat recalls a childhood in which she became enamored of literature despite and because of the fact that, in a repressive society, just to open a book was to read dangerously. She also notes that, for all the myriad misfortunes that Haiti has undergone in more than two centuries, the 2010 earthquake created a dividing point from which there is no turning back. Going forward, she states: "Perhaps we will write with the same sense of fearlessness or hope. Perhaps we will continue to create as dangerously as possible, but our muse has been irreparably altered. Our people, both inside and outside of Haiti, have changed. In ways that I am not yet fully capable of describing, we artists too have changed."

Create Dangerously comes as the partial, provisional testimony of a forty-one-year-old immigrant artist who presumably still has many more productive years ahead. In forthcoming fictions, it will be fascinating to observe the ways in which her artistry changes. In the final paragraphs of this book, Danticat describes her return to Miami after visiting Haiti immediately after the earthquake. After producing her American passport, she boards a plane at the Port-au-Prince airport named for Toussaint-L'Ouverture, the leader of the Haitian rebellion against France. When the flight attendant proclaims: "God bless America," Danticat cries out: "God bless, Haiti, too." As the plane gains altitude, she bids farewell to Haiti, but qualifies her valediction with the final words of the book: "At least for now." She is still a work in progress.

Steven G. Kellman

Review Sources

The Guardian, November 6, 2010, p. 8.
Library Journal 135, no. 17 (October 15, 2010): 76.
Miami Herald, October 24, 2010, p. M6.
New Statesman 139, no. 5022 (October 11, 2010): 56.
The New York Times Book Review, October 10, 2010, p. 14.
Publishers Weekly 257, no. 34 (August 30, 2010): 42-43.
Santa Fe New Mexican, September 17, 2010, p. PA16.

THE CROSS OF REDEMPTION
Uncollected Writings

Author: James Baldwin (1924-1987)
Edited by Randall Kenan, with notes and an introduction
Publisher: Pantheon Books (New York). 304 pp. $26.95
Type of work: Essays, literary criticism, philosophy
Time: 1947-1987
Locale: United States

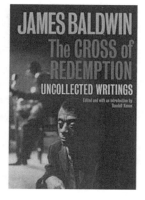

A collection of essays, reviews, interviews, and speeches by James Baldwin, including early essays from the 1940's and later writings through the 1980's, with emphasis on Baldwin's works of explicit social criticism

James Baldwin is not usually cited in first breath as a philosopher, but what stands out in sharpest relief in *The Cross of Redemption* is his intricate grappling with deeply philosophical questions. Taken as an anthology, the book offers readers a chance to see how Baldwin developed over many decades his profound social critique of American and Western culture and how he honed that critique within multiple literary genres. The works include writings from the late 1940's through subsequent decades up until Baldwin's death in 1987.

The Cross of Redemption has reopened older critical debates about whether or not Baldwin's trajectory as an artist, intellectual, and citizen was toward "bitterness" or cynicism about the U.S. capacity to transcend the tragedies of its history. This collection offers fuel for several sides in those continued debates. Even more striking in this particular set of writings is Baldwin's philosophical preoccupation with consciousness, identity, "how and what we know," and his persistent probing after some essential quality of human "being" that is discoverable, or recoverable, from what he often portrays as the rubble of historical experience.

Baldwin never backed away from specific historical critiques of American racism, of the delusions of white supremacy, of the traps of American consumerist culture, of the moral tragedies in international politics, or of the perils of compromised art. However, within these particular critiques, and via the repeated deployment of political and philosophical metaphors, Baldwin emerges in *The Cross of Redemption* as a literary philosopher with a steady eye aimed toward revealing the heart of a more universalized human experience.

Randall Kenan's introduction to Baldwin's work provides an important opening frame for *The Cross of Redemption* and merits attention in its own terms. Kenan is probably best known for his 1989 novel *A Visitation of Spirits* and his later nonfiction exploration of African American experience published in *Walking on Water: Black American Lives at the Turn of the Twenty-first Century* (1999). Kenan has also pub-

James Baldwin was an internationally famous author and activist. His novels include Go Tell It on the Mountain *(1953),* Giovanni's Room *(1956),* Another Country *(1962), and* If Beale Street Could Talk *(1974).*

lished a young-adult biography on Baldwin (*James Baldwin: American Writer*, 1993) in a series called Lives of Notable Gay Men and Lesbians, edited by Martin Duberman, noted scholar of gay American history. Kenan has also written his own memoir with a title clearly echoing Baldwin: *The Fire This Time* (2007).

As he introduces the essays in *The Cross of Redemption*, volume, Kenan offers a brief biography of Baldwin as a literary artist. However, he also calls readers to break away from habitual expectations about Baldwin's writing:

It is easy to say that Baldwin's main message was racial equality. Surely the topic flows through its work more than it ebbs. Yet one makes a grave mistake in pigeonholing James Baldwin's worldview so narrowly, for throughout this miscellany, though racial topics and racial politics are often the touchstone, his true themes are more in line with the early church fathers, with [Desiderius] Erasmus of Rotterdam, with the great Western philosophers, with theologians such as Reinhold Niebuhr and Dietrich Bonhoeffer and James H. Cone. And though it is too broad—if not useless—to say his true topic is humanity, it is useful to see how, no matter his topic, how often his writing finds some ur-morality upon which to rest, how he always sees matters through a lens of decency, how he writes with his heart as well as his head. Baldwin left the pulpit at sixteen, but he never stopped preaching.

The Cross of Redemption offers solid evidence to support Kenan's claim, especially as he links Baldwin to humanist and political theologians such as Niebuhr and Bonhoeffer and as he invokes Cone, a key figure in the black theology movement, who like Baldwin often uses racial categories and theological language as philosophical and political metaphor.

Kenan may have more argument from readers who take Baldwin at his word when he talks in more universal terms about his central focus on "humanity." In the essay "Anti-Semitism and Black Power," for example, Baldwin says: "If one accepts my basic presumption, which is that all men are brothers—simply because all men share the same condition, however different the details of their lives may be—then it is perfectly possible, it seems to me, that in re-creating ourselves, in saving ourselves, we can re-create and save many others: whosoever will." Other interpreters of Baldwin, such as Richard H. King, in *Race, Culture, and the Intellectuals, 1940-1970* (2004), place Baldwin's work among mid-twentieth century transatlantic philosophical preoccupations with "human nature" (vs. "race" or "nation"). King sees Baldwin's work as part of an international turn toward inclusive humanism in the wake of the catastrophes of World War II. That debate aside, Kenan, in his introduction and by his choice of pieces to include in this confronts successfully the persisting tendency to typecast Baldwin solely as an "American commentator on race." This kind of reductive pigeonholing drove Baldwin to France in his early years as a writer and has continued to hinder recognition of Baldwin's international importance in the history of Western intellectual life.

Especially illuminative of Baldwin's place in broader intellectual crosscurrents are the essays "Mass Culture and the Creative Artist," "From *Nationalism, Colonialism, and the United States: One Minute to Twelve—A Forum*," "We Can Change the Country," "The Uses of the Blues," "What Price Freedom," and "Lorraine Hansberry at the Summit." As is the case for all of the works included in *The Cross of Redemption*, these pieces use a specific occasion as the stage to unfold Baldwin's theories of art, his political philosophy, and his construction of the necessary conditions for actual citizenship, for moral action, and for human freedom.

"Lorraine Hansberry at the Summit" is a remarkable short piece first published retrospectively in 1979, in which Baldwin re-creates a famous 1963 meeting among himself, then U.S. attorney general Robert F. Kennedy, and several other American cultural and political leaders who were working in the Civil Rights movement. He reconstructs the scene with the literary artistry familiar to readers of his fiction. The essay serves as not only a social portrait of moral failure in American government and society but also as a profound portrait of the existential cost of that failure to individual human beings. In one scene, using dialogue and sharp characterization, Baldwin describes how Hansberry, a playwright by then internationally famous as author of *A Raisin in the Sun* (1959), tries to persuade Kennedy to take concrete action and intervene directly in the struggle to break apart Jim Crow segregation:

> We wanted him to tell his brother the President to personally escort to school, on the following day or the day after, a small black girl already scheduled to enter a Deep South school. "That way," we said, "it will be clear that whoever spits on that child will be spitting on the nation." He did not understand this, either. "It would be," he said, "a meaningless moral gesture." "We would like," said Lorraine, "from you, a moral commitment."

As the failed meeting breaks up, Hansberry's gives her last words to Kennedy: "But I am very worried," she said, "about the state of the civilization which produced that photograph of the white cop standing on that Negro woman's neck in Birmingham." Baldwin continues:

> Then, she smiled. And I am glad she was not smiling at me. She extended her hand. "Goodbye, Mr. Attorney General," she said, and turned and walked out of the room.
> We followed her. Perhaps I can dare to say that we were all, in our various ways, devastated, but I will have to leave it at that.

As Baldwin drives away with others:

We passed Lorraine, who did not see us. She was walking toward Fifth Avenue—her face twisted, her hands clasped before her belly, eyes darker than any eyes I have ever seen before—walking in an absolutely private place.
I knew I could not call her.
Our car drove on; we passed her.
And then, we heard the thunder.

This short piece is startling in its condensed apocalyptic intensity and the depth of Baldwin's social analysis, his political indictment of white liberalism (another key theme in the collection), and his portrait of ineffable rage and loss. Readers of the piece in 1979 knew that Hansberry died soon after this meeting. The physical foreshadowing of her death here sharpens Baldwin's portrait of moral collapse on a broader scale.

Another example of philosophical texture in these pieces is Baldwin's repeated use of the auction block as a metaphor for not only African American experience under slavery but also black consciousness and "American" social psyche. The title essay of the book, "Of the Sorrow Songs: The Cross of Redemption," quite explicitly calls into mind W. E. B. Du Bois's *The Souls of Black Folk: Essays and Sketches* (1903) and philosophical double-consciousness. The essay originally appeared in 1979 as a book review criticizing a book on jazz, and Kenan's short note introducing the piece calls it a "meditation and manifesto about race and music." It is also a meditation on language and experience. The auction block becomes the central metaphor of this piece, invoking African American historical consciousness; the United States as a site of political, economic, and moral failure; and the European slave trade and colonialism as symbols for humanity's capacity for violence. In a 1982 review of Roger Wilkins's *A Man's Life: An Autobiography* (1982), Baldwin extends the metaphor: "I have earned the right, from the moment of my own stupendous performance on the auction block, to tell you that this Republic is a total liar and has never contained the remotest possibility, let alone desire, to let my people go."

Some minor troubles emerge from the structure of *The Cross of Redemption*. Since the selections are clustered according to genre, they can seem repetitive if the book is read front to back. Baldwin is often, for example, responding in a particular essay or speech to a request to address broad topics like "the social role of the artist." When read in sequence, Baldwin's voice appears overly repetitive, when in fact the repetition is the result of the clustering of selections. Also, readers less familiar with Baldwin's writing in the context of his times, especially during the height of the black Civil Rights movement during the later 1950's through the 1970's, may fail to register some of the conceptual nuance and detail in the individual selections. However, Baldwin is always opening broader conceptual vistas by his engagement with particular historical moments or texts, and *The Cross of Redemption* includes many moments that can resonate profoundly across a wide swath of time. Kenan is clearly attentive to Baldwin's philosophical technique of using historical "particulars" to grapple with "timeless" human questions.

Kenan uses the same technique when he places the publication of *The Cross of Re-*

demption within the historical context of the 2008 election of Barack Obama as the first African American president. Kenan tells the reader that students have asked him:

> "What . . . would James Baldwin think of Barack Obama?"
> Now I can tell them I think I know. In a 1961 speech for the Liberation Committee for Africa, Baldwin wrote: "Bobby Kennedy recently made me the soul-stirring promise that one day—thirty years if I'm lucky—I can be President too. It never entered this boy's mind, I suppose—it has not entered the country's mind yet—that perhaps I wouldn't want to be. And in any case, what really exercises my mind is not this hypothetical day on which some other Negro 'first' will become the first Negro President. What I am really curious about is just what kind of country he'll be President of."

Sharon Carson

Review Sources

American Scholar 79, no. 4 (Autumn, 2010): 113-114.
Booklist 106, no. 22 (August 1, 2010): 17.
Kirkus Reviews 78, no. 11 (June 1, 2010): 499-500.
Library Journal 135, no. 13 (August 1, 2010): 81.
The New York Review of Books 57, no. 18 (November 25, 2010): 49-51.
The New York Times Book Review, September 12, 2010, p. 14.
Newsweek 156, no. 7 (August 16, 2010): 46-47.
Publishers Weekly 257, no. 22 (May 31, 2010): 39.

CROSSING MANDELBAUM GATE
Coming of Age Between the Arabs and Israelis, 1956-1978

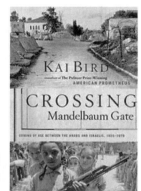

Author: Kai Bird (1951-   )
Publisher: Charles Scribner's Sons (New York). Illustrated. 424 pp. $30.00
Type of work: History, current affairs, autobiography
Time: 1938-1978
Locale: Arab East Jerusalem; Cairo, Egypt; Saudi Arabia; Beirut, Lebanon; India; Carleton College, Northfield, Minnesota; Austria; Yugoslavia; and Rome and Ferramonti, Italy

Bird's book presents itself as a combined memoir and history of the Middle East, but it is much more history than memoir, presenting a pro-Palestinian view of the Arab-Israeli conflict and also including a section on how his Jewish in-laws survived the Holocaust

Principal personages:
KAI BIRD, the author
EUGENE BIRD, his father and American diplomat
JERINE BIRD, his mother
JOY RIGGS, his girlfriend
SUSAN GOLDMARK, his wife
VIKTOR (WILLY) GOLDMARK, his father-in-law
HELMA BLÜHWEIS, his mother-in-law
LEILA KHALED, a Palestinian terrorist
GAMAL ABDEL NASSER, the president of Egypt, 1956-1970

The dust jacket for Kai Bird's latest book, *Crossing Mandelbaum Gate*, says, misleadingly, that it is a memoir about his early years in Israel, Jordan, and several other Arab countries. In fact, the book is much less a memoir than a political history; more important, Bird never lived in Israel. He did live in Jordan and other Arab countries, including Egypt, Saudi Arabia, and Lebanon, but he only visited Israel. The result, perhaps predictably, is not the evenhanded examination of the Middle East crisis one might have expected, complete with insights that someone familiar with both sides might have, but a one-sided presentation of the Palestinian cause, leavened only slightly at the end by a sympathetic presentation of Jewish suffering during the Holocaust.

Bird had an unusual childhood. His father was an American diplomat stationed in the Middle East, and as a young boy, he lived hardly at all in the United States. Indeed, on the rare occasions when the family found itself in the United States, Bird felt like a foreigner. It must have been a dislocating life, and he says his book is meant

as an exploration of identity, his own and
the identities of others in the Middle Eastern
melting pot.

Kai Bird coauthored American
Prometheus *(2006), a biography of the
nuclear physicist J. Robert
Oppenheimer, which won a Pulitzer
Prize in 2006. He has also published
biographies of John J. McCloy and
McGeorge Bundy and his brother.*

If the book had really turned out to be that
way, it might have had a great deal of interest.
Instead, it is just another example of slanted
historical writing, perhaps because Bird made
the unfortunate decision that his own autobiography would be of little interest. In any
case, he may not really be ready to write an
autobiography, because he seems still caught up in the attitudes of his youth. Though
he at times criticizes his earlier self for excessive zeal and earnestness, his views seem
essentially the same as they were then. He has not moved beyond the radical pro-
Palestinian views he espoused then, and those who come to this book expecting a mature survey of both sides of the Middle Eastern conflict will be disappointed.

It should be noted at the outset that Bird is a fluent writer; the book is quite well
written. He is also able to create a persona for himself that is appealing. Here is an
easy-to-understand, likable writer inviting the reader to journey with him through the
Middle East. It is tempting to just tag along, and frustrating only to those who expect
the tour guide to be balanced. However, once it becomes clear that Bird is presenting
only one side of the story, there is still interest in the book as a presentation of someone committed to that one side who, apparently sincerely, thinks he is being evenhanded.

Bird begins with his life as a toddler in East Jerusalem in the mid-1950's, when the
city was still under Jordanian control. His father had been posted there as a vice consul in 1956 as his first assignment in the diplomatic service. At first, says Bird, his father and mother were neutral in the Arab-Israeli conflict, but as time went on they became more and more partisans of the Arab side, which was perhaps only natural since
they lived on the Arab side and were surrounded by its version of events. This also
seems to have rubbed off on young Bird, whose childhood version of cowboys and
Indians consisted of a game between good and bad soldiers, with the Israelis cast as
the bad guys.

Bird did get some experience of life on the Israeli side of Jerusalem. Every day he
would travel through the Mandelbaum Gate of the title, the boundary between the
Israeli west and the Arab east, to go to school. However, he says nothing about what
life was like in that school on the Israeli side. That is one of the big holes in the book.
The other hole is the total avoidance of the first Arab-Israeli War, the 1948 conflict
known in Israel as the War of Independence and among the Arabs as *al-Nakba* ("the
disaster").

Bird writes at length about the Suez Crisis of 1956, detailing Israeli complicity in
the Anglo-French attack on Egypt; and he writes at even greater length about the 1967
Six-Day War, which he blames on Israel. He even looks back to Arab-Israeli conflicts
before 1948. However, he says nothing about the 1948 war itself, in which several

Arab countries invaded the territory the United Nations had awarded to Israel, perhaps because there is no way to cast Israel as the aggressor in that case.

In general, whenever it is possible to point to Israeli wrongdoing, Bird does so. If he even mentions Arab wrongdoing, it is generally excused, explained away as the unfortunate result of something done by Israel or the United States. It is true that he also tries to explain what Israel does, but there is a subtle difference in these sets of explanations. With the Arabs, Bird seems indulgent, seeking to excuse. With the Israelis, the attempt is not to lessen the evil, but to analyze why it is there. Israeli actions tend to be pathologized in this book, made to seem like the distorted product of trauma, primarily the trauma of the Holocaust.

Indeed, the whole section at the end of the book, sympathetic as it is to Jewish victims of the Nazis, seems to be there mainly to explain why Israel is so oppressive. At one point late in his book Bird recounts how he walked out in disgust when an Arab leader tried to claim that the Arabs were suffering a Holocaust at the hands of the Israelis. There is no equivalence, Bird says; Arabs were never put in death camps or anything similar. Nonetheless, Bird's entire approach tends to support the idea of equivalence: The Jews suffered in Germany, in turn they are causing the Palestinians to suffer in the Middle East.

Bird quotes one family friend in Jerusalem about Jewish actions after the Holocaust, "So why did they take Palestine? Honestly, why didn't they take it out on the Germans?" This is a fascinating slant on postwar history, making it sound like the creation of Israel was some sort of punishment inflicted by Jews in revenge for Nazi atrocities. It is interesting to realize that this is the viewpoint of some Arab and pro-Arab intellectuals. For them it is not that Israel might be responding to current attacks by the Arab states or Palestinian terrorists; Israeli violence is simply a misplaced response to the Nazi horror. Perhaps as a result, in the minds of these intellectuals, Israel should be pitied rather than condemned, but certainly not supported.

After his stay in Jerusalem, Bird moved to Saudi Arabia when his father was posted there. The result in this book is a long chapter on the history of Saudi Arabia, which gives some interesting insights into that country, though colored by criticism of American policies and actions there. For Bird, the United States is there simply for the oil, which sounds like an oversimplified view of the situation. Also, he sees American policy as slowing down democratic developments.

Throughout the book, Bird adopts the position of a liberal democrat opposed to Islamic fundamentalism (and to terrorism) and one hoping for modernization and liberalization of Arab regimes he sometimes describes as backward or dictatorial. His position in relation to Saudi Arabia and the Egypt of president Gamal Abdel Nasser tends to be one of a friendly critic, hopeful that conditions will improve in Saudi Arabia and ready to defend Nasser as a great leader even while conceding his antidemocratic flaws. It is the reverse of the attitude he adopts toward Israel, and it seems just a question of attitude; whereas Nasser is described here as "intelligent," the Israeli prime minister at the time was "cunning."

Bird provides some snippets of information about his life in Saudi Arabia and later in Egypt: his swimming and horseback riding, the family's excursions to the Red Sea and into the desert, sailing on the Nile, and enjoying Arab food. He enjoyed himself even though he knew he was an outsider, the American among Arabs. The experience seems to have given him an instinctive empathy for other outsiders, for example, for Jews living in the Diaspora as minority groups in Europe or North America. This is perhaps why he was drawn to his wife, the Jewish daughter of Holocaust survivors, whom he met at college in Minnesota. It is only Jews in Israel that fail to stimulate his empathy. About one of his trips to the Israeli part of Jerusalem he comments that the Jews he saw there seemed out of place. They did not belong in the Middle East; this was the Arabs' home, not theirs. This is odd in a way, for why not identify with outsiders in Palestine the way he does elsewhere? The difference perhaps is that Israelis are not really outsiders in a land controlled by others; they control a powerful state. It is authority figures and peoples with power with which Bird finds it difficult to identify.

Later in the book Bird describes his experiences in the antiwar movement at college in the late 1960's. He became a man of the left, a protester—though a nonviolent one—and a conscientious objector during the Vietnam War. He later went on to become a writer for the left-wing magazine *The Nation*. His views on Israel and the United States remain colored by this ideological stance; in fact, at one point he says he sees nothing he would change in articles on the Middle East that he wrote for the *Nation* almost thirty years previously.

The one Arab regime that Bird has little sympathy for is King Hussein ibn Talal's in Jordan at the time of the clash between the king and Palestinian guerrillas. Here again Bird's identification with those opposing authority emerges; he is clearly on the side of the Palestinians and against the Jordanian monarchy. He thinks the Middle East situation would have been much improved if the Palestinians had won and taken over a state for themselves. He also thinks they were deprived of victory by external forces, meaning the United States and Israel, though all those two countries did was warn Syria to withdraw after the latter had entered Jordan to help the Palestinians. From his own account, the only external forces actively involved were on the Palestinian side; however, once one is committed to a cause, as Bird is, it is sometimes hard to see what is really going on.

One of the oddest sections of the book is connected to the Palestinian-Jordanian conflict. That conflict included the "Black September" hijacking of several planes by Palestinian guerrillas, one of whom was Leila Khaled, who became something of a celebrity at the time. It turned out that Bird's girlfriend, Joy Riggs, was on one of the hijacked planes, but in his account of events it is Leila Khaled, not Joy Riggs, who is the center of attention. Bird quotes her extensively, makes her into something of a hero, and at the end expresses relief not that his girlfriend survived, but that Leila Khaled did. It is as if he puts romantic identification with political revolutionaries ahead of personal connections.

In the end, this is a fascinating book, but not in the way the author intended. It reveals a certain antiauthoritarian mind-set and an identification with the Palestinian cause. Those who want to know how the liberal-left supporters of the Palestinians think will learn much here, but those expecting insights into the reality of the Middle East will be disappointed.

Sheldon Goldfarb

Review Sources

American Scholar 79, no. 3 (Summer, 2010): 106-108.
The Atlantic Monthly 305, no. 3 (April, 2010): 88-92.
Booklist 106, no. 14 (March 15, 2010): 16.
Kirkus Reviews 78, no. 2 (January 15, 2010): 67.
The Nation 290, no. 21 (May 31, 2010): 31.
The New York Times Book Review, April 18, 2010, p. 20.
Publishers Weekly 257, no. 2 (January 11, 2010): 39.

THE CRUSADES
The Authoritative History of the War for the Holy Land

Author: Thomas Asbridge
Published in Great Britain as *The Crusades: The War for
  the Holy Land*
Publisher: Ecco Press (New York). 767 pp. $34.99
Type of work: History
Time: 1095-1291
Locale: Middle East (Levant or Outremer)

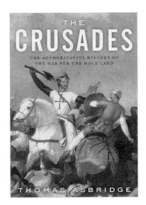

*This book provides an explanation of why and how a se-
ries of holy wars between Christians and Muslims over the
Holy Land came about, what they involved, and who really
won*

Principal personages:
> BAYBARS I (c. 1223-1277), the Mamluk sultan of Egypt (r. 1223-1277)
> CONRAD III (1093-1152), the first Hohenstaufen king of Germany
>   (r. 1138-1152)
> EUGENIUS III (unknown-1153), a Cistercian monk, pope of Rome (1145-
>   1153)
> GODFREY OF BOUILLON (c. 1060-1100), an advocate of the Holy
>   Sepulchre
> LOUIS VII (c. 1120-1180), the king of France (r. 1137-1180)
> IMAD AL-DIN ZANGI the governor of Mosul who gained control of
>   Aleppo (1127-1146)
> NUR AL-DIN MAHMUD, Zangi's youngest son and *atabeg* (governor) of
>   Mosul (1146-1174)
> RICHARD I (THE LIONHEART; 1157-1199), the king of England (r. 1189-
>   1199)
> SALADIN (SALAH AL-DIN, "goodness of faith"; 1138-1193), Ayyubid
>   ruler of Egypt and Syria (r. 1174-1193)
> 'UMAR I ('UMAR IBN KHAṬṬĀB) (c. 586-644; r. 634-644)
> URBAN II (c. 1042-1099), a former Cluniac monk and pope of Rome
>   (1095-1099)
> BALDWIN I (1058-1118; r. 1100-1118),
> BALDWIN II (unknown-1131; r. 1118-1131),
> BALDWIN III (r. 1143-1162),
> BALDWIN IV (1161-1185; r. 1174-1185), and
> BALDWIN V (1177-1186; r. 1185-1186), kings of Jerusalem

Written for general readers as well as for specialists, Thomas Asbridge's magiste-
rial tome, simply titled *The Crusades*, is an authoritative history of the crusades. It is
an evenhanded, fair, and full-blown analysis of their causes, character, and conse-

~

Thomas Asbridge began teaching medieval history at Queen Mary, University of London in 1999. He authored The First Crusade: A New History *(2004) and produced documentaries on the Crusades for BBC2 and the History Channel.*

~

quences. The story of this two-century-long violent interaction between the East and the West is terrifying and tortuous.

The book covers the history of the three principal crusades that were begun with a bang by the Western Franks, inspired by Pope Urban II in 1095, and ended with a whimper in 1291, following the fall of Acre to the Mamluks. The more than six-hundred-page long, absorbing historical narrative is flanked by an introduction that explains the importance of the idea of crusade as "sanctified violence" and a concluding chapter containing a penetrating analysis of the historical significance of this piece of history in the postmodern present.

From a metahistorical perspective, the twelfth and thirteenth century crusades were a continuation of the ongoing confrontation between the East and the West that included the Persian Wars (490-480 B.C.E.); the rivalry between the later Roman, or the Byzantine, Empire and the Iranian Sasanian Empire in the sixth century C.E.; and then, starting in the seventh century through the caliphal empire (700-950), the triumphal march of the Islamic world against the Christian West, a balance of power that held until the Franks launched Operation Cross in the late eleventh century to reclaim the Holy City of Jerusalem, which had been conquered by the second caliph, ʿUmar I (also known as ʿUmar ibn al-Khaṭṭāb), in 638.

The four-century-long Muslim occupation of the Holy City should not have been seen as Islamic aggression; nonetheless, in 1095, Pope Urban II called for a holy war for Palestine's liberation. Asbridge seeks to explain the causes of the First Crusade (1096-1099) as "one expression of a much wider drive to rejuvenate Christendom" after the reform movements of Pope Gregory VII. Urban's call for a holy war found a willing audience across Europe in the thrall of the church's teachings about the souls of sinful Christians in peril and in need of redemption. Of the two most common salvific remedies available—penance and pilgrimage—the latter was especially attractive to Western European knightly elites as a glorious occasion to fight for the liberation of Christendom's sanctum sanctorum.

The beginning of the First Crusade was marked by endemic disunity in the Muslim world. As a matter of fact, after the death of the founder of Islam, the Prophet Muhammad, in 632, Islam spread by conquest and missionary work from its headquarters at Mecca in modern-day Saudi Arabia under the relatively stable regimes of the first four *al-rashidun* or "rightly guided" caliphs or "representatives of God" (632-661). However, a significant split occurred within the Islamic world during the caliphate of ʿAlī ibn Abīṭalib (656-661), the last of the rightly guided caliphs and cousin of Muhammad (ʿAlī married Fāṭimah, Muhammad's daughter). He was assassinated by a secessionist group, the Khajirites, or the "renegades." ʿAlī's partisans came to be known as Shia.

From 661 to 750, a rival Arab clan, the Umayyads (led by Muʿāwiyah I), relocated

Muslim headquarters out of Arab borders to the Syrian metropolis of Damascus. The Umayyads and their followers became *ahl al-Sunnah*, the Sunnis, claiming to be the custodians of correct and orthodox faith and practice. Under the Umayyad caliphs the borders of the Islamic word extended to the Pyrenees in the west and the Indus River in the east.

In 750, another Arab clan, the Abbasids (begun by Abu al-Abbas Abdullah), took over the caliphate. The Abbasids were Sunnis, and they shifted the center of Sunni Islam to Baghdad, at that time a newly founded city in modern-day Iraq. Though the Shia and Sunni communities continued to live in the Middle East in relative peace for more than two centuries, in 969, a Shi'ite faction, the Fatimids (those who claimed themselves as Fāṭimah's direct descendants) set up their own caliphate not only rejecting the hegemony of the Abbasid caliph of Baghdad but also conquering a large chunk of territories on the eastern Mediterranean seaboard, including Jerusalem. "Thus," writes Asbridge, "by the time of the crusades, Islam was riven by an elemental schism—one that prevented the Muslim rulers of Egypt and Iraq from offering any form of coordinated or concerted resistance to Christian invasion."

However, the crusading zeal countered by the jihadist determination was marked by devastating sieges, and their ancillary bloodletting was motivated and legitimized by faith. For the Christians, the crusading exertions had salvific promise in contrast to the Islamic aim to fight the infidel and thus extend the ideal, pure Islam. The conflict between Christians and Muslims had been endemic, and, thus, the papal call for battle in 1095 gave no indication of a cosmic clash between two creeds or two civilizations.

The First Crusade registered a resounding victory for the Western Franks, and between 1098 and 1109 they carved out four Latin states on the eastern Mediterranean seaboard: Edessa, Antioch, Jerusalem, and Tripoli. The most important of them was the kingdom of Jerusalem, which was ruled by the crusading warlord Godfrey of Bouillon. These startling achievements of the West led to the formation of a new outpost of Europe in the Near East—the so-called crusader states in Outremer, meaning "lands overseas" in French. Chapters 4 and 5 of Asbridge's history provide a fascinating account of this "west" outside the West. His observation that the crusader states were neither shielded against the primarily Islamic world around them nor were they a multicultural utopia of tolerance, understanding, amity, and assimilation, makes his account readable as well as credible. It could be reasonable to suppose that life in Outremer revealed a state of nervous tension between a grudging but pragmatic acceptance of the infidel Franks—a sort of waiting game before the return of the rejuvenated and revanchist Hercules of the Fertile Crescent.

This savior turned out to be the charismatic *atabeg* (governor) of Mosul, Imad al-Din Zangi, who seized control of Aleppo, Syria. However, this Sunni superman was initially more concerned with annexing Syria to Baghdad than with fighting the Franks. Despite the urging of the imams (priests) of Aleppo looking up to him as a man of destiny and the new leader of the jihad, Zangi concentrated more on fighting with his Islamic foes. The only time he mounted an offensive against Outremer was in July, 1137, in his attack on Barin to the west of Hama and Orontes in Syria, but this was really for a southward expansion toward Damascus and not against the crusading states. In 1144, Zangi captured the Latin city of Edessa through a combination of diplomacy and daring. He did not, as was usual for his day, destroy the city and its population but installed a garrison to defend it.

The fall of Edessa alarmed Europe and thus sparked the Second Crusade (1147-1149). Emissaries from the Levant appealed to Pope Eugenius III; the Capetian king of France, Louis VII; and the Hohenstaufen king of Germany, Conrad III, who put together a massive force of some sixty thousand troops to defend the Outremer. Crusades were also being launched in Iberia and the Baltic. Even the pope felt the enormity of Christendom's task in 1147 in that "a multiple of the faithful from diverse regions is preparing to fight the infidel." However, the lack of cooperation from the Byzantine emperor, Manuel I Comnenus, compounded with lack of coordination between the French and German army, resulted in a lugubrious failure of the Western crusaders. Louis decided to sail to Antioch and Conrad sailed to Acre.

Following Zangi's murder by a slave in 1146, his son and successor, Nur al-Din, made a triumphal entry into Damascus in 1154. From Nur al-Din to the legendary Saladin, the Seljuk warrior, and his agonistic encounters with the absentee Angevin king of England, Richard the Lionheart, the Crusades displayed barbarous cruelty and gratuitous bloodletting pari passu valor, vainglory, and genuine virtue. However, the Third Crusade of the 1180's and 1190's, of which the Saladin-Richard encounter is the central theme, was a drab and disappointing stalemate.

The fourth crusade, called by Pope Innocent III in August, 1198, was the infamous intra-Christian violence that resulted in April, 1204, in the sack of Constantinople, the bastion of Byzantine culture and the Orthodox Church. The great city suffered as the result of a campaign to install a short-lived puppet regime intended to extend papal power over the eastern branches of Christendom. A Greek eyewitness account of the mayhem sharply contrasted the brutality of the westerners with the benevolence Saladin had accorded to the people of Jerusalem after its conquest in 1187. The Fifth Crusade (1217-1221), also preached by Innocent III, began with the siege of Damietta, foundered in the waters of the Nile Delta in August, 1221, leading to the crushing victory of the Mamluks of Egypt.

In a bid to unite Islam, Saladin had suppressed the brilliant civilization of the Shi'ite Fatimids and yet failed to complete the conquest of the Palestinian coastline. It was the achievement of the ruthless and fanatical Mamluk sultan of Egypt and Syria, Baybars, who resisted the Mongol invaders at Ain Jalut in 1260, and thereby created the conditions leading to the final expulsion of the Franks from the Holy Land in 1291. The fourteenth century marked the hegemony of the Mamluks in the Outremer.

Asbridge astutely emphasizes the equal importance of geopolitical imperatives and religious conviction in an understanding of this clash between the West and the East. The eastern coastline of the Mediterranean brought Western Christendom, eastern Christendom, and the successive waves of Near Eastern dynasties—Arabs, Seljuks, Ayyubids, Mamluks, and the Mongols—into a melee. For the Muslims their clash with Europeans was "wars of the Franks." These were defensive wars against aggression. These medieval events were reframed and rephrased as *al-hurb al-salabiyya* or "wars of the cross" in the course of the Arab nationalist struggles of the nineteenth century.

A sterling quality of Asbridge's study is its comprehensive but clear and mostly balanced treatment of a complex and controversial episode of history that continues to haunt international politics. However, its great merit notwithstanding, Asbridge's book breaks little new ground. Works of a number of scholars in the field, especially of Jonathan Riley-Smith, Jonathan Phillips, and Jill Claster, have argued over the causes and character of the Crusades, critiquing the influential but misleading "clash of civilization" thesis. Additionally, despite his conscious endeavor to remain neutral, Asbridge has, unwittingly, revealed his innate bias for Richard I, who emerges as a sophisticated and brilliant war hero and a great man, when in fact this Angevin monarch of England bankrupted his kingdom, which his unfortunate successor, King John, led to the brink of disaster.

Narasingha P. Sil

Review Sources

Catholic Historical Review 91, no. 3 (July, 2005): 517-518.
Church History 75, no. 4 (December, 2006): 895-896.
The New Yorker 80, no. 39 (December 13, 2004): 92-100.
Publishers Weekly 257, no. 5 (February 1, 2010): 43-44.
The Wall Street Journal 255, no. 59 (March 13, 2010): W8.

DEAD LINE

Author: Stella Rimington (1935-)
First published: 2008, in Great Britain
Publisher: Alfred A. Knopf (New York). 341 pp. $25.95
Type of work: Novel
Time: The present
Locale: London, Scotland, Cyprus, and elsewhere

The fourth novel in Rimington's series of thrillers featuring MI5 officer Liz Carlyle gives a scary representation of international terrorism in action

> *Principal characters:*
> LIZ CARLYLE, an MI5 officer known for her
>   success through intuition
> PETER TEMPLETON, MI6's head of station
>   on Cyprus
> CHARLES WETHERBY, Liz's boss at MI5
> MILES BROOKHAVEN, a young CIA agent
> ANDY BOKUS, Brookhaven's boss in the CIA
> CHRIS MARCHAM, a journalist specializing in the Middle East
> SAMI VESHARA, a Lebanese Christian importer
> PEGGY KINSOLVING, Liz's young research assistant
> GEOFFREY FANE, an MI6 leader
> HANNAH GOLD, a member of the peace movement whose daughter-in-
>   law is a former security agent
> DANNY KOLLEK, Hannah's suitor
> BEN AHMED, a Syrian counterterrorism expert

Over the years, a number of secret-agent books have been popular, and the best have been true literature—certainly those of Graham Greene, for example, and, arguably, of John le Carré. Stella Rimington's *Dead Line* may not be of Greene caliber, but it is perhaps as close to literature as a series book is likely to get. It provides a good dose of thrills to readers and some fascinating information about what goes on under the surface of a national security service.

In this subgenre, the plot often involves a world threat gathering momentum in the background with an agent whose job is to investigate the situation and derail the catastrophe before it occurs. This is the situation in *Dead Line*, which provides a believable main character, a credible threat, and a fine insider's look at secret agentry. A set of mysterious events occurs with no indication of how they may be related. Tension gathers well, and the conclusion is persuasive without being obvious.

Two factors contribute greatly to the success of this book. The main character is a likable, well-drawn woman, an officer of British Security Service, more commonly known as MI5, an acronym for Military Intelligence, Section 5. The insider view is

especially realistic because the author herself
was the first female head of MI5. Significantly, both Greene and le Carré had direct experience in the mysterious world of the British
secret service. MI5 is responsible for protecting the United Kingdom against threats to national security. Its current areas of concern are
terrorism, espionage, and weapons of mass
destruction. Its sister agency is MI6 or the Se-

*Stella Rimington worked for MI5,
eventually rising to the post of director-
general in 1992. She was the first
woman to hold the post. She retired in
1996, and was named a Dame
Commander of the Order of the Bath.*

cret Intelligence Service (SIS), which collects secret foreign intelligence in support of
the British government. The two agencies work with each other (with some rivalry)
and are similar to the U.S. Central Intelligence Agency (CIA) and the Federal Bureau
of Investigation (FBI).

Rimington was born in South London, but her family moved to Essex because
World War II made life in their neighborhood hazardous; therefore, she had an early
sense of national danger and international intrigue. As a young married woman she
took a job with the MI5 representative in India. After a couple of years of experience
she applied for a permanent job with MI5, and over the following thirty years, she
worked in the various branches of the security service. After a successful trip to Moscow to initiate contact with the KGB, she was promoted to director-general of MI5,
holding that position until 1996. She was known for her controversial policy of open-
ness about the Security Service, which she demonstrated by publishing her revealing
memoir, *Open Secret*, in 2001.

Rimington's first novel about MI5, *At Risk*, came out in 2004. This book introduced
Liz Carlyle, a young, intelligence agent who learns of a terrorist threat to be partly perpetrated by a young British woman classified as an "invisible," someone who can pass
borders and barriers without being noticed. The plot is complex but not obscure, and the
book received positive reviews. In the next two books of the series, *Secret Asset* (2005)
and *Illegal Action* (2007), the secondary characters are introduced and developed. In *Secret Asset*, Liz searches for a terrorist cell in London and a mole in the security system. In
Illegal Action, Liz transfers to counterespionage and unravels spy issues involved in
the global business community. *Dead Line* was published in England in 2008. It is to
be followed by *Present Danger*, which was published in England at the end of 2009.

In *Dead Line* the action begins when Peter Templeton, MI6's director in Cyprus,
gets a tip from one of his confidential sources that two people, businessman Sami
Veshara and journalist Chris Marcham, are plotting to disrupt a peace conference that
will be held at the Gleneagles resort in Scotland. They plan to disrupt it in such a way
as to blame Syria, in order to eliminate the possibility that the conference might result
in peace. Syria is planning a counter move to eliminate the threat before it material-
izes, but this action too could cause international security problems and pose a threat
to peace. Templeton is given the two names and no other information by a Syrian contact, who claims to have nothing further. It is not clear for whom the two are working,
or what form this disruption might take.

Liz is informed of the intelligence and is asked to investigate. At first, tracking down the suspects and aborting the plot appears relatively easy, but it is not: Murder intervenes; apparent clues lead nowhere; and as the conference approaches, Liz begins to understand that the stakes are far greater than anyone had suspected. A major terrorist attack on this conference—which involves heads of state from Britain, the United States, Israel, Syria, and elsewhere—could cause global disaster. However, the source and the dimension of the terrorist plot are hidden. More violence ensues. The murder victims, as is usually the case in spy novels, tend to be people who have offered or who could offer information, cut off just before representatives of MI5 could contact them. Liz's past successes have come from her intuition; this time, it seems to lead her to doors just as they slam shut.

A subplot of the novel is Liz's attraction to colleague Charles Wetherby, who reciprocates her feelings. However, Wetherby is married to a woman dying of cancer, and he is loyal to her. Liz spends time with the woman and finds her both lovely and admirable, but she is still tempted. This love interest, with all its inherent conflicts, surfaces and disappears throughout the novel as the two work together trying to get ahead of the conspiracy, their personal feelings suppressed for the sake of the project.

The action comes to a head at the peace conference. By this time Liz has learned almost enough about the plot and the plotters to put the whole scheme together. She sorts through the tangle of personal and political motives to find the final pieces of the puzzle as the presidents and leaders of nations are assembling at Gleneagles. The source of the disruption can no longer be identified as specific individuals. As the conspirators put the last touches on their complicated plan for international disaster, Liz's intuitions bring her to the truth, and she and her colleagues must race against time in an attempt to prevent the plot from succeeding.

What makes this book persuasive is the level of detail of security operations. The reader gets a realistic view of day-by-day operations in MI5. There is also a sense that no one within the agency really knows what is going on—there is no overall planner or plan, and no one has the full picture. Instead there are fragmented goals and objectives, incomplete communications, betrayals, and people and groups who have no idea whom they can trust. At times, the terrorists seem more unified than the government, but there are many reversals on both sides; finally neither the forces for order nor the forces for destruction are unified.

Another important element of this story is the buildup of tension as the action progresses. The reader may have a sense of how things will turn out, but the anxiety level is carefully raised by small discoveries and glimpses into the big picture. This is a well-plotted novel, with rising action and a strong climax without loose ends. Its plot is its selling point. It does not have an underlying perspective such as Greene's quixotic Catholicism or le Carré's nihilism; rather its plot illustrates the ironies and contradictions of the international scene and the way terrorism and intrigue pull individuals into their vortex.

The reader learns a great deal about how the British security system is ordered and how it functions, but there is never a case of "too much information"—the details are worked smoothly into the action. *Dead Line* gives a good picture of not only the agencies themselves but also of the kind of problems these groups deal with, how these issues manifest themselves, and what kind of corrupt alliances may exist between businesses and governments. When the main action ends, the writer leaves hints of future personal developments in the story that will serve to interest the reader in following the series further.

The settings are not highly distinctive—the plot evolves too quickly for much emphasis on location. The speed is emphasized by the number of scenes involving transportation. The narrative moves from one country to another as details of the plot materialize; a variety of action scenes take place in every conceivable vehicle. The main characters zip from place to place in cars, planes, and boats, always with the sense of urgency and often just too late. The complications of international security and the means of dealing with corruption and terrorism are persuasively demonstrated; this is a book that considers the possibilities and limitations of security agencies. Readers who enjoy fast-moving thrillers with a large cast of characters and an international angle will be pleased with *Dead Line*.

Janet McCann

Review Sources

Booklist 106, no. 17 (January 1, 2010): 24.
Kirkus Reviews 78, no. 9 (May 1, 2010): 391.
Library Journal 135, no. 8 (May 1, 2010): 72.
Publishers Weekly 257, no. 18 (May 3, 2010): 31.

THE DEATH OF THE ADVERSARY

Author: Hans Keilson (1909-   )
First published: Der Tod des Widersachers, 1959,
    in Germany
Translated from the German by Ivo Jarosy
Publisher: Farrar, Straus and Giroux (New York).
    208 pp. paperback $14.00
Type of work: Novel
Time: The 1930's
Locale: Germany

*Keilson's novel presents the story of how one Jewish
man feels isolated and restrained by the rise of anti-Semitism and the Nazis in the prewar Germany of the 1930's
and his particular recognition within himself of an enigmatic intimacy with the Nazis' charismatic leader*

Principal characters:
THE UNNAMED NARRATOR, ostensibly a German Jew
HIS FATHER, a photographer
HIS MOTHER
B, a charismatic leader generating an anti-Semitic fervor
AN UNNAMED FRIEND
AN UNNAMED WOMAN, his coworker

Hans Keilson's *The Death of the Adversary* was originally published in German as
Der Tod des Widersachers in 1959. Although the novel received positive reviews
when it was first translated into English by Ivo Jarosy in 1962, the novel vanished
again without much notice. In 2010, the Jarosy translation of the novel was republished by Farrar, Straus and Giroux and has received much more attention and acclaim. Born Jewish in Germany, Keilson is a survivor of the German occupation of
the Netherlands. The surge of interest in the novel is doubtless partly the result of the
author's history as well as his personal knowledge of the series of events that are the
book's central focus: the rise to power of the Nazis in Germany and the origins of
anti-Semitic policies and codes that ultimately led to the Holocaust.

Although trained as a physician, Keilson was unable to practice in Germany because of his ethnicity. He published a novel in 1933, which was soon banned, again
because the author was Jewish. Cognizant of the growing threat represented by Adolf
Hitler's rising popularity and the increase of Nazis, Keilson immigrated to the Netherlands in 1936. Within four years, however, the Germans, controlled by Hitler and
the Nazis' Third Reich, invaded the Netherlands. As shown in the famous Holocaust
memoir *Het Achterhuis* (1947; *The Diary of a Young Girl*, 1952) by Anne Frank, the
invading army and subsequent occupation required that the capitulating citizens of

the Netherlands comply with the codes of anti-Semitism enforced by Hitler's Third Reich, and so Keilson was forced to go into hiding and soon joined the Dutch resistance. Presumably, he wrote an early portion of *The Death of the Adversary* during World War II and was forced to bury it and retrieve it after the war. Although Keilson would eventually make his mark in the literary world with both

$\sim$

Jewish writer Hans Keilson was born in Berlin in 1909 but fled to the Netherlands in 1936. He joined the Dutch resistance and later became a psychiatrist, treating traumatized children after the war.

$\sim$

The Death of the Adversary and his novella *Komödie in Moll* (1947; *Comedy in a Minor Key*, 2010) his primary work after the war was in the care and counseling for the traumatized Jewish children who survived the Holocaust.

One of the most peculiar aspects of the novel is that Keilson deals with his subject matter and his characters in completely oblique ways. Not once during its length does his narrator state openly that he, his friends, or his family is Jewish. Nor, for that matter, are Nazis introduced as such. Hitler is referred to as "B" only, and neither the nation state of Germany nor the Third Reich is ever mentioned. At the same time, the Jewish identity of the narrator and his family is undeniable, and the "brown shirts" (early Nazi enforcers) are clearly identified as well.

As a small boy, the narrator hears his father and mother discussing the developing threat represented by the rise of the Nazis and B (Hitler), their leader. When the narrator interrupts his father to ask for an explanation, the father tells his son that he has an enemy. The boy is astounded to learn that he has an enemy whom he has never met, never offended, and about whom he has never previously heard. When he asks his father why these people hate their family, the father explains, "We are . . . " The trailing ellipsis seems to say many things: "We are Jews," "we are other," "we are not like them." Nonetheless, in his strange beginning is sown the initial seed of the narrator's particular obsession over B and his followers.

In addition to avoiding references to Germany, Hitler, Jews, and Nazis, the text also eschews names for all characters. Not one character in the novel is ever named, and only B is referred to by any form of address other than I, you, or other pronouns. Such a deviation from what readers expect invites them to read the novel as an allegory, drawing thematic conclusions from the novel's various departures from the norm. For example, through denying the characters their names, the narrator offers silent but implicit commentary on one of the central projects of the Nazis and the Third Reich: to deny the humanity of the Jews. A name, in some sense, constitutes an identity and, thus, an existence, and the assertion of an identity through the possession of a name in some way suggests that a life has meaning. The deliberate swerves in the narrative used to avoid identity, names, ethnicity, and nationality, echo how Hitler (or B in this novel) destroyed and denied the humanity and even the very identities of the Jews who fell victim to the Holocaust. Similarly, the Nazis themselves subjugate their own identities to the leadership of the party.

Additionally, while still a boy, the narrator realizes that his mother does not particularly respect his father, and that she regards him as a failure. A photographer at that time, he has arrived at the trade by failing at other professions such as dance instructor. Because of the allegorical nature of the text, one wonders whether or not the father, in his ineffectiveness, is supposed to represent the generation of Jews who hoped that the Nazi threat would dissipate on its own in prewar Germany.

The narrator initially does not understand the antipathy that people such as B and other anti-Semites have for him; instead, he simply knows that he is different. He is not allowed to play in the games of other children, nor is he invited into their homes. This separation from the greater community becomes most poignant to him as he grows older, however, when he and his one good friend hold debates over the danger and validity of B's rhetoric, which is spreading like flames through the tinder of the German spirit. His friend eventually explains to the narrator that he will choose the hateful and inflamed philosophies of B over the narrator, his comrade. From an allegorical stance, this would seem to be a nod to Germany's willingness to ignore the patriotic German Jews in its midst as it decided to make them scapegoats for all that had gone wrong for Germany since the beginning of World War I.

Other than the novel's intentional obliqueness, probably the other most interesting and curious characteristic of the book is the narrator's peculiar perception that he has an intimate connection with B/Hitler. He comes to believe that he and his people are defined by having enemies such as Hitler; that, in a sense, they are not persecuted because they are Jews, but, rather, they are Jews because they are persecuted. By the same token, he believes that the Hitler analogue, B, only has an identity because he has situated himself as the adversary to Jews.

The term "adversary"—*widersachers* in German—is an interesting choice for the title of the novel because of its cultural resonance. The word "Satan" in Hebrew means "adversary." The term referred not only to "the devil" as such but also to any person or group who become adversarial to the people of God. Thus, in referring to B as the adversary, the narrator is also referring to him as a Satan figure, and in some ways this seems to suggest that the narrator is himself a Job character, challenged by the adversary's primary desire to destroy his faith.

The narrator still does not truly grasp the extent of B's reach or popularity until he finds himself, almost by accident, swept into a building during a rally. Although he manages to escape the pressing crowd in the auditorium, he sits in a lounge where he can hear the words of B. He realizes the power of his rhetoric, how people can be motivated by fear and hate, and how people want a scapegoat. As much as he is repulsed by the content of B's speech, at the same time, he recognizes its allure and why the people of his homeland are so willing to fall at B's feet. His understanding of his own adversarial role in relation to B and his followers crystallizes when he is forced to spend an evening in an apartment listening to some of them tell stories. One of the young men recounts the tale of an excursion he made with a band of men to a Jewish cemetery, where they desecrated the graves of dead Jews. The sanctity of the dead, and the preservation of that sanctity, is one of the most hallowed tenets in Jewish law, and desecration of the dead is one of the most appalling offenses. In listening to the young man's story, the narrator not only realizes his own capacity for hate—a capacity perhaps as great as his enemies' own—but also the danger of hate. He understands how hate can blind one and transform from an empowering wrath to a blinding rage.

Struck by his need to join the battle against his adversaries, the narrator turns to not only his Jewish friends but also, again, his father, who has presciently understood what must be done in order to survive. Survival in itself, however, is not enough for the narrator; he has decided through logic and reasoning—and not through hate and fear—that the only solution to the problem faced by him, and his father, and indeed, all the Jews of Europe—is the eradication and death of the adversary, B. Only in his assassination will they have a chance. More important, however, is not the need to destroy B out of anger, but the need to resist and overcome evil. The novel is, ultimately, a story about the evil that dwells in every human heart and the willingness of some people to succumb to it and the strength others must find to resist its siren call.

Scott D. Yarbrough

Review Sources

Kirkus Reviews 78, no. 10 (May 15, 2010): 434.
The New York Times Book Review, August 8, 2010, p. 1.
The Times Literary Supplement, no. 5619 (December 10, 2010): 20.

DECISION POINTS

Author: George W. Bush (1946-   )
Publisher: Crown Publishers (New York). 497 pp.
  $35.00
Type of work: Memoir
Time: 2001-2009
Locale: The White House in Washington, D.C., and
  various locations throughout the world

*The forty-third U.S. president offers a vigorous defense
of his highly controversial two-term presidency*

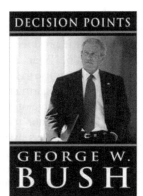

Principal personages:
> GEORGE W. BUSH (1946-   ), the forty-
> third president of the United States
> LAURA BUSH (1946-   ), his wife
> DICK CHENEY (1941-   ), the vice president during his presidential
> administration
> KARL ROVE (1950-   ), the deputy chief of staff during his
> administration
> DONALD RUMSFELD (1932-   ), the secretary of defense during his
> administration
> CONDOLEEZZA RICE (1954-   ), the national security adviser and
> secretary of state during his administration
> COLIN POWELL (1937-   ), the secretary of state during his first term

In *Decision Points*, George W. Bush, the forty-third president of the United States, provides an appealingly readable account of his troubled presidency as viewed from his own perspective. While Bush injects occasional humor, particularly at the outset, and admits an occasional regret, particularly toward the finish, the overall tone of the book is defensive, as though the author were standing trial. By the end of the book, Bush has answered just about every charge levied against him during his eight years in office, admitting to various imperfections along the way but offering a definite verdict of "not guilty."

Decision Points is organized topically rather than according to a strict chronology. In chapter 1, entitled "Quitting," Bush describes his 1986 decision to give up alcohol, citing wife Laura and his newfound religious devotion as the primary catalysts for the move, one that opened the way for his future political career to flourish. Chapter 2, "Running," recounts Bush's ultimate decision to get into politics, culminating in his ride to the presidency in 2000. Chapter 3, "Personnel," portrays the process by which Bush selected key members of his administration, including Karl Rove, Dick Cheney, Donald Rumsfeld, Condoleezza Rice, and Colin Powell. Chapter 4, "Stem Cells," presents the pros and cons that Bush weighed in coming to his decision to signifi-

cantly limit federal support of stem-cell research. Chapter 5, "Day of Fire," describes
the infamous events of September 11, 2001
(9/11), and the following days from the point
of view of the president.

Chapter 6, "War Footing," recounts the
long-term response to 9/11, including the formation of the Department of Homeland Security and the passage of the Patriot Act. Chapter 7, "Afghanistan," and chapter 8, "Iraq,"
describe the process by which Bush, and the
nation, decided to go to war in those two
countries and also the early stages of the operations. Chapter 9, "Leading," is a catchall for
a number of issues less essential to the Bush
administration than the "War on Terror" but
that Bush considers to be of substantial importance nevertheless. These issues, some of
which Bush considers successes, some of

The son of the forty-first president of the United States, George H. W. Bush, George W. Bush became governor of Texas in 1995 and served as the president of the United States from 2001 to 2009.

which he presents as failures, include the No Child Left Behind (NCLB) Act, faith-
based initiatives, Medicare reform, Social Security reform, and immigration reform.
This chapter also includes Bush's account of the 2004 election in which he won a
second term by defeating Democratic candidate John Kerry.

Chapter 10, "Katrina," gives Bush's version of the story surrounding that 2005
hurricane and its tragic aftermath. Chapter 11, "Lazarus Effect," recalls Bush's anti-
AIDS initiative and other policies aimed at spurring humanitarian gains and economic development in Africa. Chapter 12, "Surge," gives a detailed account of
Bush's decision to increase the troop commitment in Iraq in order to deal with the
country's violent civil disorder that peaked to dauntingly high levels by 2006. Chapter 13, "Freedom Agenda," describes the "liberation of Iraq" as merely one part of an
overall policy arc that also includes bringing democracy to the Middle East (most particularly to an independent Palestine), Latin America, and Asia. Chapter 14, "Financial Crisis," gives Bush's perspective on the economic meltdown that, along with his
failure to deliver as promised on the various "wars" he had started but not finished
and the federal government's budget deficit, badly marred the closing weeks of his
presidency. *Decision Points* concludes with a brief epilogue that provides a glimpse
of Bush's departure from the White House as he hands off the power and responsibility of the presidency to "number 44," Barack Obama.

Though some of the ground Bush covers in *Decision Points* has been treated in
previous books by staff members and journalists, it is generally informative, casting
light on the deliberative processes of the Bush White House as well as the president's
relationship to his family, friends, and advisers. Again, however, Bush also gives the
impression that he is testifying at his own trial. As such, he is constantly answering

charges that, in his view, have been unfairly leveled against him. These charges include that Vice President Cheney was the real power behind the throne during Bush's presidency, that Bush responded confusedly or timidly on 9/11, that Bush glibly equated patriotism with shopping after 9/11, that the Bush administration dillydallied idly while Osama Bin Laden escaped its clutches in Afghanistan, that faulty intelligence on the existence of weapons of mass destruction (WMD) was politically motivated, that Bush purposely left Saddam Hussein no other choice but to go to war with the United States and its allies, that Bush ignored the advice of military commanders in delaying the "surge" of American troops in Iraq until after civil strife had grown to intolerable levels, that National Guard units that should have assuaged the situation during Katrina were unavailable because they were deployed to Iraq, that "racist" motives informed Bush's response to Katrina, that provisions of Bush's proposed immigration reform amounted to amnesty, that Bush was turning his back on his free-market principles by passing bailout legislation for troubled banks in 2008, and that various policy decisions, such as AIDS relief in Africa and the timing of the "surge," were "politically" motivated rather than based on the desire to "do the right thing."

In all these cases, Bush believes strongly that his decisions were, at worst, both honorable in intention and rationally defensible in terms of the situation at hand. As to his overall verdict, Bush admits that he made mistakes, such as underestimating the complexities involved with nation-building in Afghanistan and Iraq, responding too slowly to the unfolding mess in New Orleans during Katrina, and less than optimal timing in proposing immigration reform. He gives himself a very high grade, however, for preventing a second attack on American soil after 9/11 (obviously assuming, along with many other observers, that 9/11 itself was unavoidable). Bush also takes substantial credit for the "liberations" of Afghanistan and Iraq, despite the higher costs—in lives and cash—than anticipated; for his Africa programs; and for NCLB. While Bush may have squandered the massive public support that came his way immediately following 9/11 and the "political capital" he claimed to have reaped from the decisive result of the 2004 election, he strongly suggests that history will greatly enhance his reputation.

The credibility of Bush's verdict to his readers will depend partly on the eyes, and political predilections, of the beholder. Bush's loyalists—including friends, family, and many members of the Bush administration, as well as many fellow evangelic Christians—will probably see Bush's self-assessment as candid and compelling. Bush's opponents—including Democrats, liberals, and the ubiquitous "left"—will be more likely to dismiss Bush as the joke they would like him to be or fasten onto apparent peccadilloes, such as Bush's claim that the low point of his presidency came not when suicide bombers crashed airliners loaded with passengers into well-populated American buildings or when the casualties began to mount in Iraq, but rather when, in response to the Katrina debacle, rapper Kanye West accused him of being a racist. Those who attempt to look at it more objectively will find a mixed bag. Bush seems convincing when he denies racist motivation, asserts his grim determination to "protect" the country after 9/11, and claims to be genuinely concerned with underachieving American students, overly burdened Africans, and hard-pressed immigrants.

On the other hand, key omissions highlight the subjectivity of Bush's perspective. For example, based on this book, one would never know that Al Gore won the popular vote in the 2000 presidential election or that the election in Florida was marred by a poorly designed "butterfly" ballot that had Gore supporters in Palm Beach County accidently casting their ballots for Pat Buchanan. Instead, all that is provided is the final official vote in Florida, together with a portrait of an unreasonably petulant Gore who fails to honor his initial concession and instead contests the election.

More to the point, Bush omits facts that reflect directly on his own standards for evaluating his presidential performance. While speaking repeatedly of the "liberation" of Iraq, he never once discusses the toll of "innocent" Iraqis killed, wounded, and displaced in the aftermath of the initial (and apparently successful) invasion. Bush also never discusses the blowback that came from the war in Iraq both in terms of the loss of global support for the U.S., which peaked after the sneak attack of 9/11 and fell rapidly with the Iraq war, and the increased recruitment of young people by our enemies in the "War on Terror." This latter point especially would seem relevant to Bush's overarching concern with national security. Then, too, Bush seems to overestimate the effects of some of his successes. NCLB has not been the "game-changer" Bush believed it to be. Reformers are still struggling to get "accountability" into American public schools in a way that amounts to more than a hopeful gesture. Likewise, Bush's African programs, though exceedingly well received by Africans themselves, seem like a drop in the proverbial bucket when matched against that continent's acute needs.

While *Decision Points* may not be as convincing a defense as Bush would like, it does reveal interesting things about him personally and about the presidency as an institution. As a man, Bush comes off neither as the bumpkin his detractors like to portray nor the inspirational leader he aspired to be. With the help of former Bush speechwriter Chris Michel and researcher Peter Rough, Bush has written a literate, well-thought-out book, one that is enhanced by many excellent photos. It is certainly not the work of a simpleton or a fool.

Bush also shows himself to possess the range of political sentiments needed to pursue the "compassionate conservatism" he promised when first launching his presidential campaign. However, there is also a negative side. Bush comes off as thin skinned and full of something uncomfortably close to self-pity. Ever anxious to liken himself to Abraham Lincoln, who also coped with public ridicule and the carnage—physical and ethical—of war, Bush fails to live up to the comparison. Where Lincoln expressed anguish at the butchery of war in a self-effacing way, Bush seems hung up on his own ego. Where Lincoln was a deep thinker who promoted a progressive and profoundly moving "new birth of freedom," Bush reduces freedom—which he no doubt loves and does sincerely want to share—to a one-dimensional platitude. Where Lincoln used religious rhetoric in a way that is spiritually moving even for those who do not share his beliefs, Bush wields the language of religion in a way that reassures fellow believers but leaves others flat. In short, Bush is no Lincoln.

Perhaps more important than this, however, is the fact that Bush describes a presidency in which even someone as great as Lincoln would struggle under the weight of endless responsibilities, constant—often corrosive—scrutiny, and a political system that seems to have become largely dysfunctional. It is no wonder that Bush has, quite admirably, sworn off of looking over his successor's shoulder. If there is nothing else he learned from his presidency, Bush knows full well what a thankless job our highest-ranking political office has become.

Ira Smolensky

Review Sources

Business Week, November 15, 2010, p. 1.
Chicago Sun-Times, November 21, 2010, p. 6.
The Economist, November 13, 2010, p. 40.
New Statesman 139 (November 29, 2010): 55.
New York 43, no. 37 (November 15, 2010): 20.
The New York Review of Books 58, no. 1 (January 13, 2011): 4-8.
The New Yorker 86, no. 38 (November 29, 2010): 72-76.
Newsweek 156, no. 21 (November 22, 2010): 20.
The Spectator 314 (November 20, 2010): 38-39.
Weekly Standard 16, no. 10 (November 22, 2010): 32.

THE DEVIL AND MR. CASEMENT
One Man's Battle for Human Rights in South America's Heart of Darkness

Author: Jordan Goodman
First published: 2009, in Great Britain
Publisher: Farrar, Straus and Giroux (New York).
  322 pp. $30.00
Type of work: History
Time: 1908-1913
Locale: Iquitos, an Amazon river town in eastern Peru;
  other locations along the Putumayo River; and London

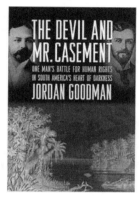

The book retells the story of the liquidation of the Peruvian Amazon Company in 1912 as the result of exposure of the company's extensive human-rights abuses

Principal characters:
> ROGER CASEMENT (1864-1916), an Anglo-Irish diplomat, famous at the time for reporting on abuses in the Belgian Congo
> JULIO CÉSAR ARANA, a despotic Peruvian rubber baron
> BENJAMIN SALDANA ROCCA, a South American journalist who was the first to publish accounts of atrocities in the Peruvian Amazon
> WALTER HARDENBERG, an American engineer who brought Rocca's accounts and his own eyewitness testimony to a receptive British audience

In the early 1900's, ownership of a rich region of more than ten thousand square miles along the upper Putumayo River was in dispute between Peru and Colombia. Although publicly both nations were committed to a "hands-off" policy until international arbitration could determine ownership, entrepreneurs and settlers from each country were combing the region. One of the most predatory of those entrepreneurs was Julio César Arana, the titular "devil" of Jordan Goodman's *The Devil and Mr. Casement.* Like others, Arana was drawn to the region by the abundance of *Hevea brasiliensis*, the world's main source of natural latex. With worldwide demand for rubber skyrocketing at the turn of the century, Arana founded the Peruvian Amazon Company (PAC), which would eventually dominate the production and transportation of latex from the jungles of eastern Peru to the markets of Western Europe.

Harvesting latex in the wild was time-consuming and demanding. The ten thousand square miles of jungle in eastern Peru might contain about one million *Hevea brasiliensis*, but only some of the trees would be suitable for harvesting at any given time. Even after locating a suitable tree, harvesters would still have to know the right method of tapping it. Most new arrivals to the region did not have this depth of knowledge, leaving the work to the indigenous people—mainly the Huitoto. To dominate the production of latex in the Peruvian Amazon, Arana sought to dominate the Huitoto.

A historian of medicine and the sciences, Jordan Goodman has held appointments at Manchester University Institute of Science and Technology and the Wellcome Trust Centre for the History of Medicine at University College London.

Although the PAC was registered in London and had a British board of directors, its operational headquarters was in Iquitos, a Peruvian boomtown along the Putumayo. Directives from the PAC went upriver from Iquitos to several company towns, then to a network of twenty-four trading stations. Each of these stations was managed by a chief, who was employed by the company on a commission basis. Each chief employed a cadre of salaried employees—many bodyguards and enforcers—who, in turn, supervised the indigenous labor force. The station chiefs gave each Huitoto worker a quota, which he was expected to fill within ten days. Once the station had met its own quota, the same indigenous workers were forced to transport the entire amount of latex to the company towns. Once in town, the latex was loaded onto company steamboats and then floated downstream to Iquitos.

The system was fraught with corruption and human-rights abuses. Competition from other companies, especially those from Colombia, was eliminated, often through murder, rape, and pillaging. Station employees were sent to round up groups of male Huitoto and force them to work by holding women and children as hostages. If the workers did not make their quotas, or resisted or tried to escape, the station employees were expected to capture, torture, and even kill. To get employees willing to commit these acts, the PAC brought unemployed men from Barbados, lying to them that they were being hired for manual labor or service jobs. Once they reached the stations, the Barbadians were in an untenable position: under contract, unable to leave their job sites, and unable to speak indigenous languages, yet expected to control indigenous workers. As was the case with the station chiefs, many of the employees turned to alcohol and abuse in response to their isolation and frustrations.

Personally, Arana wanted as little direct involvement as possible in the Putumayo region. Although he spent vast amounts of money in Iquitos, he spent little time in the PAC's corporate hometown, preferring to hobnob with the wealthy and powerful in London and Biarritz. From time to time various newspapers reported on conditions in the Peruvian Amazon, but Arana was usually able to counter criticism either by claiming that his critics were foreign agents or blackmailers or by publishing his own articles representing the PAC as a civilizing force. Even the PAC's British board members were content to ask no questions until a hardheaded American arrived in London with a suitcase full of South American newspapers and his own tale to tell.

In 1908, Walter Hardenberg and a companion had set out on an overland trip from the Andean mountains of Columbia, through the Amazon, to the coast of Brazil. The journey took them into the Putumayo. Besides collecting and reading local news accounts of the PAC's crimes, Hardenberg spoke with those who had witnessed acts of theft, brutality, sexual slavery, torture, and murder. His own trade goods, in fact, were stolen by PAC employees. In Iquitos, Hardenberg met Benjamin Saldana Rocca, a journalist who had been publishing exposés about Arana and his companies for years. Although his newspapers usually sold well, Rocca had been unsuccessful in getting Arana prosecuted; Arana represented, after all, about 7 percent of the world's latex production, and he had ample funds to derail prosecution. Aghast and angered, Hardenberg took the story to London, where in 1909, it caught the ear of an influential charitable organization, a muckraking journal, and shortly thereafter, the British Parliament.

Fortunately for thousands of people living in fear of the PAC, the time was right for the British government to launch a fact-finding humanitarian investigation. Earlier in the same decade, the British consul Roger Casement had reported on widespread human-rights abuses in the Congo Free State (now known as the Democratic Republic of the Congo), which had been committed in a similar pursuit of profit. In that instance, the profiteers were working for the Belgian head of state, King Leopold II, and there was little rationale for direct British involvement. In the latest instance, however, the PAC was at least nominally a British company, and the Barbadians who had been mistreated were British subjects.

Not only did the British government have a rationale for investigating the company, they had a hero on hand to do it. For his efforts in the Congo, Casement had been named a Companion of St. Michael and St. George. Between 1905 and 1910, he had endured a series of depressing and expensive South American postings, none of which required his considerable talents of persuasion and investigation. In mid-1910, he was asked to head a commission of investigation to look into conditions in the Putumayo.

Goodman's narrative describes the day-to-day difficulties encountered by Casement and the other commissioners. These included the enervating jungle heat and humidity, travel difficulties, lies and obfuscations, and the intrusions and schedule changes demanded by PAC-provided handlers. Despite these difficulties, the commission gathered enough evidence to conclude that the tales of atrocities were entirely accurate. Casement, who had investigated both the Congo and the Putumayo, considered the latter to be the worse of the two. He estimated that the PAC had done away with almost two-thirds of the Huitoto population; in addition to the many who were murdered or worked to death, untold thousands died as a result of starvation. In 1910, Casement completed a thorough report on the criminal actions of the PAC and submitted it to his superiors in the British government.

From 1910 to 1912, the British essentially sat on Casement's report. As Goodman points out, the reasons at first had to do with maintaining American goodwill. At the time, the United States championed the Monroe Doctrine, which had put Europe on notice that interference in Central or South America would be construed as an aggressive act against the United States as well. Perhaps a bit too circumspect, the British wanted the cooperation or at least the consent of the United States before even launching a fact-finding expedition. Later, after the facts were found, Casement's report was shared with the U.S. government, perhaps in hopes that American pressure would be enough to stop the atrocities. However, the American government was also unwilling to act on the information, largely because it in turn needed Peruvian goodwill to prevent war in South America between that nation and Colombia.

A second reason for the British government's delay in publishing Casement's report was the belief that the threat of publication could be used to force Arana to make salutary changes in his company's business practices. In 1911, increased competition from latex producers in Southeast Asia was cutting into Arana's profits, and he needed outside investment to keep the PAC afloat. Newspaper reports were making it difficult to attract investors, but an official government report would make the task impossible. In that eventuality, Arana might well liquidate the company and move his operations entirely to Peru. Such an outcome would benefit no one, least of all the Huitoto people. By 1912, however, the latter rationale no longer made sense, as Arana had liquidated the PAC.

By mid-1912, the British government published Casement's report and began a series of parliamentary hearings. Just as Arana had tried to do years earlier, he responded to charges mainly by denying them. Although he accepted the commission's evidence of wrongdoing, Arana denied any personal responsibility or knowledge. After giving his testimony to Parliament, but before the hearings were concluded, Arana returned to Peru. Although the PAC was in liquidation, it was able to stay afloat for several more years afterward. In the coming decades, there were efforts made to persuade Peru to prosecute Arana, yet he never stood trial for the crimes his company committed. In contrast, Arana enjoyed more than twenty years of business and political success until shortly before his death in the early 1930's.

From his high point in 1912, however, Casement experienced a rapid fall from grace, his life ending in execution for treason in 1916. Casement's experiences in both the Congo and the Putumayo persuaded him that no colonial power, however beneficent on the surface, could rule a colonized people ethically. By 1913, Casement had resigned his position in the British Foreign Office and was determined to work fervently toward Irish independence alongside the Irish Republican Brotherhood (IRB). Reasoning that Britain's enemy would likely be Ireland's friend, Casement met with German agents from 1914 to 1916, in an attempt to broker an agreement with Germany in the event of that nation's victory in World War I. Over the course of those two years, however, Casement's focus changed from establishing a preliminary diplomatic understanding to raising a force of Irish prisoners of war who could be landed in Ireland to reinforce a general uprising. Failing in this, Casement did persuade the Germans to ship arms to Ireland, which were to be used by Irish volunteers during a planned uprising.

Unfortunately for Casement, the other leaders of the IRB led a general uprising while he was still in Germany, and the shipment of arms was intercepted by the British navy. When Casement arrived in Ireland, he was quickly captured by police. After a short trial, he was found guilty of treason. At that point, clemency would have required either a groundswell of support from the general public or from significant numbers of Anglo-Irish public figures. Given the enormous change in popular opinion in the four years since his report on the Putumayo atrocities, neither was forthcoming.

Michael R. Meyers

Review Sources

Booklist 106 (February 1, 2010): 8.
The Chronicle of Higher Education 56 (February 26, 2010): B17.
Kirkus Reviews 77 (November 15, 2009): 1190.
Mother Jones, April/March, 2010, p. 87-88.
The New Yorker, April 26, 2010, p. 77.
Publishers Weekly 256 (November 23, 2009): 47.

DIAGHILEV
A Life

Author: Sjeng Scheijen (1972-   )
First published: Sergej Diaghilev: Een leven voor de kunst, 2009, in the Netherlands
Translated from the Dutch by Jane Hedley-Pröle and S. J. Leinbach
Publisher: Oxford University Press (New York). Illustrated. 552 pp. $39.95
Type of work: Biography, fine arts
Time: March 19, 1872-August 21, 1929
Locale: Perm and St. Petersburg, Russia; Paris; Venice; Rome; London; United States

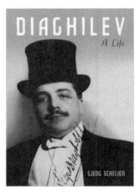

The story of Sergei Diaghilev, the art lover and impresario who committed his life to art and was the most important disseminator of art, especially ballet, in Western Europe

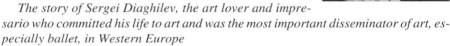

> *Principal personages:*
> SERGEI DIAGHILEV (1872-1929), an impresario, the founder of the Ballets Russes, a critic, and an art historian
> YELENA VALERIANOVNA DIAGHILEV, his stepmother, whom he always viewed as his mother
> PAVEL PAVLOVICH DIAGHILEV, his father; an army officer and amateur musician
> DMITRY (DIMA) FILOSOFOV, his cousin and first lover
> ALEXANDRE BENOIS (1870-1960), a Russian costume and set designer
> LÉON BAKST (1866-1924), a painter and Russian costume and scene designer
> IGOR STRAVINSKY (1888-1971), the composer of *Schéhérazade, L'Oiseau de feu (Firebird)*, and *Le Sacre du printemps (The Rite of Spring)*
> SERGEI PROKOFIEV (1891-1953), the composer of *Romeo and Juliet*
> MISIA SERT (1872-1950), a socialite and patroness of the arts who served as Diaghilev's confidant and adviser; the first choreographer of the Ballets Russes
> ANNA PAVLOVA (1881-1931), the first prima ballerina to appear with the Ballets Russes
> VASLAV NIJINSKY (1890-1950), a dancer and choreographer for the Ballets Russes and Diaghilev's lover
> LÉONIDE MASSINE (1895-1979), a dancer and choreographer for the Ballets Russes and Diaghilev's lover

In his biography *Diaghilev: A Life*, Sjeng Scheijen presents a detailed and comprehensive account of the life of Sergei Diaghilev in which he seeks to portray how and why Diaghilev became who he was and to give some insight into his complex and contradictory character. Scheijen opens his book with an introductory chapter "Death in Venice," which begins with a description of Diaghilev's funeral. For Diaghilev, Venice was the incarnation of art and beauty; he returned often to the city to rest and renew his creative energy, and he died there as he had wished. The chapter serves as both a summary of

∼

Sjeng Scheijen is an independent scholar and expert on Russian art. He has curated exhibitions for the Groninger Museum and the National Gallery, London. He is the consultant for the Diaghilev exhibit at the Victoria and Albert Museum.

∼

Diaghilev's life and as an invitation to find out who he was. Scheijen reveals Diaghilev, the man who determined the development of Western artistic culture in the nineteenth century, through a chronological presentation of his life from his birth to his death. Relying heavily on sources that have become available to researchers relatively recently—including Russian archives, journals, and personal correspondence—Scheijen examines Diaghilev's childhood; his experiences and discoveries as a young man; his relationship with the artists, composers, dancers, and designers with whom he interacted during his career; and his homosexuality.

Scheijen's account of Diaghilev's childhood centers on his relationship with his stepmother, Yelena Valerianovna Diaghilev, and the strong and loving bond that existed between them from their first meeting. With excerpts from Yelena's letters and memoirs, Scheijen corroborates her fondness for Diaghilev and the fact that she considered him her first born. Although she had two other children, Valentin and Yury, within four years of her marriage to Diaghilev's father, Sergei remained her favorite. He emphasizes the significance of her influence on Diaghilev through her optimism, kindness, and buoyant spirit. She instilled in him the belief that if he wanted to do something, he could. She established a household in which art, music, and literature were an important part of everyday life. Excerpts from letters and memoirs reveal that the family members gave plays, did poetry readings, and gave musical performances to amuse themselves.

In his portrayal of Diaghilev's family and his early life, Scheijen also gives insights into Diaghilev's ability to live well in spite of his financial situation. He describes Diaghilev's father as a man who enjoyed his family, relied on the family's holdings (the mansion in St. Petersburg, the estate in Bikbarda, and the distilleries) and his wealthy in-laws to maintain his lifestyle, and did not concern himself about financial matters. Unfortunately for Diaghilev's father, Pavel, his carefree attitude resulted in bankruptcy. The family's loss of its wealth did not, however, prevent Diaghilev from making the customary grand tour of Europe and enrolling at the university. His birth mother had left him an inheritance that was safe from the creditors.

In his portrayal of Diaghilev as a child and young adult, Scheijen also addresses his recurring anxiety and spells of nervous agitation. Excerpts from letters written to his mother when he was still a child make mention of a sense of dread, of an overwhelming, unidentified fear tormenting him. In recounting his brother Yury's bout of illness from diphtheria and Diaghilev's caring for him, Scheijen reveals Diaghilev's development of an extreme fear of contagious disease and his subsequent fear of being near horses, which he believed spread infection. In addition, Scheijen treats Diaghilev's fear of water, his superstitions and his belief in omens, and his paralyzing fear of traveling over water.

Diaghilev's devotion to the arts is the dominating theme of Scheijen's biography. For Diaghilev, the arts were life itself. The biography chronicles Diaghilev's activities in the world of the arts, which became the center of his life while he was still at the university and remained so until his death. In his portrayal of Diaghilev as purveyor of the arts, Scheijen explores the complexity of Diaghilev's character. Throughout the book, he insists upon Diaghilev's love of his family and of Russia, on his need to be Russian, and on his homesickness. However, as Scheijen reveals, art, artistic performance, and the exploration of new theories in the arts totally occupied Diaghilev's life and prohibited his remaining in Russia and his returning to Russia and his family. His opposition to the officially accepted art, music, and ballet of Russia eventually alienated him from the official Russian institutions and prevented his employment in Russia. Believing that Russian art needed to be revitalized, he founded the journal *Mir iskusstva* (world of art), in which he criticized and attacked the theories and judgments of Vladimir Stasov, the leading art critic in Russia.

Scheijen emphasizes the fact that Diaghilev had no private life, no permanent residence, few possessions, and no aspect of living that was not involved with the arts. All of Diaghilev's interaction with other people was an outgrowth of his involvement with the arts. Diaghilev devoted himself entirely to art in its many forms, first by founding and writing for *Mir iskusstva*, then by organizing and presenting exhibitions of art in both Russia and Paris, and finally by founding and directing the Ballets Russes from 1909 to his death in 1929.

Scheijen also treats Diaghilev's homosexuality and his need to control and create people. Diaghilev's discovery of his homosexuality occurred while he was at the university, and his first lover was his cousin Dima Filosofov. Scheijen explains that homosexuality was common among the Russian upper class and fairly accepted as long as a man eventually made an acceptable marriage. Scheijen also explains that Diaghilev's sexual relationships with his leading male dancers of the Ballets Russes was also an accepted practice. He also refutes the common conception that Vaslav Nijinsky was victimized by Diaghilev. He presents evidence that Nijinsky was as interested as Diaghilev in establishing the relationship. However, Diaghilev's involvement with his leading male dancers went beyond the sexual. Scheijen reveals Diaghilev's need to dominate, educate culturally, and in a sense create the dancer as a person. The conflicts that arose between Diaghilev and his lead male dancers (especially Nijinsky and Léonide Massine) were brought about by Diaghilev's attempt to control every aspect of their lives.

In his presentation of the Ballets Russes and his account of Diaghilev's interaction with the various artists, composers, set designers, costume designers, and dancers and his constant search for financial backing, Scheijen makes the reader fully aware of the enormous task that Diaghilev had assigned himself. He also reveals Diaghilev's faith in his own artistic judgment, his search for perfection in art, and his willingness to take risks. For Diaghilev, the final artistic creation that a ballet would become once music, costumes, set, choreography, and the execution of the dance had all been brought to a point of perfection and melded was all that mattered. As a result, his relationship with the various creative individuals who contributed to the production was more often than not discordant. He did not tread carefully and was quick to make last minute changes and replacements. Scheijen also underlines the fact that for all of his harshness in achieving a true artistic performance, Diaghilev considered his associates as a creative family. Quarrels and disagreements never really ended relationships. Scheijen's inclusion of an abundance of the correspondence that passed between Diaghilev and those with whom he worked and quarreled provides an authoritative and insightful look at how artistic creation bound them together. After the rupture between Nijinsky and Diaghilev, Nijinsky's sister Bronislava returned to be the choreographer for the Ballets Russes.

The treatment of the Ballets Russes also elucidates the enormous talent that Diaghilev possessed as an impresario and his superb judgment in matters of art. In his portrayal of Diaghilev's managing of his dance company, Scheijen also addresses Diaghilev's talent in reading the public that composed the Ballets Russes's audience. He points out that Diaghilev understood the fascination of the European, especially Parisian, audience with the quality of being Russian; thus, when he had to substitute English dancers for Russian, he created Russian names for them.

As Scheijen recounts the chaotic and complicated preparations that Diaghilev made for each season's performances, he brings clearly to the reader's attention the important role that Diaghilev played in the artistic and cultural life of Western Europe. Diaghilev enabled both established and new composers and artists to create new forms in their chosen fields and to present them to the public. Jean Cocteau, Pablo Picasso, Igor Stravinsky, and Sergei Prokofiev all worked with the Ballets Russes. Diaghilev brought the best Russian dancers and choreographers to Western Europe, as Anna Pavlova, Michel Fokine, Nijinsky, and many others were members of the Ballets Russes.

Critics have recognized the importance of *Diaghilev: A Life* in clarifying aspects of Diaghilev's life that had remained unclear or have been incorrectly represented. Scheijen's book, based on new research, has dispelled several incorrect beliefs about Diaghilev, in particular his victimizing of an innocent and defenseless Nijinsky and the story told by Diaghilev himself that his mother died from a difficult birth caused by his enormously large head. Scheijen states with corroborating evidence that his mother died from puerperal fever some weeks after his birth. The only readers who may find *Diaghilev: A Life* disappointing are those who are expecting a book about the actual performances of the dancers of the Ballets Russes; however, Scheijen's book is a biography of Diaghilev, who was neither a dancer nor a choreographer but a man who committed his life to the development and dissemination of art in all of its many forms.

Shawncey Webb

Review Sources

Booklist 107, no. 2 (September 15, 2010): 13.
Dance Research 28, no. 2 (Winter, 2010): 242-244.
Library Journal 135, no. 13 (August 1, 2010): 86.
The New York Review of Books 58, no. 1 (January 13, 2011): 24-26.
The New York Times, August 26, 2010, p. 1.
The New Yorker 86, no. 28 (September 20, 2010): 112-116.
Publishers Weekly 257, no. 27 (July 12, 2010): 37-38.
Times Higher Education, no. 1938 (March 11, 2010): 58.

DICKINSON
Selected Poems and Commentary

Authors: Emily Dickinson (1830-1886) and Helen
    Vendler (1933-   )
Publisher: Belknap Press of Harvard University Press
    (Cambridge, Mass.). 535 pp. $35.00
Type of work: Literary criticism, poetry

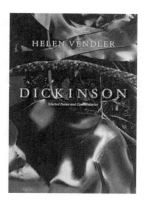

*A selection of 150 poems by Dickinson—most of the old
favorites and many rarely anthologized, this volume includes commentary on each poem by one of the premier
American critics*

By the early 1980's, Helen Vendler's name was so
prominent in bibliographies of modern poets in universities that she seemed even then a sort of established dean of
literary criticism. She seemed to be everywhere, writing about everybody. In the three
decades since, Vendler seems even more authoritative and ubiquitous. Nonetheless,
her brief explications of 150 poems by Emily Dickinson in *Dickinson: Selected Poems and Commentary* achieve an illusion of spontaneous conversation that is as accessible to the casual general reader as to the literature professor. The briefest are no
longer than the standard freshman composition: Twenty-three of the commentaries
run five hundred words or shorter, filling no more than two pages. The longest cover
six pages, some two thousand words, but there are only half a dozen of those. This is a
book admirably suited to browsing.

It is remarkable how browsable this collection of commentaries is. Despite the notion voiced by a *Los Angeles Times* reviewer of this volume, that "commentary on poetry is rarely a good idea," many of the best readers turn to commentaries for pleasure—and find it. Not the least of the pleasures of Vendler's analyses of Dickinson's
pieces—which stand with Walt Whitman's as the premier American verse of the
nineteenth century—is discovering that the art of explication de texte is alive and
well. The method of close reading recommended in the first half of the twentieth century by I. A. Richards was often scorned by the academics of the second half—though
never by Vendler, who coedited a Festschrift of essays honoring Richards in 1973.

Explication of the type Vendler showcases here—and previously in *The Art of
Shakespeare's Sonnets* (1997)—is a familiar classroom discipline, and it is clear from
the commentaries that Vendler has herself gone through the exercise with each of
these poems. Literature professors who assign explications usually have their students begin with a paraphrase of the poem, even though the clearest lesson the student
learns from the effort is the futility of paraphrase. Nevertheless, insight often comes
from the process, which can then be applied to the commentary—as Vendler does in
Poem 181 ("A wounded deer—leaps highest"). For the first two stanzas—eight lines,

~

*Emily Dickinson is considered one of
the major American poets of the
nineteenth century. She lived and
worked in Amherst, Massachusetts.
Helen Vendler is the A. Kingsley Porter
University Professor at Harvard
University. A foremost authority on
literature, Vendler has served as judge
for both the Pulitzer Prize and the
National Book Award.*

~

forty-two words—Vendler produces a 111-word prose paraphrase, and reproduces it as part of her commentary. Then she shares with the reader the prize she won from the plodding, brainstorming work of paraphrase. The next line of Dickinson's poem is "Mirth is the mail of anguish." Vendler shares her experience with the line. "In my paraphrase of the poem I wrote, 'She arms herself with the chain mail of mirth,' but that is not quite accurate. The lines offer an allegorical mirth." She goes on to add the detail that paraphrasing necessarily slights, but she shows an extraordinary humility in showing us, as it were, her rough drafts. She is taking the reader along on her journey through Dickinson's art.

After all, Dickinson's art is the primary reason most readers will come to this book. However, Dickinson looms so large in the canon, with every major American critic of the past century adding to the critical conversation, that readers might be justified in asking if the reading public really needs another book on Dickinson and, more to the point, if it needs this one. The answer is yes, both for general and specific reasons. The general reason has to do with the nature of great poetry. The best poetry is inexhaustible: each reading brings fresh insights (an observation that itself is a stale one). Because each generation brings its own concerns and presuppositions to poetry, new works of interpretation are not only inevitable but also necessary.

There is also a specific reason that Vendler has found the right moment to produce this book. Her introduction addresses the various generations, or "historical periods" of Dickinson criticism, which she terms "The Age of Publication," "The Age of Biography," "The Age of Editing," and, finally, the current age, which welcomes her book, "The Age of Commentary." Commentary abounded in all of those eras, and the work of commentary relies on the less glorious but necessarily prior labor of editing.

Vendler bases her text on Ralph W. Franklin's *The Poems of Emily Dickinson: Variorum Edition* (1998, followed by the *Reading Edition*, 1999). Because Franklin's edition could draw on nearly half a century of scrutiny of Dickinson's manuscripts since Thomas H. Johnson's *The Poems of Emily Dickinson: Including Variant Readings Critically Compared with All Known Manuscripts* (1955), it is perhaps only after Franklin's work that commentators can fully respond to these poems as Dickinson intended them to be read. Vendler identifies all poems by their Franklin numbers, though for the convenience of readers with the previously standard Johnson edition, Vendler gives the "J" numbers at the end of each commentary.

Franklin's textual work corrected more than just the readings of earlier editions. As Vendler's introduction recounts, Franklin "determined from watermarks and pinholes the order of the sheets of paper that Dickinson had folded and sewed together in the little booklets now called 'fascicles.'" Franklin completed this work in 2007, which means that the dating of many of these poems was made more secure just as Vendler was writing her commentaries.

Vendler's commentaries often refer the reader to Franklin for variant readings (she opens her comments on poem 796 by informing the reader that Franklin "spends five pages on the five variant drafts"), but only when the variants threaten to present completely different poems does she include them in this collection—only five times, in fact, for poems 124, 194, 236, 284, and 291. When the variants are the result of editorial meddling or bowdlerizing, however, they become part of the presentation history of the text, and Vendler often uses the early "corrected" versions of Dickinson's verse to comment on misunderstandings of the poet's versification and deliberate effacing of her religious doubt. With a poet as canonical and anthologized as Dickinson, textual history often intertwines with personal history; while Vendler does not dwell on the personal, she does not avoid it. Her explication of poem 800 ("I never saw a Moor") begins, "When as an adult I read this poem in Johnson's edition of 1955, I was shocked. The poem I had memorized as a girl (in the version rewritten by Dickinson's 1890 editors) had been tamer."

The selection presented in this volume is itself an editorial service, for while the "old standards" are all here—236 ("Some keep the Sabbath"), 269 ("Wild nights—wild nights!"), 314 ("'Hope' is the thing with feathers"), 340 ("I felt a funeral in my brain") 372 ("After great pain"), 383 ("I like to see it lap the miles"), 409 ("The soul selects her own society"), 448 ("I died for beauty"), 466 ("I dwell in possibility"), 479 ("Because I could not stop for Death"), 519 ("This is my letter to the world"), 591 ("I heard a fly buzz—when I died"), 620 ("Much madness is divinest Sense"), 1096 ("A narrow fellow in the grass"), 1263 ("Tell all the truth but tell it slant"), 1593 ("He ate and drank the precious words"), 1773 ("My life closed twice before its close")—there are a few gems that have remained buried in Johnson's and Franklin's editions, unmined by previous commentators. Consequently, there are two kinds of freshness in Vendler's commentary: the fresh look at an old chestnut, and the recovery of poems not found in other anthologies.

Many of the latter type—the rarely selected poems—are found in the early portion of this chronological presentation: Dickinson's earliest work. One of these shows Dickinson's own neglect: Of her early verse she selected some, presumably the best, to be copied in ink and collected in fascicles; poem 134 remains in pencil only. Vendler speculates that the exclusion may have been "Dickinson's judgment on its quality," though she explores the poem's frank but discreet discussion of sexuality. Likewise little known are Dickinson's thoughts on race and class, expressed in poem 836, "Color—Caste—Denomination." Written in 1864, while a war at least partly about racial issues was still being waged, this poem later was expurgated by the poet's niece, Margaret Dickinson Bianchi, who published the fifth line—"in sleep—all Hue forgotten"—as "in sleep—all here forgotten."

The years of the American Civil War (1861-1865) were ones of great productivity for Dickinson, and the war intruded into her poetry more than most collections indicate. Less, perhaps, than in the verse of contemporaries such as Herman Melville or

Whitman, but a few poems specifically reflected the war. Vendler selects one of them, 524 ("It feels a shame to be Alive"), dated to 1863.

> It feels a shame to be Alive—
> When Men so brave—are dead—
> One envies the Distinguished Dust—
> Permitted—such a Head

By connecting the poet with the war, Vendler acknowledges the real-life Emily in a way that early critics, obsessed with the image of a reclusive Amherst, Massachusetts, agoraphobe, did not. Nonetheless, although Dickinson did have a social circle, however small, it is undeniable that she lived largely in books ("There is no Frigate—like a book," she declared, in a much-reprinted poem Vendler did not include). Vendler's commentaries are thick with the books Dickinson read. The poet's diction is frequently checked against the 1844 edition of Webster's dictionary she owned. Echoes of earlier poets abound—William Shakespeare, certainly, but John Keats also, who is mentioned twice as often as any other poet—and the book is dedicated to Keats. More than two dozen poets are cited in the commentaries, but the citations are not, as Michael Dirda claimed in his *Washington Post* review, "quote-mongering." When Vendler suggests a parallel, it is not presented as a source; many, in fact—Wallace Stevens, Marianne Moore, Seamus Heaney—are not poets who Dickinson read, but poets who read Dickinson.

Vendler has more to say about form and metrical patterns than one might expect with a poet known for a single poetic form—a loose ballad stanza, usually related to the hymn meter New England Calvinists called "common meter." Vendler calls it "hymn meter," though Congregationalists in Amherst had a number of hymn meters. However, the critic's precise ear catches the poet's departures from the form. The form is simple and, as the Puritan name for it suggests, common. It is a four-line stanza; the first and third lines contain four stresses, and the second and fourth—the only rhyming lines—three stresses. Vendler identifies a number of variations, however: the anapests in poem 236 ("Some—keep the Sabbath—") which imitate the call (and the name) of the bobolink; the spondees that open 259 ("A clock stopped"); and the dimeter rearrangement of tetrameter couplets in 269 ("Wild Nights—Wild nights!"). Some of the metrical observations have impressionistic associations in the commentary: The rhythmic change in the fourth stanza of "A clock stopped" is "savage"; the dactyls and trochees in that stanza are "arrogant."

Dickinson: Selected Poems and Commentary presents the foremost American literary critic at the peak of her powers, training them on America's greatest lyric genius. Such a combination suggests expectations no one could possibly meet, but Vendler meets them.

John R. Holmes

Review Sources

The Christian Century 127, no. 25 (December 14, 2010): 26.
Harper's Magazine 321, no. 1927 (December, 2010): 75-76.
Library Journal 135, no. 16 (October 1, 2010): 76.
The New York Review of Books 57, no. 18 (November 25, 2010): 46-48.
Publishers Weekly 257, no. 29 (July 26, 2010): 53.

DIMANCHE, AND OTHER STORIES

Author: Irène Némirovsky (1903-1942)
First published: Dimanche et autres nouvelles, 2000, in
   France
Translated from the French by Bridget Patterson
Publisher: Vintage Books (New York). 293 pp. paper-
   back $15.00
Type of work: Short fiction
Time: 1920's to early 1940's
Locale: Paris, France

   *This collection examines the complicated relationships
between individuals that result from passion, jealousy,
greed, and self-centeredness as well as the alienation and
injustice inherent in a social system based on a hierarchy
of social class*

> *Principal characters:*
> AGNÈS, the wife of Guillaume Padouan in "Sunday"
> NADINE, the twenty-year-old daughter of Agnès and Guillaume in
>   "Sunday"
> NANETTE, the younger sister of Nadine in "Sunday"
> GUILLAUME, the unfaithful husband of Agnès in "Sunday"
> RÉMI ALQUIER, the unfaithful lover of Nadine in "Sunday"
> MME BOEHMER, Christiane's mother in "Those Happy Shores"
> CHRISTIANE, the twenty-two-year-old daughter of the Boehmers in
>   "Those Happy Shores"
> GERALD (JERRY, GÉRARD) DUBOUQUET, the lover of Christiane in
>   "Those Happy Shores"
> GINETTE, an aging tart in "Those Happy Shores"
> ANNA DEMESTRE, the matriarch of the family in "Flesh and Blood"
> ALBERT, the rich son of Mme Demestre in "Flesh and Blood"
> AUGUSTIN, the son of Mme Demestre in "Flesh and Blood"
> ALAIN, the youngest son of Mme Demestre in "Flesh and Blood"
> CLAIRE, Augustin's wife in "Flesh and Blood"
> ALIX, Alain's wife in "Flesh and Blood"
> SABINE, Albert's wife in "Flesh and Blood"
> MARIETTE, the daughter of Mme Demestre, divorced, in "Flesh and
>   Blood"
> CHRISTIAN RABINOVITCH, a Jewish immigrant who belongs to the
>   bourgeoisie and denies his Jewish heritage in "Brotherhood"
> RABINOVITCH, the poor Jewish immigrant in "Brotherhood"
> MADEMOISELLE MONIQUE, the daughter in "Don Juan's Wife"
> MONSIEUR, the father of Monique and an unfaithful husband in "Don
>   Juan's Wife"

MADAME, the mother of Monique in "Don Juan's Wife"

KLAVDIA ALEXANDROVA, a friend of Sofia Andreïevna in "The Spell"

SOFIA ANDREÏEVNA, the mother of Lola and Nina, in love with Serge in "The Spell"

LOLA, the twenty-year-old daughter of Sofia in "The Spell"

HUGO GRAYER, an affluent upper-middle-class person, from a neutral country in "The Spectator"

MAGDA, Hugo's friend who shares his lifestyle and opinions in "The Spectator"

MR. ROSE, a self-centered member of the upper bourgeoisie in "Mr. Rose"

MARC BEAUMONT, the young man Mr. Rose meets along the road in "Mr. Rose"

ROGER DANGE, a man desperately bereaved by his wife's death in "The Confident"

MADEMOISELLE COUSIN, the close friend and mentor of Dange's deceased wife in "The Confident"

CLAUDE, a French soldier in "The Unknown Soldier"

FRANÇOIS, his younger brother in "The Unknown Soldier"

In the collection *Dimanche, and Other Stories*, Irène Némirovsky examines the complexity of relationships between human beings. She treats the tensions between mothers and daughters, between husbands and wives, between family members, and between individuals of the same and different social classes. Betrayal, jealousy, envy, passion, resentment, and suffering caused by love are major themes of the stories. Descriptions of weather, nature, countryside, cityscapes, and home interiors play an important role in the stories. Némirovsky portrays her characters in settings that either reflect and enforce the emotions the characters are experiencing or that contrast ironically with these emotions. While Némirovsky writes from the viewpoint of an observer and avoids comments about her characters, the images she uses to describe them reveal significant details about their personalities and beliefs. The majority of the stories depict the French bourgeoisie and illustrate the social stratification of the time. Némirovsky is an astute storyteller; her narratives are reminiscent of those of Gustave Flaubert, Leo Tolstoy, and Anton Chekhov as they focus on individual characters but reveal ironies of human existence in general.

The first two stories, "Dimanche" ("Sunday") and "Les rivages heureux" ("Those Happy Shores"), examine the experiences of passionate love, betrayal by a lover, and suffering for love, which are common among women. These two narratives also portray the tensions and conflict that exist between mothers and daughters and between youth and age, as well as the inability of each to understand the other. In "Sunday," Agnès is envious of her daughter Nadine's beauty and vivacity and of the experiences that await her, while at the same time, she wishes subconsciously to protect her; therefore she insists upon seeing her as a child as innocent and naive as the younger Nanette. Nadine considers her mother to be dull and cannot possibly envision her involved in a love affair.

~

Irène Némirovsky, a Russian Jewish immigrant to France, was a highly successful novelist and short-story writer until her death in 1942 in Auschwitz. After World War II, several of her works were published posthumously, including La Vie de Tchekhov *(1946; the life of Tchekhov) and* Suite Française *(2004; English translation, 2006).*

~

In "Those Happy Shores," the same themes are presented but from a slightly different perspective. A mother's envy of her daughter's youth and beauty once again appears in the character of Mme Boehmer. However, here, Némirovsky uses Ginette, an aging tart, as the counterpoint to the young Christiane who is confidently and, in a sense, coldly becoming involved in a love affair. All three of the female characters wait for a man. Agnès has spent her life waiting for Guillaume, who is unfaithful as a lover and as a husband. Deceiving their parents, Nadine and Christiane wait in cafes for Rémi and Gérard, respectively. Each young woman is aware of her lover's unfaithfulness. Ginette also waits, but because her lover has died and left her without financial support, she waits for whatever man she can pick up. In her portrayals of these women, Némirovsky reveals the complexity of human emotions. Agnès envisions Guillaume killed in a car accident while with another woman and wonders if she would care. Némirovsky portrays her as preferring her solitude and the peace and quiet of the time she passes alone in the security of her home, yet she also emphasizes Agnès's pleasure in remembering how Guillaume has made her suffer. Both Nadine and Christiane envision their lovers with other women; Nadine even believes that Rémi is explaining how he can make her suffer and is mocking her.

Agnès, Nadine, and Christiane, all secure in their affluent, upper bourgeois lifestyle, exhibit frustration and resentment in regard to the men's actions, yet they enjoy their emotional suffering for love. Not a member of the bourgeoisie, Ginette is a sharp contrast to them. Her reality is different; it involves both poverty and loneliness. Her suffering is not a means of making life exciting or of passing idle time. In contrast to the lack of comprehension of Agnès and Mme Boehmer in regard to their daughters, Ginette envisions herself as a mentor to Christiane, helping her to avoid unhappiness in love.

Némirovsky also addresses the issue of class distinction in her portrayal of Christiane and Ginette. The two women become involved in a conversation while they are both waiting; Christiane buys Ginette a drink and is friendly to her. Later, Christiane and a group of friends return to the cafe and make fun of Ginette. In other stories, Némirovsky returns to this theme of the self-centered cruelty of the upper bourgeoisie.

In "Liens du sang" ("Flesh and Blood"), Némirovsky again portrays the upper bourgeoisie; however, this narrative depicts the complexities of family relationships and the love/hate relationships of siblings. Némirovsky also depicts a destructive competition among siblings as part of the lifestyle of the upper bourgeoisie. The depiction of the Demestre family is a harsh portrayal of the complex relationships of jealousy, resentment, and filial duty within the bourgeoisie.

In "Fraternité" ("Brotherhood"), Némirovsky explores the bond that links those of Jewish heritage. Christian Rabinovitch, a young, middle-class Frenchman born in France but of Jewish ancestry, meets a poor Jewish immigrant with his sick grandchild on a train platform on a cold night. Christian is uncomfortable around the immigrant but agrees to let him follow into the first-class waiting room where there is a fire. As they talk, they discover they share the name Rabinovitch. Christian insists that he is French, and as soon as he hears a train whistle gets up to leave. The poor immigrant insists upon carrying his bag. Once in the train, Christian mutters to himself, maintaining that he has no link to the immigrant; however, as he becomes more and more upset, he begins to rock back and forth in the traditional Jewish fashion. Upon arriving at his destination, he thinks less about the Jew, but shivering in the icy weather, his body once again claims its Jewish ancestry. This story is one of the best examples of Némirovsky's talent in using irony.

In "La femme de don Juan" ("Don Juan's Wife"), Némirovsky again deals with infidelity and the jealousy mothers have for their daughters. She returns also to the theme of women and suffering for love. Here, there are elements of the classical comedy of Molière. The story of betrayal and murder is recounted by a former servant in a letter written to Mademoiselle Monique, the daughter. The former chambermaid philosophizes at length about life, about relationships between men and women, and about the nature of women. She emphasizes her superior common sense about these matters. The story contains a subtle undercurrent of sarcasm as the chambermaid/narrator repeatedly explains that she is recounting all of this to Mademoiselle Monique out of concern for her well-being. The sarcastic tone reflects resentment between the servant class and the upper class.

"Le sortilège" ("The Spell"), unlike the other stories, is not set in France but rather recounts a childhood memory from the time the narrator was living in the Ukraine. The intrigue of the story centers around Russian customs and superstitions. Klavdia knows how to cast spells and read tarot cards. One summer evening in May when climatic conditions are right, she playfully casts a love spell binding Lola to Uncle Serge, the platonic lover of her mother Sofia. Sometime later Lola and Serge leave together. Sofia and Klavdia are both devastated. At the beginning of the story, Némirovsky discusses how childhood memories retain a certain magic because children do not understand the activities of adults and misread their meaning. At the end of the story, the child insists that the spell made Lola and Serge fall in love. Her nursemaid agrees but has an ironic smile on her face.

Both "Le spectateur" ("The Spectator") and "Monsieur Rose" ("Mr. Rose") are set in France during the early years of World War II. The stories depict the self-centeredness of members of the wealthier classes and the sense of superiority that permeates their thinking. In "The Spectator," Némirovsky depicts two characters, Hugo Grayer and Magda, from neutral countries. Both are wealthy and believe themselves privileged individuals who will be unaffected by World War II. Both plan to leave France at the first signs of real danger. Magda serves primarily as a means to enable Hugo to express his attitudes toward life and his place in the world. Hugo sees himself as an observer, safe from harm because he is neutral. Magda leaves first. Hugo eventually also leaves on a ship that turns out to be the first neutral ship torpedoed.

Némirovsky's descriptions of Hugo eating fruit in his cabin contrast sharply with those of him wounded and suffering on the raft after the torpedo attack. He remembers his blasé attitude toward newspaper items reporting death and suffering of others and becomes painfully aware that he has deceived himself by believing that he was safe because of his status. Némirovsky leaves the story unfinished, concluding simply with a phrase stating that the hours dragged on. Hugo remains self-oriented as it is his death that concerns him; in contrast, Mr. Rose experiences a change of attitude and escapes death.

"Mr. Rose" depicts the ordeal of a wealthy man fleeing the bombing raids in France. He expects to ride to safety in his chauffeur-driven car, stopping to eat whenever he is hungry. Refusing to believe his chauffeur's statement that there is no food to be had, he leaves his car and goes to a house along the road to request food. Having found none, he attempts to return to his car but is unable to find it. Walking along the road with great difficulty, he encounters a young man named Marc who aids him and anyone in need of help. Mr. Rose ridicules his concern for others. During an air raid, Marc shields Mr. Rose and is injured. Finally, neither Marc nor Mr. Rose can go farther; at this moment, friends of Mr. Rose appear and offer him a ride in their car. Mr. Rose asks that they take Marc too, but they refuse for lack of room. Surprising even himself, Mr. Rose refuses the ride. The car enters the bridge and is blown up. Mr. Rose has saved himself by thinking of Marc.

The collection concludes with "La confidente" ("The Confident"), a story that portrays the importance of beauty for women and the complexity of passionate love. In "L'inconnu" ("The Unknown Soldier") Némirovsky once again explores the theme of male infidelity.

Shawncey Webb

Review Sources

Booklist 106, no. 15 (April 1, 2010): 20.
Harper's Magazine 320, no. 1920 (May, 2010): 71-72.
Library Journal 135, no. 15 (September 15, 2010): 36.
People 73, no. 15 (April 19, 2010): 63.
Publishers Weekly 257, no. 5 (February 1, 2010): 32-33.

THE DISAPPEARING SPOON
And Other True Tales of Madness, Love, and the History of the World from the Periodic Table of the Elements

Author: Sam Kean
Publisher: Little, Brown (New York). 391 pp. $24.99
Type of work: Biography, history of science, science
Time: 1869-2009
Locale: Russia, Europe, and the United States

A collection of stories and anecdotes associated with the chemical elements and the scientists who developed the periodic table

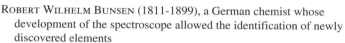

Principal personages:
> DMITRY IVANOVICH MENDELEYEV (1834-1907), a Russian chemist who formulated the first functional periodic table of elements
> ROBERT WILHELM BUNSEN (1811-1899), a German chemist whose development of the spectroscope allowed the identification of newly discovered elements
> MARIE CURIE (1867-1934), a Polish scientist who, with her husband Pierre Curie, discovered the first radioactive elements
> GLENN THEODORE SEABORG (1912-1999), an American Nobel laureate associated with the discovery and synthesis of numerous transuranium elements
> OTTO HAHN (1879-1968), a German chemist and Nobel laureate associated with the discovery of several radioactive elements
> FRITZ HABER (1868-1934), a German chemist and Nobel laureate who applied ammonium compounds for production of both fertilizer and explosives
> NIELS BOHR (1922-2009), a Danish physicist and Nobel laureate who contributed to the understanding of the atom

Sam Kean's catchy title *The Disappearing Spoon* references merely the beginning of the story of the chemical elements, totaling 118 as of 2010. The title represents an unusual characteristic associated with the metal gallium, discovered in 1875 and considered relatively harmless if ingested. Gallium has a melting point of approximately 84 degrees Fahrenheit. Spoons composed of the element melt in hot tea or coffee, allowing for an obvious practical joke or "parlor trick."

Students in science, particularly those studying chemistry, have long carried out learning with the image of the periodic table hovering over the classroom. Few have been presented with the story behind the table and the introspective initiated by Dmitry Ivanovich Mendeleyev during the 1860's in recognizing the relationship

~

Sam Kean has worked as a science writer for periodicals such as The New Scientist *and* Smithsonian Air and Space *in addition to his position as a correspondent for* Science *magazine.*

~

among the elements. Mendeleyev is merely the beginning of the story for the author, as Kean describes not only the discoveries (or creation) of the 118 known elements but also the foibles of the scientists who carried out the work. This represents the true joy of Kean's story, the ability to convey a modicum of humanity of the scientists. Even the history of gallium, the element noted above, includes an anecdotal element. Gallium was discovered in 1875 by Frenchman Paul Emile François Lecoq de Boisbaudran. He noted the unusual color bands exhibited by the mineral in the newly developed Robert Wilhelm Bunsen spectroscope—he of the "Bunsen burner" instrument used by scientists and students alike. The mineral was named gallium, allegedly for Gaul or Gallia, the Latin name for France. Suspicion exists, the author notes, that gallium was a play on his own name, Lecoq (rooster), which in Latin is the word *gallus.* Kean implies that Lecoq further demonstrated gallium's low melting point, allowing a purified sample to melt in his hands.

The Disappearing Spoon is an enjoyable read. An extensive section of notes is included near the back of the book, providing additional stories as well as useful references, allowing the reader to investigate the science more extensively. It should be emphasized, however, that the target audience is not that of professional scientists, most of whom are likely familiar with many of the stories and anecdotes. The chemistry and physics of the elements, including the basis for rows and columns found in the periodic table, are at best at the level of college undergraduate chemistry and physics courses. This statement is not meant to deride either the author's approach or the mental challenges undergone by Mendeleyev when he began his assembly using the known elements of his time. The quantum mechanics that underlie the understanding of chemical bonding and atomic orbitals presents its own challenges to both science undergraduates and laypersons, and the author's approach contributes significantly to understanding the chemical properties of the elements and the basis for their positions in the table. If the reader's interest lies in knowing more than simply a history of the chemical elements, Kean's overview of basic chemistry interspersed with physics helps clarify both the chemical properties of the elements themselves and the relationships among elements in the same row or same column.

The establishment of a sense of order to the elements does little to explain their origins directly; the two most abundant elements in the universe are hydrogen, approximately 90 percent of total atoms in the universe, and helium, nearly all of the remaining 10 percent. Kean provides a lucid explanation of the origins of the remaining natural elements. Most explanations are known to science students: The stellar nucleosynthesis model produced by Fred Hoyle and his colleagues in 1957 coupled with the larger elements created in enormous explosions of large stars (supernovas) accounts for most of the remaining elements. Interspersed throughout the book are stories of the creation of the remaining elements, generally through the radioactive decay of those that originated with stellar explosions. Hoyle is also mentioned in passing as the person who coined the phrase "the Big Bang" as an explanation of the origin of the universe, a pejorative phrase originally meant to mock the "origin theory" developed by George Gamow.

The book is not one that can be read in a single seating. Portions of Kean's story—largely the first half of the book, which consists of chapters encompassed within two larger parts—are placed in a rough time line, beginning with Mendeleyev's life and work and working toward the twenty-first century. This portion includes the laboratory synthesis of elements not known to exist in nature. Each topic is then discussed using examples of elements that fit the thesis of the story. Since chapters are based upon this time line of discovery rather than similarities of the chemical properties among the elements described, one must frequently consult the periodic table provided near the back of the book to observe exactly where these elements are situated.

The second portion of the book, consisting of parts 3 through 5, emphasizes the practical applications of individual elements within a larger theme. For example, in Kean's discussion of the "Science of Bubbles," a story beginning with a (likely apocryphal) story of how a University of Michigan graduate student conjured up the bubble chamber while observing the bubbles in his beer, the author intersperses the bubble science of elements as disparate as hydrogen, calcium, and zirconium.

Another chapter, entitled "Take Two Elements and Call Me in the Morning," emphasizes the medical applications associated with several elements. Kean begins this story with a discussion of the antibacterial properties of copper and vanadium, including an explanation as to why American coinage is unlikely to be involved in transmission of bacteria; most coins contain significant levels of copper.

Kean proceeds to explain German bacteriologist Gerhard Domagk's discovery of what was arguably the first safe broad-spectrum antibiotic, sulfonamide, weaving within the story the properties of sulfur, which provide the underlying basis for the antibacterial properties of the drug. Domagk was a German physician during the 1930's, not merely "an insignificant chemist" as implied by the author, who, as a medical student, had extensive experience serving in the German medical corps during World War I. Appalled by the high mortality that had resulted from infections rather than from the initial battle wounds, Domagk had spent much of the previous decade testing antibacterial properties of various chemicals produced by his employer, I.G. Farbenindustrie, ironically the same chemical firm that later manufactured the poison gas used in World War II death camps.

Domagk noted that one red dye, Prontosil, protected mice that had been infected with the deadly bacterium *Streptococcus*. In 1935, Domagk's daughter developed a potentially mortal streptococcal infection following a minor injury. Domagk fed Prontosil tablets to his daughter, who recovered as a result of the treatment. The active portion of the dye was subsequently determined to be the sulfur compound, sulfonamide. While later manufacturers dissolved the drug in ethylene glycol, which is used as an antifreeze, as noted by the author, it was not to "sweeten" the medicine. The use of ethylene glycol was the result of a misguided attempt to produce soluble syrup. The actual death toll that resulted from this chemical experiment was somewhat above one hundred, certainly a terrible tragedy but not the "hundreds" stated by the author.

Kean has included a number of historic ironies interwoven within the stories of discoveries. In the chapter entitled "Chemistry Way, Way Below Zero" the author describes the story of John Bardeen, who, along with his colleagues William Shockley and Walter Brattain, was awarded the 1956 Nobel Prize in Physics for his work on the development of the transistor while at Bell Laboratories. Bardeen utilized the element germanium in place of silicon, which had originally been chosen by Shockley; silicon had proven to be too brittle. In 1972, Bardeen was awarded a second Nobel Prize in Physics, the first person to be awarded the prize twice in the same field, for helping develop a theory of superconductivity. Bardeen missed the press conference being held at the University of Illinois when he was unable to open his garage door using the transistor-powered remote control. The pettiness of some scientists is also demonstrated in the same example. Bardeen's colleague Shockley attempted to steal the credit for development of the original transistor despite having used silicon in his original model. Shockley later fell into greater disrepute for his advocacy of eugenics in the "breeding" of more intelligent humans. Not surprisingly, Shockley "donated" some of his own sperm for the endeavor.

A more poignant irony is discussed by Kean in "Political Elements," a chapter dealing in part with the story of radioactivity and nuclear fission. Lise Meitner, an Austrian scientist with Jewish ancestry, had been collaborating with Otto Hahn since World War I in the identification of radioactive elements. The collaboration had benefited each, since, as a woman, Meitner was not permitted to serve as an independent researcher, but she was able to provide the scientific expertise for Hahn to develop as a successful scientist. Though not Jewish, even using the warped definition instituted by the Nazis, Hahn still resigned a professorship in protest of Nazi policies. When Germany annexed Austria in 1938 Meitner was forced to flee to Sweden, where she continued her work on radioactivity in collaboration with Hahn. It was Meitner who shortly afterward realized that the "baffling" results in experiments carried out by physicists Irène Joliot-Curie and Enrico Fermi had actually represented nuclear fission, the splitting of uranium atoms. Meitner and Hahn proceeded to publish their theoretical interpretation. However, since politics prevented Meitner's name from appearing as an author on the paper, Hahn became the author with Meitner listed as an assistant. Hahn was awarded the 1944 Nobel Prize in Chemistry for the work; his failure to acknowledge Meitner's contribution meant she never received the award. Meitner was honored, however, when element 109 was coined meitnerium in her name.

Kean's emphasis is placed on the post-World War II era, a time when politics often intervened in the application of radioactive elements in building larger and more powerful weapons. The contributions of Glenn Theodore Seaborg and his colleagues in modernization of the periodic table are highlighted in this portion of the story. Kean does refer, perhaps unfairly, to interpretive errors by scientists such as Linus

Pauling, whose (incorrect) model of deoxyribonucleic acid (DNA) resulted in James Watson and Francis Crick winning the race to understand the structure of DNA.

Kean himself makes the occasional mistake that might have been caught by an editor. For example, HIV, the human immunodeficiency virus and etiological agent of AIDS, is not a "foamy" virus. The term applies to others in that virus family. Other minor errors have been noted earlier. Despite such perceived shortcomings, Kean does provide an interesting "story behind the story" that describes the excitement and challenges underlying scientific research.

Richard Adler

Review Sources

Booklist 106, no. 21 (July 1, 2010): 15.
Chemical and Engineering News 88, no. 22 (May 31, 2010): 61-62.
Kirkus Reviews 78, no. 8 (April 15, 2010): 345.
Library Journal 135, no. 8 (May 1, 2010): 90.
Nature 466, no. 7305 (July 22, 2010): 442.
New Scientist 207, no. 2768 (July 10, 2010): 43.
The New York Times, August 5, 2010, p. C14.
The New York Times Book Review, August 8, 2010, p. 18.
Publishers Weekly 257, no. 19 (May 10, 2010): 37-38.
Science 330, no. 6010 (December 10, 2010): 1480.
Science News 178, no. 8 (October 9, 2010): 30.
Time, July 26, 2010, p. 18.

DOG BOY

Author: Eva Hornung (1964-   )
First published: 2009, in Australia
Publisher: Viking (New York). 293 pp. $25.95
Type of work: Novel
Time: Early 2000's
Locale: Moscow, Russia

Abandoned and starving in a freezing apartment build-ing in Moscow, four-year-old Romochka faces imminent death until he is taken in and raised by a feral dog pack as one of their own

Principal characters:
> ROMOCHKA, an abandoned four-year-old boy
> MAMOCHKA, the female leader of the feral dog pack that adopts Romochka
> PUPPY/MARKO, a human infant who is later brought into the pack by Mamochka
> DMITRY PASTUSHENKO, a scientist studying the socialization of feral children
> NATALYA, Dmitry's girlfriend and a pediatrician who takes a special interest in Romochka
> LAURENTIA, a kind-hearted restaurant worker who occasionally feeds Romochka and his pack
> ROMOCHKA'S MOTHER, the boy's mother, who abandons him
> ROMOCHKA'S "UNCLE," likely a boyfriend of Romochka's mother
> WHITE SISTER,
> BLACK DOG,
> GOLDEN BITCH,
> BLACK SISTER,
> GREY BROTHER, and
> BROWN BROTHER, dogs belonging to Romochka's pack

Loosely based on a real-life news story, *Dog Boy* tells the moving account of four-year-old Romochka, who is so thoroughly conditioned not to go outside without an adult that he remains huddled in a dark, unheated apartment for several days after be-ing abandoned by his mother and the man he calls "uncle." Desperate hunger finally drives him out. Therefore, because Romochka is one of thousands of homeless chil-dren trying to survive the bitter Moscow winter, nobody takes any notice of him, and he is too frightened to ask for help. As the situation becomes desperate, Romochka follows a large yellow dog that wanders by, reasoning simply that dogs too must stay warm and eat. He is briefly challenged by the female leader's two canine companions, but the leader gives the signal that the boy is to be accepted and may follow the dogs back to their lair in an abandoned church. Once inside, the leader begins nursing the four new puppies that are waiting for her and makes no objection when Romochka creeps tentatively forward to join them in suckling. Before long, without conscious thought or articulation, Romochka comes to think of the yellow alpha dog as "Mamochka," the four puppies as his littermates, and the other young pack members as his older siblings.

Eva Hornung is an Australian writer and human-rights activist living in Adelaide. Her first novel, Hiam *(1998), won the Australian/Vogel Literary Award and the Nita May Dobbie Literary Award, while her third novel,* Mahjar *(2003), won the Steele Rudd Award.*

Thus begins Romochka's gradual transformation over several harsh winters from a little boy to a potentially dangerous wild creature who is far more at home with dogs than with people. Hornung manages the difficult feat of giving each dog in the pack a distinct and identifiable personality without anthropomorphizing them, and she portrays Romochka's entry into the pack's complex social structure in a way that seems both natural and necessary. Through their behavior, Mamochka and the young adult dogs show that they recognize Romochka's vulnerability and lack of survival skills; they patiently teach him and gradually allow him increasing freedom by including him on their hunting forays as his abilities improve. Romochka often finds himself frustrated by his inadequate night vision, hearing, and sense of smell as compared to those of his packmates; however, his senses do sharpen significantly, and he eventually learns to compensate for his shortcomings by using his hands to manipulate and carry food and even to fashion a club that he can use to defend himself. Not only does Romochka survive under the dogs' loyal care, but also the pack becomes healthier and stronger as a result of his presence. Both boy and dogs instinctively recognize the mutual benefits of their relationship, and Romochka achieves some level of contentment when the hunting is good and their bellies are full.

In spite of the close and moving relationships that develop, however, *Dog Boy* can in no way be considered a "feel-good" novel. Romochka himself does not consciously recognize the grim reality of his circumstances because they are normal to him, but readers may well be horrified by the fact that Romochka eats raw rats, mice, and birds and constantly suffers from chafed and vermin-infested skin since bathing is not possible. Romochka's existence is always precarious; he must learn to avoid other dog clans, including a pack of "Strangers" who arrive to challenge his pack over territory and food. While the pack ultimately prevails in this battle, Brown Brother is killed and Grey Brother is injured, a sobering experience for Romochka. He must also learn to avoid groups of homeless people who in their desperation are as fully capable of the same violence as the most feral of dogs.

As Romochka grows and learns, Mamochka gradually yields alpha dog status to him because she recognizes his intelligence and his ability to procure food from a variety of sources. In spite of his assured position within the pack, however, Romochka cannot help but become interested in the people going about their lives in the city and the rough forest that borders it. He is alternately drawn to and repelled by the humans that he watches surreptitiously from the protection of his clan, learning through trial and error that he can better provide for his packmates if he takes up begging in subway stations. These forays are dangerous, and Romochka is caught and abused more than once by military police and vicious youth gangs, causing the reader to acknowledge that human cruelty can be far more devastating than the brutal, yet nonmalevolent violence of animals.

As Romochka continues to explore the city, Mamochka senses that he is torn between the canine and human worlds and tries to satisfy him by bringing another human infant, most likely abandoned in an alley, into the clan. This new "dog boy," whom Romochka thinks of simply as "Puppy," is far younger than Romochka was when he was taken in by the dogs. This ultimately results in further dissatisfaction, because Romochka can sense that Puppy is pure dog while he himself does not belong wholly with either dogs or humans. Romochka sometimes takes his frustrations out on the always loyal Puppy. However, when Puppy is captured by the authorities and delivered to an institution for study and rehabilitation, Romochka's own fierce allegiance emerges; he spends weeks tracking Puppy down before cautiously approaching the institution's staff, who are shocked to learn that the dog boy they have named Marko has what they assume is an older brother.

Led by Doctor Dmitry Pastushenko, an expert on feral children, the institution's staff mistakenly concludes that Romochka and Marko must have simply lived in a squalid human home that happened to have several dogs. They are not entirely sure what to do with the boys, particularly as Romochka still roams the streets in between his visits to Marko. While the younger boy is thrilled to have regular contact with his brother again, he is diagnosed with cystic fibrosis; shortly afterward he contracts pneumonia and dies. Devastated, Romochka disappears back into the canine world, but by this time, Dmitry has realized the truth: Both boys were literally raised by the same dog pack, an absolutely unprecedented event. In addition, the difference in their ages upon their "adoption," coupled with how well the socialization progress is tracked by the institute, may be the ultimate key to understanding the phenomenon of feral children. Although Dmitry had initially resented Romochka's appearance on the scene, upon Marko's death he is persuaded by his girlfriend, a pediatrician named Natalya, to become official foster parents to Romochka.

At this juncture, the reader is torn, knowing that Romochka really should be returned to human society if possible but dreading the consequences, particularly since Dmitry's interest is initially so selfish. The officials who trap Romochka do so by coercing a kind-hearted woman named Laurentia, who has long given food scraps to Romochka and his pack from the kitchen restaurant where she works, into luring the dogs back for a final, poisoned meal. The reader cannot help but speculate that this act of betrayal, however unwilling on Laurentia's part, must have some impact upon Romochka's future ability to trust humans.

In the end, Dmitry and Natalya bring not only Romochka into their home but also the three newborn puppies they were able to rescue from Mamochka's lair; they believe this will help Romochka's transition and make him understand that they want to help him. By this point, Dmitry also acknowledges that he has an emotional as well as a professional investment in this boy. Offered this sanctuary, Romochka hesitates, then decides that he will indeed remain, a decision he signifies by deliberately killing the three puppies by biting and crushing their skulls. While this act initially seems shocking and violent, the reader then remembers that Romochka witnessed Mamochka kill a litter of puppies in the same manner one winter because she knew she could not provide for and protect them. The ending is heartbreaking, leading the reader to question whether rejoining human society is truly desirable, even if the alternative for Romochka is an early death as a feral creature.

Widely praised in reviews, *Dog Boy* has also been translated into several foreign languages, which is unsurprising considering the book's universal themes and skillful execution. The reader cannot help but feel Romochka's anguish when he is separated from his pack, whether temporarily when he is lost on a subway or permanently in the end. Hornung also forces the reader to think about the concepts of kindness and cruelty, personal and cultural identify, and survival. In Dmitry and Natalya, the reader also experiences some of the hopelessness that people feel and the coping strategies they employ when faced with society's insurmountable problems, such as abject poverty and homelessness. Once Dmitry becomes aware of feral dogs, he sees them everywhere and must reflect that no matter how many strays—whether children or dogs—he helps, there are thousands more that he cannot reach.

While undeniably accomplished, *Dog Boy* is not without some minor problems. Particularly in the first of the novel's five parts, word and phrase repetition is prevalent enough to become noticeable to the reader, interrupting an otherwise gripping narrative. It is possible, however, that this is a deliberate attempt on the author's part to invoke Romochka's simplistic and quite limited view of the world in which he lives. More problematic is the somewhat jarring shift that occurs when Dmitry first appears in part IV of the book, after which significant portions of the story are then related from his point of view. Similarly, Natalya's occasional journal entries detailing her observations of Marko and Romochka feel like foreign intrusions into the canine world where not only Romochka but also the reader had become comfortable. From this point onward, much of the story is devoted to Dmitry's simultaneous elation and alarm at the prospect of studying Marko and later Romochka; he relishes the chance to prove his theories correct but fears making a fool of himself, concerns that are difficult for the reader to empathize with in comparison to Romochka's precarious existence. Fortunately, while Dmitry's initial behavior is largely selfish, at Natalya's urging, he ultimately decides to take personal as well as scientific responsibility for Romochka. Although this transformation occurs a bit abruptly and is perhaps not entirely believable, it is nonetheless moving, and the reader can believe that Dmitry is finally and firmly committed to something outside himself. It is much more difficult, however, to speculate about Romochka's fate, leaving the reader with much to ponder at this thought-provoking novel's conclusion.

Amy Sisson

Review Sources

Booklist 106 (March 15, 2010): 19.
The Guardian, February 13, 2010, p. 13.
Library Journal 135 (March 1, 2010): 74.
Publishers Weekly 257 (January 4, 2010): 28.
USA Today, March 18, 2010, p. 07d.

THE DOUBLE COMFORT SAFARI CLUB

Author: Alexander McCall Smith (1948-   )
Publisher: Pantheon (New York). 211 pp. $24.95
Type of work: Novel
Time: The present
Locale: Gaborone, Botswana

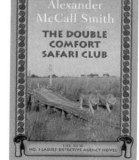

Precious Ramotswe, owner of the No. 1 Ladies' Detective Agency, takes on a case that leads her and her assistant, Grace Makutsi, to a safari camp, while Mma Makutsi's fiancé recuperates from surgery and another case involves the perfidious Violet Sephotho

Principal characters:
> PRECIOUS RAMOTSWE, the founder of the
> > No. 1 Ladies' Detective Agency; a traditionally built woman, thoughtful, patriotic, gentle, and kind
> GRACE MAKUTSI, her touchy assistant whose glasses and blotchy skin make her assertive about her excellent secretarial skills
> MR. J. L. B. MATEKONI, Mma Ramotswe's kindly husband, excellent mechanic, and proprietor of Tlokweng Road Speedy Motors
> PHUTI RADIPHUTI, Grace Makutsi's fiancé, prosperous owner of the Double Comfort Furniture Shop
> PHUTI RADIPHUTI'S NUMBER ONE AUNTIE, a dominating woman with a melon-shaped head
> VIOLET SEPHOTHO, a glamorous arch-Jezebel; the men she dominates care little about her barely passing scores at secretarial college
> MMA MATELEKE, a friend of Mma Ramotswe who doubts her husband's fidelity
> MMA POTOKWANE, the forceful director of a local orphanage and old friend of Ramotswe

At one point in *The Double Comfort Safari Club*, the detective Precious Ramotswe meditates on the world's frantic busyness. Surely, she thinks, there must be places where the old ways prevail, where people sit outdoors together and watch their cattle, talk with their friends, and support what she often calls "the old Botswana" customs, a phrase that contains a wealth of social commentary far beyond the usual meanings of "customs." To Ramotswe, it suggests an old-fashioned courtesy and respect and a general sense of gratitude for the beauties of Botswana, a world in which cattle are still the ultimate source of wealth, and where *pula*, the Setswana word for "money," is also the word for "rain," a crucial commodity in a dry country. Ramotswe herself embodies these qualities. In the old way, she reveres the memory of her father, Obed Ramotswe, a well-known judge of excellent cattle, although he is "late." Author Alexander McCall Smith uses the word "late" in Botswana fashion as a synonym

Alexander McCall Smith is the author of several series of novels as well as other short fictions. Born in Zimbabwe, he once taught law at the University of Botswana. He is professor emeritus of medical law at the University of Edinburgh.

for "dead," noting that in Botswana calling a friend or relative dead seems to suggest the late one's complete separation from the living ones, while "late" suggests their ongoing relationship.

The Double Comfort Safari Club is the eleventh volume in this popular detective series, one in which violent crime is rarely an issue and in which the detective, Ramotswe, is noted particularly for her kindness. Ramotswe's gentle attitude toward the world's evildoers—she argues that it is usually better not to humiliate the guilty—is surely part of this series' appeal, as is McCall Smith's genuine affection for Botswana, where he once taught law, and its people. This is not to say that the series ignores real problems; Botswana's many orphans are part of the series, and the poverty of some of its citizens is painfully clear. However, the No. 1 Ladies' Detective Agency mostly operates in an ordered world where solutions to bad behavior can be determined in conversations over endless doughnuts and cups of redbush tea. If that order is part of the series' appeal, so also is its gentle humor, as McCall Smith records the sometimes touchy office politics that test the usually kind relationship between Ramotswe and her assistant, Grace Makutsi, a woman with a metaphorically thin, and literally blotchy, skin; a passion for new shoes; and a sense of self-esteem based mostly on the 97 percent average with which she graduated from the Botswana Secretarial College.

In this novel, as usual, Ramotswe is faced with several problems at once. One problem is her friend Mateleke's announcement that she suspects her husband, a mild-mannered part-time radio minister, of having an affair. Indeed, Ramotswe's husband, the redoubtable J. L. B. Matekoni, opens the novel as he rescues Mateleke when her car has broken down. In the process of the rescue, he muses on something that seems curious about the incident.

A second problem rises when Ramotswe meets with a new client, Mr. Kereleng. His story is complex. His father owned a successful liquor store and had hoped that his son would run it when he retired. However, Mr. Kereleng chose biology as his career, so he left a trusted manager in charge of the store when his father retired in peace to his home village. When the manager betrayed his trust and absconded with most of the store's profits, Mr. Kereleng put his remaining funds in the bank, intending to find a wife and buy a house. Unfortunately for Mr. Kereleng, he and his money fell victim to Violet Sephotho, the glamorous seductress who has appeared earlier in this series. Like Makutsi, she also attended Botswana Secretarial College, graduating with a bare

50 percent. In the past, she attempted to capture the affections of Makutsi's fiancé Phuti Radiphuti, whose successful furniture business had come to her greedy attention. In this novel, she has turned her charms on Mr. Kereleng and seems to have succeeded in gaining the legal title to his house. Ramotswe finds a way out of this tangle, bringing along Makutsi to have a memorably satisfying confrontation with the duplicitous Violet.

The safari of the novel's title is the subject of Ramotswe's third problem. A letter from an American lawyer asks her to locate a safari guide whose kindness so impressed his client, Mrs. Grant, on her safari to Botswana's Okavango Delta that she has left him $3,000 in her will. Mrs. Grant could remember neither the name of her kind guide nor the exact name of the safari camp. However, Ramotswe has connections that help her identify the camp, which lies far in Botswana's north, and her husband has relatives in a nearby village with whom she and Makutsi can stay, calling in favors from family in the old Botswanan way. Identifying the kind guide has some complications. The real delight of this part of the novel lies in the two detectives' acquisition of safari boots in preparation for the trip and their nervous awareness of the dangers of travels on a river full of crocodiles and hippopotamuses. They are city ladies from Gabarone, not safari trekkers.

The novel's central conflict comes when Radiphuti is injured on a loading dock at his furniture store. At the hospital, his doctor performs surgery. Makutsi is understandably beside herself. She has been looking forward to the conclusion of her long engagement; recently Radiphuti has been talking more and more about marriage. Her distress is compounded when Radiphuti's auntie, an overbearing woman with a melon-shaped head, refuses to allow Makutsi to visit Radiphuti, first in the hospital and later at her house where she has taken him. She tells Makutsi that an auntie's position as blood relative outweighs the negligible position of a fiancé. Significantly, she ignores the niceties of Botswana courtesy when Ramotswe visits her in an attempt to set things right. To all appearances, Radiphuti has been hijacked by his aunt, who seems to fear that his marriage will undermine her position in his affections. It remains for the orphanage director, Mma Potokwane, a woman even more overbearing than the auntie, to put the auntie in her proper place and provide a satisfactory solution.

A leisurely pace characterizes most of the novels in this series. There always seems to be time for Ramotswe and Makutsi to discuss the topics of the day over tea, to consider Matekoni's wayward apprentices, or to talk about the mysterious appeal football offers to men. This novel seems especially given to meditative passages, some of them dealing with weightier issues than football. On the drive to the safari camp, Ramotswe provides a lengthy story of a young woman who may (or may not) have been a victim of witchcraft. At another point, as Ramotswe drinks tea near the market, an acquaintance joins her for a conversation in which the two ladies express their appreciation for the world's mechanics, people who know how to fix things and thus keep Botswana running smoothly. Also, at Sunday services at the Anglican cathedral, Ramotswe listens carefully to the message of a visiting priest. His sermon asserts that all people, both friends and strangers, are brought together by bonds of love. He goes on to say that the injunction to love one another is not simply wishful thinking; instead it is more likely to save the world than science. As he talks, Ramotswe notes how his message is received by her fellow churchgoers. When she sees a woman weeping, she starts to tell her not to cry, but on second thought she realizes that sometimes tears are right, and says instead "Yes, you can cry Mma."

If conventional detective stories find their appeal in an implied assertion that the detective's intellect can restore order to a disordered world, the No. 1 Ladies' Detective Agency novels always suggest that kindness, generosity, respect, and love are the real pathways to order. In *The Double Comfort Safari Club*, those qualities are given a helpful boost by the right connections and a level of chutzpah that can challenge even that of an ill-tempered auntie. Not surprisingly, however, the novel closes with two traditionally built women, Ramotswe and Potokwane, drinking tea and eating fruitcake. Ramotswe closes her eyes briefly, in a moment of gratitude that she lives among friends in a land she loves.

Ann D. Garbett

Review Sources

Booklist 106, no. 11 (February, 2010): 6.
Christianity Today 54, no. 4 (April, 2010): 66.
Kirkus Reviews 78, no. 4 (February 15, 2010): 110.
Publishers Weekly 257, no. 6 (February 8, 2010): 27.

DREAMS IN A TIME OF WAR
A Childhood Memoir

Author: Ngugi wa Thiong'o (1938-   )
Publisher: Pantheon (New York). 262 pp. $24.95
Type of work: Memoir
Time: Late 1930's to mid-1950's
Locale: Limuru, Kenya, East Africa

A memoir of the childhood of the noted Kenyan author, from his birth in 1938 to his coming-of-age and departure for high school in 1954

Principal personages:
> NGUGI WA THIONG'O, christened JAMES
> NGUGI, a Kenyan writer and the central
> figure in this memoir
> WANGARI, the first wife of his father and
> the family storyteller
> GACOKI, the second wife of his father
> JOSEPH KABAE, third son of Wangari and a member of the King's
> African Rifles
> LORD REVEREND STANLEY KAHAHU, an African minister trained by
> white missionaries and the family's landlord
> THIONG'O WA NADUCU, his father, husband of four wives, and father of
> twenty-four children
> KENNETH MBUGUA, his childhood friend and schoolmate
> WANJIKU WA NGUGI, his mother, his father's third wife
> NJERI, his father's fourth wife
> NGANDI NJUGUNA, a teacher at the Manguo school
> WALLACE MWANGI WA THIONG'O, known as "Good Wallace," his older
> brother, who becomes a Mau Mau guerrilla

Booklovers are generally attracted to stories about children who grow up to be writers or, more specifically, of bittersweet memoirs by writers looking back on their childhoods. Many popular examples of the genre, including Eudora Welty's *One Writer's Beginnings* (1983), Annie Dillard's *An American Childhood* (1987), and Frank McCourt's *Angela's Ashes* (1996), are aimed at readers whose lives and homes are not much different from those of the authors. Ngugi wa Thiong'o's *Dreams in a Time of War* belongs to another group of memoirs, written by major African literary figures but intended for a largely Western audience. Wole Soyinka's *Ake* (1982) is an early example of this group; more recently, Chinua Achebe published his own, *The Education of a British-Protected Child* (2009). Several reviewers of these three African memoirs have mentioned their previous ignorance of the authors and of the countries they called home; Ngugi, Soyinka, and Achebe all recognize twin responsibili-

Kenyan writer Ngugi wa Thiong'o is the author of eighteen books, including the novels Weep Not, Child *(1964); A* Grain of Wheat *(1967); and* Wizard of the Crow *(2006), nominated for the Man Booker International Prize.*

ties for their books: illuminating the unique circumstances of their younger years and educating outsiders about the cultures and the imperialism that shaped those years.

Beginning with his title and continuing throughout the book, Ngugi does offer insight into cultural and political issues in Kenya. The "time of war" mentioned in the title refers on the most literal level to the Mau Mau Rebellion, running from 1952 to 1960, while Kenya was still a British colony, during which rebels led by the author's ethnic group, the Kikuyu, battled British military and police forces. Ngugi begins his memoir in April, 1954, as he is nearing the end of his six-mile walk home from school. He is trying not to think about how hungry he is (having had only a small bowl of porridge for breakfast and a few minutes with Charles Dickens's *Oliver Twist* [1838] instead of food at lunchtime), when he meets a crowd of men talking about an exciting event from earlier in the day: A man, presumed to be a Mau Mau guerrilla, was arrested and handcuffed by the police but managed to break free and escape into the nearby tea plantations. The boy is thrilled by the story and cannot wait to share it with his family at supper. On reaching home, however, he learns that the fleeing man was his older brother, Wallace Mwangi, who has barely gotten away with his life. "It is this war," says Wanjiku, the mother of Wallace and Ngugi. The author ends the anecdote with his mother's words, not pausing to reflect that the Mau Mau Rebellion will eventually lead to independence for Kenya and inspire other African independence movements. Neither does he remind readers familiar with his career that his own first novel, *Weep Not, Child* (1964), dealt with the Mau Mau. Instead, he remains firmly within the time frame he established for this memoir; he moves backward in time and begins again at the beginning, with his birth.

"I was born in 1938, under the shadow of another war, the Second World War," the next chapter begins. This war, too, shapes his family and his people: One of his half brothers, Joseph Kabae, fought with the British in World War II and served with the colonial forces to maintain their power. As a child in this period, Ngugi was growing up as Kenya was engaged in another sort of war, making the transition from tradition to modernity—a change that will prove to be rewarding for the author but difficult for his father. Thiong'o wa Naducu, the father, is head of a traditional Kikuyu family: He and his four wives live in a compound of five huts in Limuru, in the "White Highlands" northwest of Nairobi. Each wife has her own hut, all arranged in a semicircle around their husband's. He is a wealthy man with many cows and goats and thriving crops. He acquired his land in the traditional way, with an oral agreement, but later learns that the same land has been sold to an African landlord, the Lord Reverend Stanley Kahahu, with a written contract that is determined to override the oral agreement. Ngugi's family finds themselves tenants on their own land. European-owned pyrethrum fields gradually take the place of the surrounding forests, and Thiong'o's goats and cattle are devastated by disease. Ngugi's father becomes bitter, turns to drink, and eventually forces his third wife, the author's mother Wanjiku, out of the compound.

Kahalu is a complicated figure in the author's life. He is African but also a Christian missionary, trained at the Church of Scotland Mission, and a beneficiary of the British colonial establishment and its new system of laws. When a traditional healer is unable to cure the author's persistent eye infections, Kahalu arranges for him to be treated in a hospital in Nairobi. The Kahalu children are a source of wonder and envy: They ride in cars; they wear dresses, shorts, shirts, and underwear instead of wrapping their bodies in simple rectangular cloths; and they go to school instead of working in the pyrethrum fields. Their home, next door to Ngugi's father's compound, can only be glimpsed through fences and hedges; when the local children are invited one year to a Christmas party at the Kahalu estate, they are impressed with the lawn, the iron roof, the prayer before the meal, and "the pile of jam sandwiches in huge containers." Ngugi and his brother misbehave by giggling during the prayer, eliciting a stern lecture from Kahalu's wife, who ultimately forgives them "because, being heathens, we did not know any better." In lines such as this, the author portrays powerfully, without overtly explaining, his attraction and resistance to Kahalu and his modern way of life.

The central moment of *Dreams in a Time of War* comes in 1947 after Ngugi has looked longingly at the Kahalu children returning home from school. One evening, his mother asks him a question he has assumed she could never ask: if he would like to go to school. Although some of his older half brothers have attended a few years of school each, the family is poor now, and paying tuition will be a struggle. He will have to do without lunch most days but will have to attend faithfully nonetheless. Most important, his mother asks him to promise to always try his best. "When I looked at her and said yes," Ngugi writes, "I knew deep inside me that she and I had made a pact; I would always try my best whatever the hardship, whatever the barrier." Ngugi remembers this promise and returns to it again and again through the memoir. It is this promise, he makes clear, that lies at the heart of everything he became and accomplished.

Ngugi does well in school; he is bright and hard-working and receives good advice from his older brothers. The center of the book deals with his schooling and demonstrates the cultural importance of competing educational systems. The author first attends Kamandura, one of the missionary schools known as "Kirore" schools, intended to teach Kenyan children to be useful laborers under the British colonialists. Halfway through his third year he switches to the Manguo school, one of the "Karing'a" schools that encouraged modernity, the learning of English, and a more liberal education. It is surprising that Ngugi does not step aside to contemplate the complexities or the ironies of these systems beyond a few pages of exposition. Instead, he leaves the reader to puzzle over a system that, paradoxically, moves students to develop their minds and to move into the modern world but that does so by assimilating them into British culture. Ngugi himself made the decision in the 1980's, explained in *Decolonising the Mind: The Politics of Language in African Literature* (1986), that he would never again write in English, but only in his native Gikuyu; he does not mention his decision in this book. In fact, although readers familiar with his work know that this memoir must have been written originally in Gikuyu and translated by Ngugi himself, the fact is not mentioned anywhere in the book.

Dreams in a Time of War is at its strongest when Ngugi describes his family and their way of life and shares his simple and poignant memories of home and school. He is an engaging storyteller with a sharp eye for detail and an ear for how people speak; his stories of the party at the Kahalu estate, his initiation ceremony, and his visit from the outlaw Good Wallace are clear and powerful, in large part because he does not step forward to highlight their significance. Frequently, however, particularly in the latter half of the book, he steps out of his tale to explain the history of the Mau Mau or to give background information about Kenyan historical figures. These digressions are only marginally successful, feeling like intrusions rather than illuminations. It is as though Ngugi is not sure who his audience is: Do his readers understand the historical, cultural, and political implications of these events, or do they not? Rather than commit to one readership or another, Ngugi tries to split the difference, giving enough names and dates and locations to be accurate without the maps or chronologies that would guide the uninitiated on a sure path through the thicket. But the digressions tend to be brief, and soon the author returns to his main purpose: to show how a promise to his mother set him on the road to international acclaim as the most important East African writer of the twentieth century.

The book ends at a fitting place. Having just gone through the circumcision that marks his transition into adulthood, Ngugi is accepted into Alliance High School, the most selective high school in the country. Benefactors step forward to cover the costs of tuition, supplies, and his first-ever pair of shoes and stockings. All that is left is to say goodbye to his parents and friends and then board a train for the first time, carrying him to Kikuyu Township. The final leg of the journey is by bus, and as the author rides past the sign welcoming him to school, he remembers his promise to his mother, knowing that she wants "a renewal of our pact to have dreams even in a time of war."

Cynthia A. Bily

Review Sources

Booklist 106, no. 12 (February 15, 2010): 20.
The Guardian, July 3, 2010, p. 7.
Independent, March 26, 2010, p. 26.
Kirkus Reviews 78, no. 2 (January 15, 2010): 76.
Publishers Weekly 257 (March 22, 2010): 64.
The Spectator 312, no. 9474 (March 27, 2010): 38.

DRIVING ON THE RIM

Author: Thomas McGuane (1939-   )
Publisher: Alfred A. Knopf (New York). 305 pp. $26.95
Type of work: Novel
Time: 1940's to the early twenty-first century
Locale: Livingston, Montana, and vicinity; briefly,
    Orofino, Idaho; other parts of the American West;
    Ohio; Florida; and British Columbia

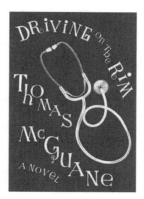

*The story of a doctor who returns to his small Montana
hometown and joins a group practice at the local clinic
and has to deal with his disreputable family background,
his own arrested development, clinic politics, assorted
girlfriends, and a charge of negligent manslaughter*

Principal characters:
> DR. I. B. "BERL" PICKETT, a doctor suffering a prolonged adolescence
> MRS. PICKETT, his mother, a Pentecostal Christian
> BOB PICKETT, his father, a World War II veteran
> SYLVIA "AUNT SILBIE," his aunt and his first sex partner
> DR. ELDON OLSSON, his mentor, a family doctor
> TESSA LARIONOV, his early girlfriend, later a patient
> DR. JINX MAYHALL, his best friend at the clinic
> DR. ALAN HIRSCH, another friend at the clinic
> NILES THROCKMORTON, his childhood friend and lawyer
> DONALD SANCHEZ, his second lawyer
> CLARICE WORRELL, his patient suffering spousal abuse
> CODY WORRELL, Clarice's abusive husband
> RAYMOND WILMOT, the chairman of the clinic's board
> JOCELYN BOYCE, a pilot who drives Berl sex-crazy
> WOMACK, Jocelyn's partner
> DANIEL BOWLES LAUDERDALE, a lawyer and later a judge
> DEANNE PERKINS, Cody's mother
> DR. GARY HAACK,
> DR. LAIRD MCALLISTER, and
> DR. ELVIS WONG, other doctors at the clinic

Driving on the Rim, Thomas McGuane's tenth novel, has a dull, slow beginning,
mixing a few narrative episodes with background from the protagonist Berl Pickett's
boyhood, teenage years, and college days. The background tends to be in expository
style, to tell rather than show, with paragraphs containing topic sentences and sentences loaded with "where" and "when" clauses. The content tends to be recursive
and repetitive: Readers are told repeatedly that Berl's parents are impecunious Pente-
costals who roam the West, try and fail at several trades, and await the Rapture.

Thomas McGuane has written nine other novels—including Ninety-two in the Shade *(1973),* Nothing but Blue Skies *(1992), and* The Cadence of Grass *(2002)—two collections of short stories, screenplays, and nonfiction works on fly-fishing, horses, and outdoor life.*

Brief relief is provided by a two-page stay with Aunt Silbie, who puts up the poor family in her double-wide trailer in Orofino, Idaho. Aunt Silbie, with a "tigerish sexual appetite," takes a liking to fourteen-year-old Berl while his parents are out trying to earn a living: "In my first six months in action Aunt Silbie taught me ninety-nine percent of everything I would ever know about sex." This incestuous fling helps explain Berl's arrested development, obsession with sex, and numerous affairs (especially with older women).

The dullness of the novel's first one-third or so can perhaps be justified by Berl's narrative point of view. His rambling first-person account is what one might expect from such a flawed protagonist, who is confused, obsessive, and ashamed of his family background. Although he is a good student and manages to earn a medical degree, even Berl is aware of his shortcomings, regularly referring to himself as an idiot, nincompoop, and dork (thankfully, the slangy American idiom adds some spice to Berl's narration).

Driving on the Rim—a title that seems to refer to Berl's precarious lifestyle, symbolized by the rattletrap Oldsmobile 88 that he drives—asks whether a dork can survive without major problems, especially as a doctor in a group practice in his small hometown. The answer seems to be no.

The action begins to pick up around page 85, on Berl's fortieth birthday, when one of his former lovers, Tessa Larionov, is brought to the emergency room after a suicide attempt, a serrated bread knife still sticking in her belly. In the intervening years Tessa has fallen on hard times, with periods of homelessness and mental instability. Although he was no longer involved with her, Berl helped her financially and tries to save her. However, after lingering four days under his treatment, Tessa dies.

The repercussions of Tessa's death are alarming. She is known to have been one of Berl's former lovers, which arouses all kinds of suspicions and rumors in the small town—not helped by Tessa's deathbed ravings. Did he kill her? Why? Was it a mercy killing or what? People around town quiz him, a few come to him for assisted suicide, and "the local Hemlock Society and its right-to-die sympathizers" hail him as a hero.

There are also repercussions within the clinic, where Berl is already embroiled in internal politics. Some of Berl's doctor colleagues consider him a scab because he did not join their boycott of the clinic during a feud with the board. Even worse, the board chairman, Raymond Wilmot (with whose wife Berl had an affair), is out to get him. Almost before he knows it, Berl is suspended without pay while an internal investigation takes place. Finally, he begins getting calls from his lawyer and visits from police officers, resulting in criminal charges eventually trimmed down to negligent manslaughter.

Complicating matters further for Berl is that he feels responsible for another suicide, that of Cody Worrell, the abusive husband of his patient Clarice. After beating Clarice up for years, Cody finally goes too far one night, kills Clarice, and calls the doctor. When Berl arrives, Cody is holding a gun to his own head, and the good doctor tells him to pull the trigger. Berl transfers his lingering guilt over this incident, which happened earlier in the novel, to the death of Tessa.

Berl's irrational transfer of guilt bespeaks the power that his Pentecostal mother still wields over his mind (his father, it turns out, was only faking belief to please the mother). On some unconscious level, Berl feels a floating guilt like the weight of original sin. The guilt seems to accrue and to include guilt over committing his mother to an asylum after she started taking to the streets and speaking in tongues. He finally seeks to shrive his guilt by attending his mother's old Pentecostal meeting and getting down with the rest of the Holy Rollers—by far the most intense and hilarious scene in the novel.

Women seem to loom over Berl's life like "the colossal statue of Our Lady of the Rockies outside Butte, a ninety-footer sitting atop the Continental Divide." The clincher is beautiful, breast-enhanced Jocelyn Boyce, who, at this worst of times for Berl, comes to dominate his mind. Jocelyn literally falls out of the sky, flies men the way she flies planes, and leaves skeletons in her wake. Berl rescues her when her crop-dusting plane crashes, and as a man of medicine, he feels obliged to follow up on her recovery at a hospital in another town. In due time her full recovery is confirmed by the intense sex they are having: If Aunt Silbie taught him "sex 101," Jocelyn instructs him in advanced techniques.

Berl thinks of Jocelyn as a gift from the gods, but she seems more like their ironic punishment. He becomes so befogged and addicted to her that he ignores, or at least does not mind, her shady sidekick Womack, even when Womack answers the knock on her hotel-room door. The only person seemingly capable of salvaging Berl, or interested in doing so, is his friend and colleague Dr. Jinx Mayhall, who calls Jocelyn a "castrating harpie." However, aside from good sense, all that Jinx has to offer Berl, in opposition to Jocelyn's feral sexuality, are their dinners and bird-watching forays together.

Another thing capable of saving Berl is the great Montana outdoors. His earlier mentor, Dr. Eldon Olsson, who saved him from his family, persuaded him to become a doctor, and funded his education, also introduced him to bird hunting and trout fishing. Later, whenever something troubles him, Berl goes fishing. Bird-watching with Jinx seems to be similarly therapeutic. Dr. Olsson himself was saved from heartbreak by coming to the great Montana outdoors, where he is able to indulge his passions for hunting and fishing.

Dr. Olsson essentially adopts young Berl as his surrogate son, since Berl's actual father is ineffectual. Bob Pickett, Berl's father, is an interesting example of someone from the "greatest generation": a small-town soldier who goes away to World War II, finds himself in the Battle of the Bulge, kills a bunch of Germans and sees death everywhere, deserts and hangs around Paris for several months, and then quietly slips back into his old unit. Anything that happens to him after these traumatizing experiences is like a footnote to his personal history. Shell-shocked, he marries a dominating Pentecostal woman and drifts through life, energized only by sharing World War II stories with other veterans.

The novel contains numerous secondary and minor characters, some of whom appear only for a page or two but who also have their stories: patients, other doctors and nurses, ranchers and ranch hands, and townsfolk. Old-style Montana ranchers are represented by Gladys and Wiley, who also take in young Berl and teach him to work and to love horses. Another old rancher is Jocelyn's father, Con Boyce. Jocelyn tells Berl that her father is dead, but she actually put him in a home and burns down his old ranch house.

Some names in the novel describe the characters. Con (he is the one conned) and Jinx (better suited for Jocelyn) are used ironically. Berl uses his nickname and initials rather than his legal name given to him by his mother: Irving Berlin Pickett, a reference to the composer of "God Bless America." Curiously, the mother is not named, perhaps to capitalize on the generic effect. Some names are used humorously: Dr. Gary Haack, an orthopedic surgeon; Dr. Laird McAllister, a patrician Yale man; and Dr. Elvis Wong, a keen-eyed radiologist. The name of Berl's gluttonous and libidinous lawyer, Throckmorton, might refer to a medical joke involving the penis, the John Thomas or Throckmorton sign.

For a novel about a doctor who works in a clinic with other doctors, *Driving on the Rim* includes few details of medical procedures and little medical jargon. No doubt the author is wise to be evasive, since medical jargon is like speaking in tongues. The novel, then, is not a medical drama but an exploration of personal development and interpersonal relationships.

It is hard to believe that men such as Berl are out there, still dealing with adolescent issues in midlife—and practising as doctors, no less. However, novelists from T. Coraghessan Boyle to McGuane keep depicting dorky guys as a genuine American type, and this type is commonplace in films, television shows, and advertisements. Are these men simply caricatures for entertainment purposes? Are the female types also caricatures? It makes one wonder whether there are smart, well-educated, mature adults somewhere in the United States.

Harold Branam

Review Sources

Booklist 106, no. 17 (May 1, 2010): 6.
Kirkus Reviews 78, no. 16 (August 15, 2010): 754.
Library Journal 135, no. 12 (July 1, 2010): 76.
The New York Times Book Review, October 24, 2010, p. 12.
Publishers Weekly 257, no. 32 (August 16, 2010): 29.

EELS
An Exploration, from New Zealand to the Sargasso, of the World's Most Mysterious Fish

Author: James Prosek (1975-   )
Publisher: Harper (New York). 287 pp. $25.99
Type of work: Natural history, science
Time: 2000-2010
Locale: New Zealand, the Pacific Ocean, New York, the
    Sargasso Sea

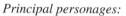

The natural history and cultural importance of the biology of freshwater eels, fish that spend most of their adult lives in freshwater ecosystems but migrate to the oceans to reproduce and probably to die

Principal personages:
> JAMES PROSEK, the author and principal
>   character, seeking to understand the freshwater eels
> RAY TURNER, the operator of an eel weir in the Catskill Mountains of
>   New York
> STELLA AUGUST, the author's guide to New Zealand, the Maori, and
>   their eels
> BILL RAYNOR, the author's guide to the Island of Pohnpei and the
>   Lasialap of U and their eels

In *Eels*, James Prosek describes freshwater eels as snakelike, slimy, and not especially lovable to most people. However, he became fascinated with the creatures; the mysterious lives they lead, especially their life cycle, aspects of which are still unknown; and their revered status in some Pacific Island cultures.

Prosek discusses his friendship with Ray Turner, an individualistic man who operated an eel weir on the Delaware River in New York's Catskill Mountains. When they are ready to reproduce, adult eels swim down freshwater streams to the ocean where they spawn. In spawning, the females lay eggs and the males deliver sperm to the eggs. The union of one egg and one sperm in fertilization produces an individual eel, a member of the next generation, in the form of the zygote or fertilized egg. A tiny larva hatches from the egg after a certain amount of cell division, growth, and specialization of the cells. The eel passes through several larval stages as it migrates to the mouth of a freshwater stream and eventually becomes an adult after it enters the fresh water. It swims up the stream, settles into a pool or other protected aspect of the upper reaches of a stream and grows into a mature adult in the freshwater ecosystem.

Prosek makes it a point to contrast eels with the more familiar salmon. Eels are catadromous fish because they move downstream to reproduce. Their life cycle contrasts with that of salmon, which are anadromous fish. Salmon spend most of their

~

*James Prosek illustrated his first book,
Trout: An Illustrated History (1996),
with his own paintings of the different
species of trout. He has written several
other books on fish and has shown his
paintings in several museums. He
cofounded* World Trout, *a trout
conservation organization.*

~

adult lives in the ocean and migrate up freshwater streams to spawn and die. "Cata-" is a word root meaning to break down or go down, while "ana-" means to synthesize, build up, or go up. The two fish types refer to the migration patterns each has to reach their spawning grounds: Catadromous fish (eels) go downstream to reproduce in the ocean, anadromous fish (salmon are the most familiar examples) swim upstream to spawn in freshwater streams.

Turner's weir is an elaborate funneling system across the Delaware River. It funnels the adult eels into a trap, interrupting their trip downstream, a trip intended to end when the eels spawn in the ocean. However, the trapped eels never finish the journey, they are processed and sold as food. At several junctions in the book, Prosek declares eel flesh to be quite good. Each declaration accompanied a different processing and cooking method. Turner's preparation and the eel preparations of various Pacific Islanders all pleased him.

Turner's interaction with eels is interesting enough: He makes a living capturing, processing, and selling eels. However, in much of the rest of the book Prosek deals with the much more elaborate relationship of some Pacific Island peoples and their eels. To them the eels, some individual eels at least, are sacred, or something close to sacred. The Maori, native New Zealanders, hold the eels in high regard. They harvest them for food but also consider the possibility that an eel, especially a large eel, may be a *taniwha,* a supernatural being. Prosek was not completely satisfied with the definitions of a *taniwha* that he obtained from the Maori, and he concluded that one probably has to be Maori to really appreciate the meaning. However, he reports several Maoris' attempts to explain the phenomenon. *Taniwha* can take a number of forms according to the Maori. They often take the form of a shark in salt water and that of an eel in fresh water. If a *taniwha* in eel form is captured, for food during the eel harvest for example, it will identify itself as a *taniwha* by behavior that is not typical of eels. Barking like a dog or crying like a baby are two examples given. The captor is thus warned that the eel is a *taniwha* and should be treated gently and released. If it is not released, something bad, death for example, will happen to the person. A *taniwha* can be a guardian, protective of and beneficial to a person, or it can be a monster and a serious detriment to a person's well-being.

Stella August was Prosek's guide to New Zealand, the native Maori people, and their eels. She was half Maori and was studying eels for her graduate degree; she agreed to introduce him to various New Zealanders who had information and stories about eels. She, and essentially all the Maori Prosek interviewed, seemed defensive of Maori culture and resentful of the British and other foreign influences on New Zealand and the Maori lifestyle. The resentment extended to Prosek in several instances. For example, in response to Prosek's expressed wish to know the location of the eels' spawning grounds, one interviewee told him that he hoped the location was never found. Another asked why it was necessary or even important to know the exact spot. He intended the comment as a criticism of Prosek's desire to know the location of that spot. One Maori interviewed expressed chagrin at the amount of Maori culture and tradition exposed in the film *Whale Rider* (2002), suggesting that the Maori were compromised in some way when outsiders were given access to such information. Even Stella, his guide, reprimanded Prosek for interrupting the Maori as they told their stories, although he was only interrupting to ask questions and gain clarification. Prosek does not express the frustration he must have felt at this reluctance to accept him and to share information with him. He simply reports it as part of the Maori persona.

Prosek reports the same reluctance to share cultural information, including information on eels, among the Lasialap of U, on the Micronesian island of Pohnpei. He again acquired the services of an insider, Bill Raynor, to introduce him to people on the island who had eel stories or eel experiences to tell about. As with the Maori, he encountered resentment of the scientific approach and his desire to know more about the eels than can be easily observed. Again, he treats this reluctance on the part of Lasialap of U to share their experiences simply as a characteristic of the people, not as a vindictive behavior.

Back in North America, Prosek explores Tim and Doug Watts's attempt to get American eels listed as an endangered or threatened species by the U.S. Environmental Protection Agency. In many North American streams the number of mature eels migrating to the sea to spawn has declined to nearly zero. This is especially true in the streams farthest from the spawning grounds. Despite this well-documented observation, the appeal for endangered status was not granted. The decision was apparently based on the also well-documented observation that American eel populations in streams closer to the spawning grounds were doing reasonably well, and so the species was in no danger of extinction. The populations of some streams, however, are in danger of suffering extinction. This is true of the different eel species and populations in many streams outside North America as well.

Prosek identifies hydroelectricity-producing dams and overfishing as the primary causes of the eels' decline. The impact of overfishing is obvious, if more eels are taken by eel weirs and other collecting systems than are produced by the eels' complex reproductive cycle, the population will decline. Of course, collecting large numbers of adult eels on their way to the spawning beds will tend to bring about exactly that result. Not only are the captured eels that are killed and eaten removed from the population but also are the products of their potential reproduction, their offspring. If these conditions continue long enough, the population of the species will decrease in numbers until it suffers extinction.

Dams impact the eels by retarding the travel of the larvae and young eels to fresh water to grow and mature but, more important, by blocking the mature, reproductively capable adults from reaching the spawning grounds and by killing many of them as they attempt to pass the dam and find their way to the ocean to spawn. Dams may bring a stream's population to extinction even more efficiently than overfishing. In the face of these factors, Prosek expresses concern for the future of freshwater eel populations throughout the world.

Unfortunately for the reader, the book has no index. Prosek introduces several native terms and explains them the first time he uses them, but if the reader forgets the meaning by the time a subsequent use is encountered, the reader will spend an appreciable amount of time trying to find the word's first use and its meaning. Had the word been indexed, or included in a glossary, reading the book would be streamlined. Initially, transition from chapter to chapter, which is often also from one location to another, seems disjointed. However, the eel life cycle links some chapters and acts to unify the book and smooth the transitions. Proofreading was carefully done, and few errors were discovered in this reading. The book is illustrated with several of the author's drawings.

Prosek has not written a scientific study of eels, and the reader would do well to look elsewhere if interested in detailed and specific eel biology. However, he does expose the reader to all stages of the intriguing eel life cycle and presents enough information to integrate the stages into a general life cycle. In addition to the lives of the eels, Prosek's interests include the lives and attitudes of the Maori, the Lasialap, and Ray Turner. He sacrifices some eel detail to include information on the people who interact with them. The cultural roles eels play in different societies, their mythical roles in some cultures, and their important contribution to the nutritional needs of some groups, including the different means by which they are captured and prepared for consumption, result in an interesting picture of the diversity (and similarity) of eel-human interactions in different cultures.

The book includes some eel connections that must surprise nearly every reader. One example is that Sigmund Freud's first scientific publication was a failed attempt to identify the male eel's gonad. Freud looked for the testes and associated tubing in freshwater eels, but the testes of these catadromous fish do not develop until the male is in marine waters, headed for the spawning grounds. Just as other scientists did at the time, Freud assumed that the eels spawned in fresh water and so expected the gonads to be present and well developed in freshwater eels. Freud's error was a reflection of the eels' mysterious life cycle, which, though clarified in some ways, continues to puzzle scientists in other ways; for example, the exact location of many eel species' and populations' spawning sites are still unknown, and the processes that guide their migrations between freshwater streams and these unknown locations are still only partly understood. Prosek suggests that Freud's eel studies may have impacted his views of human sexuality, which developed later in his career and for which he is much better known.

The book can be seen as a collection of interesting threads, more or less held together by the incompletely understood life cycle of the "world's most mysterious fish." That arrangement works well, and reviews of the book have been favorable.

Carl W. Hoagstrom

Review Sources

Booklist 107, no. 4 (October 15, 2010): 7.
Economist 396 (September 25, 2010): 106.
Kirkus Reviews 78, no. 13 (July 1, 2010): 610.
Library Journal 135, no. 13 (August 1, 2010): 105.
Nature 468, no. 7326 (December 16, 2010): 894-895.
New Scientist 207, no. 2778 (September 18, 2010): 3.
The New York Times Book Review, May 10, 2009, p. 17.
Outside 35, no. 9 (October, 2010): 28.
Publishers Weekly 257, no. 22 (May 31, 2010): 34.
Science News 178, no. 11 (November 20, 2010): 30.

ELEGY FOR APRIL

Author: Benjamin Black (pseudonym of John Banville, 1945-   )
Publisher: Henry Holt (New York). 336 pp. $25.00
Type of work: Novel
Time: 1950's
Locale: Dublin, Ireland

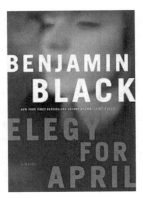

Dublin pathologist Quirke is asked to investigate the disappearance of his estranged daughter's best friend, revealing corruption in high places

Principal characters:
>QUIRKE, a middle-aged pathologist at the Holy Family Hospital
>INSPECTOR HACKETT, the detective inspector of the Dublin police force
>PHOEBE GRIFFIN, Quirke's daughter, adopted by his stepbrother after Quirke's wife's death
>MALACHY GRIFFIN, Phoebe's adoptive obstetrician father whose own father, Judge Garret Griffin, adopted Quirke as a child
>APRIL LATIMER, a young doctor and friend of Phoebe's who is missing
>CELIA LATIMER, April's wealthy, pretentious mother
>OSCAR LATIMER, April's older brother and obstetrician
>WILLIAM LATIMER, April's uncle and minister of health in Ireland
>CONOR LATIMER, April's dead physician father
>PATRICK OJUKWU, a Nigerian medical student studying in Ireland
>ISABEL GALLOWAY, an actor and friend of April
>JIMMY MINOR, a journalist friend of April

Concerned because she has not heard from her best friend, April Latimer, for more than a week, Phoebe Griffin contacts her pathologist father, Quirke, and requests his help in finding her at the opening of *Elegy for April*, by Benjamin Black, the nom de plume for John Banville. Quirke is not a private investigator, though he has worked on a pair of earlier cases with Detective Inspector Hackett of the Dublin police force, and the two begin inquiries. When they contact Oscar Latimer, April's older brother, he hardly seems concerned, regarding the disappearance as typical behavior for his erratic sister. The next day Quirke and Hackett are summoned to Celia Latimer's house and warned to mind their own business.

Quirke is a recovering alcoholic desperately trying to resume his duties as a pathologist and support his daughter from whom he has been estranged for years. Comic relief is provided by Quirke's sudden decision to buy an Alvis Super Graber Coupe, an expensive, exclusive automobile he does not know how to drive. Throughout the novel he careens through the Dublin streets, narrowly avoiding one accident after another yet persuaded he has mastered the machine.

Quirke and Hackett continue their investigations, finding traces of blood between the
floor boards of April's apartment, while her
uncle, the minister of health, further attempts
to dissuade the investigators. Quirke meets
other of April and Phoebe's friends and begins a short, romantic affair with actor Isabel
Galloway. At the same time Phoebe notices
that someone is spying on her, and in spite of
Hackett's best efforts, no one can identify the
voyeur.

*Benjamin Black is the pen name of
John Banville, an Irish novelist known
for dense, intricate novels full of
postmodern indeterminacies. His four
Benjamin Black novels, however, can
be described as literate entertainments,
detective stories set primarily in Dublin
during the 1950's.*

Patrick Ojukwu, a Nigerian medical student studying at the College of Surgeons,
admits he had a nonsexual relationship with April and that he discovered her bleeding
in her apartment after a self-inflicted abortion. After being abducted by Oscar Latimer, Quirke and Phoebe learn that April and her brother Oscar were sexually abused
as children, that Oscar impregnated his sister, and that he is responsible for her disappearance. Oscar then shoots himself while driving Quirke's uninsured car off a cliff.

The novels written under the pen name Benjamin Black offer detailed investigations of setting in ways Banville's other novels rarely do. Although he was born in
Wexford, Banville considers himself a Dubliner, and no other novelist since James
Joyce offers such a minute, comprehensive view of the city's neighborhoods, bars,
and monuments as Black.

Like each of the other two Quirke novels—*Christine Falls* (2006) and *The Silver
Swan* (2007)—atmospherics define the sense of place. *Elegy for April* opens in the
dead of winter:

> "It was the worst of winter weather, and April Latimer was missing. For days a Feb-
> ruary fog had been down and showed no sign of lifting. In the muffled silence the city
> seemed bewildered, like a man whose sight has suddenly failed. People vague as inva-
> lids groped their way through the murk, keeping close to the housefronts and the railings
> and stopping tentatively at street corners to feel with a wary foot for the pavement's
> edge."

The fog creates the perfect ambiance for crime—nothing and no one are as they appear. Clues, such as the forms in the fog, are shrouded and indistinct, discovery becomes perilous, and some answers are impossible. Readers never learn, for example,
where April is, dead or alive, and who the enigmatic voyeur, man or woman, may be.
The fog is further intensified by coal dust from the city's chimneys—"they could feel
the grit of it on their lips and between their teeth." The distasteful filthiness of the surroundings only accentuates the dirtiness of the crime and the efforts of the most
powerful to keep matters under wraps.

The temporal setting plays a particularly significant role in the novel as well. The
story takes place in the 1950's, the post-World War II era and only a few years after
the Irish Republic had gained official independence from Great Britain in 1949.

Banville has admitted his fascination with the period: "It was a remarkable time, here and in America, paranoid, guilt-ridden, beset by fear and loathing, and still shuddering in the after-effects of the war. A perfect period for a novel, if you incline toward a dark view of human beings." Ireland's economy is moribund and its population demoralized; crime is a perfect expression of the quiet despair that hangs over the place.

As Banville has pointed out in another interview, the period allows him to explore social issues that he rarely examines in his "Banville" novels. "One could not attempt to write about Ireland in the 1950's without banging one's head very hard indeed against the themes of religion and warped politics. . . . The Catholic Church ran this country for decades . . . controlling the private lives of every citizen in the state. . . . In other words, the Fifties were a noir-writer's dream." The Irish constitution enshrined Roman Catholicism as the nation's official religion and defined female experience in narrowly maternal ways. April has a reputation for sexual promiscuity, and for that reason and because of her independent spirit, she is shunned by her family and regarded as expendable.

April's wealthy mother, her father who fought in the Easter Rebellion in 1916, and her politically influential uncle wield a power that few can oppose. The real corruption in the novel rests not with April's morality but with the influence of her relatives who ruin lives and reputations, doing so not only with impunity but also without a shred of conscience. Just as the fog obscures and confines, so the church and the political status quo control and restrict individual lives. Like other colonized peoples, the Irish had learned the lessons of colonization well and, after their independence, continued to limit their own citizens.

A number of years ago, Banville began reading some of Georges Simenon's *roman durs*, his "hard novels," and was thoroughly impressed. "These are masterpieces of what one might ill-advisedly call existential fiction, and far better, less self-consciously literary, than anything by Sartre or even Camus. I thought, if this kind of thing can be achieved in simple language and direct, lightweight narrative, then I want to try it myself." The quality of existential experience is certainly apropos to Black's performance in this novel. Quirke is a fundamentally existential hero, a loner who lives one day at a time. His romantic attachments are largely circumstantial and temporary, and his life is one of containment and asceticism.

Quirke lives in a condition of almost complete alienation. Women befuddle him; he feels he has been a failure as a father, has made no amends for his mistakes, and doubts he can ever help his daughter. He has an abiding contempt for and dread of officialdom. His time in an orphanage has impressed on him the transitoriness of deep emotional connections and the harsh treatment an outsider can expect. He feels particularly well suited to his job as pathologist, "Give me the dead . . . the dead whose brief scenes on the stage are done with, for whom the last act is over and the curtain brought down." Although they are friendly and have worked together on other cases, Quirke rarely exchanges anything intimate with Hackett and does not even know the man's address.

Quirke often finds himself contemplating the difference between solitude and loneliness: "Solitude he conjectured, is being alone, while loneliness is being alone among other people. . . . He had been solitary when the bar was empty, but was he lonely now that these others had appeared?" When asked by his one confidant, Rose Crawford, if he is lonely, he quickly confirms he is and then asks, "'Isn't everyone?'"

The root of his sorrow and alienation lies in his past. He can remember only one time he ever experienced happiness and security, and those were the days when he drew pictures on the study floor of the judge who rescued him. Most of his childhood is a bad dream, and his problems with alcohol arise from a desire to escape those memories. For him the present hurries on, becoming the past all too quickly, an irretrievable experience that plagues him. His relationship with the past is also profoundly contradictory—it is a source of scalding pain yet a condition to which he returns again and again. "That was Quirke, looking back longingly to a past where he had been so unhappy."

In writing the three Quirke novels—a fourth novel, *The Lemur* (2008), is set in New York—Black has settled on a time-honored convention of the mystery writer: the serial protagonist, but with a significant difference. The tendency for too many writers, once they arrive upon a hero, is to freeze that figure. The protagonist rarely ages, their lives become a static sameness, and their cases eventually seem a round of all-too-familiar circumstances. Raymond Chandler realized this trap, and as his novels developed, his hero, Philip Marlowe, became increasingly more world-weary, but his life was largely changeless. Dissatisfied with this monotony, Chandler sought to shake his hero up by marrying him in the unfinished "The Poodle Springs Story." Black refreshes readers' memories with details from earlier novels but also develops Quirke in each new installment. The angst, for example, that plagues the pathologist only deepens in each new installment, and the complexity of his relationships with his daughter, Inspector Hackett, and his stepbrother get more complex.

While the critical reaction to the Black's novels has been largely laudatory, some reviewers have complained that Banville is slumming it by writing genre fiction. The charge is groundless. As Banville has pointed out, the Black novels give him an entirely different creative outlet. Where the Banville fictions are written slowly and with arduous care, the Black novels come in a rush and allow him a freedom to create plot-driven stories. *Elegy for April* is an accomplished, satisfying read from an adroit stylist.

David W. Madden

Review Sources

Booklist 106, no. 14 (March 15, 2010): 25.
Christianity Today 54, no. 6 (June, 2010): 54.
Kirkus Reviews 78, no. 4 (February 15, 2010): 97.
Library Journal 135, no. 5 (March 15, 2010): 94.

Los Angeles Times, April 16, 2010, p. D14.
The New York Review of Books 57, no. 18 (November 25, 2010): 39-41.
The New York Times, April 5, 2010, p. 1.
The New York Times Book Review, April 11, 2010, p. 26.
Publishers Weekly 257, no. 8 (February 22, 2010): 38.
The Times Literary Supplement, no. 5618 (December 3, 2010): 25.

THE ELEPHANT'S JOURNEY

Author: José Saramago (1922-2010)
First published: A Viagem do Elefante, 2008, in Portugal
Translated from the Portuguese by Margaret Jull Costa
Publisher: Houghton Mifflin Harcourt (Boston). 205 pp.
$24.00
Type of work: Novel
Time: 1551-1552
Locale: Beginning in Lisbon, Portugal; progressing
through Spain, the Mediterranean, Northern Italy, and
the Alps; and ending in Vienna, Austria

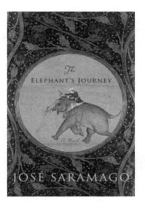

*The story of the journey of an elephant and his mahout
from Lisbon to Vienna after King João III decided to give
the animal as a wedding present to Archduke Maximilian*

Principal characters:

SOLOMON, later renamed "Suleiman," an Indian elephant
SUBHRO, later renamed "Fritz," Solomon's mahout, or keeper and trainer
DOM JOÃO III, the King of Portugal during the middle of the sixteenth
century
DONA CATARINA, the Queen of Portugal, wife of João III
PÊRO DE ALCÁÇOVA CARNEIRO, the secretary to the King of Portugal
ARCHDUKE MAXIMILIAN, the regent of Spain, later Holy Roman
Emperor Maximilian II; the cousin of the Portuguese king and queen
ARCHDUCHESS MARIA, daughter of the Holy Roman Emperor Charles V
and cousin of Maxmilian, whom she married four years before the
time in which the novel takes place

José Saramago was known for writing short novels that had the quality of parables, for his reflections on history, and for his unconventional prose style. *The Elephant's Journey*, like many of Saramago's other novels, uses long, apparently rambling sentences. Saramago distinguishes between narrative and direct conversation among characters only by context, abjuring the use of indents and quotation marks. Though set in the sixteenth century, the novel intentionally includes anachronistic comments and does not pretend to create the impression of realistic settings. He uses frequent digressions to comment on the story itself or make ironic observations about the storyteller's art and the limitations of narrative.

The novel opens in the bedroom of the king and queen of Portugal, Dom João III and Dona Catarina. The king is concerned that the marriage gift they gave their cousin, Maximilian of Austria, was inadequate. Since Maximilian, as regent of Spain, is in the city of Vallodolid, the king believes they could give the Austrian something larger and more impressive. After some thought and discussion, the queen hits

Widely regarded as Portugal's
greatest modern author, José
Saramago achieved an international
reputation only at the age of sixty,
with the publication of the translation
of Memorial do convento *(1982)*
into English in 1988 as Baltasar
and Blimunda.

on the idea of giving Solomon to the arch-duke. The king is confused at first, believing that the queen is referring to the ancient bibli-cal monarch but finally realizes that she is talking about Solomon the elephant, an ani-mal brought from Goa in India about two years before. Solomon is largely ignored in Lisbon, and he eats a great deal. Thus, not only would he be an impressive gift and serve to cement political relations among royal houses, but also giving him away would solve the problem of what to do with him.

With the help of his secretary, Pêro de Alcáçova Carneiro, the king manages to write the proper letter offering the elephant to the archduke. The back and forth ex-change between the king and his secretary gives Saramago an opportunity to poke fun at the artificiality and vanity of political hierarchy. The absurdity of power relations among people is one of the main themes running through the book. Finally, the king and his secretary receive an official letter from the archduke accepting this unique gift.

Solomon arrived in Lisbon with Subhro, his Indian mahout, or trainer and keeper. The mahout has also been living a purposeless life in Portugal, and when he enters the story he is dressed mainly in rags, some of which are the remains of the clothes he had brought with him from his homeland. After a change in outfits, Subhro sets out on the road to Valladolid with Solomon and a troop of accompanying soldiers. Subhro's conversations with the commanding officer of the troops give Saramago a chance to make wry observations on social relations of authority and regimentation. References to Subhro's Hindu heritage and to Christian beliefs provide an opportunity for ironic comments about religion.

The company stops in a village to requisition extra oxen for Solomon's fodder in order to keep the caravan moving quickly along. After moving through a number of small adventures, the Portuguese troop reaches the town where they meet the Aus-trian forces. There, a standoff occurs. Although allies, neither the Portuguese nor the Austrians trust their opposites. The Austrians, on the principle that Solomon has been given to their archduke, want to take control of the great beast for the trip to Valladolid. The Portuguese soldiers, sensitive to slights from their better-equipped opposites, believe that they will be disgraced if they cannot accompany Solomon all the way to Valladolid. After heroic speeches and promises to fight to the death, the Portuguese triumphantly carry their point and are allowed to ride with the Austrians to the archduke.

In Valladolid, the Portuguese and Austrians meet Solomon's new owner. The archduke decides that he wants to rename Solomon "Suleiman." He also finds Subhro's name hard to pronounce and announces that the surprised mahout will henceforth be called "Fritz." Even identities are subject to the whims of the rulers.

The archduke does dress up Subhro, or Fritz, in a suit of elegant clothes and has an vast, ornate saddlecloth made for Solomon, or Suleiman, thereby provoking the envy of the local clergy who would have liked the cloth for their own purposes. The arch-duke announces that the elephant and his mahout will march in a place of honor in the convoy, in front of the archduke and his bride, the Archduchess Maria. Soon, how-ever, he changes in mind. He learns that elephants relieve themselves whenever they wish, and he and the archduchess tire of traveling immediately behind a defecating elephant. The saddlecloth, too, seems to make the elephant uncomfortable and it is sent back to the Bishop of Valladolid, leaving Saramago to muse appreciatively on the prospect of leaders of the church progressing beneath a canopy made from a saddlecloth.

After an uncomfortable sea voyage, the caravan arrives in Genoa, where they are greeted by crowds of people eager to see the elephant. The procession braves rain as it rides away from Genoa, and the mahout begins to wish that Suleiman still had the saddlecloth. Making their way through the cities of northern Italy, they reach Padua, where Solomon/Suleiman and Subhro/Fritz have one of their most notable picaresque adventures. A priest from the basilica of Saint Anthony asks if the mahout can arrange a miracle. The holy man wants the elephant to kneel spontaneously in front of the ba-silica. At first, the mahout balks, but threats and inducements persuade him. The priest confides that the rise of Lutheranism has necessitated miracles to confirm the dedication of the faithful. The elephant performs so convincingly that he almost starts his own cult. Subhro/Fritz seeks to earn a little profit from credulity by selling hairs from his holy elephant that will grow hair on bald men. However, the Lutheran-lean-ing archduke learns of the mahout's small business, and this puts the Indian on the bad side of his powerful patron.

As the procession makes its way through the Alps, the mahout worries about how to recover the archduke's favor, while the elephant suffers the agonies of the ele-ments. The great animal struggles through the tough Isarco pass, only to face the even more difficult Brenner pass. Solomon/Suleiman barely makes it through the icy per-ils. Maximilian and Maria, meanwhile, make the journey in relative comfort and rush ahead through the passes, leaving their retainers and their wedding gift behind. Ulti-mately, though, everyone succeeds in going through the mountains in a kind of satiri-cal reversal of the classical crossing of Hannibal.

Finally, the company reaches Vienna. Subhro/Fritz finds himself briefly at the center of the celebrations. The elephant is a novelty for the Viennese. The triumphant end of the journey is an anticlimax, though, no more significant than any other part of the ultimately pointless adventure. Less than two years after the arrival in Vienna, a brief conclusion tells us, the elephant dies of unknown causes. The humans, having once cheered the huge beast, skin him and cut off his legs to make receptacles for canes and umbrellas. Subhro goes back into historical obscurity. After receiving pay-ment from the archduke, the mahout buys a mule and announces his intention to ride back to Lisbon. However, there is no report of his having entered Lisbon, so, Saramago tells us, Subhro must have either died on the route or changed his mind.

The Portuguese queen reacts to the news of Solomon's death with weeping, but in the end nothing much has changed. It is as if the author wants to use the novel to point out the sad absurdity of human affairs.

Solomon, the elephant, is the central character throughout *The Elephant's Journey*, but it would be difficult to describe Solomon as the protagonist. Saramago continually recounts the thoughts of Subhro/Fritz, but the elephant remains a cipher. The author occasionally speculates about what the wedding present may or may not see of the strange world of humans, but there is no effort to actually get inside the animal's thoughts. Solomon mainly trudges through a series of trials and does his best to keep up with human demands, while concentrating his attention on bathing and eating enormous amounts of fodder.

The best of Saramago's books have the quality of parables, simple tales that hint at large meanings. *The Elephant's Journey* is not among his best works. The antiauthoritarian and antireligious jokes are not particularly daring or especially shocking. The ruminations on writing and on the nature of fiction that Saramago intersperses throughout the narratives do not constitute an original narrative strategy. Self-referential novels that make their writing part of the story are too common to pass as particularly inventive. As a historical novel, it is too thin in detail to evoke an era or reimagine events of the past. Political events in Europe, the Inquisition, and the Council of Trent receive mentions, but these are all offstage, and their connections to the happenings in the novel are tenuous. Still, although this is definitely one of the author's minor works, it can be judged a modest success. A gentle humor graces the book and it presents great and small people alike with a tolerant skepticism. It gives an interesting twist to the traditional fictional theme of the journey and leaves the reader with sympathy for an elephant of centuries past.

Carl L. Bankston III

Review Sources

Booklist 106, no. 22 (August 1, 2010): 23.
The Guardian, July 24, 2010, p. 5.
Library Journal 135, no. 15 (September 15, 2010): 63.
Maclean's 123, no. 36 (September 20, 2010): 88.
The New York Times Book Review, September 19, 2010, p. 19.
The New Yorker 86, no. 32 (October 18, 2010): 81.
Publishers Weekly 257, no. 27 (July 12, 2010): 25.
Sunday Times, August 15, 2010, p. 41.
The Times Literary Supplement, no. 5599 (July 23, 2010): 19-20.
Toronto Star, September 19, 2010, p. IN7.

EMPIRE OF THE SUMMER MOON
Quanah Parker and the Rise and Fall of the Comanches, the Most Powerful Indian Tribe in American History

Author: S. C. Gwynne (1953-   )
Publisher: Scribner (New York). Illustrated. 371 pp. $27.50
Type of work: History
Time: Primarily 1836-1911
Locale: United States

A violent account of the Southwest's most feared warriors and the mixed-blood chief who guided them to glory during their last desperate days on the Texas plains before they made a remarkable adjustment to reservation life

Principal personages:
QUANAH PARKER, a Comanche chief who
   battled settlers on the Great Plains then
   led his people to settle on a reservation in Texas
CYNTHIA ANN PARKER (NADUA), his mother, a Caucasian raised as an
   American Indian
PETA NOCONA, his Comanche father
JACK HAYS, the innovative leader of the Texas Rangers
SUL ROSS, the man who killed Peta Nocona and "rescued" Cynthia Ann
ISA-TAI, a Comanche medicine man and prophet
RANALD S. MACKENZIE, a commander who conquered, then befriended
   Quanah

In *Empire of the Summer Moon*, S. C. Gwynne relays the following details: On December 10, 1910, at a ceremony reinterring Cynthia Ann Parker's remains at Post Oak Mission in Cache, Oklahoma, Quanah Parker said, "Forty years ago my mother died. She captured by Comanche, nine years old. Loved Indian and wild life so well, no want to go back to white folks. All people same anyway. God say. I love my mother."

In 1836, a Comanche band attacked Parker's Fort, a virtually undefended compound in East Texas (approximately 90 miles south of present-day Dallas). They kidnapped nine-year-old Parker after torturing and slaughtering members of her family, practices commonly meted out against settlers foolish enough to settle on Comanche traditional lands. They dragged off two other children never heard from again and a pair of older women: Elizabeth Kellogg, who was traded to the sedentary Kichai tribe and ransomed three months later, and seventeen-year-old Rachel Parker Plummer, who was abused for thirteen months before she was exchanged for emoluments. Surviving her harrowing ordeal, Parker eventually assimilated into the world of her captors, a culture, Gwynne writes:

∼

A former Time *magazine senior editor and executive editor for* Texas Monthly, *S. C. Gwynne wrote* Selling Money: A Year *(1987) and coauthored with Jonathan Beaty* The Outlaw Bank: A Wild Ride into the Secret Heart of BCCI *(2004).*

∼

of pure magic, of beaver ceremonies and eagle dances, of spirits that inhabited springs, trees, rocks, turtles, and crows; a place where people danced all night and sang bear medicine songs, where wolf medicine made a person invulnerable to bullets, dream visions dictated tribal policy, and ghosts were alive in the wind.

After Parker was captured she was renamed Nadua (Someone Found); she wed warrior Peta Nocona, destined to become successor to Chief Pobishequasso (better known as Iron Jacket because in battle he wore an ancient piece of Spanish armor). Nadua gave birth to sons Quanah and Peanuts and a daughter Topsana (Prairie Flower). While the men hunted or went on raids, the tribal women cooked, tended the animals, packed every few weeks when the band relocated, and dismantled 1,500-pound buffalo, messy labor that left one covered in fat, marrow, tissue, and blood. As Gwynne observes:

> Comanche women cut the meat into strips for drying. They tanned the hides and made the robes and harvested the paunch and the sinew and the marrow from bones and the ground-up brains and every other part of the huge beasts that were, collectively, the foundations of Nermernuh existence.

"Nermernuh," meaning simply "The People," was what Comanche called themselves. The Spanish derivation of the Ute word "Komantcia," Comanche meant, aptly, anyone who opposes me all the time. As hunter-gatherers, their culture and political organization were primitive compared to most Plains tribes. The secret of their dominance was unsurpassed horsemanship in breeding and riding, especially their ability to unleash arrows accurately at full gallop. In the late seventeenth century, bands migrated south from present-day Wyoming to more temperate lands and quickly overcame the Apache, Ute, Osages, and lesser rivals. They often attacked under a full summer moon, and adversaries came to fear those nights. In the eighteenth century, Comanche clashes with the Spanish were common. In 1758, an attack on the Mission San Sabá left three priests and a handful of soldiers dead, their bodies mutilated. An abortive punitive expedition left the Comanche in de facto control of Texas country. The risk for settlers should have been obvious, but they came nonetheless. The situation became even more perilous during the war for Texas independence. The Parkers were on their own. Indeed, Antonio López Santa Anna's defeat at the Battle of San Jacinto occurred less than a month before Parker's life was irrevocably transformed.

Imperceptibly but irrevocably, the balance of power shifted. In 1844, Comanche forces clashed with troops commanded by Felix Huston, whose bold horseback charge caused the Comanche to retreat. With Huston was John Coffee Hays, who would transform the Texas Rangers from undisciplined marauders into an efficient fighting machine by understanding, and in some cases, emulating Comanche battle tactics, which were ritualized and predictable. Warriors became demoralized if their leader was killed or wounded. Hays also fathomed the potential of the Colt six-shooter.

In 1845, with the Lone Star Republic (Texas) having become part of the United States, U.S. agent Leonard H. Williams opened peace talks with the Comanche. Coming upon nineteen-year-old Nadua, Williams attempted to purchase her; she was uncooperative, and the Indians refused an offer of twelve mules and merchandise. Five years later, a similar scenario occurred with trader Victor Ross. Again Parker entertained no thought of abandoning her family. In 1858, using tactics learned from Hays and armed with Colt six-shooters and breech-loading carbine, John S. "Rip" Ford defeated a numerically larger force in the Battle of Antelope Hills. Peta Nocona was still at large, however, and in November, 1860, he carried out raids that left dozens dead. In the twenty-four years after Nadua's captivity, the state's white population had swelled from 15,000 to more than 600,000. Meanwhile, a cholera epidemic had decimated the Comanche. In December of 1860, some forty Texas Rangers led by Sul Ross attacked Peta Nocona's camp near the Pease River. When Ross came upon his adversary, according to Gwynne:

> He was nude to the waist, his body streaked with bright pigments. He wore two eagle plumes in his hair, a disk of beaten gold around his neck embossed with a turtle, broad gold bands on his upper arms, and fawn-skin leggings trimmed out with scalplocks.

Nadua's husband was on foot, having been dragged off his horse when the American Indian riding with him was shot. On horseback and avoiding a stream of arrows, Ross wounded Peta Nocona in the elbow and then shot him twice more before an underling finished him off. Two men fought over Peta Nocona's scalp before agreeing to split it. Twelve-year-old Quanah escaped the ensuing butchery; Nadua and her daughter Prairie Flower were spared when the troops realized that the "white squaw" had blue eyes. Though subsequently reunited with the Parker family, Nadua was miserable. She often tried to escape and was sullen and hostile when not weeping or practicing Comanche rituals, including self-flagellation. She refused to speak English and hid from gawkers. In short, being "rescued" ruined her life. After Prairie Flower died in 1864, Nadua was utterly disconsolate and eventually starved herself to death.

The bloody American Civil War offered a reprieve of sorts for the Comanche and delayed their inevitable removal from the open range. Quanah's fierce band of raiders, called the Quahadi (antelope eaters), stole cattle and sold the livestock to unscrupulous middlemen in exchange for guns and ammunition. In October, 1867, at Medicine Lodge Creek in Kansas, numerous chiefs signed treaties that established a three-million-acre reservation in southwest Oklahoma and promised generous annuities in return for their Texas hunting grounds. Eighteen-year-old Quanah attended the council but refused to sign. Those who did were quickly disillusioned, as corrupt Office of Indian Affairs (now known as the Bureau of Indian Affairs) officials profited at their expense. Young braves left the reservation and joined the Quahadi, whom federal government officials were determined to eradicate.

The Battle of Blanco Canyon was the opening salvo in a four-year antiguerrilla campaign of attrition against those few thousand holdouts living free on the plains. Fourth Cavalry commander Ranald S. Mackenzie used scouts from the Tonkawa tribe, cannibalistic and deadly enemies of the Comanche, to track down the Quahadi. At midnight on October 3, 1871, Quanah's forces caught Mackenzie's troops napping and stampeded their horses and mules. The ensuing victory only forestalled the "final solution" (Gwynne's words). Mackenzie relentlessly attacked enemy camps on the North Fork Red River, killing more than 50 braves and taking 124 prisoners, mostly women and children.

In May of 1874, incensed that buffalo hunters were depleting herds at an obscene rate, Quanah's 240 warriors attacked a trading post at Adobe Walls, urged on by the prophet Isa-tai, who predicted that they would be immune to the white man's bullets. It was an utter failure. Defenders armed with Sharps .50-caliber rifles tore them to pieces. The prophecy failed, Isa-tai rationalized lamely, because braves had skinned a skunk the day before. The enraged Quahadi went on a rampage that only intensified Mackenzie's resolve. Near Palo Duro Canyon his troops rousted the Comanche from their camp, then destroyed supplies left behind, including a thousand horses, their carcasses left to rot. In the aftermath, writes Gwynne, a majority of Comanche returned to Fort Sill in the following weeks, demoralized and forced to become wards of the state. Quanah's renegades, numbering around four hundred with only a minority of seasoned fighters, evaded pursuers for seven months, then suddenly accepted peace terms that included promises of amnesty for past crimes. Beforehand, Quanah prayed for guidance from the Great Spirit and saw an eagle fly in the direction of the reservation. Slowly proceeding to Fort Sill, the proud band killed wild game, danced around their campfires at night, and accepted their fate stoically. Colonel Mackenzie kept his promises, and his interest in Quanah turned into a warm relationship.

On the reservation Quanah rose to a position of power. He brought back fifty-seven hot-blooded holdouts and arranged amnesty for them, winning praise from both government agents and tribal leaders. He bargained with cattlemen who paid to graze herds on reservation lands. They had been doing it illegally already, so it made sense to demand compensation. He built up a personal herd of five hundred cattle and oversaw forty-four thousand acres of pastureland. On high ground near the Wichita Mountains he built "Star House," a two-story, ten-room residence.

Saddened to learn of his mother's death, Quanah sought contact with Parker relatives. He supported eight wives and kept his hair long and braided. Tribal members pitched tepees near his house and intermingled with Quanah's family. Generous to a fault, he welcomed houseguests whom he hardly knew. Among the visitors who dined at Quanah's formal dining room table were such luminaries as General Nelson A. Miles, President Theodore Roosevelt, and Apache warrior Geronimo. He bought a car; rode locomotives belonging to the Quanah, Acme, and Pacific Railroad; participated in Roosevelt's 1905 inaugural parade; and had a bit part in a Western film. Eschewing alcohol, he started the Native American Church and believed peyote allowed one to convene with the Holy Spirit. Avoiding self-aggrandizement (unlike Geronimo), he refused an offer to tour with a carnival show, and be, in his words, on display like a caged monkey. At the time of his death in 1911 he had sired twenty-five children. Mackenzie, the "anti-Custer" as Gwynne called him, had died twenty-two years before in an insane asylum, his passing virtually unnoticed.

Employing an occasionally hyperbolic and overblown journalistic style, Gwynne occasionally reveals ethnocentric biases in the use of such loaded words as "squaw," "primitive," and "savage." Though he admires many aspects of traditional Comanche culture, his detailing of atrocities, particularly toward women, seems at times unnecessarily sensationalistic. That said, the author's narrative is entertaining and his facts are generally accurate, impressively so concerning the topography of the Southwest. *The New York Times* reviewer Bruce Barcott praised the book's "forceful argument about the place of Native American tribes in geopolitical history." Those desiring a more scholarly treatment of Quanah's paternal ancestors should consult Pekka Hämäläinen's *The Comanche Empire* (2008), while Jo Ella Powell Exley's *Frontier Blood: The Saga of the Parker Family* (2001) provides comprehensive details about Quanah's maternal lineage. Barcott concluded, "Thanks to Gwynne, the story of Quanah Parker may assume a more fittingly prominent role in the history of the American West."

James B. Lane

Review Sources

American Heritage 60, no. 2 (Summer, 2010): 52.
Booklist 106, no. 16 (April 15, 2010): 20.
Kirkus Reviews 77, no. 4 (February 15, 2010): 119.
Library Journal 135, no. 15 (September 15, 2010): 37.
The New York Times Sunday Book Review, June 13, 2010, pp. 1-6.

ENCOUNTER

Author: Milan Kundera (1929-   )
First published: Une rencontre, 2009, in France
Translated from the French by Linda Asher
Publisher: Harper (New York). 179 pp. $23.99
Type of work: Essays, music, literary history
Time: 1968 to the present

This collection contains essays and reviews on a variety of authors, composers, painters, and other topics

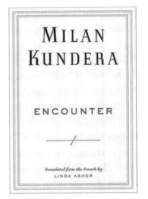

Principal personages:
FRANCIS BACON (1904-1992), a British painter
FYODOR DOSTOEVSKI (1821-1888), a Russian novelist
FRANÇOIS RABELAIS (c. 1494-1553), a French writer
LUDWIG VAN BEETHOVEN (1770-1827), a German composer
JOSEF ŠKVORECKÝ (1924-   ), a Czech novelist
LEOŠ JANÁČEK (1854-1928), a Czech composer
ARNOLD SCHOENBERG (1874-1951), an Austrian and American composer

Milan Kundera has written on various topics in this collection aptly entitled *Encounter.* The essays gathered here are mainly about his encounters with a wide selection of mostly twentieth century European writers, composers, and artists of different kinds. The book is divided into nine sections, some of them containing only a single essay; others a group of related ones.

The volume opens with an essay on the British painter Francis Bacon. Kundera admits, however, that the best criticism of Bacon's work is by Bacon himself and cites, for example, his comment regarding an organic form that relates to the human image but is a complete distortion of it (which describes many of Bacon's portraits). Kundera goes on to consider the nature of the "self" in painting, or rather the limits of the self. "Up to what degree of distortion," he asks, "does an individual still remain himself? To what degree of distortion does a beloved person still remain a beloved person? . . . Where is the border beyond which a self ceases to be a self?" Kundera lets the questions remain unanswered, leaving it up to the reader to ponder them.

Later in this essay, Kundera says, all of Bacon's reservations notwithstanding, he continues to see him in relation to Samuel Beckett, the Irish playwright. They are both located at about the same point in the respective histories of art; both are solitary figures; neither has illusions about the future of the world or of art. For them, Kundera maintains, "the ultimate brutal confrontation is not with a society, with a state, with a politics, but with the physiological materiality of man."

The next section, "Novels, Existential Soundings," contains seven brief essays or reviews on such topics as "The Comical Absence of the Comical (Fyodor Dostoevsky's *The Idiot*)," "Love in Accelerating History (Philip Roth's *The Professor of Desire*)," and "The Novel and Procreation (Gabriel García Márquez's *One Hundred Years of Solitude*)."

Born in Brno, Czechoslovakia (now in Czech Republic), Milan Kundera has lived in France since 1975. He is the author of many novels, such as L'Insoutenable légèreté de l'être (1984; The Unbearable Lightness of Being, 1984) and five collections of essays.

In the first of these, Kundera notes the paradox that the characters who laugh the most in *Idiot* (1868; *The Idiot*, 1887) do not have the greatest sense of humor; they have none at all. He then recalls sitting before a television set where a number of dignitaries seem to be having a great time laughing at each other's remarks and imagines Evgeny Pavlovitch in *The Idiot* suddenly landing among them. Noticing that their laughter has no comical cause, Pavlovitch is at first horrified, but he gradually discerns the comical absence of the comical, which causes him to burst into laughter himself. His laughter wins the acceptance of the others who earlier were suspicious of his silence.

Writing about Roth, Kundera observes that in the twentieth century the novel "discovered" sexuality, gradually and in all its dimensions, whereas in the nineteenth century "love stretched over the vast terrain from first encounter to the brink of coitus; that brink was a frontier not be crossed." He cites Roth as "a great historian of American eroticism." However, he is also, Kundera adds, "the poet of that strange solitude of man left alone to face his body." Regarding García Márquez's novel *Cien años de soledad* (1967; *One Hundred Years of Solitude*, 1970), Kundera says that scarcely 1 percent of the world's population is childless, but at least 50 percent of the characters in great fiction have no offspring. "This infertility is not due to conscious purpose of the novelists," he says; "it is the spirit of the art of the novel (or its subconscious) that spurns procreation."

Encounter's third section is devoted entirely to paying homage to Anatole France, particularly his novel *Les Dieux ont soif* (1912; *The Gods Are Athirst*, 1913), set at the time of the French Revolution. It was this novel that awakened in a young Kundera an awareness of what his world was coming to after World War II. At that period, people in his country, he says, were shedding their ideological illusions, and "the existential enigma . . . disappeared behind political certitude." Hence, he concludes, "people emerge from a historic ordeal still just as stupid as they were when they went in." In *The Gods Are Athirst*, France explores the mystery of his character Gamelin, who fascinates Kundera because he sees what happens to him as directly parallel to the rhythm of history. Moreover, part of the novel's greatness lies in "a *cohabitation of unbearably dramatic history with unbearably banal dailiness*, a cohabitation that sparkles with irony, given that these two opposite aspects of life constantly clash, contradict, and mock each other" (italics in original).

Part 4, "The Dream of Total Heritage," focuses first on François Rabelais and *Gargantua et Pantagrue* (1532-1564, 1567; *Gargantua and Pantagruel*, 1653-1694) a novel from before novels existed. According to Kundera, this was a "miraculous moment, never to return, in which an art had not yet come into being as such and therefore was not yet bound by any norms." Kundera celebrates this moment because afterward, when the novel began to assert itself as a special genre or autonomous art, its freedom shrank and aesthetic censors began to decree what does and does not fit the norms of that art. "Because of that *initial freedom* of the novel, Rabelais's work contains enormous aesthetic possibilities" (italics in original). Some of those possibilities have been realized in other novels, others have not. Louis-Ferdinand Céline was one of the few French writers who drew explicitly from Rabelais. However, the formal richness of Rabelais's novel, which stands without equal, was mostly forgotten in the novel's evolution and was only rediscovered centuries later by James Joyce.

It is to Ludwig van Beethoven, and especially his late piano sonatas, that Kundera finds the resurrection of polyphony in music. When he says, "I imagine that Beethoven wrote his sonatas dreaming he was heir to the *whole* of European music since its beginnings," the reader can understand what Kundera means by the title of this section, which ends with two more essays. The first is a tribute to the Mexican writer Carlos Fuentes; the second is an essay on "The Rejection of Heritage: Or, Iannis Xenakis." A few years after the Russian invasion of Czechoslovakia, Kundera found in the Franco-Greek composer's music a "strange consolation." In was a dark time in his life and in the lives of many other Czechs. Kundera later recognized that Xenakis's music reconciled him to the inevitability of change.

"Beautiful Like a Multiple Encounter," the fifth section, turns to the Caribbean, specifically Martinique, and to the poet Aimé Césaire, the founder of Martinican politics and Martinican literature. It is he that André Breton first encountered in 1941 while he was en route to the United States. Kundera considers Césaire's poem *Cahier d'un retour au pays natal* (1939, 1947, 1956; *Memorandum on My Martinique*, 1947; better known as *Return to My Native Land*, 1968) utterly original and a foundational work for the literature of Martinique and all the Antilles. Césaire is a modern poet and heir to Arthur Rimbaud and Breton, whose work comes together in his.

Kundera then focuses on the stories of the Haitian writer René Depestre, whose eroticism is amazing. Of the collection *Alléluia pour une femme-jardin* (1973; hallelujah for a woman-garden), Kundera says that "all women overflow with so much sexuality that even the traffic lights are aroused and twist around to watch them pass. And the men are so randy that they're ready to make love during a scientific conference, during a surgical operation, inside a spaceship, on a trapeze. All for pure pleasure; there are no problems psychological, moral, or existential; we're in a universe where vice and innocence are one and the same." Kundera confesses that this sort of lyrical intoxication usually bores him, but he did not know what he was in for when he began reading the stories and fell in love with them, even though he knew that they were something he should not have loved. Nonetheless, he describes his reaction as the best thing that can happen to a reader. In this section Kundera also discusses other Caribbean work, particularly the paintings of Ernest Breleur and Patrick Chamoiseau's novel *Solibo magnifique* (1988; *Solibo Magnificent*, 1998).

In the sixth section, "Elsewhere," Kundera returns to discussions of Rabelais and Breleur, but he also includes essays on the Czech novelists Bohumil Hrabal and Vera Linhartova, the Polish Lithuanian poet Oscar Milosz, and the Yugoslavian writer Danilo Kiš. Perhaps the most interesting essay, however, is on Josef and Zdena Škvorecký, whom he met in Paris and where together they compared the "two great springs" of 1968—the one in Paris and the other in Prague. The former was unexpected and explosive, brought about by the young inspired by revolutionary lyricism; the latter, a long time in coming, was rooted in the Stalinist terror after 1948 and inspired the postrevolutionary skepticism of older people. Kundera suggests further apt comparisons and then goes on to discuss Josef Škvorecký's first novel, *Zbabělci* (1958; *The Cowards*, 1970), hated by the authorities. Kundera regards the novel as a great literary moment, describing a great historical turning point, the emergence in 1945 of the Third Republic in Czechoslovakia.

"My First Love," the subject of part 7, is not about Kundera's first girlfriend; it is about Leoš Janáček and his music, which Kundera says was the feature of his native land most indelibly written into his aesthetic genes. The essay is a tribute to an often underrated musician, whom Kundera regards as an older brother to other great twentieth century composers such as Béla Bartók, Arnold Schoenberg, and Igor Stravinsky. A good part of the essay is on five of Janáček's operas, particularly *Jenůfa* (1904) and *Příhody lišky bystroušky* (*The Cunning Little Vixen*). Kundera acutely observes that many operagoers are distracted from the music by the dramatic action, for which the music is mere illustration. Janáček therefore renounced story making and placed music in the forefront of his operas. In *The Cunning Little Vixen*, for example, Janáček's music becomes the "fourth dimension" of a situation—"the unbearable nostalgia of insignificant talk at an inn"—that only an opera can convey.

Part 7, "Forgetting Schoenberg," contains another essay on a great composer and extols the German American's oratorio *Ein berlebender aus Warschau* (*A Warsaw Survivor*), which Kundera regards as the greatest piece of music ever dedicated to the Holocaust. "The whole existential essence of the drama of the Jews in the twentieth century is kept alive in it," he says; "In all its fearsome grandeur. In all its fearsome beauty." However, he concludes, sadly: "People fight to ensure that the murderers should not be forgotten. But Schoenberg they forget."

The final section, "*The Skin* Malaparte's Arch-Novel," is another tribute to the Italian writer Curzio Malaparte. Kundera focuses on his two important novels, *Kaputt* (1944) and *La pelle* (1949; the skin). In addition to being a novelist, Malaparte was a journalist, and *Kaputt* recounts his adventures during World War II, when he had access to many German and Italian notables as well as to the dictators of satellite countries of the Axis powers. Kundera finds it astonishing that no historian has cited Malaparte's experiences or the quoted remarks of those he records in his book, explaining that this is because Malaparte's reportage is something different: "[I]t is a *literary work* whose *aesthetic intention* is so strong, so apparent, that the sensitive reader *automatically* excludes it from the context of accounts brought to bear by historians, journalists, political analysts, memoirists" (italics original). The aesthetic intention, furthermore, is evident in the originality of the book's form, which Kundera then analyzes.

If *Kaputt* is ambiguous regarding the historical characters and situations—how close to reality are they, or are they the author's fantasy vision, the product of poetic license?—in *La pelle* all ambiguity disappears. There are no historical figures in the fashionable gatherings the novel recounts, and whether the names of the Italian and American characters are real or not becomes unimportant. The war is still on, but its end is certain. The difference between this novel and the earlier one is that in *La pelle* good and evil are no longer as clear as they were in *Kaputt*. Malaparte uses irony in both novels, but it is different in *La pelle*, rather more desperate, even overwrought, Kundera says. Malaparte is no longer the "engaged" writer, but a doleful man speaking. The structure of the novel is also unusual. Its form is radically different from what one expects, insofar as it does not rely on narrative or any causal sequence of events. Between its start and finish exists a heterogeneity of events, places, times, characters, and memories, which nevertheless does not weaken the unity of the novel, for the same breath, or spirit, blows through all twelve chapters. Like other modern novelists, Malaparte abandoned the necessity of plausibility that the nineteenth century novel maintained. In its place is what Kundera refers to as "The poetry of the improbable." In sum, *La pelle* captures in complete authenticity Europe as it emerged from World War II. The liberators—Americans and Russians—occupied Europe and everything changed. Malaparte saw this and became fascinated by the new way of being and feeling European, which his novel *La pelle* reveals.

Encounter is a rich collection of critical insights into the work of many important, if forgotten, intellectuals and artists. It serves to introduce the reader to them in a prose that is lucid, stimulating, and totally free of jargon.

Jay L. Halio

Review Sources

The Australian, October 30, 2010, p. 18.
Booklist 107, no. 1 (September 1, 2010): 28.
Kirkus Reviews 78, no. 10 (May 15, 2010): 449.
New Statesman 139, no. 5014 (August 16, 2010): 55.
The New York Times Book Review, August 29, 2010, p. 14.
Publishers Weekly 257, no. 26 (July 5, 2010): 36.
The Sunday Times, August 15, 2010, p. 37.
The Village Voice 55, no. 49 (December 8, 2010): 33-34.

EXTRAORDINARY, ORDINARY PEOPLE
A Memoir of Family

Author: Condoleezza Rice (1954-   )
Publisher: Crown Publishers (New York). 342 pp.
  $27.00
Type of work: Biography, current affairs, memoir
Time: 1954-2000
Locale: Birmingham and Tuscaloosa, Alabama; Denver,
  Colorado; South Bend, Indiana; Palo Alto, California;
  Washington, D.C.

Rice's account of her life through the death of her parents as well as of the lives of ordinary people who, in her opinion, did an extraordinary job of raising her

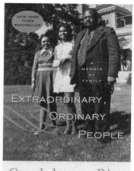

Principal personages:
  CONDOLEEZZA RICE (1954-   ), the author, an educator and public
    servant
  JOHN WESLEY RICE, JR., her father, a preacher and educator
  ANGELENA RAY RICE, her mother, an educator

Condoleezza Rice's memoir, *Extraordinary, Ordinary People*, ends with George W. Bush's election as president in 2000, which was nearly simultaneous with Rice's father's death. Presumably she will later write an account of her work in that administration; she does mention occasional incidents in the book, such as playing the piano in a joint concert with cellist Yo-Yo Ma and later doing a concert for the queen of England. For this book, she relied not only on memory but also on her father's papers and other documents, interviews with a large number of people, and several books cited at the end of the acknowledgments section. She includes a helpful index.

There are several themes that dominate this account. Education plays a major role, starting with Rice's great-grandmother, Julia Head, who somehow received an (illegal) education even as a slave. John Wesley Rice, Sr., Rice's paternal grandfather, considered himself an educational evangelist and founded several schools in the vicinity of Baton Rouge, Louisiana. Her parents were teachers, and made sure that Rice received as good an education as they could manage in the Deep South of the Jim Crow era. She would eventually become a college professor herself, including one term as provost of Stanford University.

Another theme of the book is music. Rice's mother used the Italian musical term *con dolcezza* ("with sweetness") as the basis for her daughter's name, modifying it slightly because she thought few people would pronounce it correctly otherwise. Rice spent many years playing piano (her parents eventually supplied her with a grand piano) and even started as a music major in college before deciding that she lacked the determination and skill to become a professional player and would thus end up a mu-

~

Condoleezza Rice is a college professor and former provost at Stanford University and has served in a number of public positions; she was the national security adviser and then secretary of state under President George W. Bush.

~

sic teacher. She disliked the notion, though before she found her calling she was a teacher for a while. She has continued to play piano at the level of a talented amateur.

Another theme of the book is sports. Her father was a big sports fan, and Rice joined him in this passion, eventually saying that she could enjoy being a spectator of anything that kept score. While working in Japan, she demonstrated this by becoming a fan of sumo wrestling. She also was personally involved, first with ice skating (she was good at figure skating, but her height made her a poor jumper) and later with tennis (she found tennis courts more enjoyable to play on in the mild weather of Denver and Palo Alto than in steaming Birmingham). Her mother was less interested in sports but still encouraged one of her young pupils, future baseball great Willie Mays, in his pursuit.

Such connections to future celebrities happened on other occasions as well. The Rices later lived next to Benzion Netanyahu, father of future Israeli leader Benjamin Netanyahu. Later still, Condoleezza took a course on international politics by former Czech diplomat Josef Korbel, the father of future secretary of state Madeleine Albright. Rice makes no mention of meeting any of these future celebrities during those years.

Religion is another major theme of the book. Rice's paternal grandfather became a Presbyterian minister because that enabled him to receive a scholarship at Stillman College. He combined both preaching and teaching. Later, his son, Condoleezza's father, did the same, making Westminster Presbyterian Church an important community center in Birmingham and reaching out (as much as his middle-class congregation allowed) to the poorer neighborhoods. Rice's father was rather unorthodox in his theology, viewing Judas sympathetically and regarding Thomas the doubter as his favorite apostle. He was a firm believer that faith depended on reason, and doubts must be confronted.

Finally, the book confronts the biggest issue of all in Rice's life, the problem of race. She grew up in Birmingham (and later Tuscaloosa), a descendant of slaves at the tail end of the Jim Crow era. Segregated neighborhoods enabled her to ignore this most of the time, though not always; she knew some of the girls killed in the 1963 bombing of the Sixteenth Street Baptist Church in Birmingham. (Because of these experiences, she is a strong opponent of gun control, knowing too well that a reliance on authority for protection can be foolhardy.) Her maternal grandfather, Albert Ray, always tried to make sure they had a car so they could avoid riding at the back of the bus, as required by law, and avoided segregated restrooms and water fountains by making his family wait until they were home to use such facilities. Her father's church provided some entertainment, including showing films—which enabled them to avoid the segregated movie theaters. Taking occasional vacations in the Northeast, he sought to drive all the way to Washington, D.C., in one day because of the lack of hotels available to his family.

Although a Republican, John Rice, Jr., was also a friend of radical race activist Stokely Carmichael and occasionally brought him to speak when he was at Stillman College in Tuscaloosa. Later, teaching the course "The Black Experience in America" at Denver University, he brought in many noted figures, including Carmichael and other radicals as well as more mainstream figures, to speak.

An interesting aspect of the Rice family is that the degree of darkness of skin color was important even intraracially. Angelena Ray Rice, her mother, was a light-skinned woman of mixed race—Rice suspects at least some Italian ancestry based on the frequency of Italian names in the family—which often made it easier for her to get around. When she and her husband registered to vote as Democrats in 1952, the literacy test she got was to identify the first president; his was to guess correctly how many beans were in a jar. After being informed that the Republicans had a more reasonable literary test, he registered and remained one for the rest of his life. (As a child in Baton Rouge, he and his family rather liked the populist governor and senator Huey Long and were saddened by his assassination. Rice's father later admired Senator Robert F. Kennedy and was especially saddened by his assassination.) Condoleezza herself was a Democrat until she compared the foreign policies of Presidents Jimmy Carter and Ronald Reagan and decided to switch.

Race continued to play a role even after the Rices moved to Denver. There was her father's role at Denver University, which included increasing student diversity as well as teaching about race. There was also affirmative action; Rice was the beneficiary of a mild form in her initial acceptance at Stanford. She supports such programs, unless they go too far. Outreach is noncontroversial, and she also supports at least a limited degree of preferential treatment. (She points to her own mediocre performance on standardized tests to explain her doubts about them.) However, she opposes more extreme measures, such as quota systems. All of this comes up extensively in her coverage of her years at Stanford.

The book starts with a look back at Rice's families, the Rays and the Rices, and how they made their way in the Jim Crow-era South. Many thought her mother would never marry, and, in fact, she and John Rice, Jr., had a long courtship of three years. Rice was their only child. She grew up in Birmingham and was lucky enough to encounter the obsessive racism of Jim Crow only occasionally until the civil rights issue really erupted into local violence in 1963. Later, the Rices moved to Tuscaloosa, and then to Denver. In all of this, she discusses her parents and her relationship with them. They were not always perfect; her earliest memory is her negative reaction to their attempt to send her to the elementary school on the campus where her mother taught high school—at the age of three. Nonetheless, she emphasizes repeatedly her parents' willingness to sacrifice for her, and her own childhood selfishness in accepting these sacrifices without thought. This lasted all the way into college and beyond; while she was figuring out what to do with her life after a career in music went by the wayside, she lived with them. The book is filled with details of her family life. (She had many boyfriends, but as of 2010 had not married.)

As mentioned, Rice started out in college planning to be a professional pianist, then decided otherwise. She studied various subjects until she happened on Korbel's class. At that point, she decided on history and political science as her field and never looked back. This eventually took her to Stanford, where she became a professor. She also had various stints at other institutions—three weeks as a visiting professor at the National Defense Academy of Japan (its first female teacher), six weeks at the Center for International Affairs at Harvard, a fellowship at the Hoover Institution and with the Council on Foreign Relations, and a year at the Pentagon working in the Nuclear and Chemical Division. This got her some modest national attention.

Rice then resumed work at Stanford, receiving tenure, but she left in 1989 to work at the National Security Council under President George H. W. Bush as a Soviet specialist during an interesting period in history. She returned to Stanford in early 1991 after advising a moderately hard line in the Baltic crisis. She later served a term as provost of Stanford, running day-to-day administration, during which she was confronted with such problems as maintaining an adequate curriculum dealing with Western civilization, affirmative action, and other problems involving racial identity politics (her status as a rare-for-Stanford Republican made this especially interesting). After that, she was a foreign policy adviser during the 2000 presidential campaign of the junior Bush.

Meanwhile, there were family problems. Her father had diabetes and high blood pressure. Her mother had a mastectomy in 1970 because of cancer and recovered from a small lung tumor in 1984 through chemotherapy; however, a year later she developed brain cancer and soon died. Her father was badly stressed by this, though moving to Palo Alto to be near Rice helped. A year later, she needed surgery to remove uterine fibroids, and had a difficult recovery because of a temporary digestive collapse. This may have helped lead to congestive heart failure in her father shortly afterward. Later he remarried and began to resume teaching activities. Rice got along well with her stepmother and was pleased that she did her father so much good. He finally died in December, 2000, and the book closes with his funeral.

Timothy Lane

Review Sources

Booklist 106, no. 22 (August 1, 2010): 4.
Essence 41, no. 6 (October, 2010): 102.
Jet 118, no. 20 (November 15, 2010): 49.
Kirkus Reviews 78, no. 13 (July 1, 2010): 610.
Library Journal 135, no. 14 (September 1, 2010): 115-116.
The New York Times, October 13, 2010, p. C1.
The New York Times Book Review 115, no. 42 (October 17, 2010): 24.
Publishers Weekly 257, no. 27 (July 12, 2010): 35.

THE FALL OF THE HOUSE OF WALWORTH
A Tale of Madness and Murder in Gilded Age America

Author: Geoffrey O'Brien (1948-   )
Publisher: Henry Holt (New York). 337 pp. $30.00
Type of work: History
Time: 1873-1952
Locale: Saratoga, New York; New York City; and
Washington, D.C.

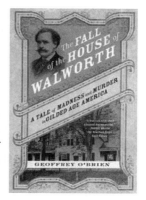

*O'Brien describes the decline of the prestigious Wal-
worth family, culminating in the murder of a father by his
son; he uses the true crime story to illuminate aspects of
the social and cultural history of the nineteenth century
United States*

Principal personages:
> REUBEN H. WALWORTH (1788-1867), the chancellor of New York State,
> 1828-1848
> MANSFIELD TRACY WALWORTH, his son
> SARAH HARDIN WALWORTH, his second wife
> ELLEN HARDIN WALWORTH, the daughter of Sarah Hardin and the wife
> of Mansfield Tracy Walworth
> FRANK HARDIN WALWORTH, the son of Ellen and Mansfield Tracy
> Walworth
> CLARA GRANT WALWORTH, the daughter of Frank, great-granddaughter
> of Reuben

On the surface Geoffrey O'Brien's *The Fall of the House of Walworth* is simply a
true crime story of a shocking parricide. On June 2, 1873, Frank Hardin Walworth
traveled to New York City from Saratoga, New York, in order to talk to his father,
Mansfield Tracy Walworth, who was sending threatening letters to his estranged
wife. Mansfield was not at home, so Frank took a hotel room and asked his father to
meet him. When Mansfield entered the next morning, Frank took out a pistol and
fired four times, killing him.

Cultural historian O'Brien goes well beneath the surface in this fascinating narrative of a family that in four generations went from wealth and social and political
prominence to extinction. He starts long before the crime with the career of Reuben
H. Walworth and continues after it to the death of his great-granddaughter. Along the
way the reader learns about Saratoga, as it rose to prominence as a society resort before the Civil War then declined into a tourist attraction. Examining New York State
politics and law helps explain the rise of Reuben; considering changes in the legal
definition of murder help understand his grandson's fate. The reaction to the murder
in the New York press illuminates the nature of journalism during the 1870's.

Cultural historian Geoffrey O'Brien is editor in chief of the Library of America. He has published Dream Time: Chapters from the Sixties *(1988),* The Phantom Empire *(1993),* Hardboiled America *(1997),* The Times Square Story *(1998), and* The Browser's Ecstasy *(2000).*

The founder of the family, Reuben H. Walworth was a homeschooled farmer's son who attended a law school in Troy before establishing a practice in Plattsburg, New York. After serving meritoriously in the Battle of Plattsburg during the War of 1812, he allied himself with Martin Van Buren's faction in New York's Democratic Party, winning political favor and access to profitable investments. He was elected to one term in Congress (1821-1822) and then served as a circuit-court judge until he was chosen chancellor of the state in 1828. Mention of a sentencing decision the patriarch Walworth made as judge provides O'Brien with the opportunity to vividly describe early nineteenth century executions as public spectacles.

In 1828, New York still had a system of chancery courts dealing with such matters as wills, property and contract disputes, and guardianship of orphans and incompetents. As chancellor, Walworth had the final word in the system, subject only to appeals to the "court of errors," which overwhelmingly sustained his decisions. One of his rulings allowed railroads to override property rights of landowners in the public interest. Walworth's arrogant treatment of lawyers arguing before his court and his slowness to decide cases is credited with leading to the abolition of chancery courts in 1846. Walworth was nominated for the Supreme Court of the United States in 1844 but failed to win Senate approval. In 1848, after retirement, he ran unsuccessfully for governor.

In 1832, the chancellor—as he was always referred to—moved the court from Albany to his mansion in Saratoga. This historical instance provides O'Brien with the opportunity to give a quick, fascinating history of Saratoga Springs, from its rise to a favorite summer resort of wealthy southerners to its takeover by gamblers during the Civil War and its decline thereafter.

After the death of his first wife, Walworth traveled to Kentucky in 1850, where he met and successfully wooed Sarah Hardin, the widow of a Mexican-American War hero, setting in motion events that would lead to the destruction of his family. Both had adult children; Ellen Hardin, Sarah's daughter, was attracted to Mansfield Walworth, the chancellor's son, despite his reputation as someone with a strong sense of entitlement, an arrogant pride in his position in the town, and a tendency to violent outbursts and abrupt shifts of mood when his desires were thwarted. Their parents married on April 19, 1851; by December, Ellen considered herself engaged to Mansfield. The two were united in a fashionable marriage on July 29, 1852, and their first child, Frank, was born the following August.

Despite earning a law degree from Harvard, Mansfield refused to follow the career his father had chosen for him. He decided to become a writer and had several novels published, but he never earned enough to support himself, much less his family. O'Brien describes the novels as ostentatiously written, sensational and sentimental fiction, and indicates the level of the literary world Mansfield inhabited by quoting

Mansfield's publisher boasting that he never bothered to read books he offered the public.

Mansfield began to spend more and more time in New York City, renting rooms where he could work undisturbed. The Civil War accentuated the separation when Ellen moved with her children to Kentucky, where she would have the support of her relatives. Mansfield went to Washington, D.C., where his activities led to his brief arrest on suspicion of being a Confederate spy. The war was a time of great anxiety for Sarah. Her daughter and grandchildren were living near actual battlefields. One son joined the Kentucky irregulars harassing Union forces; the other, an officer in the Union army, lost an arm at the Battle of Gettysburg and ended the war a brigadier general.

There were early marital problems between Ellen and Mansfield, who indulged in verbal abuse whenever affairs did not go as he hoped, but not until the family was united in Saratoga in 1865 did he escalate to physical violence. His outbursts intensified after the death of the chancellor in November, 1867, when he learned that his father had not willed his 23 percent of the estate to him directly but instead had put it into a trust under the control of his older brother, Catholic priest Clarence Walworth. After he heard the will read, Mansfield cursed his father and started kicking furniture and smashing small objects.

Ellen tried to keep the marriage going despite severe beatings until Mansfield bit her finger through to the bone in January, 1871. In October, she opened a girl's school in the big Saratoga house, which had become the property of her mother. A separation degree in April, 1872, ordered Mansfield to pay $1,100 a year alimony and child support. When Ellen failed to modify the terms of the settlement to Mansfield's satisfaction he began deluging her with threatening letters, full of obscenity, and promised to kill or maim her and her children. Frank tried to protect his mother by intercepting and hiding letters from her. On May 30, 1873, after a quiet period in which no missives appeared, another vicious letter arrived, and Frank decided to go to New York City and confront his father.

After shooting his father, Frank went to the hotel desk, paid his bill, told the clerk what he had done, and asked him to call the police. Newspaper coverage of the crime was voluminous and intensely hostile; the press tried and sentenced Frank long before the trial began. Reporters described him as disdainful and haughty when he failed to answer questions to their satisfaction, labeling him an obviously unrepentant murderer. Popular papers enjoyed exposing the hidden past of a prominent family.

Twenty-first century readers may be amazed at the speed with which the trial progressed. From the commission of the crime to the day of conviction scarcely more than eight weeks passed; one week later Frank was on his way to prison. Frank shot his father June 3, the trial began July 24. The defense had difficulty getting extenuating evidence admitted. Ellen testified to Mansfield's treatment of her, but the judge reluctantly permitted reading of Mansfield's letters, saying Frank, not his father was on trial. The letters, with their obscene and violent language, which the popular press gleefully reported, began to shift public opinion in Frank's favor. The defense argued Frank shot his father because he feared for his life when Mansfield moved toward him and also tried to prove Frank was not mentally responsible for his actions, citing past epileptic episodes. On August 1, the case went to the jury, which, after four-and-one-half hours of deliberation brought in a verdict of guilty of murder in the second degree.

O'Brien notes that the law defining murder in the second degree had only been enacted in May of that year. Previously, juries had to choose between murder, punishable by hanging, and manslaughter, punishable by a short prison term. Concerned over the reluctance of juries to sentence convicted murderers to death, the legislature added a new definition of murder, punishable by life at hard labor. In his charge to the jury the judge explained that murder in the second degree applied if there was a clear intent to kill, but without deliberation or premeditation.

Although Frank decided not to appeal the conviction, newspapers cynically predicted the son of such a prominent family would shortly receive a pardon. They were mistaken. Ellen organized a campaign seeking his release, but neither the governor nor his successor responded to family pleas or the urging of prominent supporters. The poet and newspaper editor William Cullen Bryant urged clemency, arguing that two insane men had met in the hotel room that day, one of whom survived. In December, Frank collapsed and was hospitalized with an illness diagnosed as pleurisy. While in prison his epileptic symptoms got worse, leading to his transfer in September, 1874, to the Auburn Asylum for Insane Convicts, a move the newspapers criticized as a too-easy treatment of a privileged prisoner. Not until 1877 did a newly elected governor issue an unconditional pardon for Frank.

Since he was writing a history of a family as well as a crime story, O'Brien includes what happened later. Frank married after his release and fathered a daughter. The lung problem contracted in prison became severe in 1886; he died on October 29, the cause listed as acute bronchitis. After Frank's death, his mother, Ellen, closed the school she had been operating to support the family, leased the Walworth mansion to a hotel, and moved to Washington, D.C., where her activities were sufficiently distinguished to warrant inclusion in the authoritative, multivolume *American National Biography*. In 1890, she was one of the founders of the Daughters of the American Revolution and served as its secretary-general and editor of its monthly magazine. During the Spanish-American War she was director general of the Women's National War Relief Association. She died in 1915 of a stroke.

Frank's wife and his daughter, Clara, returned to the huge Saratoga house during the 1930's. Her mother died in 1937, but Clara continued living there alone until her death in 1952, carefully preserving family manuscripts and records, which were transferred to the Saratoga Historical Society. The documents provided O'Brien with the raw materials to which he applied novelistic techniques of pacing and structure in this fascinating book. After Clara's death the house was torn down and replaced by a gas station. Both the Saratoga Walworths and the chancellor's mansion had become extinct.

Milton Berman

Review Sources

Booklist 106, no. 21 (July 1, 2010): 20.
The Boston Globe, August 1, 2010, p. C6.
Kirkus Reviews 78, no. 8 (April 15, 2010): 347.
Los Angeles Times, August 23, 2010, p. E7.
The New York Review of Books 57, no. 13 (August 19, 2010): 30.
The New York Times Book Review, July 25, 2010, p. 17.
Publishers Weekly 257, no. 21 (May 24, 2010): 47.
The Washington Post, July 30, 2010, p. C2.

THE FLIGHT OF THE INTELLECTUALS

Author: Paul Berman (1949-   )
Publisher: Melville House (New York). 299 pp. $26.00
Type of work: Current affairs
Locale: Switzerland, New York, and Egypt

A critical examination of the positive reception of Muslim philosopher Tariq Ramadan among influential Western intellectuals

Principal personages:

TARIQ RAMADAN (1962-   ), a philosopher from an Egyptian family but raised in Switzerland, whose writings deal with Islam in the modern world

ḤASAN AL-BANNĀ' (1906-1949), his grandfather and founder of the Muslim Brotherhood

SAYYID QUṬB (1906-1966), an influential Egyptian thinker affiliated with the Muslim Brotherhood, often regarded as one of the founders of the radical Islamic movement

HAJ AMIN AL-HUSSEINI (c. 1895-1974), the Grand Mufti of Jerusalem, opponent of Jewish settlement in Palestine, and German conspirator in World War II

IAN BURUMA (1951-   ), British-Dutch writer who wrote a generally favorable profile of Tariq Ramadan in *The New York Times Magazine* in 2007

AYAAN HIRSI ALI (1969-   ), a Somali-born activist, writer, and former Dutch politician

Two criticisms lie at the heart of Paul Berman's *The Flight of the Intellectuals.* First, Berman criticizes the work of prominent Muslim philosopher Tariq Ramadan. Second, he criticizes the generally favorable reception of Ramadan by the non-Western press. Throughout the book, Berman tends to move back and forth between these two issues. He clearly regards Ramadan as an attractive but troubling figure. Ramadan, according to Berman, rose to public prominence in 1993 during controversy over the performance in Geneva of a play about the Prophet Mohammad written by Voltaire. Since then, Berman maintains, Ramadan has managed to present himself as a moderate reformer to non-Muslims while retaining support among many Muslims from a range of ideological perspectives. Berman's main objection to Ramadan is that the philosopher maintains a highly flexible program, supporting moderation or radicalism depending on the audience. Berman sees the central event in the reception of Ramadan by non-Muslim intellectuals as an article by Ian Buruma, published in the February 4, 2007, issue of *The New York Times Magazine.*

The British-Dutch author Buruma had recently published a book on the murder of Dutch filmmaker Theo van Gogh by an Islamic radical incensed by a short film Van Gogh had made about the treatment of women in Islam. Despite this background, Buruma treated Ramadan too favorably in the magazine article, in Berman's view. The magazine did present Ramadan as a complex individual, combining a leftist perspective on issues

Paul Berman is a senior fellow at the World Policy Institute and a professor of journalism and writer-in-residence at New York University. He is best known for his writings on the appeal of totalitarianism for modern liberals and on Islamic fundamentalism.

such as globalization with social conservatism. Still, Buruma found Ramadan to be a sympathetic and moderate spokesman for Islam. Berman asks whether Ramadan is really a moderate, though. If he is not, then Berman wants to consider why Buruma and other intellectuals are so eager to see the Swiss-Egyptian thinker in this way.

The investigation into Ramadan's supposed moderation leads Berman to Ramadan's maternal grandfather, Ḥasan al-Bannāʾ. He was the founder of the Muslim Brotherhood, an organization long at odds with the Egyptian government and one of the most influential groups in the rise of Islam as a modern social movement. Ramadan wrote his doctoral dissertation and a later book on the reformism of al-Bannāʾ. In these works, he portrays his grandfather as a champion of anticolonialism and as the humane, visionary leader of a social-reform movement. Ramadan also treats other leading figures of the Muslim Brotherhood, most notably Sayyid Quṭb, a Muslim writer who became an intellectual inspiration for the radicals of al-Qaeda. In Ramadan's version, Quṭb is also much more moderate than generally portrayed and has been misinterpreted by Osama bin Laden and his followers.

Berman argues that Ramadan's presentation of al-Bannāʾ and other prominent Muslim leaders is inaccurate and plays to European and American wishes for a moderate Islam. Berman points out actions and statements made by al-Bannāʾ that were utterly inconsistent with Western ideas of liberal democracy and that many of the influences on Ramadan, including al-Bannāʾ, have held political values and ideals dramatically at variance with those generally accepted in North America and Europe. In questioning the implications of Ramadan's intellectual heritage, Berman considers the connections between al-Bannāʾ and Palestinian leader Haj Amin al-Husseini. This last individual opposed Jewish settlement in Palestine, as well as British colonial policy in the area, and allied himself with Nazi Germany. This alliance was not simply tactical, but shared an anti-Jewish ideology with the Nazis. Al-Husseini collaborated in forming troops under the Nazis and in encouraging the mass killing of Jews.

Even apart from a misleading reinterpretation of his own intellectual background, Ramadan has offered questionable views on current international events according to Berman. In his responses to allegations of the mistreatment of women and the denial of women's rights under Islamic law he has failed to take any definite moral positions. His criticisms of the defenders of Israel have unreasonably dismissed anti-Jewish prejudices, in Berman's view, and he has been too ready to accuse those defenders of raising anti-Judaism as a false issue. Ramadan's views of Israel are especially troubling to the author. These views are almost uniformly negative and they tend to lay all responsibility for problems of terrorism and violence in the region at Israel's door. Ramadan does express disapproval of Palestinian bombings and acts of violence. However, he describes these types of actions as those of an oppressed people who have no other way to strike back at their oppressor. Thus, even when Palestinians kill Israeli civilians the killings have ultimately been produced by Israeli state terror.

The flight referred to in the title of the book is one from the clear position on terrorism of intellectuals in an earlier time. When the Iranian religious authorities issued a death sentence against author Salman Rushdie, Western intellectuals largely rallied to Rushdie's defense, according to Berman. Later, however, the support for Ramadan by Buruma and others represents desperate efforts to come to terms with radical Islam by looking for someone who can present radical ideas in a mild and moderate form. Berman contrasts the support for Ramadan with the hostility of many intellectuals for the writer and activist Ayaan Hirsi Ali, who is in some respects a version of Rushdie. Hirsi Ali, the daughter of a prominent Somali political opposition leader, fled to the Netherlands in 1992 to avoid being forced into an arranged marriage. There, she became a prominent feminist and an outspoken critic of Islam and of the treatment of women within Muslim cultures. Hirsi Ali began receiving death threats for her statements of her views. She worked with Dutch filmmaker Van Gogh on the controversial film *Submission*, which condemned what Hirsi Ali and Van Gogh saw as the oppressed status of women within Islam.

On November 2, 2004, the Moroccan-Dutch Muslim Mohammed Bouyeri murdered Van Gogh and stuck a letter to the filmmaker's body with a knife. The letter was addressed to Hirsi Ali and threatened her and other supposed enemies of Islam. Since then, Hirsi Ali has had to live under constant guard. Her situation became worse when the Dutch government threatened to take away her citizenship on the grounds that she had given false information when she first applied for asylum. Although she retained her Dutch passport, she left the country for the United States.

Despite Buruma's book on the Van Gogh assassination, Buruma has been consistently unsympathetic toward Hirsi Ali, even while he has portrayed Ramadan in a highly favorable light. Buruma's fellow intellectual, the political writer Timothy Garton Ash, joined Buruma in a series of disparaging statements about the Somali-born feminist. In Berman's view, the persecution of Hirsi Ali has been a clear case of a public figure threatened with death for exercising the right to freedom of thought and freedom of speech. Therefore, Berman believes that all supporters of liberal democratic values should support her, whether they agree with her views on Islam and feminism or not. He argues that modern Western intellectuals have fled to a relativistic multiculturalism.

In accepting the differences of cultural and religious groups, writers such as Buruma have concluded that they must not judge other cultures in universal moral terms. Individuals such as Ramadan, who offer the appearance of moderation, give

Buruma and his colleagues a way of avoiding the aspects of Islam that may contradict liberal democracy. Hirsi Ali, on the other hand, presents them with a stark choice: They can either support her and the right to free speech or they can oppose her and abandon liberal democratic values. They avoid doing this, in Berman's opinion, by describing Hirsi Ali as too strident or too outspoken about her own ideas. In this way, the supposed enemy of Islam becomes the opponent of the intellectuals who are reluctant to criticize Islam.

The Flight of the Intellectuals is clearly a polarizing book and one that will evoke both strong agreement and intense disagreement from readers. This response may depend largely on the preexisting views of readers on relations among cultures and world religions. The book sometimes comes across as a ramble, moving from meditations on Ramadan to more general thoughts on the roots of Islamic radicalism to criticisms of the responses of Western intellectuals. It therefore often falls short of a completely coherent organization or a clear line of argument. In his objections to Ramadan, Berman may obscure the very real differences between this philosopher and more radical advocates of a militant Islam. If there are genuine distinctions between Ramadan and exponents of European and American liberal democracy, there are also distinctions between Ramadan and various other Muslim thinkers and activists. Ramadan's ambiguity is not necessarily a result of being two-faced or of showing different sides of himself to different audiences but could be the consequence of attempts to tread carefully through sensitive and complicated issues. Readers may also wonder at times whether Berman makes too much out of the single 2007 article by Buruma and a few other published pieces, since in several places Berman also refers to other intellectuals who have been quite critical of Ramadan. Even if the reader accepts the argument that Buruma has let his own reason become tainted by excessive multiculturalism, it does not necessarily follow that this represents a more general flight from liberal democratic principles by twenty-first century writers and thinkers.

While Berman should be read critically, he makes valuable contributions. He brings the work of Ramadan, an influential thinker about the direction of Islam and about the relations between Muslims and non-Muslims, to wide public attention. He raises the general question of the problematic relation between a religiously inspired view of human society and secular political values, as well as the more specific question about the consistency between modern Islam as it is practiced and liberal democratic values. Perhaps most important, he causes the reader to ask whether the eagerness to be open and tolerant toward religions and cultures may have led to acceptance of intolerance and persecution. The failure of many intellectuals to protest the persecution of Hirsi Ali and to defend her right to free speech may strike readers as one of Berman's most significant points.

Carl L. Bankston III

Review Sources

The American Prospect 21 (June, 2010): 34-5.

Biography: An Interdisciplinary Quarterly 33, no. 3 (Summer, 2010): 603.

Christianity Today 54, no. 7 (July, 2010): 54.

Commonweal 137, no. 13 (July 16, 2010): 23-24.

First Things: A Monthly Journal of Religion and Public Life, no. 205 (August/ September, 2010): 65-67.

Foreign Affairs 89, no. 4 (July/August, 2010): 138-147.

Kirkus Reviews 78, no. 5 (March 1, 2010): 179.

The National Interest 108 (July/August, 2010): 58-66.

The New York Review of Books 57, no. 13 (August 19, 2010): 84-88.

The New York Times Book Review 115 (May 16, 2010): 26.

The New Yorker 86 (June 7, 2010): 68-73

FOREIGN BODIES

Author: Cynthia Ozick (1928-   )
Publisher: Houghton Mifflin Harcourt (Boston). 255 pp.
    $26.00
Type of work: Novel
Time: 1952
Locale: Paris, New York, Los Angeles

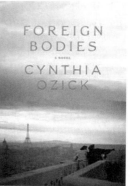

Ozick's sixth novel takes the plot of Henry James's The
Ambassadors *(1903), changes the gender of its main char-*
acter, and sets the action in a decidedly less romantic post-
World War II Paris some fifty years later

Principal characters:
> BEATRICE NIGHTINGALE, né NACHTIGALL,
>   the middle-aged protagonist, a divorced vocational school English
>   teacher
> LEO COOPERSMITH, her former husband, a composer of musical tracks
>   for Hollywood films
> MARVIN NACHTIGALL, her brother and major antagonist, a successful
>   Los Angeles businessman
> MARGARET NACHTIGALL, né BRECKINRIDGE, Marvin's wife,
>   institutionalized at a high-end retreat for the mentally ill
> JULIAN, Marvin and Margaret's son, a would-be writer, living a
>   bohemian life in Paris
> IRIS, Marvin and Margaret's daughter, a chemistry student who follows
>   her brother to Paris
> LILY, Julian's wife, a wounded refugee from Eastern Europe, who has
>   lost her former husband and son

Bea Nightingale, the central consciousness of *Foreign Bodies*, like Henry James's
Lambert Strether in *The Ambassadors*, has been asked to intervene in the life of a
young man living abroad, in this case, her nephew Julian. Also like Lambert, Bea will
ultimately find her own passive and lonely life strangely altered by the mission she
has reluctantly undertaken. Cynthia Ozick's first unpublished novel was also based
on *The Ambassadors*, she wrote her master's thesis on James, and she has often discussed his work in her essays on writers and writing. Though it is not necessary to
have read James in order to appreciate *Foreign Bodies*, Ozick clearly wants this novel
to be both a tribute to James and a revision of his worldview.

The novel begins with a brief letter from Bea to her brother returning his check and
explaining her failed efforts at tracking down his son. Marvin's response is to berate
her at length for her failure. Similar letters will continue to play a major role in deter-
mining plot and character throughout the novel. These first two are separated by one
of the few authorial intrusions, a description of Paris gripped by unbearable heat and

*Cynthia Ozick's best-known works
include* The Pagan Rabbi, and Other
Stories *(1971);* The Shawl *(1989); her
novel* The Puttermesser Papers *(1997);
and several collections of essays,
including* Art and Ardor *(1983).*

populated by two groups of foreigners—the
would-be American bohemians playing at ex-
istentialism and the Eastern European refugees displaced by war and politics. Thus, the
novel's opening pages accomplish several
important purposes. They present Beatrice
Nightingale as the principal actor, both en-
voy and spy. They establish the centrality of
place to a narrative whose action will alternate among Paris, New York, and Los Angeles. They introduce the theme of dysfunctional family relationships epitomized by the
use of letters in lieu of face-to-face communication. Finally, they set up a striking contrast
between privileged Americans and Holocaust
survivors, each seeking meaningful ways to
live their lives.

Geography and Jewish identity are closely
allied in this novel. Marvin chooses to live in
Los Angeles, as far away from his New York
immigrant parents as he can possibly get, both literally and figuratively. His Princeton degree and blue-blood wife facilitate his assimilation. He goes so far as to search
out a long-forgotten Breckinridge family crest for his letterhead though he, unlike his
sister, chooses not to change his name and though his in-laws never fully accept him
into their clan. Marvin cannot understand his son's desire to live in a Europe his family once fled and is disgusted by his marriage to a Romanian refugee, Lily. If Marvin
can be seen as the novel's villain, given his arrogance and despicable behavior toward
his wife, sister, and son, Lily is clearly its most positive and heroic figure. Bea at first
distrusts Lily, assuming that she is only using Julian as a substitute for her lost child
and husband, yet later comes to accept what Lily insists—that she is in fact quite good
for Julian and that the terrible knowledge she brings him will help make him a man.
Though Lily herself had hoped to move to Israel, she knows that Julian would not be
happy there. Ultimately, they will end up in Texas, a place of infinite possibilities
inhabited by exiles and misfits.

Ozick uses two institutions to epitomize the inhumanity of 1950's Paris and Los
Angeles. Lily works at a Centre des Emigrés, funded by a wealthy French baron
whose generosity masks his anti-Semitism and ultimate goal of ridding Paris of all its
foreign Jews. He will cruelly demand that Lily be fired for arriving late just once despite the protests of her on-site boss. Bea tracks down Lily at the center and is overwhelmed by a stench she cannot place. As if looking through her brother's eyes, she is
initially disgusted by its gypsy swarms—"homeless tramp birds, with eyes like the
eyes of fish, feeding on scraps"—and tells Lily that Julian is too young to know such
sadness. A few days later, Bea makes a surprise trip to Los Angeles, a place that is a

continent away from New York and one that she describes as broken into widely dispersed pieces lacking any core or coherence. Her first stop is the ironically named Suite Eyre Spa, a sanatorium pretending to be an English manor but populated by women "medicated into torpor, self-lulled into immobility," a wealthy horde as haunting and helpless as the immigration center's impoverished refugees. Here too there is a stench that Bea finds difficult to identify until Margaret proudly presents the painting she has produced with her own human excrement.

Lily survives; Margaret does not, in one of the novel's most dramatic juxtapositions. Bea's interactions with each of these women is key to her own sense of self and to the redefinition of her relationship with her brother, nephew, and former husband. Margaret, apart from the painting, seems quite sane in her discussion with Bea; it is she who defines Marvin as dominated by hate and explains the degree to which he must fear Julian somehow returning to the ghetto. However, when she inadvertently mentions that Marvin has been to see Leo, Bea turns on her in anger announcing what she had kept secret: Julian's marriage to Lily and his decision never to return home. The spite continues as Bea seeks out Leo in his fancy but strangely lifeless Hollywood home. In quick response to his immediate mockery of her, she manages to humiliate him by insisting that she hears the true Leo in his extraordinarily popular film scores, a betrayal of the true musical genius he still dreams of being. Finally, she will drive to her brother's home, and without letting him know she is there, she will spy on him walking to his pool with a young, attractive woman at his side, observing for herself the hypocrisy behind his professed concern for his wife.

Bea returns to New York and immediately sells Leo's piano, finally understanding that he will never return for it. Rather than continuing to idolize its unfulfilled potential, she hopes to be free at last to reclaim her apartment as her own space. It will not be so easy, however, to rid herself completely of Leo, her brother, or her sense of inadequacy, and to make of this space a home. When her friends come for dinner, they inadvertently bring with them a children's book that Bea realizes was originally a gift from Leo's mother. Then Marvin unexpectedly stops by in an attempt to involve Bea still deeper in his plans for his son. Several days later Julian and Lily arrive. Bea has been preparing for their stay and is disappointed to learn they no longer need her help. Still, even in this brief visit, Lily has lessons to offer. Bea has destroyed the check Marvin left for his son and lies to Julian about his mother's insanity and demise. She feels guilt about both of these actions and believes, as Marvin cruelly suggested, that a letter she wrote to Margaret might have in some way contributed to her death. Lily's sage words enable Bea to forgive herself and to look at her nephew through less judgmental eyes, to see him as just another "soft" boy like Leo, searching for a way to make his life matter.

Julian's search for meaning has led him to intense obsessions with a variety of literary texts, from his mother's favorite psalms to Søren Kierkegaard. Ozick has often warned about the dangers of idolatry and, at the same time, insisted on the significance of literature. Even as she may mock her own youthful worship of James, and Leo's worship of the nineteenth century concert grand piano he has imported from

Vienna, she seems sympathetic to Julian's search for a voice that speaks to him directly. His father scorns all such reading and dismisses as youthful idiocy his son's few publications in Paris. Bea is an English teacher, and the novel is filled with Shakespearean allusions. In its last pages, as she returns to her classroom to take up *King Lear* (pr. c. 1605-1606, pb. 1608) with her "antic" young vocational students, she thinks to herself: "How hard it is to change one's life. . . . How terrifyingly simple to change the lives of others." So many of her actions, whether intentional or inadvertent, have had consequences she may or may not have been able to anticipate.

It is not at all clear how Ozick expects her readers to judge Bea; *Foreign Bodies* literally ends with a question mark. Leo has finally written his symphony, inspired out of a desire to prove Bea's assessment of him wrong, and named it *The Nightingale's Thorn: A Symphony in B Minor*. Bea is not sure why he has mailed it to her—she cannot make sense of the notes on the page, though the title is clearly enough a slap in her face—but it may be he cannot escape her anymore than she could escape him. Both Marvin and Iris also send messages from California. Marvin announces his decision to put his faith in his daughter, his true child, the one who has always taken him as her model. Iris announces that though she is living with her father she wants to be "free like Bea," brave enough to lead the unencumbered single life that she mistakenly assumes her aunt has chosen. These are victories of a sort over brother and former husband to which Bea will gladly cling.

As a young woman Bea had high hopes of leaving a mark on the world. She married Leo because she was infatuated by his ambitions despite the fact that he laughed at her own dreams and was quick to mock most everything she did and said. When she explains her vision of creating a dictionary of seemingly hidden things, he jokingly suggests "cloud shapes" or "famous crooks." She cannot help but respond in earnest with an idea about collecting "Moods. Smells. Feelings that everyone's somehow felt only there's no name for them." His rebuttal is that she is well on her way to being a mediocre high school English teacher, a prediction that proves only too true.

Bea's earliest dreams were of being a detective or foreign correspondent digging up old secrets; in a sense that is what she ends up doing during the course of the novel. Ironically, it is in obeying her brother's demands despite her own misgivings that Bea begins to take the actions that allow her to reengage with the world and eventually rid herself of her suffocating, idolatrous ties to the past. She also begins to observe in others and experience for herself a wide variety of feelings that she struggles to name and understand. Maybe this is the real message Ozick intends, that in desiring to avoid messy relationships or to block out unpleasant smells, such as those in the Centre des Emigrés or the Suite Eyre Spa, rather than seeking out and sympathizing with their source, one risks replacing emotion with cynicism. Ozick chooses to end the novel ambiguously so her readers can draw their own conclusions about what Bea might do with her new knowledge, what kind of dictionary she might one day attempt to write.

Jane Missner Barstow

Review Sources

Booklist 106, no. 21 (July 1, 2010): 7.
Kirkus Reviews 78, no. 21 (November 1, 2010): 1080.
The New Yorker 86, no. 36 (November 15, 2010): 91.
Publishers Weekly 257, no. 42 (October 25, 2010): 30-31.
Weekly Standard 16, no. 12 (December 6, 2010): 34-35.

FOUR FISH
The Future of the Last Wild Food

Author: Paul Greenberg (1967-   )
Publisher: Penguin Press (New York). 284 pp. $25.95
Type of work: Nature, environment
Time: The present, with historical flashbacks
Locale: Connecticut; Long Island, New York; Alaska;
   Vietnam; Norway; Newfoundland; and the South
   Pacific

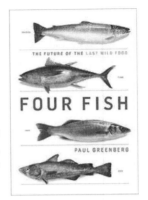

*Greenberg's boyhood interest in fishing has led him to
explore the status of the four major species of fish—salmon,
sea bass, cod, and tuna—that constitute most of the worldwide commercial supply of fish*

Principal personages:
   PAUL GREENBERG, a novelist and an essayist deeply concerned with the
      diminishing supply of fish in the world
   JAC GADWILL, his host in Emmonak, Alaska
   MARK KURLANSKY, a fisherman and a journalist who focuses primarily
      on cod
   THIERRY CHOPIN, a significant aquaculturist in Newfoundland who
      focuses on cod
   YONATHAN ZOHAR, a sea-bass aquaculturist
   SIVERT and
   OVE GRØNTVEDT, brothers and Norwegian aquaculturists

Enthusiastic about fishing and about the animals that inhabit the world's seas,
rivers, and lakes, Paul Greenberg, author of *Four Fish: The Future of the Last Wild
Food*, spent his early years in Greenwich, Connecticut, where he fished in the Byram
River near the property where his mother rented a small cottage. He often ventured as
well—usually with his father—into Long Island Sound, where, as predictably as the
seasons, nature's bounty included flounder in mid-March; mackerel, menhaden, and
blackfish in April; and in May or June the bluefish that swam into the sound's waters
to devour the fish that had arrived earlier. By autumn, the surviving blackfish and
flounder returned before the fallow months of winter. Far out in the sound, some
miles beyond Montauk, one could fish for cod, as Greenberg sometimes did when his
father agreed to pay for the rental of a seaworthy fishing boat for the day.

Eventually the harvest of the river and of Long Island Sound diminished dramatically, and fishing in these bodies of water became unproductive. Salmon, which has
been on earth for more than fifty million years, became increasingly scarce and virtually disappeared from some of its early habitats.

Years later, however, when Greenberg returned to Long Island Sound, there was

convincing evidence that nature was healing itself. Writing in 2009, Greenberg notes,
"There is still a remarkable amount of diverse
life in Long Island Sound. In fact, after catch-
ing one bluefish myself, I felt an unusual tug
on my bait and then the telltale first run of
something uncommon yet familiar. Within
a few minutes, the mate helped me net a ten-
pound striped bass." Remarkably, striped
bass did not inhabit the sound at all during

*Paul Greenberg has traveled
throughout the world in his attempts to
understand the worldwide status of
fishing and fish as a food supply. He
frequently writes articles on seafood
and conservation for* The New York
Times.

Greenberg's adolescent forays into its waters, nor were seals and dolphins found
there, although both were evident there at the time Greenberg was writing.

In *Four Fish*, Greenberg focuses on the four species of fish upon which the world
food supply is most dependent. Each of these species has a unique relationship to humans and each has characteristics that set it apart. One of these species, salmon, lends
itself remarkably well to being farmed. Sea bass, although it adapts less well than salmon to fish farms, is farmed in many areas with a modicum of success. More than
one-half of the salmon and sea bass available commercially is raised in fisheries.

Wild salmon that swim upstream to spawn still exist, but as civilization encroaches
increasingly upon their habitats, their numbers have fallen dramatically. Where, in
the past, rivers ran unimpeded to the sea, many have been dammed; thus, the salmon's
natural course upriver to their spawning grounds has been obstructed.

Salmon in the wild exist most productively in cold waters with high oxygen content. When they swim upstream to spawn, they depend upon their high fat content to
sustain them because, once they have laid their eggs, they cease eating, living solely
on the fat reserves they have built up prior to spawning. As civilization encroaches on
the swift streams and waterfalls that they require if they are to spawn in the wild, it is
increasingly difficult for egg-laying salmon to live through the normal life cycle necessary to sustain the wild salmon population.

Greenberg observes that "Pollution and dams ha[ve] ruined any salmon river that
was unfortunate enough to be near a large human population center. Industrialized
human societies and wild salmon have, with very few exceptions, never found a way
to live harmoniously in proximity to one another." He continues, "And so, in the
prefarming days, the only way wild salmon could reach the majority of consumers
was in a can from Alaska."

Fortunately for humans, salmon adapt well to being farmed in fisheries, from
which much of the salmon available for human consumption is derived. Whereas
most of the fish that humans consume is hatched out of microscopic eggs, the microscopic food required to nourish such eggs in their earliest stages is fragile. Efforts to
fertilize and nourish such eggs until they hatch is so difficult that many species of fish
simply cannot be produced profitably on a large scale. The mortality rate among such
fish is estimated at 99 percent.

Salmon eggs, unlike those of many other species, are large. When they hatch, they are rich in nutrients. They are nourished in their earliest few weeks of life by the oily yolk sac with which they are born, and they adapt quickly to taking additional nourishment from the small quantities of chopped-up fish, mostly herring, that they are fed in captivity.

Even though large numbers of salmon do not survive to become adults, a single female can produce more than one thousand offspring in a lifetime, so a healthy salmon population can live to maturity in fisheries. Wild salmon, frequently found in the Pacific Ocean, suffer a devastatingly high mortality rate, but even they, because of the size and nutrient content of the eggs from which they are hatched, exist in formidable numbers.

In some Norwegian fisheries, crossbreeding has produced salmon of nearly twice the normal size in one-half of the time it takes salmon in the wild to mature. The revolutionary methods pioneered by Norwegian aquaculturists have been adopted widely in other countries. Chile alone produces almost as much farmed salmon as all the wild salmon harvested worldwide.

Less adaptable to aquaculture is the sea bass, although the demand for such fish is enough to persuade many aquaculturists, especially those working around the shores of the Mediterranean Sea, to go to exceptional measures to raise the fish commercially. Initially, sea bass were taken from the shallow Mediterranean waters that were their natural habitat.

Greenberg undertook considerable research in Mediterranean countries to assess the current status of sea-bass populations. He traced early efforts to raise sea bass in fisheries to the historic fishermen of the pre-Christian Roman era. As sea bass have become a significant economic factor in the modern food industry, fisheries have raised them in nets, but such efforts have been fraught with difficulties. Greenberg compares the farming of sea bass to the farming of salmon: "Unlike salmon, which adapt relatively easily to a farmed environment, sea bass and the wide range of ocean fish that we eat are difficult to master. Their early lives are microscopic, their breeding habits complex, and they seem inherently resistant to our designs of putting them into our underwater mangers."

Greenberg cautions that, in the long term, raising fish in fisheries simply to meet the demands of a public hungry to buy them, is an activity fraught with hazards and destined to ultimate failure. He points to the activities of two brothers, Sivert and Ove Grøntvedt, in the Norwegian town of Hitra, as models of how fisheries can best be run, although he notes that these brothers are concerned solely with farming salmon.

Referring to the research of Mark Kurlansky into the history of the cod as a popular food source since ancient times, Greenberg offers an interesting theory that Kurlansky advances: North America might have been discovered, long before 1492, by Basque fishermen who found the cod-fishing fields of the New World but did not reveal their existence to anyone lest these rich waters be descended upon by European hordes out to get rich from the harvests of these fishing fields.

In the pre-Columbian era, cod were abundant and were viewed as commonplace. Their abundance, according to Kurlansky, permitted the population of the Western world to increase by an astounding twentyfold. All went well as long as the cod could be part of a wild harvest, but the cod population began to decline rapidly when attempts were made to raise cod in fisheries. Cod were not amenable to being confined in cages or surrounded by nets. Left in their wild state, they prospered, but attempts to domesticate them and raise them in cod farms proved futile. These fish are overly sensitive to their surroundings and are virtually impossible to breed outside their natural environment, making it necessary to control the depletion of the species by imposing international limits on cod fishing. During the 1960's and the 1970's, the rich cod fields around Newfoundland and Nova Scotia were in danger of being fished out.

Almost as unsuited for aquaculture as cod is the tuna, particularly the bluefin tuna that is valued for its dark-red, solid flesh, which has become a component of sushi. The demand for such tuna and the price it commands on the open market make it a tempting product for fishermen. As the wild varieties of bluefin tuna have diminished alarmingly since the early 1990's, desperate attempts have been launched to raise the fish in captivity; such attempts have been almost uniformly unsuccessful. Greenberg warns throughout the book that efforts to raise fish unsuited for domestication for the sole purpose of cashing in on them as commodities will predictably cause frustration. These failures, however, will not discourage avaricious fishermen from attempting to find new means of achieving their economic ends.

Greenberg draws interesting parallels between aquaculture and the breeding of such common protein sources as beef, lamb, pork, and poultry. He reminds his readers that the farm animals that people know and that are the major sources of the animal protein that nourishes large populations became domesticated because they were suited to domestication. They became even more suited to it through centuries of breeding. It is doubtful that fish such as cod and bluefin tuna are likely to be domesticated in the way that farm animals have been because they were not initially suited to domestication.

Greenberg warns that under current conditions the bounty of the sea is being squandered, but he is ever optimistic in his belief that nature can heal itself over time. The revival of the Long Island Sound during his lifetime is encouraging to him, but nature has sent out frightening signals that danger lurks, at least in the immediate future. Passionate about his desire to preserve natural fishing beds, the author urges immediate action to prevent overfishing and the destruction of the waters that fish require in order to survive. As human populations make inroads upon wilderness areas, Greenberg questions whether or not humans in industrialized societies can live in harmony with nature.

Four Fish is extremely well written. Although it is solidly and dependably accurate in presenting salient information about the status of worldwide fishing, it avoids diatribe and generally reads like a well-written memoir. Its narrative style is enticing, reminiscent of the best of such nature writers as Barry Lopez, Jonathan Safran Foer, and Rachel Carson.

R. Baird Shuman

Review Sources

Audubon 112, no. 4 (July/August, 2010): 62-66.
Booklist 106, no. 21 (July 1, 2010): 13.
Discover 31, no. 6 (July/August, 2010): 26.
The Economist 396 (July 24, 2010): 82.
Kirkus Reviews 78, no. 10 (May 15, 2010): 448.
Library Journal 135, no. 12 (July 20, 2010): 106.
Nature 466, no. 7304 (July 15, 2010): 319.
The New York Times Book Review, July 25, 2010, p. 1.
Publishers Weekly 257, no. 20 (May 17, 2010): 40.

FREEDOM

Author: Jonathan Franzen (1959-   )
Publisher: Farrar, Straus and Giroux (New York).
  562 pp. $28.00
Type of work: Novel
Time: Post-September 11, 2001
Locale: Minnesota, New York, and Washington, D.C.

Franzen's saga about the Berglund family explores American life in the tumultuous first decade of the twenty-first century, focusing on the deceptions and dangers that lurk in freedom's hopes and desires

Principal characters:
> WALTER BERGLUND, a native Minnesotan in his late forties, whose domestic and political life leads to alienation and loneliness but is infused with glimmers of hope
> PATTY EMERSON BERGLUND, his wife and the mother of their two children; a former basketball star from Westchester County, New York, and the University of Minnesota
> JESSICA BERGLUND, their first child, whose loyalty to both her parents helps them to find and to love each other anew
> JOEY BERGLUND, their rebellious son, who redeems at least some of the wreckage caused by his ambition
> RICHARD KATZ, an erratic but eventually successful musician who has been Walter's best friend and Patty's lover

The national anthem of the United States affirms that the American people in-habit—indeed constitute—"the land of the free and the home of the brave." Nine years in the writing, Jonathan Franzen's best-selling *Freedom* questions the banal optimism that often infects the singing of those words. Set in the United States after the terrorist attacks of September 11, 2001 (9/11), Franzen's novel depicts a dysfunc-tional nation. As the rich get richer, the economy declines, sapped by unemployment-producing greed and corrupting aspirations for political control that put the nation's unhealthy fate increasingly in the clutches of the self-serving wealthy. American mil-itary power can neither quell the terrorist threats of al-Qaeda that continue to haunt the nation after 9/11 nor obtain credible victories against insurgencies in Iraq and Af-ghanistan. Indifference to impending ecological disasters is matched only by ignorant belief that a consumption-driven American Dream is indefinitely sustainable, even though many Americans doubt that a fundamental assumption in that conviction—an ever-better life for their children—is true. In the world of *Freedom*, "the land of the free" has become a place where people's choices have fragmented and trapped them and where it is questionable that "the home of the brave" has the courage needed to

Jonathan Franzen has published three previous novels, including The Corrections *(2001). His literary credits also include a collection of essays called* How to Be Alone *(2002) and* The Discomfort Zone: A Personal History *(2006), a memoir.*

make Americans more than an inchoate "collection of contradictory potential someones," as Joey Berglund's musing puts the point.

This portrayal, however, is not *Freedom*'s whole story about American life in the first decade of the twenty-first century. Franzen's narrative is not primarily a survey of the United States but a detailed, carefully nuanced story about the Berglunds, an American family—immediate and extended—as unexceptional as the country itself is becoming. In ways reminiscent of John Updike, the American novelist he most resembles, Franzen invests the typically American Berglunds with such resilience and tenacity in the midst of their folly and failure that readers, at least the Americans among them, are likely to care much what happens to them. Franzen's picture of the Berglunds and their country becomes a mirror in which most Americans can see themselves, warts and all. Thus, the Berglunds' rollercoaster lives invite reflection on how well American life is doing individually and nationally, and what it would take to make life better in both of those ways.

Freedom identifies what it would take when Patty Berglund flies from Minnesota to Philadelphia to visit her daughter, Jessica. Old-fashioned words carved in stone on the main building of Jessica's college catch Patty's eye: "Use Well Thy Freedom." None of the Berglunds can honestly say that they have done so consistently, although at the time choices big and small were made, those decisions seemed alluringly desirable and good. Patty Emerson, for example, rode her basketball skills to star status at the University of Minnesota, a journey that distanced her from the scene, if not the memory, of the rape she had experienced in her New York suburb; separated her from a family she resented; and eventually led to marriage with Walter Berglund, the kind, decent, but also angry man who adored her. By the time of her campus visit to Jessica, however, Patty felt deeply the sting of the words on the building wall. Betrayed by her affair with the musician Richard Katz, Walter's former college roommate and long-time best friend, Patty's marriage has soured—too much free time and drinking are additional causes and effects of that—and so have her relationships with Jessica and Joey, the younger child, whose choices often aim at sexual conquest and selfish moneymaking. In Patty's autobiographical journal, composed, the novel says, at the suggestion of her therapist and titled with the understatement "Mistakes Were Made," Patty acknowledges that "by almost any standard, she led a luxurious life" and yet "she pitied herself for being so free" because "all she ever seemed to get for all her choices and all her freedom was more miserable."

If Patty's autobiography shows how freedom's hopes and desires can be a snare and delusion resulting in disappointment and self-loathing, Walter Berglund's entanglement with freedom's fickle and ambiguous ways involves a web spun of frustrated ambition and disillusionment produced by stymied idealism. As Walter learns, to his sorrow, his love, esteem, and passion for Patty are greater than she (rightly) thinks she deserves and can give in return, although her love and admiration for him are real. His ambitions to improve the world do not fare much better. Determined to forestall environmental disaster, Walter finds that working for the Nature Conservancy is not enough. Relocating from Minnesota to Washington, D.C., he decides to support a dubious scheme to facilitate devastating mountain-top-removal (MTR) coal mining in West Virginia and then to turn the condemned wasteland into a refuge for migratory birds. Work on this project leads Walter to fall in love with Lalitha, the vivacious, intelligent young woman who is his assistant. She fills his need as Patty no longer can, and their passion for each other finds a political outlet as Walter and Lalitha move beyond the West Virginia project and devote themselves to Walter's even larger cause: curbing the world's out-of-control population growth. However, "Free Space," as the population-control initiative was named, dead ends for Walter when a car crash takes Lalitha's life. Earlier, when Walter had been trying to decide whether to "throw away his marriage and follow Lalitha," he had felt "he didn't know what to do, he didn't know how to live. . . . There was no controlling narrative." With Lalitha's death, Walter's prospects become even bleaker, for he eventually reads Patty's "Mistakes Were Made," learns about the betrayal that Patty has dealt him, and cuts his ties to her.

Once, while considering the American obsession with "personal liberties," Walter remarked that "you may be poor, but the one thing nobody can take away from you is the freedom to f——k up your life whatever way you want to." Variations on that theme govern much of Franzen's novel. Freedom, no doubt, is precious, but Franzen's narrative shows that it guarantees little, least of all happiness. Even when braced by discipline and hard work, freedom easily results in depressing downward spirals because human choices, particularly in American form, are easily lured and tempted by aims that have unintended consequences and are laced with the seeds of their own destruction. Not accidentally Franzen's telling of the Berglund's story coincides and intersects with the tumultuous first decade of the twenty-first century. The context for his narrative is that countless choices made by Americans in the post-9/11 era have been riddled with ambiguity and fraught with ruin. When it comes to using freedom well, Franzen's assessment of American life echoes, at least in part, a comment made to Patty Berglund by her mother, Joyce Emerson, after Ray, her husband and Patty's father, has died: "At a certain point, I just have to try not to think too much about certain things, or else they'll break my heart."

Six years after their separation, life goes on for Patty and Walter. Renewing the meaning she had experienced mothering her children when they were young, Patty, at fifty-two, lives in Brooklyn and has restored some order in her life by teaching first-graders and, especially, by coaching middle-school softball and basketball teams. As she updates her autobiographical "Mistakes Were Made," she reflects on her efforts to help her students and players achieve success, concluding that "a universe that permits her to do this, at this relatively late point in her life, in spite of her not having been the best person, cannot be a wholly cruel one."

Meanwhile, Walter has retreated to the Minnesota lake cottage that has long been in his family. He knows that the cottage was one of the places where Patty's ruinous affair with Richard Katz occurred, but he chooses to live there, overseeing property for the Minnesota chapter of the Nature Conservancy and trying to protect the birds in his neighborhood from the cats that are part of Canterbridge Estates, the upscale housing development—destined for a wave of foreclosures—that has sprung up on the opposite shore of the lake.

Patty and Walter only hear about each other through their children. Joey has matured into a socially responsible international businessman, and his marriage to a boyhood sweetheart, Connie Monaghan, seems to be surviving their many indiscretions. Jessica experiences ups and downs, but a renewed relationship with her mother helps them both. Mostly by telephone, Jessica also keeps in contact with her father, who resists her efforts to reestablish contact between her parents or at least to obtain the official divorce that would set them free, a step that neither Patty nor Walter has initiated. Even Richard Katz, who has achieved big-time musical success, encourages Patty to break the silence. Eventually that—and more—takes place.

Wisely, Franzen resists giving *Freedom* a full-fledged happy ending, but in predictable American fashion, this novel does not end without glimmers of hope. Especially in the United States, freedom lures people toward new beginnings, offering second chances if people can find the courage not to give up, the strength to keep trying, and a willingness to forgive at least some of the harm that people do to one another. Whether such hopes are credible is less than certain, but Patty and Walter need them. As the novel draws to a close, they are headed for New York. What awaits them remains in suspense, but they have turned the Minnesota lakeside property into a bird sanctuary. With human access granted only to the residents of Canterbridge Estates, the preserve is named in memory of Lalitha.

Before it was too late, *Freedom* suggests, Patty and Walter came to see that in "the cold space of the future in which they would both soon be dead . . . the sum of everything they'd ever said or done, every pain they'd inflicted, every joy they'd shared, would weigh less than the smallest feather on the wind." Sealing that recognition with a kiss, they choose each other again, using the freedom that remains theirs to embrace one another as they are and may yet become. So, as the year 2010 draws to a close, Patty and Walter are on their way again. For their country, that year, a painful ending to a dismal decade in American history, was scarcely a good one. For Jonathan Franzen, however, the story was different. *Freedom*'s sales soared, making a fortune for its author, propelling him to cover-story status in *Time* magazine, and opening the possibility that he is destined to be the greatest American novelist of his generation. How well Franzen uses his freedom is one of *Freedom*'s important and yet-to-be-written sequels.

John K. Roth

Review Sources

The Atlantic Monthly 306, no. 3 (October, 2010): 114-120.
Booklist 106, no. 21 (July 1, 2010): 7.
Kirkus Reviews 78, no. 15 (August 1, 2010): 693.
Library Journal 135, no. 13 (August 1, 2010): 68.
London Review of Books 32, no. 19 (October 7, 2010): 12-13.
The Nation 291, no. 20 (November 15, 2010): 33.
National Review 62, no. 19 (October 18, 2010): 46-47.
New York 43, no. 26 (August 23, 2010): 154-155.
The New York Review of Books 57, no. 14 (September 30, 2010): 12-13.
The New York Times, August 16, 2010, p. 1.
Publishers Weekly 257, no. 26 (July 5, 2010): 25.
The Times Literary Supplement, no. 5608 (September 24, 2010): 19-20.

FREEFALL
America, Free Markets, and the Sinking of the World Economy

Author: Joseph E. Stiglitz (1943-   )
Publisher: W. W. Norton (New York). 361 pp. $27.95
Type of work: Current affairs, economics, history
Time: Late 2007 to late 2009
Locale: Washington, D.C.; the United States; and most of
  the rest of the world

The book is the study of the financial crisis that began in 2008, discussing what happened, the long-term causes, how it was dealt with, what should have been done, and what should be done in the future

Principal personages:
　　GEORGE W. BUSH (1946-   ), the
　　　　president of the United States, 2001-2009
　　BARACK OBAMA (1961-   ), the president of the United States
　　　　beginning in 2009
　　ALAN GREENSPAN (1926-   ), the head of the Federal Reserve Board,
　　　　1987-2006
　　BEN BERNANKE (1953-   ), the head of the Federal Reserve Board
　　　　beginning in 2006
　　HENRY PAULSON (1946-   ), the secretary of the Treasury under
　　　　George W. Bush
　　TIMOTHY GEITHNER, the head of the New York Federal Reserve from
　　　　2003 to 2009, then secretary of the Treasury

In *Freefall*, Joseph E. Stiglitz covers complex economic issues with a writing style accessible to the informed layperson. He traces the financial crisis that exploded in 2008 to its roots, showing why it happened and providing some suggestions for how to prevent it from recurring. There is much of great interest in the book. However, there are also flaws, starting with the most obvious: Stiglitz fails to include an index, making it difficult to check out specific points in different chapters that might be linked together in some fashion. He also occasionally contradicts himself. For example, near the beginning he admits the market self-corrects with regard to bubbles, though often too slowly and at too high a cost. On the next page, he points out that he and his fellow Keynesian economists agree that the market is not self-correcting at all.

The most serious problem is the subsidiary purpose of the book: an apology for Keynesian macroeconomics and a critique of other theories. This leads to failing to point out when non-Keynesian economists agreed with his views on specific issues, such as corporate welfare and the various 1990's bank bailouts caused by debt crises in foreign governments, and to ignoring the difficulties Keynesian economics has had, for example, explaining the stagflation of the late 1970's, which, according to their theories, should never have happened. In both the preface, which Stiglitz would be well advised to replace with a reasonable one, and a chapter discussing economic theories, he describes many idiocies of opposing economic theorists but usually does so without citing sources.

Joseph E. Stiglitz is an economics professor at Columbia University and was chairman of the Council of Economic Advisers from 1995 to 1997. He shared the Nobel Prize in Economics in 2001 and has written several books on globalism and economic crises.

Otherwise, the book is generally well provided with endnotes. When Stiglitz is not trying to push his theory, he makes a great deal of sense and is worth reading.

Stiglitz starts by studying what led to the crisis. One problem he points out is that the United States had an economy built on debt at all levels, not only for capital purchases (such as new homes) but also for ordinary living. The bulk of the economy involved housing, buying goods to put in houses, or borrowing against houses to pay for ordinary consumption. Extremely low interest rates and lax regulations fed a housing bubble. Furthermore, most banks had securitized their housing loans, which were thus spread to other financial institutions around the world. It was inevitable that the bubble would burst. It was also inevitable that the economy would eventually go into a recession, which was made worse because the economy had depended on debt-fueled consumption that collapsed when the economy soured. Combining the two created a major crisis.

Stiglitz is critical of the mortgage market in general. Banks created products that were certainly convenient for them but not good for those who took out mortgages. In particular, there were high transaction costs, which were made worse if people frequently refinanced. Variable interest rates also created a problem: People would budget for the initial low rates, then face a serious shock when the rates inevitably shot up. The securitization of mortgages created several problems. For one thing, this meant the initial creditors had little incentive to make sure that the debtors really could pay off the debt, because the mortgage would be divided up and sold to others. These buyers had no way of rating the large number of tiny pieces of mortgages in their derivatives. This led to an increasing accumulation of dubious financial assets.

Stiglitz sees the crisis as a failure of the financial markets, which was abetted by deregulation. His main example of this is the repeal in 1999 of the Glass-Steagall Act separating investment and commercial banks, but his main complaint is that this helped create "too-big-to-fail" banks. Much of the problem came from poor incentives, especially basing top executive pay on short-term rather than long-term returns; one serious problem is the disconnect between management and ownership (shareholders) regarding executive pay. The economy was also dependent on aggregate demand based on an unsustainable debt bubble (a consequence of stagnant personal income).

Stiglitz is strongly critical of certain aspects of dealing with the crisis. In a series of financial crises in other countries during the 1990's, the International Monetary Fund (IMF)—created by John Maynard Keynes, ironically—had pushed austerity policies on various governments, such as Mexico, with disastrous debt levels in return for bailing them, and thus their creditors, out. However, when the crisis hit the United States, the IMF suddenly favored the opposite, though bailouts were still popular. Stiglitz opposes such bailouts; whatever might be said of robbing the rich to pay off the poor, many people consider it unconscionable to rob the poor to pay off the rich or to reward bankers for failing grossly. Even worse, the bailouts came with no restrictions, such as forcing the executives of failed firms to disgorge some of their bloated paychecks in return, and were allocated arbitrarily. This started under President George W. Bush and continued after Barack Obama took over. (The fact that both economic teams had a large number of financiers associated with firms such as Goldman Sachs does much to explain this.)

Like his fellow Keynesian Paul Krugman, Stiglitz believes the 2008 stimulus was too small and too focused on tax cuts, too much of which would be saved rather than spent—although in other places he contradicts this, pointing out that Americans need to save far more. He felt the 2009 stimulus was also too small. This book was written in late 2009, before the 2010 Greek debt crisis, which was caused by the sort of massive deficit spending Stiglitz favors, and the continued failure of the economy to recover significantly largely because major corporations are reluctant to invest their money. Keynesians also fail to consider that the money government spends must come from somewhere, at some cost to society, reducing, or even eliminating, the benefit of spending.

On several occasions, Stiglitz discusses the need for more regulation of the financial industry. The purpose of such regulations would be to cause the financial industry to serve the public while receiving its fair rewards. Clearly, in the first decade of the twenty-first century the industry failed grossly to serve the public interest—whether defined as the public in general, depositors, or borrowers—while the executives who failed both the public and their own firms reaped excessive rewards instead of being punished. Auditors became closely entangled with the firms they audited, so that their reports were unreliable. This made the fraudulent marketing of dubious mortgage securities much easier, which spread the disaster around the world. These risky securities had worse returns, long term, than more normal securities, but this only became clear when the downturn finally hit; their returns were better in good times, and the unreliable audits hid the risk.

Stiglitz recommends reforms in corporate management, allowing shareholders more control, particularly over executive pay. This is one key area in which the interests of management and the interests of the owners differ. If executives receive incentive pay, it should be based on long-term rather than short-term profits. Better transparency in finance is needed. Caveat emptor ("let the buyer beware") may be reasonable for the wealthy who can afford losses but not for firms deceived by fraudulent audits or for customers who have no way of understanding the real value of their investments. Stiglitz thinks banks also were too ready to make risky investments. This banking philosophy comes from prior bailouts, which persuaded bankers that the government will cover any disastrous losses while letting them keep any profits. He thinks the Gramm-Bliley repeal of the Glass-Steagall Act contributed to this, partly by creating excessively large, too-big-to-fail banks, but also because combining commercial and investment banks together resulted in banks that placed their priorities on investment, and especially on high returns. Stiglitz thinks Glass-Steagall may have needed reworking as the twenty-first century dawned but should not have been totally repealed.

Derivatives are a major target in *Freefall*, and at one point Stiglitz brings up a peculiar aspect noticed by billionaire investor Warren Buffett: Some derivatives have an inherently devastating potential. AIG insured major financial firms against disaster, wrongly believing that firms such as Bear Stearns and Lehman Brothers could not possibly be in danger. Then it sold derivatives based on these policies, in the form of credit default swaps. If the insured company got into trouble, AIG would have to post collateral; when several ran into trouble simultaneously, AIG was unable to do anything. In addition, the derivatives meant that those who purchased them had an incentive to drive the insured companies to bankruptcy. Stiglitz thinks derivatives are useful for risk management but need to be carefully regulated.

Although Stiglitz's main concern is the American economy, he also looks at the global situation. He sees a serious global gap between demand and supply because of underused resources. There is also the imbalance that a large part of the world lives far beyond its means, with another supplying the excess. The recession of the early twenty-first century has reduced American consumption, which mitigates the problem, but it may only be temporary. Stiglitz is also concerned with the problem of manufacturing more goods with less labor. As a liberal Keynesian, he naturally frets about income inequality as well. He also sees financial instability as a major global concern.

Stiglitz sees a number of specific, long-term problems for the United States also, among them an aging population, a fragile manufacturing base, an inefficient health care system, and poor education below the university level. In his search for answers, he falls back on standard Keynesian economics. This presents a problem: Macroeconomists look at one aspect of economic policy and treat it as virtually all that matters. Stiglitz's blind spot is especially severe, so his solutions are based entirely on heavy government intervention in society. Though claiming to support capitalism, he claims government actually runs things better and cites several examples, carefully leaving out boondoggles such as the giant hole at the former World Trade Center and the failures of public education and Veteran's Administration hospitals.

Timothy Lane

Review Sources

The American Prospect 21, no. 1 (January/February, 2010): 33.
Business Week, no. 4164 (January 25, 2010): 66.
The Economist 394 (March 20, 2010): 91.
The National Interest, no. 106 (March 4, 2010): 64.
The New York Review of Books 57 (April 8, 2010): 54.
The New York Times Book Review 115, no. 6 (February 7, 2010): 6.
The New Yorker 86, no. 3 (March 8, 2010): 75.
Time 175, no. 4 (February 1, 2010): 18.

FUN WITH PROBLEMS

Author: Robert Stone (1937-   )
Publisher: Houghton Mifflin Harcourt (New York).
    195 pp. $24.00
Type of work: Short fiction

A collection of seven short stories by a writer better known as a novelist

One of the most critical differences between the novel and the short story is that whereas in the former the plot can wander and the writer can ramble almost aimlessly, in the latter, the action must have some end-oriented intention on which the writer focuses scrupulously in order to give the story a unified thematic significance. The reader can perceive this difference immediately when reading a short story by a writer who is more comfortable writing novels. Such is the case with several stories in Robert Stone's *Fun with Problems*. Stone has written some impressive novels in his career, such as *Dog Soldiers* (1975), but only one very good short story, "Helping" from his other story collection, *Bear and His Daughter* (1997).

Most of the stories in *Fun with Problems* are peopled by unpleasant drinking and drug-taking male throwbacks to the old days when Stone hung out with Ken Kesey and his Merry Pranksters in the 1960's: "Wine Dark Sea," about a freelance journalist who gets drunk by 6 P.M. and often overlooks deadlines and entire assignments; "The Archer," about an artist and university professor who goes after his wife and her lover with a crossbow while dressed in jockey shorts; and the title story, wherein an aging attorney seduces a young woman trying to stay sober into drinking again. More important, however, they seem haphazardly and indifferently written.

If there is thematic significance in Stone's new stories, it might best be summed up as "an uppity man gets what he deserves"—not because of any serious specific misdeed that he commits but just because he is not very nice. The most obvious example is the story "From the Lowlands," in which a man named Leroy, who has somewhat ruthlessly made a lot of money in the Silicon Valley technology boom, travels, with "little sense of sin," to a vacation home that he has had built in the mountains. When he stops at an old general store for some supplies, on a perverse whim, he steals a candy bar and gives it to a young boy who is in the store with his parents. The owner stops the boy on the way out and causes a scene, while the mother screams that Leroy gave the candy to her son, but Leroy only shrugs, walks out, and "puts the scene behind him."

When he stops in the local post office and sees a Wanted poster for a murderer named Alan Ladd and later sees a construction worker whose brutal face reminds him of the poster, he becomes unsettled by the coincidence and begins to notice what he

Robert Stone is the author of seven novels, including Dog Soldiers *(1974), for which he won the National Book Award. His earlier short-story collection,* Bear and His Daughter *(1997), was a finalist for the Pulitzer Prize.*

takes to be portents of evil and disaster. He is frightened by seemingly minor things; a plastic bag knotted on a tree branch seems a symbol of something ominous, as does another plastic bag lapping against the tile of his swimming pool. When he breaks an egg in a frying pan, he sees a bright spot of blood that also disturbs him, and he tries to think of what it might signify. A call to his girlfriend, whose nickname for him is "king," since *le roi* is the French word for king, is further alarming, for she has discovered that he has a less flattering name for her and angrily tells him that the red spot in the egg probably looks like a skull, cursing both his money and his fancy house.

Leroy, who continues to see the face of the fugitive Alan Ladd, uses a magnifying glass to look at the blood spots in the eggs and thinks they might be skulls. In his usual cocky and blustering way, he tries to dismiss all this by reminding himself that he is the king and that all others are losers who cannot compete with his superior mind. However, the signs and portents he has seen are fulfilled when a panther with a skull-like face appears by his pool. Leroy leaps into the water and clings to a huge beach ball to stay afloat. The ball drifts toward the cat, however, and the story ends with Leroy singing a song that he and his partner used to sing to deride the "IBM types" about drowning in the lowland sea. Because the story provides no background about Leroy's character that would account for his seeing portents in the world around him, its conclusion seems forced and unconvincing.

Another story about the comeuppance of a successful man is "Charm City." At a classical music concert, Frank Bowers meets a psychiatrist named Margaret who asks to buy him a drink afterward. He calls his wife to make an excuse for being late, and they leave together for what he hopes will be a one-night stand. However, Margaret has no intention of going to bed with him and, much to his embarrassment, makes him drive her home. The reader then discovers that Margaret and her daughter are thieves who deal in meth. She calls in a couple of criminal helpers, saying she has identified this "awful man" whom they can easily rob. They go to Bowers's house and steal furniture and bric-a-brac, carrying it all away in a rental van, but not before Margaret slashes his paintings and other possessions with a razor. This is the least motivated story in the collection, for only Bowers's feeble attempt to have sex with Margaret seems to justify the wanton destruction she brings about at the end of the story.

The title story centers on an aging attorney with the public defender's office named Peter Matthews, another of Stone's gratuitously mean men, but one who this time escapes retribution. Visiting a young burglar whom he thinks the police are trying to railroad into a confession, Matthews meets a young psychologist named Amy Littlefield, who reads tarot cards with prisoners to get them to talk about themselves. When Matthews takes the young woman for a drink, he learns that she has a second career in off-Broadway plays and does not drink because it makes her forget her lines. However, Littlefield, who is bored and lonely and whose attraction to the woman is "sensual, sexual, and mean," which is the way he wants it, flatters her and gets her to drink margaritas, stopping at a liquor store for more tequila when he takes her home. As she gets drunk, he senses her weakness and abasement and slaps her on the bottom "as hard as she might reasonably require," after which they go to bed. The next morning when she cries, he shrugs and walks away, saying nothing. Matthews's attitude, typical of many of the men in these stories, is best expressed by his former wife, who once told him that he did not even care if had sex with a woman as long as he could make her unhappy. It is not clear what the purpose of this story is, except to exhibit the crassness of the central character.

The shortest story in the collection, and perhaps as a result the most carefully written, is "Honeymoon," in which a man, on his honeymoon with a young woman in the Caribbean, calls his former wife to tell her how lonely he is. When he tells her that he wants to come home, the former wife hangs up on him, reminding him that he was the one who wanted to leave. Later, when the man and his bride go deep sea diving, he takes off his oxygen tank and drops it. As he sinks in the water, he watches the desired form of his bride swim above him. The story lacks credulity because Stone fails to provide background to the man's breakup and any sense of what feelings he has for his bride. Because of its shortness, however, the result is a tight little tale about the basic mystery of the difference between love and desire—the kind of universal mystery that the short story form handles best.

"High Wire," in which a screenwriter named Tom Loving on drugs, drink, and the skids cannot get over his obsession with an old actor lover named Lucy, replays a Hollywood cliché that Stone developed at length in his novel *Children of Light* (1986). In "High Wire," however, the restrictive first-person point of view is more believable than the rambling third-person perspective of the other stories. Although Loving tells Lucy that he loves her and she tells him that he is the only one she knows who is real, nothing ever comes of the relationship. In fact, the more he sees her, the more unreal she seems to him. At one point, when she is seeing another man, she tells him that they are sleepwalking, unconscious, living parallel lives. The story ends with Lucy spiraling downhill and Loving left alone.

"The Archer," perhaps the most absurd story in the collection, begins with a recounting of a legendary incident when Duffy, a university art teacher, once threatened his wife with a crossbow. Although Duffy says the story is pure invention, the way that the ballad (as it is termed by his students) is usually told is that Duffy came home when he knew that a man was having his way with his wife. He took off all of his clothes except for his jockey shorts and a tweed angler's hat and charged into the parlor with the bow cocked, screaming dementedly, "Cupid is here."

After the two separate, Duffy begins traveling the academic craft lecture circuit, going from campus to campus teaching art classes. At one such guest lecture gig in a state university on the Gulf of Mexico, Duffy becomes so disgusted with the cheesy hotel where he is staying that he considers jumping off the balcony and killing himself. When the professor who has invited Duffy to give the lecture comes to the hotel with his wife and children and takes him out to dinner, Duffy begins drinking, quickly passing what he describes as an undetectable line between inebriation and riot. After a young waitress serves them crab, he becomes belligerent and out of control, claiming that it is some rotten thing out of a tube and not crab at all. He creates such a fuss that the furious cook comes out of the kitchen, and a noisy scene ensues. Duffy curses and screams, calling the cook names, telling him the only crabs he has are in his pubic hair. He is arrested for assault and must call his estranged wife for bail.

When he is finally released, Duffy sits on a park bench facing the Gulf of Mexico with a sketchbook, drawing what he sees. The next day when he takes a taxi to the airport, he happens to run into the young waitress who served him the disputed crab and gives her the picture he drew the day before, leaving feeling much better than when he had arrived. The story seems to exist mainly for the sake of Duffy's outrageous antics.

When he is demonstrating reporting and research skills in long novels about the complexities of America's involvement in Southeast Asia, Latin America, and the Middle East, Robert Stone is at the top of his form. The problem with *Fun with Problems*, however, is that he seems to lack the creative control required to write effective short stories.

Charles E. May

Review Sources

The International Herald Tribune, January 30, 2010, p. 18.
Los Angeles Times, January 10, 2010, p. E11.
The New York Times, January 26, 2010, p. 1.
The Toronto Star, March 7, 2010, p. INO7.
The Washington Times, February 19, 2010, p. B7.

GEORGE, NICHOLAS, AND WILHELM
Three Royal Cousins and the Road to World War I

Author: Miranda Carter (1965-   )
First published: The Three Emperors: Three Cousins,
  Three Empires, and the Road to World War One,
  2009, in England
Publisher: Alfred A. Knopf (New York). 498 pp. $30.00
Type of work: Biography, history
Time: 1859-1918
Locale: England and the European continent

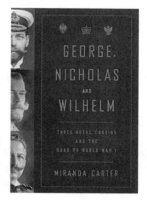

Three cousins who were monarchs of great powers but little more than bystanders to the political turmoil of the period are the focus of this study of the background to World War I, which resulted in the downfall of the old European political/military order and of two of the three monarchies

Principal personages:
  GEORGE V (1865-1936), king of Great Britain
  WILHELM II (1859-1941), German kaiser
  NICHOLAS II (1868-1918), csar of Russia

World War I has engaged many historians, and there is a plethora of biographies of key players in the 1914-1918 conflict. Miranda Carter's *George, Nicholas, and Wilhelm: Three Royal Cousins and the Road to World War I* takes a different approach to this oft-told tale, focusing upon the roles of three monarchs—first cousins and personally close—in the run-up to a conflict that brought down two of the dynasties. Carter's first book, *Anthony Blunt: His Lives* (2001), about the longtime Surveyor of the Queen's Pictures who also spied for the Soviet Union, won the Royal Society of Literature Award and the Orwell Prize. This biography about the three royal cousins, her second book, is a worthy follow-up, though her game plan for the book eludes her.

Carter's title suggests equivalence among her three subjects, but Germany's Kaiser Wilhelm II is the dominant character, having ascended the throne in 1888, whereas Nicholas II of Russia became csar eight years later and George V of England was crowned in 1910. Further, overshadowing them in the first half of the book are Queen Victoria—in the twilight of a long reign but still meddlesome in matters of state and persistently active as Europe's matchmaker—and her eldest son, who in 1901 succeeded her as Edward VII.

Barely a pretender to statesmanship for much of his life, Bertie, as Edward was called by his family, was a playboy prince who set social standards for the age on the European continent and in Great Britain. As king, however, he became intimately involved in international matters and served as a useful front man for a government that,

∼

Miranda Carter worked as a journalist before embarking in 1994 on the research for her first book, Anthony Blunt: His Lives *(2001), a biography of the art historian and spy, for which she received the Royal Society of Literature Award and the Orwell Prize.*

∼

according to Carter, "was notably lacking in charismatic public figures or statesmen." Edward "had a real talent for personal relationships. His effect was almost Reaganite," and following the promulgation in 1904 of the Entente Cordiale, "it was Edward who went round Europe reassuring the various monarchs and presidents that it had only peaceful implications." In sum, says Carter, "within his own limitations and because of the needs of the time, he made a significant contribution to the furtherance of British foreign policy, the consequences of which would be by no means all benevolent." Edward VII reigned until 1910, so George V—unlike his father, a paragon of morality and asocial to a point of dullness—is a latecomer to Carter's triumvirate and is mainly a bystander, a ceremonial figurehead watching ministers squabble and vie for power.

George's primary decisions during this tumultuous period were to change his Germanic family name from Saxe-Coburg to Windsor and to deny refuge in England to his Romanov cousins in 1917. His parents' second son, he became heir when Albert, his older brother and closest friend, died in 1892 of influenza at the age of twenty-nine. Whereas Albert was sent to Cambridge University, George had only a brief stint as a naval man (he suffered from seasickness). Having become Prince of Wales and a married man, wedding his late brother's fiancé, he lived happily as a country gentleman on his parents' estate, carrying out occasional public engagements, hosting frequent hunting parties, and tending to his stamp collection. Carter quotes George's biographer Harold Nicolson: "For seventeen years [until he came to the throne in 1910], he did nothing at all but kill animals and stick in stamps." This was an exaggeration, for his father kept him up-to-date on matters of state, he was a trustee of the British Museum, and in 1901, he and his wife went to Australia for the opening of its new parliament and transition from a group of six colonies to a single country.

The Australian trip lasted eight months, with the royal couple also visiting Canada, New Zealand, and South Africa. Despite his required public duties, George, like his cousin Nicholas, was almost reclusive. The Edwardian world he inherited upon his father's death in 1910 "left him bewildered and alarmed," says Carter. Hopelessly conservative, even reactionary, he looked upon socialists, trade unions, and the radical part of the ruling Liberal Party as the enemy. He was against the right of workers to strike and even prompted his prime minister to propose a law prohibiting peaceful picketing. He often lectured his ministers at great length about domestic issues (to no avail); however, foreign affairs did not interest him, for he favored "splendid Isolation" rather than alliances with other countries. He did, however, believe that the monarch could bind together a sprawling empire. He persuaded a skeptical cabinet to let him go to India, restive with an independence movement, and be proclaimed its emperor. Despite a massive spectacle and throngs at the durbar, this expensive royal visit did little to advance the imperial cause or diminish India's increasing nationalism.

Faced with historic limitations on his authority, and lacking the personal dynamism necessary to overcome such constraints, George settled in to become a model constitutional monarch: "a layer of foundation stones, a visitor of schools, mining towns, railway works and occasionally workers' cottages." Under George, Carter says, "the British monarchy really would become . . . 'dignified' and 'symbolic.'" George's throne, though an anachronism, remained a potent symbol that was unthreatened by the turmoil of World War I and, in fact, was strengthened by the cataclysm. "By the end of the war, *The Times* would write of 'the wonderful popularity with Londoners—as we are convinced, with the whole country—of THEIR MAJESTIES the KING and QUEEN . . . this signal outburst of loyal feeling is born of the conviction that the CROWN, well-worn, is the symbol and safeguard of unity, not only here in England, but in the free dominions overseas, and in India.'" Carter also states that "It was George who established the British monarchy as the domestic, decorative, ceremonial, slightly stolid creation it is today."

By contrast, Nicholas had unlimited authority, for Russia had not even the facade of a representative government until after the fiasco of the Russo-Japanese War (1904-1905). Nicholas lived a cloistered family life and was oblivious to the simmering civil unrest that would eventually end his dynasty. With the most isolated upbringing of the three cousins and poorly educated by inept tutors, he had little idea of life beyond the royal estates: a vast realm spanning 8.5 million square miles inhabited by 120 million people, most of whom were peasants, who pretty much bore the country's tax burden. With the war debacle of 1905, events in Russia—factories closing, trains not running, riots rampant—made it clear that the country was on the cusp of revolution. Out of this chaos came the October manifesto, largely the work of an enlightened government minister, Sergey Yulyevich Witte, which promised "civil liberties—freedom of religion, of speech, of assembly, of association—as well as an elected assembly, whose consent would be required for laws to come into force, and universal male suffrage," albeit with the csar retaining the right of veto over everything. While reluctant to endorse what amounted to a constitution, Nicholas recognized the ramifications of a refusal: To "crush the rebellion by sheer force . . . that would mean rivers of blood and in the end we should be where we started," he wrote to his mother. He signed it, though doing so meant to Nicholas "absolute failure, and the abandonment of a 600-year-old sacred birthright," says Carter.

Though aware that it was the weakest of the three powers, Russia determined to restore its imperial glory by expanding its empire and asserting its influence in the Balkans, but Nicholas and his ministers neither reckoned with an aggressive Austria nor with the fact that Russia's army, however massive, lacked the ability and materiel to engage in a war. Economic shortcomings including famine; brutal police actions against the populace; an erratic empress who was under the sway of a religious charlatan, Grigori Yefimovich Rasputin; and, once hostilities began, hundreds of thousands of battlefield dead combined to erode the credibility of the csar's increasingly fractious government and eventually led to calls for his abdication. After he signed the document on March 15, 1917, "the end of aristocracy was greeted with bells, songs, cheering and flags."

Because Wilhelm is first among these cousins, and he was on the throne longer than the others, Carter devotes more time to him and Germany's role in the war. Twenty-nine years old when he succeeded his father, he intended to rule but was confronted by Otto von Bismarck, who had been chancellor and putative ruler for almost thirty years. While Wilhelm seemed to prevail early on, he was temperamentally unsuited for leadership, for he had been poorly educated (by equally weak English and German tutors alternatively representing the two aspects of his paternity), had suffered from depression since childhood, and was hopelessly narcissistic.

In the rivalries among the powers, he favored England and was hostile to Russia. Once war broke out, his already limited authority was further proscribed. "I may as well abdicate, he complained, but in the event remained as the front man for a military dictatorship . . . a virtual prisoner of the army . . . shuffled from front to front, pinning on medals, then dining at some grand aristocrat's large estate." Indeed, this was a role for which he was best suited. Years earlier, his grandmother Victoria had made him an honorary admiral in the Royal Navy, and he reveled in the ceremonial occasions when he could sport the same white and gold dress uniform that Lord Nelson had worn years earlier. When he loses his authority because of emotional instability, what remain are the rituals, titles, and uniforms that always fascinated him.

All three monarchs, cousins who genuinely liked one another, believed naively that maintaining amiable familial relationships could temper and neutralize the political conflicts festering on the continent and threatening war. Nonetheless, however much the personal and political intersected during the years before and during World War I, the three had little influence on the events that led to war. When the June 28, 1914, assassination of the heir to the Austria-Hungary throne stoked fires of militancy that already had been burning across the continent, the cousins were otherwise occupied—Wilhelm at a yachting regatta, Nicholas on a Baltic cruise, and George with the Irish Home Rule problem—and doubted, unrealistically, the imminence of war. These men were swept along by social, political, and economic forces they did not control; though royalty seemed to matter during this era, World War I shattered what had always been at least partly an illusion.

The cousin's limited engagement in the major international issue of their time neither diminishes the scholarly importance of Carter's book nor lessens the pleasure her narrative imparts. She does not present the balanced tripartite narrative her title promises, but by focusing upon personal correspondence among the principal subjects, she develops a dramatically compelling, and sometimes mordantly humorous, narrative of weak men nominally presiding over a politically unstable continent. The stories of these lives has been told before, but rarely as well.

Gerald H. Strauss

Review Sources

Booklist 106, no. 12 (February 15, 2010): 22.
Library Journal 135, no. 5 (March 15, 2010): 109.
The New York Times Book Review, April 4, 2010, p. 19.
The New Yorker 86, no. 9 (April 19, 2010): 115.
The Wall Street Journal, May 5, 2000, p. W10.

THE GIRL WHO KICKED THE HORNET'S NEST

Author: Stieg Larsson (1954-2004)
First published: Luftslottet som sprängdes, 2007, in
  Sweden
Translated from the Swedish by Reg Keeland (pseud-
  onym of Steven T. Murray)
Publisher: Alfred A. Knopf (New York). 563 pp. $27.95
Type of work: Novel
Time: 2005
Locale: Stockholm and Göteborg, Sweden, and their
  environs

The final volume of Larsson's Millennium trilogy, in which he explores social conditions, particularly those of women, in Sweden at the beginning of the twenty-first century

Principal characters:

    LISBETH SALANDER, a brilliant computer hacker with a photographic
        memory
    ALEXANDER ZALACHENKO, her father and a Soviet spy who defected to
        Sweden
    RONALD NIEDERMANN, her half brother, who works for Zalachenko
    MIKAEL BLOMKVIST, an investigative journalist and publisher at
        Millennium magazine
    RICHARD EKSTRÖM, the prosecutor at her trial
    ANNIKA GIANNINI, her attorney and Blomkvist's sister
    EVERT GULLBERG, a retired leader of the secret security police section
        and a conspirator against her
    ERIKA BERGER, editor of *Millennium* and one of Blomkvist's lovers
    JAN BUBLANSKI, a Stockholm police inspector
    FREDERIK CLINTON, the acting chief of the secret security police section
        and Gullberg's fellow conspirator
    ANDERS JONASSON, a doctor who attends her at Sahlgrenska Hospital in
        Göteborg
    PETER TELEBORIAN, a psychiatrist who assisted in the conspiracy against
        her
    TORSTEN EDKLINTH, a government official in charge of investigating
        crimes against constitutionally guaranteed freedoms
    MONICA FIGUEROLA, Edklinth's coworker and one of Blomkvist's lovers

A publishing phenomenon, Stieg Larsson's Millennium trilogy has sold more than 27 million copies in forty countries. Each of the three volumes has been filmed in Scandinavia, and a Hollywood remake of the first volume, *Män som hatar kvinnor* (2005;

The Girl with the Dragon Tattoo, 2008), was scheduled to be released in 2011. Centered on his protagonist Lisbeth Salander, each volume in Larsson's Millennium trilogy—the second one was titled *Flickan som lekte med elden* (2006; *The Girl Who Played with Fire*, 2009)—explores both Lisbeth's personal history and the late twentieth century and early twenty-first century history of Swedish society. Without disturbing contradictions, Lisbeth is presented both as an exceptional individual and as a prototypical postmodern "every woman," whose personal experiences both typify and exceed those of women in general in postindustrial Scandinavia, and, by extension, become indicative of the place of women in a globalized world.

> ～
> *Stieg Larsson was known chiefly as the author of the Millennium trilogy and received several awards both in his native Sweden and abroad. As a magazine editor and expert on right-wing extremism and racist organizations, he was an important political activist also.*
> ～

Named for the monthly magazine *Millennium*, where Larsson's lead male character and alter ego, Mikael Blomkvist, works as an investigative reporter, an editor, and a publisher, the trilogy as a whole constitutes an inquiry into what has gone wrong not only in the private sphere but also in business and government during Sweden's final decades of the twentieth century. Larsson's indictment of contemporary society is severe and is advanced on several fronts, but the linchpin of his analysis is the irrational manifestation of male thinking called misogyny. In fact, the Swedish title of the first volume translates directly into English as "Men who hate women," and the trilogy can be read as an exploration both of the reasons for this hatred and the various ways it manifests itself both privately and in society as a whole.

Larsson is an heir both to the practice of the Western mystery novel, associated with such outstanding female writers as Agatha Christie and Dorothy Sayers, and to a Scandinavian narrative tradition that offers a plethora of strong female characters. In the twentieth century, the Scandinavian novel was dominated by the style of psychological realism, which clearly has had a strong impact on Larsson. So also have such novels as the socially conscious police procedurals of Maj Sjwall and Per Wahlöö, as well as perhaps Henning Mankell's relentless questioning of what went awry in Swedish society, presented through the work of his fictional police inspector Kurt Wallander. A possibly unlikely—but palpable—model for Lisbeth is the archetypal Swedish good-and-bad girl Pippi Longstocking, created by the children's writer Astrid Lindgren. Pippi has bequeathed both some of her physical strength and her resourcefulness to Lisbeth; indeed, Lisbeth may be viewed as a grown-up Pippi who has acquired a variety of piercings and tattoos and whose bisexuality is an affront to traditional patriarchy.

The story in *The Girl Who Kicked the Hornet's Nest* begins where the previous volume left off. Lisbeth has been nearly killed by her father, Alexander Zalachenko, and his sidekick, Lisbeth's half brother, Ronald Niedermann, who operate a crime ring involved with trafficking and money laundering. Zalachenko hates his daughter because as a young teenager she doused him and set fire to him in an attempt to stop his physical abuse of her mother. Zalachenko, a Soviet spy who relocated to Sweden and enabled several employees of the Swedish security police to build successful careers for themselves, has lured Lisbeth to his home, a small farm outside Göteborg, where he and Niedermann almost manage to shoot her to death; in fact, Niedermann buries her, thinking that she is dead. After regaining consciousness and clawing her way out of her shallow grave, Lisbeth tries unsuccessfully to kill her father again. When the police finally arrive on the scene, Lisbeth is airlifted to the Sahlgrenska hospital in Göteborg, where she is placed under guard as the prime suspect in a murder actually committed by Niedermann.

Throughout the trilogy Larsson's voice is largely indistinguishable from that of his omniscient narrator, carefully feeding the reader information about Lisbeth's personal history, particularly as it relates to her father Zalachenko. In the first two volumes the reader has been told about Lisbeth's troubled youth, including a forced stay at a mental hospital where she was under the care of Dr. Peter Teleborian, and the fact that she has been declared incompetent, as the medical authorities believe her to be mentally deficient. In *The Girl Who Kicked the Hornet's Nest* Larsson reveals additional details about Lisbeth's background by placing her personal experiences in a broader social and historical context.

As it turns out, Zalachenko's defection was a godsend for some of the employees of the so-called Section, an entirely secret division of the Swedish security police headed by a man named Evert Gullberg. Antidemocratic to the core, Gullberg has no qualms about illegally shielding Zalachenko from the consequences of his criminal activity—Zalachenko is essentially a Soviet thug who, after the fall of the Soviet Union, has only crime as an outlet for his destructive personality—as long as Gullberg and his men can take credit for obtaining potentially valuable information furnished by the former spy. As a result of their task of cleaning up Zalachenko's messes, they sacrifice Lisbeth, conspiring with Teleborian to confine her to a mental institution in order to shut her up. While later unable to keep Lisbeth from being released, they manage to keep her under guardianship; consequently, she is both physically and sexually abused by her guardian.

When Gullberg, who is long retired, learns about the shootings at Zalachenko's farm, he springs into action, leaving his home for Stockholm and essentially taking away command of the Section from Frederik Clinton. Motivated more by professional pride than by his desire to avoid any of the unpleasant legal ramifications of his past decisions, Gullberg's objective is to prevent any information about the Zalachenko affair from becoming public. Therefore, he must neutralize the threats represented by both Zalachenko and Lisbeth. The former is more easily contained than the latter. Gullberg, who has cancer and only a short time to live, goes to the hospital, assassinates Zalachenko, and then kills himself. Clinton is left to manipulate the Swedish police and court system so that Lisbeth can be declared insane and again placed in the care of Teleborian, who has treated her sadistically in the past and fantasizes sexually about her. Their strategy is to frame Lisbeth for Niedermann's murder of one of Blomkvist's associates at *Millennium*.

Most of the action in *The Girl Who Kicked the Hornet's Nest* concerns the investigative and legal maneuvering aimed at keeping Lisbeth from being committed. The characters involved in a rather complicated series of events divide neatly between heroes and villains. Chief among the heroes is Blomkvist, whose friendship with and past efforts to help Lisbeth were detailed in the previous two volumes. Through the cooperation of Anders Jonasson, Lisbeth's physician at the Sahlgrenska hospital, who has successfully removed a bullet from her brain, Blomkvist manages to smuggle a handheld computer and a cell-phone modem into her room. This enables her to communicate with her friends in the hacker community as well as with Blomkvist, which again allows her to spy on the activities of those who are out to get her. Blomkvist's sister, the women's-issues lawyer Annika Giannini, whose first name is possibly an allusion to Pippi Longstocking's friend in Lindgren's books, agrees to provide Lisbeth with legal representation.

In addition to Clinton, most of those who are certain that Lisbeth is guilty of murder, a threat to society, and insane are found in the police department and prosecutor's office. Larsson offers narrative snapshots of stupidity, prejudice, and incompetence on the part of several male police officers, whose common trait is that they all have problems relating to women. Some members of the police, however, are fair-minded seekers after the facts. Among them is the Stockholm police inspector Jan Bublanski, who is central to the investigation into how Lisbeth has been treated by the security police; in one instance, she leads a crucial raid on their offices. Other champions of justice are found at a government office that is charged with investigating violations of people's constitutional rights, where the pair Torsten Edklinth and Monica Figuerola show themselves as fully worthy of the trust placed in them.

After the case against Lisbeth collapses and she is released from custody, she reconnects with former friends but has an important piece of unfinished business to take care of. Her half brother, Niedermann, has been hiding out in an isolated industrial building where Zalachenko's gang has been keeping women brought illegally to Sweden from the Baltic states. When Lisbeth finds him there, he manages to lock all exit doors and is about to put her in a vat with a murdered prostitute. Lisbeth's chances at defeating him in the ensuing game of cat-and-mouse are slim at best, for Niedermann is both physically strong and has a medical condition that renders him incapable of feeling pain. Lisbeth outwits him, however, and manages to fasten his feet to the floor with a nail gun. Struggling to overcome the urge to kill Niedermann, she then demonstrates that her rationality is in full control of her behavior by calling some of Niedermann's former partners in crime and the police, resulting in the arrest of Niedermann and others.

Both suspenseful and action-packed, *The Girl Who Kicked the Hornet's Nest* is more than just an entertaining read. Larsson's indictment of the arrogance, stupidity, and sheer malevolence of some of those in society who have been entrusted with great power and influence has a message that transcends time and place. This fundamental point coincides with the justice-as-fairness tradition of Scandinavian democracy and the comparatively high regard in which women were held in traditional Scandinavian

society. Above all, however, Larsson shows that men have no special claim to rationality and that his talented and decent female characters are frequently better at
promoting truth and justice than their male counterparts.

Jan Sjåvik

Review Sources

Booklist 107, no. 1 (September 1, 2010): 60.
The Daily Telegraph, February 20, 2010, pp. 4-5.
Kirkus Reviews 78, no. 7 (April 1, 2010): 280.
Library Journal 135, no. 15 (September 15, 2010): 35.
Los Angeles Times, May 24, 2010, p. D1.
The New York Times, May 21, 2010, p. 21.
The New Yorker 86, no. 20 (July 12, 2010): 87.
Publishers Weekly 257, no. 13 (March 29, 2010): 37.
The Times Literary Supplement, October 16, 2009, p. 21.

GLOBISH
How the English Language Became the World's Language

Author: Robert McCrum (1953-   )
Publisher: W. W. Norton (New York). 331 pp. $26.95
Type of work: History, language
Time: From the early middle ages to the present
Locale: Great Britain, the United States, Australia, India, and various other countries

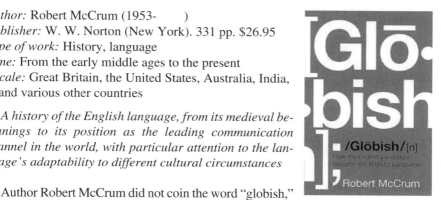

A history of the English language, from its medieval be-ginnings to its position as the leading communication channel in the world, with particular attention to the language's adaptability to different cultural circumstances

Author Robert McCrum did not coin the word "globish," which he uses as the title of this book about the history and development of the English language. The credit for coining and popularizing the word goes to an amateur, French-speaking linguist named Jean-Paul Nerriere, who noted in 1995 how influential English had become as a global language. McCrum dates his own interest in this phenomenon to a time when he overheard a conversation in an airport between an Indian man who spoke no Spanish and a Spaniard who spoke no Punjabi. The men communicated in "a highly simplified form of English, without grammar or structure" and based on "a utilitarian vocabulary of some 1,500 words." This form of English, McCrum asserts, has developed in the increasingly interconnected world specifically to allow nonnative speakers to communicate with one another and with native speakers of English.

McCrum is perhaps best known as the coauthor of the well-received 1986 book and public television series *The Story of English.* This new book, while more than simply a rehash, shares some of the scope and ambition of that project: It seeks to explore what makes English unique and dominant without resorting to jingoistic claims about the strength and character of the English people. Culture and language are not easily separable, so this book is as much about culture (English, American, and world) as it is about language, especially in early sections of the book. Much of the material in this book will be familiar to students of English history, language, and literature. Still, the story of English remains a fascinating one, and *Globish* is loaded with facts and has a distinctive spin.

McCrum does not celebrate the conventional strength and stability of the language. His idea, rather, is that English gains its edge through adaptability. To demonstrate this point, the French language provides an enlightening contrast. Decisions about what constitutes "proper" French have, since the seventeenth century, been made by the learned body known as the Académie Français. English has no such arbitrating body. At about the same time as the academy was established, French was

~

Robert McCrum is associate editor of the Observer *newspaper in London. His previous books include* The Story of English *(1986), cowritten with William Cran and Robert MacNeil;* My Year Off: Recovering Life After a Stroke *(1998); and* P. G. Wodehouse: A Life *(2004).*

~

adopted as the language of diplomacy, used in official documents and international communications throughout Europe. "French," writes McCrum, "would be the language of international relations, but its influence would always be top-down and not, like English, bottom-up." This bottom-up quality is among the attributes of English that McCrum most celebrates. Indeed, the oft-repeated drumbeat of *Globish* is that English is "contagious, adaptable, populist, and subversive." Contagion and adaptability, at least, are amply demonstrated throughout the book.

Globish is divided into five sections, each devoted to a different phase in the development of English as a global language. The first section, called "Founders," begins with the Germanic dialect known as Old English, or Anglo-Saxon, and carries the story of English through to the amazing literary flowering of the Elizabethan period in the late sixteenth and early seventeenth centuries. In a relatively short space, McCrum chronicles the series of invasions on the British Isles from 55 B.C.E. to 1066 C.E.—Romans, Saxons, Vikings, and Norman French—each of which left a mark on the culture and language of the land that would become known as England. By 1100 C.E., under the influence of a French court and increased international trade, Old English had transformed into a new language, known as Middle English.

To demonstrate the beauty and flexibility of this evolving language, McCrum discusses the contributions of great literary figures. Though the author claims he is interested in the "populist" and "subversive" qualities of the language, the illustrations he uses are quite conventional, drawn straight from the established English literary canon. Geoffrey Chaucer serves as the primary representative of the Middle English period, and William Shakespeare plays that role for Early Modern English. In addition to literary figures, though, McCrum takes time to appreciate the influence of William Caxton, who introduced the printing press to England, thereby helping both to stabilize the language and to make books and literature more affordable to everyday Britons.

Part two of *Globish* locates a power shift toward American English, not in the twentieth century (as is often suggested) but in the seventeenth century and the eighteenth century, where McCrum sees "the world's English in its infancy." The Declaration of Independence (1776) is one powerful example of American writing, and the proudly Americanizing dictionary maker Noah Webster gets credit for being as important to the development of English as Caxton had been in an earlier century. By the nineteenth century, the writings of Abraham Lincoln and Mark Twain provide examples of American English at its finest. Again, these choices are quite conventional, but McCrum also shows how the slave trade contributed to the beginnings of African American slang, which would have a major impact on the world's English by the middle of the twentieth century. Though many Britons have long been dismayed at the

American "contamination" of their language, McCrum sees things differently. The rise of American English is simply another stage in the exciting linguistic evolution that began with the fifth century Anglo-Saxons.

The third section of *Globish* focuses on the rise of the British Empire and the effect of imperial expansion on the language, with special attention to the former colonial possessions of Australia and India. In the eighteenth and nineteenth centuries, Australia's principal function in the empire was as a penal colony, where large numbers of convicts were transported to relieve overburdened correctional facilities at home in Britain. The sparse aboriginal population was, for the most part, simply pushed aside or subjugated, their land appropriated to make room for British prison populations. Native languages and culture, therefore, had relatively little impact on the varieties of English spoken in Australia. India, on the other hand, was a more conventional imperial possession, with trade and resource exploitation as its main rationale. Here the native populations were courted as allies (although generally of lesser status than their British counterparts) and encouraged to reproduce aspects of English high culture— including language and literature—in an Indian context. Different still is the role the English language played in Africa, where British settlement was often connected as much with Christian missionary activity as with colonial settlement in the traditional sense.

Each of these examples of imperial expansion, as well as others McCrum discusses in less detail, provides evidence of his point about the adaptability of English. New vocabulary was needed to describe features of landscape and culture unknown in England, and this vocabulary needed either to be invented or adopted from local languages. At the same time, in isolation from the stabilizing effect of the home culture, novel grammatical features and forms of slang were free to develop. In some cases, these new words and styles of speech returned to England, where they had an effect on the mother tongue, even as it was spoken at home. Among McCrum's examples, the word "kangaroo" provides an intriguing example. Though originally believed by the English to be an aboriginal word, no native Australian peoples have ever claimed it as their own, and the assumption is that it was so corrupted from the original that it is no longer recognizable. On the other hand, words from various Indian languages—"calico," "curry," "mantra," and "pundit," among many others—had a much greater impact on English vocabulary.

Leaving the farther flung parts of the empire behind, part four of *Globish* returns to England and the United States in the twentieth century. Winston Churchill, who began his adult life as a journalist and later rose to prime minister of the United Kingdom, is seen as the quintessential example of English eloquence during the period when the empire was in decline. The twentieth century, though, is sometimes called the "American century," with the United States exercising both hard (military and political) and soft (pop-cultural) power over the rest of the world. McCrum acknowledges that by this point in history, American English had become the dominant form. By the last two decades of the twentieth century, the expansion of American-dominated, global mass communications and capitalism meant that English had become the most important language on the planet. The power of American English was further solidified by the beginning of the twenty-first century, when the Internet had become a worldwide phenomenon. The United States was at the forefront of this communications revolution, and more than 80 percent of Internet content was written in English.

In the final section of the book, which is considerably briefer than the other four, McCrum asserts that English has come completely unmoored from the Anglo-American cultures that were originally responsible for its rise. He believes English belongs to the whole world. Nations from Chile to Singapore have official state policies promoting bilingualism. Even in the absence of such policies, English is simply the default language in many international relations, including those that involve neither England, its Commonwealth partners, nor the United States. McCrum seems nothing short of delighted to report that English has become "a lingua franca . . . unhindered by the Anglo-American past." The idea that the language was once "hindered" by its connection to particular cultures suggests how deeply the author believes in a global exchange made possible by a common language.

This utopian notion of a world language, though, is not really elucidated by the examples in *Globish*. McCrum writes occasionally of a single language, but he also acknowledges how the expansion of English has led to Creoles such as "Spanglish" (Spanish and English), "Franglais" (French and English), "Chinglish" (Mandarin Chinese and English), and many others. In the end, then, English does not really constitute a world language, because many of these half-English dialects are mutually unintelligible. Furthermore, McCrum never seems to lose his great faith that "globish" is a positive force that can bring the world closer together.

The question of whether "globish" is one or many languages leads to perhaps the greatest shortcoming of the book: The key term does not remain stable from one chapter to the next. Having used Nerriere's definition early on—"globish" as a utilitarian communication channel with a radically limited vocabulary and simplified grammar—McCrum spends relatively little time discussing that phenomenon. Rather he devotes most of the book to other varieties of English, both traditional and emerging. Also problematic is the fact that he does not prove so much as repeatedly assert the "subversive" nature of English, though he clearly demonstrates its ability to adapt. Still, the history and evolution of the language is a subject of almost infinite interest, and McCrum's clear expertise on, and enthusiasm for, the subject means that *Globish* will find many enthusiastic readers.

Janet E. Gardner

Review Sources

Booklist 106, no. 16 (April 15, 2010): 11.
The Economist 395, no. 8684 (May 29, 2010): 83.

Kirkus Reviews 78, no. 5 (March 1, 2010): 186.
Library Journal 135, no. 8 (May 1, 2010): 75.
New Statesman 139, no. 5007 (June 28, 2010): 51.
The New York Times, May 26, 2010, p. 6.
The New York Times Book Review, June 20, 2010, p. 10.
The New Yorker 86, no. 15 (May 31, 2010): 76.
Publishers Weekly 257, no. 11 (March 15, 2010): 47.
The Times Literary Supplement, no. 5602 (August 13, 2010): 22.

GOLD BOY, EMERALD GIRL

Author: Yiyun Li (1972-   )
Publisher: Random House (New York). 221 pp. $25.00
Type of work: Short fiction
Time: The 1960's-2010
Locale: China

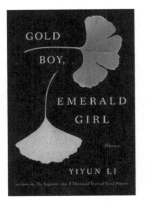

Nine pieces of short fiction about the experience of ordinary people living in mainland China during the late twentieth century and early twenty-first century

Not two weeks after *Gold Boy, Emerald Girl* was released by its publisher in September, 2010, its author Yiyun Li was awarded a half-million-dollar MacArthur Fellowship. Of course, the award was not for Li's accomplishment and promise in this book only. *Gold Boy, Emerald Girl* was preceded by Li's prize-winning short-story collection *A Thousand Years of Good Prayers* (2005) and her highly regarded novel *The Vagrants* (2009).

Like Li's earlier fiction, the stories of *Gold Boy, Emerald Girl* illuminate with unblinking realism and uncommon insightfulness the lives of ordinary people in the People's Republic of China during the far-from-ordinary historical period spanning the Cultural Revolution of the 1960's through the tumult of the prodemocracy Tiananmen incidents of the 1970's and 1980's to the accelerating economic and social changes at the beginning of the twenty-first century, as a new, more capitalistic China is being realized.

Though Li's narrative gaze has focused upon mainland Chinese, several of her stories have also broadened to include the transnational experience of overseas Chinese in the United States and Portugal. Also, like Li's earlier books, the stories in *Gold Boy, Emerald Girl* address a classic theme of Chinese fiction, that of family. This theme had been inaugurated by Cao Xueqin's *Hongloumeng* (pb. 1792; also known as *Hung-lou meng*; *Dream of the Red Chamber*, 1958; also translated as *A Dream of Red Mansions*, 1978-1980, and *The Story of the Stone*, 1973-1982), the Ching Dynasty family epic that rivals world literary masterpieces about family, such as Aeschylus's *Oresteia* (458 B.C.E.; English translation, 1777) or Leo Tolstoy's *Anna Karenina* (1875-1877; English translation, 1886). In *Gold Boy, Emerald Girl* the family theme is also frequently entwined with that of human interconnection; hence it explores the obstacles to communication, the fault lines in relationships, and the hunger for community.

The themes of family and human interconnection are developed exquisitely and complicatedly in the book's opening story, "Kindness" (an eighty-page novella, really). The difficulty of human interconnection is embodied by the narrator-protagonist Moyan, a forty-one-year-old spinster teacher of mathematics who has willed herself

into a cocoon of isolation from personal relationships. Her misanthropy resembles that
of Fyodor Dostoevski's "Underground Man"
from *Zapiski iz podpolya* (1864; *Letters from
the Underworld*, 1913; better known as *Notes
from the Underground*) but her calm and reasonable narrative voice is a contrast to Dostoevski's ranting and manic character, and
the reader becomes sympathetic and curious
about Moyan's reclusiveness. Her family circumstances are also important formative factors.

*Yiyun Li has received many prestigious
prizes, including a Frank O'Connor
Award, the Hemingway Foundation/
PEN Award, and a MacArthur
Fellowship. In 2010,* The New Yorker
*listed her among the top twenty fiction
writers under forty years old.*

Moyan's family originates in kindness, but a kindness that results in ironic out-
comes. Moyan's caring, fifty-year-old janitor father marries her beautiful, twenty-
year-old mother out of kindness, for she was stigmatized as a nymphomaniac by the
neighborhood after she fell in love with a married man. Reciprocating her husband's
kindness, she kindly promises to give him twenty years of her life, one that she would
rather not live. In kindness and to strengthen their marriage, they adopt Moyan, an orphan. The adoptive mother loses herself in romance novels, hardly noticing Moyan.
The father strives to parent Moyan, but he is a night-shift janitor who sleeps during
the daytime (when he uses their bedroom, his wife leaves home on endless errands,
and when he works, she sleeps). Twenty years after their wedding, the wife promptly
commits suicide.

It is not simply her family that conditions Moyan's loneliness. A kind neighbor,
Professor Shan, befriends her and tutors her in English until college. Shan is herself a
beneficiary of kindness, having been an adopted orphan. She and Moyan start by
reading Charles Dickens (the novelist of orphans requiring kindness), proceed to
Thomas Hardy (whom Moyan loves), then to D. H. Lawrence (whom Moyan considers mad, such as her mother). Moyan forms a teenage infatuation for an older unhap-
pily married man and grieves when he leaves their neighborhood. Shan advises: "The
moment you admit someone into your heart you make yourself a fool. . . . When you
desire nothing, nothing will defeat you"—the first sentiment reeks of the mean spirit
of Dickens's Miss Havisham and the second is as enlightening as Buddha. Among
other things, then, Li's "Kindness" also ponders this quality in human feeling,
thought, and action, a quality that is kin to the compassion desired by Buddha and
Confucius, and cousin to St. Paul's Christian charity.

Moyan's acting on Shan's advice is vividly captured in the account of her year in
military service, when camaraderie in the face of hardship can be so strong. However,
even in the bitter cold of winter, when the women are permitted to bunk together for
warmth, Moyan refuses. When her officer, Lieutenant Wei, becomes concerned about
Moyan and asks how she can be helped to be happy, Moyan rejects her overture.

The novella closes on an exquisite image of isolation when Moyan walks past a
shop window through which she sees a television showing one of her former fellow
soldiers who has become an internationally famous soprano. Moyan cannot hear her,

but remembers the day when she sang "The Last Rose of Summer" at a suddenly hushed firing range. It is a telling image of possibilities forever missed. Moyan is excruciatingly like the J. Alfred Prufrock of T. S. Eliot's poem, who has heard the sirens singing each to each but then, either through diffidence or cynicism, has willed herself to walk away from the feast that life may offer.

The themes of family values and communication also provide the initial impetus for "A Man Like Him." Teacher Fei, aged sixty-six, attempts to stop a nineteen-year-old girl from persecuting her father for alleged marital infidelity—her instrument is the worldwide communication of vitriolic postings on the Internet. Fei champions the father (with whom he fails miserably to communicate) because Fei's own career had almost been ruined by false accusations of pedophilia and because Fei's own father, a leading philosopher and eventual suicide victim, had been demoted from professor to toilet cleaner by the Red Guard youths of the Cultural Revolution. Ultimately, the story may be read as a critique of the Cultural Revolution's excesses; the zealous daughter's pillorying of her father on the neocapitalist Internet is an ironic parallel to the Red Guard's denunciation and execution of intellectual "capitalist roaders" during the 1960's.

Though the notoriety brought through communication is unwanted in "A Man Like Him," it is actively sought in "The Proprietress" and "House Fire," stories that also deal with family. "The Proprietress" is a woman who aspires to be interviewed and featured in a prominent magazine for helping (and, incidentally, controlling) the wife of a jailed inmate who wishes to conceive his child. In "House Fire," six women become television celebrities by banding together to investigate marital infidelities, ostensibly to cleanse society and strengthen family values (though the women themselves are deeply flawed individuals).

Courtship and clear communication during courtship are necessary preliminaries to family formation. Li's "Souvenir" is a brilliant tour de force about a man coming on to a woman and of both interacting at cross purposes. The man, a querulous elderly widower, is intent on reliving memories, and his ludicrous pickup line for courting the young woman is that she resembles his dead wife. The young woman, who is painfully shy, is intent on discreetly purchasing condoms to make love with a male student whose memory has been befuddled by his imprisonment and reeducation after (presumably) the Tiananmen incident.

"Number Three, Garden Road" tells a tale of a courtship extending over several decades. In it, a woman nurses a girlhood crush on a neighbor man many years her senior, an attraction that persists through her two failed and childless marriages, his widowerhood and philandering, and even through the gentrification of their humdrum Garden Road properties into an upscale neighborhood in twenty-first century capitalist China.

The book's title story, "Gold Boy, Emerald Girl" (a metaphor for the perfect wedded couple), is a novel courtship tale describing the genesis of a family. In a deliciously surprising way it mingles traditional Chinese matchmaking with modern tolerance of homosexuality to accomplish an unusual ménage à trois. The protagonist,

Siyu, is a thirty-eight-year-old female librarian who, since her student days, has harbored an unspoken attraction to another woman, seventy-one-year old Professor Dai. Tenacity and devotion mark Siyu's character—when a student, she spends half an hour daily for two years seated in front of Professor Dai's office memorizing Dickens's *Great Expectations*. Professor Dai has a forty-four-year-old gay son, Hanfeng, who has lived twenty years in the United States; San Francisco's gay scene lacks attraction for him, and he decides to repatriate to Beijing (much to his friends' amazement). Mother and son are affectionate, and they are model practitioners of "don't ask don't tell": He has not come out to her, but one gathers she knows. Professor Dai fixes up Siyu and Hanfeng on a date, and it is soon understood that they will marry and that all three will live together in separate bedrooms, each person complementing the others like gold and emerald in jewelry, never melded into an alloy, but each discretely enhancing the other.

Partially set in the United States, "Gold Boy, Emerald Girl" gestures to the transnational experience of overseas Chinese. Two other stories in this collection also contain transnational overtones. Both concern family, and both are told in the ironic mode. "Prison" is about a well-educated, middle-aged Chinese couple who immigrate with their only child to the United States to better their family. Ironically, the husband, a high-status doctor in China, lacks the English skills to pass the board exams and must work as a low-status laboratory assistant in the United States. Then their Harvard-bound daughter is killed in a typical American auto accident, effectively shattering their family dream since the wife is past childbearing age. Attempting to revive their dream, the couple visit China to employ a surrogate mother. They feel guilty for exploiting the naïveté of the poverty-stricken, downtrodden woman they select from the many applicants. However, this seemingly tractable surrogate becomes increasingly empowered, demanding, and even threatening as her pregnancy progresses—her hostage, their fetus. The irony thus deepens for the transnational couple imprisoned by the means by which they sought to shape their family fate—migration, science, and exploitation.

"Sweeping By" is the other story with transnational resonance. It begins during the age of innocence of three women, girls during ante-Cultural Revolution times who are best friends; they take a professional photograph to seal their sisterhood. Their interconnectivity persists as they mature and marry; when one woman has a daughter and the other a son, the third plays matchmaker for the youngsters to cement their bond with a family tie. In a wrenching irony, however, the son accidentally strangles the daughter, and the effort at interconnectivity explodes into bitterness and incrimination. Ironically, also, the matchmaker's granddaughter has "photoshopped" the fifty-year-old photograph of the three women during their salad days of innocence, and she hangs it in her Chinese restaurant in Lisbon, Portugal, where she has migrated. There her customers will gaze upon it as an orientalized scene of Chinese communality, blissfully unaware of the tragic events that have swept away the camaraderie, unaware that even the photographer had been swept away during the Cultural Revolution for having used a capitalist German-made camera.

Li's remarkable facility in English, her second language, should be noted. She has been favorably compared with Joseph Conrad and Vladimir Nabokov, both fiction writers who wrote in their nonnative English. It should also be noted that Li typically eschews the sometimes convoluted syntax of a Conrad and the stylistic pyrotechnics of a Nabokov; instead, Li writes a lean, spare prose, clear as a windowpane through which her unflinchingly realistic narrative compels her readers to share so profoundly in the full humanity of her characters.

C. L. Chua

Review Sources

Booklist 106, no. 22 (August 1, 2010): 22.
Kirkus Reviews 78, no. 13 (July 1, 2010): 591.
Library Journal 135, no. 11 (June 15, 2010): 69.
The New York Times Book Review, September 19, 2010, p. 10.
People 74, no. 11 (October 4, 2010): 50.
Publishers Weekly 257, no. 19 (May 10, 2010): 24.
San Francisco Chronicle, September 12, 2010, p. FE2.

THE GRAND DESIGN

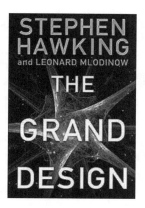

Authors: Stephen Hawking (1942-   ) and Leonard
  Mlodinow (1954-   )
Publisher: Bantam Books (New York). 198 pp. $28.00
Type of work: Science, history, philosophy, religion

*Presenting recent findings in modern physics, Hawking
and Mlodinow address fundamental questions about the
origins of the universe and life itself and propose M-theory
as the most viable candidate for a complete theory of everything*

How did the universe begin? What is the nature of reality? Why are the laws of nature so finely tuned as to allow
the existence of creatures such as humans? Is a creator responsible for drawing the blueprint of the cosmos? Throughout human history, esteemed thinkers have wrestled with these perplexing questions. The answers have
proven illusive until now—at least according to renowned physicist Stephen Hawking and his colleague Leonard Mlodinow. In their lavishly illustrated handbook, *The
Grand Design*, they attempt to provide a fresh perspective on what Douglas Adams,
author of *The Hitchhiker's Guide to the Galaxy* (1979), called "life, the universe, and
everything." Hawking and Mlodinow claim, however, that their answer "won't
simply be '42'."

Unlike Deep Thought, the megacomputer in Adams's science-fiction saga, which
sifted through billions of computations to come up with "42" as a theory of everything, Hawking and Mlodinow eschew the dense and confusing equations that sometimes appear in popular science books. Instead, they offer general readers a succinct
nontechnical survey of the history of scientific thought regarding the origins and
maintenance of the universe, as well as a lively analysis of the latest theories that
dominate the field of modern physics.

Hawking and Mlodinow begin by examining the scientific breakthroughs of the
Ionian Greeks who, throwing myth and theology out the window, believed that nature
was governed by fundamental laws and not by the whims of gods and goddesses. The
approach of these early observers was reasoned and rational and led to significant contributions to the ancient world's understanding of scientific principles. One of the most
lauded of these intellectual pioneers is Pythagoras (c. 580-c. 500 B.C.E.), who is credited
with discovering the "numerical relationship between the length of the strings used in
musical instruments and the harmonic combinations of sounds." Although Hawking
and Mlodinow claim that it is doubtful that Pythagoras actually "discovered" the law of
strings, they state that the mathematical formula attributed to him is "the first instance
of what we now know as theoretical physics." Archimedes (c. 287-c. 212 B.C.E.) fares
better in the opinion of the authors. Hawking and Mlodinow call him "by far the most

~

Stephen Hawking was the Lucasian Professor of Mathematics at the University of Cambridge and is the author of numerous books, including A Brief History of Time *(1988). Leonard Mlodinow is a physicist at Caltech and the author of* Feynman's Rainbow: A Search for Beauty in Physics and Life *(2003).*

~

eminent physicist of antiquity" and credit him with describing three physical laws—the laws of the lever, buoyancy, and reflection—first known in the ancient world.

Other observers influenced by the Ionians' rational approach also contributed key discoveries. Based on his observations, Anaximander (c. 610-c. 547 B.C.E.) proposed that humans must have evolved from other animals. Empedocles (c. 490-c. 430 B.C.E.) conducted experiments that confirmed the existence of air. Democritus (c. 460-c. 370 B.C.E.) postulated the existence of "uncuttable" fundamental particles he called atoms. Finally, Aristarchus of Samos (c. 310-c. 230 B.C.E.) analyzed the relationship between the sizes of Earth and the Sun and concluded that not only was the Earth much smaller than the Sun but also that the stars shining in the night sky are also suns.

Many of the Greeks' findings were temporarily lost to history and then rediscovered and elaborated upon later. For example, Anaximander's conjecture about the possibility of evolution lives on in Charles Darwin's theory; Democritus's atom is still considered a basic building block of material reality; and Aristarchus's findings presage Nicolaus Copernicus's heliocentric model of the universe.

Unlike many of the Ionians who had little association with theology, later observers held various religious beliefs. René Descartes, an important figure in seventeenth century rationalism, was the first to articulate the laws of nature as they are understood in the twenty-first century. He was also a devout Catholic who held that God set the world in motion and then had nothing more to do with it. Johannes Kepler based his laws of planetary motion on the idea that God had created the world according to a specific plan that could be discovered through reason. Sir Isaac Newton deduced a God-ordained design behind the laws of motion and universal gravitation. The theories of these and other scientists held sway until the advent of the twentieth century, when special and general relativity and quantum mechanics upended classical physics and introduced the scientific community and general public to a bizarre, Alice-in-Wonderland-like cosmos.

Newton's theories reflect human experience of day-to-day life, in which one perceives material objects as having definite locations, a traceable history, and a tangible existence. Quantum mechanics, on the other hand, describes events from an atomic and subatomic point of view and is far less concrete. In 1905 and 1916, respectively, Albert Einstein published his theories of specific and general relativity, which were the first steps in the quantum-mechanics revolution. Demonstrating how relativity describes the interplay among the speed of light, time, and the observers' frame of reference, Hawking and Mlodinow give the example of two people watching a pulse of light zooming from the tail of an airplane to its nose. Both may agree on the speed at which light travels, but because one observer is on the ground and the other is traveling on the jet, their frames of reference are different. Therefore they will not perceive the time it took for the light to travel the length of the aircraft in the same way. In fact, the authors point out, the measurement itself is determined by the person doing the measuring.

If Einstein's theories of relativity loosened the cords of causality that bound classical physics, quantum mechanics severed them, giving way to seemingly contradictory theories. For example, the uncertainty principle conceived by Werner Heisenberg in 1926 states that the position and velocity of a particle cannot be known simultaneously. An observer may be able to observe the position of a particle, but he or she will not be able to determine its spin and vice versa. The wave/particle property of light has also become an accepted axiom of quantum mechanics, where the nature of individual photons can behave as both a wave and a particle. The dual characteristics of electrons and photons also figure into a formulation conceived by Richard P. Feynman, which he called the "sum over histories." In Feynman's view, an individual electron does not just travel in a straight line from point A to point B as Newtonian physics would have it do. Instead, in the topsy-turvy world of quantum mechanics with its weird probabilities, subatomic particles can take any number of probable paths before reaching their target, including ones that go to the "restaurant that serves great curried shrimp, and then circle Jupiter a few times before heading home; even paths that go across the universe and back."

Much of the historical and technical information Hawking and Mlodinow present in their breezy survey has appeared over the years in books such as Carl Sagan's *Cosmos* (1980), Timothy Ferris's *The Whole Shebang: A State-of-the-Universe(s) Report* (1997), Christopher Potter's *You Are Here* (2010), and Hawking's own *A Brief History of Time* (1988). By offering a concise chronology, however, the authors lay the groundwork for their main discussion concerning how the coming together of quantum mechanics and gravity is responsible for the universe spontaneously springing into existence out of nothing. In the opinion of the authors, the best candidate for explaining why the universe—and humans exist—is M- or multiverse theory. Echoing the Copernican idea that the solar system is far from unique, M-theory predicts the probability that an unlimited number of universes have arisen that may support life. Hawking and Mlodinow comment:

> The multiverse idea is not a notion invented to account for the miracle of fine tuning. . . . The strong anthropic principle can be considered effectively equivalent to the weak one, putting the fine-tunings of physical law on the same footing as the environmental factors, for it means that our cosmic habitat—now the entire observable universe—is only one of many, just as our solar system is one of many. That means that in the same way that the environmental coincidences of our solar system were rendered unremarkable by the realization that billions of such systems exist, the fine-tunings in the laws of nature can be explained by the existence of multiple universes.

Because quantum mechanics predicts the probability that universes spontaneously arise as the result of quantum fluctuations, no divine creator is necessary to explain why there is something instead of nothing.

That humans are here by chance and not design is the real point of Hawking and Mlodinow's book. Although they offer an engaging, easy-to-understand explanation of the history of physics and the latest discussions dominating the field, they admit to an underlying agenda in the first chapter when they discuss the role of philosophy—their euphemism for religion—in speculating about the origin of the cosmos:

> Philosophy is dead. Philosophy has not kept up with modern developments in science, particularly physics. Scientists have become the bearers of the torch of discovery in our quest for knowledge. The purpose of this book is to give the answers that are suggested by recent discoveries and theoretical advances.

By the last chapter, they are quite confident that they have provided a satisfactory answer for "life, the universe, and everything" when they assert "M-theory is the unified theory Einstein was hoping to find. . . . If the theory is confirmed by observation, it will be the successful conclusion of a search going back more than 3,000 years."

Nonetheless, there are those who would beg to differ. Because *The Grand Design* was written by two authors, one may assume that they speak with one voice. However, their claim that the universe created itself with no help from a deity signals a shift in Hawking's thinking. When he published *A Brief History of Time* in 1988, he left open the question of whether God created the cosmos. Now he seems to have gone in the opposite direction. His stance has disappointed people of faith, who claim that Hawking's insistence on a universe birthed by natural law does not undermine the argument for the existence of a creator God. Other critics point out that although both science and religion pursue truth, the two disciplines take divergent paths when it comes to delving into the fundamental questions of existence and therefore cannot be fairly compared.

Believers in God are not the only ones dismayed by the authors' endorsement of M-theory. There is disagreement concerning the validity and usefulness of the approach among physicists as well, and Hawking and Mlodinow's claim that M-theory is a complete theory of everything is viewed as overblown by many in the scientific community. Some have noted that the theory is incomplete and must remain so given that science does not have the tools to test or confirm it. Others have criticized Hawking and Mlodinow for bringing God into the discussion at all, saying that it would have been enough to stick to explaining the particulars of the theory and let readers come to their own conclusions.

Hawking and Mlodinow's straightforward text and helpful color illustrations make *The Grand Design* a useful introduction to physics and quantum mechanics for a general audience. However, readers would do well to take the authors' conclusions with a grain of salt and to read perspectives on M-theory from other scientists.

Pegge Bochynski

Review Sources

Booklist 106, no. 22 (August 1, 2010): 5.
Library Journal 135, no. 20 (December 1, 2010): 78.
National Review 62, no. 22 (November 29, 2010): 54-55.
Nature 467, no. 7316 (October 7, 2010): 657-658.
New Scientist 207, no. 2778 (September 18, 2010): 1.
The New York Times, September 8, 2010, p. 1.
Publishers Weekly 257, no. 29 (July 26, 2010): 65.
Science 330, no. 6001 (October 8, 2010): 179-180.
Science News 178, no. 6 (September 11, 2010): 30.
Scientific American 303, no. 4 (November, 2010): 21.

A GREAT UNRECORDED HISTORY
A New Life of E. M. Forster

Author: Wendy Moffat (1955-   )
Publisher: Farrar, Straus and Giroux (New York).
  404 pp. $32.50
Type of work: Literary biography
Time: 1879-1970
Locale: England, Italy, Egypt, India, and the United
  States

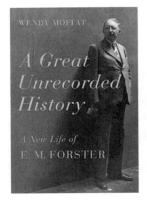

*Concentrating on Forster's sexual orientation and its
effect on his life and literary endeavors, Moffat's lively biography provides fresh insights into this master of the English novel*

Principal personages:
  E. M. FORSTER (1879-1970), eminent English novelist of the early
    twentieth century
  LILY FORSTER, Forster's strong-willed, widowed mother
  MOHAMMED EL ADL, Alexandrine tram conductor who was Forster's
    first great love
  BOB BUCKINGHAM, married London policeman who was Forster's
    greatest love
  MAY BUCKINGHAM, Bob's patient wife and Forster's understanding friend
  FLORENCE BARGER, Forster's chief female confidant throughout his
    adult life

Wendy Moffat's new life of Edward Morgan Forster, better known as E. M.
Forster, entitled *A Great Unrecorded History*, does not pull any punches. The book
opens with a prologue titled "Start with the Fact That He Was Homosexual," words
borrowed from another prominent gay English writer, Christopher Isherwood. Isherwood proffered them in 1970, just after Forster's death, as theoretical advice to future
biographers and critics. All of the earlier books devoted to Forster would have to be
rewritten; because they did not take Forster's homosexuality into account, they were
meaningless. The occasion of Isherwood's pronouncement was his receipt of Forster's long-suppressed unpublished novel devoted to homosexual love, *Maurice*,
which had for decades circulated among the authors' gay friends like a samizdat text.
For more than twenty years, Isherwood had importuned Forster to publish *Maurice*,
and in 1954, Forster finally agreed that the novel could be released posthumously—
despite his view that it was "unpublishable until my death and England's."

Forster was by nature a profoundly shy and private person, so much so that the English critic and biographer Lytton Strachey, nicknamed him "the Taupe," French for
mole. However, Forster was also a shrewd observer of society and its mores, and he

feared exposure for both personal and practical reasons. Once, when a friend pointed
to French author André Gide's publication
of his frankly homosexual memoirs, Forster
quipped, "But Gide hasn't got a mother!"
Forster, who had come of age during Irish
aesthete and playwright Oscar Wilde's sod-
omy trials and subsequent imprisonment, had
good reason to believe that English law and
society would be slow to accept and decrimi-

∽

*Wendy Moffat was born to British
parents, received a Ph.D. in English
from Yale University, and has taught
English at Dickinson College in
Carlisle, Pennsylvania, since 1984. A*
Great Unrecorded History *is her first
book.*

∽

nalize homosexuality. He knew he was not alone, but he also knew that his life and the
lives of thousands of others like him constituted "a great unrecorded history."

Forster seems also to have known from an early age that he was attracted solely to
men; however, in 1891, when he was a mere schoolboy, he had an encounter with a
pedophile that permanently impressed upon him the dangers associated with homosexual activity. After he dutifully told his mother and his schoolmaster about his encounter, Forster was quizzed and harassed to the point that he was obliged to withdraw from boarding school and return home. The lesson Forster took away from the
whole experience was that speaking openly and honestly about the things that affected him most brought danger and persecution. He recorded his understanding in
his diary by writing the word "Nothing" to remind himself that something important—but unspeakable—had happened. As Moffat rightly observes, the pedophile incident was for Forster a kind of parable both of finding himself as a writer and of losing faith in social systems. Around this time, he lost his faith because, he later
claimed, he could find no evidence in the Bible that Christ had a sense of humor. Furthermore, although until the age of forty-five he had a prolific career as a novelist, after the publication of *A Passage to India* (1924), there would be no more novels. Exhausted by the charade of writing about heterosexual love and marriage, Forster spent
the second half of his life writing, rewriting, and suppressing *Maurice*. The final
novel was intended to be revolutionary, in that it portrayed for the first time a homosexual love story that ended happily; however, because it concerned what Wilde's
lover Alfred Lord Douglas called "the love that dare not speak its name," *Maurice*
could not even be published.

The origins of *Maurice* lie in a 1912 trip Forster took to visit with the English socialist Edward Carpenter, who lived openly with his working-class lover George
Merrill. Unbeknownst to Carpenter, Merrill approached Forster, touching him "just
above the buttocks" with a gesture that seems to have affected the writer both physically and spiritually. As Forster wrote fifty years later, "It was as much psychological
as physical. It seemed to go straight through the small of my back into my ideas, without involving my thoughts." Physically, things went no farther. However, the simple
but profound experience of having been intentionally, intimately touched by another
man—together with his observation of Carpenter and Merrill's easy domesticity—
inspired him to conjure up his gay love story with a happy ending.

Forster did not have any genuine sexual experience until the age of thirty-seven, and then it was in another country. Stationed in Alexandria, Egypt, as a Red Cross functionary during World War I, he met and was further inspired by the originality and self-possession of openly gay, Greek expatriate poet, Constantine P. Cavafy. Determined finally to experience sex with someone, Forster first had a furtive encounter with an anonymous soldier, then fell deeply in love with an Egyptian tram conductor, Mohammed el Adl. This was not, for all Forster's willing it to be, the blissful gay love story he had imagined. Mohammed soon married, fathered two children (one of them named after Forster), and then died at the tender age of twenty-three after contracting tuberculosis.

After his sexual initiation in Egypt, Forster experienced many types of homosexual activity with many partners in many locales. Often the sex was anonymous and self-serving. Always, though, Forster craved genuine love and commitment, seeking to combine his gift for friendship with his physical cravings in a lasting, same-sex relationship. Forster did eventually find the kind of comfortable, fulfilling domesticity he craved; once again, he found it in a triangulated relationship. In 1920, he met Bob Buckingham, a London policeman of lower-class origins who became Forster's greatest love. Theirs was a relationship that resembled a marriage, or would have, had it not been for Buckingham's marriage in 1932 to the already heavily pregnant May Hockey. After a stormy period of adjustment, the threesome did, nonetheless, settle into a loving relationship that lasted nearly four decades. While Forster and Bob maintained a sexual relationship, it was May who held Forster's hand as he lay on his deathbed.

Although readers can never again view the great lesson of Forster's great novel *Howards End* (1910)—"Only connect!"—in the same light, the author himself seems to have lived what he so memorably wrote. He lived it nowhere more committedly and completely than in his bifurcated partnership with the Buckinghams.

Forster chose to live a double life. Even as he was crawling through the lower depths of London's gay pubs with his friend, the editor and memoirist J. R. Ackerley, Forster continued to live quietly with his mother until her death in 1945, when he was sixty-six. Although other homosexuals of his time, including Ackerley, managed to live openly as gay men, Forster never could reconcile the two halves of his being. Moffat has done a superior job of combing through her subject's many "sex journals" and reviving and rehabilitating *Maurice* and Forster's other homoerotic writing, but in a sense, she mimics him by giving short shrift to his more conventional, more established work. While it could be said that her goal was to write a "new life" of Forster by revealing the whole man for the first time, the balance in her biography shifts so far toward revisionism that her book somewhat lacks balance. While Moffat's revelations do cast some new light on *A Passage to India*, for example, this novel's significance fades from view, apparently having little connection with Forster's real life. However, few would question the superiority of this work—or of *Howards End* or even *A Room with a View* (1908), a work Forster apparently came to dislike—to *Maurice*. Moffat seems disinclined to consider the reasons for this disparity, other than entertaining the obvious explanation that *Maurice*, like the rest of Forster's sex life, remained repressed. Moffat's book mimics Forster's double life in yet another respect: Nearly one-quarter of this most personal of biographical investigations of the man Moffat refers to by his "intimate name," Morgan, is given over to scholarly apparatuses such as notes and acknowledgments.

Quibbles aside, *A Great Unrecorded History* is a good, entertaining, and often illuminating read. Moffat, who was among the first to have access to some of her subject's diaries, has been justly hailed for covering new territory. She has forever changed readers' perceptions of this tweedy, retiring Edwardian, whom readers know to have been both generously humanitarian and sexually rapacious. Had Forster lived in a different time, perhaps the schism between his public and his private selves would not have been as profound. Moffat seems to argue that a modern Forster would be remembered for the eroticism of *Maurice*, rather than for the nuances of *A Passage to India*. This is thoroughly debatable. It could well be argued that Forster's most pronounced characteristic, his reticence, was the quality that both kept him closeted and kept him writing. Furthermore, the more closeted he was, the more he sublimated his desires, channeling them into art. It is notable that at the outset of his career, Forster published four accomplished novels in five years: *Where Angels Fear to Tread* (1905), *The Longest Journey* (1907), *A Room with a View*, and *Howards End*. Only one novel, *A Passage to India*, appeared after he began to express his sexuality physically, and that book took more than a decade to write. To be sure, Forster continued to be a prolific writer throughout his life, but what he produced, with the notable exception of *Maurice* and some minor homoerotic fiction, was mostly nonfiction. Also, while *Maurice* may serve to make Forster a pioneer of gay writing, it is hard to imagine this work ever marking him as a literary immortal. Given his determinedly dual nature, Forster probably wished to be both.

Lisa Paddock

Review Sources

Booklist 106, no. 13 (March 1, 2010): 40.
Gay & Lesbian Review 17, no. 6 (November/December, 2010): 36-37.
Kirkus Reviews 78, no. 4 (February 15, 2010): 125-126.
Library Journal 135, no. 4 (March 1, 2010): 84.
The New Republic 241, no. 11 (July 8, 2010): 29-34.
The New York Review of Books 57, no. 15 (October 14, 2010): 18-22.
The New York Times, May 18, 2010, p. 7.
The New York Times Book Review, July 25, 2010, p. 22.
The New Yorker 86, no. 17 (June 14, 2010): 137.
Time 175, no. 22 (June 7, 2010): 60-61.

HARVESTING FOG

Author: Luci Shaw (1928-   )
Publisher: Pinyon (Montrose, Colorado). 89 pp. $15.00
Type of work: Poetry

Shaw's latest collection of poetry combines natural beauty and religion in an appealing mixture of good humor, speaking images, and praise

"Spiritual poetry," "transcendent poetry," "Christian poetry"—these terms lead to controversy, especially the last. Some who are identified as Christian poets create generally spiritual work, not dogmatic in any way—poems often containing lucent nature images that may suggest the world is more than it seems. On the other edge are poems that turn belief systems into rhyme, presenting dogma as traditional verse. The former have an appeal far beyond Christian readers but may not fulfill the hopes of those who turn to poetry as an aid to faith. The latter are "preaching to the choir"; the poems may come across as empty doggerel for those who are not on the same spiritual channel. Even some who are may find them uninspired, like Sunday sermons cribbed from preachers' manuals.

Luci Shaw is a spiritual writer whose work, including *Harvesting Fog*, avoids these extremes. Its surface is rich enough to please even those who have different beliefs or none at all. Her work is undeniably and unashamedly Christian, but it demonstrates rather than preaches. It uses the rich and varied textures of the world not so much to preach as to explore Christianity. Always thoughtful, never intrusive, the poems invite a sense of participation and peace. They provide glimpses of far and near places that serve as stimuli for meditations that are intellectually teasing and spiritually satisfying.

Shaw has been a poet, retreat facilitator, and lecturer for many years. She has held workshops on poetry writing, on the Christian imagination, and on using the journal as an aid to creative writing. She has eleven books of poetry and has published in other genres as well; also, she has collaborated with Madeleine L'Engle and others. Her style as a poet is usually a musical free verse, although she sometimes uses rhyme and meter. Many of her poems have been set to music by composers in the United States and internationally.

Her work is widely known among Catholic and Protestant circles. She is an Episcopalian; therefore, her poetry has the "sacramental vision" highly valued by Catholic readers and writers, but it also explores Protestant themes and concerns. Some poems are on Biblical themes; others use form in some way to underscore Christian theme, such as "Crossways," a cross-shaped poem reminiscent of the work of George Herbert.

Harvesting Fog is rich in natural imagery, approaching the spiritual through the physical in the manner of Mary Oliver. Shaw explains the title in an introduction that tells a lot about her creative writing process. In Lima, Peru, where there is very little rain but a lot of heavy fog, the inhabitants hang rags and nets on clotheslines until they are saturated and then wring them out to use the water. Shaw compares this practice to writing poems: "Something's in the air, a word, an impres-

∼

Cofounder and later president of Harold Shaw Publishers, Luci Shaw has also been a writer-in-residence at Regent College, Vancouver, Canada. In addition to her many poetry collections, Shaw has published essays, autobiography, study guides, children's books, and mixed-media work.

∼

sion, a rhythmic phrase, a sound, a small connection. You grab it and then you catch more drops and pool them all together, and wring some fresh meaning out of them, and as if by miracle this mystery, this moisture becomes a new entity that satisfies a thirsty imagination. Sometimes, in the process, the words themselves tell you where they want to go." Wallace Stevens said "Thought tends to collect in pools"; these poems are collections of thoughts, ideas, and images, sometimes seemingly wrung from the air.

The book is divided into two sections, "Harvest" and "Fog." The poems in "Harvest" are deeply rooted in nature and provide vivid snapshots of places the poet has visited, but the images are seen through the eyes of a committed Christian who views the world as the handiwork of God. Often the natural details take on transcendence, but in doing so, they do not lose their nature; they remain both themselves and representatives of the divine. The divine nature of things is not hidden, as it tends to be in the work of many contemporary religious poets, but is patent, as it was in the works of the metaphysical poets.

Poems in the first half are of many scenes and events but hold a meditative, quiet wisdom. The speaker is sometimes in the forefront, other times almost hidden. Shaw is a precise observer for whom every detail is lovingly described, because the vision of the writer is a persistent faith that sees wholeness rather than fragmentation and locates each particular within its framework. Even those touched with sadness place the sense of loss or grief within the larger context of faith. "The Voice in the Pines" begins, "The pine-tops start to stir to sway their pencil trunks/ and waken the soft sound of breath, silk on sadness." The speaker goes on to ask, "How does air make music? Does it seek/ a solid thing to rub against and send a sigh that is a song?" The air/music then requests the poet take it in, suggesting that this music in spending itself causes a transformation in the poet that lifts the spirit.

"The Generosity of Pines" is typical of Shaw's melding of nature and divinity. It suggests that the pine logs retain a kind of life: "Even after/ months stacked in the pile in the yard, open-hearted/ host to spiders and small rodents." The burning of the logs is "piney essence . . . gathering itself." The burning is telling those who gather around it that it is as if "the long years/ of achieving dense and muscular and tall/ could be summed up in these joyous needles/ and cones of flame, and the vitality of resin spit and split." The pine's imagined joy in being consumed, fulfilling its destiny, suggests the purpose Shaw finds in all nature and the happiness even inanimate objects seem to feel in fulfilling the purpose not their own. In this natural world, everything is intended, and joy lies in recognizing and celebrating this intention. Like Stevens, a master "as if" poet, Shaw does not want to make blunt statements. Her poems suggest and explore the dimension of divinity in the natural world. They start with concrete objective detail, which then becomes touched with illumination.

The poems in the second part, "Fog," include memories of a rich family life often interwoven with natural images. These poems seem more varied in form and content than those in "Harvest." Nature to Shaw is sentient, echoing human life as well as experiencing its own. "Leaf, Fallen" compares the leaf to the speaker's dying mother, but manages to avoid the obvious in the comparison. Of the leaf, she comments, "How ineluctably sap left the veins,/ the spine curled." She segues into her experience of her mother's last years: "I hear again my mother's complaint/ on each of her fifteen years' visits from me,/ I've lost a lot of ground this week." The mother had a different way of seeing: "She wore the russet color well but never sang." The child grew away from the woman for whom "duty rallied" rather than love. Finally the relationship is severed: "In the cold's wither she finally let go/ let go of me. Clipped by a biting wind from a naked stem/ she fell to that ground she thought she'd lost." Subtle differences between mother and child, and their potential for conflict, are all developed through the images.

Not all the poems are of nature; some are related to science, art, the media, or technology. "New Yorker, Dec. 7, 2009" plays with the "double spread" pairings of photographs of Mahmoud Ahmadinejad and Barack Obama, Muammar al-Qaddafi and Benjamin Netanyahu, and others in the "line-up of leaders putting/ their best faces forward." The speaker imagines the dialogue going on between pages when the magazine is closed and the leaders are locked together. It is a playful poem, teasing the reader with its imaginary, intimate politics. Another poem of sheer enjoyment is "Odd Angel," in which the speaker looks at illustrations in the De Lisle Psalter, finding the humor in the nonstandard image of "this aberrant angel" who does not look as though he is promoting anything holy, but has a sneer and a glare: "One more vigilante for original sin."

The poems in *Harvesting Fog* are Christian poems and they inhabit a Christian world, where churches and cathedrals are at home and where nature is often another kind of church. However, they have a freshness to them that renews; when they use nature as metaphor, they do so in original ways. Shaw's animate natural world commands attention—whether she is providing crows as world leaders in summit or remembering "how every spreading/ fingerling of ocean inscribes a beach with its/ unique story." The ways in which the observer encounters nature are sacramental; each contact and scene reveals something of the immanent presence and divine plan. The poems seem filled with grace. B. H. Fairchild commented on her work, "For a poet of profound religious sensibility such as Luci Shaw, whose poems so brilliantly and movingly locate authentic Being in the forms and processes of nature, the lyric impulse often approaches the incarnational."

The very last poem of the collection is a tour de force. "Attendez!" is subtitled "The Buildings of Languedoc." Each element of the scene is named and then followed by lists of evocative descriptive verbs—the castle walls, for example:

> crenellated, cloven,
> carved, chiseled, sloping, slipping, blackened, blank,
> grooved

She proceeds from the castles, to the churches, to the martyrs:

> —Armand, Luce, Audalde, Alacandre—
> burned, decapitated, tortured, flesh flayed raw as
> the blood-red marbles of Caunes Minervois. Lives built
> spent, spilled, splendid. Here words fail. All that comes
> is what they were singing—Glory! Glory! Glory!

Her piles of adjectives build up a fervent emotion as they give a sense of continuity, history, the holiness of place, and the source of that holiness. The poem bursts forth in a climax of praise, allowing that all the nightmarish history of Languedoc still points to the glory of God.

Shaw sees writing as a gift, and in her introduction, she gives a good sense of how she writes and what the inception of a new poem is for her. "It's as if some transcendent transaction lies in wait for me to recognize it, pluck it out of this other world, and begin to record it. It comes with a sense of availability, of given-ness, and a generosity that enlarges my understanding of the cosmos." "Generosity" is a good word to describe the sense of these poems. They imply that God is generous, nature is generous, and the poet's vision is generous, too.

Janet McCann

Review Sources

Christianity Today 54, no. 6 (June, 2010): 54.
Englewood Review 3, no. 23 (June 18, 2010).

HE CRASHED ME SO I CRASHED HIM BACK
The True Story of the Year the King, Jaws, Earnhardt, and the Rest of NASCAR's Feudin', Fightin' Good Ol' Boys Put Stock Car Racing on the Map

Author: Mark Bechtel (1971-   )
Publisher: Little, Brown (Boston). Illustrated. 308 pp. $25.99
Type of work: Current affairs, history
Time: Primarily 1979
Locale: United States

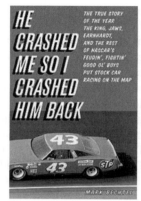

An intimate look at the colorful characters who popularized stock-car racing, the fastest-growing sport in the United States, during the tumultuous year of 1979, when the country embraced Southern culture despite the waning popularity of Georgia-born President Jimmy Carter

Principal personages:
> RICHARD PETTY (1937-   ), "The King" of stock-car racing
> DALE EARNHARDT (1951-2001), the heir apparent to "The King"
> JUNIOR JOHNSON, a legendary racer turned owner
> "BIG" BILL FRANCE, the founder of the National Association for Stock Car Auto Racing (NASCAR)
> BOBBY ALLISON (1937-   ) and DONNIE ALLISON, the leaders of the "Alabama gang"
> DARRELL "JAWS" WALTRIP and CALE YARBOROUGH (1939-   ), challengers to "The King"

On Sunday February 19, 1979, the only readily identifiable stock-car-racing driver in the United States was forty-two-year-old Richard Petty, who appeared in commercials on behalf of STP automotive maintenance products. However, as Mark Bechtel points out in *He Crashed Me So I Crashed Him Back*, Petty had gone a total of forty-five races—more than one year—without getting to "victory circle," and his lucrative corporate sponsorship was in peril.

On that Sunday, Daytona Beach, Florida, was one of the few locales east of the Mississippi River where snow was not falling. Millions of households were searching for something to watch on television. It so happened that the Columbia Broadcasting System (CBS), taking a corporate gamble, was carrying the Daytona 500 live for its entirety, using nine cameras, less than one-fourth of the number employed at major races in the twenty-first century. It was unprecedented; as Bechtel quipped, stock-car racing highlights only appeared on the *Wide World of Sports* on the American Broadcasting Company (ABC) somewhere between barrel racing and Mexican cliff diving.

The CBS network's only major competition was college basketball on the National Broadcasting Company (NBC) since ABC affiliates were airing local programming. ESPN, so vital to NASCAR's future, did not go on the air for another seven months. Almost nobody anticipated that the Daytona 500 and the brawl afterward would catapult NASCAR from a regional phenomenon into big-money spectacle.

~

A senior editor for Sports Illustrated *who has covered NASCAR for that magazine, Mark Bechtel wrote the narration for* NASCAR 3-D: The IMAX Experience *(2004).*

~

Organized auto racing in Daytona dates to the 1903 Winter Speed Carnival, which took place near the lavish Ormand Hotel. The beach surface was ideal: The sand, emanating from coquina clamshells, was packed hard as asphalt. The first fatality occurred two years later. Swerving to avoid a bicyclist, New Yorker Frank Croker flipped over. Eclipsed by the Indianapolis Motor Speedway, which opened in 1911, Daytona Beach made headlines as the site of English playboy Malcolm Campbell's 1935 attempt to surpass 300 miles per hour (mph). He only reached 276 mph but had later success at Utah's Bonneville Salt Flats.

Inspired by Campbell, "Big" Bill France started promoting competitive races on a makeshift oval, utilizing the shoreline and an adjacent highway. In 1947, France founded the National Association for Stock Car Auto Racing (NASCAR). Because some people thought the name sounded too much like "Nash car," the now-famous moniker originally was passed over for NSCRA (National Stock Car Racing Association). Then someone discovered that an organization with that acronym already existed in Georgia. An autocrat whom one could count on to keep his word, France curtailed gate-receipt skimming, improved payouts, and instituted safety standards. Learning that drivers were contemplating joining the Teamsters, he vowed to shoot any union driver daring to compete in a NASCAR event.

Thanks to France, the Daytona International Speedway opened in 1959. Petty won the first 500 before forty-one thousand fans in a photo finish with Johnny Beauchamp. Legendary racing promoter Humpy Wheeler, who inherited the nickname from his Camel-cigarette-smoking dad, said of France, "He was tough, with a one-track mind when it counted." NASCAR's pioneers allegedly honed their skills outrunning revenue agents on treacherous mountain roads.

Contributing to the Southern "good ol' boy" stereotype was a mid-1960's *Esquire* article by Virginia-born "New Journalist" Tom Wolfe entitled "The Last American Hero Is Junior Johnson. Yes!" Johnson served prison time for moonshining before finding competitive racing more lucrative; he invented the 180-degree "bootleg turn" as well as the "slingshot" gambit of "drafting" behind faster cars and then "slipstreaming" to the finish line. Johnson's contemporaries included Tim Flock, "Little Joe" Weatherly, and Curtis Turner. Searching for new worlds to conquer, Johnson retired from competitive driving in 1967 at the age of thirty-five, after winning nearly twice as often as his nearest rival. Assembling a team of experts, Johnson mentored

LeeRoy Yarbrough, Bobby Allison, and Cale Yarborough, who instigated the altercation that put NASCAR on the map.

The 1979 Daytona 500 climaxed a week that included qualifying runs, the ARCA 200, won by Petty's son, Kyle; the Busch Clash, a fifty-mile sprint featuring nine pole sitters from the previous year, including winner Buddy Baker; and the Sportsman 400, marred by a fiery crash that left Don Williams in a near-vegetative state. When skies cleared miraculously at noon in response, legend has it, to France's entreaties, actor Ben Gazzara assumed his place as grand marshall, and the show began. On turn two of the final lap frontrunner Donnie Allison went low to cut off Yarborough, who did not back down. Their cars locked together, hit the outside wall, and slid to a halt in the infield. Both frontrunners were finished, although some old hands thought Donnie should have tried harder to restart his engine.

Suddenly Petty had a slight lead going into the final stretch. Darrell Waltrip tried the slingshot maneuver, but Petty outsmarted him, using a strategy that his son, Kyle, had employed a few days earlier. What made the finish truly memorable, however, was a postrace fight between Yarborough and Donnie Allison. Following an exchange of expletives, Yarborough struck Allison in the nose with his helmet and then attempted a karate kick. Allison grabbed the offending leg, and the protagonists rolled around on the ground. "The Thrilla in Manila it wasn't," Bechtel quipped in a reference to the championship boxing bout between heavyweights Muhammad Ali and Joe Frazier. Nevertheless, the media ate it up.

Most newspapers ran photographs of the combatants rather than the winner, Petty. Two weeks later during the Carolina 500, Yarborough's car slammed into Allison's; both careened off the fence, causing six others to crash, including Petty and Waltrip. Fearing suspension, both Yarborough and Allison claimed that the crash was inadvertent. A week later, a record press contingent descended upon Richmond Fairgrounds Raceway, eager for "round three." Alas, it turned out to be, in Petty's words, the cleanest race he ever saw.

The leading NASCAR drivers returned to Daytona on July 4, for the Firecracker 400. The heat was so oppressive that winner Neil Bonnett collapsed afterward. The feet of second-place finisher Benny Parsons were so blistered that, eyeing a crewman with an artificial leg, he said, "That's just what I need now." Dale Earnhardt felt so woozy during the last laps, he later admitted, that "my brain wouldn't work." Observing Petty seemingly unscathed, the rookie exclaimed, "Boy, you're the toughest old man in the world." Waltrip eschewed postrace interviews and submerged himself in a tub of ice. Having gained 92 points in the season standings on the strength of a fourth-place finish, he led nearest rivals Bobby Allison by 133 points and Petty by 198. A triumph in the Talladega 500 a month later stretched Waltrip's lead to more than 200 points.

Then Waltrip's troubles began, some of which were self-inflicted. Harboring resentment against Petty personally and NASCAR officialdom in general, Waltrip vowed to be the cause of Petty retiring. After Talladega he suggested that his aging rival might need a prescription windshield. During the Southern 500, despite protestations from his pit-crew boss, Waltrip tried to embarrass Petty by lapping him twice and for his trouble hit a wall, costing him dearly. Then at North Wilkesboro, North Carolina, he bumped Bobby Allison and got bumped back, resulting in a disastrous spin out. Black-flagged during the American 500 for leaking oil, which cost him eight laps, Waltrip was persuaded that enemies were conspiring against him.

Entering the season finale, Waltrip's lead over Petty had shrunk to a mere two points. Whoever finished higher in the *Los Angeles Times* 500 would win the Winston Cup. Prior to the November 18, "shootout" in Ontario, California, Petty, an expert at mind games, claimed that all the pressure was on his rival. On the defensive, Waltrip complained that Petty had been getting away with "bumping and banging and spinning out, doing everything." On lap nine Waltrip deliberately went into a spin to avoid the smoke and fire caused by a crash. The ploy averted disaster but flattened his tires. CBS announcer David Hobbs, an Englishman, intoned: "They'll change all four tires on this. Possibly change the driver's underwear."

Later a miscalculation caused Waltrip to lose a lap on a pit stop, dropping him to eighth place. Petty finished fifth and thereby won the Winston Cup by 11 points. Rookie of the year Earnhardt finished ninth. For nine months he had inspired countless fans with his fearless style and working-class persona. The following year he won his first of seven Winston Cups, ultimately equaling Petty. Earnhardt died of a broken neck in 2001, just ten months after Petty's grandson, Adam, succumbed on the track.

As the twenty-first century began, NASCAR signed a television deal with Fox and NBC, netting $2.47 billion over six years, a fourfold increase over the previous contract. NASCAR was big business. Reared in Alabama, Bechtel admits that the stories he collected were often embellishments and exaggerations. After postrace melees, one could find as many explanations as participants. Leaning heavily on interviews and racing magazines, the author demonstrates familiarity with the secondary literature in the field and gained insights from James Webb's *Born Fighting: How the Scots-Irish Shaped America* (2005) and Bruce J. Schulman's *The Seventies: The Great Shift in American Culture, Society, and Politics* (2002). *Publishers Weekly* concluded that, "What could have been a painful juggling act becomes an illuminating, informative, and entertaining read, as the engaging and droll Bechtel is in complete control from start to finish." Steady at the wheel despite the glib tone, Bechtel treats the antiestablishment superstars of arguably the most dangerous sport in the United States with respect. A consummate journalist and oral historian, Bechtel seamlessly weaves into his narrative the Islamic revolution in Iran and the long gas lines at the pump, as well as such indicators of "redneck chic" as the hoopla surrounding daredevil Evel Knievel; the hokey, moneymaking *Smokey and the Bandit* series; the mainstream breakthrough of Southern rock music; and the television hits *The Dukes of Hazzard*, in which Yarborough appeared in an episode narrated by outlaw country singer Waylon Jennings, and *Flo*, about a Houston waitress who wisecracked, "Kiss my grits."

The country seemed enamored by Southern folk ways. In 1978, President Jimmy

Carter invited NASCAR's leading lights to the White House, but a year later, with the economy moribund and Americans held hostage abroad, he lost the support of most "NASCAR dads," who found Republican Ronald Reagan's sunny optimism more appealing. The former actor, Bechtel concluded, "celebrated the rugged, God-fearing patriotic individual; NASCAR was offering up forty of them on display every weekend." With jingoism in vogue, Wheeler's lavish prerace productions at the Charlotte Motor Speedway knew no boundaries. Bechtel writes of one instance of tasteless excess: In 1984, Wheeler staged a reenactment of Operation Urgent Fury, the 1983 U.S. invasion of Grenada. The show lasted fifteen minutes and featured thatched huts being strafed by planes and palm trees splintered by simulated gunfire. On July 4, 1984, President Reagan, seeking reelection, flew to Daytona aboard Air Force One and was on hand when Petty crossed the finish line to win his two hundredth and, as it turned out, final race.

James B. Lane

Review Sources

Booklist 106, no. 12 (February 15, 2010): 19.
Library Journal 135, no. 3 (February 15, 2010): 100.
Publishers Weekly 257, no. 1 (January 4, 2010): 41.

HELLHOUND ON HIS TRAIL
The Stalking of Martin Luther King, Jr., and the International Hunt for His Assassin

Author: Hampton Sides (1962-   )
Publisher: Doubleday (New York). 459 pp. $28.95
Type of work: History
Time: 1967-1968
Locale: Memphis, Tennessee

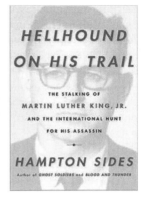

A dramatic account of the events leading up to the assassination of King on April 4, 1968, and of the FBI's efforts to identify and capture his murderer

> *Principal characters:*
> JAMES EARL RAY (1928-1998), the man convicted of the assassination of Martin Luther King, Jr.
> MARTIN LUTHER KING, JR. (1929-1968), the leader of the Civil Rights movement and the recipient of the 1964 Nobel Peace Prize
> RALPH DAVID ABERNATHY (1926-1990), King's close, personal friend and the handpicked successor to head the Southern Christian Leadership Conference
> JESSE JACKSON (1941-   ), a young, ambitious civil rights activist from Chicago who coveted a more prominent role in the movement
> CORETTA SCOTT KING (1927-2006), the wife of King; his assassination will propel her into the role as spokesperson for the civil rights movement
> J. EDGAR HOOVER (1895-1972), the director of the Federal Bureau of Investigation, who considered King a threat to law and order and pursued a personal vendetta against him
> RAMSEY CLARK (1927-   ), the attorney general of the United States, who sympathized with King's efforts on behalf of social justice
> LYNDON B. JOHNSON (1908-1973), the thirty-sixth president of the United States
> ROBERT F. KENNEDY (1925-1968), U.S. senator from New York and candidate for the Democratic presidential nomination
> GEORGE WALLACE (1919-1998), the governor of Alabama and the American Independent Party candidate for the presidency of the United States in 1968

In *Hellhound on His Trail*, Hampton Sides crafts a thrilling and suspenseful historical account of the assassination of Martin Luther King, Jr., and the pursuit of his killer. A native of Memphis, Tennessee, the city where King was killed, Sides confronts the event that forever defined the history of his city.

∼

Hampton Sides is the author of two previous works of history, Ghost Soldiers: The Epic Account of World War II's Greatest Rescue Mission *(2001) and* Blood and Empire: The Epic Story of Kit Carson and the Conquest of the American West *(2006).*

∼

Sides takes his title from a song by blues legend Robert Johnson, who came from the Mississippi Delta country, south of Memphis. As legend has it, Johnson met the devil one night at a country crossroads and sold his soul in exchange for musical immortality. Johnson died young under mysterious circumstances, perhaps the victim of poisoning, perhaps in payment of his debt. Just as Johnson's restless spirit is said to haunt that Mississippi crossroads, James Earl Ray haunts the pages of Sides's history like a proverbial ghost.

The book opens with the escape of prisoner 416-J from the Missouri State Penitentiary in Jefferson City. One of the central devices used by Sides to characterize King's assassin is his refusal to identify the man by name. Instead, the author refers to the killer by a succession of aliases and false identities used by Ray. The name James Earl Ray does not even appear in the book until page 321, when he is finally identified by agents of the Federal Bureau of Investigation (FBI). Ray drifts through the pages of the book like a wraith, assuming and discarding names like a snake sheds its skin.

After escaping prison in Missouri, Ray appears on the beaches of Mexico, with a new name, a white Mustang with Alabama tags, and a vague scheme of becoming a director of pornographic films. His trunk is filled with camera equipment and "girlie" magazines, which he uses to research his new profession. From Puerto Vallarta, Ray drifts to Los Angeles, where he lives in a succession of flophouse hotels and takes classes at a bartending school. His stories about himself vary depending upon his audience. He visits a psychologist in order to learn hypnotism, and he has plastic surgery on his nose. Otherwise, he lives alone in furnished rooms, eats cheap food from a hot plate, and watches television by himself. The only two constants from this period of his life are his apparent racism and his involvement in George Wallace's campaign for president.

In the pages of Sides's history, King is a man haunted by ghosts of his own. By the beginning of 1968, the Civil Rights movement that has propelled King to international prominence is at a difficult crossroads. After the triumphant passage of the Civil Rights Act and the Voting Rights Act, other black leaders and new agendas threaten the moral supremacy of King's mission. Black nationalists such as Stokely Carmichael are beginning to advocate direct confrontation with the majority white society in their impatience for more rapid change. For King, the urban riots of the summer of 1967 raise the specter of violence, which threatens the nonviolent character of his crusade for justice as well as his leadership of the Civil Rights movement. There is a crisis looming even within his own organization, the Southern Christian Leadership Conference, as younger leaders such as Jesse Jackson begin to emerge and push their own agendas.

King has alienated himself from former allies such as President Lyndon B. Johnson by sharply criticizing the U.S. military adventure in Southeast Asia. As 1968 begins, King is preparing to commit the movement to a new effort, the Poor People's Campaign, which will bring together representatives of all races in a march on Washington, D.C., to demand government action against the plague of poverty in the United States, an issue that King sees as transcending racial boundaries and threatening the very survival of the nation. In the meantime, King is battling personal demons as well. His marriage is crumbling as a result of his serial adultery with a succession of mistresses. He is on the verge of total physical, emotional, and spiritual exhaustion and is beginning to speak more frequently of his own death, an outcome that even he sees as increasingly probable.

These are the lives of the two men who collide in Memphis on the evening of April 4, 1968. King has come to Memphis to march with the city's striking garbage workers. Even as King links arms with black workers carrying signs that read, "I AM a man," other groups are threatening to co-opt the strike for their own purposes. King is aware of the potential for violence that lies just beneath the surface. However, he sees the sanitation workers' strike as emblematic of his own greater struggle against poverty and remains committed to the protest despite the urgings of other leaders in the movement.

Into this almost apocalyptic setting comes Ray, who has stalked King across the country, first to his home base in Atlanta and then to Memphis. As the story builds to its inevitable climax on the balcony of the Lorraine Motel, Sides drives the narrative forward with the relentless pace of a thriller.

The actual shooting of King takes place at the halfway point of the book. As King lies dying in the arms of Ralph David Abernathy and as Ray begins to make his escape, the tone of Sides's book changes from that of a suspense thriller to that of a police procedural. The details of the crime itself and the immediate aftermath of the shooting are rendered minute by minute, in stark journalistic detail. Sides's aim here is to shift the reader's attention from the twin stories of Ray and King to the other major participants in the book, the FBI and the literally thousands of agents who are engaged in the largest single investigation in the agency's history and arguably one of the greatest success stories in modern criminal annals.

In a rare spirit of ideological bipartisanship, the liberal attorney general of the United States, Ramsey Clark, joins forces with the reactionary J. Edgar Hoover at the FBI to spearhead an international manhunt for King's killer. While Clark engineers the federal government's takeover of the criminal investigation from the local Memphis police department, Hoover insists on deploying the full resources of the agency he has single-handedly built into a modern, scientific national police force. After years of hounding King with wiretaps and surveillance, Hoover is intent on avoiding the appearance of the FBI's complicity in King's murder by utilizing all the means at its disposal to solve a crime that threatens to plunge the nation into new depths of civil unrest.

As Hoover's investigators perform countless interviews and conduct ballistic and fingerprint analyses, Ray continues to shift identities in an attempt to escape. Sides follows Ray's steps from Memphis to Atlanta, Toronto, Montreal, and, finally, London. Alongside the progress of the FBI's investigation and Ray's flight, he also recounts the familiar stories of King's mule-drawn cortege, Johnson's decision not to seek the Democratic nomination for the presidency, the failure of the Poor People's Campaign to re-create the glories of the 1963 March on Washington, and the assassination of Robert F. Kennedy. Sides's narrative captures dramatically the sequence of events that began on the balcony of the Lorraine Motel in Memphis and that will end later that summer in the streets of Chicago, as the hope and idealism with which the decade of the 1960's began degenerates into madness and nightmare.

Although Sides is clearly aware of the conspiracy theories that have sprung up around the King assassination and led to the hearings of the House Select Committee on Assassinations during the 1970's, his history steers clear of those controversies while presenting succinctly the evidence that has given them credence. Sides acknowledges two incontrovertible facts that have produced much of the continuing speculation: the lack of a clear motive on the part of Ray and his lack of a visible means of financial support in the months leading up to and following King's death. Although Ray is clearly a rabid racist, he lacks a clear political motivation for the crime. Ray was at least tangentially involved in Governor Wallace's campaign for president and seemed to entertain some fantasy of escaping to central Africa and finding employment with a mercenary army. However, he left behind nothing that points to a clear political vendetta against King or the Civil Rights movement. Also, throughout his stalking of King and his subsequent flight from the United States, Ray seems to have a ready supply of cash on hand that only begins to run out once he reaches London. Sides refuses to engage in any conjectures about the source of Ray's money. He only briefly glosses over Ray's story of the mysterious "Raoul," who supposedly was the true perpetrator of the King assassination.

Sides's book ends with a brief account of Ray's escape from Tennessee's Brushy Mountain State Prison in 1977, which further fueled the fires of the conspiracy theorists because it occurred just as the U.S. House of Representatives was beginning to conduct interviews for its own investigation into the assassination of King. The panicked search for the fugitive quickly ends in Ray's recapture but also supports the overall impression of Ray that emerges from this narrative. As difficult as it is for one to believe, even after the passage of decades, Ray was a petty criminal and thug who succeeded in killing an American icon. In the end, the author shows, the greatness of individuals such as King is susceptible to the whims of lesser human beings.

Tony Rafalowski

Review Sources

American Scholar 79, no. 3 (Summer, 2010): 108-110.
Booklist 106, no. 15 (April 1, 2010): 8.

Kirkus Reviews 78, no. 4 (February 15, 2010): 131.
Library Journal 135, no. 4 (March 1, 2010): 92.
The New York Times, April 22, 2010, p. 1.
The New York Times Book Review, May 16, 2010, p. 27.
Newsweek 155, no. 19 (May 10, 2010): 52.
Publishers Weekly 257, no. 6 (February 8, 2010): 37.

HERE

Author: Wisława Szymborska (1923-   )
Translated from the Polish by Clare Cavanagh and
  Stanisław Barańczak
Publisher: Houghton Mifflin Harcourt (Boston). 85 pp.
  $22.00
Type of work: Poetry

A collection of poems by the 1996 Nobel laureate, gath-
ering poems from two volumes published in Poland

Although fifteen years have passed since Wisława
Szymborska went from national renown to international
attention with the award of the Nobel Prize in Literature,
her poems remain so singular in style and attitude that her
work remains as immediately engaging as it did when she was introduced to a much
wider audience than existed for her in Poland. Part of this is the way her work seems
to have a continuing relevance for the modern world, even as it is grounded in the human history of an older civilization, and for the Anglo-American reader, an important
part is the superb translations that Clare Cavanagh and Stanisław Barańczak have
provided. As an example of what can be done with the extremely difficult task of conveying all of the elements of a poem from one language (and its cultural matrix) to another, Cavanagh and Barańczak have given Szymborska a "voice" in English that is
recognizable as her own, while the translator's names on the cover—not that common
a practice—are an appropriate testament to what should also rightly be recognized as
a kind of collaboration. Nonetheless, the poems are Szymborska's in ways that are
unmistakable and, for that matter, inimitable. Szymborska's life in Poland through
the years leading to World War II, when she was in her teens; followed by the devastation of the nation, as Adolf Hitler's and Joseph Stalin's forces ravaged the country;
and then on the long, painful path through the Cold War until a democratic form of
government gradually emerged gave her a full view of humanity at its worst.

Whether from an inextinguishable impulse toward expression, or a compelling desire to speak from and to history, Szymborska managed to publish a book of poems in
1948 when she was in her mid-twenties. The Soviet-directed government censors
suppressed the book as "too obscure for the masses," a typically preposterous distortion since one of the most captivating qualities of Szymborska's work is its lyric mo-
dalities. Adam Gopnik, in an article in *The New Yorker* about Nobel Prize winners in
literature, referred to her as a "reticent lyricist" and it is this reticence—an aspect of
understatement, comportment, and control of tone—that is one of the key compo-
nents of her voice. It is also one of the reasons that Benjamin Paloff cites her as an exception as he begins an essay "Polish poets publish too much."

Here includes the entire contents of that volume published in Poland in 2009, and "some of the poems in *Duwkropek*" (2005), which is translated as "Colon." There is no poem with that title in the volume, but it is the last word in the collection, and a central principle of structure for Szymborska is the syntax of expansion that a colon can create, and beyond that, the impulse toward continuance that its placement implies.

Wisława Szymborska's poetry, acclaimed in Europe through the last decades of the twentieth century, reached an Anglo-American audience in 1996 when she was awarded the Nobel Prize in Literature.

Barańczak uses this formulation as a means of explaining Szymborska's strategy of composition, noting "the confrontation between directly stated or implied opinions on an issue and the question that raises doubt about its validity," which is echoed by Szymborska's comment that "In every possible answer there should be another question." This is the perspective of someone who has lived in a country where the authorities claimed to have all the answers to the extent that the population was not supposed to have any questions at all. For Szymborska, the interrogative form is fundamental, even in terms of the essence of poetry itself. In "An Idea," Szymborska utilizes the dash for pause and follow-up to arrange a dialogue between the poet and an embryonic "poem" awaiting gestation. This kind of conversation is one of the defining forms of the poems in *Here*, and it stands as a variant to the shape posited by the title of her previous collection *Monolog psa zaplątanego w dzieje* (2002; *Monologue of a Dog: New Poems*, 2006). The introduction of the second voice reinforces the instinct to ask "another question" somewhat in the manner of Robert Frost's comment that "There is always something more to everything."

Szymborska begins "An Idea" with an ambiguous image of inspiration that launches an inquiry with the potential for invention. "An idea came to me/ for a rhyme? a poem?" is her way of entering into the process of production. Her interest engaged, she establishes an ethos of creative interaction: "Well, fine—I say—stay awhile, we'll talk./ Tell me a little more about yourself./ So it whispered a few words in my ear./Ah, so that's the story—I say—intriguing." The use of the word "it" retains the uncertainty that the poet is probing, and the confidentiality of the address suggests that the reader is being allowed access to a construction of consciousness that will permit the poem to take shape. The poet is wary but eager, considering how each option might suit her capabilities. "You're wrong—I say—a short, pithy poem/ is much harder than a long one," she insists, explaining a crucial feature of an aesthetic credo. Each section of the poem begins with the phrase "So it whispered a few words," a version of a stanza, but with no line breaks to maintain a continuous flow until the potential "poem" vanishes.

As if it would be almost easier to accept the offering in the classic spirit of a gift from the muse (with all its implications of obligation), the poet agrees "All right then, I'll try, since you insist/ But don't say I didn't warn you." Then, instead of encouragement, "it" points out that this precious offering might be welcomed by "other poets" and as the poet acknowledges, "Some of them could do it better," although she has been sufficiently involved to envision a poem that would satisfy her expectations. "But this one should . . . it ought to have," she ponders, expecting to continue deliberating, but "It just sighed./ And started vanishing./ And vanished."

As an allegory of an encounter with the energizing impulse of inspiration, "An Idea" combines Szymborska's ideas about origins with her analytic reflections on how query and application are an essential part of the poet's craft. In her Nobel lecture, she touched on "inspiration" saying "contemporary poets answer evasively when asked if it actually exists. It's not that they've never known the blessings of this inner impulse. It's just not easy to explain something to someone else that you don't understand yourself," which makes the poetic process a kind of continuous dialogue with the self. Szymborska both personalizes and generalizes this by saying "Whatever inspiration is, it's born from a continuous 'I don't know,'" which she takes further by explaining "as soon as the final period hits the page, the poet begins to hesitate, starts to realize that this particular answer was pure makeshift that's absolutely inadequate to boot."

The last poem in *Here*, "In Fact Every Poem," begins "In fact every poem/ might be called 'Moment' [because] one phrase is enough/ in the present tense,/ the past and even the future;"—with the semicolon, which concludes every stanza, indicating the pause prior to a development of the concept. The body of the poem intermixes images of the quotidian ("about Sally who has a kitty") with musings on the metaphysical ("an author places temporary hills/ and makeshift valleys") until the poem's last word, the crucial "dwukropek:" (colon), which acts as a conclusion without finality, the epitome of all for which Szymborska has been aiming.

While "An Idea" is presented in the tangible terms of an actual deliberation, it has manifestations of the metaphysical, a prominent feature of Szymborska's poetry. In "Before a Journey" she wonders why "They call it space" when it is "Empty and full of everything at once"and "Shut tight in spite of being open." In "Dreams" she describes how "in a split second/ the dream/ piles before us mountains as stony/ as real life." In the inward spiral of detail that depicts a "Labyrinth," she asserts:

> There must be an exit somewhere,
> that's more than certain.
> But you don't look for it,
> it looks for you,
> it's been stalking you
> from the start

In the poem "Metaphysics," she summarizes the perplexing nature of existence: "It's been and gone./ It's been, so it's gone." In the same irreversible order in this fashion until the last line where, with a nod to all the philosophers who have answered theories about the phenomenology of perception with the explicit, she points out the fact that even today you had a side of fries.

The metaphysical can offer access to "the something more" that is so important for Szymborska, as well as a substantiation for the inventive images that are the ways that the imagination extends the literal toward the plausible and, perhaps, beyond to the threshold of the exceptional—a means of framing the next question after any answer.

Although the philosophical cast to Szymborska's poetry is one of its more distinctive features, Gopnik's categorization of Szymborska as a "reticent lyricist" calls attention to a stylistic inclination that accounts for comments such as Robert Hass's admiration for poems he calls "accessible and deeply human." The poem "Vermeer," the most compact in the collection, illustrates the lyric facility that Szymborska employs to vivify the metaphysical:

> So long as the woman from the Rijksmuseum
> in painted quiet and concentration
> keeps pouring milk day after day
> from the pitcher to the bowl
> the World hasn't earned
> the world's end.

The poem is a part of a tableau of human existence, actually a single statement of faith and conviction, arranged in six lines of accumulating intensity. It is a tribute to the powers of artistic imagination to justify the value of human endeavor on a planet where much of human activity has been destructive. The well-known and beloved image of maternity and fertility, rendered with the kind of attentive care that poetry shares with painting, emphasizes a way of seeing—"quiet and concentration"—so vital for a truly civil way of living.

A longer poem with a narrative design, "In a Mail Coach," imagines a journey with Juliusz Słowacki ("One of Poland's greatest Romantic poets . . . 1809-1849," as a note informs) that takes the reader into the coach with the poet and:

> a nursemaid [who] holds an infant red from bawling,
> a tipsy merchant with relentless hiccups,
> a lady irritated for all the reasons above,
> furthermore a boy with a trumpet,
> a large fleabitten dog,
> and a caged parrot.

The evocative language is considerably more effusive than the lean lines of "Vermeer" (even more apparent in the multisyllabic lines of the Polish). The catalog of images places the poet amid the vibrant vulgarity of the immediate present, a ground for the poet's active imaginative excursions beyond the bounds of any historical era. This coalescence of the metaphysical mode with a lyric voice enables Szymborska to respond appropriately since "whatever else we might think of this world—it is astonishing" (as she exclaimed in her Nobel Lecture, also ably translated by Cavanagh and Barańczak).

To be astonished is, at its linguistic root, to be struck so powerfully that a strong response is inevitable. For a poet, this likely results in an effort to capture in suitable language the lineaments of the phenomenon itself. Szymborska does not move toward the melodic aspects of the lyrical often, which makes those instances even more striking, as in the twelve-line last stanza (no other stanza among the eight is more than six) of "Dreams," which builds toward a crescendo of closely rhymed plural nouns expanding "our dreamings" by the measure of looking:

> in their shadowings and gleamings,
> in their multiplings, inconceivablings,
> in their haphazardings and widescatterings
> at times even a clear-cut meaning
> may slip through.

One can appreciate the zeal with which Cavanagh and Barańczak tackled these lines since they had to find a series of rhymes in English to render:

> *w ich cieniach i lśnieniach,*
> *w ich zatrzęsieniach, niedoprzewidzeniach,*
> *w ich odniechceniach i rozprzestrzenieniach*

and their pleasure in the way they found plausible English terms to contrast darkness and brightness to carry the close rhyming of the first line, words with additional syllables for the second, and then creative coinings to adequately approximate the dense inner rhyming of the third.

In the fifth stanza of the title poem of the collection, Szymborska lists various defining attributes of the human, including the "astounded head," recalling her reference in the Nobel Lecture. The next stanza, balancing positive and negative elements "here on earth" as she has throughout the poem, declares "Ignorance works overtime here." So do her poems, calling attention to matters too astonishing to ignore, maintaining and demonstrating, in spite of ample evidence to the contrary, "Life on Earth is quite a bargain."

Leon Lewis

Review Sources

Booklist 107, no. 1 (September 1, 2010): 29.
Los Angeles Times, November 28, 2010, p. E11

HERO
The Life and Legend of Lawrence of Arabia

Author: Michael Korda (1933-   )
Publisher: Harper (New York). 762 pp. $36.00
Type of work: Biography, history
Time: 1888-1935
Locale: England, France, Egypt, Arabia, Italy, and India

T. E. Lawrence evolves from a young archaeologist into an unlikely and charismatic war hero

> *Principal personages:*
> T. E. LAWRENCE (1888-1935), the leader of the Arab revolt during World War I
> THOMAS CHAPMAN (LAWRENCE), his father
> SARAH LAWRENCE, his mother
> DAVID G. HOGARTH, an Oxford don, an archaeologist, a soldier, and his main mentor
> LORD ALLENBY (1861-1936), his commanding officer
> DAHOUM, his closest Arab friend
> GEORGE BERNARD SHAW (1856-1950), an Irish playwright and his literary adviser
> CHARLOTTE SHAW, his wife, one of Lawrence's closest friends
> VYVYAN W. RICHARDS, an Oxford friend of Lawrence
> JANET LAURIE, a family friend to whom Lawrence proposed
> HUSSEIN BIN ALI, the sharif of Mecca
> FAISAL I (1885-1933), his son, an organizer of the Arab revolt
> EMIR ABDULLAH, Faisal's brother
> AUDA ABU TAYI, the tribal leader of the Howeitat
> LOWELL THOMAS (1892-1981), American journalist and documentary filmmaker
> WINSTON CHURCHILL (1874-1965) and DAVID LLOYD GEORGE (1863-1945), British prime ministers

T. E. Lawrence was one of the most analyzed and romanticized historical figures of the twentieth century. Biographers and historians have attempted to portray the World War I soldier as almost a superhero, have debunked his accomplishments, and have subjected him to intense psychoanalysis. Michael Korda, author of *Hero*, whose previous subjects have included the war heroes Ulysses S. Grant and Dwight D. Eisenhower, attempts to synthesize the many views of Lawrence into a coherent whole, while placing his achievements in the context of World War I and in the history of the Middle East.

Korda eschews a strictly chronological approach, beginning with a lengthy account of how the relatively untested young Lawrence molded a group of untrained

~

*Michael Korda is one of the legends of
American publishing. His books
include* Charmed Lives: A Family
Romance *(1979), recalling his family's
adventures in the film business, and*
With Wings Like Eagles: A History of
the Battle of Britain *(2009).*

~

Arabs into a guerrilla army to combat the Turkish forces occupying much of the Middle East in 1917. In an attack on Aqaba, in what is now Jordan, Lawrence lost only two men while killing or capturing more than twelve hundred Turks. Korda wants to illustrate what made Lawrence special before venturing into his early life. In painstaking detail, Korda divides Lawrence's life and legacy into prewar, war, and postwar segments, all the while looking at all sides of his complex, contradictory, and elusive nature.

Central to understanding Lawrence is his odd family background. Thomas Lawrence, his father, whose real name was Thomas Chapman, was a wealthy landowner in Ireland who left his wife and four daughters to run off with the governess, Sarah Lawrence, who soon gave birth to Robert Lawrence. Although Thomas made frequent visits to Ireland to attend to "family business," he was cut off from most of his fortune, and his second family made do with less lofty circumstances, eventually settling in Oxford. The second son, Thomas Edward Lawrence, known as Ned, grew up idolizing his father, who was adept at shooting, carpentry, and photography, while fearing his deeply religious mother. Korda theorizes that Ned accidentally learned of his parents' secret and resented his mother for stealing away his father's birthright. Lawrence and Sarah never became reconciled to each other, though he reportedly said that he inherited her intensity and strong will.

Korda constantly debates earlier biographers, as when he argues that Sarah Lawrence was not the dominant parent in shaping her son's character, but that Thomas Lawrence was the role model for his heroic ideals. Young Ned always sought his father's approval, not his mother's. Thomas persuaded Sarah that Ned required different treatment than his brothers did. Many observers felt that Lawrence was conducting himself in a lordly manner in Arabia, as if he were trying to make up for his father's disappointments.

Korda examines how Lawrence's time at the University of Oxford prepared him for his Middle Eastern adventure and how David G. Hogarth, the keeper of Oxford's Ashmolean Museum, became the young scholar's mentor in archaeology and the closest of his several surrogate fathers. Korda describes Hogarth as the aspiring hero's Merlin. Lawrence's work with Hogarth at Carchemish, now on the frontier between Turkey and Syria, from 1911 to 1914, gave him a solid grounding in Arab culture and the geography of the region. Almost everyone who encountered Lawrence during this period recognized that he seemed destined for greatness.

Lawrence's initial role in the war was as a liaison between military intelligence and the Arab Bureau, which studied and developed British policy in the Middle East. The British knew that the only way to defeat Turkey, their biggest foe after Germany, was to orchestrate an Arab revolt in the territories included in the Ottoman Empire. These territories would become Iraq, Jordan, Lebanon, Palestine, and Syria. It became increasingly clear that not only was Lawrence the best man for the job but also the only one knowledgeable enough about the Arabs and the vast deserts they inhabited to bring off the revolt. Korda's account of how the revolt came to pass might be criticized for its lack of linear development, but his point is that considerable luck and trial and error were involved to get the right Arab leaders in place at the right locations and the right times.

Lawrence had to consider carefully each of the four sons of Arab leader Sharif Hussein bin Ali before settling on Faisal I as possessed with the intelligence, courage, and calm diplomatic resolve to achieve the goals of both the Arabs and the British: Faisal had "everything he had been searching for, not only politically, but personally. If it was not love at first sight, it was something very much like that." Lawrence and Faisal, who was impressed by the Englishman's commitment to the Arab cause, collaborated closely throughout the war and came to express identical thoughts as if they were two halves of the same person.

The army assembled by Temporary Second-Lieutenant and Acting Staff Captain Lawrence, eventually to be Colonel Lawrence, was not one his superiors could easily understand. On one hand were sophisticated leaders such as Faisal and on the other were relentless warriors such as Auda Abu Tayi, leader of the bedouin tribe the Howeitat. Korda claims that Lawrence may have more closely resembled the brutish Auda; they were united by their indifference to danger and their cool judgment under fire. Untrained, undermanned, and badly armed, Lawrence's forces could not engage in conventional battles but had to learn how to strike quickly, quietly, and unexpectedly, specializing in blowing up rail lines and trains. Korda connects what Lawrence taught the Arabs about guerrilla warfare to more recent unrest in the Middle East.

Korda's Lawrence was wracked by guilt throughout the war for encouraging the Arabs to fight, even though he knew the British and French would not grant them the lands and independence they wanted. Such was Lawrence's "self-disgust and shame" that he declined all honors and decorations at the end of the fighting. In becoming the first white man to lead the bedouin into battle, "he gave up some part of himself that he never recovered, eventually becoming a stranger among his own countrymen." The paradox of Lawrence's nature is that each of his achievements was accompanied by an almost equal sense of loss.

Lawrence tried to make up for his failures after the war by getting Faisal involved in the diplomatic negotiations over the future of the Middle East. He wanted to keep the British and French out of the region, create autonomy for the Arabs, and define the relations between Arabs and Jews in Palestine, but agreements were made behind his back. After the peace conferences, however, he continued advising Prime Minister David Lloyd George about British policies in the Middle East and had his friend Winston Churchill placed in charge of these policies. Churchill promptly hired Lawrence as his adviser and emissary to the Arabs. Lawrence succeeded in creating the borders of Iraq and what was then called Transjordan with Faisal and his brother Abdullah as their kings.

Korda contends that Lawrence decided at an early age he had to be a hero, hoping to become a general and be knighted before he was thirty, and that he waited patiently for the opportunity to present itself. He achieved his heroic status during the fight against the Turks not only through his ability to unite disparate Arab tribes into a surprisingly effective army but also through the quality of his mind, which allowed him to recall the details of terrain he had traveled only once and plan his attacks accordingly, and through the wealth of information he included in his reports, some as long as seventeen-thousand words, to his British superiors. While many officers were appalled by Lawrence's donning Arab dress, most "discovered the most striking thing about Lawrence: however far-fetched his ideas might seem at first, he usually knew what he was talking about."

Korda frequently addresses Lawrence's sexual nature, concluding that his parents' sin made him afraid of sex. Though others have assumed Lawrence was homosexual, Korda can find no convincing evidence. Lawrence had homosexual friends, notably Vyvyan W. Richards, an Oxford classmate, and had a strong attachment to Dahoum, his servant during his time at Carcemish: "Lawrence would seek throughout his adult life the company of men, and . . . it was only during the few years he spent with Dahoum that he ever found somebody he loved who could share it." According to Korda, Lawrence "might have been homosexual had he allowed his sexual instincts to emerge." His uncertainty about his sexuality may have led to an impulsive proposal to family friend Janet Laurie, later engaged to his brother Will.

While on an undercover mission in Deraa (now in Syria), Lawrence was arrested, brutally beaten, and sexually assaulted by the Turks. Korda sees Lawrence as torn between the masochistic pleasure he took in his rape and his shame in this pleasure, never reconciling the two. For Korda, Deraa is the central event in Lawrence's life, breaking his spirit, convincing him he had not lived up to his own standards, and resulting in his withdrawal from society after the war.

Lawrence's postwar retreat into the anonymity of an enlisted man in the Royal Air Force, which he loved, and the Royal Tank Corps, which he abhorred, was complicated by his immense fame. American journalist and documentary filmmaker Lowell Thomas spent time with Lawrence during the war and then exploited him with a wildly popular series of illustrated lectures and a biography. Lawrence was both distressed and flattered by his fame, mastering "the art of seeking to avoid the limelight while actually backing into it."

Lawrence used his fame to advance his causes and contributed to it by writing the limited-edition *Seven Pillars of Wisdom* (1922, revised 1926, 1935) and a popular abridgement of his story, *Revolt in the Desert* (1927). Korda, a former editor and publisher, clearly enjoys recounting the lengthy, agonizing process of the book's composition ("perhaps trying too hard to produce a masterpiece"), and its uniquely complicated publication history. During this process Lawrence became close friends with George Bernard Shaw and his wife, Charlotte, and relied upon their advice, while ignoring much of it.

Although Korda is constantly debating his predecessors throughout *Hero*, he admires *Colonel Lawrence: The Man Behind the Legend* (1934) by Basil Liddell Hart for having the best insight into Lawrence as a military strategist and Jeremy Wilson's *Lawrence of Arabia: The Authorized Biography of T. E. Lawrence* (1990) for its thoroughness. Korda regrets the popular image of Lawrence as portrayed by Peter O'Toole in *Lawrence of Arabia* (1962). While he considers David Lean's film a "masterpiece," he still thinks "it misses the point."

Korda's goal is to present a more complete picture of Lawrence than his predecessors, accumulating the qualities that made him special: "his curious mixture of shyness and vainglory, of heroism on the grand scale and self-doubt about his own feats, of political sophistication and occasional naïveté." Korda seems to feel that the most common misconception of Lawrence is that he was a neurotic loner, perhaps even a misanthrope, so he emphasizes Lawrence's unusual gift for friendship and his equal comfort with the working class and the ruling class. *Hero: The Life and Legend of Lawrence of Arabia*, without melodrama, sentimentality, or too much psychoanalysis, succeeds in creating a multifaceted view of a highly complex person.

Michael Adams

Review Sources

Booklist 107, no. 1 (September 1, 2010): 31.
Kirkus Reviews 78, no. 16 (August 15, 2010): 771.
Library Journal 135 (September 1, 2010): 115.
The New York Times, November 22, 2010, p. C1.
Newsweek 156, no. 20 (November 15, 2010): 53.
Publishers Weekly 257, no. 33 (August 23, 2010): 37.

THE HILLIKER CURSE
My Pursuit of Women

Author: James Ellroy (1948-   )
Publisher: Alfred A. Knopf (New York). 203 pp. $24.95
Type of work: Memoir
Time: 1955-2010
Locale: Los Angeles and surrounding suburbs

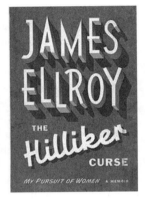

Revisiting the traumatic experience that brought an abrupt and premature end to his childhood—the brutal murder of his mother, Jean Hilliker, in 1958—Ellroy offers a harrowing account of the ways in which this event has shaped his life and resulted in his protracted and obsessive search for "atonement in women"

Principal personages:
> JAMES ELROY, the author and narrator
> JEAN HILLIKER, his late mother, a nurse
> ARMAND ELLROY, his late father, an accountant
> MARY DOHERTY, his first wife
> HELEN KNODE, his second wife
> JOAN KLEIN, his former mistress
> KAREN SIFAKIS, his former mistress
> ERIKA SCHICKEL, his mistress at the time the book was written
> ELIZABETH ("BETTY") SHORT, known as "THE BLACK DAHLIA," the
>   victim of a notorious unsolved murder in Los Angeles
> BILL STONER, a retired LAPD homicide detective

Since the mid-1980's, James Ellroy has earned a reputation as a major innovator in crime fiction of the "noir" school. Author of thirteen novels, including the highly regarded "L.A. quartet" (comprising *The Black Dahlia*, 1987; *The Big Nowhere*, 1988; *L.A. Confidential*, 1990; and *White Jazz*, 1992) and the even more ambitious Underworld U.S.A. trilogy (*American Tabloid*, 1995; *The Cold Six Thousand*, 2001; and *Blood's a Rover*, 2009), Ellroy has garnered both critical and commercial success with his stentorian and increasingly convoluted tales of the American criminal underbelly. Though most of his fiction is set in the past—the late 1940's and 1950's in the L.A. quartet, and the 1960's in the Underworld U.S.A. trilogy—this success derives in part from his uncanny ability to immerse readers in a world that is at once nightmarish and familiar.

Indeed, Ellroy's fictional canvas in the aggregate is so large, his vision so sweeping, that it may at first seem odd that its catalyst is fundamentally personal, in effect a gut-wrenching variation on the Freudian "primal scene." As those familiar with his work are well aware, he returns over and again—explicitly in nonfiction and interviews, implicitly in fiction—to the traumatic impact of losing his mother when he was just ten years old. In *The Hilliker Curse*, however, Ellroy takes pains to trace the etiology of his obsession not simply to Jean Hilliker's murder on June 22, 1958, but to an encounter a few weeks earlier, when he dared to defy her openly for the first time. In an unguarded moment she had asked him whether he wished to continue living with her or to move in with his father, whom she had divorced two years previous. When he blurted out his preference to be with his father, she struck the boy in the face, causing him to instantly wish her dead. In less than a month, his wish was fulfilled.

James Ellroy is the author of thirteen novels, two autobiographical memoirs, and three collections of short stories and journalism. Several of his novels have been adapted to the screen, the most successful being L.A. Confidential *(1990), which won an Academy Award in 1997.*

Notwithstanding his undemonstrative reaction to the news of his mother's murder (she was raped, beaten, and strangled to death, and her body was dumped at a high school near their home in El Monte, California), the burden of guilt was immediate and unshakable. Undoubtedly this "curse" was the chief psychological source of the aberrant behavior that ensued as well as the imaginative stimulus for the fiction that he would eventually produce. "My storytelling gifts are . . . rooted in the moment that I wished her dead and mandated her murder," he writes. "The Curse incubated my narrative gift." The distinction is significant in that, unlike a horrific event perpetrated by an unknown assailant for mysterious reasons (the murder was never solved), the invocation of a curse is at least an act of volition, however impulsive and freighted with remorse after the fact. It would seem to follow that if the ten-year-old Ellroy could "mandate" her murder by invoking a curse, the sixty-two-year-old author could similarly use his "narrative gift" as a kind of verbal incantation intended to break the curse once and for all and thereby effect a rapprochement with the spirit of Jean Hilliker—or her living surrogates. That, at least, is the book's ostensible aim.

Between the trauma of his tenth year and the beginning of his career as a novelist in his early thirties there was a protracted period of rebellion, experimentation, failure, and solipsistic withdrawal. Presented rather elliptically in *The Hilliker Curse*, these years are more fully explored in Ellroy's previous memoir, *My Dark Places* (1996). There the character and influence of his father, Armand Ellroy, are more clearly delineated. In both books the contrast between the child's views of his father and the mature adult's retrospective views is stark. To the boy, the father was a kind of pal. He was a lot of fun; he did not really care to discipline the boy (or himself); sometimes he even shared his wine and girlie magazines with him; he took pleasure in calling his former wife a drunk and a whore and encouraged the boy to spy on her for him. When Ellroy saw her in flagrante delicto with another man, "her first post-divorce squeeze," he duly reported the fact to his father. To the adult, however, the father's laziness and irresponsibility, along with his flagrant racism and homophobia, were all too clear.

Armand's health began to decline. He had a stroke in 1963, after which he was generally unemployed, living on Social Security. Meanwhile Ellroy was expelled from high school and joined the Army; he was discharged after only three months because of wildly erratic behavior. His father had a second stroke and died in June of 1965. Although his maternal aunt provided him with some financial support, Ellroy was basically on his own from the age of seventeen. He often slept in parks and stole food, liquor, and books. He developed addictions to alcohol, marijuana, and a variety of uppers. When he could afford it, he slept with prostitutes. He became adept at breaking into the homes of wealthy Hancock Park girls, sniffing and stealing their underwear and other personal items. After a few years, he was jailed for petty burglary and later admitted to the drunk ward of the state hospital. He did manage, in the meantime, to earn some income as a caddy. Eventually, with the help of Alcoholics Anonymous and his own nascent determination "to give my mental stories to the world," he was able to pull himself together and undertake his life's work. His first novel, *Brown's Requiem* (1981), finally set him on course at the age of thirty-three.

Ellroy describes the L.A. quartet as his "home-town elegy," all four novels featuring "Bad Men in Love with Strong Women." *The Black Dahlia* in particular he considers his "breakthrough book." Dedicated to his mother, the novel grew out of an article he wrote for *GQ* magazine dealing with the notorious unsolved murder of Betty Short, a wannabe film actor brutally killed in Los Angeles in 1947. The parallels between the Short and Hilliker cases were simply too abundant and too suggestive to deny. In an afterword to the novel, written in 2006, Ellroy sees the two women as "one in transmogrification," together comprising "the central myth of my life. . . . I want to close out their myth with an elegy. I want to grant them the peace of denied disclosure and never say another public word about them." In effect this was a trial run at breaking the curse, though it is significant that the longed-for rapprochement could not be attempted directly but only by proxy at this time. As he put it in his afterword to the novel, "I could not openly grieve for Jean. I could grieve for Betty. I could divert the shame of incestuous lust to a safe lust object. I could dismiss Jean . . . and grant a devotional love to Betty." Seen in this light, the *GQ* article, *The Black Dahlia*, *My Dark Places*, the 2006 afterword to the novel, and *The Hilliker Curse* are all attempts to approach and ultimately embrace Jean Hilliker by channeling her through Betty Short.

Though the two memoirs, *My Dark Places* and *The Hilliker Curse*, go over much of the same ground, there are interesting differences between them. *My Dark Places* is a much longer, more detailed, and linear account, focusing not only on Ellroy's dilatory process of maturation but also on his attempt, with the help of a retired Los Angeles Police Department homicide detective, to solve the nearly four-decades-old mystery of his mother's murder. The Betty Short murder is one of several other cases invoked as parallels to that of Hilliker, including the O. J. Simpson murder trial, which was underway at the time of Ellroy's investigation. Ellroy's formal search for Hilliker's killer, which lasted no less than fifteen months, proved fruitless, as both investigators determined that the evidence was spotty and inconclusive, and any possible suspects were likely dead in any event. However, in looking closely into Jean's background and interviewing her friends and relatives, he learned more about her life than about her death. That in itself should have been salutary. Unsatisfied with this discovery though, Ellroy ends the memoir by insisting that the case is ongoing. "The investigation continues," he says in a notice appended to the end of the book, and he provides a telephone number and an email address through which readers may forward leads. For his part, Ellroy confesses that he "didn't want it to end. I wouldn't let it end. I didn't want to lose her again." He concludes: "I know myself well enough to state that I will never stop looking."

It is worth noting that Ellroy once told an interviewer that if he "could abolish one concept from the parlance, it would be closure." For him the aversion to closure is both a technical and a psychological imperative. As a writer he considers the forced resolution putatively mandated by conventional narrative a kind of aesthetic fraud, an unwarranted imposition of "form at the expense of content." As a bereaved son he considers the ultimate acceptance of Hilliker's loss—and the open acknowledgment that her murder cannot be solved—a kind of betrayal. He must continue the investigation, prolong the story, and find more and more avatars of Hilliker so that he will never lose her again and so their bond will endure.

The Hilliker Curse shows rather decisively how problematic this unwillingness to let go and accept closure (whether narrative or psychological) can be. Ellroy enumerates an extensive series of romantic and/or sexual encounters with various women spanning more than four decades. The book's subtitle, *My Pursuit of Women*, obviously looms large here. They include, in chronological order, women named Marcia, Penny, Karen, Marge, Mary Doherty (his first wife), Helen Knode (the second), Joan Klein, Karen Sifakis, and finally Erika Schickel, the current embodiment of "Her, She, The Other" who inspires in him hopes of breaking the Hilliker curse. The final pages of the book celebrate his dream of merging with Erika "into a symbiotic and noncodependent whole. . . . We were united for that express purpose. It eclipsed sexual conjunction and anointed us with a solar-system-high calling." While the longing for such atonement is fully understandable, Ellroy's assumption that its attainment will put the Hilliker Curse to rest is surely belied by the evidence that the curse still has him in its power. The fact that similar rhapsodies about a dream woman appeared in the final chapters of *My Dark Places*, in that instance describing his "symbiotic" bond with Knode, would seem an ominous precedent, as they were to divorce fourteen years later. In *The Hilliker Curse* Ellroy cannot resist including an observation of Erika "stepping out of the shower yesterday morning. . . . She looked startlingly like Jean Hilliker." It is a chilling moment. Fans of Ellroy will doubtless be grateful for this latest addition to his canon, while even those who have reservations about its more grandiose claims will welcome another fascinating installment in his ongoing obsession with the "Great Mother."

Ronald G. Walker

Review Sources

Booklist 106, no. 21 (July 1, 2010): 4.
Kirkus Reviews 78, no. 14 (June 15, 2010): 652.
Library Journal 135, no. 15 (September 15, 2010): 72.
Los Angeles Magazine 55, no. 9 (December 2, 2010): 120.
Los Angeles Times, September 15, 2010, p. D1.
The New York Times Book Review, September 26, 2010, p. 8.
Newsweek 128, no. 20 (November 11, 2010): 79.
Publishers Weekly 257, no. 47 (November 29, 2010): 46.
The Spectator 314, no. 9499 (September 18, 2010): 48.

A HISTORY OF CLOUDS
Ninety-nine Meditations

Author: Hans Magnus Enzensberger (1929-   )
*First published: Die Geschichte der Wolken: 99
Meditationen,* 2003, in Germany
Translated from the German by Martin Chalmers and Es-
ther Kinsey
Publisher: Seagull Books (New York). 137 pp. $18.00
Type of work: Poetry

*Enzensberger uses clouds as a symbol for, among other
things, the transience of human life and revels in the significance of the seemingly mundane details of modern existence*

Hans Magnus Enzensberger is a prolific German writer,
with several collections of poetry, as well as novels and nonfiction books, to his
credit. He is known for his ironic, often wry, explications of the human condition, and
A History of Clouds, translated by Martin Chalmers and Esther Kinsey, highlights his
strength as a poet: the ability to write about complex themes with deceptively simple
rhythms and word choice.

The collection hinges on the eponymously titled twelve-part poem that composes
the last section of the book. Though not as abstruse, "A History of Clouds" is reminiscent of Wallace Stevens's iconic poem "Thirteen Ways of Looking at a Blackbird"
(1917), in which the poet uses an identifiable and relatively simple natural object to
ruminate on movement as representative of time and of the ephemeral qualities of existence, on epistemology, and on both the similarities and differences among living
organisms. For Enzensberger, the human spirit, in its myriad emotional states, is reflected in the actions of the clouds; in addition, the poet implies, clouds have the ability to teach: "They do not need historians/ henchmen, medics . . . / Their wanderings
high up/ are quiet and inexorable." Enzensberger illustrates that human lives are just
as fleeting as clouds, but that humanity clings to ideas and actions that seek to disguise this fact; clouds are unimpeded, forming and fading, immune to the problems
that encumber people.

A History of Clouds is separated into six sections that, except for the last, appear to
be only tenuously concerned with a central theme or set of themes. As an octogenar-
ian, Enzensberger has a lifetime of memories, and his age grants him a long view of
significant aspects of existence. In the first section, he focuses on memory, playfully
deflating the egocentric tendencies that define identity and writing bittersweetly
about what each person loses over the passage of time. In perhaps the strongest poem
of the first section, entitled "Sins of Omission," he examines the often difficult process of taking action: "I didn't hurry over/ when the need was greatest . . . / shied

~
Hans Magnus Enzensberger is a
German poet, translator, and
intellectual. He has written numerous
books, including Civil Wars: From L.A.
to Bosnia *(1994) and* Lighter than Air:
Moral Poems *(2000).*
~

away/ from improving the world/ never dropped out or in at the right time . . ./ Yes, I abstained from killing people." Enzensberger highlights the inertia of modern life; most First World individuals do not do much more than subsist, superficially content in a life that is uninterrupted by either great success or calamity.

Enzensberger echoes the theme of the average person's lack of utilitarian abilities in "Division of Labour," in which he focuses on "everything you can't do," listing individuals—such as "the man/ with the insulated pliers, the fortune-teller/ the dustman, the medicine man"—who perform tasks in other individuals' lives that they are either too busy or lack the skills to perform themselves. They all "contribute/ to your maintenance." Aided by Chalmers's jocular translation, Enzensberger does not come across as chastising or reproachful but rather as seeking to put modern humanity in its proper place. Though Enzensberger writes in the second person, as an academic focused on abstract ideas often without practical application, he mocks his own notion of self-importance. Because of Enzensberger's lighthearted use of language, his philosophical point about the inconsequence of human existence does not come across as morbid but instead has the effect of causing one to laugh at oneself.

Enzensberger's thoughts on human inconsequence are tempered by his ability to find revelation in simple pleasures and observations as well as in people and incidents that are often taken for granted. In "My Wife's Merits," he states that "each and every hair is dear to me," and after praising her unique and idiosyncratic attributes, he ends by stating, "I am amazed that here,/ where I happen to be, is where she usually is." From his perspective he is able to laugh at human shortcomings but also spotlight the sturdy edifice of emotions, in this case love for a spouse, that underpin and create meaning. Perhaps the most enlightening aspect of his poetry is its ability to underscore the complex spectrum of experience, embracing the aspects that speak to positive truths while lightheartedly discarding the imperfections that beget confusion and chaos.

The purpose for the way in which the second section is structured is not as easily discernable as that of the first section. In these poems, Enzensberger tends to focus on historical figures, though not ones of any great fame, perhaps in an attempt to illustrate that humans, though transient by nature, have made lasting contributions to the progress of society. Enzensberger features inventions that appear commonplace and, at the same time, have helped compose the substructure on which Western civilization stands. He refers cryptically to Joseph von Eichendorff, a German poet who dealt thematically with the goodness of nature; Steinar Pétursson, an Icelandic carpenter who invented a wooden band saw with an iron blade; and Andreas Heinrich Contius, an organ builder who constructed the "biggest mechanical organ in the world." By writing poems about these relatively obscure historical figures, Enzensberger illustrates humanity's innate capacity for greatness as well as how an individual life can alter the course of a larger group. The stories represent examples of the depth of the inspired human spirit. Therefore, the first and second sections butt up against each other, revealing Enzensberger's inherent ambivalence toward humans: He speaks to their shortcomings but also accentuates their strengths.

In the third section, Enzensberger discusses confounding existential topics, pondering the roles that God, religion, and evolution play in modern life. In "Malfunction," he traces evolution from its primordial coincidences to its modern implications.

> already
> there's a creature standing
> on two feet, starting to talk,
> even worse—to think!
> in the beginning
> they still plead,
> smoke rises from their altars,
> but no sooner do they have more or less
> enough to eat, than they get cocky
> . . . .
> Billions saying me-me-me.

He mocks both the notion of evolution as a somewhat flawless hypothesis about the origin and meaning of human life and the misnomer that people worship God for spiritual transcendence. In reality, he seems to state, primitive peoples turned to religion out of hunger and confusion, not in a quest for enlightenment. At the same, by addressing evolution, he is in fact communicating with scientists who cling to their theories as infallible interpretations of biological development. Because religion and science are both contrivances of an imperfect species, the validity of each is inherently dubious.

When pondering the possibilities for meaning in the universe, Enzensberger vacillates. In "Little Theodicy," he again addresses the subject of religion and its inevitable dissolution as a manmade creation.

> First you invent Him,
> then you try
> to devour each other
> mutually,
> in His name
> . . . .
> Who'd be surprised
> that His interest
> in such pompous asses
> is limited?

Positioning himself as an outside observer, Enzensberger can toy with ironic notions of religion—if God is a human invention, then, in reality, he does not exist; therefore, he could not have any interest in humanity. A God that has made a species in his image, a premise that underlies the very existence of Judeo-Christianity, would have an implicit interest in his creation; therefore, letting humanity run amok and perpetrate atrocities in his name would seem contrary to divine desire or purpose, possibly implying the lack of a divine ruler of the universe. Enzensberger's comic take on the nature of religion and the portrayal of God in religion presents a deep, theological quandary that does not offer an easy explanation.

Despite his mockery of entrenched ideas about meaning, in "Astronomical Sunday Sermon," Enzensberger asks the reader to consider the fortuitous circumstances in which humans find themselves: "A madhouse!/ But please permit me/ to remark in all modesty/ that all in all/ it's quite a favorable planet/ on which we find ourselves." This sentiment appears to enforce much religious thinking about humanity's unique inhabitation of this realm, as if it were created specifically for the species. Again, Enzensberger exposes his ambivalence, juxtaposing blind chance with cosmic convenience.

Enzensberger begins the fourth section of his book with a poem about death and ends it with several ditties that analyze the ephemeral qualities of wordplay and the creation of, deliberation over, and acceptance of written works. In "Parliamentary," he compares the process of writing poetry to the introduction and passage of a legislative bill. The rather challenging topics of death and artistic creation represent ironic bookends to the section because the general focus of the chapter is on everyday objects and technical implements. In "An Earth-Coloured Ditty," Enzensberger asks, "Another poem about death, etc.—/ certainly, but what about the potato?" He goes on to discuss the beneficial attributes of this specific tuber and its apparent absence from poetic or literary endeavors. This sentiment provides a metaphor for Enzensberger's overarching purpose: to highlight the sacred and philosophical significance of common people, places, and objects. The lofty or cryptic language that often characterizes poetry can alienate the general reading public; Enzensberger illustrates that poetic references to arcane or esoteric tenets are no more penetrative than odes to the average lives that most people live.

"Rusty fish knives, jagged lids of pocket watches/ refuse to perish. Polished and cleaned/ refurbished and desired they resurface,/ antiques/ Just like obsessions," Enzensberger writes in "Fish Knives and Ideas," again utilizing common objects to highlight a human state. In this case, he uses antique items to illustrate how emotions and states of mind can resurface, as the past manifests itself in the present. In another poem in this section, "Superfluous Elegy," items such as an "old tin locomotive" and an "egg timer, never . . . used" are called upon to unveil the human tendency to hoard, highlighting the undercurrent of greed and fear that possession can represent.

Enzensberger uses the fifth section to highlight science, reason, and understanding (or the lack thereof). From black holes and dark matter to a *"Theory of Everything,"* Enzensberger juxtaposes the finite with the eternal. Though not condemning science, as a poet Enzensberger sees the world as open to many interpretations. In poems such as "Questions for the Cosmologists" and "If You Believe It," he questions the ability of humans to understand the workings of the universe, whether through religion or science—"I do not know what I prefer:/ the promises of the initiated/ or the miracles of science." Though much of Enzensberger's book is a rumination on the metaphysical, he retreats from any form of belief system that codifies the universe. By juxtaposing the seemingly simplistic endeavors of common people with grand schemes of universal order, and by essentially endorsing neither, he prepares the reader for his treatise on transience in the final section of the book.

Enzensberger states that, in contrast to how humans perceive themselves—solid, existing, present—clouds "can hardly be considered/ as being born" and that "they have no notion of dying." This affords them a sort of freedom unavailable to the human race, caught as it is in self-referential exercises. Enzensberger dedicates the first four parts of the final poem to the fleeting beauty of clouds. They are a panacea for "stress, grief . . . [and] depression"; they are "intangible" and "non-violent." However, in the fifth part he says, "they have another face too./ Out of anger or exuberance/ they bunch together, fist-clenching clusters,/ threatening." Here, his description illustrates how humans mirror the clouds: Intricacy of emotion is part and parcel of the species.

Enzensberger's comparison of clouds to humans is subtle because he spends much of the poem contrasting the two. Clouds are "a separate species./ transient, but older than our kind./ And it will survive us by/ plus minus a few million years." However, when the book is viewed holistically, Enzensberger's thesis becomes more clear. His often humorous analysis of the human condition—from the endless, recurring foibles to the subtle, significant progress over the course of time—reveals the complexity of the species, in all its transience. Like the clouds, the human race seems to be both here and not here, appearing and reappearing in recognizable, but distinct, forms. In the end, clouds are Enzensberger's metaphor for all aspects of life, those that are infused with meaning and those that remain beyond the reach of rationality.

Christopher Rager

Review Source

The Guardian, May 15, 2010, p. 12.

HOPE IN A SCATTERING TIME
A Life of Christopher Lasch

Author: Eric Miller (1967-   )
Publisher: Wm. B. Eerdmans (Grand Rapids, Mich.).
    394 pp. $32.00
Type of work: Biography
Time: 1932-1994
Locale: Omaha, Chicago, Boston, New York City, and
    Rochester, New York

Miller's book on Lasch is less an intimate biography of the influential late twentieth century social thinker than an intellectual history of the development of his essential ideas

Principal personages:
> CHRISTOPHER LASCH (1932-1994),
>   American historian and social theorist
> ZORA SCHAUPP LASCH, his mother, a teacher and social worker
> ROBERT LASCH, his father, a journalist and editorial writer
> WILLIAM E. LEUCHTENBURG (1922-   ), the noted Columbia
>   University historian under whom Lasch studied for his Ph.D.
> EUGENE D. GENOVESE (1930-   ), a friend and colleague in the history
>   department at the University of Rochester

Christopher Lasch, the subject of Eric Miller's *Hope in a Scattering Time*, was one of the most important American social critics in the second half of the twentieth century. For more than thirty years, he wrote intellectual wake-up calls—the most important of which was *The Culture of Narcissism* (1979)—to rouse Americans from what he saw as their political and cultural lethargy. In May of that year, he was invited to a private dinner at the White House with President Jimmy Carter and a handful of leading American thinkers and activists, including Jesse Jackson and Bill Moyers; in July, he was featured in *People* magazine. Few American intellectuals have achieved such celebrity. He also helped to reinvigorate the study of American history, especially in the new emphasis he brought to social and cultural history, and he helped train a generation of historians in his distinguished, nearly twenty-five-year career at the University of Rochester.

Miller's biography is the first full-length treatment of this influential teacher and cultural theorist—a man whose life reflected many of the central tensions of twentieth century American life, as Miller argues. Miller charts Lasch's intellectual development in a detailed analysis of his books, articles, and correspondence. Readers curious about Lasch's personal life, however, will be disappointed in this biography, for Miller focuses almost exclusively on Lasch's thoughts and words; biographical details, such as psychological, financial, and sexual, that overwhelm many other biographies are absent here. This is intellectual history channeled through biography. Lasch's life becomes a framework for Miller's explication of Lasch's ideas, their many sources, and their impact on American life and thought.

∼

Eric Miller is associate professor of history and humanities at Geneva College, in Beaver Falls, Pennsylvania, and has a Ph.D. in American history from the University of Delaware.

∼

Lasch grew up in Omaha and Chicago, the precocious only child of parents who were products of Progressive Era populism and who gave him a strong intellectual background. His mother, Zora, had a Ph.D. in philosophy from Bryn Mawr College and was a teacher and social worker. His father was a journalist who won a Pulitzer Prize in 1966 for his editorials in the *St. Louis Post-Dispatch*, opposing Lyndon B. Johnson and the Vietnam War. Miller spends some time on Lasch's upbringing because the historian spent a lifetime coming to grips with his parents' liberal legacy. After four years at Harvard (where he roomed with the future novelist John Updike), Lasch gained his Ph.D. in American history at Columbia University, working with giants William E. Leuchtenburg and Richard Hofstadter. After short teaching stints at Williams College, the University of Iowa, and Roosevelt University and Northwestern University in Chicago, Lasch settled into the history department at the University of Rochester in 1970, where he spent the remainder of his career.

Lasch's first book, *The American Liberals and the Russian Revolution* (1962), was his Ph.D. dissertation only slightly revised. It indicated the direction of his intellectual progress for the rest of his prolific career, which entailed confronting his own, and his country's, liberal legacy and grappling with its political and cultural consequences, in this case what he saw as the sentimental belief in "the inevitable spread of democracy throughout the world, by orderly change or revolution, as circumstances might dictate." This book had sold only 318 copies by the end of a year.

Lasch's next book, *The New Radicalism in America, 1899-1963: The Intellectual as Social Type* (1965), turned the young historian into a star. The change coincided with the shift in Lasch's writing from political and intellectual history to social history, in which he drew on sociology and psychology in an attempt to get beneath the surface of American history as it had previously been studied to uncover the larger themes and patterns he discovered there.

Lasch felt that the failure of American intellectual leaders was evident in the Cold War culture of the 1950's and 1960's and in the deepening morass in Vietnam. According to Miller, Lasch contended "American intellectuals must recover a truer understanding of how to carry out what he termed their 'vocation' if the follies of contemporary liberalism were to be corrected and the nation's course righted." Increasingly, Lasch turned to emerging neo-Marxist thought of the time—the early Karl Marx, translated through later European thinkers such as Theodor Adorno and Antonio Gramsci—in critical essays he wrote for *The Nation* and *The New York Review of Books*, collected in 1969 in *The Agony of the American Left*.

During the 1960's, as Lasch was analyzing the failures of American politics and culture—and coming to a deeper understanding of the country's fragmentation—he was also wrestling with his own sense of isolation. In 1970, he moved permanently to Rochester, in hopes of finding the social and intellectual community he sought. He was increasingly alienated from the political left during the 1970's for his criticism; Lasch argued for a freedom based not on some countercultural, personal liberation but on "the dignity of privacy, kinship ties, moral order, and civic duty." His *Haven in a Heartless World: The Family Besieged* (1977) confirmed his emergence as a conservative radical who was building a case against "a dominant tendency among Americans: the instinct to assume a basic, elemental wholeness, even goodness, at the heart of their national life and indeed their national history." It was this new critical stance that was the underpinning of Lasch's 1979 best seller, *The Culture of Narcissism: American Life in an Age of Diminishing Expectations*. In four months, the book sold forty-five thousand copies and triggered articles on its author in both *Time* and *Newsweek*. Like social critic David Riesman before him (*The Lonely Crowd*, 1950) and Robert Bellah after (*Habits of the Heart: Individualism and Commitment in American Life*, 1985), Lasch was diagnosing American ills and explaining why the society failed to provide the moral and spiritual sustenance its members required.

Drawing on both psychology and sociology, Lasch analyzed what had turned Americans from community members into narcissists, and he "prob[ed] the connections between particular social structures and the shaping of personality, seeking to detail the human toll of what he termed 'the wreckage of capitalism.'" His analysis struck a chord with intellectuals and critics everywhere. Carter appropriated some of the more negative ideas from *The Culture of Narcissism* for speeches that Lasch felt misread his text, but Lasch was already moving toward higher, more constructive ground. Going beyond the Marxist and Freudian ideas he had earlier been building upon, Lasch's work in his last fifteen years was marked by a search for connections, by a neohistorical writing that looked for moral and religious traditions on which to build. *The Minimal Self: Psychic Survival in Troubled Times* (1984) displayed a "persuasive set of assumptions on the nature and interrelations of personhood, culture, and politics," Miller argues.

In 1985, Lasch assumed the chairmanship of the history department at Rochester, in a parallel search for the home in history teaching he wanted to find. His quest for intellectual community at Rochester did not end successfully. The collapse of the Soviet Union in 1989 coincided with the completion of what Miller considers the most important book of Lasch's prolific career. Miller is not alone; Bellah hailed *The True and Only Heaven: Progress and Its Critics* (1991) as an "extraordinary" work, and Lasch's "masterpiece." Thinking people, Lasch argued, should "cultivate an independence of mind and spirit that, structured within and by the community, could give a person the keenness to detect and strength to resist the political and economic powers that sought always to enthrone themselves as the necessary ends of human life." However, intellectual critics and other readers failed to respond to Lasch's message. Perhaps Lasch's defection from the Left and his turn to more traditional and conservative values had alienated too many readers. Perhaps, also, the nation itself was turning in another direction, as the "dot.com" revolution of the 1990's and the 1994 conservative congressional revolt indicated. Whatever the reason, Lasch had ceased to be the leading social critic everyone read.

Along with a serious falling out with his friend the historian Eugene Genovese, Lasch found other colleagues at Rochester unwilling to move in the directions he wanted the history department to go, considering the overspecialization of scholarship in his and other disciplines a dangerous trend. As he wrote to his father about the university in 1989, "There is a permanent sense of grievance; the whole institution is built on the politics of envy. It's a poisonous atmosphere, ruinous to any serious pursuit of learning."

Lasch was diagnosed with cancer in 1992 and was dead by February of 1994, at the age of sixty-one. His last book, *The Revolt of the Elites and the Betrayal of Democracy* (1996), appeared posthumously. Still, as Miller amply demonstrates, Lasch's career was a triumph of a sort. His books were clarion calls to the complacent, almost somnolent United States. His teaching, likewise, was an inspiration to his students. "It was his courageous willingness to give himself over to both the search for wisdom and the casting of judgment, public judgment," Miller writes, that made Lasch "the magnetic figure he, for a time, was. Scores of students landed on his doorstep hoping to discover what he knew and how he saw, and left his care having written remarkable books, on technology and industry, on love and feminism, on race and democracy, on intimacy and reticence, on handicrafts and politics, and more."

Miller's respect for Lasch shines through on every page of this study, and he does an estimable job of boiling down Lasch's often dense and complex ideas into manageable prose. The writing here is good, often sprightly, but it is also academic; Miller's (or his editors') decision to place footnotes on the bottom of the page (rather than in end papers, as most studies of this sort do) further slows down the narrative pace. Finally, the biography is hardly, as Miller claims in his subtitle, *A Life of Christopher Lasch*. Lasch's wife and four children appear only when they intersect with his intellectual development. His parents play a far more central role because Lasch grappled with their liberal legacy throughout his career.

Hope in a Shattering Time is about ideas and about their development in the thinking and writing of one of the twentieth century's most important social critics, a historian who was simultaneously a pessimist and an idealist. Miller concludes, Lasch provided "intelligent, insistent probing of the nation's political and cultural terrain," and "sought to move past the mood and measures of the moment to a place of political and spiritual renewal."

David Peck

Review Sources

Commonweal 137, no. 18 (October 22, 2010): 21-28.
Dissent 58, no. 1 (Winter, 2011): 99-104.
The New Republic 241, no. 7 (May 13, 2010): 30-34.
Weekly Standard 16, no. 7 (November 1, 2010): 35-37.
World Affairs 173, no. 1 (May/June, 2010): 81-89.

HOW TO READ THE AIR

Author: Dinaw Mengestu (1978-   )
Publisher: Riverhead Books (New York). 305 pp. $25.95
Type of work: Novel
Time: The mid-1970's to the early twenty-first century
Locale: Ethiopia, Sudan, and the United States

A young man of Ethiopian descent struggles to understand his own life and the stormy relationship between his emotionally damaged parents

    Principal characters:
        JONAS WOLDEMARIAM, a repressed young
            Ethiopian American
        YOSEF WOLDEMARIAM, his immigrant
            father
        MARIAM WOLDEMARIAM, his self-effacing mother
        ANGELA WOLDEMARIAM, his African American wife
        ABRAHIM, Mariam's father and Yosef's friend

Dinaw Mengestu's second novel, *How to Read the Air*, is not for readers who prefer clarity tied up in a neat little package. The author offers multiple, conflicting versions of events, perhaps none of which are true.

Although Jonas Woldemariam, the American-born son of Ethiopian immigrants, relates the story in his own voice, he is clearly an unreliable narrator. Little in his past is certain, but whatever he does not know, his agile imagination willingly supplies. Because his parents do not reveal much about their prior lives to him, he must envision scenes that he did not witness and tell stories he may have invented. Every scrap of information in the novel is filtered through him.

Jonas's narrative follows three paths: his relationship with his parents, the unfortunate American honeymoon journey that his father Yosef insisted on making and that his mother Mariam did not want, and his own uneasy relationship with Angela, his wife. There is also a dramatic plot: Yosef Woldemariam overcomes a series of obstacles, struggling to save his own life as he escapes from the military overthrow of Emperor Haile Selassie I's government into the further chaos of Sudan. However, the real, more subtle story examines not only the actions of these four characters but also the characters themselves, none of whom feels comfortable in their own skin.

Chapters alternate between Jonas's present life and his imagined version of his parents' earlier lives, as he attempts to reconstruct the belated honeymoon in the United States, three years after their marriage in Addis Ababa and six months before his own birth. He has to reinvent his father through stories in order to understand him, but his reticent mother remains more of a mystery, even though there is a tacit bond between them. This novel is really about Jonas's attempt to make sense of his fam-

~

*Dinaw Mengestu came to the United
States from Addis Ababa, Ethiopia, at
the age of two. His first book,* The
Beautiful Things That Heaven Bears
(2007), has received numerous awards.

~

ily history and thereby understand and heal
himself.

In Ethiopia, Yosef and Mariam Woldemariam were together only briefly before they
were separated. After the emperor was de-
posed in 1974, the young Yosef, among others, called for a revolution. First imprisoned
then released, and fearing a second arrest and
probable death during the political upheaval,
he fled the country for neighboring Sudan, hidden in the back of a pickup truck. Fortunately for him, he had sensed "the abrupt and dramatic shift in the air that precedes
any violent confrontation" and learned "to read the air" to protect himself.

In an embellished version of his father's life that Jonas later offers his students,
Yosef encountered Abrahim, a friendly Arab, in a large port city (probably Port Sudan), where he hoped to find passage out of Africa. Abrahim helped Yosef evade the
police, who could have sent him back to Ethiopia; found him a job delivering tea to
dock workers; and eventually arranged for him to stow away on a freighter bound for
Europe. Once Yosef arrived at his ultimate goal, the United States, he was expected to
send for Abrahim's daughter Mariam after showing immigration authorities falsified
documents to confirm that she was his wife. Thus Mariam would be protected from
further political uprisings. (Eventually, Mariam herself will tell her son a different
story.)

After stowing away on another ship to reach the United States, Yosef began to
dream frequently of boxes large enough to contain him and those that were small, like
the cubbyholes in which he had hidden on the ships: "He was always crouching, curl-
ing, trying to reduce himself into a package smaller than the one he was made of."
Once he reached the United States, he found himself working in the shipping department of a factory in Peoria, Illinois, again surrounded by boxes. (Ironically, he will
even die in a boxlike room at the YMCA.) By the time Mariam joined him, he had already begun to plan their honeymoon. He intended to drive five hundred miles to
Nashville, Tennessee, home of the country music he had loved even in Ethiopia. As a
boy, Yosef was drawn to this music after his mother's death because it expressed the
loneliness he felt. He made a careful list of historical sites to visit along the way, to
share all this with his wife.

Meanwhile, Mariam had become an independent woman in Ethiopia, holding a responsible job, employing servants, and essentially controlling her own life. In Peoria,
she discovers that she has no control. She seeks it, making Yosef wait in his red Monte Carlo while she pretends to retrieve something she forgot to pack. Yosef realizes
what she is doing and, without warning, strikes her viciously. Having grown up with a
violent father, he lashes out physically when angered. Mariam does not resist—she
wants to escape but dares not.

In her life, passive Mariam tries many times to leave Yosef but never really can until Jonas goes off to college. Instead, she will teach her son that it is wiser "not to

translate emotions into actions, to let them lie dormant, because once . . . expressed, there was no drawing them back." Jonas learns this lesson well, and his ability to repress emotion becomes a problem in his marriage. The lack of passion in his early narrative voice makes any sudden violence even more unsettling.

Only forty miles from Peoria, Yosef and Mariam stop first at Fort Laconte, the scene of a crushing seventeenth century attack on French troops by Tamora warriors. This is the first place Yosef wants to visit, believing that if he becomes familiar with American history it will make him more American. Afterward, he misses the exit to the freeway and becomes lost. Mariam knows he is driving in the wrong direction but says nothing. When they reach the western Illinois border, Yosef realizes his error and, furious, hits her again. Their journey is not completed, but this event will change both their lives and, thus, their son's. Eventually they will separate.

In some ways, the adult Jonas's relationship with Angela mirrors his parents' dysfunction. She is a young African American lawyer who comes from southern poverty, working with him as a summer intern at a Manhattan immigration center. For the previous ten years he has held a variety of temporary jobs while he considers a postgraduate degree in English. Angela and Jonas share a common bond as the only persons of color in this office, other than their clients, and both assist refugees who seek asylum in the United States. Jonas's particular job is to edit the clients' petitions to make them more effective. Like Winston in George Orwell's *Nineteen Eighty-Four* (1949), Jonas rewrites their history, just as he continues to rewrite his parents' history.

When he learns that Angela's father left her and that her mother frequently disappeared, their bond is strengthened even more. After Angela begins a real career at a law firm, she gets her own apartment, which they soon share. Both invent fantasy histories for themselves, lives neither has lived. In the meantime, Jonas is dismissed from the immigration center because it has run out of funds. He avoids telling Angela that he has lost his job, knowing she will be angry when she finds out. Both of them are wounded; they seem to circle each other warily. Nevertheless, she helps him to find a part-time position at a private school, where he is hired to teach literature and composition.

Jonas guards his emotions carefully from his students; he suspects that he "had gone numb as a tactical strategy" in childhood. At the academy, his students question him about his recent marriage to Angela, but he reveals little about himself or his previous life. He still has no clear sense of self, having learned to blend into the background to avoid his father's anger.

In May he completes his first year of teaching, which has begun to transform him, even though he does not feel ready for a Ph.D.; nonetheless, he still withholds himself emotionally from Angela. When she has an extramarital affair, he pretends not to care. After they begin to separate, Angela describes them as "two damaged little kids trying to heal each other's wounds." Once again, his parents' estrangement forms a model for his own. He completes another year of teaching, gradually gaining self-confidence around his students.

Jonas senses that something significant happened on his parents' honeymoon, and whatever it was permanently affected their relationship. As a child, he compulsively built tiny forts (his versions of a safe home) as symbolic sanctuaries from his unhappy parents, but he hid them away, often under the bed. He still dreams of them. In the summer, he drives to Fort Laconte, the first stop on his father's original list, the scene of a brutal battle between the French and Native Americans, as well as a scene of conflict between his parents in 1977. He suddenly realizes that the construction of the fort is faulty—it would have been impossible to shoot at an advancing enemy from inside the fort. This is a fort that does not protect; one that does not symbolize safety for Jonas, his mother, or for the dead. When he returns home, he and Angela make their peace, although they will still divorce; shortly after his estranged father's death, Jonas begins to tell a new class the story of Yosef's journey to the United States—a posthumous tribute to his father.

The use of alternating chapters, past and present, make *How to Read the Air* rather difficult to access at first. Also, the time sequence of past events is often hard to follow, especially when the past is part memory and part imagination. Mengestu deliberately withholds a good deal of information, perhaps to mirror Jonas's own struggle to make sense of things. What is presented as fact is frequently erroneous, making it difficult to distinguish what is true or false when even the unreliable narrator is not certain.

Each major character undergoes a separate, symbolic journey that effects a significant change. Yosef's excruciating exodus—from the chaos of Ethiopia to Sudan, Italy, England, and the New World—is a process that embitters him for life. Although Mariam does not know what happened to her husband until three years after his sudden disappearance from Ethiopia, she obediently follows him to the United States when he sends for her; however, her life alters dramatically. Their doomed honeymoon leads her to another journey, from passivity into action, but this action only happens once and is nothing she can sustain. Her life has exhausted her, and she becomes an isolated woman. Jonas also goes on the road alone, traveling to visit each of his parents, who live separately but not happily, as well as retracing the honeymoon trip to Fort Laconte in an attempt to understand them. Even Angela, the daughter of an unstable and frequently absent mother, manages to escape her impoverished childhood to become an attorney in a well-connected Manhattan firm.

A number of critics have already praised this novel for its ability to re-create the immigrant experience and the alienation that can follow. Mengestu offers a stunning and disturbing glimpse into this clash of cultures.

Joanne McCarthy

Review Sources

Booklist 107, no. 4 (October 15, 2010): 19.
Kirkus Reviews 78, no. 21 (November 1, 2010): 1079.

Library Journal 135, no. 10 (June 1, 2010): 82.
The New York Times, October 16, 2010, p. C1.
The New York Times Book Review, October 10, 2010, p. 18.
Newsweek 156, no. 17 (October 25, 2010): 69.
Publishers Weekly 257, no. 30 (August 2, 2010): 27.
Rolling Stone, no. 1115 (October 14, 2010): 90.

HUMAN CHAIN

Author: Seamus Heaney (1939-   )
Publisher: Farrar, Straus and Giroux (New York). 85 pp.
  $24.00
Type of work: Poetry
Time: The present
Locale: Ireland and worldwide

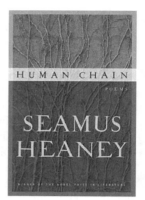

Heaney's first book after his stroke in 2006 meditates on his near-death experience yet conveys the solidarity and continuity available in life; it proclaims the imaginative potential of every verbal nuance and constructs a distinct sense of Heaney's own poetic tradition

The reaction to Seamus Heaney, whose 2010 book of poetry is collected in *Human Chain*, since the mid-1990's has been two parts awe and one part resentment. He has not just gained a world audience but done so in such an effortless and scrupulous manner that fellow poets and critics feel the need either to praise him vociferously or to try spitefully to find flaws in his work. Even without this, there is an inevitable tug in criticism toward the early and midcareer work of a writer, especially one as laureled as Heaney, who won the Noble Prize in Literature in 1995 and has garnered myriad other awards. However, Heaney's poetry in the twenty-first century has been not only as strong as ever but also innovative in its reliance on an unobtrusiveness, a trust in language, and the poet's own ability to inhabit language so resolute that the sort of emphasis or declamation other poets might need falls by the wayside.

Electric Light (2001) and *District and Circle* (2006) were at once typical of Heaney's style and also attained, in each case, a distinct register; each of Heaney's books is indeed like an individual province of the same country, with an overall national aura but with a distinct local feel. The same is true with *Human Chain*. As many critics have noted, mortality is a theme. The one poem literally about Heaney's stroke, "Chanson d'Aventure," pictures the poet and his wife in an ambulance, at a loss for words, knowing the right poetic allusions to speak but not mentioning them—in the poet's case because the stroke had robbed him of speech. This momentary suspension of speech at once calls attention to the wonders of the world's tangible realities and brings alive a realm of absence, a sense of the decorum of withdrawal and departure. The first note is sounded by the book's opening poem, "Had I Not Been Awake," speaks simply but beautifully about the delight in each moment; had the poet been asleep, a rustle of the wind that occurred just then would have passed unnoticed. Though the stroke is not mentioned overtly, the presence of "Chanson d'Aventure" a few pages later suggests that this vulnerability to the smallest moments of grace is induced by the more proximate awareness of death that such an ex-

perience would generate. "Miracle," with the
sense that those who help save a life are as miraculous in their compassion as is the resusci-
tated survivor, can also be seen as a stroke
poem, as can the volume's title poem, "Human Chain," which concerns a crew of relief
workers handing bags of meal to one another;
the act of one worker handing off a bag to another is a premonition of relinquishing life
in which the final casting off is not one of
interconnection but departure.

Readers would be mistaken to see death
as a new theme in Heaney's work. Heaney
became famous writing about violence and
burial in prehistoric northern Europe. The
sense of withdrawal and absence is not new
either. The poet speaks of himself and his
peers when young as "White-night absen-
tees," open to hear the freshness of beauty

*Seamus Heaney's first poetry
collection,* Death of a Naturalist,
*appeared in 1966, and since then, he
has published poetry, criticism, and
translations that have established him
as one of the leading poets of his
generation.*

and music in youth. This strain of absence and withdrawal being positive has been a
staple in Heaney's work as far back as the 1970's diptych "Mossbawn." Absence is as
old a trope for Heaney as the more visible motifs (elderberries, blackberries, the de-
lectably resonant place names of Lough Neagh and Anahorish), and its salience in
this volume is not a radical departure.

Heaney is often seen as a pastoral poet, a poet of the earthly, the tangible; but he
has never relied on these elements alone. Time and distance have also been elements.
Even in his earliest poems from the 1960's, Heaney was evoking his childhood in Ireland at the same time as he was recognizing and valuing his distance from it. This distance has accelerated as the poet has advanced to genuine old age, with youthful
memories, though vivid, beginning to seem like a reach across an extended chasm.
However, a moment that is wholly present cannot be valued; in "The Baler," the poet
listens to the humdrum sound of the straw baler and appreciates its resonance only in
the evening when he knows it is about to cease. Heaney is a poet of joy in landscape
and sensation, but he is also a poet of loss.

Heaney is also—more than is usually represented—an ambitious and cosmopolitan poet who reaches with ease across centuries and around any different poetic traditions to conjure his moods and reveries. "Lick the Pencil" is most likely about a
school colleague of Heaney's; however, with only a few details changed, it could
readily have been about a medieval monk in the company of his peers, a point driven
home by the references to Colmcille (Saint Columba, the important leader of the early
medieval Celtic church) and a saint's life. "Colum Cille Cecinit" and "Sweeney Out-
Takes"—the latter presumably an addendum to *Sweeney Astray: A Version from the
Irish* (1983), Heaney's notable translation of the medieval Irish tale *Buile Suibhne—*

dip into this medieval Irish/Latin register more overtly. This register is always latent in Heaney's poetry, and the reverberation of this latency is not so much Heaney's nostalgia for the rural Ireland of his youth, nor any sort of pious Catholicism (as is curiously alleged by some of Heaney's detractors), but a vivid sense of the continuity between medieval Latin culture and the Irish present; children who went to school in Heaney's youth were not living lives far different from young medieval novitiates in the same place, in days of yore.

The living link, through religious tradition, to Latin makes the two poems that allude to Vergil's *Aeneid* (29-19 B.C.E.; English translation, 1553) powerful. "The Riverbank Field" is not so much a translation of the famous "golden bough" passage in the sixth book of the *Aeneid* but a meditation on what it might be to translate the poem and a claim by the poet that he possesses the terms—in the affective vocabulary of his daily living—to mount such a translation. "Route 110," referencing a Dublin bus route, is a full-scale adaptation of Aeneas's pilgrimage to the underworld in book 6, as the poet meets shades both of important people in his own past and anonymous victims of violence and asserts that "Venus's doves" are readily translatable into "McNicholl's pigeons." Heaney possesses a particular affinity for Vergil because his lightness and verve can accommodate and transform the Latin poet's gravid melancholy, and also because Heaney's imagination is both credulous and somber enough to have known "the age of ghosts."

The volume's most striking translation, though, is the one that closes the book. "A Kite for Aibhín" is a free rendering of "L'Aquila" by the Italian poet Giovanni Pascoli. Both are about kite flying in youth, both the exhilaration of the flying kite soaring in air above the ground and among the elements and the astonishment felt by the adult poet in recalling that long-ago event "from another life and time and place." This is a translation between languages and between settings, as Heaney substitutes Anahorish for Urbino, but it is more thoroughly a translation between moods. Heaney's canny exuberance is far from Pascoli's alert melancholy, but Heaney respects the old poem and signals his personal presence by the very nature of the new. In this volume, Heaney displays to particular effects his immersion in Italian poetry. The reader trusts that "the very word is like a bell" in "Chanson d'Aventure" cites the very phrase in John Keats's "Ode to a Nightingale," but the reader also may assume that the eels in "Eelworks" allude to the Italian Nobel laureate Eugenio Montale's great poem "The Eel" and that the disregarded broom in "A Herbal" is written with knowledge of Giacomo Leopardi's nineteenth century poem "La Ginestra" (the broom sprig).

"A Herbal" is another fascinating free rendering, this time of a poem by the Frenchman Eugène Guillevic. The taut, hermetic style of Guillevic's poetry is not an immediately obvious candidate for reference for Heaney. Granted, Heaney is noted for his translations—the best-selling *Beowulf: A New Verse Translation* (1999), but also the equally superb, if less heralded, works such as his versions of the sixteenth century Polish poet Jan Kochanowski and the fifteenth century Scotsman Robert Henryson. To reiterate, what is more remarkable, however, is Heaney's ability to adapt different sensibilities to his own without engorging them. In "A Herbal" a dense thicket of plants limns the loss of human consciousness: "No way have plants here/ arrived at a settlement." The highest compliment one could pay to this poem is to say it is unlikely a reader shown it afresh would ever guess it was by Heaney. The same could not be said of what is already one of the most popular poems in the volume, "The Conway Stewart." Here, a luxury pen is described in gnarled, tangy detail. The dialectical relation to Heaney's early "Digging," in which the poet resolves to do with his pen what his farmer father had done with a spade, is both evident and gratifying. "Hermit Songs," a long sequence of twelve-line poems, has an analogous, if more oblique, relation to Heaney's remarkable midcareer sequence "Alphabets." Heaney's form and meter are less discussed than they should be—the critical consensus considers him a poet of reference and diction—but these unrhymed stanzas—largely of eight beats but sometimes as few as seven and as much as nine—conjure a process of learning, which is both the poet's personal one and that of human culture as a whole, conducted through the remote rigors of medieval Ireland, as, like in the biological thesis of old, ontogeny recapitulates phylogeny. Motifs from other poems in the volume—Columcille, pencils and pens—reappear, but this poem stitches them into an ample, overall tableau.

A poet of Heaney's age will likely have many friends who have died. However, each of the elegies herein preserves its own terrain of experience. "Death of a Painter," in memory of Nancy Wynne-Jones, takes note of what Wynne-Jones's paintings were like—not only their colors and aura, but also the painter's own process and the landscape in which she worked—while drawing a general lesson about the courage and persistence needed to produce art that matters. A potentially dolorous note becomes more of a fitting tone, a suitable chord. When one can match language to mood this readily, serenity, even ebullience, becomes as fit a subject for verse as nostalgia and loss. "Canopy" was originally written in 1994, set amid an art installation in Harvard Yard. Its language of miracle and revelation is so buoyant that one can imagine a child enjoying it, and, properly anthologized, this could become a popular poem for elementary school children. If so, Heaney will have diligently schooled others as he himself was so diligently schooled and transmitted the wholesome cheer he has so clearly drawn from others and anchored in his own ingrained mastery, which persists in being astonishing.

Nicholas Birns

Review Sources

Booklist 107, no. 2 (September 15, 2010): 17.
Library Journal 135, no. 13 (August 1, 2010): 87.
New Statesman 139, no. 5018 (September 13, 2010): 45-47.
The New York Review of Books 57, no. 17 (November 11, 2010): 20-21.

The New York Times, September 17, 2010, p. 26.
The New York Times Book Review, September 26, 2010, p. 18.
Newsweek 156, no. 15 (October 11, 2010): 58.
Publishers Weekly 257, no. 32 (August 16, 2010): 36.
The Times Literary Supplement, October 15, 2010, p. 10.
The Washington Post, September 21, 2010, p. C03.

HUMORISTS
From Hogarth to Noël Coward

Author: Paul Johnson (1928-   )
Publisher: Harper (New York). 228 pp. $25.99
Type of work: Essays, fine arts, film, music

Johnson discusses creativity from eighteenth century painting and engraving through early film comedy to twentieth century fiction, art, and drama

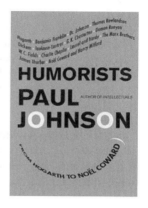

Since 1988, among his many other publications, conservative British Roman Catholic journalist and popular historian Paul Johnson, author of *Humorists*, has published four volumes of companion essays. Each illumines a specific way of behavior or thought dangerous to humankind, universal among humans, or valuable for human life. The first volume, which is the lengthiest at 342 pages of text, is *Intellectuals: From Marx and Tolstoy to Sartre and Chomsky.* In it, Johnson denounces intellectuals or experts who value ideas more than human lives and who create havoc among family members, lovers, and sometimes even whole populations. Among these figures, Johnson includes philosophers Jean-Jacques Rousseau and Karl Marx, novelist Leo Tolstoy, and playwrights Henrik Ibsen and Lillian Hellman.

More positively, in *Creators: From Chaucer and Durer to Picasso and Disney* (2006), Johnson explores some of creativity's many manifestations, from the works of the ancient Egyptian priest and architect Imhotep to the attitude of a London bus-ticket collector. To Johnson, creativity is universal because humans were created in God's own image. In a chapter that displays his remarkable ability to see similarities and differences across distance and genre, Johnson compares the use of nature in the art of Pablo Picasso to that of Walt Disney. Disney studied nature: He brought animals to his studio to help his cartoonists draw the musculature and motion found in life. Picasso instead reduced nature to the dimensions of his own ego. Johnson compares Disney, with his staff of cartoonists, to a seventeenth century painter such as Guido Reni, whose name made his work marketable although much work was done by assistants.

Heroes: From Alexander the Great and Julius Caesar to Churchill and De Gaulle (2007) similarly shows manifestations of heroism rather than defining the term, although the figures Johnson selects consistently show courage, concentration, and determination. Johnson finds his first heroes in the Bible, where, startlingly, he sees the biblical Samson, shorn of hair and strength by the treacherous Delilah, as the first Mideast suicide terrorist. He includes actors Mae West and Marilyn Monroe; gives a chapter to a society hostess; and, less surprisingly, includes U.S. president Ronald Reagan, British prime minister Margaret Thatcher, and Pope John Paul II.

∿

Paul Johnson began with the English liberal New Statesman. *By the 1970's, he had become a conservative and was an adviser to Conservative British prime minister Margaret Thatcher. President George W. Bush awarded him the Presidential Medal of Freedom in 2006.*

∿

Although Johnson claims that humorists are more valuable than intellectuals, creators, and heroes, *Humorists* is the shortest volume, with only 214 pages of actual text (excluding an introduction, a brief bibliographic essay, and an index) divided into fourteen chapters. As in the previous volumes, Johnson is erudite, opinionated, and idiosyncratic, but brevity creates problems. Developing tentative definitions of humor in his introduction, Johnson later divides humorists into those who attempt hopelessly to create order from chaos and those who turn whatever order they encounter into chaos. Nonetheless, Johnson's impressive knowledge of and affection for many humorists—including artists, writers, and talkers—makes it impossible for him to confine his discussion to specific categories.

Not surprisingly, Johnson's attempt to explain briefly the complex nature of humor works best with subjects whose approach to humor is relatively simple. His essay on Benjamin Franklin is excellent. In a few pages, Johnson brings Franklin to life as a businessman, political leader, inventor, publisher, and sensualist. As publisher of *Poor Richard's Almanack* (1732-1757), Franklin, Johnson writes, originated the use of the "one-liner, the quintessential form of American humor." (Actually, Franklin admittedly borrowed his proverbs from a variety of sources, adapting and polishing them.) Published under the pseudonym Richard Saunders, the almanac achieved a circulation of ten thousand, remarkable for its time and place. Johnson provides examples of Franklin's witty maxims and interesting information about early almanacs. Similarly excellent is a chapter on Damon Runyon, best known posthumously for the stories that became the musical *Guys and Dolls* (1950). Johnson rightfully compares Runyon with British humorist P. G. Wodehouse. In their different ways, both were remarkable prose stylists. Runyon turned the grim reality of Broadway into a kind of magic world populated by larger-than-life gamblers and gangsters (Hot Horse Herbie, The Lemon Drop Kid, Dave the Dude), much as Wodehouse transformed the nobility and already vanishing landed estates of England into a magic world where a nobleman's main concern might be not taxes but his prize pig.

Johnson's approach also works well with silent and early talking film comedy stars, in part because comedians of this era were vaudeville veterans who tested their material on live audiences before the invention of microphones. Of necessity, the successful among them learned to rely on instantly recognizable, and easily described, sight gags that would quickly establish their identities. W. C. Fields became the angry, prejudiced, and hard-drinking man who hated such manifestations of respectability as babies and dogs. Charles Chaplin invented the Little Tramp. Groucho Marx was identified by his moustache, glasses, and leers.

In his chapter on Noël Coward and Nancy Mitford, Johnson assumes that sexual warfare in the United States is the equivalent of class warfare in England. This may be why Johnson focuses on Chaplin's personal life and Stan Laurel and Oliver Hardy's many marriages, rather than on their concerted attacks on the forces of respectability. Mack Sennett's Keystone Studios, where Chaplin began his film career, was the home of the oafishly ineffective figures of authority, the Keystone Kops. The Marx Brothers rioted destructively through such bastions of middle- and upper-class respectability as department stores, transatlantic ocean liners, and the opera, places where the early film audiences, mostly working class and immigrant, would not have been welcomed.

Johnson also discusses visual art. Unfortunately for readers, the book contains no illustrations; one needs prior familiarity or other sources to follow Johnson's arguments. Johnson regards the eighteenth and early nineteenth century painter, printmaker, and pornographer Thomas Rowlandson as "England's most perfect artist." He appreciates Rowlandson's earthy humor; probably Rowlandson's best known work is "Exhibition Stare Case" (c. 1811), featuring the bare thighs and broad bottoms of ladies upset on a staircase at a Royal Academy of Art exhibit. Johnson's comments on printmaker and painter William Hogarth are inadvertently slightly deceptive. As Johnson points out, in Hogarth's works, a tragic or horrifying figure may be placed in the foreground, but figures surrounding it are comic. Then Johnson immediately cites Hogarth's best-known work, *Gin Lane* (1751); the reader may assume that the print illustrates Johnson's generalization. It does not. The central image is horrifying enough: A drunk woman sprawls on a steep staircase, her breasts bare. The child she has been nursing has fallen from her arms over the staircase; his face registers his terror. A corpse lies at the woman's feet. Other background figures include two young girls wearing the badges of a charity as they sip their gin, a woman quieting a child by forcing gin through a funnel down its throat, a hanged man, an advertisement for coffins, and a naked woman being placed in her coffin. A man holds a pole; a child is impaled upon it. As Johnson notes, Hogarth was a moralist; this is the angry art of a man involved in attempts to establish a foundling hospital for shelter of London's needy infants.

Less satisfactory are chapters in which Johnson attempts to briefly explain writers of considerable complexity. Johnson provides an excellent introduction to G. K. Chesterton's life and thoughts and talks about Chesterton's humor, quoting some of Chesterton's maxims. Primarily interested in Chesterton's beliefs after his 1922 conversion to Roman Catholicism, however, Johnson only superficially analyzes the nature of Chesterton's humor, a complex matter involving remarkable control of language, especially visual imagery, and a gift for paradoxes and multiple levels of meaning as in *The Man Who Was Thursday: A Nightmare* (1908), which is simultaneously a spy story, a detective story, a biblical parable, and pure fantasy. Johnson mentions Chesterton's poetry, citing a few stanzas, but makes little attempt to explain why the poetry is either humorous or good. Citing some lines from Chesterton's poem "The Rolling English Road" (*The Flying Inn*, 1914), Johnson regards them only as part of a drinking song; the poem actually shows a mature man wistfully remembering the outrageous behavior of his youth when the defiance of convention and even common sense represented the Englishman's traditional hatred of conformity. Johnson's readers need more development than he provides.

In the case of *The New Yorker* cartoonist and writer James Thurber, the situation, not the artist, is complex. In accepting Thurber's *The Years with Ross* (1959) as his primary source, Johnson does less than justice to the magazine's founder and first editor Harold W. Ross. While continually acknowledging his respect and affection for the editor, Thurber cannot resist the humorist's gift for exaggeration and presents Ross as a clownish yokel, a depiction resented by many of Ross's colleagues and friends and refuted by later writers. The reader is asked to take Thurber's portrayal at face value, not as comic exaggeration.

The most serious problem occurs with Charles Dickens, whose works are vast and their humor complex. Some characters fit into Johnson's categories. For example, in *Great Expectations* (1861), John Wemmick, Jr., completely separates his personal life from his dubious professional life. His home is quite literally his castle, complete with moat and cannon. His opposite is Wilkins Micawber (*David Copperfield*, 1850)—acted splendidly by Fields in Metro-Goldwyn-Mayer's 1935 film—whose financial optimism results in chaos. There is much more, however. Faced with such abundance, Johnson concentrates on *Pickwick Papers* (1837), in which Dickens's work is simplest, and then picks out a few of Dickens's techniques, such as his gift for naming characters and his running gags. Inexplicably, Johnson argues that Dickens found amusement in "disfigurement" and "disability," giving only the one-legged figure of Silas Wegg from *Our Mutual Friend* (1865) as evidence. He offers no evidence for his theory that, for Dickens, disability was a cause of evil. Dickens's own views are implicit in his fiction; for example, he shows tenderness toward the illiterate and unwanted crossing sweeper Jo in *Bleak House* (1853), and his views are explicit in *American Notes* (1842), written hastily after his return from the United States. There, he records his fascination with the education of Laura Bridgman, who lacked sight, hearing, and speech, commenting on the child's high moral character. He is sickened and disgusted, not amused, by fugitive slave advertisements, with their listings of maiming and mutilation as a way of identification.

Johnson admits that Dickens's characters were based on reality. Probably Dickens's reality is itself unimaginable to later generations. He did not need a specific model for Silas Wegg, as Johnson supposes. The wealthy might avoid some accidents and hide scarred victims at home, but, in the streets, Dickens would have seen the mutilated and amputated victims of the Napoleonic conflicts; of industrial accidents as London became modernized; of fires spread by candles and fireplaces; and of the collisions, in increasingly crowded streets, of humans with carts, carriages, and the flailing hooves of horses. Malnutrition and disease left their marks. Medicine could do little. Such figures as Jo and personifications of ignorance and want in *A Christmas Carol* (1843) are dangerous because of the possible blight they inadvertently spread, as Jo spreads smallpox. To Dickens, always a reformer, they represent the dangers of life itself if not corrected by human benevolence and social reform. They are not themselves malevolent.

In these books, Johnson's flaws and idiosyncracies may be weaknesses, but they point to Johnson's strengths, which include his profound courage in speaking his mind. Because he is deeply interested in his subjects and unconcerned with others' reactions, he writes with passion and vitality. His people are humans, not merely numbers in sociological or government surveys. As a result, Johnson brings them to life. Even when shocked by some of Johnson's conclusions, the reader may well find that Johnson's energy and love of life are, despite everything, somehow contagious.

Betty Richardson

Review Sources

Booklist 107, no. 7 (December 1, 2010): 12.
Publishers Weekly 257, no. 38 (November 27, 2010): 47.
The Wall Street Journal, November 20, 2010, p. C6.

IF THE DEAD RISE NOT

Author: Philip Kerr (1956-   )
Publisher: G. P. Putnam's Sons (New York). 437 pp.
    $26.95
Type of work: Novel
Time: 1934-1954
Locale: Berlin, Germany, and Havana, Cuba

*Bernie Gunther finds a reason to continue his troubled
life in the sixth novel of Kerr's noir mystery series, even as
he realizes that fighting evil has left him morally corrupted*

Principal characters:
    BERNIE GUNTHER, a private investigator in
        Berlin and former homicide detective
    MAX RELES, an American gangster
    NOREEN CHARALAMBIDES, an American writer
    DINAH CHARALAMBIDES, Noreen's nineteen-year-old daughter
    ALFREDO LÓPEZ, a Cuban lawyer and dissident
    MEYER LANSKY, an American gangster

If the Dead Rise Not, the sixth mystery novel in the Bernie Gunther series, opens
with a murder and draws to a close after another murder, both committed by Gunther.
The killings constitute the end points of a line of change in Philip Kerr's noir detective from a man of principles in an era of fascist inhumanity to a man who realizes that
his brushes with human evil have blackened his soul. It is the darkest novel of the series, yet it ends with a glimmer of purpose for Gunther, an unexpected reason to be
more than a mere survivor of political lunacy.

Gunther is among the most hard-boiled detectives in mystery fiction. The times
make him so. The novel opens in 1934 in Berlin, as the Nazi regime is preparing to put
on a showpiece Olympics in order to impress the world with Germany's superiority.
Gunther has been forced out of his job as a senior detective in Berlin's police department, KriPo, because he will not join the Nazi Party. He has become the house detective at the ritzy Adlon Hotel, where he is a steady, if thoroughly dismayed, German.
The cause for dismay is apparent everywhere. On the street Gunther listens to a man
loudly denounce the Nazis. Instead of squealing on this critic to the nearest policeman, as is Gunther's duty in the new Germany, Gunther walks away. However, a policeman notices this and tries to arrest him for it. The scene seems contrived despite
the atmosphere of paranoia and fear that Kerr evokes, but the outcome has a purpose.
Reacting with anger and disgust, Gunther sucker punches the policeman, who later
dies. While Gunther avoids arrest for the crime, it marks him. He feels outrage that
German politics have created the possibility of such an incident but also feels intense
guilt for having killed a man, even a Nazi toady. His attitude at this point is important

to a principle theme of the novel: the effects on conscience of compromise.

The compromises start with help from former KriPo colleagues, who are, at least, token Nazis. They provide him with an alibi so that, although a suspect, he is not arrested for killing the policeman. More important for his survival, he obtains forged papers that hide the fact that he had a Jewish grandmother.

Philip Kerr is the author of historical mysteries, thrillers, film scripts, and young adult books, as well as the Bernie Gunther series, and was the recipient of the Ellis Peters Historical Award.

Even being one-quarter Jew is dangerous in Germany, but this compromise with his identity is a step toward losing it and the conscience that comes with it.

With these secrets hanging over him, Gunther meets two Americans at the Adlon Hotel, both Jews but of polar opposite temperaments. The first is Noreen Charalambides. She is a playwright and journalist who has come to Germany to expose its official anti-Semitism and suppression of dissent in hopes that an article she plans to write will provoke an American boycott of the upcoming 1936 Berlin Olympics. The second is Max Reles, a Chicago mobster who bribes and threatens German businessmen and politicians so that he can receive lucrative construction contracts to build facilities for the Olympics.

Charalambides is a crusader, Reles a profiteer, and they naturally come into conflict—via Gunther. Charalambides hires him to investigate the deaths of Jewish workers hired illegally to build the Olympic stadium. He finds plenty of evidence and learns of Reles's role in corrupting Nazis on the German Olympic committee. He also learns that Reles is Jewish, something the gangster has to hide from his Nazi cohorts. What Gunther does not learn, until too late, is that Reles is aware of his investigations and has powerful friends among the German police. Reles has Gunther whisked away to a provincial prison to shut him up; when that fails, Reles kidnaps Gunther in order to murder him and dump his body in a harbor. Gunther, however, is always able to talk his way out of a fix. He makes a bargain with Reles: He agrees not to divulge Reles's Jewish heritage to the Nazi authorities (exactly how is a bit murky), and in return, Reles agrees not to act on his threat to have Noreen Charalambides killed.

Charalambides and Gunther have fallen in love. The end of the first part of the novel separates them. Charalambides goes back to the United States and her husband, while Gunther returns to private investigations in the knowledge that his pact with Reles is a step further into moral compromise, even if it saves his lover.

The second part opens twenty years later, in 1954, and in Havana, Cuba. Gunther is hiding there under a pseudonym, Carlos Hausner. He is trying to reinvent himself as a businessman when he runs into Charalambides. Now a celebrated author and a leftist under investigation by the U.S. House Un-American Activities Committee, she is staying in the house of her friend Ernest Hemingway (off hunting in Africa) to escape persecution. With her is her wild daughter, Dinah, who is nineteen. At this point, no one involved in the novel, reader or character, can fail to conclude that Dinah is Gunther's daughter except the world-weary detective himself. He has to be told by a friend (and sometimes lover) of Charalambides, Alfredo López, although the reader is not informed of this until almost the last page.

In the meantime, Gunther has also run into Reles, who co-owns a casino in Havana with Cuba's dictator, Fulgencio Batista y Zaldívar. Reles, who has always liked Gunther despite kidnapping him and trying to kill him, now offers him a job managing the casino. Reles is also engaged to Dinah. Kerr diverts readers from this sheer unlikeliness with a flashy backdrop of Cuban revolutionaries, Chinese celebrations, murderous militias, and American Mafia-run casinos. Kerr is brilliant at creating vivid settings.

By this point the theme of anti-Semitism that gave the novel's first part a chilling impact fades. Jewishness only appears in the persons of American gangsters who control many of the Havana casinos. Among them is the real-life kingpin Meyer Lansky. Gunther is not through making compromises with evil to survive—or help others do so—and here Lansky becomes important to the plot. Reles is mysteriously murdered. Not trusting the local police, Lansky hires Gunther to find the murderer, an offer he can hardly refuse. After a short, astonishingly perceptive examination of evidence and suspects, he succeeds. Lansky is impressed, too much so. He insists on hiring Gunther to run one of his Las Vegas casinos. Gunther finds himself doing deals with another devil, but it gets worse. A Cuban intelligence agent has discovered that Gunther is wanted for murder in Vienna and uses the fact to blackmail Gunther into spying on Lansky.

These events probably look toward the next novel in the series, but readers may well feel unsatisfied and confused near the end. It all seems so aimless. A final scene, however, firms up the motivations. Dinah has been sent packing to college in the United States, and Gunther has a frank talk with Charalambides. When she reveals to him that Dinah is his daughter, he admits to already knowing. He admits also to having killed Reles in order to stop Dinah from marrying him. He admits feeling no guilt about it, either. In a speech that summarizes the theme of compromise and corruption, Gunther says, essentially, that some people have to be murdered to allow better people to live. He recognizes, almost despairingly, what this has done to him: "I used to think I could stand apart from it. That I could somehow inhabit a nasty, rotten world and not become like that myself. But I found out you can't."

The Bernie Gunther novels are carried along primarily through two stellar qualities: first, the detective's personality, both romantically attractive and harshly wise, and, second, Kerr's remarkable capacity to re-create historical settings with visceral force. Plot plays a strong supporting role, usually. In *If the Dead Rise Not* it seems more a distraction. Readers may want to cheer Gunther for killing a man to save his daughter from a disastrous marriage, but all that has gone before the murder has to be overlooked if readers themselves do not want to feel corrupted by approving the chain of events. The murders are troubling even when they are for survival's sake. Not all of them appear justified, and there are a lot. Being around Gunther is not safe for friend or foe. In fact, the only characters who are safe are those based on historical persons (such as Hermann Göring, Juan Perón, Adolf Eichmann, and Lansky), whose murders would outrage the historical record.

It is not so much credibility that is strained by the novel as the reader's goodwill. At times Kerr seems almost to be kidding his audience. Gunther is super-hard-boiled. He so often and so hyperbolically "cracks wise," even to those about to maul or murder him, that he sounds like a parody. That and occasional scenes thrown in just for the sake of atmosphere take some of the edge off the moral dilemma that he faces as a maverick, smudged-white knight.

At the end of the story, when Gunther has become Lansky's employee and a stool pigeon for Cuban spy masters, he has his lingering love for Charalambides and his nascent concern for his daughter to move him forward in life despite all his compromises with evil. A large portion of the dialogue revealing his emotional state takes place in Hemingway's house, and during it Gunther sometimes descends into self-pity. That is almost understandable. He is a man apart and alone morally, emotionally, and intellectually. It is a pity, then, that Hemingway does not return before the end of the novel to give Gunther a punchy dose of masculine advice about the futility of keeping company with tyrants, mobsters, secret police, and crusaders. He needs a pal who cannot be killed off.

Roger Smith

Review Sources

Booklist 106 (January 1, 2010): 18.
Kirkus Reviews 78 (February 15, 2010): 105.
Library Journal 135 (February 1, 2010): 57.
Los Angeles Times, March 20, 2010, p. D10.
The New York Times Book Review, March 28, 2010, p. 26.
Publishers Weekly 257 (January 18, 2010): 28-29.
The Times Literary Supplement, June 11, 2009, p. 21.
The Washington Post, March 22, 2010, p. C2.

ILUSTRADO

Author: Miguel Syjuco (1976-   )
Publisher: Farrar, Straus and Giroux (New York).
  306 pp. $26.00
Type of work: Novel
Time: Last half of the twentieth century and the begin-
  ning of the twenty-first century
Locale: New York City, Vancouver, and Manila

*When famous expatriate and Filipino author Crispin
Salvador drowns mysteriously in the Hudson River, young
Filipino author Syjuco is determined to investigate both
his life and his death*

Principal characters:
  MIGUEL SYJUCO, aspiring young Filipino writer
  CRISPIN SALVADOR, legendary and world-famous Filipino author

This novel's intriguing title, *Ilustrado*, describes both of its major characters. Following in the footsteps of a nineteenth century group of cosmopolitan intellectuals
and activists in the Philippines known as the Ilustrado, or the "enlightened," the two
major characters in this novel—each a novelist and an intellectual—have similarly
gone abroad with the purpose of bringing back the advances of the world to the Philippines as well as to bring the Philippines into the modern world community.

The story tracks the struggles of the young Miguel Syjuco and the older, established Crispin Salvador in their efforts to revolutionize both the literature and the social fabric of their homeland through the written word. Even more powerful is the
metafictive way in which Syjuco makes central his novel's radical narrative strategies
and his own identity as an author, so that this innovative novel itself is representative
of the mission of a twenty-first century "Ilustrado," that is, Syjuco himself.

The novel's experimental narrative strategies are as important as traditional elements, such as character or turn of plot, so that the reader becomes transfixed by the
novel's processes as much as by its messages. Made up of a large number of different
story lines woven together into a patchwork pattern that is tenuously coherent,
Ilustrado challenges the reader to reconsider the premise of the entire novel form.

Throughout the novel, narrative continuity is sacrificed to a surfeit of fragments,
compared by the character of Miguel himself to a mirror that has been shattered
into many pieces. Despite this fragmentation, however, it is clear that one major
plotline concerns the life of the legendary Salvador, which is set as both a parallel
and a counterpoint to the story of young Miguel. Miguel's own story is further shattered into two perspectives, one told in an intimate first-person voice, the other in a
detached third-person voice. Miguel's unsettled childhood, love life, and identity are
further complicated by the reader's understanding that the fictional Miguel merges

easily into the author himself. Indeed, the entire novel mixes the factual and the invented in a disarming way, so that real history and real people are blended with imaginative possibilities and probabilities.

The novel also includes the fictional Miguel's own unfinished writing project, a biography of his mentor and teacher Crispin Salvador called *Eight Lives Lived*. Furthermore, Miguel is combing through Salvador's own autobiographical work *Autoplagiarist*, as well as samplings from Salvador's imaginative fiction, which further fragments the elusive Salvador into many different literary personae. His identity is shattered into that of thriller writer (*Manila Noir*), historical novelist (*Kaputol Trilogy*), socially conscious castigator of the Marcos regime (*Because of You*), sea-saga writer (*Master of the Seas*), and fantasy novelist, librettest, poet, and travel writer. Salvador's protean literary identity serves as a mirror for Miguel's own uncertain sense of self; but, in addition, all the possible types of work Salvador produces are exuberant examples of the kind of free-spirited creativity Syjuco admires and wishes for Filipino writing in general.

Miguel Syjuco received the 2008 Man Asian Literary Prize and the Philippines's highest literary honor, the Palanca Award, for the unpublished manuscript of Ilustrado. *Born and raised in Manila, he lives in Montreal.*

In addition to the welter of works by Salvador, Syjuco also includes newspaper articles and interviews, all of which are organized more as a collage than as a conventional narrative sequence. Additionally, Syjuco incorporates into his narrative new media, such as blogs, tweets, and emails, complete with its familiar companions, spam, bad spelling, and bad grammar. Syjuco not only saturates his text with various forms of written communication but also spends about four pages describing the content of the television channels as Miguel flips through them, adding to the reader's sense that the young, bemused Miguel is overloaded with information, but perhaps not with clear meaning.

Aware of the way his variety of narrative threads may tax the concentration of the reader, Syjuco will periodically lighten the mood through humor; the novel's beginning is an especially amusing look at the career of Salvador that becomes increasingly parodic of the career of any modern literary lion. Salvador himself is celebrated in this prefatory encomium as "the lion of Philippine Letters" in a way that manages to be both sincere and ironic. Syjuco will also often deploy humor with regard to the young Miguel's courtship of his maddening inamorata, Madison Liebling, who leads him on a merry chase. More promising perhaps is a Filipina named Sadie he meets at a nightspot in Manila called the Club Coup D'Etat, and who, providentially, was named after a redoubtable female character in one of Salvador's novels. Miguel also manages to father a daughter, who, rather like most of the other women in his life, has somehow got lost in the shuffle in a way that gives the absurdity of his situation a bittersweet edge.

The complicated, confusing quality of so much of Miguel's life lends its humorous treatment an angry edge; this anger is also present in the novel's satiric look at the ruling class of the Philippines and those who serve its interests. Miguel's acid humor can be suggested here by the way in which he notes that those who now serve the interests of the ruling class include the deferential, prosperous literati of Manila—who had formerly identified themselves as Maoists. Perhaps the most memorable use of humor in *Ilustrado*, however, is through its series of well-worn and sometimes raunchy Filipino jokes, most of which feature a legendarily gullible dupe named Erning and all of which serve as commentaries on what Philippine society finds funny and also what it takes seriously. The agile, antic manner in which Syjuco digresses into jokes and then returns to further the progress of Miguel's story is reminiscent of Laurence Sterne's classic narrative jumble *The Life and Opinions of Tristram Shandy, Gent* (1759-1767). However, Syjuco's stories-within-stories also call to mind the metafictive, metaphysical puzzles of Jorge Luis Borges.

Many characters come and go within what may seem to be a bricolage of bits and pieces, but the deeper story that is developed concerns the only two true enduring characters in *Ilustrado*, namely Miguel and his mentor Salvador. Although the genesis of this novel is Miguel's attempt to figure out Salvador, it is the younger, bewildered Miguel who emerges as this novel's major presence. To further confound things however, Miguel's hero Salvador functions not simply as a separate entity but as an alter ego for the thirty-three-year-old Miguel. Their identities merge into each other: Each was from a politically connected, privileged Filipino family; each was expected to be in the running as a future president of the country; each lives in voluntary exile in New York City; each has a distant daughter; and each is committed to enriching the literature of their homeland through experimentation and fearless social consciousness. In this way each resurrects the legacy of the Ilustrado in Filipino culture within a revised historical context that urgently requires national reform.

In carrying on Salvador's ambitions, Miguel is finally able to secure his vocation as an author, which suggests that at its heart this novel is a portrait of the artist. Miguel begins to shape his identity as both an author dedicated to the people of the Philippines and a global author who embraces the world. On his return to the Philippines, Miguel fulfills the purposes of Salvador's final bridge-burning novel, the vanished *The Bridges Ablaze*.

Because Miguel spent much of his childhood in Vancouver and at the Trump Tower in New York City when his activist, guardian grandparents were exiled for political reasons, his return to the Philippines after the death of Salvador becomes the occasion for his exposure of the selfish, cold, corrupt elite that has dominated Filipino life for many decades, perpetuating economic and social inequities as well as human-rights abuses. The moral insensitivity of the small circle of families who have ruled the country for years is especially revealed when Miguel interviews Salvador's pampered sister, Lena, whose cosseted existence is suggested by the two uniformed maids who take turns protecting her from the tropical heat by means of a large handheld fan. Lena becomes a symbol of the perpetuation of the Philippines' colonial past, which Miguel understands has sustained a situation in which destitute workers are exploited by wealthy and punitive employers. Miguel observes that the poor enjoy little protection either from the weather or by the police. For Miguel, the victimized poor bear witness to the criminality of the elite, who are invariably connected to various scams and scandals, and who preside indifferently over a society beset by drugs and other social problems, including terrorism.

Miguel's raised political consciousness is in some ways a return to his earlier troubled relationship with his domineering, politically powerful grandfather, known as Grapes, who had expected Miguel to follow in his footsteps and to rise even higher. Miguel's parents were murdered during a period of political unrest. Therefore, Grapes has become the formative influence in his life. Miguel's quest for the reasons behind Salvador's death leads him to rethink his home country and his identity as a Filipino.

As playful as this novel is on one level, it is also a book that engages seriously with politics. While avoiding the polemical or the didactic, *Ilustrado* follows in the footsteps of the earlier Ilustrados in Philippine history by approaching the novel as a vehicle for social change. As a result, Miguel's quest for Salvador's missing novel, *The Bridges Abaze*, said to have held the ruling class accountable for the evil concealed under its comfortable surface, has been realized not only in the quest of his character Miguel but also in the context of the novel.

As Miguel explores modern Manila, Syjuco includes Salvador's history of the modern Philippines, touching on his own family history but also on the colonial period, the Ilustrado-inspired fight for independence from Spain, and the Japanese occupation during World War II. Embedding Salvador in a historical context is yet another way Syjuco's story broadens the scope of his novel, lending it a certain epic quality. It is also one way Syjuco manages to persuade the reader that "world-famous Filipino writer" is not simply an imaginative construction, but somehow a real figure. Paradoxically, the presentation of this character is written is such a way as to lead the reader to believe there is such a Filipino author, while simultaneously suggesting contrariwise that he is a supreme fiction.

Salvador himself begins this story as a dead body, having been fished from the Hudson River as an apparent suicide and a possible murder victim. Thus, it seems Salvador, "the savior" of Philippine literature, has failed to fulfill his promise. Nonetheless, Salvador is reanimated as the novel unfolds, given new life by Miguel's postmodern assemblage of narratives. The reality of Salvador lives on in Miguel; this psychic convergence is *Ilustrado*'s deep subject, offering the reader a perfect explanation for its title, and is the means by which this fascinating, peripatetic novel finds its way home.

Margaret Boe Birns

Review Sources

Booklist 106, no. 15 (April 1, 2010): 24.
Library Journal 135, no. 3 (February 15, 2010): 91.
The New York Times, May 9, 2010, p. A12.
The New York Times Book Review (June 13, 2010): 8.
Publishers Weekly 257, no. 29 (July 26, 2010): 67.
The Times Literary Supplement (June 4, 2010): 21.
The Wall Street Journal, May 7, 2010, p. W12.

THE IMMORTAL LIFE OF HENRIETTA LACKS

Author: Rebecca Skloot (1972-   )
Publisher: Crown (New York). 370 pp. $26.00
Type of work: Science, biography
Time: The 1920's-2010
Locale: Primarily Baltimore, Maryland

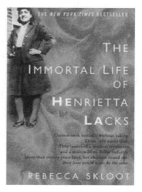

*A meticulously researched book on the ongoing exis-
tence of aggressive cancer cells that took the life of an
anonymous African American women in 1951*

Principal personages:
> HENRIETTA LACKS, the woman whose
> cancer cells have helped scientific
> research for decades
> DEBORAH, her daughter

For decades after Henrietta Lacks's death, her seemingly immortal cells have continued to reproduce. A young and vibrant wife and mother, Lacks died of cervical
cancer in 1951. Her abnormal cells, known in the scientific community as HeLa,
proved extraordinarily useful as well as lucrative to medical science. Before HeLa,
human cell cultures quickly died. Hers did not. They continue to generate millions of
dollars in profit. Lacks's heirs have never seen a penny from her cells. The book includes excellent and generous notes; Rebecca Skloot has carefully documented her
story, the story of her cells, and the ongoing saga of the surviving family.

A poor African American tobacco farmer with a houseful of children, Lacks went
to Johns Hopkins physicians in hopes of eliminating her cervical cancer. Although
treatment at the charity hospital for nonwhite patients was initiated, the aggressive
cancer did not respond. The plan of care was appropriate to the time, but the disease
had advanced too far to stop its growth. Lacks died, with severe radiation burns. She
left husband David, her children, a large extended family, and a sample of her
extraordinary tissue.

The cells from the malignancy proved to be more viable than their unlucky host.
They were given to a scientist, Dr. George Gey, who had been attempting unsuccessfully to grow human cells. Nevertheless, he was able to get this new crop of cells to
grow in vitro as vigorously as they had grown in vivo of Lacks. This was the first time
researchers had been able to keep human cells alive and reproducing. The medical
breakthrough that HeLa represented continues to be an efficacious and profitable tool
for research. For a price, researchers can order a batch of the cells for their own use.
Gey, who was responsible for this marvelous research tool, never profited from his
work. He gave the cells away, even in the face of financial exigency in his own life.
Never a rich man, he experienced periods when he could not even pay the mortgage.

Although much has been made of the fact that the tissue was taken from the patient

~

A prolific and award-winning science writer, Rebecca Skloot holds a degree in biological sciences and an MFA in creative nonfiction. The Immortal Life of Henrietta Lacks *is her first book.*

~

without her permission, consent has never been required for disposition of tissue obtained from surgery. Placentas, appendices, and other surgical detritus are considered waste material. Generally they are examined by the hospital pathologist and discarded. In some cases such biological by-products have proven useful for medical advances. Lacks's case is not the only one of its kind; Skloot documents a similar situation in the case of the removal of a California patient's spleen more than thirty years after the Lacks case.

The issue of financial benefit from Lacks's cells continues to be raised. Her heirs are the antithesis of a Norman Rockwell American family. Since many of them live at a subsistence level and often without health care, there is considerable irony in the fact that millions of dollars have been made on Lacks's genetic material. Those who carry her genes have not seen one cent of that windfall. Decades passed before the family even knew of the continued existence of their mother, in her extraordinary cells. Not only is this famous woman buried in an unmarked grave, but also her family is "unmarked" with the monies her cells have generated.

The first portion of the book, titled "Life," is not about the cells but about the person. Lacks was a tiny woman, just five feet tall. Her photograph, displayed on the book's dust cover, shows a happy, vital lady with her hands posed confidently on her hips. Although she had only a sixth- or seventh-grade education, she was the person who discovered the "knot" in her cervix. Although she was barely thirty, her life had already been a chronicle of pain. Her mother died when she was a child, which caused her and her siblings to be distributed among relatives to be raised. She milked cows, worked in the tobacco fields, and endured the stifling summer heat in tiny Clover, Virginia.

Even though science is her professional specialty, Skloot does not limit her account to the story of the HeLa cells themselves. She thickens the scientific account skillfully with a real-life story. She demands that the reader first know the woman from whom the cells were removed. As Lacks lay buried for decades, so did the human source of the vital material that proved to be such a scientific bonanza. Skloot ushers Lacks from behind the curtain of anonymity—the cells had been attributed for years to a number of fictitious persons (Helen Lane, Helen Larson). The reader walks with Lacks through her childhood, her marriage and motherhood (including the story of an institutionalized epileptic daughter who died shortly after Lacks), her relationships, and, finally, her horrendous death. The HeLa cells are no longer a disembodied scientific curiosity; they have coalesced into a palpable person. The reader comes to know Lacks.

The second part of the book, "Death," narrates Lacks's second life: the amazing survival of her cells. A riveting section concerns what happened just after her death. Gey requested an autopsy of the body stored in the "'colored' freezer." He hoped to obtain samples of the dead woman's other organs, those not from the primary cervical cancer. The author describes in detail the gruesome process of dissecting organs covered ubiquitously with small pearly tumors.

Soon after, the National Foundation for Infantile Paralysis contributed monies to build a factory to reproduce the precious HeLa cells. They would be used to test the vaccine for polio, a debilitating and sometimes deadly disease of the mid-twentieth century. The first yield from an ongoing financial gold mine was realized.

The third section of the book is, interestingly, "Immortality." The book chronicles not only the medical history of Lacks and her cancer cells, but also it tells the story of her large and extended family. One of the most interesting vignettes concerns how the family found out that Lacks's cells were still alive, decades after her death. In 1973, through an unlikely series of coincidences, Lacks's daughter-in-law learned that a researcher was using HeLa cells in his lab. He had gotten them from a research supplier, as had many others for years. The family's reaction was paranoia. If they took the cells from the mother, how long will it be "before they come for Lacks's children, and maybe her grandchildren."

The notorious Tuskegee syphilis study made many poor black families wary of medical studies and research. Skloot encountered this attitude when she first contacted the family. She was viewed as just another white person come to exploit the family—probably for money. It took her a long time to build the bond that would translate into a book that was more than a disinterested science report.

The author devoted many years to her work, some of which were spent interviewing the remaining members of Lacks family. While the family was initially resistant to her intrusion, she became more than an external observer. She spent many days and sometimes even nights with family members. She researched hospital documents and records connected with Lacks and her many relatives living and dead. She visited the grave of Lacks's mother and walked on the streets where Lacks had walked.

One of the incidents Skloot relates concerns her ongoing relationship with Lacks's youngest daughter, Deborah. When Skloot began her research, Deborah was in her sixties. Deborah's approach to the revelation about her mother was mixed. On one hand, she had many sober questions about her mother's illness, her ongoing "life," and its contributions to science as well as about the implications for her own health. On the other hand, she feared that her mother's cells felt the effects of the diseases they were employed to study. At times Deborah believed her mother to be, in some sense, alive and capable of feeling the pain and other accompanying effects of AIDS, Ebola, and other diseases. She had read that her mother's cells had been used for researching cures for these diseases. She vacillated between a cooperative and friendly attitude toward the author and a paranoid and distrustful stance. Skloot stuck with Deborah through her bouts with depression, hysteria, and a severe cases of hives. The author once even came to blows with Lacks's daughter, and she was present when Deborah was exorcized. By the time the book was published, Deborah had died.

The rich back story of this dysfunctional Southern clan will rivet readers. The family saga tells not only the story of Lacks's unfortunate daughter, Elsie, who was committed to a state hospital for "idiocy," but also other dirty laundry, including incest, crime, and addiction. In places, the book reads like a novel, rather than a work of nonfiction.

The book includes dog-eared, sepia pictures of Lacks and color photos of her surviving relatives; scenes of where she lived; and people involved early in the scientific project that the HeLa cells spawned. The author handles deftly the different threads of her research. She uses language that is accessible to an audience beyond the scientific community. She maintains a delicate membrane of objectivity with the family, even as she is drawn into their lives. This is a gripping story of the complex and often tragic Lacks family, of the birth and ongoing life of the HeLa cells, and of the scientific world that continues to use the cells, seeking cures and knowledge. As the chapter groupings suggest, this is a story of life, death, and immortality.

Dolores L. Christie

Review Sources

Booklist 106 (December 1, 2009): 18.
Kirkus 78 (January 1, 2010): 37.
Library Journal 134 (December 15, 2009): 130-131.
Nature 463 (February 4, 2010): 610.
The New York Times, February 3, 2010, p. 1.
The New York Times Book Review, February 7, 2010, p. 20.
Publishers Weekly 256 (October 5, 2009): 40.
Science News 177 (March 27, 2010): 30.

IMPERFECT BIRDS

Author: Anne Lamott (1954-   )
Publisher: Riverhead Books (New York). 278 pp. $25.95
Type of work: Novel
Time: Early twenty-first century
Locale: Landsdale, California

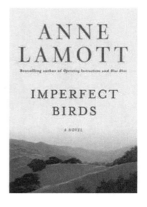

Lamott's bittersweet story of an accomplished seventeen-year-old young woman who is a drug abuser explores the effects of her addiction and deceptive behavior on her relationship with her unsuspecting parents

Principal characters:
> ROSIE, a high school senior who leads a double life as a model teenager and a drug abuser
> ELIZABETH, Rosie's mother and a recovering alcoholic
> JAMES, a writer and Rosie's stepfather
> RAE, Elizabeth's best friend
> LANK, Rae's husband
> JODY and ALICE, Rosie's best friends
> FENN, a drug dealer and Rosie's boyfriend

Shortly after her novel *Crooked Little Heart* was published in 1997, Anne Lamott told Malcolm Jones, Jr., of *Newsweek* that main characters Elizabeth, James, and Rosie "were closest to my heart. And of course secretly facets of myself." The trio was first introduced in Lamott's second novel, *Rosie*, published in 1983. The plot revolves around widow Elizabeth Ferguson and her bright young daughter of the title. After the sudden death of her wealthy husband, Andrew, in a car accident, Elizabeth tries to assuage her grief in alcohol while leaving Rosie to fend for herself. When Rosie becomes friends with Sharon Thackery, Sharon's mother provides Rosie with the parental love she lacks in her own home. Meanwhile, Elizabeth finds companionship with Rae, a bohemian weaver. Recognizing that Elizabeth's alcoholism is a symptom of depression, Rae suggests that they go on a camping trip, where they meet fellow hikers James, a writer, and Lank, a teacher. James and Elizabeth connect on a deep level when they discover they share similar tastes in reading. Eccentric, compassionate, and caring, James supplies the emotional support Elizabeth and Rosie have lacked since Andrew's death, which helps Elizabeth to achieve sobriety.

In *Crooked Little Heart*, Elizabeth is happily married to James. Thirteen-year-old Rosie is struggling with the trials of adolescence in spite of her achievements as a young tennis champion. Her insecurities, especially those concerning her body image and budding sexuality, are exacerbated by her friendship with her buxom tennis part-

Anne Lamott has written several novels, including Hard Laughter *(1980) and* Crooked Little Heart *(1997). She is also a nonfiction writer; her book* Traveling Mercies: Some Thoughts on Faith *was published in 1999.*

ner, Simone, who becomes pregnant. The pressure to succeed in tennis and her own teenage angst lead her to lose confidence in her abilities and to cheat. She is confronted by Luther, a down-and-out former tennis star, who helps her come to terms with her self-doubt and indiscretions.

In both novels, Lamott explores crucial issues as Rosie travels from childhood to early adolescence. In *Rosie*, she focuses on the impact of the death of a family member, the ramifications of alcohol addiction, and the repercussions of sexual abuse. In *Crooked Little Heart*, Lamott examines the bumpy transition to adolescence, dealing with loss, morality in competitive sports, and the challenges of parenting in a changing world. *Imperfect Birds* echoes themes from the previous two books in the trilogy but also incorporates the new elements of teenage drug addiction, promiscuity, and rebellion.

Seventeen-year-old Rosie and her family live in a toney small town in the San Francisco area where yoga studios, health food stores, and coffee bars dot the landscape. The atmosphere of carefree affluence, however, masks a dark underside that nobody wants to acknowledge. Lamott exposes it in an ominous opening paragraph: "There are so many evils that pull on our children. Even in the mellow town of Landsdale, where it is easy to see only beauty and decency, a teenager died nearly every year after a party and children routinely went from high school to psych wards, halfway houses, or jail. Once a year a child from the county of Marin jumped off the Golden Gate Bridge." Carefully cultivating various self-images—"punk, funk, hippie, straight"—the teens of Marin County live double lives, but their parents rarely catch on unless a disastrous event occurs. James and Elizabeth are among their number.

Elizabeth's character has changed little since *Crooked Little Heart.* She is a devoted wife and overprotective mother who loves to garden, to cook organic gourmet food, and to hang out with her best friend, Rae. Still sober, she attends Alcoholics Anonymous meetings. She does not work and, approaching fifty, has no desire to find a job. She loves James, but her world revolves around Rosie. In spite of her discovery of Rosie's secret journal entries detailing her sexual exploits and the rolling papers she finds in Rosie's purse, nothing shakes Elizabeth's conviction that her gorgeous daughter is a "good kid."

James is more realistic about Rosie's risky behavior, but only slightly so. He also loves her but is quicker than Elizabeth to see that she is headed for trouble. Although James occasionally sets boundaries for Rosie, his preoccupation with his writing career, which includes a weekly stint as a radio commentator on National Public Radio, prevents him from effectively curtailing his stepdaughter's increasingly out-of-control conduct.

If Elizabeth and James are in denial about Rosie's troubling lifestyle, Rosie is also in denial about how successfully she is deceiving her parents. She is a strikingly beautiful young woman, a straight-A student, a vacation Bible school volunteer, and a talented tennis player who hopes to gain admittance to an Ivy League school. She is also an accomplished liar and a master manipulator who experiments with cocaine, marijuana, mushrooms, and Ecstasy; washes down her drugs with alcohol; and is intent on seducing one of her high school teachers. Her cocksure attitude combined with her frequent disdain concerning James and Elizabeth's naiveté is in stark contrast to the charmingly precocious young girl introduced in *Rosie* and the insecure adolescent of *Crooked Little Heart.*

Rosie's choice of friends only serves to drag her deeper into addiction and deceit. Jody, though "rehabbed," occasionally takes drugs. Alice feeds Rosie's habit by slipping her Adderall, and Fenn, Rosie's boyfriend, is a dealer. The three are members of a larger group of young people who frequent the Parkade, a large parking lot in the center of town, where drugs are bought and sold. James and Elizabeth rationalize Rosie's drug abuse, trying to persuade themselves that Rosie's reckless behavior will pass. Even when Rosie is arrested at a party in the hills surrounding the Parkade, Elizabeth is still reluctant to admit that her daughter has a drug problem. Nonetheless, she forces Rosie to adhere to strict curfews, attend support groups, and submit to regular home drug tests. Rosie, who knows how to mask evidence of drugs in her system, goes along but continues to abuse drugs and often skips meetings to be with Fenn. When Rosie's grades begin to slip, Elizabeth talks to one of Rosie's teachers and then confronts Rosie, who sweetly replies:

> Mommy . . . it's humiliating that you called . . . I'm happier than I've ever been. I'm doing fine in school. I gave you a clean urine test. I'm going to meetings with Fenn. Will you please be a little happy for me? . . . I'm a good kid, Mom.

In spite of Rosie's reassurances, Elizabeth and James know she's lying. Finally accepting that Rosie's problem is bigger than the three of them can handle, the parents make the emotionally difficult and financially demanding decision to send her to a rehabilitation wilderness camp in Utah to cure her of her habit.

Lamott is a recovering alcoholic and former addict herself. Therefore her comment that Rosie, James, and Elizabeth are "secretly facets of myself" is no surprise given that she often draws on her own experience to create her fictional characters. Her three spiritual memoirs, *Traveling Mercies: Some Thoughts on Faith* (2000), *Plan B: Further Thoughts on Faith* (2006), and *Grace (Eventually)* (2007), detail her recovery from addiction, offer insight into her growth as a writer, and reveal the challenges she has faced as a single parent. She draws on those experiences—with varying success—to portray Rosie's addiction and Elizabeth and James's struggle to come to terms with their daughter's deceptive behavior.

One of the hallmarks of Lamott's writing is her penchant for unflinchingly telling the truth as she sees it. Her intimate portrayal of Rosie and her friends certainly reflects the raw realities of her own bout with drug abuse. Rosie is the poster child for teenage addiction as she straddles the line between the sunny world of the "good kid" her parents believe her to be and the dark existence of a child trapped by the Parkade drug culture. James compares the plight of the drug abuser to "dancing with an eight-hundred pound gorilla: you were done dancing when the gorilla was done." Rosie and her friends are so enthralled by the gorilla's monkeyshines that they not only deceive their parents about their habit but also lie to themselves.

Rosie, however, is not the only one who is in denial about her drug use. Elizabeth and James catch on slowly—too slowly in terms of character and plot development. A few pages into the story, after Elizabeth reads in Rosie's diary that she has tried marijuana and cocaine, she refuses to engage in speculation about "grisly teenage possibilities" and chooses to believe that Rosie "had apparently dodged a bullet when it came to drugs." As the narrative progresses, James and Elizabeth continue to reject the likelihood that Rosie is a user, even when circumstances strongly point to that reality. The reader wonders how the two parents could so blind themselves to the facts, even taking into consideration their pride in their daughter. Elizabeth's lack of awareness is particularly puzzling given that she resorted to similar subterfuge while she was addicted to alcohol. Finally, when Elizabeth writes to Rosie in Utah, she looks at the list she made of Rosie's lies and betrayals and wryly confesses to James, "It's starting to occur to me that our child *may* have had a little problem." Although her admission indicates a turning point in Elizabeth's attitude, it comes too late in the novel to make much of a difference in Rosie's recovery.

Community and connectedness are frequent themes in Lamott's work, and the community of the family is often an important influence on her characters. Elizabeth and James obviously care about their daughter's welfare, but they are also afraid that if they discipline Rosie too harshly they will lose her love. Their reluctance to intervene in Rosie's life contributes to her downward spiral. In contrast, Jody's family is much more involved in her rehabilitation and recovery, even though Jody sometimes relapses. Elizabeth and James's hesitancy to recognize that Rosie has a problem is in stark contrast to the way Rosie views Jody's home life:

> Rosie liked watching Jody's family because you could see that they cared about one another. They pulled together for Jody, like a web around her. She felt a pang of jealousy, because she had such a tiny pathetic family herself, but she was relieved that the parents stepped in . . . Jody had been on perilous ground before . . . now she was back and people wanted her to be safe and well, and maybe they felt like if they were toxic and fake around her, she would get sick again. So they reflected their very best at her and she was reflecting it back.

On a deeper psychological level, Rosie realizes that she requires somebody to administer the tough love her parents are incapable of providing to help her face the truth of her addiction. She finally gets what she needs when she participates in the wilderness rehabilitation program.

In Utah, Rosie meets belligerent young addicts such as herself who rebel against the demanding outdoor regimen of hiking in the snow, eating spartan meals, and learning to make fire by rubbing sticks together. As Rosie struggles with symptoms of withdrawal and the arduous physical challenges of the camp, she lashes out at her comrades and counselors. After one such episode, Bob, one of her advisers, says, "We're not drug bounty hunters. This is a place where we try to leave you better off than we found you. That's all we can do. And no matter what, we love you."

Although some of her characters are two-dimensional—most notably Elizabeth and James—Lamott offers astute insight into what it is like to be a teenage drug abuser. She also explores the ways in which a community can either help or hinder an addict as he or she struggles to kick the habit. Her heart-wrenching tale of a young woman trying to liberate herself from addiction offers a disturbing yet hopeful portrait of what it means to live and love honestly and truly, even when it hurts.

Pegge Bochynski

Review Sources

America 73, no. 14 (April 26, 2010): 38-39.
Booklist 106, no. 11 (February 1, 2010): 6.
The Christian Science Monitor 78, no. 2 (April 15, 2010).
Entertainment Weekly, no. 1097 (April 9, 2010): 79.
Kirkus Reviews 135, no. 3 (January 15, 2010): 59.
The New York Times Book Review, May 25, 2010, p. 22.
Library Journal 257, no. 4 (February 15, 2010): 90.
People 175, no. 14 (April 12, 2010): 55.
Publishers Weekly 202, no. 13 (January 25, 2010): 90-91.
Time, April 12, 2010, p. 72.

THE IMPERFECTIONISTS

Author: Tom Rachman (1974-   )
Publisher: Dial Press (New York). 272 pp. $25.00
Type of work: Novel
Time: 1953-2007
Locale: Rome, Paris, Geneva, Cairo, and Atlanta

This book charts the lives of the staff members of an English-language newspaper in Rome at work and at home

> *Principal characters:*
> LLOYD BURKO, a Paris correspondent
> ARTHUR GOPAL, an obituary writer
> HARDY BENJAMIN, a business reporter
> HERMAN COHEN, a corrections editor
> KATHLEEN SOLSON, an editor in chief
> WINSTON CHEUNG, a Cairo stringer candidate
> RICH SNYDER, Cheung's competition
> RUBY ZAGA, a copy editor
> CRAIG MENZIES, a news editor
> ORNELLA DE MONTERECCHI, a loyal reader of the newspaper
> ABBEY PINNOLA, a chief financial officer
> CYRUS OTT, the founder of the newspaper
> BOYD OTT, his son and successor as publisher
> OLIVER OTT, Boyd's son and successor
> BETTY LIEB, the original news editor
> LEO MARSH, the original editor in chief
> DARIO DE MONTERECCHI, Kathleen's former lover and Ornella's son
> JIMMY PEPP, Herman's lifelong friend

Newspapers are endangered species in the Internet age, with publications all over the world struggling to compete. *The Imperfectionists*, Tom Rachman's first novel, takes a comic look at one such newspaper, an unnamed English-language periodical based in Rome whose mostly American staff consists of eccentrics and ne'er-do-wells. The paper's fate is doomed from the beginning of the novel because it has stubbornly chosen not to have a Web edition. Rachman combines the details of the newspaper's daily routine with those of his expatriate characters using irony and pathos.

The Imperfectionists consists of eleven chapters, each focusing on a different character and serving as self-contained stories, with brief glimpses of the history and development of the paper between chapters. Characters mentioned in passing in the early chapters receive full exposure later on, with narrative strands overlapping and Rachman presenting his protagonists from multiple perspectives.

Unable to come up with any ideas for stories, Paris correspondent Lloyd Burko is tricked by his son, who claims to have a high government post, into filing a false story and subsequently loses his job. Obituary writer Arthur Gopal experiences a family tragedy that spurs him to become one of the few characters to improve his status. Business reporter Hardy Benjamin is unlucky in love. Corrections editor Herman Cohen delights in mistakes his three copy editors let slip. Editor in chief Kathleen Solson longs for Dario, a former lover. Auditioning for a stringer post

Tom Rachman was born in London in 1974 and grew up in Vancouver. After studying film at the University of Toronto, he received a master's degree in journalism from Columbia University in 1998.

in Cairo, young Winston Cheung allows himself to be duped by veteran foreign correspondent Rich Snyder. While the private life of copy editor Ruby Zaga is a disaster, she consoles herself through knowing she is good at her job. Pudgy, bald news editor Craig Menzies is embarrassed when the entire staff receives a nude photograph of his much younger lover, Annika. Dario's mother, Ornella de Monterecchi, is several years behind in her reading of the paper. Chief financial officer Abbey Pinnola is humiliated by an employee she has just had fired. Publisher Oliver Ott is lazy and ineffectual, unable to halt the paper's demise.

Between these stories Bachman builds a history of the paper, started on an apparent impulse by Oliver's millionaire grandfather, Cyrus Ott, in 1953. Cyrus abandons his family in Atlanta to live alone in Rome, building an art collection to impress Betty Lieb, his first news editor, with whom he is secretly in love. Betty and her husband, Leo Marsh, the editor in chief, are oblivious to Cyrus's motivations.

The Imperfectionists is as much about the vagaries of romance as it is about the newspaper business. Lloyd Burko's much younger wife, his fourth, has a French lover who lives across the hall. At seventy, Lloyd is finished with sex. Kathleen lives with Dario when in her twenties, leaves him and Rome, and returns years later with some regrets only to discover her former lover is no longer sexually attracted to her.

Meanwhile, Nigel, Kathleen's house husband, commits adultery. Ruby secretly loves Dario, and rather than spend New Year's Eve alone, she checks into a hotel and pretends to be a businesswoman stuck overseas for the holidays. Ornella's beloved husband goes mad and tries to choke her to death. She hides from the present to remain in the past with him. Against her better judgment Abbey decides to have sex with her fired employee with disastrous results. Oliver's family fears he is gay because he does not have a girlfriend, but he is too passive to contemplate romance with anyone.

Bachman's protagonists are relentlessly out of touch with their times. Lloyd has no computer, using a 1993 word processor instead. For Ornella the world has not changed since 1994: "Modern technology is not allowed in her house." Herman's rationale for not having an online presence is that "The Internet is to news what car horns are to music."

The characters in *The Imperfectionists* lead sad, little lives, recalling the pathetic self-deception of T. S. Eliot's "The Love Song of J. Alfred Prufrock" (1915). For Lloyd the grandeur of Paris "resides elsewhere. His own is smaller, containing himself, this window, the floorboards that creak across the hall." He is so out of touch with his milieu that he cannot recognize half the names in a French current-affairs magazine. If he does not earn money soon, he will lose his apartment, his refuge, and his unfaithful wife.

The son of a famous journalist, Arthur is forced to perform menial tasks he despises: "His overarching goal at the paper is indolence, to publish as infrequently as possible, and to sneak away when no one is looking." His goal is to live a quiet life of simple pleasures without anything unpleasant happening. Kathleen sends him to Geneva to interview a dying writer, making him extremely uneasy about confronting his subject with her impending death.

Thirty-six-year-old Hardy, "pinkish, geeky, [and] short," has been on a diet since she was twelve. A young man to whom she is kind steals her belongings at a police station after they have been recovered from other thieves, one of several instances in which Rachman twists a commonplace occurrence into an absurdity.

Herman has contributed 18,238 entries to the paper's style guide in an effort to impose order on a world stubbornly resistant to his conception of the way things should be. Disappointed in his own life, Herman has always considered his boyhood friend Jimmy Pepp the more talented of the two, expecting him to become a famous writer. When Jimmy visits, Herman learns the sad truth, while his friend praises him for having done "useful work."

On the other hand, Dario challenges Kathleen's choices: "Couldn't you have done better than the paper?" Kathleen, Dario, and Ruby all worked there together when they were younger, but only Ruby has remained throughout at the only job she has ever had. However, she has never truly fit in, and her fellow copy editors are repulsed by her attempts at humor. No one notices that she is the only one actually doing the work for which she is paid. She fears considering a future outside the newsroom. Ruby sadly inserts herself into tourists' photographs to achieve a sort of immortality in their pictures.

Insecure Craig, whose only friend is Arthur, is the first to arrive at work and the last to leave; his devotion to the paper creates a barrier between him and any other possible existence. Like Ruby, he is stuck: "I have no alternative to this life." Ornella begins reading every word in the paper in 1976, when her ambassador husband is posted to Saudi Arabia. Her reading is so slow that she has reached only 1994 by 2007. In "her slow drift from the present," she is puzzled by references to events she has not yet encountered. Oliver Ott, who never reads the paper he publishes, thinks he can hide from his responsibilities, only to have the ugly truth disrupt his life.

Miscommunication is a consistent theme. One of Lloyd's daughters refuses to speak to him in English, and his son speaks little of his father's native language. Arthur's cubicle is moved away from the water fountain so that his bosses do not have to speak with him. Herman has spent a lifetime misreading his best friend's character. Craig refuses to learn Italian even though his lover is a native of Rome.

The Herman Cohen chapter is one of the best in *The Imperfectionists* because Herman learns painfully necessary truths about himself and the life he has considered disappointing. Likewise, Arthur Gopal is strengthened by a shocking turn in his existence. The best and most comic episode is Winston Cheung's. He has no clue how journalism works but simply wants an interesting job; veteran reporter Rich Snyder takes advantage of his innocence, manipulating the young man into doing his bidding, such as library research, treating him more as a servant than a rival. Much of the humor comes from the fiftyish Snyder's talking like a much younger person, freely injecting "like" into his comments and saying things such as "Dude, let's commit some journalism."

Humor also occurs in Rachman's use of newspaper headlines as chapter titles. Such headings as "World's Oldest Liar Dies at 126," "Europeans Are Lazy, Study Says," "Global Warming Good for Ice Creams," and "The Sex Lives of Islamic Extremists" help establish the comic tones of the chapters. The ways in which the chapter plots tie in with their titles exemplify Rachman's consistent cleverness.

The Imperfectionists is part of a venerable Anglo-American tradition of comical expatriate novels, many of which deal directly or indirectly with journalists. The travails of Americans and British abroad appear in Anthony Powell's *Venusberg* (1932), Evelyn Waugh's *Scoop* (1938), Joyce Cary's *Mister Johnson* (1939), Kingsley Amis's *One Fat Englishman* (1962), Paul Theroux's *Saint Jack* (1973), William Boyd's *Stars and Bars* (1984), and Martin Amis's *Money: A Suicide Note* (1984).

Like his predecessors, Rachman can be somewhat dyspeptic at times, treating his characters as ironic victims of his whims. The deaths of two loved ones, coming within the novel's comic context, are a bit jarring. Rachman creates a formula for each chapter, building slowly toward the humiliation of a character, and the repetition of this pattern might make some readers uneasy. The pattern is broken occasionally, as when Ornella tosses her newspapers into a chaotic pile to demonstrate her new freedom from the past.

What is finally significant, however, is that Rachman writes firmly in the tradition of the British comedy of manners, especially as practiced by Waugh, in which characters commit follies because they make false assumptions about themselves and others, especially in matters of the heart. In his hands the decline of print news merges with the ineffectuality of characters unable or unwilling to understand the increasing complexities of the modern world. Rachman's skills at delineating the daily routines of his characters at work and at home and his talent for comic dialogue invigorate *The Imperfectionists*.

Michael Adams

Review Sources

The Economist 395 (May 15, 2010): 91.
Kirkus Reviews 77 (December 1, 2009): 26.
Library Journal 135 (January 1, 2010): 92.

The New York Times, May 6, 2010, p. C1.
The New York Times Book Review, May 2, 2010, p. 1.
The New Yorker 86 (May 3, 2010): 77.
Publishers Weekly 256 (November 30, 2009): 25.
The Times Literary Supplement, April 9, 2010, p. 21.
The Washington Post, May 1, 2010, p. C3.

THE INFINITIES

Author: John Banville (1945-   )
First Published: 2009, in England
Publisher: Alfred A. Knopf (New York). 279 pp. $25.95
Type of work: Novel
Time: Indeterminate
Locale: Irish countryside

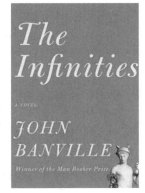

The relatives of an internationally famous mathematician gather at the family home in the Irish countryside awaiting his death after he has been felled by a stroke

> *Principal characters:*
> ADAM GODLEY, the patriarch of the family, who lies in a coma after succumbing to a stroke
> URSULA GODLEY, his distraught, alcoholic wife
> ADAM GODLEY II, his ungainly, self-doubting son, who worries about his wife's devotion and his mother's emotional health
> HELEN GODLEY, the actor wife of Adam II
> PETRA GODLEY, the psychologically disturbed daughter of Adam Godley
> HERMES, the messenger god from Greek antiquity
> ZEUS, Hermes's father
> BENNY GRACE, Pan in human disguise
> RODDY WAGSTAFF, Petra's feckless boyfriend who seeks to become Adam's biographer

John Banville's *The Infinities* begins somewhat elliptically with the nameless narrator announcing that he has delayed the dawn so that his father can make love to a sleeping Helen while her husband putters about in the kitchen. Gradually the narrator identifies himself as the god Hermes, and his father is Zeus, up to his old tricks of seducing humans. The family of Adam Godley, a theoretical mathematician who has suffered a debilitating stroke and lies comatose in his bedroom, has gathered at their country estate somewhere in Ireland.

Gradually each member of the Godley family is introduced: son Adam, a large, self-conscious man who doubts his wife's love; his wife Helen, a beautiful, self-involved actor; Petra, the emotionally troubled daughter; Ursula, the alcoholic, yet devoted wife; Ivy Blount, the housekeeper whose family once owned the estate; and Adrian Duffy, the estate's cowman. Hermes introduces each figure and reveals their differing attitudes about the patriarch and his death. While this is hardly a dysfunctional family, the members are beset by doubts, faults, and emotional limitations. They are at once sources of amazement and confusion for Hermes, who uses their temperaments to discourse widely on the differences between humans and the gods.

Hermes also allows access to the patriarch's dimming consciousness as he reviews

~

John Banville is known for dense, intricate novels full of recondite allusions and postmodern indeterminacies. His novel Kepler *(1981) was awarded the Guardian Fiction Prize and the Allied Irish Bank Fiction Prize.* The Sea *(2005) won both the Man Booker Prize and the Irish Book Award.*

~

his life, his attitudes about each family member, and his estimation of his career and revolutionary ideas. While the family believes he is beyond consciousness, Godley actually knows all that is taking place, and the counterpoint in views is often revealing. The family has two visitors—Roddy Wagstaff, Petra's boyfriend who hopes to become Godley's biographer, and an enigmatic figure named Benny Grace, who is eventually revealed to be Pan. After various travails and confusions, the novel ends as darkness approaches with the assurance that all will be resolved happily—Ursula abstaining from drink, Adam and Helen living on the estate, Petra healing, Blount and Duffy marrying.

In an age divided between pure secularism and doctrinaire fundamentalism, Banville proposes an ancient notion of divinity—multipersonal and interpenetrating with the human realm. Although the novel teems with references to many gods, only three actually appear; in each case they are divinities particularly concerned with the human experience—a libidinous Zeus, a puckish Pan, and Hermes, the creature of many names and duties.

However it is as a trickster god that Hermes is most significant. He is a shape-shifter who inveigles his way into the affairs of others, gods and humans. As Carl Jung pointed out, he is a "psycho-pomp" or "soul-guide," leading people to greatness or destruction. In this capacity he is the one who guides souls to the underworld; as he awaits Adam's death, he acts as the reader's tour guide through the patriarch's past and through the fates of the survivors.

As a narrator Hermes is ceaselessly arch and playful. He discusses serious subjects in an offhand manner, frequently interrupting himself and the narrative with asides and digressions. He often addresses the audience directly, suggesting that readers are his intimates or immediately in his presence. In some cases he anticipates the reader's disbelief, in others he will chastise his impatient father, "All right, all right, all *right*! Keep your curls on," or discusses the delusion of believing in a single deity, as Christians do. At other moments he loses track of his narrative and either announces a pause or redirects attention to get his bearings, "Where were we? At the lunch table, among these people. All I am doing is passing the time here, flicking these polished playing cards into the upturned silk hat."

As the story progresses, the narrative voice slips increasingly between Hermes and the dying Adam and briefly to the visiting physician, Dr. Fortune. At one point the narrative confusion is foregrounded with the question, "Who am I now?" The technique can be explained in a couple of ways, the most obvious of which is that Hermes controls everything to the point that he can completely penetrate the consciousness of others.

Another explanation, however, may be tied to the novel's title. Adam's abstruse mathematical calculations have shattered traditional notions of reality and time. Adam has proved that infinity is plural, reaching out across the known universe and time itself and suggesting eternalness. "Since there are infinities, indeed, an infinity of infinities, as he has shown there to be, there must be eternal entities to inhabit them. Yes, he believes in us [the gods], and takes it that the hitherto unimagined realm beyond time that he discovered is where we live."

Thus Adam and Hermes exist in these eternal infinities—Hermes by virtue of his divinity and Adam as a result of his coma—each neither here nor there entirely. Adam's discoveries make "all the bits seem to cohere in a grand amalgam wrought by the mumbo-jumbo of mere numbers." The result of such speculation is the phenomenon of multiple or parallel universes. If worlds are encapsulated in other worlds—"the world has many worlds" as Adam proclaims—the boundaries of experience dissolve, identities shift and blend, and long-standing notions of fiction, such as that of a stable narrative voice, also dissolve. With worlds morphing into one another, the shift in characters' experiences becomes more comprehensible and believable.

The themes of time and temporal dislocation lie at the center of the novel. Time, the novel suggests, is a convenient fiction—immeasurable, forever eluding and mystifying. A provisional title of Vladimir Nabokov's *Ada or Ardor: A Family Chronicle* (1969) was "The texture of time," and such a phrase well describes Banville's concern here. Since time cannot be seen, it can only be apprehended through the sensation of living within it. Hermes and Adam are alike in their fingering the fabric of time, commenting on its feel and meditating on its changing constancy.

The novel's many temporal shifts become especially evident in the numerous, outrageous anachronisms. These include mail delivery by Thurn and Taxis carriers; reference to a recent English pontiff, when the only English pope was Adrian V in the twelfth century; the beheading of Elizabeth Tudor; a car powered entirely by salt water; Johann Wolfgang von Goethe's reputation entirely forgotten; and Sweden's becoming an aggressive, belligerent country. The fluidity of time underscores the notion of universes sliding into one another until all realities become contemporaneous.

The myth of Amphitryon, which is also central to the novel, concerns a husband whose wife, Alcmene, is impregnated by Zeus and later gives birth to Heracles. The story has been told and retold as a supposedly lost tragedy of Sophocles' by Molière in 1668, by John Dryden in 1690, and by Heinrich von Kleist in 1807, in perhaps the most popular version of the story. Other versions appeared in the twentieth century, including a famous Nazi-era film. Banville's Helen is excited because she will be starring as Alcmene in a modernized interpretation, though she has had an unwitting rehearsal that morning when Zeus, appearing as her husband, ravages her in much the same way as the classical Alcmene is tricked in cuckolding her husband.

These deceptions, while amusing, lead to some of the novel's most serious reflections on human and divine life. Although Hermes frequently mocks humans for their inarticulate gruntings compared to his rarefied speech and for all the complications of love they endure, he also admits to the "sad silence of our envy." He admires the human fascination with the dawn and admits the intrusion in human affairs results from a divine desire for new sensations that are occasioned by birth, death, and love, none of which the eternals can experience. Loss and the tragedy of human existence, which are so foreign and incomprehensible to the gods, constitute the very formulas for meaning in human life.

At the same time, the myth of Amphitryon provides an ironic aside to another aspect of the author's career. In 2000, Banville adapted Kleist's play as *God's Gift*, and the novel's reworking of that story stands as a witty piece of self-referential irony. As in many of his other novels, which also concern themselves with serious philosophical and metaphysical questions, Banville relishes undercutting the mordancy of his subjects with often surprising humor. In *The Infinities* events take place in a single day amid the bucolic splendor of an estate named Arden in the middle of summer. Those general outlines invite comparison with one of Shakespeare's most buoyant comedies, *A Midsummer Night's Dream*. Hermes's flippant remarks, Zeus's pouting over Helen's attraction to her husband, and the porcine Benny Grace ingratiating himself with the family suggest a comic spirit at play.

Classic comedy, from the Greeks through the moderns, often hinges on the creation of an alternative to the status quo, which is depicted as crushing, even life-denying. The triumph in these fictions comes with the alternative either prevailing or surviving, and the notion of a virtual future is crucial to the mode of comic reconciliation. Marriage is typically the classic illustration of the comic alternative, asserted here in Blount and Duffy's imminent union and the decision of Adam and his now-pregnant wife to inhabit the old house. Even Petra and her mother are destined for their own happiness.

Banville has the reputation of being an austere, challenging writer, more concerned with arcane wordsmithery than with the dramatization of human experience. Such is really not the case, and *The Infinities* is clearly one of his most amusing, life-affirming fictions. Typical concerns with art (Banville's novels abound with allusions and direct references to many artists and works) and philosophical complexity are certainly present here, but the overriding attitude of this novel is gentle acceptance and even a celebration of life.

David W. Madden

Review Sources

America, April 26, 2010, p. 34.
Booklist 106 (January 1, 2010): 42.
The Boston Globe, April 4, 2010, p. C5.
Kirkus Reviews 78 (February 15, 2010): 96.
Library Journal 135 (January 1, 2010): 85.
London Review of Books, March 11, 2010, p. 17-18.

New Statesman, September 7, 2009, 46-47.
The New York Times, April 5, 2010, p. 1.
The New York Times Book Review, March 7, 2010, p. 10.
The New Yorker 86 (April 5, 2010): 74-79.
Publishers Weekly 256 (November 23, 2009): 1.
The Times Literary Supplement, September 18, 2009, p. 21.
The Washington Times, March 19, 2010, p. B6.

INNOCENT

Author: Scott Turow (1949-   )
Publisher: Grand Central (New York). 416 pp. 27.99
Type of work: Novel
Time: The present
Locale: Kindle County, fictional midwestern location

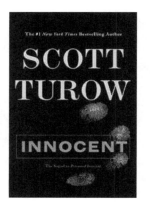

The sequel to the blockbuster Presumed Innocent
*(1987) finds Rusty Sabich again accused of murder and
facing down the same prosecuting attorney, Tommy Molto*

Principal characters:
> RUSTY SABICH, a sixty-year-old appellate
> court judge, former prosecuting attorney,
> and accused murderer
> BARBARA SABICH, his mentally unstable
> wife
> NAT SABICH, his quiet son who is a law student
> SANDY STERN, his attorney
> MARTA STERN, Sandy's daughter and Rusty's attorney
> ANNA VOSTIC, a clerk in Rusty's court
> TOMMY MOLTO, Kindle County acting prosecuting attorney
> JIM BRAND, chief deputy prosecuting attorney

In his ninth work of fiction, Scott Turow returns to the characters who made him famous. In Turow's first novel, *Presumed Innocent*, Rusty Sabich has an affair with a woman who is later murdered. Prosecuted for her murder by Tommy Molto and defended brilliantly by Sandy Stern, Rusty beats the accusation. The book, later adapted for a popular film, is still in print.

Turow remains a practicing lawyer with a large firm in Chicago, and his work is reflected in both *Innocent* and *Presumed Innocent*, where the wheels of justice can crush an innocent man as easily as a guilty one. When an innocent person is caught in the system, getting out is no small matter. Wondering whether the system has implicated an innocent man makes for much of the books' appeal.

Rusty is still married to Barbara, his unbalanced, bipolar wife, who is both brilliant and beautiful. However, she also is prone to rages and disturbing behavior. Rusty has been resigned to his personal life primarily because of his son, Nat. At his sixtieth birthday party, Rusty contemplates his life, which, while professionally satisfactory, is personally difficult, thinking "at the heart of my heart, I will still not have the unnameable piece of happiness that has eluded me for sixty years." He and Barbara have a difficult and strained relationship, no surprise to any reader of *Presumed Innocent*.

In *Presumed Innocent*, Rusty was forced to stand trial for a murder he did not commit, and most of the prosecutors in the office believe he was guilty. Somehow, though, in *Innocent*, Rusty is now a judge on the appeals court and is standing for election to the state supreme court. Soon it becomes clear he is also drawn to his senior law clerk, Anna, who is thirty years his junior. Anna makes clear she is attracted to him; even though Rusty tries to rationalize his way out of the attraction, they find themselves consummating an affair. Given that his affair twenty years previously landed him in the middle of a murder investigation and pushed his wife to the edge of a mental breakdown, Rusty knows the affair is doomed, but cannot bring himself to leave. Indeed, the affair takes up only a small portion of the book, but shifts the destiny of all the major characters. Rusty's quest for happiness through this affair leads to the death of his wife, his son's eventual bittersweet contentment, and the reappearance of Tommy Molto.

Scott Turow is a practicing attorney and writer. He has written nine novels, including Presumed Innocent *(1987), and two nonfiction books, including* One L: An Inside Account of Life in the First Year at Harvard Law School *(1977). He won* Time *magazine's Best Work of Fiction in 1999.*

Rusty's actions are increasingly self-destructive, as Rusty subconsciously seeks to end the unhappiness in his personal life. However, every decision he makes as the story progresses also undermines his legal career. He and Anna are indiscreet in the hotels they use and the emails they send. In addition, during the timeframe of the affair, the appeals court is considering the criminal appeal of John Harnason, who is accused of murder. Contrary to all ethical rules, Rusty speaks with the defendant outside the courtroom about the case, which leads to the defendant running away while his case is on appeal. While he may have destroyed his personal life, his actions in the *Harnason* case are far more likely to jeopardize his judgeship.

Nat, Rusty and Barbara's son, initially appears fragile and confused. Both Rusty and Barbara feel guilty about the way the earlier murder trial and their short separation affected their son. Now a grown man, he can be paralyzed by indecision, a trait perhaps brought on by years of psychoanalysis. He continues, however, to follow in his father's footsteps as he finishes up law school and plans to clerk in the same court his father did. Indeed, later in the novel he starts a relationship with Anna, heartbroken over the end of the affair with his father. Once able to present his own perspective, however, Nat becomes a fully fleshed-out character, who has learned how to protect himself from the destructive tendencies of his mother and the lack of love between his parents.

In one of the most memorable chapters, the tension is ratcheted up when Barbara insists on meeting Anna, now her son's girlfriend. Anna herself has problems, claiming that all her life she has "seemed to have a talent for catastrophic blunders." She recognizes her dual relationship with Rusty and Nat certainly has the potential for disaster. Nat narrates the chapter, unaware that Anna and his father had an affair and that Anna believes Barbara knows about it. None of the people at the dinner know what the reader knows, that this is Barbara's last meal, and the food Rusty serves will become significant evidence in the coming trial. Anna, sick to her stomach, manages to make it through the meal, certain Barbara has discovered her affair with Rusty. Turow's style of alternating narratives and time lines means that the reader doubles back on this meal with different characters.

The novel opens with Barbara's death. With Nat narrating, he tells the story of his father sitting next to his mother dead in her bed, waiting twenty-four hours before calling anyone. Nat, innocent in many ways, is the most sympathetic character, standing by his father though not persuaded of his innocence. Barbara's family is known for their weak hearts, and the coroner believes she died of natural causes. However, by waiting so long to call the authorities, the prosecuting attorney's office, stung by their actions in Rusty's first murder trial, uses this as an excuse to open an investigation into Barbara's death.

Tommy Molto, the acting prosecuting attorney, married with a young son, initially resists the investigation. His deputy, Jim Brant, persuades him that the investigation is necessary. Brant is still trying to get revenge on behalf of Tommy, who ended up humiliated at the end of the first trial. Tommy, on the other hand, has found satisfaction in his beautiful wife and child and can see the problems inherent in going after Rusty a second time. The evidence continues to mount against Rusty, and with Brant's encouragement, Tommy decides to prosecute the case. However, Brant's single-minded determination to convict Rusty leads him down an ethically compromised path. Tugged reluctantly into the case, Tommy is less dogmatic than he was twenty years ago, but remains certain Rusty murdered Carolyn Polhemus back then. Eventually, however, he is convinced of Rusty's guilt in the second death, "*He did it again.* The words, the idea, stretched out through Tommy like a piano key with the damper pedal compressed. Rusty did it again."

The murder investigation ultimately leads to evidence of the affair between Rusty and Anna, which provides a motive for Barbara's murder. The police soon arrest Rusty and the remainder of the novel is taken up by the trial. Deoxyribonucleic acid (DNA) evidence unavailable twenty years prior shows that Rusty did have an affair with Polhemus, a fact he denied in the first trial. In addition, on the night of Barbara's death Rusty bought specific groceries that would cause death when the ingredients interacted with a drug Barbara took. This evidence, plus his odd actions after his wife's death, his affair, and his interactions with Harnason provide enough for the prosecution to make their case. Luckily for Rusty, he is again defended by Sandy Stern, who is stricken with cancer. Once a vital and energetic defense attorney, Stern is now a shadow who manages to return for one last murder trial. Aided by his daughter, Stern pulls out a few of his old tricks, but remains in the background for much of the book. The trial ends with a surprise, but the book continues longer than expected and eventually loses some momentum.

Turow uses any number of twists and turns common to murder novels, but the most interesting one is the way he manipulates both the time lines and the perspectives. Starting with Barbara's death, Turow moves back in time eighteen months to Rusty's birthday party. Using alternating perspectives among Rusty, Nat, Anna, and Tommy, and alternating time lines moving forward from both the sixtieth birthday party and Barbara's death, information is revealed slowly. The reader doubles back through events that carry different meaning after the murder. This technique makes the first half of the book particularly compelling as the prosecuting attorney's office re-creates Rusty's actions leading up to the murder at the same time the reader is discovering them from Rusty's perspective.

The different time lines merge by the time of the trial, which works for part three, the trial, but means the long denouement of part four slows down considerably. In addition, only Tommy's perspective is written in the third person, which, in addition to all of the other narrative switchbacks, can make for an odd reading experience. Finally, while Turow's reflections on aging and personal satisfaction are interesting, Rusty's actions are frustrating. Appearing to bow to self-destructive tendencies more than to any other motivation, Rusty knows his actions could be ruinous. Still, he cannot control himself and justifies his behavior by referring to the last time he had an affair, "What has lain between then and now—because that time is not fully deserving of being called living." This is especially difficult when considering his affair is with a woman thirty years his junior and his subordinate. While his wife is indeed difficult, his justifications for his affair come across more as whiny than sympathetic. Indeed, the voice that may have provided the interesting perspective in this book, especially given the ending of *Presumed Innocent*, would be that of Barbara, the one character not given an opportunity to explain herself.

Kathryn E. Fort

Review Sources

Booklist 106, no. 22 (August 1, 2010): 64.
Chicago Sun-Times, May 2, 2010, p. D6.
Kirkus Reviews 78, no. 7 (April 1, 2010): 274.
Library Journal 135, no. 8 (May 1, 2010): 72.
Maclean's 123, no. 19 (May 24, 2010): 57.
Minneapolis Star Tribune, June 30, 2010, p. 6E.
The New York Times, April 30, 2010, p. C23.
The New York Times Book Review, May 16, 2010, p. 1.
Publishers Weekly 257, no. 34 (August 30, 2010): 46-47.
USA Today, April 29, 2010, p. 6D.
The Washington Post, May 2, 2010, p. B8.

INSECTOPEDIA

Author: Hugh Raffles (1958-   )
Publisher: Pantheon Books (New York). 465 pp. $29.95
Type of work: Science, sociology, nature
Time: The relative present
Locale: China, Niger, and other countries

The twenty-six essays in this collection proceed alphabetically by a key title word and illuminate in sometimes startling ways the world of insects and their interrelationships with humans

Principal personages:

P. A. GLICK, the first entomologist to organize insect collections by using an airplane

CORNELIA HESSE-HONEGGER, a determined researcher into the possible effects of the Chernobyl disaster on insects

JEAN-HENRI FABRE, a French "insect poet" who tended a large house and garden that is now a national museum

DR. LI SHIJUN, "the cricket professor," one of Raffles's guides to cricket lore

JORIS HOEFNAGEL, a Flemish naturalist and miniaturist who wrote *The Four Elements* (1582), a magnificent compendium of the world's animals

ALFRED NOSSIG, a controversial Jewish sculptor arrested in the Warsaw ghetto in 1943 and executed for treason by a Jewish underground group

KARL VON FRISCH (1886-1982), German entomologist who won a Nobel Prize for his discovery of "the language of bees"

KARIM, the author's tutor in the complexities of life in Niger

JEFF VALENCIA, a founding father of the "crush freaks" brotherhood

DAVID DUNN, the recorder of "the music of the phloem"

All of the essays in Hugh Raffles's *Insectopedia* are unfailingly interesting in their diversity and originality. The breadth of Raffles's subjects and the detail he musters in expounding them reveal a mind of considerable sophistication.

The essay "Air" describes how August 10, 1926, marked the first attempt to collect insects with airplanes, an experiment that P. A. Glick and his government research colleagues in Tallulah, Louisiana, hoped would help thwart the many insect enemies of agriculture. More than thirteen hundred sorties over the following five years yielded tens of thousands of specimens, including ladybugs at six thousand feet, a fungus gnat at ten thousand feet, and a ballooning spider at fifteen thousand feet. All told, thirty-six million insects were estimated to be in the air over one square mile of countryside. Researchers identified the "aerial plankton" that floated around in involuntary paths above three thousand feet and the larger ones, like monarch butterflies, that were strong enough to control their course at less than three thousand feet. Years before the airplane studies, William Beebe (of bathysphere fame) had reported seeing huge swarms of many species passing through a migration flyway.

~

Hugh Raffles teaches anthropology at the New School in New York City. His book Amazonia: A Natural History *(2002) won the Victor Turner Prize in Ethnographic Writing. He is also the recipient of a Whiting Writers' Award.*

~

According to the essay "Chernobyl," Cornelia Hesse-Honegger is probably the world's leading authority on leaf bugs, the tiny insects of the suborder Heteroptera that she has been painting and studying for more than thirty years. When asked by a teenage girl how to become someone like her, she advised her to "always listen to her heart and never worship a human being. If she wanted to find solace, she had to turn to an animal or a tree for help." The advent of nuclear power plants, followed by the disaster at Chernobyl, has given her a fresh impetus for research. Working from her home in Zürich, Hesse-Honegger has written several articles for the Swiss newspaper *Tages-Anzeiger* about "When Flies and Bugs Don't Look the Way They Should," presenting illustrations of deformed specimens from the area of eastern Sweden where fallout from Chernobyl had been most intense. On the whole, however, her collections have been inconclusive; even at Chernobyl the insect life was no more "disturbed" than in Switzerland.

The essay "Evolution" explains how Jean-Henri Fabre, known as the "insect poet," began creating his naturalist's laboratory, l'Harmas, in Provence in 1879. Among other achievements, Fabre painted six hundred "luminous aquarelles of local fungi." He died in 1915 at the age of ninety-two after writing his ten-volume *Souvenirs entomologiques* (1891-1909), a tremendous labor of scholarship that he intended to refute "transformism," his term for evolution by means of adaptive transformation. Fabre was especially drawn to wasps, whose behavior he saw as entirely instinctive and devoid of intelligence. However, instinct yielded during the 1920's to behaviorist theories and returned to favor only during the 1950's. Fabre is now largely forgotten except in Japan, where he is prominent in the elementary school curriculum and has devoted intellectual followers in the labor leader Osugi Sakae and the founder of Japanese primatology, Imanishi Kinji.

In the essay called "Generosity (the Happy Times)," the "happy times" are the months August through October in Shanghai when crickets mature and get busy with sex. The males start to sing and get ready to fight. Cricket lovers then pack the trains to Shandong Province where the smartest, most macho crickets thrive; everyone anticipates the three-week Golden Autumn Cricket Festival at nearby Qibao.

The classic text on crickets is the thirteenth century *Book of Crickets*, by Jia Sidao, with an elaborate taxonomy featuring body colors. For fighters, "The quality of the jaws is decisive." A later manual identifies such iconic heroes as Ying Yang Wing and Strong Man That Nobody Can Harm. Master Fang, the director of Shanghai's fighting cricket museum, is an authority on cricket training. Raffles explains Fang's teachings: "A cricket knows when it is loved, and it knows when it is well cared for, and it responds in kind with loyalty, courage, obedience, and the signs of quiet contentment." A bustling (and illegal) cricket gambling industry flourishes in Shanghai; through the good offices of Boss Xun, a cricket casino owner, Raffles is lucky enough to witness some premier matches.

In the essay "The Ineffable," Raffles is entranced by the Flemish miniaturist Joris Hoefnagel's masterpiece *The Four Elements*, a compendium of the world's animals completed in 1582. The animals are in four groups, depending on which of the elements—earth, air, fire, and water—they inhabit. Insects claim the first volume, *Ignis*, a tribute to Aristotle's cosmology that gave fiery bodies the most elevated position in nature, from which they aspired toward the celestial realm. Raffles interprets *Ignis* as a work of homeopathic magic, an exercise in penetrating "the gap between the visible and the intuited universe." Thus, Hoefnagel's tremendous skill at representing his subjects, his "mimetic magic," in Sir James Frazer's epithet, achieves a miracle in which, as the anthropologist Michael Taussig says, "Imitation becomes immanence." Hoefnagel's genius is not imitation, Raffles opines, but "philosophical art in the service of something greater and more mysterious," such as the ineffable.

In the essay "Jews," Raffles tells the story of Alfred Nossig, contextualizing it in an account of the rise of racial theories that identified Jews as parasites, which culminated in Heinrich Himmler's remark that "Antisemitism is exactly the same as delousing." Nossig was seventy-nine years old in 1943 when he was executed in the Warsaw ghetto by the ZOB, the Jewish underground group that led the uprising. His execution was described as necessary to purge the Jewish population of "hostile elements," but precisely what his offenses were is not completely clear. He had led a remarkable life as a sculptor but had insisted that assimilation made Christians insecure and encouraged anti-Semitism; in 1887, he had proclaimed, "The average Jewish type exhibits strength in the struggle for survival but is morally on a lower level than the non-Jew; he possesses more shrewdness and endurance, but at the same time more ambition, vanity, and a lack of conscience." Such remarks made him an ambiguous figure.

The essay "Language" describes how Karl von Frisch won a Nobel Prize in 1973 for discovering "the language of the bees." Von Frisch began his studies of bees during the 1920's, identifying two "dances" that he called the round dance and the waggle dance. The bees were communicating symbolically, but modern researchers think that both dances relate the same information. In his book *The Dancing Bees* (1955), Von Frisch explains that bees are such intensely social creatures that a lone bee, kept to itself, would quickly die. As Raffles puts it, "In his version, the hive is the expression of a culture of cooperation among its thousands of distinct individuals." Von Frisch gained recognition for questioning simple stimulus-response models of animal behavior and for allowing for "a precise and highly differentiated sign language." Raffles rejects Jacques Lacan's understanding of honeybee behavior as programmed and mechanical, preferring to celebrate their mystery and accomplishments: "What pitiful poverty of imagination to see them as resources merely for our self-knowledge!"

In the essay "On January 8, 2008, Abdou Mahamane Was Driving Through Niamey . . . ," the *criquets* of the Sahel belong to the Acrididae family, the short-horned grasshoppers. All twenty species of locusts are in this group. Locusts are *Schistocerca gregaria*, known as the *criquet pèlerin*, or desert locust. They change form when crowded, and the nymphs march in thousands—even millions—for as many as two thousand miles in a season. One swarm in Kenya numbered fifty million, each eating the equivalent of its own weight in vegetation every day. Besides crops, they also consume plastics and textiles; most dreaded of all is a grasshopper, the *criquet sénégalais*. In Niger, Raffles travels with his guide, Karim, to Maradi, the nation's commercial center, where they meet Zebeirou, the leading *criquet* broker. The *criquets* (or *houara* in Hausa) are a major food source, and when Raffles and Karim are invited to a naming ceremony, they watch masses of the insects turning pink as they are boiled in a big pot. Then they share the feast. Despite their value as food, *criquets* are an enormous pest, as the *criquet pèlerin* extends over eleven million square miles in sixty-five countries. Nobody seems optimistic about controlling them.

Jeff Valencia, profiled in the essay "Sex," is the author of *The American Journal of the Crush-Freaks* and the producer of fifty-six titles in the *Squish Playhouse* series of videos featuring well-pedicured young women trampling various small critters: "crickets, snails, and pinkies [small mice] as well as worms"—into a mushy mess. Valencia explains quite frankly the appeal of watching barefoot women crushing insects: For its male addicts, the practice leads to sexual release. Just what psychological factors dominate remains murky. Jeff fantasizes about being ground into the rug by his lady, and Raffles consults Sigmund Freud, Leopold von Sacher-Masoch, and the French philosopher Gilles Deleuze in a search of a motive. None of these thinkers advance the reader's understanding noticeably. However, to California's U.S. representative Republican Elton Gallegly, Valencia's work was not art but pure smut, and he campaigned against it in Congress. Legal problems complicate the issues: There are no laws preventing killing—even torturing—insects and vermin.

In the essay "The Sound of Global Warming," David Dunn is the composer of *The Sound of Light in Trees.* He uses transducers to make audible the racket created by beetles, ants, and others such as the piñon engraver beetle that has thinned millions of piñon pines in northern New Mexico. Dunn listens to it and to the aquatic insects in his composition "Chaos and the Emergent Mind of the Pond," hearing, Raffles says, "patterns comparable only to the most sophisticated computer compositions and the most complex African polyrhythmic drumming." Raffles explains how global warming results from the interaction between trees and their insect predators: As winter and summer temperatures have increased, precipitation has decreased; freezes have become shorter, and plants and insects have "fallen out of step." Animals adapt faster than trees and so the beetles flourish, eating more and developing faster. In the last decades of the twentieth century and into the twenty-first century, Alaska has lost 4.4 million acres of boreal forest to the spruce bark beetle, and British Columbia has lost 33 million acres to the mountain pine beetle. Raffles concludes, "Repression is futile. Somehow, we will have to cohabit. Somehow, we will have to make friends."

Frank Day

Review Sources

Anthropological Quarterly 83, no. 3 (Summer, 2010): 701-703.
Audubon 112, no. 4 (July/August, 2010): 64.
Library Journal 135, no. 2 (February 1, 2010): 89.
New Scientist 205, no. 2754 (April 3, 2010): 43.
The New York Times Book Review, May 2, 2010, p. 18.
Publishers Weekly 256, no. 51 (December 21, 2009): 51-52.

JACK KEROUAC AND ALLEN GINSBERG
The Letters

Authors: Jack Kerouac (1922-1969) and Allen Ginsberg
  (1926-1997)
Edited with notes and an introduction by Bill Morgan and
  David Stanford
Publisher: Viking (New York). 500 pp. $35.00
Type of work: Letters, literary history
Time: 1944-1963
Locale: New York City and Ozone Park, New York; San
  Francisco and San Jose, California; Patterson, New
  Jersey; Denver; Mexico City; Rocky Mount, North
  Carolina; Orlando, Florida; Paris; Northport, New
  York

*This collection of correspondence tracks the friendship
and literary evolution of two essential founders of the Beat movement*

> *Principal personages:*
> JACK KEROUAC (1922-1969), the author of *On the Road* (1957), *Doctor
>   Sax* (1959), and other major twentieth century novels
> ALLEN GINSBERG (1926-1997), the author of *Howl, and Other Poems*
>   (1956), *Kaddish, and Other Poems, 1958-1960* (1961), and many
>   seminal Beat poetic works
> LUCIEN CARR (1925-2005), a journalist, an editor for United Press
>   International, and a lifelong comrade of Kerouac and Ginsberg
> EDIE PARKER (1922-1993), Kerouac's first wife
> WILLIAM S. BURROUGHS (1914-1997), the author of *The Naked Lunch*
>   (1959) and a central Beat movement figure
> HERBERT HUNCKE (1915-1996), a street denizen, thief, and friend of the
>   Beats
> CARL SOLOMON (1928-1993), a fellow mental patient with Ginsberg who
>   became the starting point for *Howl*
> NEAL CASSADY (1926-1968), a close companion to Kerouac and
>   Ginsberg and inspiration for many of their works
> GARY SNYDER (1930-   ), the author of *The Back Country* (1967) and
>   a leading figure of the San Francisco poetry renaissance

    In 1944, the year Jack Kerouac and Allen Ginsberg, whose letters are the subject
of *Jack Kerouac and Allen Ginsberg: The Letters*, began to correspond, the chance
intersection of three aspiring writers in New York City would spark a significant
post-World War II American literary movement and thereby shape bohemian youth
for decades to come. The year before, Kerouac, the son of French Canadian immigrants and a Columbia University dropout, met Lucien Carr through Kerouac's

~

Jack Kerouac and Allen Ginsberg are
among the most notable founders of the
Beat literary movement. Their works
include Kerouac's On the Road *(1957)*
and Visions of Cody *(1960) and*
Ginsberg's Collected Poems, 1947-
1997 *(2006).*

~

lover and future wife, Edie Parker. As 1944 dawned, Carr introduced Kerouac to William S. Burroughs—drug aficionado and heir to the declining Burroughs Adding Machine Company fortune—and Allen Ginsberg—a seventeen-year-old communist, poet, and brilliant intellectual. The three formed an enduring friendship based on literature, music, the arts, and the exploration of the far edges of experience. As the Beats, they went on to write some of the most exciting and influential works of the postwar United States.

Covering the years 1944 to 1963, *Jack Kerouac and Allen Ginsberg: The Letters* is a fascinating and essential artifact of that movement. Epic letter writers, Kerouac and Ginsberg's correspondence possesses much of the stylistic fire and grace of their finest works. There is depth of content as well, as the two ponder everything from Fyodor Dostoevski to LSD, not to mention describing the major moments of their lives and the creation of such literary masterworks as *On the Road* (1957) and *Howl, and Other Poems* (1956).

The book begins rather dramatically. David Kammerer, an older friend of Carr's, has been pursuing him with pleas of love for years. On the night of August 14, 1944, Carr, pushed past endurance by Kammerer's obsessive attention, stabs and kills him. Kerouac aids Carr in getting rid of evidence: the murder weapon and Kammerer's blood-flecked glasses. As a result, the police arrest Kerouac as a material witness when Carr turns himself in. Thus, the book's first letter is from Ginsberg to Kerouac, incarcerated in the Bronx County jail, awaiting Parker, his new bride, to bail him out. In the letter, Ginsberg expresses his delight at Parker's bringing Kerouac a copy of the Nikolai Gogol's *Myortvye dushi* (part 1, 1842, part 2, 1855; *Dead Souls* 1887) to read in his cell.

An incarceration of another kind occurs five years later. Early in 1949, Herbert Huncke, a street criminal and member of the Kerouac-Ginsberg-Burroughs circle, appears on Ginsberg's doorstep fresh out of jail, broke, his feet frozen and bleeding from wandering New York's February streets. Ever compassionate, Ginsberg allows Huncke to stay in his apartment, but soon, Huncke's friends Vickie Russell and "Little Jack" Melody move in as well. Russell is a heroin addict and Melody a petty thief, so it is not surprising they join with Huncke in a robbing spree, using Ginsberg's apartment to store the loot, which includes two stuffed chairs, a wooden cabinet, and a cigarette machine. When police arrest Melody driving a stolen car, papers found in the vehicle reveal Ginsberg's address, leading officers to the stash of stolen goods and Ginsberg.

The court decides that Ginsberg, a Columbia University graduate with a full-time job at the Associated Press, must be literally insane to allow the likes of Huncke to live with him and take advantage of his good nature. Instead of prison, the judge commits Ginsberg to the New York State Psychiatric Institute. There, he meets Carl Solomon, the inspiration for Ginsberg's most acclaimed poem, *Howl*. In a letter dated July 13-14, Ginsberg describes Solomon, noting that he is "the most interesting of all" the inmates, whose "madhouse humor" creates "a perfect opportunity here for existentialist absurdity."

Kerouac's response to Ginsberg's letter arrives from Denver, for Kerouac is in the midst of the many journeys that become the subject of his most famous novel, *On the Road*. In 1948, his letters begin to arrive from places as disparate as North Carolina, Colorado, Mexico, and California. The muse of these road trips is Neal Cassady—a former Denver street kid who merges a hunger for cars, kicks, and women with a poetic soul and a fascination for wild flights of intellectual discovery. Cassady first appears in a Kerouac novel as Dean Moriarty, Sal Paradise's companion of the highway in *On the Road*, but he is also a central character in *Dharma Bums* (1958), *The Subterraneans* (1958), *Visions of Cody* (1960, 1972), *Book of Dreams* (1961, revised 2001), *Big Sur* (1962), and *Desolation Angels* (1965).

Kerouac's adoration of Cassady shines through a letter dated December 6, 1948, in which Kerouac gleefully announces that Cassady is on his way to New York in a 1949 Hudson. "[H]e long-distanced me from San Fran," Kerouac writes, "and I heard his mad Western excited voice over the phone." Kerouac then goes on to relate the entire conversation. Despite significant strains to their relationship, such as Kerouac having an affair with Cassady's wife Carolyn, Kerouac and Cassady would remain friends until Cassady's death from exposure on a set of Mexican railroad tracks in 1968.

Ironically, while the best-selling *On the Road* would become Kerouac's iconic novel, even his closest friends declared it a failure at first. On June 12, 1952, Ginsberg expresses his reaction to the manuscript of *On the Road*. While he praises it as the best contemporary writing in the United States, he predicts that its private mythology and sexual material doom it to unpublished obscurity. Kerouac's response is swift and vitriolic. He accuses Ginsberg not only of hating *On the Road* but also of despising Kerouac himself, and the letter closes with Kerouac's proclamation that their friendship is at an end. Nonetheless, the friendship lives on, for Ginsberg calms Kerouac with his next letter, which praises Kerouac's *Dr. Sax* (1959) as truly brilliant, "a Beethovenian-Melvillian triumph."

The Beat movement reached a pivotal climax in the mid-1950's. On October 7, 1955, the famous Six Gallery poetry reading—featuring Ginsberg, Philip Lamantia, Philip Whalen, Michael McClure, and Gary Snyder—fully energizes the San Francisco Beat literary scene. Snyder, the model for Japhy Ryder in Kerouac's *The Dharma Bums* (1958), becomes that year the focal point for the Beats' growing interest in Buddhism.

A year later, on August 12, merchant seaman Ginsberg, off the coast of Alaska aboard the USNS *Sgt. Jack J. Pendleton*, writes a long missive to Kerouac in his fire lookout tower on Washington's Desolation Peak, the setting for the opening chapters of *Desolation Angels*. The letter proudly announces the publication of *Howl* from City Lights Books. The title poem, with its Whitmanesque vision of America's spiritual and social ills, became a classic of postwar literature. In 1957, while Ginsberg's letters to Kerouac travel their way across the Atlantic from Morocco and the Nether-lands, San Francisco police arrest Lawrence Ferlinghetti, the founder of City Lights Books, on obscenity charges for publishing *Howl*. However, the court case resulted in both a victory for Ferlinghetti and national fame for Ginsberg.

That year also brought fame for Kerouac when, in September, Viking Press pub-lished *On the Road*. The book was an immediate, stratospheric triumph, and when Kerouac writes to Ginsberg on October 1, the letter brims with the novelist's new-found success—sales of *On the Road* running strong, Marlon Brando expressing in-terest in playing Sal Paradise in a potential film version, *The Subterraneans* sold to Grove Press, articles on Kerouac planned for *Playboy*, *Saturday Review*, *Life*, and *Harpers Bazaar*.

At first, the success invigorated Kerouac, and he continued writing at a furious pace, pounding out *Dharma Bums* in mere weeks. However, fame soon took its toll. *On the Road* is a joyous novel of youthful freedom and travel, but the author who had experienced its adventures had aged. The public expected him to be the vital young Sal Paradise of the novel, or worse yet, Dean Moriarty, whom Kerouac based on the untamed Denver wild man Cassady; these expectations wore at Kerouac. Also, *On the Road* became the vortex of the growing Beat culture maelstrom, and Kerouac re-sented being hailed as the "King of the Beats," or accused of leading to the corruption of teens. What hurt most, however, was not being taken seriously as a writer. Kerouac mentions a typical assault in a letter dated January 8, 1958: "Big attack against me in *Nation* saying I a fool boy poet and Richard Wilbur a heroic man poet."

In reaction to the empty whirlwind of fame, Kerouac began drinking heavily, his writing slowed, and he became increasingly bitter toward his life and friends. A letter of June 18, 1959, states, "I saw a snapshot of myself taken recently in which I could see with my own eyes what all this lionized manure has done to me: it's killing me rapidly. I have to escape or die, don't you see?" A year later, in another letter he ques-tions why he is alive. For Kerouac, the publication of *On the Road* was both the apex of his literary career and the beginning of a decade-long decline, ending with his death on October 21, 1969, from stomach hemorrhages caused by excessive drinking.

In sharp contrast to Kerouac's spiral down after *On the Road*, the success of *Howl* stoked Ginsberg's love of life and creative fires. In the ten years after *Howl*, while continuing to travel the world, having spiritual and sensual adventures, Ginsberg published *Empty Mirror: Early Poems* (1961), *Kaddish, and Other Poems, 1958-1960* (1961), *Reality Sandwiches* (1963), and *Planet News, 1961-1967* (1968). Also, while Kerouac vehemently rejected the Beat and hippie labels, Ginsberg joyously embraced them, reveling in being a countercultural hero associated with fellow 1960's icons such as Bob Dylan, John Lennon, and Timothy Leary.

The final letters of the volume, both written in 1963, display this contrast with star-tling clarity. Kerouac's letter, written from the home he shares with his mother on Long Island, is filled with regret and loss and stories of fights in bars. He expresses the desire to weep and go on a good whiskey drunk, although he has been doing this already for days on end. Ginsberg, on the other hand, is in San Francisco, just returned from a voyage across Asia with Snyder and Joanne Kyger, exploring Buddhist temples and encountering bohemians from Japan to India. Toward the end of the letter, Ginsberg declares, "Now we go out save America from lovelessness." Thus, *Jack Kerouac and Allen Ginsberg: The Letters* is a powerful portrait of a literary friendship that, despite two different life arcs, produced some of the most vibrant and enduring literature of the mid-twentieth century.

John Nizalowski

Review Sources

Booklist 106, no. 21 (July 1, 2010): 19.
College Literature 37, no. 2 (Spring, 2010): 187-195.
Georgia Review 64, no. 4 (Winter, 2010): 745-749.
Kirkus Reviews 78, no. 12 (June 15, 2010): 530.
Library Journal 135, no. 10 (June 1, 2010): 86.
Los Angeles Times, July 18, 2010, p. E7.
The New York Times Book Review, August 8, 2010, p. 12.
Publishers Weekly 257, no. 20 (June 17, 2010): 37.
The Washington Post, July 29, 2010, p. C1.

A JOURNEY
My Political Life

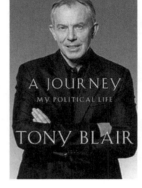

Author: Tony Blair (1953-   )
Publisher: Alfred A. Knopf (New York). 700 pp. $35.00
Type of work: Current affairs, history, autobiography
Time: 1997-2007
Locale: Great Britain

Personal account by Blair of the decade in which he was prime minister of Great Britain, including his domestic reforms and his support of the wars in Iraq and Afghanistan

Principal personages:
> TONY BLAIR (1953-   ), the prime
> minister of Great Britain,
> 1997-2007
> ALASTAIR CAMPBELL (1957-   ), one of his advisers
> CHERIE BLAIR, his wife
> GORDON BROWN (1951-   ), the Chancellor of the Exchequer,
> 1997-2007
> BILL CLINTON (1946-   ), the president of the United States,
> 1993-2001
> GEORGE W. BUSH (1946-   ), the president of the United States,
> 2001-2009
> ELIZABETH II (1926-   ), the queen of Great Britain, 1952-
> DIANA, PRINCESS OF WALES (1961-1997), daughter-in-law of the queen,
> killed in a car accident

It is predictable and expected that former presidents, prime ministers, and other important statespeople will, shortly after their departure from office, write their memoirs with the goal of ensuring their historical legacy. However, some memoirs obfuscate parts of the political past, and others are so bland and unrevealing that few other than political junkies or members of the author's immediate family or entourage would find them rewarding. Tony Blair's *A Journey* rises above the usual run of political memoirs. It is a self-serving justification of his many decisions and actions during his years as prime minister of Great Britain, from 1997 to 2007, which included three electoral victories over the Conservative and Liberal Democratic parties. It is also a revealing account of the uses of political power as well as its limitations.

Blair has been called the most brilliant progressive politician of his generation. However, his opponents were often not his Conservative political rivals but members of his own Labour Party. That party, which traces its origins back to the beginning of the twentieth century, was ideologically working-class based, albeit with many middle-class intellectual adherents, particularly in leadership roles. According to Blair, the party had more success in opposition than in governing. There were exceptions, notably the Clement Attlee government from 1945 to 1951, which established many of the pillars of Britain's welfare state. Blair's personal background was not working class but firmly middle class. His father had been a member of the Conservative Party, and Blair matriculated at a "public school" (or what would be a private school in the United States) and at Oxford University. Trained as a lawyer, or barrister (although his wife Cherie would have a much more distinguished career at the bar), he joined the Labour Party and was elected to Parliament in 1983. As he admits, in his early campaigns he positioned himself as a traditional Labourite, using a class-based appeal. By the early 1990's, he had doubts about the traditional Labour Party philosophy, with its working-class bias. He was not the first member of the party who believed that the party should modernize, but he was the most successful.

Tony Blair was prime minister of Great Britain from 1997 to 2007. After his resignation, he established the Tony Blair Faith Foundation, dedicated to furthering understanding and respect between the world's major religions, and was engaged in several international challenges.

Blair's political rival during his years as prime minister, and even before, was Gordon Brown, a fellow member of the Labour Party. With the death of John Smith in 1994, both Blair and Brown had hopes of becoming the leader of the party, but Blair won out. Something of a Faustian bargain was made at the time, an agreement that Blair would serve first as prime minister when the Labour Party came to power, but Brown would succeed him. In the interim, Brown became the prospective, or the "shadow," Chancellor of the Exchequer and then chancellor, the second most powerful position in the government, when Labour was victorious in the 1997 parliamentary elections. It proved to be a difficult relationship, with Brown eagerly anticipating his turn in the premiership and Blair reluctant to give up the position.

In 1997, Blair campaigned on the slogan of "New Labour," an attempt to distance himself from many of the traditional Labour shibboleths. In Blair's view, Labour had been focused upon working-class needs for too long. His own approach, as he explains, was that government policy should be focused upon the individual and that politics should be focused upon raising up the individual, not just to benefit a particular class. His aim was to satisfy through government actions the aspirations of those who hoped to rise into the middle class.

The labor unions had been a powerful force in British politics during much of the twentieth century but less so by the time Blair founded "New Labour," in part because of the reforms instituted by the controversial Conservative prime minister Margaret Thatcher. The unions tended to view the middle class as an enemy, as did many left-wing intellectuals who never understood the issue of aspiring upward, something Blair very much admired in the American experience. One of the icons or totems of "old" Labour was "clause 4," dating from 1918, which committed the Labour Party to the "common ownership of the means of production, distribution and exchange," or public ownership of the means of production, a policy implemented by the Attlee government after 1945 but later broadly reversed by Thatcher's Conservative government. Some Labourites believed that public ownership was outmoded and unworkable, but Blair took a considerable risk when he appealed to the party to abandon clause 4 in 1995. He won, and it was a major symbolic victory for his "New Labour."

Like most politicians, in Great Britain and elsewhere, Blair campaigned for office mostly on domestic issues, promising to modernize and reform his own Labour Party as well as rectify the domestic decisions of the previous Conservative government under Prime Minister John Major, Thatcher's Conservative successor. During his premiership, Blair instituted many domestic reforms, some more successful than others. Blair argues that it was important to change structures and not just tinker around the edges, and he claims that too many British citizens had taken unfair advantage of welfare-state benefits. Individual responsibility was paramount in his vision of an upwardly aspirational Britain, making Blair sound like a less abrasive Thatcher in some of his statements. Many of the reforms required additional government funds, and here Brown, as Chancellor of the Exchequer, was crucial. Blair respects Brown's financial astuteness, and although they frequently differed over monetary issues, Brown generally went along with Blair's New Labour programs.

When Labour assumed power in 1997 there were 1.3 million patients who had been waiting a minimum of six months for an operation; the National Health System was underfunded, and its service was uneven. Forty percent of eleven-year-old children were leaving primary school without the necessary reading and writing skills, and intercity secondary schools were failing. At the bottom of society crime and other antisocial behaviors were widespread. The immigration system was broken, with too many seeking unjustifiable political asylum. Reform with increased investment did improve education and medical care, but, in general, the changes were more incremental than fundamentally transforming. Perhaps Blair's most controversial proposal was national identification cards for everyone. Some objected to the costs, others feared a weakening of civil liberties, and the proposal was subsequently abandoned.

If "New Labor" was mainly concerned with domestic reforms, once in office, Blair, like many other successful politicians, was faced with numerous foreign policy challenges. In Northern Ireland he inherited "the Troubles" between Catholics and Protestants and between those that demanded that Northern Ireland become part of the Republic of Ireland and those that wished it to remain in the United Kingdom. Here he was largely successful, with the assistance of U.S. president Bill Clinton, exhaustion with the violence perpetrated by both sides, and lucky timing. The result was a coalition government between the republican Sinn Féin and the Protestant party of Ian Paisley. By the time Blair left office in 2007, the bombings and other acts of violence had largely disappeared, and the coalition still continued to govern in spite of issues dividing the two communities.

Blair was also a central figure in responding to the ethnic cleansing that took place in Kosovo between the Serbs and the majority Muslim population. He was an early advocate of sending in North Atlantic Treaty Organization (NATO) ground forces if needed, and he claims stiffening Clinton's support of the NATO effort. He also successfully backed the government of Sierra Leone, a former British colony in Africa, against the brutal Revolutionary United Front, by sending in British soldiers to restore order. However, it was in the aftermath of the September 11, 2001 (9/11), terrorist attacks in New York City and elsewhere that came to define and to dominate Blair's foreign policy agenda and his legacy.

Blair states that the terrorist attacks of 9/11 made him a "revolutionary." He immediately saw it as war, not just some limited action to be finessed and brushed aside. Although acknowledging that the terrorists represented only a minority of Muslims, he states that many Muslims had yet to face seriously the implications of modernism; thus, he sees a continuing battle for the mind and soul of Islam.

Immediately after 9/11 he publicly vowed to "stand shoulder to shoulder" with the United States. Britain was involved militarily in the initial assault against Afghanistan's Taliban and al-Qaeda, which began in October, 2001. Blair admits that the Western allies could have done things better in the War in Afghanistan, but he argues that on balance, the decision was correct and justified, as was the later war in Iraq against Saddam Hussein, on the grounds of "human freedom." When, at the 2010 British Chilcot Inquiry into the Iraq War, Blair was asked if he had any regrets, he responded that he accepted full responsibility for the decisions that were made. He argues that the evidence that Iraq had weapons of mass destruction (WMDs) seemed overwhelming. He admits that in retrospect that evidence was wrong, but he strongly denies the accusation that the evidence had been falsified or manipulated to justify war against Iraq, and he claims that Hussein was committed to eventually restoring his WMDs program once the United Nations sanctions had been removed. In any event, the removal of Hussein, regardless of costs, ultimately benefited Iraq and its peoples, and he blames the costs of the war in human and economic terms and the long duration of the Iraq campaign on outside forces, particularly al-Qaeda and Iran. Although on opposite polls politically—Blair a progressive and U.S. president George W. Bush a conservative—Blair liked Bush personally but also admired Bush's leadership abilities and his focus on the issues. He claims that the pressure of war against Iraq was less from Bush and more from some of his advisers, and that he was able to persuade Bush to go to the United Nations for support and not act unilaterally. Also, allying with the United States gave Britain, a secondary power in the twenty-first century, "a huge position" and an "immediate purchase" on events, or as a prior prime minister had stated, Britain could be a Greece to an American Rome. In the crucial parliamentary vote for war against Iraq, Blair prevailed, 412 to 149, with much of the opposition coming from his own Labour Party. However, the length of the war in Iraq, the number of civilian and military casualties, and the bloody insurgency eroded support in Britain for both the war and for Blair himself.

Blair claims that he was reluctant to step down as prime minister because of his doubts that Brown would continue Blair's New Labour policies. Also, it is always difficult to give up power. After considerable divisions within the party and the cabinet and critical commentary from the media, of which Blair is damningly critical, he resigned in June, 2007, still persuaded that he was the most qualified person to lead

Britain. Although in *A Journey* Blair focuses upon Brown's political and philosophical differences rather than his somewhat difficult personality, others have noted that when Brown did become prime minister after Blair's resignation in 2007, he was deemed to have been a failure and was badly defeated in the 2010 elections. Like most autobiographies, *A Journey* is a self-justification for Blair's premiership, but it is well written and gives considerable insight to arguably the most important British politician of the early twenty-first century.

Eugene Larson

Review Sources

New Statesman 139 (September 13, 2010): 39.
The National Review 62 (October 4, 2010): 10.
The New York Times Book Review, October 10, 2010, p. 22.
The New Yorker 86, no. 27 (September 13, 2010): 70.
The Spectator 314 (September 11, 2010): 48.

JUST KIDS

Author: Patti Smith (1946-   )
Publisher: Ecco (New York). 278 pp. $27.00
Type of work: Memoir
Time: 1946-1989, primarily the late 1960's and 1970's
Locale: Primarily New York City

A gripping and intriguing story of two talented and sensitive young people who find themselves and fame in New York City

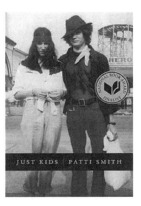

Principal personages:
> PATTI SMITH (1946-   ), a poet, artist, and musician who was both lover and lifelong friend of Robert Mapplethorpe
> ROBERT MAPPLETHORPE (1946-1989), an artist and photographer who gained notoriety for his homoerotic photographs
> ANDY WARHOL (1928-1987), an influential pop artist
> BOB DYLAN (1941-   ), a brilliant singer-songwriter who inspired a generation, including Smith
> ALLEN GINSBERG (1926-1997), an influential Beat poet
> WILLIAM S. BURROUGHS (1914-1997), an influential Beat writer
> SAM SHEPARD (1943-   ), a playwright
> JIM CARROLL (1949-2009), a poet
> JANIS JOPLIN (1943-1970), a rock singer
> KRIS KRISTOFFERSON (1939-   ), a singer-songwriter
> JIMI HENDRIX (1942-1970), a brilliant rock guitarist

Patti Smith and Robert Mapplethorpe have become larger-than-life iconic figures, but at one time, they were merely two young people trying to find themselves in New York City. Patricia Lee Smith and Robert Michael Mapplethorpe were both born in 1946. She was born during the great blizzard of 1946 in Chicago. He was born and raised in the Floral Park section of Queens in New York City. Smith is the only one of the pair left who can piece together the story of their relationship.

The photograph on the cover of this mesmerizing memoir is one of the pair attending the Coney Island funfair in 1969. Both in their early twenties, they had been lovers for two years at the time of the photograph. That they even would become a couple in the first place was made possible only by a chance meeting. Was it fated to be? For Smith it must have been difficult at every turn in the writing of this extraordinary memoir to not just print the myth and let the truth fade to black. Attempting to squeeze out a living in New York was not an easy proposition for either of them. It must have felt like it was them against the world.

Although born in Chicago, Smith was raised in Deptford, New Jersey. She grew

> ~
> *During the 1970's, Patti Smith
> established herself as a seminal punk
> rocker as well as a critically acclaimed
> poet. While her first love was poetry,
> she found that the combination of rock
> and poetry could make for a potent mix.*
> ~

up in fits and starts. During these years, Smith was "transformed" by art. She wanted to be a part of the art world. She "hungered" to be a real artist, a human being who could create. Not popular in high school, Smith immersed herself in drawing, writing poems, dancing, reading, and listening to rock music. In 1966, Smith got pregnant and gave birth to her child on "the anniversary of the bombing of Guernica." She states that on "that same day, in Brooklyn, Robert dropped acid." Each would have to come to terms with where they were in life and decide which direction they should take.

After attending Glassboro State College (now Rowan University), in Glassboro, New Jersey, for a short period of time, Smith eventually came to the conclusion that she had to move to New York City in order to find her way. She was living in the United States of the late 1960's. During the spring of 1967, she had to take a close look at her life and decide where she wanted to go. She gave up her child for adoption. Smith also came to the conclusion that she was not cut out to be a teacher. At this point in time, she recognized that she did not have "the discipline, the focus, nor the money to continue" her stint at college. There was change and confusion seemingly on every street corner. She took "solace" in the French Symbolist poet Arthur Rimbaud. It was time to make a major move in her life. It was time to enter the cauldron that was New York City. Smith and Mapplethorpe first met in 1967 while she was working at the Gotham Book Mart. They commenced on a journey together, first as lovers and then as lifelong friends who only wanted the best for the other.

For all the roadblocks that stood in the way, Smith found a way to eventually become the "godmother" of punk music and produced one of its seminal albums in 1975 with *Horses*. The iconic cover photograph was taken by Mapplethorpe. The Patti Smith Group included Lenny Kaye, Ivan Kral, Jay Dee Daugherty, and Richard Sohl. Before she could get to this point in her development, she had to grow up in the everchanging world around her. Part of the myth that Smith creates is how she sees Mapplethorpe and herself as the Rimbaud/Paul Verlaine of modern-day New York. However, the reader clearly understands that there is something beyond the myth. Their first apartment together was located in Brooklyn and was extremely small. It was all that they could afford. Eventually, they ended up living in the Chelsea Hotel in Manhattan. This move put them at the epicenter of the counterculture. The young, innocent Smith came face-to-face with a crazy world with which she was not familiar. Because of her fear of dying, she never became a user of dangerous drugs. She would have to learn how to survive in an environment where there were few boundaries on what was allowed.

While Mapplethorpe had been experimenting with collages, installations, and drawings during his time with Smith, after he was given a Polaroid instant camera, his whole approach to art changed. He almost immediately turned to photography. As she saw it, he was "smitten with the elasticity" of it. Mapplethorpe also began to evolve into a photographer who was more than casually interested in the male body. He was in the process of realizing that he was gay, and he needed to find how he fit in with the emerging gay consciousness that was surrounding him. The love affair that had brought them together had to end. A bond of respect for each other took its place. While she thought of herself as "a bad girl trying to be good," she saw Mapplethorpe as "a good boy trying to be bad."

In his search for recognition as a photographer, he found his way into the pop-art world of Andy Warhol. Smith was not fond of Warhol and his approach to art. Mapplethorpe also gained entrance into the "sadomasochist community." This was a completely foreign world for Smith. It became Mapplethorpe's mission to "take very difficult pictures with the same classic view as he would taking flowers or a portrait." Smith had to come to terms with the realization that her devotion to him would not save her onetime partner from himself or the world around him. She could not alter that Mapplethorpe was a gay man in the United States and that a horrific thing like AIDS would eventually take his life. Smith was forced to conclude that her "comprehension" of homosexuality was "narrow and provincial." While she "needed to explore beyond" herself, Mapplethorpe "needed to search within himself." They threw themselves into their art and the cultural milieu that surrounded them. Smith could tell that Mapplethorpe believed in his abilities as an artist. He had a shyness, yet he was sure of himself. She admired him, wanted the best for him, and wanted him to succeed. They leaned on each other for whatever was needed. However, love could not insulate the lovers from the consequences of their actions, from the cruel luck that seemed to rule the world.

Making ends meet was not always easy for either of them. There was a certain androgyny that ended up advancing their celebrity. They soaked up the vibrations that permeated the Chelsea Hotel and the streets of Manhattan. There was both grit and innocence in abundance. Smith describes the Chelsea as "a doll's house in the Twilight Zone, with a hundred rooms, each a small universe." The "shabby elegance" of the hotel seemed to suit her. First and foremost, she had been a poet. This was her foundation. Smith first wrote "Fire of Unknown Origin" to be a poem and not a song. She worked on learning a few guitar chords as she went through a book of Bob Dylan songs. The poem was turned into a song after Smith met Dylan. This seemed like the appropriate leap to make. She tried out the song on Mapplethorpe with the lyrics "Death comes sweeping down the hallway in a lady's dress/ Death comes riding up the highway in its Sunday best/ Death comes I can't do nothing/ Death goes there must be something that remains/ A fire of unknown origin took my baby away." She took inspiration from Dylan, John Lennon, Neil Young, and others who were finding their voice in rock music. She wanted to merge the poetic with the energy of rock and roll.

There also was a political component, a search for social change, and a sexual energy from the rock performers whom she admired. Along the way a multitude of extraordinary figures crossed Smith's and Mapplethorpe's paths, including Jimi

Hendrix, Kris Kristofferson, Janis Joplin, Allen Ginsberg, William S. Burroughs, Gregory Corso, Jim Carroll, and Sam Shepard. At one point she was asked "to keep an eye" on Joplin at the Chelsea. Joplin was crushed after "a good-looking guy she was attracted to" decided to leave with another—more attractive—female. During this time together, Smith wrote "a little song" for Joplin that included the lines "I was working real hard/ To show the world what I could do" and ends with "When the crowd goes home/ And I turn in and realize I'm alone/ I can't believe/ I had to sacrifice you." Joplin recognized herself in the lyric. As Smith left her on this occasion, Joplin was looking in a mirror and "adjusting her boas." She wanted Smith to tell her how she looked and her response was "Like a pearl." In addition to finding her way as a rock performer, she wrote for such rock publications as *Rolling Stone*, *Circus*, and *Crawdaddy*. For all the youthful exuberance that existed in this cultural milieu, there was also a fragility that lay just beneath the surface. These young performers, artists, and vagabonds could be easily driven to tragedy, easily broken at the drop of a word or a glance.

While Smith had brief but intense relationships with both Shepard and Carroll, they could not compete with the ghost of Mapplethorpe. For all the success that came Smith's way, it was Mapplethorpe who was her "partner in crime" and partner in art. It was their love for the multitude of creative possibilities that had first brought them together and allowed them to endure the multitude of hardships and the fact that they were not meant to be lovers forever.

Mapplethorpe died in a Boston hospital on March 9, 1989, from complications related to AIDS. He was only forty-two years old. Although Smith knew that her "soul mate" would not survive, she was devastated by his death. Smith was inducted into the Rock and Roll Hall of Fame in 2007. The groundwork for success, fame, and iconic status was laid during the 1970's when she and Mapplethorpe linked arms, linked souls, and took a chance. *Just Kids* is the fascinating story before the avalanche of fame and notoriety and rightfully won the 2010 National Book Award for nonfiction.

Smith was "so excited" to win, "so happy," but she did not write the book hoping to win an award. To do "good work" was what she had set out to do. Ultimately Smith is happy "to give Robert to the people, really give the people a more holistic image" of him. As she looks back, Smith recognizes that she was his first model and he was her first muse. She wrote a memorial song for Mapplethorpe that incorporates the images of a "Little emerald bird" wanting "to fly away." She asks the questions "If I cup my hand, could I make him stay?" and "Little emerald bird, must we say goodbye?" *Just Kids* is a touching tribute from Smith to her friend and to their relationship. It is also a telling tribute to the sometimes crazy and harrowing process of becoming an artist.

Jeffry Jensen

Review Sources

The Boston Globe, January 17, 2010, p. C6.
Chicago Tribune, January 17, 2010, p. 5.
The Globe and Mail, March 13, 2010, p. R9.
The Guardian, February 13, 2010, p. 6.
The New York Times, January 18, 2010, p. C1.
The New York Times Book Review, January 31, 2010, p. 1.
Publishers Weekly 256, no. 49 (December 7, 2009): 43.
Sunday Times, February 7, 2010, p. 39.
The Village Voice 55, no. 49 (January 26, 2010): 34.
The Washington Post, January 26, 2010, p. C4.

JUSTICE BRENNAN
Liberal Champion

Authors: Seth Stern (1975-   ) and Stephen Wermiel
(1950-   )
Publisher: Harcourt (Boston). 674 pp. $35.00
Type of work: Biography, law
Time: 1906-1997
Locale: United States

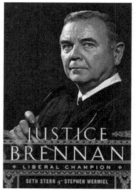

A fascinating and scholarly account of William J. Brennan, the liberal Supreme Court justice who is considered by many legal scholars to have been the most influential member of the Court during the entire twentieth century

Principal personages:
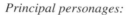

WILLIAM J. BRENNAN (1906-1997), an
associate justice of the Supreme Court, 1956-1990
MARJORIE LEONARD BRENNAN, his wife until her death in 1982
MARY FOWLER BRENNAN, his wife from 1983 to 1997
FELIX FRANKFURTER (1882-1965), a conservative associate justice and
his former teacher
EARL WARREN (1891-1874), the chief justice of the United States, 1953-
1969
WILLIAM O. DOUGLAS (1898-1980), a liberal and temperamental justice,
who was brilliant but often unreliable
WARREN E. BURGER (1907-1995), a moderately conservative justice
whose relationship with Brennan was strained
WILLIAM H. REHNQUIST (1924-2005), a conservative chief justice,
whom Brennan personally liked and respected

This magnificent biography, *Justice Brennan: Liberal Champion* by Seth Stern and Stephen Wermiel, was the product of more than fourteen years of serious research and writing. In 1986, lawyer-journalist Wermiel was a reporter for *The Wall Street Journal* when he had the opportunity to meet with William J. Brennan to discuss the possibility of working on a book about Brennan's life and judicial career. At the time, Brennan was interested in cooperating on such a project, and he was looking for a legal scholar who was also a competent writer able to communicate with non-legal professionals. During the following five years, Wermiel interviewed Brennan in sixty recorded sessions, and he had unrestricted access to thousands of pages of Brennan's personal papers, including draft opinions and memos exchanged with other justices.

Following Brennan's retirement in 1990, Wermiel continued his research and wrote a few articles on Brennan's jurisprudence, but after Brennan's death in 1997, teaching and other obligations forced him to put the project aside. Returning to the project in 2006, Wermiel decided to work with Stern, another experienced journalist-lawyer. After four additional years of research, interviews, and writing, the long-awaited *Justice Brennan: Liberal Champion* was finally published.

Stephen Wermiel covered the Supreme Court for the Wall Street Journal, *and he has written numerous scholarly articles for law journals. Seth Stern, a Harvard Law School graduate, has been a writer and reporter for* Congressional Journal *since 2001.*

A large percentage of the biography is devoted to Brennan's work on the Supreme Court, but it nevertheless includes considerable information about his personal life, even though Brennan placed a high value on his privacy and was always reluctant to openly discuss his personal opinions and experiences. Raised in a struggling middle-class, Irish Catholic family, he witnessed a great deal of poverty and social unrest during his youth in Newark, New Jersey. By his own account, he was particularly influenced by his father, a labor leader and city commissioner who had left-of-center ideas about economic issues but relatively conservative views on issues such as free speech and pornography. Although Justice Brennan gave the impression of thinking only about judicial questions during his tenure on the high court, the authors make it clear that his family relationships and personal problems occupied much of his time and energy. He struggled with his first wife's alcoholism, experienced major problems with two of his three children, and had long periods of debt that kept him at his "wit's end."

In hindsight, it is amazing that a moderately conservative president such as Dwight D. Eisenhower nominated Brennan. Wermiel and Stern observe that the selection was a result of particular circumstances and took place in "a rather cursory fashion." When an unexpected opening on the Court occurred during the election year of 1956, Eisenhower instructed his advisers to look for a judge who was Catholic, a member of the Democratic Party, and a person relatively young and of good moral character—criteria that narrowed the number of qualified persons. Eisenhower's moderate Republican advisers were also impressed with Brennan's work in reforming the New Jersey courts to make them more efficient. Some of his writings for the New Jersey Supreme Court, according to the authors, should have set off alarm bells to conservative Republicans. In the midst of an election, however, Eisenhower was not preoccupied with the ideologies of his judicial nominees, despite his dissatisfaction with some of the decisions of his earlier choice, Chief Justice Earl Warren, as in *Brown v. Board of Education* (1954). Within a few years, Eisenhower would refer to his nominations of Warren and Brennan as the two greatest mistakes of his presidential decisions.

Brennan is frequently characterized as the most prominent practitioner of "free-wheeling judicial activism," an expression that usually refers to the practice of boldly and broadly interpreting the Constitution according to the judge's own moral values, without proper respect for textual exegesis or legislative discretion. Both critics and admirers recognize that Brennan was the Court's leading advocate of the notion that the Constitution was produced in order to promote the dignity, freedom, and equality of individuals and oppressed groups. Nevertheless, in a 1963 speech, he declared that the Court was not a "council of Platonic Guardians" with authority to decide questions based on "the justices' own notions of what is just or wise or politic." His critics accuse him of doing just this. On issues such as capital punishment, for example, legal journalist Stuart Taylor wrote that Brennan tended to find constitutional rights "that can honestly be found neither in the language of the document, nor in the records left by those who wrote it, nor in any broad national consensus that has evolved since then."

As soon as Brennan became an associate justice of the high court, his relationships with other justices were of crucial importance; sometimes they influenced the development of his judicial philosophy. Serving as Warren's "chief unofficial adviser," Brennan held meetings with the chief justice to discuss the docket before conferences. Like several other justices, Brennan's relationship with Felix Frankfurter, who had been his teacher at Harvard, was frequently confrontational and tense, in part because of Frankfurter's rather heavy-handed attempts to guide his former student in a more conservative direction. However, Brennan was an outgoing man who maintained friendly relationships with John Marshall Harlan as well as several other conservative justices. Wermiel and Stern observe, moreover, that he complained about the intransigence and work habits of justices who shared his liberal ideology, particularly William O. Douglas and Thurgood Marshall. During the 1980's, when Brennan experienced the frustrations of frequently voting with the minority, he often took walks with his most outspoken antagonist, Antonin Scalia, and he admired and praised the work of Chief Justice William H. Rehnquist.

A remarkable number of landmark opinions written by Brennan continue into the twenty-first century as established constitutional law. Whenever he was asked which of his opinions were the most important, he answered that he did not like to choose among his children, but he nevertheless pointed to two cases: *Baker v. Carr* (1962), when the Court held that the federal courts had the authority to decide whether legislative districts violated the principle of "one person, one vote," and *Goldberg v. Kelly* (1970), the decision establishing that government assistance was a form of property, so that an evidentiary hearing was necessary before the termination of benefits. Wermiel and Stern suggest that two other cases were of equal validity: *New York Times v Sullivan* (1964), which established that public officials could not collect damages for libel unless they were able to demonstrate a reckless disregard for the truth, and the controversial *Texas v. Johnson* (1989), when a 5-to-4 majority ruled that the desecration of the U.S. flag was a form of "symbolic speech" protected by the First Amendment.

One of the fascinating themes in the book is the inconsistency between Brennan's personal beliefs and some of his decisions. Wermiel and Stern find that it is probably not possible to entirely reconcile Brennan the judge with Brennan the person. Although he looked upon pornography as pernicious, for example, he consistently worked to expand First Amendment protection for such materials. Even after he became the Court's most vocal proponent of equality for women, he remained hesitant to appoint any female law clerks. When a University of California law professor recommended a highly qualified young woman in 1970, he wrote, "Send me someone else." Four years later, after the professor complained in a personal letter that his blanket rejection was "both unconstitutional and simply wrong," Brennan finally relented and hired his first female clerk. Wermiel and Stern observe that he compartmentalized his judicial decisions from his personal behavior to the extent that he appeared not to recognize the "profound disconnect" of practicing gender discrimination while denouncing it as unconstitutional in Court opinions.

The tension between Brennan's personal beliefs and his judicial rulings is especially interesting in the area of religion. Although he retained his Catholic identity until his death, he attended mass infrequently during several periods of his life. Never did he appear to be particularly concerned about the details of the Church's dogmatic theology, as articulated in councils and papal encyclicals. Wermiel and Stern concede that it is difficult to discern the extent to which his Catholic faith influenced his judicial philosophy, but they observe that his decisions often mirrored the Sunday school lessons he had learned about "taking care of the poor and weak." His emphasis on human dignity, moreover, echoed the social-gospel version of liberal Catholic intellectuals, as expressed in *Commonweal* magazine and by liberal priests such as John A. Ryan. Although Brennan sometimes rendered decisions that contradicted the Church's doctrines (for example, on abortion), he was concerned about the judgments of Church officials.

When Brennan read the journalistic account of the men on the Supreme Court in *The Brethren* (1979), by Bob Woodward and Scott Armstrong, he was apparently appalled by the way in which the book portrayed him as an "Irish ward boss" exchanging votes to score as many victories as possible. Although Wermiel and Stern insist that he would not compromise his fundamental principles, they describe numerous instances in which he patiently rewrote his drafts and modified his language in order to accommodate his colleagues' concerns, with the goal of reaching a majority consensus, usually in order to obtain as liberal a decision as possible. A tactician who kept his eyes on the practical consequences of decisions, he had the habit of holding up five fingers for his clerks, indicating the importance of getting five votes for the positions he favored. Among his various techniques, he learned to lace his writings with "time bombs," which were seemingly harmless statements that he would utilize in later cases. His intellectual opponent Scalia called him "the most skillful general on the Court," and further remarked, "He is the epitome of skill, subtlety, and yet tenacity and he's always going somewhere."

Wermiel and Stern clearly admire Brennan, and they do not try to conceal their sympathy for his "living Constitution" approach to constitutional interpretation. In several places they remark that the meanings of the general terms of the Constitution, such as "cruel and unusual punishment," are not static according to their original meanings—that they change as societal conditions change. Their biography, despite their admiration for Brennan, is generally balanced, fair-minded, and evenhanded, with the possible exception of the celebratory final chapter. It is a superb example of readable and interesting scholarship. It is unlikely that any writer will ever be able to write a better account of Brennan's life and judicial career, and certainly no other writer will ever be able to rival Wermiel's direct access to the man. In order to benefit from the book, readers probably need to have a degree of informational background about the nature of the U.S. Constitution and the Supreme Court, although it is certainly not necessary for a reader to possess any specialized knowledge.

Thomas Tandy Lewis

Review Sources

Kirkus Reviews 78, no. 15 (September 1, 2010): 720.
Library Journal 135, no. 15 (September 15, 2010): 87.
The Nation 291, no. 23 (December 6, 2010): 31-34.
The New York Times Sunday Book Review, October 8, 2010, p. BR20.
Publishers Weekly 257, no. 30 (August 2, 2010): 40.

THE KING OF TREES

Author: Ah Cheng (Acheng Zhong; 1949-   )
Translated from the Chinese by Bonnie S. McDougall
Publisher: New Directions Books (New York). 196 pp.
    $14.95
Type of work: Novellas
Time: Between 1968 and 1976
Locale: Rural China, resembling the mountainous
    Yunnan Province

Told from the perspective of three educated young men sent to the countryside during the upheavals of China's Cultural Revolution, all three novellas highlight some of the paradoxes, absurdities, and acts of small resistance during this Communist mass social experiment that negatively affected millions of Chinese people

Principal characters:
> KNOTTY XIAO, called the KING OF TREES, a former soldier turned logger and farmer who feels protective of a massive old tree the students want to cut down
> LI LI, the leader of the students, who wants to cut down the tree in the spirit of Communist ideology
> WANG YISHENG, called the CHESS FOOL, a deprived youth whose single talent is his mastery of Chinese chess
> NI BIN, called TALL BALLS, a young chess player from a privileged background who seeks to enter Wang into a local tournament
> THE SECRETARY FOR CULTURE AND EDUCATION, willing to enter Wang into the tournament for a bribe by Ni Bin
> BEANPOLE, a young student asked to teach rural village children
> LAIDI, Beanpole's friend, who works as a cook and dreams of being a music teacher
> CHEN LIN, the principal of a rural junior high school
> WANG FU, a bright and ambitious pupil

The King of Trees makes available again in English the three key novellas of Ah Cheng, which cast a clear light on the human cost of China's devastating Cultural Revolution. Originally written at a moment of political liberalization in China in 1984 and 1985, Cheng's three stories look back at the fate of the so-called Educated Youth. These were young people from the schools and universities of mainland China who were sent to the rural countryside to promote Mao Zedong's brand of communism. The three stories look at the issues of ecological destruction in the name of modernity, the value of friendship in adversity, and one young man's heartfelt struggle to teach his rural students something of value and meaning in their lives instead of rote

~

Ah Cheng is the pen name of Chinese writer Acheng Zhong, who rose to literary fame in China and was recognized abroad on the basis of his three "king" novellas collected in The King of Trees. *He cowrote the script for the film* Wu Qingyuan *(2006;* The Go Master, *2006).*

~

memorization of bland, standardized propaganda texts.

In the title novella, *The King of Trees*, the unnamed narrator, along with other young people yanked out of city schools, is sent into a mountainous countryside that strongly resembles China's southern province of Yunnan, which borders Laos. Their task, encouraged by Communist propaganda slogans, is to chop down old-growth trees to make room for supposedly more modern tree plantations meant to yield more valuable forest products.

Arriving at his destination, the narrator witnesses the power struggle among the students' ideological leader, the dedicated young cadre Li Li, and the logger and farmer Knotty Xiao. While Li Li spouts slogans and is determined to fell each and every old-growth tree according to the party's mandate, Knotty Xiao shows an appreciation for nature and tradition.

A clash erupts about the felling of one remaining, massive old-growth tree the local loggers have left standing out of reverence for its natural beauty. Cheng shows the strength of the spiritual alignment of that tree with the traditional beliefs represented by Knotty Xiao when both share the same honorific title. For while even Li Li refers to the tree as "the King of Trees," the locals call Knotty Xiao "King of Trees" for his skill and willingness to fell all but that magnificent exception. On a symbolic level, Li Li and Knotty Xiao stand for opposing elements in China, modernization at all costs or an appreciation of tradition, harmony, and spiritual balance between humanity and nature.

Li Li triumphs in alliance with the local Communist Party secretary. Knotty Xiao watches the felling of the old tree, which is told in agonizing detail. After a forest fire is set to clear the denuded mountain, leading to the death of forest animals, which is witnessed by students and villagers, Knotty Xiao falls ill and dies.

Knotty Xiao's death and burial within the roots of the old tree's remaining stump clearly signal the defeat of traditional China at the hands of zealous cadres spurred on by the Communist Party hierarchy. The novella has been widely praised by Chinese and foreign critics for its depiction of the human cost of radical modernization without concerns for traditional beliefs or economic sustainability.

The King of Chess is Cheng's first and most widely known and critically discussed novella. It was written in 1984, a few years after the author was permitted to return to Beijing in 1979 after spending eleven years in the rural Yunnan Province. Its plot tells the story of the life of the Educated Youth at their remote destination. The novella begins when the unnamed narrator is about to leave by train from a major city, most likely Beijing, for a long journey to the countryside. He is invited to a game of chess by another young man, Wang Yisheng.

When the narrator makes his first move, telling how "I picked up my cannon and moved it toward the center line," a footnote would have been warranted to explain that this game is not Western chess, as the title seems to imply. Instead, the game is a different version, called *xiangqi*. Literally, this can be translated as "elephant chess"—named after the piece *xiang*, elephant, and *qi* for chess—or, more commonly, as Chinese chess. Given that translator Bonnie McDougall dedicated her translation to "readers with little or no Chinese or expertise in Chinese history and culture," an explanation of this difference should have been given. Ironically, Western scholars who have analyzed this novella in academic journals have not yet pointed out this key difference.

The "Chess Fool," as Wang is known, possesses one unique talent—mastering this game that has sustained his otherwise deprived young life so far. However, his talent has been exploited by others, most recently by a band of pickpockets who rob Wang's spellbound audiences during intense matches. The narrator feels ambiguous toward Wang. Their ensuing conversation introduces the story's key topics of hunger and the question of whether a spiritual pastime, like chess, can sustain a person in times of great physical adversity.

At their destination, the narrator and Wang are split into different labor camps. When Wang visits later on, the narrator and his young comrades prepare a communal feast based on the meat of a freshly caught snake. They watch as Wang plays Ni Bin, called "Tall Balls" in the somewhat crude style of the exiled youths. As Ni Bin is beaten and impressed by Wang's ability as a chess prodigy, he hatches the plan to enter Wang in a local tournament to get both out of camp.

As Ni Bin comes from a previously privileged bourgeois family that still holds some power, he has access to the local Communist Party secretary for education and culture. That man agrees to enter Wang for the price of a gift of "an ebony chess set dating from the Ming" Dynasty from Ni Bin's father to the secretary. However, when Wang learns of the deal, he adamantly opposes it. His rejection, based on the traditional Confucian command to value one's parents' gifts, is underlined by the fact that Wang holds dear a set of homemade, still blank Chinese chess pieces his late mother made for him out of discarded plastic toothbrush stems. While Wang bestows great value on this set for spiritual reasons, Ni Bin would easily discard a much more valuable patrimony for the sake of bettering his present life, obtaining a desk job, and the chance to profile himself as Wang's manager.

Finally, Wang plays nine local players simultaneously, defeating all but the reigning district master. That old man is given a gracious tie by Wang. Dramatizing again that Wang prefers spiritual values over material ones he declines the old man's offer to leisurely discuss chess moves at the man's comfortable home for a few days. Instead, Wang seeks the company of his peers, sharing meals and facing hardships together.

The *King of Children* tells the poignant tale of a young teacher going against stale Communist Party instructions to provide his village pupils with a meaningful education instead. One day Beanpole, nicknamed for his skinny stature, is appointed replacement teacher at a rural junior high school by the disillusioned principal Chen

Lin. He is given the position because he is the only one among the Educated Youth who had finished the first year of senior high school before being sent to the countryside.

Beanpole's assignment causes the envy of his friend Laidi, a young woman employed to cook at the labor camp, who dreams of becoming a music teacher. When Beanpole starts teaching, he quickly resents the mortifying task of having his students copy into their exercise books what he writes on the blackboard from the only official textbook the school possesses for his class. Edged on by the ambitious young pupil Wang Fu, Beanpole changes the curriculum without permission. He also writes the lyrics for a song Laidi composes to take the place of the old Communist Party songs at school.

When the local authorities learn of Beanpole's insubordination, they send an official to relieve him of his duties. Sensing the hopelessness of his position, Beanpole resigns himself to his fate and returns to the forest labor camp. Before leaving, he makes a present out of the Chinese dictionary Laidi gave him in exchange for writing the lyrics to her song. This he leaves for Wang Fu, his best and most challenging student.

This poignant tale of one young man's rebellion against a stultifying official curriculum that is euphemistically designed to teach "character building" but that is meaningless in reality caught the attention of Cheng's readers and admirers. It was made into a screenplay for Chen Kaige's successful film, *Hai zi wang* (1987; *King of Children*, 1987). The film resonated with Chinese audiences wary of the more dreary aspects of their education experience.

In all three stories collected in *The King of Trees*, Cheng's impassioned prose lets young cadres, peasants, middle-aged Communist officials, and the young people removed from their urban homes speak for themselves. The conflicts are narrated in a neutral voice so that readers are invited to draw their own conclusions. Cheng's portrayal of his young protagonists and the people with whom they interact is open and balanced, juxtaposing acts of friendship with those of politically motivated actions.

Chinese readers immediately treasured Cheng's clear accounts of the many pitfalls of the Cultural Revolution's quixotic idea of sending young students from their schools and universities to labor in the countryside, a mass movement motivated by an inner power struggle in Mao's China. *The King of Chess* was republished in Chinese in Hong Kong. The summer, 1985, edition of the magazine *Chinese Literature* carried a first translation in English. It was done by W. J. F. Jenner, translated as *The Chess Master*, and gave the author's name as "Ahcheng." Western scholars immediately began writing analyses of the story, focusing on the Daoist strategy of Wang Yisheng to defeat his opponents. The novella *The King of Trees* was translated first by Gladys Yang and published in the Winter, 1986, issue of the same magazine.

This edition of *The King of Trees* and its translation by McDougall is based on the Chinese texts of the novellas as collected in Ah Cheng's *A Cheng xiaoshuo* (1985; stories by Ah Cheng), which differs slightly from their magazine versions. In 1990, McDougall published her first translation of the three novellas in the United Kingdom as *Three Kings* (1990). This translation has been revised from that British book, most noticeably using pinyin throughout and making minor stylistic changes. It is a welcome publication that makes Ah Cheng's most famous and successful novellas available again to an audience that has appreciated it for Ah Cheng's focus on the survival of human decency in a politically charged environment.

R. C. Lutz

Review Source

Library Journal 135, no. 15 (September 15, 2010): 57.

KRAKEN
An Anatomy

Author: China Miéville (1972-   )
Publisher: Del Rey/Ballantine Books (New York).
    509 pp. $26.00
Type of work: Novel
Time: The 2000's
Locale: London

When a giant preserved squid inexplicably disappears from the museum at which he is a curator, Billy Harrow is astounded to learn that several competing factions, including the Church of God Kraken, believe that the squid is a prophet who may either hasten or prevent the coming apocalypse

Principal characters:
> BILLY HARROW, a museum curator who specializes in preserving marine specimens
> DANE PARNELL, a museum guard and member of the Church of God Kraken
> WATI, a spirit and the leader of the Union of Magicked Assistants, who can only manifest within statues or other inanimate figures
> THE TATTOO, a villain whose essence has been imprisoned inside a tattoo on another man's body
> PAUL, the person whose tattoo The Tattoo inhabits
> GOSS and SUBBY, a pair of The Tattoo's brutal henchmen
> PATRICK VARDY, a psychology professor and cult profiler who becomes a temporary true believer in every cult he encounters
> LEON, Billy's friend
> MARGINALIA ("MARGE"), Leon's girlfriend
> SAIRA and FITCH, Londonmancers, or individuals who consider themselves "cells" of the living city of London
> KATH COLLINGSWOOD and BARON, investigators in the Fundamentalist and Sect-Related Crime Unit

Considered a novel in the "New Weird" tradition of speculative fiction, *Kraken*, by China Miéville, is the story of Billy Harlow, a museum curator who catalogs and preserves marine specimens. In particular, he has worked on Architeuthis dux, an approximately thirty-foot-long giant squid that is the museum's main attraction. While conducting a routine tour for museum visitors, Billy is flabbergasted to find that the squid, its tank, and thousands of gallons of the preservative formalin have simply vanished, with no physical evidence to suggest how someone could have gotten the intact tank out of the building. Along with the other museum employees, Billy is in-

terviewed by the police, but it is not until he
is summoned to a remote location by the mysterious Baron and Kath Collingswood, who
claim to be police officers in the Fundamen-
talist and Sect-Related Crime (FSRC) Unit,
that Billy realizes he is irrevocably involved
in these strange events.

*A British writer and three-time winner
of the Arthur C. Clarke Award, China
Miéville has also won the British
Fantasy Award. His writing is
considered by some to characterize the
"New Weird" movement in science
fiction and fantasy.* Kraken *is his
seventh novel.*

After a dissatisfying interview that leaves
Billy more confused than ever, he returns to
the museum only to discover that a man has
been murdered and somehow been placed in a
jar of preservative fluid, even though the body could not possibly have fit through the
jar's neck. The FSRC escort Billy back to his apartment and create protective magical
wards to guard him, but a strange and brutal pair named Goss and Subby manage to
kidnap Billy after Goss literally swallows Billy's friend Leon whole.

A museum guard named Dane Parnell rescues Billy just as Goss and Subby deliver
him to the monstrous the Tattoo, an evil spirit imprisoned within the tattoo on an innocent man's back. Dane, a member of the Church of God Kraken, becomes frustrated
with his cult's lack of initiative in solving the mystery of the missing squid, so he
drags Billy on a desperate race throughout London, during which they try to determine friend from foe and ascertain the greater implications of this strange crime. Billy
cannot understand why Dane's church and various other factions believe he possesses secret knowledge of the kraken, but he gradually accepts his own connection to
the events, persuaded in part by the strange prophetic dreams that he experiences under the influence of squid ink. Billy and Dane's encounters with the normally unseen
inhabitants of London grow more and more peculiar, making it difficult for them to
determine who is behind the disappearance and what the thieves intend to do with the
stolen kraken.

Undoubtedly, Miéville's greatest strength lies in his vivid imagination. The creatures that populate this strange London that Billy is just beginning to know are
grotesque and fascinating. In addition to the Tattoo, Billy encounters Wati, a well-
meaning spirit who performs his work as leader of the Union of Magicked Assistants
by leaping from one inanimate figure to another, including statues, action figures, and
garden gnomes; Grisamentum, a creature that manifests itself in ink and therefore
may have a particular interest in squids; and the Londonmancers, who literally consider themselves to be cells that make up the living city of London. In addition to
these odd creatures, Miéville sprinkles interesting thought experiments throughout
his narrative, such as animal familiars, consisting primarily of cats and birds, who under Wati's leadership go on strike and march in picket lines that largely go unnoticed
by most of London's inhabitants. This particular tidbit upends the common trope in
fantastic literature that magical creatures rarely seem to object to their indentured service, allowing *Kraken* to simultaneously exist within yet stand apart from common
fantasy conventions.

In another interesting episode, Miéville refers to a form of spatial origami that allows practitioners to fold objects and even people into extremely small sizes. Perhaps not surprisingly, Miéville often interjects humor into the middle of a fascinating concept, such as when a minor practitioner of this spatial origami shrugs matter-of-factly and says he mostly uses it to cram extra clothes into his carry-on bag while traveling. While some readers may find it frustrating that such an intriguing concept is introduced only to be treated somewhat facetiously, others will appreciate the absurdity, which is reminiscent of Douglas Adams's *The Hitchhiker's Guide to the Galaxy* (1979).

Indeed, another of Miéville's strengths is the way in which he deliberately recalls so many conventions and styles from the speculative fiction tradition. For example, the kraken's tentacled nature and the book's horrific overtones immediately bring H. P. Lovecraft's Cthulhu mythos to mind, while Billy's sudden submersion into a world he could not have imagined evokes Alice falling down the rabbit hole in *Alice's Adventures in Wonderland* (1865). In addition, Miéville liberally sprinkles popular-culture references throughout the novel, some of them quite subtly. He includes a mention of Mr. Miyagi from the film *The Karate Kid* (1984); hints at *The X-Files* (1993-2002) in relation to Baron and Collingswood's special investigative unit; gives a nod to Narnia's magical wardrobe; and even makes an allusion to the brooms that carry water buckets in Johann Wolfgang von Goethe's poem "Der Zauberlehrling" ("The Sorcerer's Apprentice"), which was popularized in the 1940 Disney film *Fantasia*. Some references, such as a line stemming from a 1970's British television police drama called *The Sweeney*, will be unfamiliar to American audiences, but most will be widely recognizable.

One of Miéville's largest nods in *Kraken* is to *Star Trek*, and it is quite funny, although some might not consider it entirely complimentary. In a humorous but ghastly incident, Billy and Dane encounter a man named Simon, who is haunted by all the ghosts of himself that he unwittingly created when traveling via a *Star Trek*-style transporter device. In a combined book review and interview in *The New York Times*, Miéville declared that he was horrified as a child when *Star Trek* characters "beamed" from one place to another, because he thought it was self-evident that the original person would die from being disassembled. Therefore, the person who emerges on the other end would be a copy with the original's memories, which does not negate the original death. The encounter with Simon, then, is Miéville's tongue-in-cheek way of registering his complaint, years later, with the *Star Trek* franchise. His use of Simon also seems to poke fun at the clichéd obsessive *Star Trek* fan who wants to "live the show." At the same time, however, the reader senses the author's affection for *Star Trek*, which obviously was an important part of his formative years. At one point, for example, Wati occupies a Captain Kirk action figure, and Billy uses a working phaser to fight the bad guys, thus implying that Miéville considers *Star Trek* to have positive elements upon which to draw.

While Miéville's work routinely receives both critical and popular acclaim, it cannot be denied that *Kraken* is a difficult book to read. Both the reader and Billy are kept in the dark about what is going on for a long time, to the point that some readers may find it frustrating. Conversations work at cross purposes, and there are several repetitive chapters in which Billy swears that he does not understand what is happening while everyone around him insists just as strenuously that he does. Many of the characters do not even bother responding to Billy's direct questions but rather come out with nonsensical statements that seem to belong to a different conversation entirely. Much of the dialogue has a *Monty Python* quality, which can be entertaining at times, but which is also confusing. In addition, Billy and Dane seem to run from one brief encounter to another, to the point where much of the action tends to blur together.

Much of the novel's characterization is also somewhat lacking. Even Billy is difficult to get to know, and therefore, he is unlikely to engender a great deal of sympathy. Many of the supporting characters seem interchangeable throughout the first half of the novel before they ultimately distinguish themselves, although the unusually colorful villains may mitigate most readers' dissatisfaction in that regard. In addition to the individual villains, Miéville incorporates a plethora of rival cults and factions, including the Chaos Nazis, the Jesus Buddhists, and the aforementioned Londonmancers, which readers are likely to find interesting.

In the context of the author's larger body of work, *Kraken* continues to explore one of Miéville's favorite concepts, that of an unseen city that exists alongside or underneath the one that most of the world sees. In *The City and the City* (2009), Miéville takes this idea to an extreme, writing of two cities occupying the same geographical space whose citizens are not permitted to acknowledge the existence of the city to which they do not belong. In his young-adult novel *Un Lun Dun* (2007), Miéville creates "unLondon," a mirrored version of London primarily populated by the "real" city's discards, in terms of actual garbage as well as the people outcast by society. While the alternate city in *Kraken* is not quite as literal as those in *The City and the City* and *Un Lun Dun*, it nonetheless conveys the same sense that strange creatures are lurking and odd occurrences are happening right under the noses of everyday people who do not see them. That, combined with the bizarre and sometimes bewildering atmosphere of the book, helps place this novel within the realm of the "New Weird" subgenre so often used to categorize Miéville's work.

Amy Sisson

Review Sources

Booklist 106, no. 18 (May 15, 2010): 7.
The Guardian, May 15, 2010, p. 10.
Kirkus Reviews 78, no. 10 (May 15, 2010): 442.
Library Journal 135, no. 11 (June 15, 2010): 66.
Publishers Weekly 257, no. 21 (May 24, 2010): 41.
The Times Literary Supplement, no. 5610 (October 8, 2010): 19-20.

THE LAKE SHORE LIMITED

Author: Sue Miller (1943-   )
Publisher: Alfred A. Knopf (New York). 270 pp. $25.95
Type of work: Novel
Time: 2000-2008
Locale: Vermont and Boston

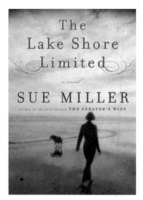

The production of a play about a terrorist attack be-
comes the link for four people and raises questions about
the importance of relationships

> Principal characters:
> BILLY GERTZ, the former lover of Gus; a
>   playwright who wrote *The Lake Shore*
>   *Limited* and who becomes the connecting
>   character in the story
> LESLIE, the sister of Gus, her life changed when Gus died
> RAFE DONOVAN, an actor who plays the main role in Billy's play
> SAM, a friend of Leslie's, potential partner for Billy
> GUS, Leslie's younger brother who lived with Billy and died in the
>   September 11, 2001, terrorist attacks
> PIERCE, Leslie's husband
> LAUREN, Rafe's dying wife

Sue Miller's ninth novel, *The Lake Shore Limited*, received varied critical reception. Most reviewers have commented positively on the depth of characterization as she explores the repercussions of illness, death, grief, and violence on her four main characters. At least one reviewer suggested that the novel's main focus was on brief glimpses into the characters' lives rather than a unified story. Less favorable observations argued that the plot lacked the suspense of and moved more slowly than Miller's previous works.

The story is centered around a fictional play titled *The Lake Shore Limited*. The play has been written by Wilhemina "Billy" Gertz, a tiny but tough playwright. Attending the play are Leslie, the sister of Billy's former lover; her husband, Pierce; and their family friend, Sam. The play tells the story of a man, Gabriel, who hears that his estranged wife, Elizabeth, may have been killed in a terrorist attack on a train. After he is confronted by their adult son, Alex, about his seeming lack of concern over his wife's possible death, he must quickly determine the meaning behind his marital relationship. Gabriel and his son have an argument. To complicate the relationships further, Gabriel's lover turns up at his door; he realizes that the human condition is one of desiring what is missing. Now that he believes Elizabeth is dead, he no longer wants his lover, but he does want his wife. He sends the lover away, knowing that his life has been irreparably altered. As the play draws to a close, Gabriel's wife enters the stage, and he turns to her with tears on his face. The audience, Leslie in particular, is left wondering what the tears mean.

The novel is broken into sections that revolve around the four main characters: Leslie, Rafe, Billy, and Sam. The play is embedded in a segment about Leslie, and she is the first portrait that Miller paints. Leslie, a graceful, gentle woman, draws the love of those who surround her. She is a supportive wife to Pierce, a potentially romantic figure to Sam, and a friend to Billy. However, it is her connection to Billy, through the death of her brother and Billy's lover, Gus, that brings her to the play and introduces the connecting thread in the novel.

Gus, younger than Leslie by fourteen years, became the replacement of the child Leslie and her husband, Pierce, could not have. She lavishes love and attention on him, and she comes to life in his presence. However, on September 11, 2001 (9/11), Gus was on one of the planes that hit the World Trade Center towers. After her brother's death, Leslie puts her life on hold. She cannot see beyond her own grief to understand that Billy may not be feeling the same depth of despair. Leslie interprets the play as Billy's way of working through her feelings for Gus, and Leslie is forced to acknowledge that Billy is more like Gabriel than Leslie would have anticipated. When the novel cycles back around to Leslie, she admits to herself that she has set limitations on her world to make it livable, and she can find contentment, if not happiness, with the safety she feels in that small space.

Sue Miller is a professor of creative writing at Smith College in Massachusetts. Her previous novels include The Good Mother *(1986),* The Senator's Wife *(2008), and six additional titles. She has also written a collection of short stories and a memoir.*

The next player in the novel is Rafe, the actor who portrays Gabriel in Billy's play. Rafe has meandered through life immersed in his work and driven by his own desires. His acting career is comparatively steady, but he has never achieved stardom; *The Lake Shore Limited* is a big break for him. As he begins to take over the part, he also begins to come to an understanding about his own life and marriage. Rafe's wife, Lauren, is dying of amyotrophic lateral sclerosis. He has tried to be a good husband to her, staying with her through the worst of the disease and caring for both her physical and emotional requirements, but, like Gabriel, he wants more. He is greedy for freedom from the burden of a dying spouse, yet he carries guilt over his desire for a life without that burden. The night he recognizes that the ambiguous feelings he has harbored during his wife's illness are not important when faced with her impending death, he becomes Gabriel on stage and gives the best performance of his life.

Rafe's portrayal of Gabriel on that night enlightens Billy to something she possibly did not conceive of when she created the part. However, when she realizes that

Rafe has left the theater before she can congratulate him, Billy reveals her own self-ishness. She asks her director where Rafe has gone and states, "'I should have slept with him much, much sooner.'" The director's horrified response to her flippant atti-tude about sleeping with the troubled actor does not upset Billy, but it does make her think about her own motivations as she goes to meet with Leslie. The meeting with Leslie forces Billy's relationship with Gus to the surface. As Billy remembers it, she and Gus were awkward at best as a couple. She was six years older and much more mature than he. She was bothered most by his childlike happiness and was deter-mined to leave him. Unfortunately for Billy, 9/11 happened before she could take that final step. His death plunged her into the role of the grieving lover that Leslie pro-jected upon her. Love for Leslie keeps Billy tied to this role, but she is left with anger toward Gus for leaving her in it. The guilt over that anger limits her from being able to move on with her life, but she revels in using it as a shield to protect her from deeper relationships.

The final character in the quartet is Sam, an architect and friend of Leslie's. Sam has attended the play at Leslie's request. He is to be Leslie's gift to Billy, a suggestion that it is acceptable for Billy to finally move forward with a new relationship. Sam feels awkward about being used in this way, but he cares too much about Leslie to point this out. He and Billy skate around in a discomforted effort, testing whether their interaction can be more than a well-intentioned but clumsy blind date. While Sam works through his ambiguous feelings for Billy, he reminisces about his mar-riages. His first wife, Susan, was perfect for him. She lifted him into an elegant upper-class society, and their union was a solid one until she got breast cancer. While she was ill, he became the caretaker in their family, pushing aside his own desires to be what his wife and children needed. Years after his wife's death, he remarried in an at-tempt to fill his own needs, but that turned out badly. A brief unconsummated infatua-tion with Leslie further illustrates that he is selfless enough to choose what the other person needs above his own desires.

From a literary standpoint, the most important element in the novel is characteriza-tion. Miller cycles through these four characters twice in the novel as their connec-tions to the play, to the death of a loved one, and to one another bring them to a point of healing. Each character provides a limited omniscient focus, and each succeeding section adds something new to the other characters' inner struggles. Within the seg-ments of the novel, Miller skillfully combines flashbacks with present-tense events to provide further psychological depth. As a result, Leslie, Billy, Sam, and Rafe provide fascinating contrasts for the themes of death, guilt, and grief.

An additional thematic idea that the novel suggests is the creative process. Billy continually struggles with the way she writes and where she finds time to put her ideas into words. Her early plays, briefly mentioned as Miller develops her character, display a level of fury toward the world and turn her family away as a result. Once she has exorcised the demons of her family life, her plays become less adventurous in tone. The writing process itself is one of her main reasons for wanting to leave Gus; with him she does not feel that she has the freedom to express herself, but when she leaves their apartment or is away from him, her words soar again. One of the major reasons for her guilt, and part of the reason that the play took longer than any other play to write, is she was savoring the peace of an empty apartment on the day he died.

Another area of literary study might look at the historical and cultural aspects of the terrorist attack in Billy's play. The most obvious link is 9/11 because of Gus's death in the attacks. Billy clearly admits that she spent years writing and rewriting the play after the tragedy. However, the terrorist situation in the fictional play is not on an airplane; rather, it is in a train station. Train attacks have taken place in several European and Asian countries. On March 11, 2004, Madrid, Spain, suffered an attack on their Cercanías system; on July 7, 2005, London's public transportation system was struck by suicide bombers on three underground trains and one double-decker bus. In 2006, Mumbai, India, became the target of numerous explosions, on commuter trains and at train stations. Then, in November, 2009, a terrorist plot resulted in the derailment of a train in Russia. These four attacks, whether they were directly influential on Miller's side plot or not, can be connected to the event that so affected Elizabeth and Gabriel.

Further connections can be taken from a literary history standpoint. The play within the novel is strongly reminiscent of Kate Chopin's short story "The Story of an Hour," in which a wife is told that her husband has died in a train accident. Just when she comes to a point of awakening about her own life after her husband's death, her husband enters, and she dies of a heart attack. The train accident, the potentially dead spouse, and the awakening of their own true desires offer close ties between these two pieces.

Theresa L. Stowell

Review Sources

Booklist 106 (February 1, 2010): 6.
Entertainment Weekly, April 23, 2010, 118.
Kirkus Reviews 78, no. 4 (February 15, 2010): 107.
Library Journal 135 (April 15, 2010): 75.
The National Post 12 (April 12, 2010): p. WP14.
The New York Times, April 23, 2010, p. C24.
Publishers Weekly 257 (January 18, 2010): 26.

LAST CALL
The Rise and Fall of Prohibition

Author: Daniel Okrent (1948-   )
Publisher: Charles Scribner's Sons (New York). 469 pp.
$30.00
Type of work: History
Time: 1870's-1930's
Locale: United States

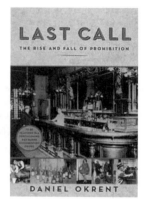

This book offers a panoramic history of Prohibition that emphasizes the broad and transformative aspects of the struggle surrounding the Eighteenth Amendment

Principal personages:
>NEAL DOW, an early prohibitionist businessman responsible for the Maine Law
>"MOTHER" ELIZA THOMPSON, a temperance activist and leader of the Hillsboro Crusade
>FRANCES WILLARD (1839-1898), the leader of the Women's Christian Temperance Union
>MARY HANCHETT HUNT, a lobbyist for temperance education
>HOWARD HYDE RUSSELL, the founder of the Anti-Saloon League
>WAYNE BIDWELL WHEELER (1869-1927), the chief lobbyist and general counsel for the Anti-Saloon League
>CARRY NATION (1846-1911), an antialcohol militant known for attacking bars with a hatchet
>ADOLPHUS BUSCH (1839-1913), a brewing magnate
>RICHMOND HOBSON (1870-1937), the Alabama congressman famed for "The Great Destroyer" speech
>REVEREND JAMES CANON, JR., the "Dry Messiah," who preached Prohibition to Southern Democrats
>MORRIS SHEPPARD (1875-1941), a Texas senator and "dry-dry" who sponsored the Eighteenth Amendment
>BILLY SUNDAY (1862-1935), an evangelist and a Prohibition advocate
>ANDREW J. VOLSTEAD (1860-1947), the Minnesota congressman who penned the legislation that enforced Prohibition
>ROY HAYES, the first head of the Treasury Department's Bureau of Prohibition
>MABEL WALKER WILLEBRANDT (1889-1963), the assistant attorney general in charge of Prohibition enforcement
>SAMUEL BRONFMAN (1889-1971), a Canadian bootlegger
>PAULINE MORTON SABIN, the founder of the Women's Organization for National Prohibition Reform

JAMES A. REED, a Missouri Senator who became the leading wet
  politician of the 1920's
GEORGES DE LATOUR, a California vintner famed for his sacramental
  wines
PIERRE DU PONT (1870-1954), a wealthy benefactor of the Association
  Against the Prohibition Amendment

Prohibition began on January 16, 1920, exactly one year after the ratification of the
Eighteen Amendment to the Constitution, and ended on December 5, 1933, when the
Twenty-first Amendment relegalized the sale of intoxicating beverages; it has long
been a subject that has captured the public imagination. From the bootlegging mafia
fiefdom that Al Capone established in Chicago to the Jazz Age parties immortalized
by F. Scott Fitzgerald in *The Great Gatsby*, the iconic images and myths of the U.S.
failed social experiment have spawned countless Hollywood films—*Scarface* (1932)
and *Some Like It Hot* (1959), for example—and an equal number of unsubstantiated
myths, such as the widely held belief that Joseph P. Kennedy made his fortune trading
in illegal liquor.

Serious historical writing on Prohibition has lagged behind the popular interest. Several excellent studies have tackled aspects of Prohibition, such as David Kyvig's *Re-
pealing National Prohibition* (1979), Austin Kerr's *Organized for Prohibition: A New
History of the Anti-Saloon League* (1985), and Catherine Gilbert Murdock's analysis
of the leading role played by women in the temperance movement, *Domesticating
Drink: Women, Men, and Alcohol in America, 1870-1940* (1998). Starting with Richard Hofstadter's *The Age of Reform* (1955), historians have also attempted to situate
Prohibition within the context of larger political and social developments, which, for
Hofstadter, meant identifying the battle between "wets" and "drys" as part of a broader
struggle between parochial rural populists and cosmopolitan urban elites. However,
strikingly missing from the historiography of Prohibition is a comprehensive and
synthetic work that weaves a single, analytic narrative out of its many disparate stories and legends. Daniel Okrent's *Last Call* is an effort to condense into a complete
and coherent story the diverse ways in which Prohibition reshaped American life.

One of Okrent's goals in *Last Call* is to present a cogent explanation for how Prohibition evolved from earlier temperance movements and how such a transformative
and radical agenda became law. He starts with the Washingtonian movement of the
1840's, which focused on voluntary abstinence, and the Maine Law of 1851, which
was the nation's first statewide (albeit short-lived) alcohol ban. He explores the influence of Frances Willard's Women's Christian Temperance Union and Mary Hanchett
Hunt's Department of Scientific Instruction in placing Prohibition on the national
agenda.

Okrent's gift for analysis becomes most clear when he elucidates the complex political and social alliances that propelled the dry forces to legislative victory. At the
core of the Prohibition movement was Wayne Bidwell Wheeler, the de facto director
of the Anti-Saloon League (ASL) and arguably the most powerful man in the United

≈

*Daniel Okrent served as the first public
editor of* The New York Times *from
2003 to 2005. He previously served as
an editor at large at* Time *magazine.
His history of the development of
Rockefeller Center,* Great Fortune, *was
a finalist for the Pulitzer Prize in 2004.*

≈

States. Okrent certainly makes a compelling
case that Wheeler was one of the best-known
figures in the nation during his heyday, probably the most famous American ever to be so
decisively forgotten by the general public.
Wheeler developed two key strategies that
made the ASL the most influential lobbying
organization ever to wield power in Washington, D.C. The ASL confined itself to only one
issue and willingly embraced any individual
or organization, including the Ku Klux Klan, that shared its goals. It also kept itself
nonpartisan, enabling it to focus on marginal and swing voters who could shift elections between candidates, enabling the ASL to wield far greater power than its
numbers would otherwise have yielded.

Okrent explains how the ASL and hardcore dry activists joined forces with advocates for women's suffrage, as women were expected to vote in favor of Prohibition.
According to Okrent, the resulting Nineteenth Amendment, granting women the right
to the ballot, was inextricably bound to the Eighteenth. He also makes a persuasive argument that the Sixteenth Amendment, legalizing income taxes, resulted from Prohi-
bitionists' effort to find an alternative source of revenue for the federal government,
which prior to 1913 had relied heavily on alcohol taxes, in order to make Prohibition
economically viable. Similarly, efforts to curtail immigration stemmed from fears of
potentially wet Catholic and Jewish voters.

The origins of the anti-Prohibition forces, which have been given much less attention by other historians, are also explored extensively in Okrent's study. He depicts
the surprise, and often willful blindness, with which many wet Americans greeted the
coming antialcohol tsunami. The beer-brewing industry and the liquor-distilling industry, which seemingly should have been political allies, viewed each other as adversaries in the years leading up to the dry victory; many brewers hoped that any ban
would apply to hard alcohol only. Okrent emphasizes the role that anti-German sentiment, generated by World War I, played in demonizing the brewing concerns, whose
most prominent face had been the German-born magnate, Adolphus Busch.

While most previous studies of Prohibition have focused primarily on beer and liquor, Okrent also tackles the unique problems facing the wine industry. He follows
the rise of Georges de Latour, a California vintner who made his fortune selling sacramental wines to Catholic churches. He also explores the widespread planting of
alicante grapes, a low-quality breed well suited for transnational shipments, from
which the fruits were fermented into homemade wines. Okrent even discusses the industrial uses of alcohol products and the relationship between Prohibition and medical prescribers of alcohol. However, in a rare oversight, he passes over some relatively recent scholarship in the history of medicine that suggests that Prohibition
played an important part in shaping the cohesive identity of the modern medical
profession.

A second aspect of Okrent's volume tackles efforts to enforce Prohibition, at both the national and the state levels. He assesses the key portions of the Volstead Act, the statute that fleshed out the specifics of the new national alcohol ban, including the decision to include wine and beer among the "intoxicating beverages" banned by the Eighteenth Amendment. The reader learns that Wheeler resisted efforts to criminalize the purchase of alcoholic beverages, fearing the buyers would never be willing to testify against their providers if they feared criminal penalties. Okrent also discusses the widely despised Jones Law, named after Senator Wesley L. Jones of Washington, which turned Volstead violations from misdemeanors into felonies punishable by long prison sentences. The most famous of these sentences was that handed down to Etta Mae Miller, a Michigan housewife and mother of ten, who was sent away for life in 1928 for selling two pints of liquor to an undercover cop. (Her sentence was later commuted.)

Last Call highlights the celebrated career of Mabel Walker Willebrandt, the nation's highest-ranking female official during the 1920's, who defended Prohibition in the courts. At the same time, Okrent narrates the saga of Sam Bronfman, the Seagram founder (and father of entrepreneur Edgar Bronfman) whose audacity enabled him to build a bootlegging empire in Canada via the French overseas port of Saint Pierre. While Okrent discusses both Capone and the role that Prohibition played in the growth and nationalization of organized crime, he emphasizes that Prohibition made lawbreakers out of millions of ordinary citizens as well. Among the most vivid and memorable passages in the work are the descriptions of "rum row," a series of vessels stationed just outside the boundaries of U.S. waters, where seagoers could stop to wet their throats and refill their alcohol stores.

If Okrent's volume provides a nuanced and analytic history, the work also offers a series of minibiographies of the key players in the Prohibition saga and follows them through the course of the 1920's. In addition to Bronfman, Willebrandt, and Wheeler, Okrent covers Pauline Morton Sabin, a wealthy matron and committed Republican dry who embraced the wet cause after the failures of Prohibition became apparent; she eventually became a rallying force for the backers of repeal by making the goal respectable. In the process, she became a thorn in the side of dry politicians such as President Herbert Hoover. Another of Okrent's fascinating dramatis personae is industrialist Pierre Du Pont, who purportedly funded the Association Against the Prohibition Amendment with the primary goal of creating an alternate source of revenue, in alcohol taxes, that would lead to the reduction or repeal of the graduated income tax. In addition to these colorful characters, the narrative portrays the leading political figures of the day, from the arch-dry William Jennings Bryan to the sopping-wet Alfred E. Smith, carefully exploring the nuances of their positions and the consequences of their exploits, such as Bryan's threat to invade the Bahamas to suppress the illegal liquor trade.

Last Call also presents a serious scholarly argument about the political forces surrounding Prohibition and offers a popular history replete with entertaining and informative anecdotes—such as the origins of the word "scofflaw," which was the winning entry in a 1923 contest sponsored by a Boston newspaper in which readers were challenged to coin a term for illegal drinking. He peppers his prose with material from sources as disparate as the literary critic Van Wyck Brooks and the lexicographer Stuart Berg Flexner and uses apt quotations from Ernest Hemingway, H. L. Mencken, Will Rogers, Malcolm Cowley, and many others. The breadth of Okrent's material renders the work not merely authoritative, but likely definitive.

The success of *Last Call* lies foremost in the author's ability to draw insightful connections, often unexpected, between seemingly unrelated events. For example, he points out that the novel idea of a ratification time limit, first introduced into the Eighteenth Amendment as part of a compromise to permit brewers and distillers to adjust to Prohibition, did little to help the alcohol industry at the time but later played a role in the failure of the Equal Rights Amendment. Such connections abound in *Last Call*. He also acknowledges the greatest irony of the Prohibition story: While the effort to ban alcohol failed, the result was that Americans in the post-Prohibition era consumed far less in the way of intoxicating beverages than they did before 1920. Okrent's larger message is that Prohibition transformed American society radically, in ways large and small. He makes his case convincingly in a volume worthy of one of most significant American social movements.

Jacob M. Appel

Review Sources

Booklist 106, no. 13 (March 1, 2010): 34.
Kirkus Reviews 78, no. 4 (February 15, 2010): 127-128.
Library Journal 135, no. 1 (January 1, 2010): 120-121.
The New York Times Book Review, May 23, 2010, p. 20.
Publishers Weekly 257, no. 2 (January 11, 2010): 40.
The Wall Street Journal, May 14, 2010, p. W15.